BLACKS IN WHITE AMERICA
Before 1865
Issues and Interpretations

BLACKS IN WHITE AMERICA

Before 1865

Issues and Interpretations

Robert V. Haynes
UNIVERSITY OF HOUSTON

E 70

DAVID McKAY COMPANY, INC.
New York

BLACKS IN WHITE AMERICA: Before 1865
Issues and Interpretations

LIBRARY OF CONGRESS CATALOG CARD NUMBER: 78–185137

MANUFACTURED IN THE UNITED STATES OF AMERICA

Contents

BLACKS IN WHITE AMERICA
Before 1865
Issues and Interpretations

I

Black History and the Historian

Despite the erroneous impressions left by the recent requests for Black Studies, scholarship in Afro-American history did not suddenly spring into being to satisfy these demands. Instead, the writing of black history, like American history in general, dates from the mid-nineteenth century. In contrast to later students of Negro history, the earliest writers were usually amateurs or non-professionals and almost always Afro-Americans who were politically active in promoting the interests of black people. Among the most prominent of these early black authors were William Wells Brown, an abolitionist who wrote *The Black Man* (1863); George Washington Williams, another veteran of the Civil War whose *History of the Negro Race in America from 1619 to 1880* ranks among the best histories written in the nineteenth century; and Benjamin Griffith Brawley who was best remembered for his popularly written *A Social History of the American Negro* (1921). All of these black Americans were motivated by a common desire to demonstrate the patriotic and heroic efforts of Afro-Americans, to condemn the injustices inflicted upon them by white Europeans, to dispel the myth of racial inferiority, and to "give the world more correct ideas of the colored people, and incite the latter to greater efforts in the struggle of citizenship and manhood." *

In the early twentieth century, a small but growing band of university-trained scholars launched the Negro History Movement. While their objectives were similar to those of nineteenth-century writers, they placed greater emphasis upon the rigorous standards of academic scholarship then in vogue among professional historians. They optimistically predicted that proof of past achievements and contributions of black people would erase the stain of white prejudice against the Negro. Since bigotry was for them more the result of ignorance than of conviction, they viewed education as the most realistic panacea for America's racism.

* George Washington Williams, *A History of the Negro Race in America from 1619 to 1880* (New York: G. P. Putnam's Sons, 1883), p. v.

1

The father of the Negro History Movement was Dr. Carter G. Woodson. Shortly after obtaining his doctorate from Harvard University, Woodson founded in 1915 the Association of Negro Life and History, a vehicle with which he hoped to realize his goal of transforming "his historical training and preparation to the best racial account." Not only did Woodson further the cause of Negro history by authoring some ten scholarly monographs, but he was also largely responsible for the Association's decision to launch in 1916 the invaluable *Journal of Negro History*, a gold mine of black scholarship, which he edited until his death in 1950. Other black scholars active in this movement were Charles H. Wesley and Monroe M. Work.

During the 1940s, the Negro History Movement was replaced by a group of second generation black professional historians who were less interested than their predecessors in combatting anti-Negro propaganda and more concerned with producing what they regarded as more objective history. Although smaller in numbers and productivity than their white counterparts of the same period, several were recognized as outstanding historians. Rayford W. Logan, Lorenzo Johnston Greene, John Hope Franklin, and Benjamin Quarles produced studies which were well received by their professional peers.

Concomitant with the appearance of these black historians was a group of liberal white historians and social scientists who were strongly influenced by the Swedish scholar, Gunnar Myrdal, and his massive study of the American race problem which he entitled *The American Dilemma*. They questioned the older interpretations of American history which had stressed the influence of impersonal forces such as geography and economics upon men and which treated Afro-Americans either as nameless slaves who tilled southern soils or unskilled workers who blighted northern cities. In either case, they were part of what white Americans meant by the "Negro problem." Typical of the type of history to which they objected was U. B. Phillips' *Life and Labor in the Old South*, a classic work which stands as a paragon of scholarship except for the author's obvious bias against Negroes.

By viewing the Negro as a white man with black skin, these more liberal historians sought to make Afro-American history "relevant to men of all races." History was to serve the purpose of promoting integration of American society. Together with the second generation of black professional historians, they denied that the historical record of Afro-Americans could be used to justify racial discrimination. They hoped, as many scholars have before and after them, that history would serve as an antidote to hysteria. Their studies lent support to the integration movement by chronicling how blacks had participated willingly and in some cases enthusiastically in the mainstream of American development. Not only had Afro-Americans fought to establish and maintain American independence, but they had also joined with compatriots in the systematic annihilation of the American Indian.

Proud of this heritage and anxious to publicize it, black Americans expected to gain access to the benefits of an advanced technological society as soon as they proved themselves capable. History was one means of convincing white America of their ability to share in the largess. This view of black history, best exemplified by John Hope Franklin's encyclopedic *From Slavery to Freedom*, held sway as long as the Civil Rights Movement was in vogue.

During the 1960s, black Americans increasingly lost faith in integration as an immediate goal or in the willingness of a majority of white Americans to accept black people for what they were. Convinced that integration on white terms meant rejecting their blackness and sacrificing their cultural heritage, many young blacks espoused the doctrines of Black Power and Black Nationalism.

Several young black scholars not only have denounced earlier attempts at ascertaining the place of black Americans in the context of United States history, but they have also begun to redefine as well as to reinterpret black history. No longer accepting the values and goals of white America as necessarily valid for black people, they insist upon writing history from a black perspective. To them emphasis must be placed on events and concepts important to black people and not on how Afro-Americans participated in historical movements controlled and directed by white people. They call for a realistic appraisal of the manner in which blacks have been profitably exploited, continually oppressed, and systematically reduced to a state of dependency. The purpose of their study was not self-pity but black freedom. Only by a thorough knowledge of where they have been and where they are now, they insist, can Afro-Americans begin the process of Black Liberation.

The following selections reveal the present ambiguity of historians about the purpose of black history and the place of Afro-Americans in United States history. In the first selection the author traces the changes in interpretation of historians from a tendency to ignore the black man altogether to a view which places him at the center of American history. The other two articles illustrate the divided mind of black scholars. Earl E. Thorpe, representative of more traditional black historians, espouses an interpretation more akin to the Negro History Movement and more attuned to the Civil Rights Movement. The purpose of history for him is the critical study of past achievements in order to provide black people with a sense of identity. On the other hand, John Henrik Clarke expresses a viewpoint popular with many young scholars who see history as a component of Black Nationalism and Black Liberation. History should do more than provide people with a knowledge of where they have been, it should also instill in them a determination for freedom and suggest guidelines for achieving control over their own destinies. More than earlier writers, Clarke attempts to redefine black history from the black perspective.

1. ROBERT STAROBIN, The Negro: A Central Theme In American History (1968)*

Robert Starobin was formerly an associate professor of history at the State University of New York at Binghamton until his untimely death in 1971. He received his Ph.D degree from the University of California at Berkeley where he studied under Kenneth M. Stampp. Oxford University Press recently published his dissertation, *Industrial Slavery in the Old South,* which corrects the old myth that black slaves could be profitably used only as plantation laborers. In this essay Starobin summarizes contemporary scholarship about the importance of the Negro in American history. Unfortunately Starobin emphasizes the works of white historians to the neglect of the few black scholars who have also published in the field.

In the United States, Negro history has been characterized, until very recently, either by traditionalism or by revisionism. The traditionalist historians held, in brief, that Negroes were of little consequence to the American experience. Revisionist historians, on the other hand, hold that Negroes have made some important contributions to the American heritage. Within the last decade, however, a new group of scholars has challenged both these views, and Negro historiography has begun to undergo a radical shift in interpretation. For the latest studies stress the centrality of institutions like slavery to long periods of American history, and regard the Negro as a key to the meaning of the American experience.

Traditionalist historiography viewed Negroes as altogether passive in the American story. It ignored, distorted, or disparaged the contributions of blacks to the shaping of American institutions. The Negro's presence in America was an unfortunate mistake or at best a nuisance. Least of all did the traditionalists see American development as dependent to any extent upon the position of the Negro.

The traditionalists dominated American historical writing on slavery and the Reconstruction period after the Civil War from the turn of the twentieth century until about the Second World War. Products of an age when Negroes were being more and more segregated, disfranchised, and denied human dignity, the traditionalists tended to exhibit white supremacist attitudes towards Negro history. Pseudo-scientific theories of race also provided neat justifications for consigning blacks to an inferior caste. American overseas penetration, based on the concept of the "white man's burden" to "civilize" his "little brown brothers" in Latin America and Asia,

* Robert Starobin, "The Negro: A Central Theme in American History," *Journal of Contemporary History* 3 (April 1968): 37–53. Reprinted by permission.

corresponded to Negro proscription at home. Many of the old abolitionists and radical Republicans, who had become disillusioned with the Reconstruction experiment and with the Negro's capacity for self-government, abandoned the freedmen to southern whites. The rapid influx of new immigrants from Southern and Eastern Europe into urban centers made Northerners more understanding of southern attempts to cope with their blacks. Not surprisingly, many traditionalists displayed racism when they wrote about Negro history.[1]

The traditionalist historians never really took Negroes seriously. If they considered the Negro at all, they generally depicted him as a Sambo —shiftless, docile, happy-go-lucky, intellectually incompetent, and almost sub-human. Africa was a land of dark tribal savagery, and therefore slavery had been absolutely necessary to civilize the black barbarians. Slaveowners were benevolent masters who maintained slavery not because it was profitable, but because it was the only conceivable system of race relations. Since slavery was dying out by itself, the Civil War was a needless bloodbath caused either by fanatical abolitionists or by southern fire-eaters, or by both. Reconstruction was likewise a "tragic era" of proscription of natural southern white leaders, corrupt government, and the amalgamation of the races. The Redeemers, those white Southerners who overthrew Radical Reconstruction, were the ultimate saviours of the South, since they restored the Negro to his proper place in southern society.

By the 1930s, a reassessment of the role of the Negro in American history was clearly under way. Unlike the traditionalists, the revisionist historians emphasized the outstanding contributions of Negroes to, and the success of their progress in, American life. As much inspirational as it was informational, revisionism urged both whites and blacks to appreciate Negro achievements and to revere famous Negroes in order to integrate Negroes into the American heritage. Whereas the traditionalists ignored Negroes, the revisionists ardently praised them and attempted to bring them into the American family. *The Negro, Too, in American History* [2] was the title of a typical revisionist survey.

Revisionism differed strikingly from traditionalism in almost every respect. Revisionists regarded Negroes as full human beings, and they conceived of slavery as a profitable system of labor exploitation, which the blacks heroically resisted. The Civil War was necessary to abolish slavery as well as to preserve a model republican Union. Reconstruction was a time of great hope and of positive participation by Negroes in the democratic experiment. It failed because the freedmen were not given sufficient economic power to secure their political rights. Despite some corruption and many mistakes, however, Reconstruction was not a complete disaster, since the Fourteenth and Fifteenth Amendments promised a later fulfilment of legal equality after the Second World War. Even so, the Compromise of 1877 between northern Republicans and conservative white southern Democrats led directly to the nadir of the Negro's experience at the close of the nineteenth century.

Revisionism was in part a response to current political events and to new intellectual trends. Anthropological conceptions of race underwent a dramatic shift, so that Negroes could be regarded as full members of the human family. Their image was upgraded at home, in order, first, to defeat fascism, then to counter Soviet propaganda, and finally to woo the black nations emerging from European colonialism. It became public policy to integrate blacks into the national labor force, the market economy, the military, and into electoral politics. The beginnings of the civil rights movement in the Roosevelt, Truman, and Eisenhower administrations tended to accelerate this integration of Negroes into American historiography. As a result of these trends, traditionalism was submerged beneath an outpouring of revisionist writings.

Pioneer black historians who attempted to demonstrate the contribution of their own race to American development greatly promoted the revision of Negro history. W. E. B. DuBois's classic *Souls of Black Folk* (1903) was followed in the 1920s by scholarly writings by such outstanding Negro historians as Carter Woodson and Charles H. Wesley. In particular, Alrutheus A. Taylor published carefully documented works on *The Negro in South Carolina during the Reconstruction, The Negro in the Reconstruction of Virginia*, and *The Negro in Tennessee, 1865–1880.*[3] Similarly, worthy Negro educators like Luther P. Jackson and Horace M. Bond produced histories of ante-bellum free Negroes and of black education and Reconstruction, respectively. The Association for the Study of Negro Life and History, which began publishing the *Journal of Negro History* in 1916, also accelerated the revisionist trend, which was reinforced by sociological studies, such as E. Franklin Frazier's *The Negro Family*, his classic critique of the *Black Bourgeoisie*,[4] and Gunnar Myrdal's *An American Dilemma*,[5] to which many Negro scholars contributed.

Marxist and communist writers greatly stimulated the revision of Negro history. Dubois's *Black Reconstruction*[6] stressed the unity of black and white proletarians, as well as black accomplishments during the postwar years. Herbert Aptheker's *American Negro Slave Revolts*[7] catalogued the unrest permeating slavery, and zealously traced the tradition of black militancy. In 1955 Philip Foner brought out his edition of *The Writings of Frederick Douglass.*[8]

Liberal white historians—North and South—also participated in the revision of Negro history. Charles S. Sydnor's *Slavery in Mississippi*[9] provided an early case study in the nature of bondage in a key state. Kenneth

M. Stampp's *The Peculiar Institution* [10] demolished the traditionalist views and is the best and most comprehensive study of plantation slavery to date. Stanley Elkins' *Slavery* [11] attempted a psychological analysis of the impact of enslavement on the personality of American Negroes. Vernon Lane Wharton's study of the *Negro in Mississippi, 1865–1890*, [12] and Francis B. Simkins' and Robert H. Woody's *South Carolina during Reconstruction*, [13] presented well-balanced views of Negro participation in Radical Reconstruction governments. C. Vann Woodward's well-known studies of the New South period attempted to account for the failure of black-white cooperation during the 1880s and for the beginnings of segregation and disfranchisement in the 1890s. [14]

Despite its integration of Negroes into American history, revisionism suffers from grave shortcomings. First, elitism and political conservatism tend to characterize much, but not all, of revisionist Negro historiography. It glorifies those blacks who tried to integrate into the mainstream of American society. Benjamin Banneker, the Jeffersonian architect, Phillis Wheatley, the Revolutionary poet, Frederick Douglass, the fugitive slave abolitionist, George Washington Carver, the peanut scientist, and Booker T. Washington, the accommodationist educator, are thus elevated to the pantheon of acceptable American Negro heroes. Those blacks who advocated the violent overthrow of bondage, those who became militant nationalists or Pan-Africanists, and those who embraced socialist alternatives, are neglected. David Walker and Henry Highland Garnet, the revolutionists, Bishop Turner and Marcus Garvey, the militant nationalists, DuBois, Washington's great antagonist, and Malcolm X, the Muslim internationalist, have received little scholarly study. [15]

These limitations are clearly revealed in Richard Bardolph's *The Negro Vanguard*. [16] Posing as a social historian of black "movers and shakers," Bardolph attempts to update the *Dictionary of American Biography*, which included only one hundred Negroes in nearly sixteen thousand entries and furnished no index to the Negroes included. Though he rescues many blacks from oblivion, Bardolph's account is frankly elitist: "This study is offered . . . as an attempt to identify the most celebrated Negro Americans in the country's past," he writes. "The Negro's heroes . . . afford a convenient medium for studying the history of the whole American group. . . . I have tried to assemble a list of those persons who appear most prominently in the written historical record." To be sure, this Negro elite deserves study, but not at the expense of the black masses—those field hands, factory workers, house servants, and artisans who certainly "made" as much history as Bardolph's "talented tenth." They were of course illiterate, as Bardolph acknowledges, but this does not mean that their traces do not survive. If historians and graduate students spent as much time collecting the records of plain people as they do of business and religious leaders, would we not have a better picture of them?

A similar elitism plagues August Meier's *Negro Thought in America, 1880–1915*,[17] which concedes in a "Methodological Note" that "Naturally, in a study of this sort one is largely limited (by the material available) to the expressed ideas of the articulate, who are ordinarily among the prominent people, and usually of the favored social and economic classes." Though he fails to analyze what the common black folk thought or did, Meier does patiently assess some, but not all of the programs for racial advancement put forward by the Negro elite during the period. Such plans ranged from Bishop Turner's colonization schemes to DuBois's political activism. But Meier is at his controversial best when he dissects Washington's grand strategy of political and social accommodation combined with training for Negroes in agricultural and mechanical pursuits, and backroom dealing with conservative politicians and business leaders.

Problems of a different sort burden the Marxist biographers. Foner's work on Frederick Douglass, for example, not only magnifies the ex-slave's heroism out of all proportion to his contribution to "the struggle," but also fails to grapple with Douglass's human weaknesses. Foner ignores his early idiosyncrasies and excuses his later conservatism. Douglass certainly made an enormous contribution to the abolitionist movement, but in the 1870s and 1880s he became a hack Republican Uncle Tom. Foner neither accounts for this transformation nor fully admits that Douglass failed to build a real political base in the community of common Negroes—slave and freedmen—at the time. Is it not conceivable that Douglass "sold out" in his later years and catered to liberal white abolitionists earlier precisely because he originated in the bourgeoisie of *his* day, that is, in the slave artisan group? A more comprehensive study would have done Douglass and black history better service.

Similar weaknesses are apparent in Herbert Aptheker's approach to W. E. B. DuBois. Few doubt DuBois's contribution, but Aptheker's extreme hero-worship interferes with his understanding of the strengths and weaknesses of the man. ". . . DuBois was a Renaissance Man who lives in our own era . . . and chief founder and inspirer of the liberation movements of peoples of African descent now shaking and remaking the globe from Mozambique to Mississippi," he writes. "DuBois's range was as wide as that of Leonardo da Vinci. . . . No doubt some day, somewhere, all papers relevant to Dr. DuBois will be gathered together in a fitting hall of learning and research. Such a collection will rival in quantity and in significance any other collection of the papers of any individual anywhere in the world; none will surpass [them] in breadth and grandeur." [18] In short, the communist historians and many other revisionists worship Negro heroes blindly and write almost exclusively the history of Negro success, without accounting for the failure of the majority of blacks to integrate into American life.

The revisionist writers are also preoccupied with organizational and military history. The first volume of Charles F. Kellogg's *NAACP: A History of the National Association for the Advancement of Colored People*, covering the years 1909–20,[19] and the forthcoming volume on the Congress of Racial Equality by August Meier and Elliott M. Rudwick, are typical of this trend. While the history of these inter-racial organizations is important for the background of the Civil Rights Movement, it may be argued that these studies are too narrowly conceived. Kellogg's book rests on a thorough study of the NAACP papers, but it is weakened by its concentration on the internal structure and leadership of the group, rather than on what the typical member was thinking and doing at the time of the First World War. Concerning the Negro in the military, Benjamin Quarles has written on *The Negro in the American Revolution* and on *The Negro in the Civil War*.[20] Though Quarles praises the sacrifices made by the blacks for independence and reunion, it is still true that in the Revolution blacks bled for whites who either owned slaves or supported slavery and the slave trade. In the Civil War, whether they knew it or not, Negroes fought to preserve a racist Union; in later conflicts they would die to safeguard the Caribbean and Asia for American penetration.

In short, the revisionists stress the contributions of Negroes to American history in an attempt to integrate blacks into the American story. This leads them to concentrate on the biographies of outstanding Negroes, on organizational and military history, and to study conservative Negro elites to the neglect of the bulk of the black population. They are almost wholly preoccupied with the history of Negro success, without fully acknowledging the history or roots of black failure. Most important of all, they hardly appreciate that slavery and Negroes were, over long spans of time, central to the development of American political and economic institutions.

The new group of scholars who challenge the interpretations of both traditionalists and revisionists stress the *centrality* of the Negro, the South, and of racism to American development. They do not contend that *all* American history turned upon the "Negro Question," but that long periods of American history were largely shaped by the problem of slavery and of the freedmen. Relating slavery directly to the formation of basic political institutions, such as the Constitution and parties, these scholars view late eighteenth and most of nineteenth-century American politics as determined by issues concerning Negroes. In the new studies early nineteenth-century trade and industrialization are shown to depend mainly on the growth of the slave economy of the South. Territorial and economic expansionism was also a direct function of slavery and racism. The anti-slavery politics of the 1840s and 1850s were of course related to slavery itself. The roots of segregation lie more in the Reconstruction and ante-bellum periods than they do in the 1890s. In short, the most recent scholarship begins to view the Negro as a key to the meaning of the American experience.

The new interpretations respond to new political and intellectual trends as well as to some of the factors which led to revisionism in the 1930s and 1940s. First, the failure of the Civil Rights Movement of the 1950s and 1960s to make significant changes in the lives of most Negroes has demonstrated how deeply entrenched discrimination and racism are in American society. As a result, the new scholars have a deeper understanding of how firmly embedded slavery was in the social order of the nineteenth century. They therefore regard slavery not as an American anomaly, but as central to American society from its early beginnings. Moreover, the wars of national liberation overseas and the corresponding call for "Black Power" by ghetto and delta Negroes in the United States, have led many post-revisionists to question older revisionism and to undertake more realistic assessment of the Negroes. Finally, they tend to reject crude Marxist frameworks of interpretation, adopting instead a more free-wheeling historical materialism, which can account for the psychological and sexual origins of racism, as well as for the role of slaves and freedmen in the society. They therefore reject many of the simplistic formulations made by the early revisionists. Thus while the continuity with early revisionism is clear, the new scholars have so deepened their insights that their work is qualitatively and radically different.

Though the new Negro historiography is just getting under way, it is not too early to discuss some of its most important contributions. For the 1780s, Staughton Lynd provocatively argues in "The Compromise of 1787"[21] that slavery was as central to the compromises of the Constitutional Convention as the traditional conflicts between big states and small states, monarchists and democrats, and real property and personal property. Lynd suggests that the famous "three-fifths" clause, which added part of the slave population to the southern white population for the purposes of taxation and representation and which increased southern power, was of primary importance. Furthermore, the issue of western lands was part of the sectional conflict between northern and southern states. The clauses providing for federal suppression of insurrections and capture of fugitive slaves, as well as for postponing the abolition of the slave trade, were all integral to the framing of the new government. Since they expected pro-slavery Southerners to settle in the Northwest Territory, slave-state representatives at the last Continental Congress acceded to the Northwest Ordinance, despite its anti-slavery proviso. Moreover, the Ordinance was probably construed by Southerners as a tacit endorsement of slavery in the Southwest Territory, and seemed to involve an agreement to speed the admission of new states from the Northwest by lowering population requirements. Combined with the continued stalemate on the Mississippi navigation issue, the Northwest Ordinance seemed like a southern victory to the slave-state congressmen. News of the Ordinance apparently reached the Constitutional Convention in Philadelphia in time to persuade Southerners there to incorporate the three-fifths clause into the constitution so long as it applied equally to representation and taxation. Then, late in the summer of 1787, Georgia and the Carolinas completed the compromise after Northerners had yielded on the issues of the slave trade and fugitive slaves. Thus, on 30 June, James Madison stated "that the States were divided into different interests not by their difference of size, but by other circumstances; the most material of which resulted partly from climate, but principally from the effects of their having or not having slaves." It was "pretty well understood," said Madison on 14 July, that the "institution of slavery and its consequences formed the lines of discrimination" between the contending states at the Constitutional Convention. In short, according to Lynd, slavery was "an independent force in the shaping and ratification of the Constitution." The Compromise of 1787 was reached by men who for the most part disliked slavery, but who acted ambivalently on it because of their desire to keep the Union together, their belief in the sacredness of private property, and their "inability to imagine a society in which Negroes and whites could live together as citizens and brothers."

For the early decades of the new republic, Robert McColley's *Slavery and Jeffersonian Virginia* [22] broadens the concept of the centrality of slavery to American politics. Whereas most revisionists did not question the theory that slavery was moribund until the cotton boom after 1815, McColley believes that "the slave-based plantation system was . . . fundamental in the large economic affairs of Virginia." Describing Jefferson as "the father of slavery in Louisiana," McColley argues that "the Virginia dynasty in national politics . . . pressed the claims of American planters for wider access to world markets and opened up the rich lands of the lower Mississippi Valley to plantation agriculture." Moreover, "the Virginia influence on the Old Northwest was a pro-slavery influence, and nothing was done by the national government under the Virginians Jefferson and Madison to restrain the pro-slavery efforts of their migrated countrymen" to capture Indiana and Illinois. Refuting the myth of Jeffersonian liberalism on slavery, McColley concludes that, along with the axioms of democratic republicanism, the Virginians worked out and transmitted "the model theory of American racism."

Continuing this line of reinterpretation, Richard H. Brown's "The

Missouri Crisis, Slavery, and the Politics of Jacksonianism" [23] contends that "the central fact" of American history from the inauguration of Washington until the Civil War was that the "South was in the saddle of national politics." From the outset, southern participation in national affairs was governed by "one single compelling idea" which united all Southerners despite their diverse social and economic interests. This was that the institution of slavery, whatever its faults, should not be handled by outsiders. "The presence of the slave was a fact too critical, too sensitive, too perilous for all of Southern society to be dealt with by those not directly affected. Slavery must remain a Southern question." Like Lynd, Brown emphasizes that slavery and southern power underlay the framing of a constitutional government with limited powers. Then, in the 1790s, Jefferson and Madison sought to protect that Constitution from "change by interpretation" by creating a national party based mainly on an alliance of Virginia planters and New York farmers whose requirements from the federal government were then minimal. This formula for political ascendancy converted a southern minority into a national majority and assured slave-state pre-eminence until the Civil War.

The Jeffersonian Republican success was also, however, its undoing. As the Federalists declined, the Republicans became more nationalistic, adopted some Federalist programs, and became an "amalgamated" party of the whole nation. As a result, they ceased to be responsive to any particular elements in their constituency and became unresponsive to the South. This, according to Brown, invited the Missouri Crisis of 1819–20 over whether the federal government had the constitutional power to exclude slavery from the territories. Southerners believed that this debate caused the Denmark Vesey slave revolt conspiracy in Charleston, South Carolina, in 1822.

These crises led to an urgent and finally successful attempt to revive the old Jeffersonian party with its political formula for southern control. The new Jacksonian coalition rested on slave-owning planters of the older South and the newer Southwest *and* "plain Republican" farmers and planters of New York and Pennsylvania. It depended upon the election of presidents who were either Southerners with a western image (Jackson and Polk), or northern "doughfaces" with southern principles (Van Buren, Pierce, Buchanan). As before, the price of southern participation was, first, the suppression of any discussion of slavery which might endanger southern interests by forcing the South into a permanent minority in the Union; second, it was necessary to interpret the Constitution more strictly, so that the federal government would never gain the power to deal with slavery.

According to Brown, the architect of the new Democratic party was Martin Van Buren. Combining Jackson's western constituency of 1824 with the old Republican voting strength of the South Atlantic states and his own New York, he engineered Jackson's victory in 1828. The two most important examples of Van Buren's policy were the veto of the Maysville Road Bill, which provided federal support for a local Kentucky section of a national highway, and the destruction of the Bank of the United States. Despite their economic consequences, these two vetoes were *political* measures designed to consolidate the new party on the basis of strict constitutional construction. In sum, Van Buren created a party predicated on limited government powers over both the economy and slavery, but at the same time flexible enough to serve the interests of its constituents.

In contrast to Van Buren's essentially political solution stood Calhoun's constitutional formula for southern control—the nullification of obnoxious measures. However, Calhoun's remedy was defeated by Van Buren's, which offered more vote control, albeit less theory. In any event, after 1844 the growth of northern anti-slavery and free-soil sentiment forced Van Buren to relinquish his leadership and compelled the Democratic party to sustain itself solely by territorial expansion.

William W. Freehling's *Prelude to Civil War: The Nullification Controversy in South Carolina, 1816–1836*,[24] brilliantly demonstrates that suppression of debate on slavery was crucial to the politics of the Jackson period. In the 1820s, most South Carolinians were experiencing their first and longest economic depression, while in the low-lying parts of the state there was great nervousness about recurrent malaria epidemics. In 1822, Denmark Vesey's slave conspiracy severely distressed most low-country planters. Then, in 1831, Nat Turner's Virginia slave revolt frightened whites all over South Carolina. To these causes of unease, Freehling adds the feeling of guilt among Southerners resulting from the discrepancy between Jefferson's declaration that "all men are created equal" and the existence of slavery, as well as from the contrast between the harsh reality and the myth of the mellow plantation.

These tensions in the Carolina mind and economy produced recurrent uproars over slavery by coastal Carolinians in the 1820s. Partly for economic purposes, but mainly to win constitutional protection against the abolition challenge, they advocated tariff nullification. Freehling contends that though the anti-slavery crusade remained "relatively undeveloped" and a "distant threat" in 1832, Carolina politicians responded "hysterically" to slavery and delivered fire-eating harangues at any mention of abolition. They decided to fight the abolitionists indirectly by fighting against the tariff. "Put in simple terms, the nullification crusade was produced by two acute problems: protective tariffs and slavery agitation," which "had long since intermeshed in a single pattern of majority tyranny" over the state.

For various reasons, other states did not follow South Carolina down the road to nullification. In the late 1820s, most other southern regions were either accustomed to hard times, were enjoying economic prosperity, or were not so distressed by tariffs. Regions possessing a less concentrated Negro population were less tense about slave revolts, had less experience with slave conspiracies, and were not so worried about abolitionists. Finally, other regions lacked the close relationships between the coast and the interior which helped to inflame citizens of these regions in South Carolina.

Nullifiers, then, considered protective tariffs not only an inherently onerous economic burden but also an integral part of a pattern of sectional exploitation which would lead to slave revolts, colonization schemes, and ultimately the abolition of slavery. The nullification impulse was both a result of the severe pecuniary distress which afflicted many Carolinians in the 1820s and an expression of the anxiety, surrounding the discussion of slavery in South Carolina. . . . Depressed economically, frightened by recurrent slave conspiracies, disturbed by nagging qualms about slavery, threatened by rising worldwide moral condemnation, South Carolinians had every reason to dread an encounter with the abolitionists. To leading Carolina nullifiers, the chance of avoiding the encounter, lowering the tariff, and winning permanent security seemed worth the risk of provoking an American civil war.[25]

Since the relationship between slavery and the coming of the Civil War has always been clear, even to the traditionalists and revisionists, the events of the 1840s and 1850s have not yet received as much attention from the new scholars as those of the earlier decades. It is generally held that slavery was, as Kenneth Stampp writes, "above all a labor system" vital to southern economic development at least from 1815 on. Since, however, slavery was also a system of race relations and a way of life for most Southerners, it was unthinkable that slave-owners and their supporters would willingly abandon slavery without a struggle. The Civil War came when southerners believed that their "peculiar institutions" were no longer safe within the Union.

If the broad outlines of the coming of the war are clear, the new scholars have nonetheless reconsidered some significant themes. One of these is abolitionism and the politics of the anti-slavery movement during the last ante-bellum decades. Here the general trend has been to refurbish the image of the abolitionists. They are no longer seen as fanatics, neurotics, and impractical reformers, but as sincere humanitarians responding to real injustices in American society and to what appeared to be the strengthening of the "slave power conspiracy." Though no one has yet transcended the "good guy–bad guy" dichotomy which plagues abolitionist historiography in order to see abolitionism as a case study in American reformism, the neo-revisionists have at least shown that many anti-slavery men were practical politicians.[26]

Another theme reconsidered by the new scholars is that "historical perennial," the profitability of slavery, which bears greatly on the importance of slavery to American economic development. Alfred H. Conrad's and John R. Meyer's "The Economics of Slavery in the Ante-Bellum South" [27] argues persuasively that most slave-owners could expect to receive a reasonable rate of return on their investment in slaves. Not only was it profitable to grow cotton with slave labor, but slavery's intermediate product—marketable human offspring—could be efficiently sold to newer regions of the South. Similarly, Douglass North's *Economic Growth of the United States, 1790–1860* [28] demonstrates that slave-grown cotton exports were the main stimulus to economic growth during most of the antebellum period, despite the expansion of the domestic market. Slavery was therefore essential to the rapid "take-off" of the national economy. If this is true, then there was good reason for the South's being, as Richard Brown says, in the saddle of national politics.

The neo-revisionists have also re-examined the relationship between slavery and territorial expansionism. Rejecting traditional interpretations,[29] Eugene Genovese's *Political Economy of Slavery* [30] holds that slavery had not reached its natural geographical limits of expansion of cotton planting. Since bondsmen could perform a variety of tasks, slavery could easily have spread into the mining regions of Mexico and California, and slave-owners were aware of these prospects. Moreover, Southerners attempted to annex Cuba to extend sugar production, to obtain new slaves, and to increase their political power. If northern Free Soilers had not interfered, slaves might also have been used in hemp production in eastern Kansas, in California agriculture, and (according to my own research) in western lumbering, and transcontinental and isthmus railroad-building. To the post-revisionists, the traditionalist view that the territorial issue of the 1850s was phony is therefore dubious; the North fought the Civil War in part to scotch southern and slavery expansion.

Unlike the ante-bellum period, the post-bellum period has hardly been touched by the new scholars. However, C. Vann Woodward's interpretation of the origins of segregation and disfranchisement has come under close scrutiny. Woodward holds that from the 1870s to the 1890s there was rough legal equality between the races. Segregation, disfranchisement, and discrimination against Negroes stemmed not from Reconstruction, but from the politics of the 1890s. In that decade, southern white conservatives responded to the Populist threat of a new coalition between Negro and white farmers and workers. This alliance rested on radical anti-monopolism and political equality of the races which raised the spectres of racial miscegenation and "nigger rule." To defeat Populism, Negroes were first disfranchised and then socially segregated in the period from 1890 to 1910.

Woodward's account of the origins of segregation has been implicitly challenged by many recent studies. Leon Litwack's *North of Slavery: the Negro in the Free States, 1790–1860*,[31] for example, demonstrates that, before the Civil War, racist bigotry had already pervaded every sector of northern society. Except for a handful of equalitarian abolitionists, most northerners treated free Negroes with contempt. Segregation originated in ante-bellum northern cities and most "free states" disfranchised Negroes before 1861. Similarly, Richard Wade's *Slavery in the Cities: the South, 1820–1860* argues that segregation of free Negroes and of slaves was also beginning in the South's largest cities before the Civil War:

> Even before slavery had been abolished, a system of segregation had grown up in the cities. Indeed, the whites thought some such arrangement was necessary if they were to sustain their traditional supremacy over the Negroes. . . . Segregation sorted people out by race, established a public etiquette for their conduct, and created social distance where there was proximity. Urban circumstances produced this system long before the destruction of slavery itself.[32]

Finally, Joel Williamson's *After Slavery: the Negro in South Carolina During Reconstruction, 1861–1877* holds that the "physical separation of the races was the most revolutionary change in relations between whites and Negroes" during Reconstruction. Williamson concedes that "formal discrimination" was not practiced by railway operators, for example, but he nonetheless strongly contends that "unofficial racial separation did occur on a large scale." In any event, he concludes:

> The real separation [of the races] was not that duo-chromatic order that prevailed on streetcars and trains, or in restaurants, saloons, and cemeteries. The real color line lived in the minds of individuals of each race, and it had achieved full growth even before freedom for the Negro was born. . . . Well before the end of Reconstruction, this mental pattern was fixed . . . and South Carolina had become, in reality, two communities—one white and the other Negro.[33]

Clearly, then, segregation and disfranchisement of Negroes did not begin suddenly in the 1890s; racism has long roots in nineteenth-century northern and southern society.

In conclusion then, it can be seen that the contours of the new Negro history have already been delineated, and that the works of the new scholars are leaving their mark. Slavery was an integral institution in American political and economic life at least as early as the 1780s. An important sectional conflict characterized American politics long before the 1840s. Slavery and the position of the Negro seemed to determine important political decisions and party formations from the framing of the Constitution until the Civil War. The abolitionist movement therefore should be taken more seriously; it should be understood that racism was characteristic of American society from its early beginnings. The proper role of the freedmen was as central an issue from Reconstruction until the early twentieth century as it is in the 1960s. In short, the Negro is becoming recognized as a key to American history and one of its most distinctive themes.

NOTES

1. Their chief spokesmen were Ulrich B. Phillips, whose *American Negro Slavery* (New York: D. Appleton and Company, 1918) was the first systematic study of slavery, and William A. Dunning and his students, who undertook research into the Reconstruction era. Since Phillips was a Louisianian and Dunning a Northerner, the traditionalist scope was national, not peculiarly southern.

2. Merl R. Eppse, *The Negro, Too, in American History* (Chicago: National Educational Publishing Company, 1939). Racism still pervades elementary school, high school, and college textbooks in most states—North and South. As late as 1947, E. Merton Coulter could still publish a frankly racist study of the *South During Reconstruction* (Baton Rouge: Louisiana State University Press, 1947) for the otherwise excellent "History of the South" series.

3. Alrutheus A. Taylor, *The Negro in South Carolina During the Reconstruction* (Washington: Association for the Study of Negro Life and History, 1924); *The Negro in the Reconstruction of Virginia* (Washington: Association for the Study of Negro Life and History, 1926); *The Negro in Tennessee, 1865–1880* (Washington: The Associated Publishers, 1941).

4. E. Franklin Frazier, *The Negro Family* (Chicago: University of Chicago Press, 1939); *Black Bourgeoisie* (Glencoe, Ill.: The Free Press, 1957).

5. Gunnar Myrdal, *An American Dilemma* (New York: Harper and Brothers, 1944).

6. W.E.B. DuBois, *Black Reconstruction* (New York: Harcourt, Brace and Company, 1935).

7. Herbert Aptheker, *American Negro Slave Revolts* (New York: Columbia University Press, 1943).

8. Philip Foner, ed., *The Writings of Frederick Douglass* (New York: International Publishers, 1955).

9. Charles S. Syndor, *Slavery in Mississippi* (Washington: D. Appleton-Century Company, 1933).

10. Kenneth M. Stampp, *The Peculiar Institution* (New York: Vintage Books, 1957).

11. Stanley Elkins, *Slavery* (Chicago: University of Chicago Press, 1959).

12. Vernon Lane Wharton, *The Negro in Mississippi, 1865–1890* (Chapel Hill: University of North Carolina Press, 1947).

13. Francis B. Simkins and Robert H. Woody, *South Carolina During Reconstruction* (Chapel Hill: University of North Carolina Press, 1932).

14. C. Vann Woodward, *The Strange Career of Jim Crow* (New York: Oxford University Press, 1955, 1967); *Tom Watson, Agrarian Rebel* (New York: Rinehart, 1938); and *The Origins of the New South* (Baton Rouge: Louisiana State University Press, 1951).

15. E. David Cronon's *Black Moses: The Story of Marcus Garvey* (Madison: University of Wisconsin Press, 1955), is one of the few recent biographies which contribute to an understanding of Negro militancy and black nationalism.

16. Richard Bardolph, *The Negro Vanguard* (New York: Holt, Rinehart & Winston, 1959).

17. August Meier, *Negro Thought in America, 1880–1915* (Ann Arbor: University of Michigan Press, 1963).

18. Quoted in *Political Affairs,* the "theoretical journal of the Communist Party, U.S.A.," March 1966. Aptheker's hero-worship was also apparent in his paper on the Niagara Movement, in which DuBois participated, delivered at the annual meeting of the Organization of American Historians, Cincinnati, April 1966. Despite Aptheker's possession of DuBois's papers, his presentation made no new contribution to scholarship on black movements, but was rather a sermon on the infallibility of the "good Doctor."

19. Charles F. Kellogg, *NAACP: A History of the National Association for the Advancement of Colored People* (Baltimore: Johns Hopkins Press, 1967).

20. Benjamin Quarles, *The Negro in the American Revolution* (Chapel Hill: University of North Carolina Press, 1961); *The Negro in the Civil War* (Boston: Little, Brown & Company, 1953).

21. *Political Science Quarterly* 81 (1966): 225–50; complemented by Lynd's earlier formulation, "The Abolitionist Critique of the United States Constitution," in Martin Duberman, ed., *The Antislavery Vanguard* (Princeton, N.J.: Princeton University Press, 1965), and his "Turner, Beard, and Slavery," *Journal of Negro History* 48 (1963): 235–50.

22. Robert McColley, *Slavery and Jeffersonian Virginia* (Urbana, Ill.: University of Illinois Press, 1964).

23. *South Atlantic Quarterly* 65 (Winter 1965–1966): 55–72.

24. William W. Freehling, *Prelude to Civil War: The Nullification Controversy in South Carolina, 1816–1836* (New York: Harper & Row, 1966).

25. Ibid., p. 259.

26. See, for example, the essays in Martin Duberman, ed., *The Antislavery Vanguard* (Princeton, N.J.: Princeton University Press, 1965); James McPherson, *The Struggle for Equality* (Princeton, N.J.: Princeton University Press, 1964); the excellent biography by Richard Sewell, *John P. Hale and the Politics of Abolition* (Cambridge: Harvard University Press, 1965); and Dwight L. Dumond, *Antislavery* (Ann Arbor: University of Michigan Press, 1961).

27. *Journal of Political Economy* 66 (1958): 95–122. Cf. Robert W. Fogel and Stanley L. Engerman, eds., *The Reinterpretation of American Economic History* (New York: Harper & Row, 1971), introduction to part VII on the economics of slavery.

28. Douglass North, *Economic Growth of the United States, 1790–1860* (Englewood Cliffs, N.J.: Prentice-Hall, 1961).

29. For example, C. W. Ramsdell, "The Natural Limits of Slavery Expansion," *Mississippi Valley Historical Review* 16 (1929): 151–71.

30. Eugene Genovese, *Political Economy of Slavery* (New York: Pantheon Books, 1965).

31. Leon Litwack, *North of Slavery: The Negro in the Free States, 1790–1860* (Chicago: University of Chicago Press, 1965).

32. Richard Wade, *Slavery in the Cities: The South 1820–1860* (New York: Oxford University Press, 1964).

33. Joel Williamson, *After Slavery: The Negro in South Carolina During Reconstruction, 1861–1877* (Chapel Hill: University of North Carolina Press, 1965).

2. JOHN HENRIK CLARKE, The Meaning of Black History (1971)*

John Henrik Clarke, presently an associate editor of *Freedomways*, is one of the most active spokesmen for a new black consciousness. In addition to his work as a historian, Clarke has written numerous short stories and is editor of several anthologies on Black America, including one on Malcolm X. In this essay, Clarke suggests a reinterpretation of black history and urges scholars to combine knowledge with activism. Students interested in this viewpoint should also consult Vincent Harding's incisive essay entitled "Beyond Chaos" in the first volume of *Amistad*.

In many ways all history is a current event that relates to the past, the present and subsequently the future. All history teaching, if it is done with honesty and imagination, reflects this fact and shows the influences of history on our day-by-day lives. The demand for Black history is really a demand for self definition, direction, and a decision-making role in the structure of power that determines the destiny of men and nations. When a people know who they are, they will know what they have to do to make themselves free. A people who have found themselves can not be easily conquered. In the book, *Tom-Tom*, the writer John W. Vandercook has said, "A race is like a man, until it uses its own talents, takes pride in its own history and loves its own memories, it can never fulfill itself completely."

To some extent, Black history is a restoration project. The honest teachers of this subject are using history to show Black people how to apply their talent more creatively as an instrument of their liberation. In doing this, a new concept of history is being developed. The intent is to move Black people beyond the "black and beautiful" stage where they are now, and project them into the more important area of nation building. In this country, the proving ground for nation building is the Black community. The institutions in this collective community must be controlled on all levels by Black people. The role of history and the history teacher in

* John Henrik Clarke, "The Meaning of Black History," *Black World* (February 1971): 27–36. Copyright February 1971 by Black World. Reprinted by permission.

this restoration project is to give Black people a sense of pride in their past and memories that they can love and respect. The fulfillment will be in the total restoration of the manhood and nationhood of Black people, wherever they live on this earth.

The people of African descent are not entering history for the first time, but are reentering the mainstream of history. They have never left the mainstream as an influence in history, but now they are seeking a decision-making position in world history and in world direction. This is beginning to annoy quite a number of people, but I think we should understand that the people of African descent are not young people in the world, not by any stretch of the imagination . . . they are an old people and, perhaps, the oldest people in the world.

I remember a few years ago, speaking to one of the Jewish groups that might be called conservative. I had worked out a very good lecture and, no doubt, it was the wrong lecture and the wrong audience, because the talk was on the historical relationship of the Jewish people to the African people. They seemed rather shocked that we have had a very long and a very good relationship in history; we have not always been in opposite camps at each other's throats. We have met many times on the crossroads of history and we have complemented each other. My point in the lecture that surely wasn't appreciated was that, out of this past, we can build a present relationship that is meaningful, one that can contribute to the new age of man, principally because we are not strangers. Like all peoples, we have had our Golden Ages, our ups, our downs, our Renaissances . . . in fact, the Italian Renaissance is not as Italian as one might think it is when examined carefully. Africans had some influence on this Renaissance.

The relationship between the Africans and the Jews started long before this time. It also started before the beautiful romance between King Solomon and the remarkable Ethiopian Queen named Makeda, who is better known as the Queen of Sheba. The Jewish leader, Moses, who was born in Africa, married an Ethiopian woman named Zeporah. There is a strong relationship between the teachings in the early Egyptian books called "The Mysteries" and the Hebrew religion. During the Roman occupation of North Africa, a small colony of Jews went to live in the Kingdom of ancient Ghana. They lived peacefully in this Black nation until the year 770 A.D., when internal pressure within Ghana forced most of them to return to Europe.

The Africans who played a major role in the conquest of Spain in 711 A.D. took a large number of North African Jews into Spain. They stayed in Spain and participated in the cultural and commercial life of that country until the beginning of the rise of modern Europe and the expulsion of the Moors in the year 1492.

I have been alluding to these facts merely to illustrate, again, that Black people are very old in the world and their history relates, in some way, to all of the world's peoples.

In these remarks, I am going to see if I can address myself to how a whole people got lost from the respectful commentary of human history, and how, at the present juncture of history, they are finding themselves and demanding things it was never dreamed they would demand. These demands and this self-assertion are the basis of a whole lot of problems that need not be problems.

Now let us look at how and why the slave trade came, because it was during this period that the African people were lost, consciously, from the commentary of human history. It is necessary to study something other than the slave trade as such. As a teacher, I never teach this area of history and call it the slave trade, because this is not what it's about. My subject is, "The Consequences of the Second Rise of Europe." Until we study the consequences of the second rise of Europe, we are not going to understand current events, because during the first rise of Europe, after the first decline of Africa, the European, the Greco-Roman, was not a racist. There were many African Emperors of Rome. This might come as a complete surprise. There were many African fathers of the early church. There were many African leaders of Islam, and the original conqueror of Spain was a black African, not an Arab, Berber or Moor, but a black African who came from inner Africa.

My point is that we have played a major role in human history, in the shaping of the destiny of man before the coming of the slave trade. To understand what did happen to us, it is necessary to understand once more certain things that happened in Europe between the decline of Rome in the seventh and eighth century and the resurgence of Europe in the fifteenth and sixteenth century. When Europe reasserted itself and reentered the world and began to expand into the broader world, Europe had endured a number of family quarrels; and not only did Europeans have no attachment to the non-white world, Europeans also didn't have too much of a sentimental attachment to each other. The Crusades, the famines, the internal disputes within the Church—all of this had drained Europe of sentiment. Thus, the decline in the agricultural output and the need to project on the broader world in search of something to eat.

There was Henry the Navigator, who never went to sea, incidentally. He began to send his captains down the west coast of Africa in search of gold and new allies. When Columbus stumbled quite by accident upon what is called the New World and introduced the idea of using African labor to develop the New World, this came at a time when the

Africans had had a number of family disputes which had weakened the structure of the African countries.

Then the Berbers, the Moors, and settlements of Arabs came back into Africa. As Africans with no sentimental attachment to Africa, they began to prey upon the independent states in East Africa and West Africa. Finally, they broke the structure of these states and made Africa vulnerable to the slave trade.

Europe needed a rationale to oppress that many people, to destroy civilizations that were old before Europe was born, to destroy a people who had contributed to the early development of Europe, so they turned to the Church, and the Church obliged them. In 1455, Portugal and Spain went to Pope Callistus III to settle a dispute. The Pope told them: "As for the lines of demarkation, you take the East and you take the West." They didn't quite know who was supposed to take what, because the Pope's gestures were somewhat ambiguous. Finally, Spain began to gravitate toward the West and Portugal toward the East, and Europe began to expand into the broader world.

Another fight ensued in 1493, and they went back to the Pope. This time, Alexander VI said, "You are both authorized to reduce to servitude all infidel peoples." It just so happened that most of the so-called infidels were non-white people. Europe had its rationale now to go out and subjugate most of the people of the world.

You cannot subjugate a man and recognize his humanity, his history and his personality; so, systematically, you must take these things away from him. You begin by telling lies about this man's role in history. You deny that from time immemorial you married into royal families of the very people that you are now enslaving; you deny that you accepted their scholars and gave them homage in the universities of your country. You now set out to prove that they never had any universities, they never had any scholars, they never had any kings, they never had any structured country or any country that's worthy of respect.

It is necessary to take this man out of consideration as a fellow and as a brother under humanity, because, if you acknowledge a man as being totally a man, served by the same humanity that you are served by, no matter what his color may be, you are saying, "That man is an extension of me"; and if the man is an extension of you, there is nothing you can do to him lest you do it to yourself. So, the idea of oppressing people is first to reduce them to non-men, to insignificant cipher statistics; and this is how African history was lost. Many African history books were gone through and stripped of everything complimentary to Africa; many Africans were turned white. All of a sudden, we see many Africans who were Black in history portrayed in the movies as white. The mass media began, when they came into being, to contribute greatly to reading the African out of human history as a hero.

Let me mention a recent example. In a silly movie called "Khartoum," the leader of the rebellion in the Sudan is a babbling Arab and an idiot. In real life, he was a black African, a Dongula from the Sudan, not an Arab at all. At issue was a people of the Moslem faith fighting a war against England. The people of the Sudan have never been Arabs and are not Arabs now. I say this not to degrade or denigrate the Arab in the slightest. My point is that when an African rises to great magnificence he is depicted as anything but black African. He has to be something else; he has to be Hamitic or Semitic, and these are linguistic terms, not ethnic terms. It took evil genius to set this trend in motion and to set the world up the way it is now. You will not understand it or our present conflict until you understand the rise of a monster called racism.

Nature created no races. Nature created people and people did not refer to themselves as belonging to a race until the rise of the colonial system and of the slave trade concurrent with that system. People belonged to groups and religions, they belonged to clans, they belonged to regional groupings, they belonged to blacksmith guilds and carvers' guilds, but they did not belong to a race in the general sense that we are now talking about. This concept was created to justify European colonialism. I am not saying that prejudice is a European invention but I am saying the Europeans began prejudice based solely on color of the skin. The European could not acknowledge the role that the African played in the making of the "New World."

But for the exploitation of African labor, the capitalist system could never have emerged the way it did. The first large-scale investment in anything—this inter-continental investment—was investment in the slave trade. This was an investment touching three continents, South America, Europe and Africa. The development of embryo technology, principally the gun, gave the Europeans an advantage over most of the peoples in the world.

What we are witnessing now is a people who have been systematically read out of history demanding reentry into history and demanding compensation. This demand is at the basis of so much of the dissension between Black people and white people. And white people, who have lived so long thinking and seeing Black people in an oppressed servant role, are not ready to see them in a decision-making position affecting paramount change and making the whole new Age of Man.

The reaction of white people is somewhat tragic, because they are throwing away the best possible ally they could ever have—this newly emerged man reentering the mainstream of history and demanding, at the very base, the respect for his dignity and his stakes as a human being. This reaction contributes to the conflict in the school system and is part of what is going into the cry for Black history and Black power—which is somewhat "old hat" with us. A negative reaction to this cry proves how little is known about the fight Black people had in the latter part of the eighteenth and the whole nineteenth century to regain our total self and to restore the history that has been taken away from us.

This is not a new fight at all, and Black power is neutral; but we put a word *Black* together with *power* and start frightening people. Then we say, "Well, now, that's a new weapon so we might as well use this new weapon." But David Walker, in his dramatic "appeal" to the colored people of the world in 1829, laid the theoretical basis for what is being called Black power. And the Black petitioners of the latter eighteenth and throughout the nineteenth century, up to the Civil War, were demanding the same thing many of our youth are demanding today—that we must be treated and regarded as total human beings.

We seem to have come to some kind of crossroads in our relationship because of this demand, and yet the demand is not monumental at all. The demand is that when a Black child goes to school and reads about heroes, he be able to read something about heroes of his own people who look like him.

It might break a lot of people's hearts to know that America has been set up as a white Anglo-Saxon Protestant country. A careful scrutiny of the founding fathers, nearly all slave-holders, and of the direction of America, shows this is what this country was intended to be. It was intended to be a haven for the white Anglo-Saxon Protestant and the people not falling into this category seem to have upset the basic pattern of the country.

I tend to believe that the American promise was made only to that branch of America, and that this fact is what makes America such a contradiction at this juncture in history—because this is a multi-ethnic nation. It is a multi-ethnic nation that has never made the best use of the fact that it is multi-ethnic. It is throwing away its golden opportunity in the world. Because this country ethnically relates to most of the people in the world, we have some kind of calling card on most of the people of the world, and we will be in serious trouble so long as some Americans keep thinking of America as not only a white nation, but as a white Anglo-Saxon Protestant nation. This description is not true; and if it ever was, it is no more.

America must bring all of these components together into some kind of concerted effort that can be used for America's projection on the world; and that projection cannot be solely under our present economic system, which is not good for most of the people in the world. Africans have no money to buy out gold mines and oil fields! They have no choice but to nationalize; and no matter what I personally believe, there is absolutely no road for them other than socialism—and I am *not* speaking of communism. I am speaking of a socialism that would be based on the best socialist values of an African communal society. If this leads them to cooperation with communism, it is a decision for them to make, but that is not really what I am talking about.

Let me see if I can conclude this by explaining what, then, is the meaning of African history and Afro-American history today.

The young Black students demanding Black Studies Programs, even Black dormitories, are saying to America and the world, "I am a total human being and I want the respect that is due a total human being." This being the case, one might wonder, why are they demanding Black dormitories when their families fought for generations to get integrated dormitories? They are not demanding Black dormitories in the general sense. They need to go through a period when something is being done on their terms. They live in a world and a country where everything is being done on somebody else's terms. They want to make the decision. Now, once they are given the Black dormitory, chances are most of them won't even live in it; but they would have participated in the decision-making apparatus.

I remember the case of two girl students in one of the smaller colleges in New England, an Afro-American student and a white student, who were roommates. In jest, the Afro-American girl put on the door, "In this room lives one piece of white trash and black me." She was kidding. The white girl, a nice, naive, middle-class girl said, "Why would you do this? I accept you, I like you." The Black girl answered, "Who gave you permission to like me? You are under consideration as a friend and I haven't finished deliberating on it. I'll let you know whether you'll be accepted or not."

What are they doing? Reversing the procedure. They want to make the decision about whether you should or should not be their friend —because decision-making is adulthood and this is the basis of what they are claiming. It is not really monumental at all.

A people in search of themselves and their history are not looking for concessions—concessions can always be taken away. They are seeking acknowledgement of their inalienable right to certain things, the right to make mistakes and to correct them and to suffer from them—even this.

We are going to enter the mainstream of history. We are going to enter it as some of the decision-makers. I am not saying all of these decisions are going to be good. I am saying that, in the light of some of the decisions made by others, they probably could not be worse.

The role of history in the life of a people is to give them a kind of measurement as to where they have been and where they are; and, if they understand history correctly, they will have some definition of what they still must be. At this juncture in history, this is the major search of the Black people—finding out where they have been, where they are and what they still must be. This search is going to cause even more trouble before it is finally settled, but it can be settled comparatively easily. If others are to accept our total human beingness, then they must accept the fact that our good is equal to their good and, at least sometimes, our bad is equal to their bad.

And what does this prove? Nothing more or less than that we are human beings—and, as human beings, we are now demanding the right to reenter world history, and this is what most of the fight is all about. The tragedy of the fight is that *it need not be a fight at all.*

Let me see whether I can conclude this definition of Black history by calling attention to an aspect of the Black-white conflict that is generally neglected. When the Europeans began to reemerge on the world scene in the fifteenth and sixteenth centuries, they colonized most of the world. Then, in their new institutions, they colonized the interpretation of history. They began to interpret history as though the world waited in darkness for them to bring the light. Non-European scholars, and non-European people in general, are now engaged in a fight to decolonize history. This is what the Black scholars mean when they demand consideration from an Afro-centric view of history. In many ways this is history told from the point of view of the victims—in essence, the other side of the story. This is the basis of the fight between the Black and white scholars that split the African Studies Association into two factions that developed into two separate organizations; the African Studies Association, ASA, and the African Heritage Studies Association, AHSA. Because there is still some confusion about what AHSA is and what it hopes to accomplish, I would like to conclude by calling attention to its ideological framework:

"The intent of the African Heritage Studies Association is to use African History to effect a world union of African people. This association of scholars of African descent is committed to the preservation, interpretation and creative presentation of the historical and cultural heritage of African people both on the ancestral soil of Africa and in diaspora in the Americas and throughout the world. We interpret African history from a Pan-Africanist perspective that defines all Black people as an African people. We do not accept the arbitrary lines of geographical demarcations that were created to reflect colonialist spheres of influence. As scholar-activists, our program has as its objective the restoration of the cultural, economic and political life of African people, everywhere.

"In our ideological perspective, we are committed to taking the concept of Pan-Africanism into another dimension beyond its present meaning. We recognize the need for the cultural unity of the black peoples of the world, and we are committed to all sincere efforts that will make this unity a reality, but this is only the beginning. We know that there is no way to move a people from slavery to freedom and self-awareness without engaging in political expedience and revolutionary coalitions. As scholar-activists, our primary role is to define the historical currents relating to this action in such a manner that when this inevitable action occurs it can proceed with a maximum of involvement of the people and a minimum of confusion."

The essence of what our ideological perspective is, is contained in a recent poem, "On Pan-Africanism," by Carolyn F. Gerald, a young Afro-American poet, essayist and teacher. Mrs. Gerald says:

Pan-Africanism means an inner need in us which has finally surfaced on the world, after decades of fermenting in the ground. It's not the whole thing (though it has to be part of it) to fight with our black brothers in other parts of the world, to fight with our Bandung brothers all over the world (though the fight helps us to redefine ourselves) against a common, rampant, raging enemy. We'll keep looking at each other, examining each other's tools and comparing artifacts we make with them, testing them out on ourselves—each other. 'Til we annihilate our own suspicious moods and recognize the same images looking back at all of us from over the seas and the centuries.

In a word, the ideological perspective of AHSA will have to define the method and importance of putting a fragmented African people back together again, and in finding a way to heal the deep psychological wounds that are the legacy of the slave trade and the colonial system.

In our search for definition, unity and identity, we will have to evolve to Pan-Africanism and go far beyond that. It is not enough just to be united unless that unity has some meaning and some goal. We had a common heritage before and after the slave trade. We will have to make creative uses of this heritage. First we will have to define heritage itself.

Saunders Redding has said, in effect, that heritage is reflected in how a people have used their talent to create a history that gives them memories that they can respect and use to command the respect of other people. The ultimate purpose of heritage, and heritage teaching, is to use a people's talent to develop an awareness and a pride in themselves. This sense of identity is the stimulation for all of a people's honest and creative efforts. A people's relationship to their heritage is the same as the relationship of a child to its mother.

It will be our function as scholar-activists to put the components of our heritage together and weld it into an instrument of our liberation.

3. EARL E. THORPE, The Central Theme of Black History (1969)*

Earl E. Thorpe, professor of history at North Carolina Central University in Durham, is representative of that second generation of black professional scholars who followed in the footsteps of such pioneers of the Negro History Movement as Carter Woodson. A native of Durham, North Carolina and recipient of the Ph.D., from Ohio State University, Professor Thorpe has published widely in the field of Negro history including *Negro Historians in the United States*, and *The Mind of the Negro*. The following selection is the lead essay in his latest book, *The Central Theme of Black History*.

Black history may be defined as American history with the accent and emphasis on the point of view, attitude, and spirit of Afro-Americans, as well as on the events where Black Americans have been either the actors or the objects of action. Because Blacks have been forcibly kept in a subordinate degraded status, so that they have held a much smaller portion of America's wealth and power than their numbers would command, the point of view, attitude, and spirit of Black Americans are often different from those held by white Americans. In similar vein the history of the South or West is American history with a primary focus on the South or West, while North Carolina history is American history with a primary focus on North Carolina. The national—and even the international context—must not be lost.

Black history is that American history which, until the 1960s, largely was either viewed by White America with contempt and disdain or ignored altogether. This history was viewed and treated with contempt and disdain because Blacks themselves largely were so viewed and treated. It was ignored for this reason, plus the factor of psychological repression. Men tend either to deny or force out of consciousness the evil that they do. Much of Black history, then, is the story of the cruelties and inhumanities which a powerful White majority has inflicted on a defenseless Black minority.

* Earl E. Thorpe, *The Central Theme of Black History* (Durham, N.C.: Seeman Printery, 1969), chapter I, pp. 3–17. Reprinted by permission.

As fields of historical specialization, before 1945 Afro-American history and the history of Africa shared the common fate of not having won wide respectability and acceptance. In Service Center for Teachers of History Pamphlet No. 56, entitled, *African History*, Philip Curtin makes the statement: "Before the Second World War, most of the important contributions to African history were made by non-historians." Today, the fact that one can earn the Ph.D. with a specialty in African or Negro history is perhaps the strongest proof that these fields have won wide acceptance. This has been a source of both pleasure and concern for the pioneers in these fields. At annual meetings of the Association for the Study of Negro Life and History since 1945, lengthy discussions have centered about the question of whether the new acceptance of Negro history makes the work of the Association obsolete.

The black scholars who pioneered in establishing Afro-American history as a respectable field of historical endeavor had motivations which stemmed in large part, but by no means completely, from the condition and status of their race in this nation. Negro history is still studied, taught, and written, by both white and black Americans, in part for these reasons. But more than ever, today Black history is studied, taught, and written for the same reasons that all other fields of historical specialization are studied, taught, and written.

The forces of industrialization and urbanization which were changing the South during the 1920s and 30s caused Southerners to become more concerned than ever with the question of their identity. The blurring of regional lines led to a search for the central theme of southern history. The famous essay on this subject by Ulrich Bonnell Phillips has been supplemented with essays by C. Vann Woodward, David Potter, George B. Tindall, and others.

A similar situation exists where areas of historical specialization are concerned, for here, too, when one area comes close to others the problem of identity becomes more acute. Before 1945 there was less need for a discourse on the central theme of Black history. Today, this need exists.

The central theme of Black History is the quest of Afro-Americans for freedom, equality, and manhood.

It is not necessary to cite many instances where black spokesmen before 1865 used the words "freedom" or "liberty." "Free Negroes" and "freedom" were terms of pride. The first Negro newspaper was called *Freedom's Journal*. Recently the "Freedom Riders" had their busses burned as they made sacrifices in the cause of advancing civil rights. "Freedom" has been one of the black American's most often-used words.

Nor is it necessary to recite many instances before and since 1865 when black spokesmen used the word "equality." In Georgia, near the opening of this century, Negroes called one of their organizations "The Equal Rights League." Among other things and along with other groups, the National Association for the Advancement of Colored People has fought for equality before the law, while the National Urban League has sought equal employment opportunities. "Equality" has been among the words most often-used by black Americans. The same is true of the words "manhood" and "dignity."

The Negro male is unique in the extent to which he has been subjected to female authoritativeness in the home. Throughout the Caribbean area and in North America, the slave family was often a matriarchy. The husband was less respected by his wife and children because slavery prevented him from playing the role of a real authoritarian father-figure. Since 1865, due to low wages often paid Negro males, their wives have been forced to work more. Also, more Black households have had female heads than has been the case among white Americans.

In addition to the Negro male being subjected longer to female authoritativeness in the home, he has been subjected to unique forces of emasculation outside the home. Throughout the United States of America, ideology and practice in the Black-White relationship often have tried to deny the Black male the right and opportunity to be a man, to be aggressive, competitive, and to hold high positions.

Manhood means to have freedom, pride, and courage for maximum growth, self-expression, and personal and social health. Slavery was manhood's greatest antithesis.

A Kentucky court ruled in one case that "a slave by our code, is not a person, but a thing." But the law of slavery was ambiguous, and in practice there were both ambiguity and consistency. The main recognition of slaves as persons was in the area of crime—to protect the white man's life and property. In other words, it was largely for the white man's convenience that the black man was ever regarded or treated as a person.

A judge in a Georgia court stated in 1854:

. . . it is not true that slaves are only chattels, . . . and therefore, it is not true that it is not possible for them to be prisoners . . . The Penal Code has them in contemplation . . . in the first division . . . as persons capable of committing crimes; and as a consequence . . . as capable of becoming prisoners.

A few years later, another southern judge declared:

Because they are rational *human beings*, they are capable of committing crimes; and, in reference to acts which are crimes, are regarded as *persons*. Because they are *slaves*, they are . . . incapable of performing civil acts; and in reference to all such, they are *things*; not persons.

By law, a male slave was a more degraded being than a female slave, for the latter could be legally recognized as a mother. Since marriage between slaves had no legal standing, no offspring of slaves was ever recognized as having a legal father.

The speeches and other statements of black Americans reveal the extent to which they have felt that slavery and compulsory racial segregation and discrimination constituted denials of their manhood.

Concern about manhood is seen in Frederick Douglass's description of slaves as "beings deprived of every right, stripped of every privilege, ranked with four-footed beasts and creeping things, with no power over their own bodies and souls, . . . compelled to live in grossest ignorance, herded together . . . without marriage, without God, and without hope." The same is true of the statement by Douglass that nothing could keep the Negro satisfied in slavery. "Give him a *bad* master," Douglass declared, "and he aspires to a *good* master; give him a good master, and he wishes to become his *own* master."

In his famous 1829 appeal to the slaves, David Walker said several times to white America: "Treat us like men." At one point Walker added to this: "Treat us like men and we will like you more than we do now hate you." In an 1843 address to the slaves, made at the National Convention of Colored Citizens convening in New York, Henry Highland Garnet said many times: "You had far better all die—*die immediately*, than live slaves." To this he added, "Let your motto be resistance! *Resistance!* RESISTANCE!" Many times he recounted the evils borne by the slave. "In the name of God," Garnet cried, "We ask, are you men?"

The Fugitive Slave Law of 1850 so angered Charles Lenox Remond that he hoped for the breakup of the Union. Yet, in an 1854 speech before the New England Anti-Slavery Convention, Remond could say to white Americans: "Friends! God has made us men. If you will recognize us as such, we will conduct ourselves in a manner worthy of your regard and protection." Adult Black males long have resented being referred to as "boy," and of course, "a nigger" is not a man.

Although the Thirteenth Amendment to the federal Constitution lifted black Americans above the level of chattel, they were far from their goal of equality of status and opportunity.

In an article entitled, "The Relation of the Whites to the Negroes," published in the July, 1901 issue of *The Annals of the American Academy of Political and Social Science*, the president of North Carolina's white land-grant college expressed the long-prevailing views of many white Americans. Throughout a lengthy article this southern leader repeated such statements as the following: "The Negro is a child race . . . the Negro here is bound to be under the tutelage and control of the whites."

He continued:

> It would be a cruelty greater than slavery to leave this helpless race, this child race, to work out its own salvation . . . the Negro . . . must aim at white civilization, and must reach it through the support, guidance, and control of the white people among whom he lives.

At another point, this college president repeated once more: "The Negro race is a child race and must remain in tutelage for years to come." It is noteworthy here that, in such minds as this one, the Negro had progressed from being classified as chattel—along with horses, cows, and barns—to the classification of a *child*. How much good would it have done to point out to this college president that there never has been any such thing as child races and adult races—and that during the ninth, tenth, and eleventh centuries of the Christian era, highly civilized, independent, affluent black kingdoms and empires existed in Africa? How much good would it have done to tell this college president that he—and many other persons who thought as he did—were rationalizing to justify the degradation and exploitation of Black Americans?

The black educator, J. C. Price, declared: "Freedom implies manhood." In his 1903 book *The Souls of Black Folk,* W. E. B. DuBois attacked Booker T. Washington's philosophies of education and racial progress, and based his case on Negro manhood. He said that Washington's thinking overlooked the "higher aims of life" in favor of making money. On this, DuBois declared:

> If we make money the object of man-training, we shall develop money-makers but not necessarily men: if we make technical skill the object of education, we may possess artisans but not, in nature, men. Men we shall have only as we make manhood the object of the work of the schools.

In his last speech in Congress, delivered in 1900, George White, the last Black Reconstruction Congressman, urged his white colleagues to stop maligning the Afro-American and to help him in his efforts to rise. "Treat him as a man," White urged.

Restoring to health the crippled manhood of many Negro males has been a central concern of the so-called Black Muslims and other nationalist-oriented groups. When in his great eulogy at the funeral of Malcolm X, the actor Ossie Davis sought the central meaning of the life of this remarkable man, he found that meaning in Afro-American manhood. Davis declared: "Malcolm was our . . . living, black manhood!" But, as was Marcus Garvey before him, Elijah Muhammed was also a symbol of manhood to thousands of Black Americans. In this regard Malcolm and his mentor "made each other." The big objection which many young Blacks had with the non-violent philosophy of Martin Luther King, Jr. was their conviction that not to strike back when hit is unmanly. Even though many felt that Dr. King compromised when he would not strike back, because he fearlessly, willingly, and continuously, offered his body to be bruised, arrested, and murdered, he too, was a true symbol of manhood to millions of Black Americans.

Some persons contend that the young Black male of the ghetto participates in riots because he is not allowed enough other means of asserting his manhood. Consider also the "Deacons" of the South, and the Black Panthers, and their concern with Black manhood. Also, read Eldridge Cleaver's book, *Soul on Ice*, and note his great concern with Black manhood.

Even a superficial reading of the documents of Afro-American history reveals that the central theme of Black history is the quest of Black Americans for freedom, equality, and manhood. This can be further seen when one surveys the development and philosophy of Negro history.

Because of the experience of slavery, when George Washington Williams, the first serious student of Negro history, appeared in the early 1880s, white America already had produced such eminent historians as Francis Parkman, William H. Prescott, both Bancrofts, and Charles Gayarré. Among earlier Blacks who wrote history, such as William Cooper Nell, James W. C. Pennington, Robert Benjamin Lewis, James Theodore Holly, Joseph T. Wilson, and William Wells Brown, the latter had the greatest success.

Carter G. Woodson is often called the Father of Negro History. Woodson was born in Virginia, December 19, 1875. In 1912 he received the Ph.D. in history from Harvard University. Three years later, in Chicago, he started the Association for the Study of Negro Life and History. In 1916 he founded the *Journal of Negro History*. Later he started the *Negro History Bulletin* and the Associated Publishers. The latter firm published all of the many books written by Dr. Woodson, as well as numerous books on Negro history written by others. After a long life devoted almost exclusively to studying and popularizing Afro-American history, Dr. Woodson died in 1950. When Dr. Woodson launched the Negro History Movement one of his chief aims was to use history to replace ethnic shame with pride of race. By reminding young Blacks of men and women of their race who had made notable contributions, Dr. Woodson hoped to inspire them to high achievement. In 1923 he published a book entitled *The Mis-Education of the Negro*, in which he pointed out that modern culture has systematically exalted the white race and denigrated the colored races. Later W. E. B. DuBois echoed this theme in a book entitled, *Color and Democracy;* and still more recently this was the theme of E. Franklin Frazier's book, *Black Bourgeoisie*, and Nathan Hare's book entitled, *The Black Anglo-Saxons*. All of these scholars contend that their race has been brain-washed into a blind glorification of whiteness and European values, and that, as a consequence, Negroes not only lack sufficient pride in their own identity and potentialities, but they are overly imitative rather than creative. These scholars contend that there can be no fullness of maturity where there is insufficient self-acceptance.

In 1915 Dr. Woodson launched the modern Negro History Movement to correct the thinking of both races. Although over fifty years had passed since he began this great work, 1969 found the nation in the throes of a mighty effort to complete the task which he began.

In 1969 the movement of black consciousness or black awareness or black affirmation was one of the dominant concerns of colleges and universities, and this movement affected the materials and methods and other aspects of education in the elementary and high schools. Through painfully slow growth many Black Americans had acquired such a high level of pride and self-respect that they could no longer tolerate age-old indignities, insults, and obstacles to opportunity and achievement. As the nation learned during the 1960s in such places as Watts, Detroit, Newark, Orangeburg, and Memphis, involved here is considerable pain and agony for the total population. A central concern was the task of ending racism in the nation, and despite the danger of the assassin's bullet, no American could escape involvement in this task.

There are at least three basic reasons why the Negro History Movement began and continues to exist. The first is related to the fact that historical writing has been slow to shed its aristocratic tradition and bias of being almost exclusively concerned with the affairs of the ruling class or elite. Even after written history shifted from its aristocratic-political emphasis, it long neglected numerous segments of society. Thus it is that even today there is too little writing on the role of women in history. Thus it is, too, that the Negro History Movement came into being because Blacks, as human beings, had been left out of history. Dr. Woodson called the Association for the Study of Negro Life and History "the first systematic effort . . . to treat the records of the race scientifically and to publish the findings to the world." He gave this same justification for the founding of the *Journal of Negro History*, but, to this he added that the *Journal* was also dedicated to "the promotion of harmony between the races by acquainting the one with the other."

A second reason that the Negro History Movement came into being was the prominence of racial prejudice and stereotypes. To justify slavery and the system of degradation which followed emancipation, many people found it convenient to argue that Blacks belonged in a degraded social position because they were biologically inferior. A highly articulate and influential segment of Occidental civilization long has depicted Blacks as being emotional, impulsive, non-rational, childish creatures. This, of course, was the judgment which was pronounced by the ante-bellum slave owners and their apologists, and it has been the judgment of numerous racist social scientists who have written in more recent times. James Schouler, a noted American historian of the Nationalist School, described Negroes as being "a black servile race, sensuous, stupid, brutish, obedient . . . and childish." Ulrich Bonnell Phillips described the Negro as innately stupid, docile, submissive, unstable, and negligent. William A. Dunning, John Fiske, J. G. Randall, and Claude H. Van Tyne are also among the sizeable number of American historians who have depicted Blacks in this vein. Well-known is the manner in which such European writers as Houston Stewart Chamberlain and Count de Gobineau told the world that such was indeed the scientifically verified picture of the mentality, personality, and character of Blacks.

The Negro History Movement came into being to combat this image and to correct a serious sin of omission made by Caucasian historians. Disbelief of this so-called science, plus a desire to round out and complete the record, and to set the record straight, caused Drs. Woodson, DuBois, and other scholars to concentrate on studying and popularizing the truth about the Afro-American past.

In a multi-ethnic society like the United States of America, every public school and college graduate should know that when white Christian Europe was living in her Dark Ages, there were great Black kingdoms and empires and high civilizations in Sub-Sahara Africa; that the successful revolt of black people led by Toussaint l'Ouverture was a major reason why Napoleon I sold the Louisiana Territory to the United States. They should know that this nation probably would have lost its War for Independence if George Washington had stuck to his early decision not to use Black soldiers; that Andrew Jackson praised the service of the Black troops who fought in the battle of New Orleans; and that Abraham Lincoln admitted that the Union could not have been preserved without the service of the Black soldier. They should know that Black men and women have made outstanding contributions not only in music, entertainment, and sports, but in such fields as scholarship, literature, medicine, invention, and science—and they should know the names and achievements of some of these men and women.

They should know that in recent years a number of books have been published which not only revise old views and attitudes, but fill gaps in our knowledge of the history of this nation. Thus it is, for example, that there now exists a book on the Negro cowboy, and a volume on slavery in the cities. Thus it is, too, that there is, in Kenneth Stampp's book *The Peculiar Institution*, a more favorable view of the slave than that given in the books of Ulrich Bonnell Phillips. Also, Stampp, John Hope Franklin, and others, have caught the spirit of W. E. B. DuBois's book, *Black Reconstruction*, and have assaulted the old myth that black people and so-called Radical Republicans were responsible for all of the evils of a supposedly bleak and barren Reconstruction period.

History is the memory of mankind and all men need and use it. The question is not whether men know some history and use it, but rather how well they understand and use history. Especially are professional historians aware that, because everyone needs and uses history, everyone should not only seek a fuller understanding of it, but should be concerned that the history he knows is as free as possible from class, racial, religious, or national bias.

A third reason why the Negro History Movement came into being was to inspire Blacks to high achievement. People always have sought to inspire the young by telling them of the outstanding achievements of their ancestors. Evidence that leaders of the Negro History Movement hoped and sought to use history to bolster the race's self-esteem and self-confidence is abundant. This is seen in the fact that until around 1920, many histories of the race were largely biographies of outstanding Blacks. Writing in the year 1931, in a volume entitled, *The Negro Author*, Vernon Loggins observed this tendency. "A characteristic of much Negro history," he wrote, "is that the historian seems to arrive at a point beyond which he cannot go without bringing before us, in catalogue order, the main facts in the careers of illustrious members of his race." In the preface to his *History of the Negro Race in America*, George Washington Williams stated that one of his reasons for writing the book was to "incite the Negro people to greater effort in the struggle of citizenship and manhood." W. E. B. DuBois states that he studied and wrote history, in large part because he felt that to do so would help elevate the race through re-educating both black and white Americans toward a greater respect for the Black race. "The world was thinking wrong about race," he wrote, "because it did not know. The ultimate evil was stupidity. The cure for it was knowledge based on scientific investigation." While he is not generally known as an historian, Booker T. Washington produced a two-volume history of the race which has been widely read. In the preface, Washington expressed the hope that the book would "inspire" some Negro "to make himself useful and successful in the world."

Carter G. Woodson's life was devoted to correcting the false image of Blacks so that, as he put it, his race might "escape the awful fate of

becoming a negligible factor in the thought of the world." In the introduction to his little book entilted *The Mis-Education of the Negro*, Dr.
Woodson said: "When you control a man's thinking you do not have
to worry about his actions." One of Dr. Woodson's often-repeated
themes was the power and importance of faith and self-affirmation. In
effect, he said to his race: "Yes, your ancestors were slaves, but they had
a distinguished history *before America was discovered,* and even as slaves,
they never stopped loving freedom!" And in spite of the long dark night
of bondage, they still produced the poetry of Phyllis Wheatley, Paul
Laurence Dunbar, James Weldon Johnson, Margaret Walker, Gwendolyn
Brooks, and Langston Hughes; the scientific genius of Benjamin Banneker,
George Washington Carver, Daniel Hale Williams, Ernest Just, and
Charles Drew; the novels of Richard Wright, Ralph Ellison, Ann Petry,
and James Baldwin; and the eloquence and saintliness of Frederick
Douglass, Medgar Evers, and Martin Luther King, Jr. Dr. Woodson
reminded men that the Afro-American has been much more in history
than a hewer of wood and drawer of water, and that there is nothing
wrong with Black affirmation.

The popularity of certain aspects of history has some relationship to
social conditions and usefulness. When it was true that the sun never went
down on British soil, the history of England was more popular than it is
now. When President Franklin D. Roosevelt was promoting the "Good
Neighbor" policy, the history of Latin America acquired greater popularity. In 1969 the fact that the so-called Black Revolution was one of the
nation's major domestic issues presented an added reason why both white
and black Americans should look to Afro-American history for whatever
inspiration, mutual respect, and sense of direction they can acquire from
this history.

During the summer of 1967 Martin Luther King, Jr. announced
that his organization was newly committed to the Black History Movement. Such organizations and groups as the Congress of Racial Equality,
National Association for the Advancement of Colored People, municipal
and state boards of education, and colleges and universities made similar
commitments during that and subsequent years. These people knew
that history inspired such men as Winston Churchill, and that history
may be used to liberate as well as to oppress. These people knew that
many Blacks have been ashamed of their history—and of themselves—only
because degrading propaganda and mythology have been fed to them as
scientific truth, and they knew that even if accentuating the positive also
is sometimes myth and propaganda, it is better to inspire than to discourage.

Both black and white Americans need an acquaintance with Black history. Unless they, too, can endorse the Black History Movement, white Americans of this generation cannot have respect for black Americans of this generation. It is impossible to think positively about any group whose past you view negatively. The negative view can never predominate if we will always keep in mind that the central theme of Black history is the Afro-American's quest for freedom, equality, and manhood.

II

Black Americans and Africa

While scholars have always acknowledged the importance of European influences upon American life and culture, only a small number have recognized any traces of African heritage in the United States and, apart from the slave trade, most writers have ignored the long history of contact between black Africans and Afro-Americans. In emphasizing the odious slave trade, historians have been particularly fascinated with the infamous "middle passage," so called because it constituted the middle portion of the triangular trade from New England to Africa to the New World. The middle passage specifically involved the purchase of slaves along the African coast, their transportation across the Atlantic Ocean, and their sale in the Americas, generally in the islands of the Caribbean. At the height of this trade in the eighteenth century, profits were so enormous that Eric Williams, a black historian who is currently the Prime Minister of Trinidad, has dated the emergence of modern capitalism from wealth obtained from the slave system.

In addition to acting as an important stimulus to European development, black slavery provided a feasible solution to the European dilemma of how to exploit the rich natural resources of the New World in the shortest time possible and at a maximum profit. Black Africans proved better able to survive the rigors of slavery than the native American Indians because they had already acquired a greater immunity to European diseases through long years of contact with Europeans prior to 1500 and because they were more accustomed in West Africa to an organized system of plantation labor. The lack of any desire on the part of Africans to migrate voluntarily to the New World compelled slave dealers to resort to coercive methods for the forced removal of millions of black slaves.

While these aspects of the slave trade have been rather thoroughly documented by historians, other more significant facets have received less attention. Most curious of all, perhaps, is the absence of detailed studies of the effects of the trade upon Africa itself, the total number of slaves involved in the long history of this trade, and the specific areas from which most of the slaves were originally taken. In part, the failure of historians to deal thoroughly with these questions is due to the lack of reliable source material. Unfortunately, however, historians have been too prone to repeat the conjectures of earlier writers rather than to engage in the painstaking research necessary in order to make positive assertions. Consequently, both white and black historians have monotonously insisted that the vast majority of slaves came from the Guinea coast of Africa and that at least twenty-five million and possibly as many as sixty million were uprooted from their homeland during the course of this trade.

Among recent studies of the effects of this trade on Africa, there are two conflicting points of view. One group of historians, consisting largely of European liberals, has emphasized the gross injustices committed against black Africans by white Europeans, beginning with the Portuguese explorations of the fifteenth century and continuing through twentieth-century imperialism. They have reserved their harshest criticism for the slave trade. Not only was the New World demand for black slaves insatiable, but also the odious European traffic promoted vicious inter- as well as intra-rivalries which disrupted peaceful relations among African states. The inevitable results were a cycle of bloody warfare which depopulated West Africa and an unhealthy exchange of trade which robbed Africa of its youth and natural resources in return for manufactured articles which proved useless in developing the continent. This situation eventually left Africa vulnerable to European conquest in the nineteenth century. In addition to this harmful legacy, European imperialists were able, from profits obtained from black labor, to finance the exploitation of New World resources as well.

Although this interpretation was clearly more critical of than apologetic for imperialism, the European remained at the center of history. Not only did he control the course of his own history for greedy ends but he was equally the determinant of African destiny. Indeed the African emerged as little more than a pawn in the hands of white capitalists. This white perspective was evident despite the fact that historians acknowledged the inability of the Europeans, except in the Congo, to penetrate the African interior until the nineteenth century and the necessity for slave dealers to trade on African terms.

Recently a small but growing number of scholars have raised important questions about this orthodox interpretation of West African history. Viewing African history from inside the continent rather than from without, they have minimized the disruptive effects of European commerce and the enormous influences assigned to the traffic in firearms by earlier historians. Along with this tendency to downgrade European influences, they have insisted that the number of Africans transported to the New World was much smaller than previously believed. For example, Paul Curtin of the University of Wisconsin argued that the twenty-five to sixty million figure was highly inflated. In his most recent study, *The Atlantic Slave Trade*, Curtin placed the number at no higher than ten million and perhaps as low as six million.

An equally unfortunate misunderstanding about Africa has been the tendency among scholars to insist that Afro-American slaves brought nothing with them to the New World. Traditionally historians have argued that they were stripped of their culture, language, and history through the operation of a brutal slave system that reduced them to a state of complete dependency and compelled them to adopt the characteristics and habits of their masters and oppressors. In the process, they were transformed from black Africans into black Europeans who accepted the goals and aspirations of the white man even though they were systematically denied participation in the society he developed.

Prior to the 1960s only two scholars, William E. B. DuBois, a black historian and sociologist, and Melville J. Herskovits, a white anthropologist at Northwestern University, questioned this interpretation. In *The Myth of the Negro Past*, published in 1941, Herskovits attempted to dispel certain false notions shared by most Americans about Africa and Afro-Americans. He tried to demonstrate not only that ancient Africa's history was as glorious as Europe's and that Africa had produced a culture worthy of study but also that the Africans brought to the New World retained enough of this culture to make important contributions in the Americas.

Herskovits' study received, however, a rather lukewarm reception from both his academic colleagues and the general public. Unfortunately Herskovits frequently overstated his case and occasionally utilized faulty methodology and field techniques. But a more important reason for its poor reception was the unfortunate timing of the publication. It appeared at a time when Americans were rather sharply divided into segregationists and integrationists. Neither group appreciated the implications of Herskovits' findings. Segregationists took exception to his study because it attacked the myth of Anglo-Saxon superiority, while integrationists found unacceptable those parts of the investigation which suggested the existence of significant cultural differences between blacks and whites. Both Negroes and white intellectuals, anxious to prove their contention that Afro-Americans could assimilate into American society, were embarrassed by Herskovits' efforts to reveal the survival of Africanisms, especially when a few of these characteristics such as emotionalism in religion and promiscuity in sexual relations, were viewed by middle class scholars as undesirable cultural traits.

E. Franklin Frazier, an outstanding black sociologist at Howard University, led the attack against Herskovits. Instead of viewing these traits as cultural "retentions of Africanism," Frazier saw them as direct results of long years of slavery and oppression at the hands of white America. In addition, Frazier denied that the black African could possibly have maintained any cultural traits in the face of an oppressive slave system in which all vestiges of Africanisms were systematically destroyed.

So long as most scholars remained adherents of both integration and assimilation, Frazier had the better of the argument. The demise of the Civil Rights Movement and the concomitant emergence of the Black Power Movement with its stress on cultural nationalism have made Herskovits' observations more relevant to the current aspirations of some black Americans. One of the principal emphases of the new black thrust is rejection of white America's system of values. By stressing African continuity, young black scholars have provided the black community with an alternate set of values. No longer apologetic about cultural differences or ashamed of their ancestral homeland of Africa, these Black Nationalists proudly point to the accomplishments of black people rather than demonstrating what the white man has done to them. Instead of seeking assimilation into American society, these black intellectuals call for cultural pluralism where black values will be esteemed as much as white ones. One result of this change of orientation should be a renewed scholarly interest in African survivals within a pluralistic America.

Even though blacks were not anxious to trace the influences of African culture until recently, they never completely lost interest in Africa. One of the most obvious indications of this interest has been the continuous desire of at least a few black Americans to rescue Africa from white imperialism, and to assist in developing black African governments equal to any in the world. By these means they hope to demonstrate the capabilities of black people as well as to build a base for the liberation of all black peoples. This identification with the mother continent extends backwards at least into the late eighteenth century when a few wealthy Afro-Americans advocated emigration to Africa.

In part, this early interest in redeeming Africa sprang from a feeling of superiority on the part of black Americans who had also bought the prevailing notion of African backwardness. Consequently they regarded it as their duty to transmit the superior western civilization which they had acquired in the United States to their less fortunate brothers in the Old World. More often, however, identification with Africa has been most pronounced in periods of greatest oppression against black Americans. Despairing of ever obtaining justice or freedom in a white dominated society, black consciousness leaders from Paul Cuffee to Marcus Garvey have called for a return to the ancestral homeland.

In the period before the Civil War, black Americans were least optimistic about their future in America during the 1790s and 1850s. Emigration was attractive not only to free blacks in the North who faced constant hardships and few opportunities, but more especially to black slaves caught in the web of a vicious and oppressive slave system. For instance when a Mississippi planter offered his more than 700 slaves the choice of transportation to Africa or sale to a master of their own choosing, all but one selected migration. Denmark Vesey, the remarkable free black of Charleston, South Carolina, seemed to have had migration ultimately in mind when he plotted a black take-over of that city in the early 1820s. Pan-Africanism was hardly a twentieth-century phenomenon of black Americans; instead it has had a long and continuous history.

The following selections from the writings of contemporary scholars indicate the state of scholarship about Africa and Afro-Americans. The articles by Professors Davidson and Fage illustrate the conflicting viewpoints of historians about the effect of the slave trade upon Africa itself. Davidson stresses the destructiveness of European imperialism while Fage indicates some weaknesses in this argument. On the other hand, the studies by Professors Turner and Lynch describe the interrelationships between Africa and the New World. Turner insists that there were important African survivals among Afro-Americans, especially in the areas of language, literature, religion, art, music, and dance. Finally, Professor Lynch provides a comprehensive survey of the interest of black Americans in Africa before 1860 and offers some reasons for this continuous attachment.

4. BASIL DAVIDSON, A Period of Great Change (1966)*

Basil Davidson's *A History of West Africa*, from which this selection comes, is an excellent example of recent scholarship by the liberal school of historians. Davidson emphasizes the disastrous effects which the introduction of European weapons had on West African society and the helplessness of African governments to alter trade patterns established and dictated by European nations. In addition to this study, Davidson is the author of several popular accounts of African history including *Lost Cities of Africa*, *Black Mother*, and *The African Past*.

It is reasonable to think of the years around 1600 as a turning point, as the outset of a major epoch of transition that was to steer West Africa by many paths out of Iron Age civilization into the very different civilization of our own times.

Across the far plains and slow ascending hills of the Western Sudan the authority of the old empires was now at an end. By 1600 the imperial power of Mali had practically disappeared; only its ancient and imposing reputation lingered in the minds of men. The Songhay empire lay in ruins. Even Kanem-Bornu, though embarked on a new empire under Idris Alooma (c. 1580–1617) and his immediate successors, had begun to decline by 1700.

The end of the old empires brought trouble and confusion. Especially in the western and central regions, many peoples faced the need to build a new security. Power and initiative shifted back to the pagan peoples of the countryside. Muslim influence weakened for more than a hundred years, but then, as new leaders arose, took new political shape in a wide revival that was to cover much of the eighteenth and nineteenth centuries, and would be stopped only by the machine-gun fire of European invasion.

These events were accompanied by a gradual but important shift in trade from the western routes across the Sahara to the central routes; and from the central routes to the eastern routes. The western routes, for many years so vitally important, were employed less and less; during long periods they were barely used at all. By the end of the eighteenth century a French traveller called Venture de Paradis found there was only one caravan along the main western route every two or three years, while many other trails were barred or extremely hazardous. The nomads raided as they liked; the wells fell in and were not repaired.

The rare caravans travelled usually between Timbuktu and Wadan in

---

the far west, thence passing northward by way of Wadi Nun to the cities of Morocco. One by one the market cities, which had relied on regular trade for their support, perished or declined. North of the desert, Sijilmasa, once so comfortable and prosperous, never recovered from its ruin during the conflicts and invasions of the Maghreb in the sixteenth century. South of Sijilmasa the old Saharan oasis towns of the westerly routes fell into decay or vanished altogether. The market cities of the central and western region of the Western Sudan suffered in the same way. They dwindled in wealth and power.

It was above all this decline of the cities that sent the cause of Islam into retreat, and gave the non-Muslim peoples of the villages their chance to take a lead once more, a chance that many of them seized eagerly. At the same time one should note that trade on the central routes was damaged less seriously and considerably recovered later on, while trade on the eastern routes, those going north from Hausaland and Bornu and Waday east of Lake Chad, almost certainly expanded after 1600. What had really happened, as we have noted, was that the bulk of the trans-Saharan trade had shifted eastward.

There were correspondingly large changes in Guinea, though in very different circumstances. Oyo rose to power among the Yoruba and became a strong empire. Benin city remained prosperous but the authority of its rulers seems to have steadily diminished outside its boundaries, especially after 1700.

New commercial opportunities with the sea-merchants, and notably a vast expansion of the Atlantic slave trade, deeply influenced many of the seaboard populations. In this respect, too, there came a marked shift in the weight of West African trade: increasingly, and with respect to the whole region, it shifted southward to the coast as the slow-plodding camel caravans of the north were rapidly supplanted by Atlantic sailing ships. These vessels might be very small when compared with later standards; they were none the less very large when compared in carrying capacity with a camel caravan.

These were years of tremendous expansion in the Guinea trade. Prosperous city-states were founded in the Niger delta. Others emerged along the coast of Dahomey. Almost all the populations of the Gold Coast and of what became known to Europeans as Sene-Gambia—reaching from the good harbors of Sierra Leone to those of Senegal—were active in this trade.

We shall therefore find the seventeenth and eighteenth centuries a period of great complexity and vivid interest. Many new departures make their vigorous mark upon the record. Many bold and remarkable leaders appear upon the scene, wrestling with the problems of a time of change. There are many disasters, but also many triumphs. In some ways the record of these centuries may be the most stimulating and dramatic of all West

African history. In following this intricate story we shall find it helpful to modify the geographical order used in earlier chapters. Accordingly we begin with Guinea and work from east to west, taking Guinea to include the forest and part-forest country as well as the seaboard itself, and then go on to consider the Western Sudan.

The Sea-merchants

A little has been said in these pages of the growing influence of sea-merchants from Europe and the Americas. But for a long time this influence was felt only along the coast, and even here it was often of small importance. To put all this in its perspective, it will be useful to consider just what this overseas influence was, and how it took shape.

By the early years of the seventeenth century, as we have noted, sea-merchants from several European nations were arriving on the coasts of Guinea. But they were still few and far between. They had no political or military importance in West Africa. Their ships were weak and unreliable, their sea-maps and sailing instruments primitive. They knew little of Africa, while much of what they thought they knew was wrong.

To the perils of the ocean and the fevers of Guinea there were added other risks. These Europeans were not united. They fought each other fiercely and often. At first the Portuguese had the upper hand over the English and the French. Then the Dutch, being by now the foremost trading union of Europe, came into Guinea waters and took the lead. In 1637 they attacked and captured the Portuguese castle at Elmina with the help of local Africans. Five years later they threw the Portuguese out of the Gold Coast altogether.

European Rivalries

Having broken Portuguese control of Europe's trade with Guinea, the Dutch now tried to set up their own control. They immediately found rivals in other European competitors, notably the English. There followed years of occasional battle and ambush between Europeans whose violent rivalries were watched with keen attention by coastal Africans. These sided now with one European group and now with another, according to their judgment of where their own best interests lay.

Yet the sea-merchants persevered, gradually working their way towards a peaceful partnership both with each other and with African merchants along the coast. Once again it is easy to see why. Behind these sea-merchants there were powerful political and commercial companies and interests who were now becoming strongly established in the West Indies and on the mainland of the Americas. They needed the Guinea trade as part of their system of commerce; therefore they needed peace among themselves. So the coastal trade steadily became more extensive and less violent. Soon it was being carried on peacefully at dozens of regular markets along the seaboard. Of the forty-one trading castles that were eventually built by Europeans in modern Ghana, for example, no fewer than twenty-eight were constructed before 1700. All of them were built only after local African permission was given, and their owners continued until colonial times to pay rent to the peoples on whose land these castles stood.

While the seventeenth century was thus the period of the establishment of the European-American trade with Guinea, the eighteenth was the period of its large expansion. By the year 1800 there was scarcely a single coastal people without its close interest in the trade; and by this time, too, the influence of the trade had pushed inland to many peoples who lived some distance from the coast.

Yet the Africans, though deeply influenced by this maritime trade, always retained the upper hand. If the Europeans were masters on the water, the Africans were masters on the land; and they made sure that they remained so. Not until the middle of the nineteenth century would this balance of power be seriously altered to the European advantage.

Entrepreneurs in far-away Europe, now beginning to feel strong enough with their ships and their soldiers to go anywhere they wished and do anything they liked, fell into the mistake of thinking that the Guinea trade was run by Europeans from first to last. But the truth, as the traders on the coast well knew, was quite otherwise. "There is no small number of men in Europe," a Dutch official at Elmina Castle, William Bosman, was writing home to a friend in 1700, "who believe that the gold mines are in our power, and that we, like the Spanish in the West Indies, have nothing more to do than to work the mines with our slaves. But you should understand that we have no means of getting to these treasures, nor do I believe that any of our people have ever seen a single one of these mines."

Even in modern Ghana, where so many European castles were built, the sea-merchants landed and settled only with permission from the people of the seaboard. The Europeans might sit strongly in their forts, but they still had to pay rent for the land on which the forts were built. Beyond their walls, they could dominate the country only for the range of their musket-shots. Often these Europeans were attacked in their castles, and sometimes these castles were taken by African armies. In 1693, for instance, the Danish fort of Christiansborg in Accra was seized by the soldiers of Akwamu, held for a year under the flag of Akwamu,* and given back to the Danes only after the latter had paid a large ransom in gold.

* The Akwamu flag depicted an African brandishing a sword.

Throughout this period, in short, the Africans were generally in complete control of their side of the trade. Often they were strong enough to punish European misbehavior and insist on compensation for damages, or else simply to make use of the Europeans for their own political plans and strategies.

Growth of the Atlantic Slave Trade

Yet there was one thing that the Africans could not control, and this was to prove of decisive significance. For while they could decide to some extent what the Europeans wished to *sell* them, they could not control what the Europeans wished to *buy* from them. And what the Europeans wished to buy, more and more, and soon with a driving eagerness that overcame all opposition, was slaves.

It began, as a large and regular system of trade, only in the second quarter of the seventeenth century. This was when the Portuguese were well established in Brazil; the Spanish on other parts of the mainland of South, Central, and North America; the English, French, Dutch, Danes, and Spanish on the islands of the Caribbean Sea. All these opened mines and plantations. They wanted more and more captive workers. They sent to Africa to find them, and there they obtained many millions.

Why did they succeed in this? The key to understanding why the slave trade began and grew lies in the master-servant organization which operated in many states and societies. As in other countries of the world, then or at other times, West African chiefs and kings regularly turned war-captives and certain classes of law-breakers into slaves. These slaves, as we have seen, were not very different from most other men and women except that they had fewer rights. As often as not, they were little different from servants who had special duties and obligations.

And just as in other countries, then or at other times, African kings thought it perfectly legitimate to sell, barter, or simply give away their servants or slaves. Accordingly it was easy for European kings, when they found their own supplies of European or American-Indian slaves coming to an end, to obtain more from Africa. In 1562, for instance, the English captain Sir John Hawkins was presented with several hundred war-prisoners, whom he turned into slaves and sold across the Atlantic, in exchange for military help that he gave to two kings of Sierra Leone. Slave trading was a harsh and destructive aspect of the world of that time, and many nations had their part in it.

We have seen, too, that the slavery of Africa was a much less cruel servitude than the slavery which now developed in the Americas. Yet there is little reason to think that African kings, chiefs, and merchants would have stopped selling their servants and war-captives even if they had known the fate reserved for slaves in the Americas, for these kings, chiefs, and merchants were under powerful and growing pressures to continue selling men and women. In the first place, the Europeans now began to ask for slaves more than anything else, even more than gold and ivory. If refused slaves at one market along the coast, they simply went to the next market. If opposed by one chief, they applied to his neighbor. In the second place, kings and chiefs now began to need certain kinds of goods which they could obtain only from the Europeans. Of these, the most important were firearms.

Just as iron-pointed spears had proved better than clubs and stones a thousand years earlier, so now the musket became king of battles. A situation began to arise where chiefs and kings could feel safe only when they were sure of a supply of firearms. Yet these chiefs and kings, living in a society with almost no machine production, were unable to manufacture firearms for themselves. They had to buy them from abroad. Apart from a few that came south across the Sahara, all the firearms had to come from Europe, and the Europeans would seldom sell them except in part-exchange for slaves. Under pressures such as this the overseas slave trade rapidly developed into a massive export of captive labor to the Americas.

There were many cases where African kings, chiefs, or elders, seeing how destructive this trade had become to peace and prosperity at home, tried hard to bring it to a halt. We shall look at some of these cases later on. But the pressures were too strong for them. Little by little, the overseas slave trade spread from the coastal countries to the lands behind the coast.

Firearms

This spreading influence was also linked to the changing organization of African society. The rise of professional armies came at about the same time as the arrival of the first firearms. This coincided, too, with the wars and troubles of the seventeenth century. Very large quantities of muskets now began to be imported. From England alone, at the height of the eighteenth-century Guinea trade, the gunsmiths of Birmingham were providing more than 100,000 a year.

Here also there were gains as well as losses. By selling these guns, Europeans helped to spread war among Africans, since the buying of guns called for the capture of war-prisoners. But at the same time the guns strengthened Africans against European invasion or attack. The Europeans saw this latter point very clearly. Yet they on their side were as powerless to stop the sale of guns to Africans as the Africans were powerless to stop the sale of war-prisoners to Europeans, and for the same reason: they could never win agreement among themselves. The Dutchman William Bosman, then living at Elmina, explained this in a letter written home in 1700.

"The main military weapons [of the Gold Coast Africans]," he wrote, "are muskets or carbines, in the use of which these Africans are wonderfully skillful. It is a real pleasure to watch them train their armies. They handle their weapons so cleverly, shooting them off in several ways, one man sitting, another creeping along the ground or lying down, that it is surprising they do not hurt each other.

"Perhaps you will wonder how the Africans come to be furnished with these firearms. But you should know that we sell them very great quantities, and in doing this we offer them a knife with which to cut our own throats. But we are forced to do this. For if we [the Dutch] did not do it, they would easily get enough muskets from the English, or from the Danes, or from the Prussians. And even if we governors [of the official European trading corporations] could all agree to stop selling firearms, the private traders of the English or the Dutch would still go on selling them."

Cause and Effect

Looking back today on all those confused events, one can detect a clear chain of cause and effect running through much of the story of the coastal lands of Guinea, and even to some extent of the forest lands, during these centuries.

First, there is the slow beginning of coastal trade. New markets and centers of African power appear along the coast. New states emerge. These build themselves into a controlling position, as middlemen, between the sea-merchants on one side and the inland merchants on the other.

In the second half of the seventeenth century there comes an enormous expansion in the demand for slaves for the mines and plantations of the Americas. Urged on by the sea-merchants, the coastal rulers try to supply this demand. They have to make wars in order to get hold of enough captives.

These wars are increasingly made with guns brought from Europe. But the European demand for slaves sharpens the African need for guns; and this need for guns in turn makes greater the need for captives with whom to purchase the guns. By the eighteenth century the politics of Guinea are deeply influenced by the exchange of African captives for European manufactured goods, with guns high on the list of these.

It seems worth while to have spent a little time on these matters because, although they were only a small part of the overall West African picture in the seventeenth and even in the eighteenth century, they were a part of growing importance. They set the scene for several very great developments. They show how it came about that large populations of African origin were settled in the Americas. They explain why the influence of the sea-merchants, so very small at first, should have grown so great as the years went by. They help interpret much that happened.

5. J. D. FAGE, Slavery and the Slave Trade in the Context of West African History (1969)*

In this essay, Professor J. D. Fage, formerly professor of history in the University College of Ghana and currently lecturer in history at the University of London, examines the three principal interpretations of the relationship between the slave trade and West African development. Considering all of them inadequate, Fage provides another alternative which gives greater weight to African considerations. In the process, he suggests a significant reinterpretation of West African history in general.

There have been at least three widely held and influential views about slavery and the slave trade in West Africa, and also about their relation to its society in respect both of their origins and of their effects on it.

The first is that the institution of slavery was natural and endemic in West African society, so that the coming of foreign traders with a demand for labor, whether from Muslim North Africa or from the countries of maritime Europe, led swiftly and automatically to the development by West Africans of an organized trade in slaves for export.

The second is a contrary view, that it was rather these external demands for labor which led to a great growth of both slavery and slave-trading in West Africa, and so corrupted its indigenous society.

The third view, which may or may not be associated with the second, is that the external demand for West African labor, especially in the period ca. 1650 to ca. 1850, was so great that the export of slaves to meet it had a disastrous effect on the peoples of West Africa, disrupting not only their natural demographic development but their social and moral development as well.

In this essay it is proposed to examine and reassess these views in the light of recent research and thinking, and, as a result, to offer an interpretation of the roles of slavery and the slave trade in the history of West Africa which may be more in accord with its economic and social realities.

* J. D. Fage, "Slavery and the Slave Trade in the Context of West African History," *Journal of African History* 10 (1969): 393–404. Reprinted by permission of the author and publisher.

The first view, namely that the export slave trade was possible because both slavery and trading in slaves were already deeply rooted in West African society, was of course a view propagated by the European slave traders, especially perhaps when the morality of their business was being questioned. Norris' and Dalzel's books on Dahomey towards the close of the eighteenth century are developed examples of this attitude; [1] Dalzel, for example, quite seriously argues that greater good was done by exporting slaves to American plantations than by leaving them in West Africa, where they were likely to become victims of the practice of human sacrifice. But the slave-traders' view in effect persisted into the abolitionist atmosphere of the nineteenth century and was, in fact, put forward as a principal moral justification for European colonization. To stamp out the evils of slavery and slave-trading in West Africa, occupation of its territories was thought essential; indeed, it was specifically imposed as a duty on the European powers following the Brussels Act of 1890. The view that West Africans left to themselves were inherently prone to own and trade in slaves became in fact one of the received myths of the conquering colonizers.

Analysis and criticism of this view are complicated by the problem of deciding what institution or institutions in West African societies corresponded to the European idea of slavery. Many people will be familiar with Rattray's analysis of slavery in Ashanti society, in which he defined at least five separate terms to describe the various conditions or degrees of voluntary or involuntary servitude in Ashanti.[2] Only two of these, *odonko*, a foreigner who had been purchased with the express purpose of making him or her a slave, and *domum*, a man or woman received in tribute from a subjugated foreign state, might seem to correspond more or less to what an eighteenth-century European or white American might understand by "slave." But Rattray then goes on to consider the rights of such slaves in Ashanti society, and these were far in advance of the rights of any slaves in any colony in the Americas. He concludes that the rights of an Ashanti slave were not so very different from "the ordinary privileges of any Ashanti free man, with whom, in these respects, his position did not seem to compare so unfavorably." He also states that "a condition of voluntary servitude was, in a very literal sense, the heritage of every Ashanti," and that to be masterless in that society was an open invitation to involuntary servitude. Similarly, Dalzel reports of the neighboring, somewhat more authoritarian society of eighteenth-century Dahomey, which he knew at first hand, that its inhabitants were "*all* slaves to the king." [3]

But it is not necessary here to enter into the arguments as to whether various forms of unfreedom in various West African societies should be called by the name of "slave," or by such other terms as "subject," "ser-

vant," "serf" or "pawn." It would seem possible to produce a straightfor-
ward definition of slavery that is perfectly adequate for the purposes of
this present enquiry: namely that a slave was a man or woman who was
owned by some other person, whose labor was regarded as having economic value, and whose person had a commercial value.

It is obvious enough that slaves as so defined existed in many West
African societies during the heyday of the Atlantic slave trade from
the seventeenth to the nineteenth century, though possibly not in state-
less societies or in societies that were little or not touched by the major
routes of trade. The question is, then, whether such slavery existed in West
African societies before the impingement on them of external trade.

It is impossible to answer this question with respect to those parts of
West Africa in the Sudan to which external trade came across the Sahara.
The only considerable body of evidence which is really relevant is the
accounts of the Arabic writers who were the first to describe the West
African Sudan either from their personal knowledge or on the basis of
others' first-hand experience, together with early local written histories
such as the Timbuktu *Tarikhs* or the Kano Chronicle. This evidence has
been reviewed by Mauny.[4] It may be said that both its quantity and its
quality are disappointing. The Arab authors take the existence of both
slavery and trading in slaves very much for granted, and neither seems to
them to call for very much comment. It is thus apparent that both institutions were well established in the major states and empires of the West
African Sudan from the eleventh to the sixteenth century. We cannot tell
whether these institutions were indigenous, or whether they had evolved
following the growth of trans-Saharan trade, because, of course, Arab
traders had preceded Arabic scholarship across the Sahara by about four
centuries. Furthermore, traffic of some kind across the Sahara between
North and West Africa had been in existence for something like a thousand years at least before the Arab conquests began in the seventh century
A.D. It has been shown, in fact, that a trans-Saharan trade in Negro slaves
must have existed, though perhaps in little volume, as early as about the
second century A.D.[5] However, we have no means of knowing what relation this may have had to slavery and the slave trade within West Africa
itself.

In default of evidence of the relation between the existence of an external demand for slaves and of slavery and an internal trade in slaves for
the West African Sudan, we must turn to the Guinea area, where commonly the first truly external traders were the European sea-traders, who
first arrived on the coasts in the fifteenth century. The evidence for Upper
Guinea, from the Gambia to modern Liberia, has been analyzed by Dr.
Walter Rodney.[6]

The ethnographic picture that can be built up for this part of the coastlands from sixteenth- and seventeenth-century European, especially Portuguese, accounts would seem to be good and detailed, but the references to slaves are few and far between. They indicate little more, Rodney says, than that the kings and chiefs of the area had a small number of "political clients" in their households. There is no evidence for the existence of "chattel slaves, agricultural serfs, or even household servants" in any numbers, or in any condition to differentiate them from ordinary citizens. He concludes, therefore, that there was no sizeable class of men, and no indigenous trade in men, which could serve as a launching-pad for the Atlantic slave trade. In this part of West Africa at least, a class society involving slaves and trade in them was a consequence of the European demand for slaves for the Americas, and not an indigenous feature upon which an export trade could be built up.

Rodney contrasts this picture, not only with the eighteenth- and nineteenth-century situation in his area, when specialized traders, mainly Mandingo and Fula, possessed and dealt in large numbers of slaves, but also with the sixteenth- and seventeenth-century situation farther north, in the Senegal, and also farther east, in Lower Guinea. In the latter case, he does not do very much more than refer to the fact that, as early as about 1500, the Portuguese were *selling* slaves on the Gold Coast, which of course presupposes a society knowing of the value of slaves and having a demand for them.[7] But the whole context in which the Portuguese first traded in Lower Guinea seems to have been very different from that in which they sought to trade in Upper Guinea.

We might begin by remarking that the ethnographic picture that can be built up from early Portuguese accounts of Lower Guinea is slighter, less complete and less detailed than that which can be built up for Upper Guinea. It is sometimes suggested that this is so because, after the Portuguese Crown had asserted its control over the Gold Coast trade in the 1480s, it required that its own and its subjects' doings in Guinea should be kept as secret as possible to place their foreign competitors in the Guinea trade at a disadvantage. But in fact most of the information used by Rodney is later than 1500, and it seems possible that the relative dearth of Portuguese ethnographic material for Lower Guinea may have other explanations. It seems possible that one of these may be that on the coasts of Lower Guinea, especially on the Gold Coast and in and around Benin, the Portuguese were in contact with organized kingdoms which had developed trading systems of their own and which were already engaged in long-distance trade or in trading with long-distance traders (like the Mande merchants on the Gold Coast). Whereas in the Upper Guinea coastlands the Portuguese had to deal with societies which were politically and commercially less well developed, and which therefore had to be thoroughly examined to see what prospects of profitable trade they might offer, no such exploration was necessary for the kingdoms of Lower Guinea, which already knew what commodities they had to offer to strangers and on what terms they would deal in them.

In these circumstances, for Lower Guinea it is necessary to infer local attitudes to slavery and trading in slaves from the trade which the Portuguese conducted there. It is immediately apparent not only that there was a market for slaves on the Gold Coast, but that there were communities farther east which both had slaves and knew the conditions on which they could be offered for sale. Thus as early as ca. 1500, Pacheco Pereira could write of Benin that the kingdom was "usually at war with its neighbors and takes many captives, whom we buy at 12 or 15 brass bracelets each, or for copper bracelets which they prize more; from there the slaves are taken to [the Gold Coast] where they are sold for gold." [8] It is interesting that Pacheco says nothing about the royal ban on the export from Benin of male slaves which Professor Ryder says was "imposed at the beginning of the sixteenth century." Presumably it was not yet in force when Pacheco wrote. Conceivably it may have been instituted in the belief that it was more beneficial to the kingdom to maintain than to export its manpower. Conversely, and more probably perhaps, the subsequent decline of European trade at Benin as the trans-Atlantic slave trade developed, and the need to reverse this decline when neighboring kingdoms were gaining strength through growing trade with Europeans, may well explain why the ban was rescinded in the 1690s.[9]

In general, we can be confident that what the Portuguese sought to do in Lower Guinea from about 1480 was to profit by imposing themselves (as later they were to do in East Africa and Asia) on already existing patterns of trade, and that they found there organized kingdoms in which the idea of foreign trade, carried on under royal control and in accordance with state policy by established merchant classes or guilds, was already well established. Such a system involved the use of slaves—and an appreciation of their economic value—in a number of ways: as cultivators of crops for market on the estates of kings or nobles; as miners, or as artisans in craft workshops; as carriers on the trade roads, and even as traders themselves; as soldiers, retainers, servants, officials even, in the employ of kings or principal men in the kingdom. A similar but, one suspects, less well developed pattern was evident, as Rodney admits, in the Senegal region on the western fringes of the Sudan, and it was undoubtedly from the Western and Central Sudan that it had spread into Lower Guinea some time before the arrival of the Portuguese. In this sense the area of Upper Guinea, where in the sixteenth and seventeenth centuries there was no organized slavery, was an economically little developed and backward region.

There seems in fact to be a close correlation in West Africa between economic development (and political development, because indigenous commercial activity was largely king- or state-directed) and the growth of the institution of slavery as here defined. This growth was already well advanced before European sea trade with West Africa began in the fifteenth century, and certainly before the main commercial demand of Europeans on West Africa was one for slaves—which was not really until the middle or the second half of the seventeenth century. Neither the first nor the second of the commonly held views about the relationship between the Atlantic slave trade and slavery and slave-trading within West African society is really satisfactory. Slavery and the commercial valuation of slaves were not natural features of West African society, nor was their development and growth simply a consequence of the European demand for slaves for American plantations. This last may well have been the case in Upper Guinea, but elsewhere, e.g. in Lower Guinea, all the coming of European slave-buyers meant in principle was that African kings and merchants were increasingly presented with a new element of choice— fundamentally, it would seem, an economic choice: whether it was more advantageous to them to keep their slave laborers at home, as farmers, artisans, porters, retainers, soldiers, etc., or to exchange them or some of them for other forms of wealth (or of power, e.g. guns and powder).

We arrive then at a first conclusion, that slavery and the making, buying and selling of slaves were means by which certain privileged individuals in West African society, or persons who wished to gain or to extend positions of privilege in that society, sought to mobilize the wealth inherent in the land and the people on it, and that this process had already gone some distance before the Europeans arrived. Insofar as it seems to have started in the Sudan, rather than in Guinea, it is of course still possible, even perhaps likely, that the process was sparked off by the demands of visitors coming to West Africa from across the Sahara, from North Africa. On the other hand, such evidence as there is suggests that it is *un*-likely that these first external demands were primarily or even essentially demands for labor. The prime North African demand was probably for gold and exotic produce, and the first basis of the trans-Saharan trade the exchange of salt for gold. It would thus be a demand for *commodities* which provoked the vital change by which some West Africans began to view some others not as kin or non-kin but as a means by which to obtain wealth and power.

We are still left, however, with the questions whether, and, if so, to what extent, the external demands for West African labor, especially the great European demands for labor for the Americas, may have distorted the natural economic development of West Africa, and have produced socially, economically, and even politically disastrous consequences.

Clearly we should begin by assessing, first, the actual size of this demand for labor exports and, secondly, its possible demographic effects in West Africa. Thanks to the recent researches of Professor Philip D. Curtin,[10] it is now possible to do this with rather more confidence than before in respect of the export of slaves to the Americas. The numbers of slaves reaching the Americas and so, allowing for losses *en route*, the numbers leaving Africa seem likely to have been appreciably smaller than has been commonly supposed. For the whole four centuries of the trade, Curtin's evaluation of the evidence available points to the conclusion that the number of slaves reaching the Americas cannot have been more than about 9 millions, and may well have been rather less. Furthermore, he doubts whether it would have been technically possible for the shipping resources available to Europe to have transported more. He also has evidence that suggests, too, that the losses *en route* from sickness, starvation and revolt, not more than 16 percent on average, were significantly less than the figures commonly accepted, which derive—like the earlier estimates for total volume—from the exaggerated pleadings of the abolitionist campaigners. On this basis, the total number of men and women exported from Africa during the whole period of the slave trade is unlikely to have been much more than about 11 millions. Of these, a considerable and growing proportion came from south of the Cameroons, and so from outside West Africa as commonly understood. The *West* African contribution to the Atlantic slave trade is in fact unlikely to have been much more than about 6 millions.

It would be helpful if we could compare this estimate with a figure for the number of slaves exported northwards from West Africa across the Sahara. This, frankly, is impossible: the available data are exiguous and unreliable in the extreme, as is admitted by Mauny, who, however, offers a guess of a minimum of 20,000 a year, or 2 million a century.[11] Something like the first of these figures might be reasonable for the annual capacity of the trans-Saharan caravan roads, but it would seem totally unreasonable to suppose that anything like this number crossed the Sahara every year during the seventeen centuries in which we know the northern slave trade to have existed, or even during the twelve centuries following the Arab conquest of North Africa. Thirty-four or twenty-four million Negroes would have made an impact on the population of North Africa and the Middle East quite as great as 9 million Negroes on that of the Americas, and really there is little evidence of this. It seems safer to conclude that, extending over a very much longer period, the trans-Saharan trade removed fewer Negroes than the Atlantic trade, and that its effect on the West African population during the time the Atlantic trade was operating was relatively minor.

Prior to the middle of the seventeenth century, the Atlantic slave trade was on a small scale; Curtin's figures suggest a loss of population to West Africa before 1600 of only about 200,000. The seventeenth-century figure would be nearly a million, but it was in the years from 1701 to 1810, when something like 4½ million slaves were removed, that the effect of the trade was most serious, averaging a loss of 41,000 men and women a year. The nineteenth-century loss, in so far as West Africa was concerned, was much lighter, probably of the order of only about 11,000 a year on average.

We do not, of course, know the size of West Africa's population in the eighteenth century. But extrapolation backwards from twentieth-century censuses and estimates and rates of increase suggests that the population of West Africa may have been at least 25 million at the beginning of the eighteenth century, with a rate of natural increase of about 15 per 1000 at the beginning of the century and of about 19 per 1000 at the end. If these estimates [12] are anything like right, then at first sight the effect of the export slave trade in the eighteenth century may have been more or less to check population growth, the rates of slave exports and of natural increase being of the same order. For other centuries, the effect of the slave trade would have been slight.

Various refinements can be made to such a crude calculation. For example, some allowance should be made for deaths caused directly or indirectly by the operations of the slave trade within West Africa itself. On the other hand, such a factor might be more than offset by the fact that only a third of the slaves exported were women, so that in a polygynous society the rate of natural increase by new births may not have been as much affected as would otherwise have been the case.

It is probably more important to appreciate that the incidence of the slave trade, both in time and space, was by no means even. Thus in the 1780s, for instance, about 80 percent of all slaves exported from West Africa (and nearly half of the slaves taken from *all* Africa) were taken from the coast from the Gold Coast to the Cameroons inclusive. Thus if there were serious depopulation and other destructive effects caused by the Atlantic slave trade, they might be expected to show most clearly in this region. In point of fact, they do not appear to show at all. This, by and large, remains the most densely populated part of West Africa, and the Ibo country is as thickly settled as any part of the whole continent. Moreover, this was the part of Guinea, including the Akan states, Dahomey, the Yoruba and Benin kingdoms, which was politically and economically best organized.

The conclusion to which one is led, therefore, is that whereas in East and Central Africa the slave trade, sometimes conducted in the interior by raiding and warring strangers, could be extremely destructive of economic, political and social life, in West Africa it was part of a sustained process of economic and political development. Probably because, by and large, in West Africa land was always more abundant than labor,[13] the institution of slavery played an essential role in this development; without it there were really few effective means of mobilizing labor for the economic and political needs of the state. (One may recall Charles Monteil's dictum that "a Sudanic empire is in essence an association of individuals aiming to dominate the generality for profit." [14]) But in this process the *trade* in slaves, certainly the export trade, was essentially incidental, only one of a number of ways of increasing a kingdom's wealth and power, and in the Guinea coastlands only during the eighteenth century the most important way. Whether or not to export slaves and, if so, in what quantities, seems to have been increasingly an economic choice.

It has already been suggested that this choice was exercised at Benin. Here, shortly after 1500, the authorities seem to have concluded that the kingdom and its economy would be weakened if the export of male labor were permitted. Later on, the view seems to have been taken that the resultant loss of trade with Europeans (*inter alia* the vendors of firearms), and the consequent gain to the trade and strength of neighboring African rivals, was more dangerous than the loss of manpower. Dr. Akinjogbin has suggested a similar argument in eighteenth-century Dahomey: first a refusal to export slaves (lest the kingdom be weakened), then a realization that it was only through selling slaves that the kingdom could buy the guns and powder necessary to maintain its power.[15] It may also be significant that, although the European demand for slaves for the Americas was continually growing and the price of slaves steadily increasing from about 1650 to about 1810, the numbers of slaves exported from the well-organized Gold Coast states remained more or less constant throughout the period, never really exceeding about 10,000 a year. It may be argued, then, that economic and political logic had in effect persuaded the Gold Coast authorities that this was about the number of slaves they could afford to export, in order to obtain the guns and other imports their states required, without weakening their societies. The numbers of slaves exported through the Niger delta ports did greatly increase during this period, but this too could also have been a more or less conscious economic response to a different set of circumstances. In the Ibo hinterland of the delta, where, although political authority was diffuse, economic life seems to have been well developed, it may well have been that there was already an unusual growth of population in relation to the productivity of the land, so that men of enterprise may have concluded that it was becoming more profitable to export labor for sale than to employ it at home.

But the balance should not be struck exclusively in economic terms (even if it may be suggested that at the time the economic arguments were becoming increasingly important in the minds of the ruling segments in West African societies). There is not space here to enter into a discussion of the host of moral and social issues involved in the slave trade, but there is one politico-social point that should be briefly touched upon. It has been seen that European slave-traders like Dalzel justified their activities on the ground that they were rescuing Africans from oppression and exploitation by their own rulers, and that likewise the abolitionists argued that their campaigning was needed to redeem African society from the degradations brought by the slave trade. It is therefore worth asking whether the ever-increasing American demand for slaves from West Africa from the middle of the seventeenth to the beginning of the nineteenth century led to increased slave-raiding and to more wars being fought for the express purpose of securing slaves, and so to a growing political stability which was destructive of economic and social progress.

This is a very large question, and one to which there may well be no single answer applicable to all parts of West Africa and to all kinds of West African societies. It might, however, be argued—as, for example, Professor Flint has argued [16]—that the stereotyping of such polities as the emirates of Nupe and Ilorin as "slave-raiding" was part of the apologetics by which the European colonizers justified their conquests. For one area, and for one type of West African society, namely the kingdoms of Lower Guinea, there is, however, some interesting evidence on record. Both King Kpengla of Dahomey (1774–89) and King Osei Bonsu of Ashanti (ca. 1801–24) were specifically asked by European visitors whether they engaged in warfare with the express purpose of capturing slaves for trade.[17] Both are reported as saying that they did not, that their wars were fought for political reasons, to protect, maintain or promote the power and prestige of their nations relative to their neighbors.

If it is argued that their replies may not have been properly reported by their inquisitors, who may well have had their own motives for distorting them, then attention should be drawn to the strong similarities between their reported arguments, and to the fact that their reporters had opposing biases, Absom and Dalzel (in the case of Kpengla) being partisans of the slave trade, and Dupuis (in the case of Osei Bonsu) being an opponent of it. In these circumstances, Kpengla's and Osei Bonsu's statements have the ring of truth: their own opinion was that their wars were not fought to secure slaves for sale to the Atlantic slave-traders. But the existence of the Atlantic trade did give such kings a new choice: whether it was more profitable for them to sell their war captives abroad, or to keep them at home, employed as soldiers, or as laborers on their and their generals' estates or on their trading enterprises, or, perhaps, whether they might best be used for the traditional sacrifices to their and the nation's ancestors (sacrifices whose scale may have been growing as the scale of royal and national power was itself growing). A similar choice was also intruding into more domestic spheres, whether criminal and civil malefactors should be punished by such traditional penalties as fines or execution, or whether they might best be dealt with by selling them to the Atlantic traders—in effect, by deportation. Here analogies from seventeenth- and eighteenth-century English history might suggest that the latter remedy was on the increase (but this might be thought a social good rather than an evil).

On the whole it is probably true to say that the operation of the slave trade may have tended to integrate, strengthen and develop unitary, territorial political authority, but to weaken or destroy more segmentary societies. Whether this was good or evil may be a nice point; historically it may be seen as purposive and perhaps as more or less inevitable.

One may perhaps conclude with the reflection that, in the context of the times in West Africa, by stopping the slave trade and by attacking slavery, Europeans did much to impoverish and weaken its monarchies. This was so because, on the African side, the slave trade was conducted on a large scale by a relatively small number of major entrepreneurs under state patronage or, indeed, direction. Thus, when the export slave trade was ended, the African monarchies lost a major source of revenue and a large part of the economic structure which supported them. This might not have been the case had the slaves available been put to plantation production for export—an expedient which certainly seems to have been considered, for example, by King Gezo of Dahomey in the 1850s.[18] But in practice the so-called "legitimate" trades which replaced the slave trade as the staple of West African foreign commerce tended to be based rather on production by large numbers of small-scale "peasant" farmers. The major kingdoms found difficulty in adapting their fiscal, economic and political systems so as to profit from this change in the economic structure. For this reason, as the nineteenth century progressed, they seem to have become at once less efficient in securing revenue from, and less able to provide the order needed by, their peoples' producers and traders.[19]

The steps taken by Europeans against the slave trade and slavery therefore hastened the day when, in their own economic interest, they thought it necessary first to conquer the West African kingdoms, and then to continue the process, initiated by African kings and entrepreneurs, of conquering the segmentary societies and absorbing them into unitary political structures.

Summary

This paper examines three views which have been widely held about slavery and the slave trade in West Africa, and which have tended to mold interpretations of its history, especially for the period from the fifteenth to the nineteenth century. These are:

(1) That the institution of slavery was endemic in, and a natural feature of, indigenous West African society, so that when foreigners arrived in West Africa with a demand for slaves, West Africans were able immediately to organize an export trade in slaves on an ever-increasing scale.

(2) A contrary view, that it was the external demands for labor which led to a great growth of the institution of slavery in West Africa, and so corrupted its indigenous society.

(3) A view which may or may not be combined with (2), namely that the external demand for slaves became so considerable that there was a disastrous effect on its population.

Relevant evidence is touched upon from about the eleventh century onwards, and a fourth interpretation is developed which seems better to fit the economic and social realities which can be ascertained.

In essence this is that economic and commercial slavery and slave-trading were not natural features of West African society, but that they developed, along with the growth of states, as a form of labor mobilization to meet the needs of a growing system of foreign trade in which, initially, the demand for slaves as trade goods was relatively insignificant. What might be termed a "slave economy" was generally established in the Western and Central Sudan by about the fourteenth century at least, and had certainly spread to the coasts around the Senegal and in Lower Guinea by the fifteenth century.

The European demand for slaves for the Americas, which reached its peak from about 1650 to about 1850, accentuated and expanded the internal growth of both slavery and the slave trade. But this was essentially only one aspect of a very wide process of economic and political development and social change, in West Africa. The data recently assembled and analyzed by Curtin for the volume and distribution of the export slave trade do not suggest that the loss of population and other effects of the export of labor to the Americas need have had universally damaging effects on the development of West Africa. Rather, it is suggested, West African rulers and merchants reacted to the demand with economic reasoning, and used it to strengthen streams of economic and political development that were already current before the Atlantic slave trade began.

NOTES

1. Robert Norris, *Memoirs of the Reign of Bossa Ahadee, King of Dahomy* (1789), and Archibald Dalzel, *A History of Dahomy* (1793).

2. R. S. Rattray, *Ashanti Law and Constitution* (Oxford: Clarendon Press, 1929), ch. 5.

3. Dalzel, *History of Dahomy*, p. 124.

4. Raymond Mauny, *Tableau géographique de l'ouest africain* (Dakar: IFAN, 1961), pp. 336–43, 377–9, 422–4.

5. R. C. C. Law, "The Garamantes and trans-Saharan enterprise in classical times," *Journal of African History* 8 (1967): 196.

6. Walter Rodney, "African slavery and other forms of social oppression on the Upper Guinea Coast in the context of the Atlantic slave-trade," *Journal of African History* 7 (1966): 431–43.

7. Barbot in 1682 also reported that the Dutch sometimes *sold* slaves on the Gaboon (Churchill's *Voyages*, v, p. 390).

8. D. Pacheco Pereira, *Esmeraldo de Situ Orbis*, ed. by Raymond Mauny (Bíssau: Centro de Estudos de Guíné Portugesa, 1956), p. 134.

9. A. F. C. Ryder, "The Benin missions," *Journal of Historical Society of Nigeria* 2 (1961): 237, and "Dutch trade on the Nigerian coast during the seventeenth century," *Journal of Historical Society of Nigeria* 3 (1965): 203. To Professor Ryder, the Benin refusal to supply male slaves to the Portuguese seems to be associated with the Portuguese refusal to sell firearms to the pagan Benin kingdom. But this does not seem to invalidate the argument about the economic, and therefore (in a state-directed economy) the political, appreciation of the value of slaves. By the later seventeenth century, with the growing and competitive European arms trade, Benin's rulers must have concluded that the acquisition of firearms was more vital to the strength and wealth of the kingdom than the conservation of its manpower.

10. Philip D. Curtin, *The Atlantic Slave Trade* (Madison: University of Wisconsin Press, 1970).

11. Mauny, *Tableau géographique*, p. 379. A. Adu Boahen estimates the volume for the first half of the nineteenth century at about 10,000 slaves a year: *Britain, the Sahara, and the Western Sudan, 1788–1861* (Oxford: Clarendon Press, 1964), p. 127.

12. In which I have been guided by the experience and calculations of my colleague Dr. P. K. Mitchell.

13. As was pointed out to me by my colleagues Mr. D. Rimmer and Dr. A. G. Hopkins.

14. Charles Monteil, "Les empires du Mali," Bulletin, *Comité d'etudes historiques et scientifiques de l'Afrique occidentale franchaise* 12 (1929): 312 (p. 22 in the separate (1968) reprint).

15. I. A. Akinjogbin, *Dahomey and its Neighbours, 1708–1818* (Cambridge: Cambridge University Press, 1967), pp. 73–80, 90–95.

16. John E. Flint, *Sir George Goldie and the Making of Nigeria* (London: Oxford University Press, 1960), p. 246.

17. Dalzel, *History of Dahomy*, pp. 217–21; Joseph Dupuis, *Journal of a Residence in Ashantee* (1824), pp. 163–4.

18. D. A. Ross, "The autonomous kingdom of Dahomey, 1818–94" (unpublished London Ph.D. thesis, 1967), ch. 2.

19. The only place in which this argument seems to have been developed is, with reference to Yorubaland, in an article by A. G. Hopkins, "Economic imperialism in West Africa: Lagos, 1880–92," *Economic History Review* 21 (1968): 587–92.

6. LORENZO D. TURNER, African Survivals in the New World with Special Emphasis on the Arts (1958, 1963)*

As a specialist in linguistics, Professor Lorenzo D. Turner of Roosevelt University investigated the Gullah dialect spoken by Afro-Americans in the Sea Islands of South Carolina and Georgia. He proved that their language was not a bastard form of Elizabethan English, as many authorities had conjectured, but that its peculiarities of vocabulary and syntax closely resembled speech patterns in West Africa. In this essay, Professor Turner discusses other areas where African survivals in the United States are equally apparent but seldom recognized by scholars.

For several centuries now many persons have thought of sub-Saharan Africa primarily as a land to be exploited both as regards human lives and materials. They have thought of the inhabitants of this region as not deserving the respect accorded other peoples. So inferior, they have contended, was the African's culture that it could not survive when brought into contact with the culture of the Europeans. Consequently, the African on arriving in the New World, they have said, abandoned his own culture and has not even yet been able to assimilate thoroughly that of the white man. In the United States and in many countries of the Caribbean during the period of slavery, persons favoring the continuance of that institution, in answer to the abolitionists, utilized this insidious myth of the inferiority of the Negro to jusify their holding him in subjection. Though the myth could not stem the tide of the abolition movement, it did leave in the minds of many people a stereotype of the Negro which is still prevalent in many quarters.

On the other hand, those who have taken the time to acquaint themselves with the history and culture of the Africans know well that many of the slaves brought to the New World were highly intelligent and talented people. Many were not only proficient in their own native language and culture but could write in the Arabic language and speak it fluently. Many were from the upper levels of African societies: kings, princes, chiefs of tribes, priests, military experts, artists, and others well versed in their history and folklore. Inter-tribal wars frequently resulted in the enslaving of the conquered ruler and all of his followers and subsequently in their being sold to white slave-traders and being brought to the New World. Moreover, a study of the native culture of West

* From "African Survivals in the New World with Special Emphasis on the Arts," by Lorenzo D. Turner, in *Africa Seen by American Negro Scholars*, edited by John A. Davis, Dijon: 1958; New York: 1963. Reprinted by permission of the American Society of African Culture.

Africa (the home of the large majority of Africans who came to the New World) reveals that the West Africans had a culture comparable to that of any essentially non-literate and non-machine society in the world. They had well organized economic systems, political systems adequate for the effective administration of large kingdoms, a complex social organization, intricate systems of religious belief and practice, a folk literature comparable to that of any other group, as well as music, the dance, and highly developed art forms. African languages (inaccurately called "dialects" by detractors of the Africans) are also comparable to any other languages as vehicles of aesthetic, logical, and effective expression; and as more of these languages are written, the more evident this fact is becoming. The late R. E. G. Armattoe, an anthropologist, says that "throughout the whole of the Middle Ages, West Africa had a more solid politico-social organization, attained a greater degree of internal cohesion, and was more conscious of the social function of science than Europe." [1]

A study of the influence of African culture upon the Western Hemisphere reveals that the slaves on reaching the New World did not wholly abandon their native culture, but retained much of it with surprisingly little change. Much of it also has been considerably modified by contact with Western civilization, and a good deal of it, as would be expected, has been lost entirely. Those aspects of African culture which have been most tenacious throughout the New World are survivals in languages, folk literature, religion, art, the dance, and music; but some survivals from the economic and social life of the Africans can also be found in the New World.[2]

Conditions tending to concentrate large numbers of Negroes in a given area of the New World, to segregate them from the other inhabitants, or to keep them in touch with their African homes contributed to the retention of African cultural elements. The fact that the number of Africans coming to certain countries reached considerably into the millions at a time when the European population in these regions was relatively small had important bearing upon the extent of African survivals in such places. Probably few North Americans are aware of the fact that in practically every country of Latin America between the sixteenth and nineteenth centuries Negroes constituted a large element of the population; in some parts of Latin America they outnumbered all other racial groups except the Indians. Census figures in these countries, however, are seldom accurate. This is understandable. First of all, the mixing of the races has gone so far that division into mutually exclusive groups is practically impossible. Again, in Mexico, Colombia, and Chile investigation of racial origin was for a long time officially prohibited in the taking of the census. Moreover, in some countries—Peru, for example—Africans and their children were classified as Negroes only if they were slaves; and in all of these countries many mulattoes frequently were classified as white. But in spite of these conditions, there are minimum figures which give some idea of the extent of the Negro element in the population of Latin America.[3]

As early as 1553 there were more than 20,000 Negroes in Mexico. These had been brought in from Cuba and ports of southern Spain, but before 1585 slaves were being imported there directly from Africa. Slavery was abolished in Mexico during the first quarter of the nineteenth century, but not before 200,000 slaves had been brought in. Even today there are concentrations of Negroes in several places in Mexico. As late as 1778 Negroes constituted one-third of the population of the Argentine. It has been estimated that Venezuela in 1810 had approximately 500,000 Negroes, free and slave, in a total population of 900,000. In Colombia at the end of the eighteenth century there were 210,000 Negroes. In 1817 Brazil had more than three times as many Negroes as whites. Negroes were imported in large numbers also to coastal Peru and Ecuador and to Chile. In all the Central American countries persons of African descent are numerous, as well as in Cuba, where in the first quarter of the nineteenth century there were more Negroes than whites. In Haiti and in the British and French West Indies the population is still predominantly of African descent. Even in some states in the southern part of the United States there were periods prior to 1900 when Negroes outnumbered the whites; and on the Sea Islands of South Carolina and Georgia white people still constitute only an infinitesimal percentage of the total population. Wherever Negroes were in the majority, African cultural elements had a better chance of surviving, even though frequently in a modified form, than in regions where such a situation did not exist.

Another condition that facilitated the retention of African cultural elements resulted from the physical features of certain regions. Frequently swamps, mountainous areas, or places generally inaccessible attracted run-away slaves. In such places a climate was often created which was conducive to the retention of these elements. Outstanding examples of such concentrations of slaves are the Republic of Palmares, in Pernambuco, Brazil (where for sixty-seven years the Negroes resisted all attempts to the whites to subdue them), the Maroons of Jamaica, British West Indies, and the Bush Negroes of Paramaribo, Dutch Guiana.

Still another factor affecting the retention of African cultural elements was the attitude of the whites. Generally in Catholic countries where African religious practices and certain other aspects of African these elements were more likely to survive than in Protestant countries, culture were more vigorously opposed. In Spanish and Portuguese America, where Africans were never considered inferior to other peoples, the slaves enjoyed many advantages that were denied their brothers in the United States, the British West Indies, and the French possessions in the Caribbean. In Brazil, for example, manumission for the slave was comparatively easy; and once free, he had all of the rights and privileges of any other citizen of the country. In the United States a child born of a slave mother and a white father took the status of the mother, but in Brazil a child so born took the status of the father, and thus was born free. Again, when two slave parents had ten children, the entire family was automatically free. In addition, throughout the long period of slavery in Brazil there was a government official, known as the protector of slaves, who looked after the welfare of slaves treated with cruelty and who had the authority to deprive the owners of slaves so treated. The Brazilian law also provided that slaves should enjoy special privileges on 85 (in some states 104) days out of every year. On these days they could earn enough money to purchase their freedom and their owners were compelled to permit them to do so at a price not higher than that at which they had been purchased. There were still other provisions whereby Brazilian slaves could obtain their freedom. In these ways thousands of them became free. So extensive, in fact, was manumission that by 1888, when slavery was abolished in Brazil, a large majority of the Negroes were already free and were participating actively in all phases of Brazilian life.

Large numbers of these Brazilian Negroes who had obtained their freedom prior to 1888 returned to West Africa. The experiences of this group of ex-slaves have never been adequately described.[4] They settled in various places along the coast of West Africa, and today the wide distribution of Brazilian names in West Africa throws light on some of their own and their descendants' movements. One of their largest settlements was in Lagos, Nigeria, where many of them still live and speak both the Portuguese and Yoruba languages. The first Catholic church in Nigeria was built by ex-slave mechanics from Brazil. School buildings and other structures in Nigeria, Dahomey, and elsewhere in West Africa, some of which are still standing, were built by these Brazilian ex-slaves. One of the best known of these mechanics, Marcos Cardoso, some of whose children are now living in Brazil, built both churches and schools in Nigeria and Dahomey and is also credited with having constructed the first spiral stairway in Nigeria.

When slavery was abolished in Brazil, many of these ex-slaves who had gone to Africa returned to Brazil. Frequently parts of families remained in Africa but kept in close touch with their brothers, sisters, and

other relatives who had returned to Brazil. In some cases, marriages between two Brazilian ex-slaves did not take place until they reached
Africa. There their children would be born, and after a period of years
the parents would return to Brazil with their African-born children,
some of whom would be twenty years of age or older. Many such African-
born persons are now living in Brazil and, of course, speak their native
African language fluently. Sometimes after purchasing his freedom and
that of his family, the former Brazilian slave would not be in a position
to return to Africa with his family, but would send his child or children
there to be educated in the mission schools. In numerous instances Brazilian
ex-slaves kept in touch with Africa by becoming engaged in some lucrative
trade between a West African port (most often Lagos, Nigeria) and
Bahia, Brazil. They would carry to Africa such Brazilian products as
tobacco, sugar, dry salted beef, and cachaça, a drink made from sugar-
cane. On their return they would bring to be sold in Brazil such African
products as kola nuts, palm oil, black soap, pepper, beads, baskets, cowries,
drums, and others. In fact, Brazilian Negroes were engaged in trade with
West Africa until after World War I; and at least as late as 1942, and
possibly later, many articles from West Africa could still be purchased in
the stores and markets of Bahia. Thus, interest in Africa has been kept
alive in Brazil and the retention of many elements of African culture
has been greatly facilitated. Furthermore, this influence of African culture
has spread far beyond the borders of Brazil. Similarly elements of African
culture that have been preserved in Spanish America are constantly
spreading into other New World areas, including the United States.

In the United States the policy of racial segregation (also resulting
from an attitude of the whites toward Negroes), not only in religious
worship but in other activities, has often aided in keeping alive the African
influence. This is especially noticeable in large urban centers of the North
to which Negroes from the South have migrated for better economic,
educational, and political advantages than they have access to in the South.
In the Negro sections of such cities, African survivals of several varieties
can often be found. I have selected for brief treatment here six varieties of
African cultural survivals in the New World that are among the most
prominent: those in languages, folk literature, religion, art, the dance, and
music.

Languages

African linguistic survivals are more numerous in Brazil than
anywhere else in the Western Hemisphere. My own phonograph recordings, made in connection with my field work on African survivals in

Brazil and consisting of approximately six hundred 12-inch discs, all in the African languages, reveal that at least five West African languages are still spoken in the northeastern part of the country by ex-slaves and their descendants. Of these, Nagô or Yoruba (Nigeria), Gêge or Fon (Dahomey), and Kimbundu (Angola) are used more than any others. In some homes in Bahia, I found Yoruba spoken almost as much as Portuguese. From these three languages and others, several thousand words—a conservative estimate, based upon my own findings, would be between 10,000 and 12,000—have become a permanent part of the vocabulary of Brazilian Portuguese. In Cuba, at least one African language (Yoruba) is still spoken. In other parts of the New World, including certain sections of the United States, the influence of African languages is found chiefly in vocabulary (including many thousands of African personal names), sounds, syntax, morphology, word-formations, and intonation. In the coastal region of South Carolina and Georgia, both on the Sea Islands and on the mainland near the coast, I was able to collect nearly six thousand words of African origin that represent approximately thirty West African languages.[5] The large majority of these words are heard now only as personal names, but many of them are used otherwise. Among those in fairly general use in this country, but especially in the South, are the following:

buckra, white man

bubu, insect

cooter, tortoise

cush-cush, corn meal dough sweetened and fried

fufu, mush

ganja, gingerbread

goober, peanut

gumbo, okra

jigger, a species of flea

juju, magic

juke, (as in *jukebox*)

nanse, spider

ninny, female breast

nyam, (*nyam-nyam*) to eat, to eat up

oola, louse, bedbug

oona, (*hoona*) you, your

pinda, peanut

pojo, heron

samba, a dance, to dance

sibby, lima bean

swanga, proud

tabby (as in *tabby-house*), a house made of cement oyster shells, pieces of brick, etc.

tote, to carry

tutu, excrement

voodoo, charm, witchcraft

wanga, charm, witchcraft

yam, sweet potato

Negroes from the southern part of the United States are and have been continually moving northward and westward. In doing so they carry with them many of these African words. It is not surprising, therefore, that so many Negroes in the large urban centers of the North and West still have African given names, though probably most of them are unaware of the meaning of the names and of the fact that they are

words of African origin. Among the Africans the personal name per-
forms certain important functions. For example, it may indicate the
time of the child's birth, or the physical condition or appearance of the
child, or its temperament, character, or mental capacity; it may reveal
the religious affiliation or occupation of the child's parents; or it may
give other types of information about the child at the time of its birth
or later. Among many African tribes one of the given names is that of
the clan to which the child's family belongs. These African names among
American Negroes of both the South and the North are not difficult
to discover. Lists of members of store-front and of other unsophisticated
Negro churches in the North and West, and lists of members of many
other Negro organizations, constitute only one of the many fruitful
sources of such names. The following are a few of the several hundred
African names which I have collected among Negroes on the South
Side of the city of Chicago:

Agona, a country in Ghana (Twi)
Alaiye, monarch (Yoruba)
Anyika, she is beautiful (Vai)
Asumana, a king of the Gallinas in
   Sierra Leone (Vai)
Awuna, name of a tribe in Togoland
Bangala, the season when the grass is
   burned (Congo)
Bilali, the first muezzin, son of Ali
   (Mandingo)
Bimbi, early morning (Fula)
Bobo, one who cannot talk (Vai)
Daji, to rise before day (Yoruba)
Dasi, to spare (Yoruba)
Fitima, evening, dusk (Mende)
Geeji, a language and tribe in Liberia
Hawanya, a tear (Hausa)
Ilaiya, courage (Yoruba)
Jaiya, to be afraid (Yoruba)
Kasanji, an Angola tribe
Keanu, cry mercy (Yoruba)
Kofi, name given a boy born on Friday
   (Twi, Ewe, Fante, and Gâ)

Kwasi, name given a boy born on
   Sunday (Twi and Ewe)
Lukala, name of a river in Angola
Makonya, to serve (Bambara)
Muana, "child" (Tshiluba)
Ola, that which saves (Yoruba)
Sambo, name given the second son
   (Hausa)
Sanko, name of a chiefdom in Sierra
   Leone (Temne)
Sinola, sleeping (Mandinka)
Tiemi, mine (Yoruba)
Timbo, name of a town in French
   Guinea
Tiwoni, it is yours (Twi)
Tonya, truth (Vai)
Wayiba, bad (Kimbundu)
Yetunde, name given a girl born after
   the death of its grandmother; liter-
   ally, Mother comes again (Yoruba)
Zola, to love (Congo)

In the case of many American Negroes, when the personal names
are not of African origin they are likely to be English words revealing
some of the methods employed by the Africans in naming their children.
For example, many American Negroes have such given names as the following: *Eartha*,[6] *Earthy, Freeze, Snowy, Storm, Rain, Wet*, etc. (in-

dicating the nature of the weather or the condition of the earth at the time of birth); or *Badboy, Bigboy, Bigchild, Egghead, Ugly*, etc. (indicating the appearance or temperament of the child at the time of birth or later); or *Harvest, Hightide, Evening, July, Saturday*, etc. (indicating the time of birth, etc.) Many such names among American Negroes are now considered nicknames.

Folk Literature

African folk literature has survived throughout the New World. In Brazil, African folk tales, proverbs, riddles, and other types are told not only in Portuguese but also in the African languages. The folk tales include animal stories, stories relating the exploits and supernatural powers of African deities, tales revealing various aspects of domestic life in Africa (such as the jealousy and rivalry existing among wives having the same husband), narratives of tribal wars and of the brave deeds of African heroes, and etiological tales—those that give a reason for the existence of things. This last-named group also includes cosmological myths. Though these folk tales perform fewer functions in Brazil than they did in Africa, they still play a rather important role in the lives of the large majority of Brazilian Negroes. Many of the stories have special social significance. The rights of the poor are defended against the injustices of the rich and the ruling class. In others, however, loyalty to the ruling class is expressed. Several tales are anti-slavery in sentiment. There are children's stories in which are emphasized the evils resulting from disobedience, laziness, over-eating, etc. In most of the stories some moral is drawn, but many of them, as in Africa, are told primarily to entertain. Such tales, frequently involving magic, generally make a strong imaginative appeal, their humor is often very subtle, and their plots are in most cases skillfully constructed.

In the United States, as well as in Spanish America and the Caribbean, the influence of West African folk literature is unmistakable, especially in the form of folk tales, proverbs, and riddles. Many collections of American Negro folk tales have been published, frequently with many distortions. Among such collections are those of Joel Chandler Harris, Ambrose Gonzales, S. G. Stoney and G. M. Shelby, Irwin Russell, Charles C. Jones, and others; but better examples can be obtained in the South, especially in the Gullah region of South Carolina and Georgia, directly from the Negroes themselves. Some persons have even made phonograph recordings of their own imitations of Gullah (which are poor imitations) and have called them Gullah tales.[7] Since it is not difficult for a field worker to obtain genuine Gullah tales from the Gullahs themselves, one wonders why such persons would be satisfied with issuing imitations of Gullah which are not particularly good imitations.

Many Gullah stories contain African words, phrases, and sentences. Frequently these African portions are accompanied by explanations in English. Plot structure and character portrayal in these tales told by the Gullahs remain essentially the same as in the African tales, with the exception that certain animals may be substituted for their African counterparts, such as the rabbit for the African hare and the tiger for the African leopard. Among the Gullahs the rabbit appears to be more common than the hare is in African tales, and the tortoise and spider are less common. Several of the functions which folk tales serve in African society appear to have been lost among American Negroes. One of the functions of folk tales in Africa is to teach the African child certain aspects of his native language and culture, as, for example, the significance of tone or pitch in determining the meanings of words. There has been no necessity for the retention of this function in the New World. Africans also use folk tales as social satires, employing certain animals to symbolize unjust rulers and certain others as the victims of such injustice. This function also appears not to have survived to any great extent among the Gullahs. On the other hand, such functions as conveying a moral lesson and furnishing entertainment and recreation are still apparent in Gullah tales.[8]

Religion

Throughout the New World in places where the Negro population is large, the influence of certain African religious practices can be observed among unsophisticated groups. Among these are spirit possession, which is a type of highly emotionalized religious experience achieved most easily by the aid of handclapping, singing, and the use of drums and other percussive instruments; a special type of religious dance or ring-shout in which the participants, usually moving counter-clockwise, execute a step similar to the two-step but with a distinctive arm and shoulder movement; the extraordinary degree to which the supernatural functions; the concept of the Devil as a trickster; and others.

In Brazil, African religious practices have been preserved in their purist form in the cult houses of the northeastern part of the country, especially in Bahia, Pernambuco, Minas Gerais, Maranhão, Alagoas, Sergipe, and Rio de Janeiro. Among the names given to these cult houses are Condomblé, Macumba, and Shango. Though the influence of the Catholic Church is present in the cult ceremonies, this influence is far less than is commonly supposed by observers unacquainted with the nature of religious worship in those sections of West Africa from which the Brazilian Negro came. In and around the Nagô or Yoruba cult houses of Bahia, for example, the atmosphere is so unmistakably African that one has difficulty realizing that he is in the New World. Here one can listen to genuine African drum rhythms. The melody and lyrics of the several hundred different songs sung are in Yoruba, Congo, Kimbundu, Fon, and other African languages. The same African influence is observed in the dances, the costumes and their accessories, the invocation to the African deities, the discipline imposed upon cult members, and many other important details connected with the form of worship. The musical instruments are also African. There are fewer deities worshiped today in Brazil, however, than formerly. The following are a few of the Yoruba deities or orishas still worshiped in the African cult houses of the northeastern section of the country: Oshala, the chief of the orishas, also called Oshogiyan; Shango, the god of thunder; Ogun, the god of war and iron; Omolu,[9] the god of smallpox, also called Shokpono; Osahin, one of the Yoruba gods of medicine; Oshumare, the rainbow deity; Oshun, the river goddess; Yemaja, the goddess of the sea; and many others. It should be noted that in spite of the fact that the majority of the Negroes of Bahia are worshipers of African deities, many of them are also members of the Catholic Church. As already indicated, however, the form of their worship in the cult houses is essentially African, not Catholic, even though each African deity has the name of a Catholic saint as well as an African name.[10]

Art

In Africa, the Negro's chief arts were sculpture in wood, bone, and ivory, metal-working, leather work, shell and bead work, weaving, and pottery—all combined with skillful decoration in line and color. In the United States because of conditions surrounding the slave, African art forms had less chance of survival than religion, folk literature, music, the dance, and some other aspects of African culture; yet in isolated areas, like the Sea Islands of South Carolina and Georgia, the influence of African art is still present in metal-working, wood-carving, and weaving.[11] Before the Civil War in the United States, Negro artisans played an important role in American industrial development in the South and parts of the East. They showed great skill in such trades as weaving and the making of tools and utensils, as well as in the construction and decoration of buildings. Much of this work clearly reveals the African influence.[12]

Survivals of African art can be found in other parts of the New

World. In the worship of African deities in the cult communities of Brazil, for example, the sculptor is called upon to create male and female figures which serve as intermediaries. Through them contact is made with the various deities. Moreover, in the practice of divination, the Afro-Brazilian diviner has to make use of carved objects; and in the houses in which the cult ceremonies take place, wood-carving, metal-working, and other forms are needed, as well as costumes for the dancers. Thus, the Afro-Brazilian sculptor and craftsman are almost constantly employed; and all of these creations are kept as close to the African originals as possible.

The Dance

In Africa almost every act of social life is accompanied by dance and song. Many varieties of these dances, both secular and religious, were brought to the New World by the slaves and are still popular here. In Brazil, besides the numerous religious dances dedicated to the African deities, many African secular dances have survived. Several of these were combined into a single form known as the samba (itself an African word), which became the national dance of Brazil, equivalent to the rhumba in Cuba and the tango in the Argentine. These and many others are African with some modifications because of European influence. Throughout Spanish America and the Caribbean the influence of African dances of many varieties is unmistakable.[13]

On the Sea Islands of South Carolina and Georgia several dances of African origin have been preserved. Among these are the Charleston, the black bottom, the buzzard lope, the mosquito dance, and others, including the religious dance or ring-shout. The ring-shout, previously described, is also common in some of the unsophisticated Negro churches in many sections of the South and the North.[14]

Music

Professor Richard A. Waterman, who has worked extensively in the field of African music, has pointed out several distinctive features of African folk music as contrasted with European folk music.[15] Whereas both are on about the same level in melodic structure, European folk music is more complex harmonically and simpler rhythmically. He lists such distinctive features of African folk music as predominance of percussion, multiple meter or the use of two or three time-signatures at once, the over-lapping of the call and response pattern, and the off-beat phrasing of melodic accents, resembling what one calls syncopation in jazz. All of these features are found in African music that has survived in the New World.

The African songs that are still heard in Brazil usually deal with the same subjects as the folk tales. In fact, most of the tales are interspersed with songs that are commentaries on the different parts of the story. There are religious songs (usually sung in honor of the various African deities), funeral songs (in which a moral is frequently drawn from the life of the deceased and which, to a certain extent, serve as a funeral sermon), love songs, lullabies, street cries, war songs, hunting songs, work songs, drinking songs, and many other varieties. Several of the songs, like many in West Africa, have the melody of some of the Negro spirituals, so common in the United States, and of some of the tunes of Stephen Foster, who said that he acquired some of his tunes from the Negro slaves.[16] The Calypso type of music, which reached the United States by way of the West Indies, is also of African origin, having been carried to the West Indies by the slaves.

Many rhythms that are now well known in the United States and Latin America are of African origin. Among these are the Charleston, the Juba, the Malaguenha, and several others. The Charleston rhythm is derived from the rhythm of Oshun, the Yoruba goddess of rivers; the Juba, from that of Iyansan, the wife of the Yoruba god of thunder (Shango); and the Malaguenha, from that of Oshala, the chief of the Yoruba deities.

Throughout the New World in areas where Negroes have lived in large numbers many varieties of African musical instruments can be found. Among these are drums, rattles, gongs of several kinds, the marimba (also an African word) or xylophone, and certain types of stringed instruments. Among African musical instruments used both in the cult houses and elsewhere in Brazil are the following: the double iron gong, called in Yoruba *agogô*; gourd rattles, including the *ganzu*, the *shekere*,[17] and the *chocalho*; the long drums, having various African names, such as *hun, humpri, le, illú*, etc.; a friction drum called the *cuica*; a hollow and notched rubbing instrument, known as the *ganzá*; the musical bow or *birambau*; the *balanji* or xylophone; and several others. Some of these are also found in other parts of Latin America and the Caribbean.

Today, with the rapid spread of nationalism in sub-Saharan Africa, this region is becoming better known in other parts of the world than ever before. Press coverage of African affairs and books and magazine articles dealing with Africa have increased enormously during the past few years. Today African art forms are achieving in America and Europe a recognition and status scarcely to be imagined several years ago. Each year an increasing number of African students are attending universities in

Europe, Asia, and America; and more foreigners, especially Americans and Europeans, are visiting Africa on technical and educational missions and as tourists. But to most Europeans and Americans sub-Saharan Africa is still essentially a land of mystery. Whereas research dealing with varying forms of the impact of European culture on sub-Saharan Africa is quite considerable, far too little attention is being given to objective studies of those aspects of the native culture of Negro Africa—especially the arts—which are and have been exerting, for more than four centuries, a significant influence upon Western civilization. More such studies would go a long way toward destroying in the minds of other peoples of the world the many deeply rooted stereotypes regarding Africans—stereotypes due in great part, but not wholly, to lack of knowledge of the native culture of Negro Africa.

NOTES

1. R.E.G. Armattoe, *The Golden Age of West African Civilization* (Londonderry, Northern Ireland: Pub. for Lomeshie Research Center by the *Londonderry Sentinel*, 1946), pp. 33, 35.

2. See Melville J. Herskovits, *The Myth of the Negro Past* (New York: Harper & Brothers, 1941), pp. 143–206.

3. Frank Tannenbaum, in his *Slave and Citizen: The Negro in the Americas* (New York: A. A. Knopf, 1947) gives many valuable statistics, drawn from numerous sources, on the importation of slaves both to Latin America and other parts of the New World. For an account of slave importations to the United States prior to 1808, see Elizabeth Donnan, *Documents Illustrative of the History of the Slave Trade to America* (Washington, D. C.: Carnegie Institution of Washington, 1935), vol. IV.

4. Lorenzo D. Turner, "Some Contacts of Brazilian Ex-Slaves with Nigeria, West Africa," *Journal of Negro History* 27 (January 1942): 55–67.

5. See Lorenzo D. Turner, *Africanisms in the Gullah Dialect* (Chicago: University of Chicago Press, 1949) for an account of African survivals not only in the vocabulary of Gullah but also in its sounds, syntax, morphology, word formations, and intonation.

6. Miss Eartha Kitt has been quoted as saying that her parents named her *Eartha* because they were enjoying a good harvest at the time of her birth.

7. Three long-playing records of imitations of Gullah have been issued by the Library of Congress and called "Animal Tales in the Gullah Dialect" by Albert H. Stoddard of Savannah, Georgia, and edited by Duncan Emrich.

8. For examples of the influence of African folklore on that of parts of South America and of the Caribbean, see Suzanne Comhaire-Sylvain, "Creole Tales from Haiti," *Journal of American Folklore* 50–51 (July–September 1937, and July–September 1938); Melville J. and Frances S. Herskovits, *Suriname Folk-Lore* (New York: Columbia University Press, 1936); Melville J. Herskovits, *Life in a Haitian Valley* (New York: A. A. Knopf, 1937), pp. 264–65; Elsie Clews Parsons, *Folk-Tales of Andros Island, Bahamas* (Lancaster, Pa. and New York: American Folklore Society, 1918) and *Folk-Lore of the Antilles, French and English*, Parts I, II, and III (New

York: American Folklore Society, 1933, 1936, and 1943); and Arthur Ramos, *O Folk-Lore negro do Brasil* (Rio de Janeiro: Civilizacao Brasileira, 1937).

9. The symbol *o* represents the sound of *aw* in the English word *law*.

10. For an account of survivals of African religious practices in Haiti, see Herskovits, *Life in a Haitian Valley*, pp. 139–319.

11. See Lydia Parrish, *Slave Songs of the Georgia Sea Islands* (New York: Creative Age Press, Inc., 1942), where, facing pp. 112 and 113, appear photographs showing the influence of African sculpture upon Gullah wood-carvers.

12. For an excellent discussion of these activities of Negroes, see James A. Porter, *Modern Negro Art* (New York: The Dryden Press, 1943), pp. 13–28.

13. For a list and brief description of many of the Afro-Brazilian secular dances, see Arthur Ramos, *The Negro in Brazil* (Washington, D. C.: The Associated Publishers, Inc., 1951), pp. 116–23. For an account of the role of the religious dance in the cult houses of Bahia, Brazil, see Melville and Frances Herskovits, "The Negroes of Brazil," *The Yale Review* 33 (Winter 1943): 275–79, and Donald Pierson, *Negroes in Brazil* (Chicago: The University of Chicago Press, 1942), pp. 300–04. Dr. Pierson, not well acquainted with the native culture of the Africans, has greatly underestimated its influence on Brazilian culture. For an account of the influence of African dances in other New World regions, see also Melville J. Herskovits, *The Myth of the Negro Past*, pp. 269–71, and *In a Haitian Valley*, pp. 262–64.

14. See Lydia Parrish, *Slave Songs*, where, facing pp. 128, 144, and 145, are photographs of Sea Island Negroes, participating in the ring-shout. See also in the same study (facing p. 129) photographs of participants in the buzzard lope.

15. See Richard A. Waterman, "African Influence on the Music of the Americas," in *Acculturation in the Americas*, edited by Sol Tax (Chicago: The University of Chicago Press, 1952), pp. 207–18.

16. For example, the tune of Foster's "Camp-Town Races" I found to be that of a tune sung by African (Yoruba) mothers while playing with their small children. Another of Foster's tunes is that of a canoeing song sung by the Efik people of Eastern Nigeria.

17. The symbol *e* represents the sound of *e* in the English word *met*.

7. HOLLIS R. LYNCH, Pan-Negro Nationalism in the New World, Before 1862 (1966)*

As a native of Trinidad, a specialist in modern West African history, and professor of history at Columbia University, Hollis R. Lynch brings an appropriately varied background to his keen interest in Pan-Africanism. This essay grew out of Lynch's earlier study of Edward Wilmot Blyden, one of the early patriots of Pan-Negroism. By focusing on the work of such leading Pan-Africanists as Blyden, Martin R. De-

* Hollis R. Lynch, "Pan-Negro Nationalism in the New World Before 1862," reprinted by permission of the publishers from *Boston University Papers on Africa*, Volume II, *African History*, Jeffrey Butler, editor, pp. 149–79, Boston, Massachusetts: Boston University Press. © Copyright 1966 by the Trustees of Boston University.

laney, Paul Cuffee, James T. Holly, and Alexander Crummell, he is able
not only to trace the development of Black Nationalism among Afro-
Americans but also to describe the conflicts that occurred among the
leading advocates of Pan-Africanism.

Pan-Africanism and pan-Negro nationalism are historically related
phenomena with similar origins.[1] Both grew out of resentment at the
treatment of black-skinned peoples, whether as slaves in the West Indies
and in the American South, as "free persons of color," or, later, as subjects of new European empires in Africa. Pan-Africanism as an organized
movement, concerned with the grievances of all black-skinned peoples,
and particularly involving an attack on colonialism in Africa, is a twentieth-century phenomenon: the term came into use in 1900 when Henry
Sylvester Williams, a West Indian barrister from Trinidad, organized a
Pan-African conference in London, attended by delegates from the West
Indies and the United States.[2]

Five other conferences were held, largely through the efforts of
the American Negro scholar, W. E. B. DuBois, at which delegates met
to articulate their grievances and to devise means of removing them.[3]
These delegates were almost entirely from the New World; indeed, it was
only at the last of the extra-African conferences—at Manchester in 1945—
that Africans were adequately represented.[4] No meetings had been held
on African soil, though African issues were discussed at every conference.
After Ghana gained its independence in 1957, the Pan-African movement began to take on a more African character, largely because it had the
support of the first of the new African states created after World War II.
Though New World Negroes had played, and continued to play, a part
on the African continent, the movement passed finally into the hands of
African leaders.[5]

This specifically named and organized Pan-Africanism was not the
first Negro movement with "African" and "all-African" aspirations.
There were at least two earlier such manifestations of thought and feeling, the most recent—Marcus Garvey's "Back to Africa" movement in the
nineteen-twenties—being the best known.[6] But early in the nineteenth
century there developed among Negroes in the West Indies and in the
United States a movement preoccupied with the promotion of emigration
and the creation of new states, most of them in Africa. As in the case of
Garvey's movement, these early pan-Negro nationalists were concerned
with the plight of Negroes in the New World. They failed, however,
to produce a charismatic leader or a mass movement. Nevertheless, in
their statements and actions these pan-Negro leaders anticipated many
of their twentieth-century successors,[7] particularly in their interest in
Africa, their belief in a great African past, and their dilemma of choice

between reform of the New World and "regeneration" of their ancestral home.

Haiti

Haiti had a chance to be the first state to provide a base for a pan-Negro program. The slaves of Haiti revolted in 1804 and gained their independence from the greatest military power in Europe, to become the second modern sovereign state in the Americas. The rulers of the Negro "empire" were aware of a responsibility to the Negro race when they invited Negroes to cooperate in building a model state as the final, convincing answer to assertions of Negro inferiority.[8] However, because of internal division, Haiti failed to fulfill its promise.[9] Even so, its continued existence remained for many Negroes proof of Negro ability, and a source of hope for a better future for the race.

Of course, many New World and British Negroes had maintained a sentimental attachment to, and interests in, Africa. It is noteworthy that practically all Negro organizations formed in the United States up to about the third decade of the nineteenth century had the word "African" in their titles.[10] And among the Negroes in Britain, set free by Lord Mansfield's judicial decision in 1772, there were a few who advocated what was essentially the point of view of British evangelicals and humanitarians, namely, that Britain should exert itself to stop the slave trade, replace it by legitimate commerce, and help to Christianize and civilize Africa.[11] These Negroes of Britain also played a part in inducing British humanitarian groups to found the colony of Sierra Leone in 1787. The Negroes themselves formed the great majority of the emigrants who embarked from Britain.[12] Less than two years after the first emigrants landed, the Free African Society of Newport, Rhode Island, showed an interest in the colony and in 1795 sent out a delegate to prospect.[13] Sierra Leone also attracted Negroes from Nova Scotia, where they had been settled after fighting on the side of the British in the American revolution. Anxious to leave behind an uncongenial climate and society, 1,131 of them—led by Thomas Peters, a millwright, who had negotiated with the directors of the Sierra Leone Company, and David George, a zealous Baptist preacher—emigrated to the "Colony of Freedom" in 1792. Both Peters and George can be regarded as prototypes of those Negro leaders who sought to lead Negroes out of "bondage" and back to the "fatherland" in Africa.

Moreover, the arrival of the Nova Scotians saved the colony from complete dissolution. Further reinforcements came in 1800 in the form of 532 Maroons who had taken part in a revolt in Jamaica, had been transported to Nova Scotia, and had then elected to emigrate to Sierra Leone. In 1807, the British government outlawed the slave trade and on January 1, 1808, assumed from the Sierra Leone Company direct control of the colony, which was to be used as a center for the suppression of the slave-trade in West Africa as well as for settling and civilizing liberated Africans. In 1804, the Church Missionary Society began work in the colony, and Sierra Leone became the center of British humanitarian activities in West Africa. By 1808, Sierra Leone had a population of nearly two thousand westernized Negroes and had became an obvious focus for further Negro emigration to Africa. Sierra Leone might do what Haiti was failing to do.

In the early years of the ninteenth century, there were already signs that the freed American Negro might have to seek a home outside the United States. Those years marked a sharp decline in his fortune. The invention and use of the cotton gin in the last years of the eighteenth century, and the subsequent remarkable spread of the cotton kingdom to the South and Southwest, had served to revive the waning institution of slavery. Manumission of slaves, which had been frequent in the years following the American revolution, had come to a virtual end in the South by the turn of the century. The relatively large free Negro population that had grown up was regarded by many white Southerners as an anomaly and a threat to its society.[14] In the North, Negroes fared no better: although by 1804, all slavery there had been abolished, Negroes were not accepted as an integral part of American society.[15] And as the southern states began taking measures intended to return free Negroes to slavery or to drive them out, the North, fearful of an influx, seemed to vie with the South in making their lives difficult.

Despite the growing discrimination against them, however, many American Negroes continued to assert their rights as American citizens. Many, for instance, began to look upon the efforts of the American Colonization Society,[16] founded in 1817 as a barely disguised attempt on the part of slaveholders, who were prominently associated with the organization, to rid the United States of a potentially troublesome element and thus make secure the Southern system of slavery.[17] From 1830 on, Negroes met in national conventions to denounce slaveholders and the American Colonization Society, and to declare their determination to fight for their civil rights.[18]

United States

While many Negroes in the United States sought to achieve complete integration within American society, others became pan-Negro nationalists. Despairing of becoming first-class citizens in their own country, they became advocates of Negro emigration to Africa and elsewhere, and held visions of new states on a continent regenerated by their efforts. Prominent among them were Paul Cuffee, Daniel Coker, Lott Cary, and John Russwurm.[19] All but Cuffee died in the newly established Negro settlements in West Africa.

Cuffee was a devout Quaker from Massachusetts, a prosperous trader and shipowner who, as a young man, had fought for the rights of Negroes in his native state.[20] When this met with little success, he turned to Africa, and particularly to Sierra Leone, to work for the "improvement and civilization of the blacks" of Africa, to provide selective emigration to Sierra Leone, and to seek the suppression of the slave trade and its replacement by legitimate commerce. His trader's mind was excited by the possibility of extensive commerce between Negro America and West Africa, to raise the wealth and prestige of the race. In 1808, he obtained the support of the African Institution, a British humanitarian organization comprised mainly of former directors of the Sierra Leone Company and still influential in directing the affairs of the colony. Three years later he visited Sierra Leone, where he showed considerable care in making plans for emigration. Finally, he founded the Friendly Society of Sierra Leone "to open a channel of intercourse" between Negro America and Sierra Leone; as an earnest of his good faith, he bought a house in Freetown.[21]

Long interested in Negro education in America, Cuffee also showed interest in promoting education in Sierra Leone: "Africa calls for men of character to fill stations in the Legislature," he wrote.[22] On his return to America, he sought personally to persuade Negroes in such centers as Baltimore, Philadelphia, New York, Boston, and his own town of Westport to support colonization in Africa. In 1815 Cuffee made his second trip to Sierra Leone, taking, largely at his own expense, thirty-eight Negroes in family groups. In letters to America these emigrants urged other Negroes to follow their example.[23] When Cuffee returned, he made his experience available to the founders of the American Colonization Society. Indeed, he was chosen to lead emigrants to be sent out by the society, but he died before the first expedition left for West Africa. However, shortly before this he expressed the widespread feeling Negroes shared against the society by cautioning against too eager an acceptance of its scheme.[24]

Despite Cuffee's warning, the society won the support of his friend Daniel Coker. A runaway slave who as a boy had acquired a rudimentary education, Coker had become schoolmaster and religious leader in the free Negro community of Baltimore. As a young man, he had angrily denounced the institution of slavery and asserted that, despite its handicap, "the African Race . . . had given proof of talents." [25] Coker had played a leading role in the break with the Methodist Episcopal Church, which resulted in the formation of the African Methodist Episcopal Church.[26] Elected its first bishop, he had declined the honor. Intent on emigrating to West Africa, he was among the first eighty-eight emigrants sent out by the Colonization Society. Although the expedition was led by three white officials, it seems that in the eyes of the emigrants Coker was the leader.[27] His journal shows him as keenly conscious of the possibilities of the enterprise and of some responsibility for its success. In the two years of hardship and uncertainty that followed before the emigrants finally settled at Cape Mesurado—the first beginnings of Liberia—the leadership devolved mainly on him. He later settled in Sierra Leone.

Lott Cary, who was among the second group of emigrants, played a versatile role as clergyman, doctor, militiaman, builder, and pioneer in agriculture.[28] He regarded himself as primarily a missionary to the native Africans, and from the start he was concerned that the colonists should have friendly relations with the tribes and so exert a civilizing influence. He was born a slave, and, though ignorant at twenty-seven, he acquired considerable learning and became a well-to-do Baptist preacher in Richmond, Virginia, by the age of thirty-three. Yet he gave up this relatively comfortable position to go to Liberia. He wrote: "I am an African; and in this country, however meritorious my conduct and respectable my character, I cannot receive the credit due to either. I wish to go to a country where I shall be estimated by my merits not by my complexion, and I feel bound to labour for my suffering race." [29] Cary died, in an accident, on November 10, 1828.

John B. Russwurm was born in Jamaica, and became one of the first two Negro graduates from an American college.[30] In March 1827, he founded and became the editor of the first American Negro newspaper, *Freedom's Journal*. He abandoned his opposition to the American Colonization Society, and in 1829 announced his conversion to the view that the free Negro could help himself and his race best by giving strong support to Liberia.[31] He soon left for Liberia and in 1830 founded the *Liberia Herald*. He also held the positions of superintendent of education and colonial secretary; from 1836 until his death in 1851, he was governor of Maryland, a colony adjacent to Liberia to the south, which was founded by the Maryland Colonization Society in 1834.[32] As the first Negro governor in West Africa, Russwurm felt that the conduct of his office was a test of the ability of the Negro: he seems to have ruled with substantial justice to colonists, Africans, and missionaries alike.[33]

These four leaders in the early phase of the Pan-African movement had much in common. All were men of substance, in nearly every case through their own talent and industry. All of them, including Russwurm the Jamaican, were protesting against discrimination in the United States. Indeed, Coker had taken part in the setting up of an "African" church, an early example of the use of historical origins as the basis of a protest. Although Russwurm and Cuffee showed an understandable suspicion of the white-dominated American Colonization Society, they gave Liberia their support, perhaps on the good practical ground that, whatever the motive of the society's leaders and supporters, the society was creating a Negro state in Africa.

Between 1830 and about 1850, there seems to have been something of a falling off of activity among American Negroes. No new and effective leader appeared to take up the pan-Negro cause, although there is evidence that sentiment in favor of emigration continued to grow.[34] In the West Indies, particularly in Jamaica and Barbados, there was widespread interest both in leaving the place of former bondage and continued discrimination and in taking Christianity to "benighted brothers" in Africa.[35] In Barbados, in the three decades after the abolition of slavery, at least three organizations were formed for promoting emigration to Liberia: the Barbados Colonization Society, the Fatherland Union Society, and the Barbados Company for Liberia.[36] But because of the lack of adequate financial resources among Negroes or external aid, the opposition of the still powerful West Indian sugar planters, and perhaps the absence of any oppressive discrimination, little emigration was organized.[37]

It is, however, interesting that groups in the West Indies should have looked to Liberia. After the emancipation of the slaves, there was less pressure on them in the form of discrimination than on the American Negro to seek a home elsewhere. It is significant that the three important West Indian advocates of pan-Negro nationalism discussed here—Russwurm, Edward W. Blyden,[38] and Robert Campbell[39]—had all experienced and resented the discrimination against Negroes in the United States.

The desire of West Indian Negroes who wanted to emigrate for other reasons had important consequences for West Africa. It was these people who urged the start of missionary work in West Africa by both the British Baptist and the United Scottish Presbyterian societies. West Indians played an important role in their work, as well as in that of the Basel and Wesleyan missions. They accounted also for the formation of the West Indian Church Association, whose missionaries worked in the Rio Pongo area in West Africa. The association was an autonomous body which, unlike the other missionary societies, derived its support in money and men mainly from West Indian Negroes.[40] The West Indian missionaries and teachers worked, so they felt, for the regeneration of Africa and on behalf of the Negro race.[41] Men like Joseph Fuller, Henry Wharton, and John Duport respectively spent forty, twenty-eight, and eighteen years in Africa.[42]

In the eighteen-fifties, however, there was a rapid revival of interest among American Negroes, as the conflict over slavery became more intense. Negroes were, of course, deeply involved and, as events appeared to be set on a course against them, more wanted to emigrate. In 1850, the Fugitive Slave Bill was passed giving federal commissioners virtually unlimited power for the apprehension and return of alleged fugitives. This was only the first shock in a decade of "sorrowful and unmixed gloom." [43] There followed the Kansas-Nebraska Act, the Dred Scott decision, the failure of John Brown's raid, and an apparent blow from the Republican Party when Abraham Lincoln, a compromise candidate, assumed the presidency. It would be useful to study the period between 1850 and 1862 in detail because not until Garvey's "Back to Africa" movement of the 1920s did pan-Negro nationalism seem again to possess real vigor.

The independence of Liberia in 1847 could hardly have come at a more opportune time for the cause of emigration from the New World. Congratulations to the new republic came from all major Negro groups, and many hoped with John B. Hepburn of Port-au-Prince that Liberia's course was now "onward to empire and to fame." [44] In 1848, the American Colonization Society sent out delegates to report on Liberia's possibilities as a future home.[45] West Indian Negroes, too, showed interest: the Barbados Colonization Society "for assisting in the suppression of the Slave Trade, and the introduction of civilization into Africa" received the news of Liberia's independence with "inexpressible joy" and regarded it "as another demonstration to the world, that the descendants of Africa, when placed in a fair position, are not inferior in civilization, religion, and morality, to those nations amongst whom it was their lot to be cast for a given time." [46] The new interest in Liberia reflected itself in a substantial increase in the annual number of American emigrants, which rose from 51 in 1847 to 441 in 1848. This increase in emigration was maintained throughout the next decade.[47]

Liberia

The new Liberian republic, of which so much was hoped, had a disappointing beginning. In 1850, three years after independence, it was a country of roughly 13,000 square miles, with a coastline of approximately 300 miles. Its emigrant population, depleted by a high mortality rate, was about 6,000. Since 1827 the majority of those sent out by the Colonization

Society had been slaves who were emancipated expressly for that purpose,[48] and many were unfit for pioneering.[49]

It is not surprising, then, that the sense of mission and destiny which inspired the early emigrants was largely missing among the later ones. Between its founding and 1850, Liberia seems to have produced only one outstanding champion of the pan-Negro ideology, the "poet and philosopher," Hilary Teage, son of Colin Teage, who had come from Lott Cary's congregation in Richmond, Virginia. He succeeded Russwurm as editor of the *Liberia Herald* in 1835, and for the next fourteen years used it to express his pan-Negro sentiments. He was certainly the first poet of pan-Negro nationalism: his poetry is concerned with the themes of the past achievements of his race and of a mission to fulfill.[50] He was also an accomplished orator. He said to a group of Liberians in 1846: "Upon you, rely upon it, depends, in a measure you can hardly conceive, the future destiny of the race. You are to give the answer whether the African race is doomed to interminable degradation—a hideous blot on the fair face of creation, a libel upon the dignity of human nature; or whether they are capable to take an honourable rank amongst the great family of nations." [51] In 1847 he was a representative at Liberia's constitutional conference.

On the whole, however, Liberians did not demonstrate much unity of purpose or public spirit. They were berated by their white governors and their progressive leaders for their "want of self-respect" and their easy dependence on foreign philanthropy.[52] Socially there had quickly developed in Liberia an American pattern of stratifications based on color, the mulattoes considering themselves superior to the black emigrants while the colonists, generally speaking, held the natives in contempt.[53] The Liberians exploited native labor on their plantations, but, on the whole, agriculture was neglected for trading, which brought quick profits without developing the productive capacity of the country.

Until its independence, the supreme authority in the colony was the American Colonization Society. Independence came from the demand by Liberians for, among other things, the soverign power to deal with recalcitrant European traders scornful of the developing Negro nation.[54] And so on July 26, 1847, Liberia became a sovereign nation with a constitution modeled on that of the United States.[55] Unfortunately, the constitution contained a provision which was later to keep the young nation in a chaotic political condition: the president, the House of Representatives, and half of the senators were be elected every two years. Moreover, the franchise was confined mainly to American colonists.

With renewed support from New World Negroes, however, the new nation could have retrieved itself. Such was the view of Edward Wilmot

Blyden, probably the most articulate advocate of pan-Negro nationalism in the nineteenth century.[56] Born free [57] on the Danish West Indian island of St. Thomas in 1832, and educated at the local primary school and by private tuition from his American pastor, the Reverend John Knox, and his own mother, Blyden early decided on the ministry as a career. In May 1850, Knox took him to the United States and attempted to enroll him in Rutgers' Theological College, Knox's alma mater. Blyden was refused admission because of his race, and, aware of the operation of the Fugitive Slave Law, he accepted an offer from the New York Colonization Society to emigrate to Liberia.

Even before he left the United States, Blyden expressed pride in the newly independent Negro republic: Liberia, he thought, could "include within its limits the dark regions of Ashantee and Dahomey and bring those barbarous tribes under civilized and enlightened influence." [58] In his first letter to the United States he described his pleasure at being on African soil: "You can easily imagine the delight with which I gazed upon the land of Tertullian, ancient father in the Christian Church; of Hannibal and Henry Diaz, renowned generals; yes, and the land of *my* forefathers . . . The land here is teeming with everything necessary for subsistence of man." The skeptics, he wrote, should come and see for themselves.[59] He continued his studies at Alexander High School, a Presbyterian school in Monrovia. In 1858 he was ordained a minister and became principal of the high school. From the beginning of his time in Liberia, Blyden was active in public life, both as a correspondent for the *Liberia Herald* and as editor during 1855–56. Moreover, he remained an active propagandist for Liberia and the cause of emigration, writing often for the *African Repository* (the journal of the American Colonization Society) and for the journals of the New York and Maryland Colonization societies.

Blyden was an articulate and critical defender of his new home, and from an early stage he was concerned about diverting the expected flow of emigration from the United States to Africa, particularly to Liberia. It is probable that his first pamphlet, *A Voice from Bleeding Africa*, published in Monrovia in 1856, appeared just before the emigration conference of 1856 was scheduled to meet in Cleveland,[60] though there is no evidence that it was discussed there. In the pamphlet he appealed to "colored men of every rank and station, in every clime and country" to support the colonization movement. Moreover, he urged Negroes to take the name of the new state seriously: the object of the creation of Liberia was "the redemption of Africa and the disenthralment and elevation of the African race, objects worthy of every colored man." At the same time, he attacked Liberians for a lack of dedication to the cause:

How painful is the reflection that there are but few of the young men of Liberia who seem to give the future of their country a moment's thought . . . ! O young men and women of Liberia, arise from your lethargy, shake off your puerile notions and practices! It is high time to bestir yourselves to be men and women. Let the brave achievements and noble deeds of your fathers arouse you to effort. Let the future glory that awaits your country kindle within you an honorable ambition and urge you onwards.[61]

He wanted to see "the young men of Liberia, like the youth among the ancient Spartans, exercise themselves vigorously in all things which pertain to the country's welfare." [62]

An opportunity for him to act as a defender of Liberia came in 1852. Gerrit Smith, a veteran abolitionist and member of Congress from New York, in opposing a scheme to send Negroes to Liberia, dubbed the American Colonization Society "the deadliest enemy of the Negro race," and Liberia "a frightful graveyard." [63] Blyden attacked Senator Smith for "doing . . . considerable harm . . . by blinding the minds of colored men to their true interests." Colonization in Africa, he contended, was "the only means of delivering the colored man from oppression and of raising him up to respectability." He would not accept the advice of Smith and other abolitionists that, if necessary, free Negroes should retire to Canada to await the outcome of the issue of slavery. Admitting that the mortality rate in Liberia was high, Blyden claimed that this was a temporary condition, common to all pioneer communities.[64]

While Blyden was rebuking Senator Smith, Martin R. Delaney, a Negro doctor trained at Harvard and a former newspaper editor and abolitionist, was devising a scheme based on a Negro empire in the Caribbean and South and Central America. After the passage of the Fugitive Slave Bill, he despaired of American Negroes ever enjoying the full rights of citizenship in the United States. He had grown impatient even with the white abolitionists when he realized that Negroes were "occupying the very same position, in relation to our anti-slavery friends, as we do in relation to the pro-slavery part of the community—a mere secondary, underling position, in all our relations to them, and anything more than this comes by mere sufferance." He dismissed with "contemptuous indignation the absurd idea of the natural inferiority of the African," warned Negroes not to carry their religion to the point of hoping for a divine intervention on their behalf, and urged them to support him in constructive action.[65]

His projected empire was to be formed by American Negroes emigrating to South America, an area for which he made two doubtful claims: first, that it was predominantly Negroid and, second, that there had "never existed there an inequality on account of color or race."[66] His advocacy of a Negro empire in the Americas was partly for strategic reasons: by its proximity it would, either by moral or physical force, bring about the collapse of slavery in the United States. But he also believed that Negroes, as developers of the economic base of the New World, were entitled to their full share of its fruits. Still he did not overlook Africa, which he hoped would be "civilized and enlightened," with Liberia in a "high and elevated position . . . among the nations of the earth." Yet he continued to regard the American Colonization Society as working to promote the interest of slaveholders and was, therefore, severely critical of Liberia's dependence on it.[67]

It is hardly surprising that Blyden and Delany came into conflict. Blyden defended the American Colonization Society and Liberia with some spirit. Delany's plan was a diversion, he wrote, and doomed to failure in any case. Only in Africa could the Negro race rise to distinguished achievement.[68]

Before Delany could act on his scheme, the largest Negro national conference up to that time was convened in Rochester, New York, in 1853, and the persistent division between emigrationists and anti-emigrationists was forced into the open. The anti-emigrationists, led by the Negro leader Frederick Douglass, persuaded the conference to go on record as opposing emigration.[69] But as soon as the conference was over, the emigrationists, led by Delany, James M. Whitfield, a popular poet, and James T. Holly, an accomplished Episcopalian clergyman, called a conference for August 1854, from which anti-emigrationists were to be excluded. Douglass described this action as "narrow and illiberal," and he sparked the first public debate among American Negro leaders on the subject of emigration.[70]

The conference on emigration met in Cleveland as planned. It was, according to Delany, the most widely representative one ever convened by Negroes.[71] Shortly before it met, the passage of the Kansas-Nebraska Act had provided another triumph for the supporters of slavery. Understandably, the mood of the conference was militant. Delany repeated his call for the creation of a Negro empire in the New World, where "the inherent traits, attributes . . . and native characteristics peculiar to our race could be cultivated and developed." [72] He warned that "submission does not gain for us an increase of friends nor respectability, as the white race will only respect those who oppose their usurpation, and acknowledge as equals those who will not submit to their rule." They were to take concerted action: "We must make an issue, create an event and establish for ourselves a position. This is essentially necessary for our effective elevation as a people, in shaping our national development, directing our destiny and redeeming ourselves as a race." A Negro empire was further necessary to put "a check to European presumption and insufferable Yankee intrusion and impudence."[73]

Although the conference adopted Delany's report, there were distinct territorial preferences among those who thought in terms of the Western hemisphere. Whitfield favored colonization in Central America, while Holly opted for Haiti. No public announcement about Africa emerged from the conference, but that too had been discussed. According to Delany: "The Convention . . . in its Secret Session made Africa, with its inexhaustible productions and the great facilities for checking the abominable Slave Trade, its most important point of dependence; though our first gun was levelled, and the first shell thrown at the American continent driving the slave-holding faction into despair . . . Africa was held in reserve." [74] As a result of the conference, the National Emigration Board was set up. Delany began negotiations with "several states of Central and South America as well as Jamaica and Cuba." [75] Holly left for Haiti to conduct negotiations there, which, although inconclusive, were encouraging enough to cause him on his return to begin agitating for Negro emigration to that territory.[76] In August 1856, the biennial meeting of the National Emigration Conference convened again in Cleveland; delegates supported emigration again and decided to organize a publishing company for propaganda purposes.

West Africa

As the conflict between Delany and Blyden shows, it was not merely a dispute between emigrationists and their opponents that was preventing a rapid flow of Negroes back to Africa. The emigrationists were quarreling among themselves. Fortunately for those who wished emigration to Africa, Delany abandoned his scheme for an empire in the Americas, soon after the National Emigration Conference in Cleveland. Whitfield died in California on his way to Central America, and Delany began to develop a positive enthusiasm for Africa, stimulated by the publication in 1857 of works by Thomas Bowen and David Livingstone.[77] In particular, it was Bowen's "intelligent and interesting account of Yorubaland" which spurred him to explore the Niger Valley in search of a base for a Negro nation.[78] Even when he turned to Africa, Delany persisted in looking beyond Liberia. His enthusiasm for an expedition to Yorubaland was matched by that of his assistant, Robert Campbell, a young Jamaica-born chemist. When the third National Emigration Conference met in Chatham, Ontario, in August 1858, Delany had his plans ready. The conference endorsed the expedition to the Niger Valley as well as Holly's Haitian scheme.

Those interested in West Africa received further help in 1858 when the African Civilization Society was formed, with Henry Highland Garnet as president, to support emigration to that region. Garnet was one of the most aggressive of the American Negro leaders. As early as 1843, he had called on slaves "to rise in their might and strike a blow for their lives and liberties," a counsel which, although it won the endorsement of John Brown, failed to win the general support of Negroes.[79] He left the United States in 1850 for England, where he lectured as an abolitionist for three years. On his return to the United States in 1855, he became a strong supporter of emigration. He had no sympathy for those Negro leaders who opposed free emigration to Africa simply because slaveholders promoted it, and he castigated Frederick Douglass and his associates as "humbugs who oppose everything they do not originate."[80] The main object of Garnet's society was "to establish a grand center of Negro nationality from which shall flow the streams of commercial, intellectual, and political power which shall make colored people respected everywhere."[81] Though he preferred such a center to be founded in West Africa through select American Negro emigration, he was not averse to the building of a Negro state in the Americas. Furthermore, by 1858, a few Liberian trading vessels were plying regularly between the Negro republic and eastern American ports. Garnet was impressed by this; the establishment of a vast commercial network between West Africa and Negro America, he wrote, "would do more for the overthrowing of slavery, in creating a respect for ourselves, than fifty thousand lectures of the most eloquent men of this land."[82]

In turning to West Africa as the geographical center for their pan-Negro program, the Delany-Garnet groups were not overlooking one of their major objectives: the overthrow of slavery in the United States. The new plan, in theory, represented a more effective strategy: it would bring about the collapse of American slavery as well as annihilate the slave trade at its source. The first object was to be attained by the planting of cotton in the selected sites, with the object of underselling in world markets the cotton produced in the southern states.[83] American Negroes, with their special knowledge of the cotton culture, so it was reasoned, were peculiarly well fitted to succeed in this.

Campbell, Delany's assistant, reached West Africa before his leader. On June 24, 1859, he sailed from Liverpool aboard the "splendid ship, Ethiopia," in the company of an American Negro from New York, John Bennet, who had invested $125 in two cotton gins and was on his way to Lagos to start an independent venture in cotton growing.[84] Campbell landed at Freetown, Sierra Leone, on July 12, and here met "several natives . . . of respectability and . . . education."[85] He made short stops at Cape Palmas and Cape Coast before arriving at Lagos on July 21. Through the acting British consul of Lagos, Lieutenant Lodder, Campbell met Okukenu, the Alake of Abeokuta, and found him favorable to the idea of select Negro emigration into his territory. Already in the Alake's domains were several hundred emigrants—"semi-civilized" liberated Africans from Sierra Leone who had returned to their homeland or had been re-patriated from Brazil and Cuba.[86] In Campbell's view, these emigrants "had inaugurated a mighty work, which . . . must be continued in a higher form by the more civilized of the race." He advocated that emigrants should organize on "municipal" lines. But his goal was that of a "national government" which would require the cooperation and support of native Africans. He therefore advised prospective emigrants to "remember that the existing rulers must be respected, for they alone are the *bona fide* rulers of the place. The effort should be to fit them up to the proper stand-ard, and not to supersede or crush them."[87]

Delany, leader of the Niger Valley exploring party, sailed from New York aboard the Liberian vessel, *Mendi*, on May 24, 1859, and arrived in Monrovia early in July. Also aboard the *Mendi* as an emigrant to Liberia was William C. Monroe, an Episcopalian clergyman from Detroit, a for-mer missionary to Haiti, and former president of the National Emigration Conference, who had come to believe that Liberia was "the chief instru-ment in determining the future destiny of the Negro race."[88] In Mon-rovia Delany received a hero's welcome as he reported to a large public meeting of Liberians, who had come "from all parts of the country," that "the desire of African nationality has brought me to these shores."[89] At Grand Bassa, a council of "the most eminent Liberians" approved Delany's mission and policy. This meeting gave Delany "one of the most happy hours of his life" and produced in him "an unforgettable and profound sensation."[90] On July 26, he participated in Liberia's twelfth annual Inde-pendence Day celebration, which "came off with grand effect."[91] On August 1, Delany and Blyden, now much closer together in policy, were speakers at the twenty-fifth anniversary of the emancipation of British West Indian Negroes, celebrated "with great spirit by the leading citizens of Liberia."[92]

Delany left Monrovia on August 4, 1859, for Cape Palmas, where he stayed six weeks. During his two and a half months' stay in Liberia, Delany moved even further toward Blyden's views: his opposition to the Negro republic had been transformed into support. He was especially impressed with the area up St. Paul's River—its beautiful location, its thriving sugar and coffee plantations, its "livestock of all kinds," and its neat brick houses.[93] Although still wishing to see the Negro republic more self-reliant, he was now able to recommend it to the "intelligent of the race."[94] Bly-den had also been prominent in welcoming Delany. He hailed him as "the far-famed champion of the elevation of colored men," as the "Moses" who would "lead the exodus of his people from the house of bondage."[95]

Delany reached Lagos on September 20, spending five weeks there and winning the confidence of Docemo, king of Lagos. Delany wrote to Garnet from Lagos:

Lagos is a fine, and will be a great, commercial city. It is destined to be the great metropolis of this part of the world. Entirely under a black government, it only wants a few of the right stamp of black men to make it one of the most desirable cities in the world. They bid us come, and to that end the authorities have presented me with two acres of land in the heart of the city plot on which to build any residence . . .

There will be for you and also Mr. J. T. Holly, after our return to Africa, a fine prospect in this rich city of Lagos, where Christians . . . desire to have black instead of white preachers.[96]

From Lagos he went to Abeokuta, where he joined his fellow commissioner, Robert Campbell, and together they spent six weeks touring the principal cities of Yorubaland. On their return to Abeokuta, they held talks with the obas and chiefs and, on December 27, signed a treaty that assigned to them as "Commissioners on behalf of the African race in America the right and privilege of settling in common with the Egba people, on any part of the territory belonging to Abeokuta, not otherwise occupied." [97] The signing of the treaty was witnessed by the famous African missionary, Samuel Crowther, and his son, Samuel, Jr. Delany had taken the first step, he felt, in "the grandest prospect for regeneration of a people that ever presented itself in the history of the world." [98]

The expedition had aroused great curiosity and interest in both humanitarian and commercial circles in England; men were deeply divided on the issues of the coming American Civil War, and attention was turning to sources of supply of cotton in areas outside the United States. [99] On their way back to the United States, Delany and Campbell arrived in London on May 17, 1860, and on the next day were invited to a meeting "of a number of noblemen and gentlemen interested in Africa's Regeneration," held in the parlor of Dr. Thomas Hodgkin. A series of meetings was subsequently called, from which grew the African Aid Society, founded to assist by "loans or otherwise" the emigration of Negroes from North America to Africa for the purpose of cultivating tropical products, including cotton, and of promoting "the Christian Civilization of the African Races and the annihilation of the slave trade." Though extremely cautious of any alliance with white men, Delany agreed to cooperate with the society after he had impressed upon its members that the relations between the two groups were to involve strictly business, and that Negro emigrants were to be completely free in managing their own affairs. "Our policy," Delany emphasized, "must be . . . Africa for the African race and black men to rule them." [100]

Emigration

Although Delany had abandoned his idea of an empire in Central America and Whitfield had died, James T. Holly was still active in promoting his scheme for emigration to Haiti. The scheme began to gain support even before Delany and Campbell left for West Africa. The emigrationist position was generally strengthened by the Dred Scott decision of 1857,[101] which led directly to the founding of the *Weekly Anglo-African* and the *Anglo-African Magazine* by Robert Hamilton, who in 1859 urged Negroes to "set themselves zealously to work to create a position of their own—an empire which shall challenge the admiration of the world, rivalling the glory of their historic ancestors." [102] Meanwhile Holly was leading his campaign and in 1857 wrote of Haiti's revolution: "This revolution is one of the noblest, grandest and most justifiable outbursts against oppression that is recorded in the pages of history . . . [it] is also the grandest political event in this or any other age . . . it surpasses the American revolution in an incomparable degree." [103] "Never before," he continued, "in all the annals of the world's history did a nation of abject and chattel slaves arise in the terrific might of their resuscitated manhood, and regenerate, redeem and disenthral themselves: by taking their station at one gigantic bound, as an independent nation among the sovereignties of the world."

His object in recounting this phase of Haitian history was to arouse Negroes of the United States "to a full consciousness of their own inherent dignity." They were to help in building up Haiti "until its glory and renown overspread and cover the whole earth, and redeem and regenerate by its influence in the future, the benighted Fatherland of the race of Africa." As a tactical measure, Holly was against immediate American Negro emigration to Africa: for a start, efforts should be concentrated on building a "Negro Nationality in the New World." Such a successful state would then "shed its . . . beams upon the Fatherland of the race." [104]

The Haitian emigration movement received a further fillip when the Haitian government gave it official sanction. The Haitian "Call for Emigration" was issued on August 22, 1859, by R. E. DuBois, Secretary of State for Justice and Public Worship.[105] Haiti's doors were now open to all Negroes who wished to emigrate. Fabre Geffrard, the new president who seemed bent on reforming Haitian society, joined in the appeal, inviting Negroes to bring "their arms and minds." He predicted: "Haiti will soon regain her ancient splendor . . . and . . . will be a formal denial, most eloquent and peremptory, against the detractors of our race who contest our ability to attain a high degree of civilization." [106] And F. J.

Joseph, Secretary of State for Agriculture, who was directly responsible for settling emigrants, said that "welcoming men of our blood, the victims of these outrageous persecutions, is to continue the work of rehabilitation undertaken by the Founders of the Republic, and to remain faithful to the National Traditions." [107] Among the agents of the Haitian emigration bureau were Holly and Garnet, the latter showing his willingness to support emigration both within the New World and to Africa.

Events in the United States were continuing to give impetus to the emigration movement: the failure of John Brown's raid, the split in the Democratic Party, and the founding of the avowedly anti-slavery Republican Party had both exacerbated feelings against Negroes and increased the interest in emigration. By January 1861, the Haitian emigration campaign seemed to be succeeding. After five weeks in Philadelphia, Holly reported that "the choicest spirits among our people . . . are thoroughly awake to the importance of the present movement and ready to give it their contribution." [108] Garnet also rejoiced "to see that there are more of the colored people . . . in favor of this movement than they are of any other of the present age." [109] Indeed, by 1861 almost all American Negro leaders had given some expression of support to Negro emigration. Even the formidable Frederick Douglass gave in and accepted an invitation by the Haitian government to visit that country.[110]

Thus, when Delany and Campbell returned to the United States in late December 1860, they found that the feeling for emigration was stronger than ever. But Delany did not become involved in a conflict with the Haiti group. He soon let it be known that he was preparing for "a hasty return to Africa where my duty calls me." He called for the cooperation in his venture "of intelligent persons . . . of various occupations, among whom mechanics and cotton cultivators are acceptable." Select emigration was essential, he felt, to ensure the success of his plan; for "Africa is our fatherland, we, its legitimate descendants, and we will never agree or consent to see this . . . step that has been taken for her regeneration by her own descendants blasted." [111]

Liberians, too, were encouraged by the steady, if moderate, flow of emigrants. In the 1850s, Liberia had settled a total of 5,029—almost as many as had been settled in the previous thirty years. The Negro republic's incorporation of Maryland in 1857 and purchase of territory in the area of the Mano and Gallinas Rivers had given it a coastline of 500 miles. Late in 1860, the Reverend James Payne wrote a series of articles in the *Liberia Herald* entitled "A Plea for Liberia," with a view to arresting the attention of American Negroes and directing their attention to the land of their fathers. And the vice-president, D. B. Warner, a close friend of Blyden's, wrote that he was gratified "that Liberia had begun to make a favourable impression abroad among whites and coloured." He hoped American Negroes would "reestablish themselves in this our fatherland." [112]

There is one more Negro leader who should be mentioned here, Alexander Crummell. He left the United States in 1847 at the age of thirty-six; after graduating from Queens College, Cambridge, he went to Liberia in 1853. As in the case of Blyden, he sought to bring about reform in Liberian society and to impress upon his countrymen their high responsibility.[113] He wanted Liberia to extend its influence and jurisdiction over the inland peoples, and he took a leading part in organizing schemes for exploring and opening up the interior. In September 1860 he published an open letter to win the support of all the American Negro leaders, both emigrationists and anti-emigrationists, for Africa.[114]

To appease the anti-emigrationists, he rejected the idea that America could never be the home of the Negro, but he maintained that the task of civilizing Africa was peculiarly that of westernized Negroes: "without doubt God designs great things for Africa and . . . black men themselves are without doubt to be the chief instruments." The civilizing process could be accomplished by voluntary emigration, by the pooling of economic resources and inauguration of trade between America and Africa, and by support of the missionary activities of American Negro churches. "From the port of Lagos in almost direct line through a crowded population, and passing by cities containing tens of thousands of people, a highway is now open reaching to Rabba on the banks of the Niger. All through this country the coloured churches of America can send their missionaries, build up Christian churches, and lay the foundation of Christian colleges and universities." [115] By utilizing this combination of commerce and Christianity, not only would Africa be civilized, but American Negroes would gain in wealth and respect:

> At an early date whole fleets of vessels, manned and officered from the United States and Liberia, would outrival all the other agencies which are now being used for grasping West African commerce. Large and important houses will spring into existence among you, all through the States. Wealth will flow into your coffers, and affluence would soon exhibit itself amid all your associations.
>
> The kings and tradesmen of Africa, having the demonstration of Negro capacity before them, would hail the presence of their black kinsmen from America and would be stimulated by a generous emulation . . . To the farthest interior, leagues and combinations would be formed with men of commerce, and thus civilization, enlightenment and Christianity would be carried to every state and town, and village of interior Africa.[116]

Crummell, like Blyden and Delany, had strongly supported the founding of Liberia College, on which construction had begun by 1860.

The college was to be the first modern, secular English-speaking institution of higher education in tropical Africa. Crummell and other Negro patriots hoped that the college would attract Negro scholars and students from all parts of the world.

Crummell and Blyden left Liberia in February 1861 for England and America, to win financial support for the college and to study institutions of higher learning. In England, Blyden met W. E. Gladstone, Chancellor of the Exchequer, with whom he had been in correspondence, and Lord Brougham, the great humanitarian, both of whom he sought to interest in the "little Republic" that was destined to "revolutionize for good that whole portion of Africa." [117]

When Blyden and Crummell arrived in the United States in June 1861, war had already begun between the Union and the Confederacy. But this seemed to make no difference to the plans of the emigrationists. By May, Delany and Campbell had joined forces with Garnet's African Civilization Society in an attempt to raise funds to promote colonization in the Niger Valley.[118] Campbell, "appearing in native costumes," lectured regularly on West Africa and vowed that "my home shall be in Africa though I be the only person from America." [119] Delany and Campbell had each published a book describing the expedition to the Niger Valley and propagandizing for the cause of colonization.[120] In November the African Civilization Society increased its strength by gaining the support of men who held high offices in the African Methodist Episcopal Church.[121]

Blyden and Crummell joined with the other emigrationists. Blyden himself welcomed the Civil War as the "purifier of a demoralized American conscience," [122] and no doubt as a means of bringing slavery to an end. However, he warned Negroes that they were deceiving themselves if they thought they could earn proper respect in the United States. He urged them to be makers and witnesses of history: "It need not imply any pretensions to prophetic insight for us to declare that we live in the shadows of remarkable events in the history of Africa." [123] Crummell asserted that "the free black man of this country . . . is superior to the Russian, the Polander, the Italian" and was now "in a state of preparedness for a new world's history, for a mission of civilization." He saw the decline of Anglo-Saxon civilizations in "the moral and political convulsion" within the United States. But "now the Negro is rising and will rise . . . God has destined a great future for the Negro race . . . On the continent of Africa, a civilization of a new type and more noble and generous . . . than has ever existed, is on the eve of starting a new life." [124]

When Blyden and Crummell returned to Liberia in the fall of 1861, they reported the support of American Negroes for emigration. The Liberian government decided to act: legislation was passed by which Blyden and Crummell were appointed commissioners "to protect the cause of Liberia to the descendants of Africa in that country, and to lay before them the claims that Africa had upon their sympathies, and the paramount advantages that would accrue to them, their children and their race by their return to the fatherland." [125]

The action of the Liberian government had little effect. The outbreak of the Civil War was the turning point after which there was a fairly sharp decline in pan-Negro nationalism. At the start of the war, Douglass canceled his trip to Haiti and urged American Negroes to stay and help to decide the outcome of the struggle, advice that apparently found quick response. The emigrationists, who had at first regarded the war as irrelevant to their plans, were unable to act because of lack of funds. The war apart, emigration to Haiti had by December 1861 virtually come to an end because of reports of the high mortality rate among the emigrants and unattractive living conditions.[126] There was a correspondingly swift decline in emigration to Liberia. By early 1862, Negro leaders were again united to work for the victory of the North. Indeed, when in the summer of 1862 Lincoln decided to put into effect his scheme for gradual Negro emancipation with colonization, he received no support from American Negro leaders.[127] Thus when Blyden and Crummell returned to the United States as official commissioners in the summer of 1862, to urge American Negroes to "return to the fatherland," they found "an indolent and unmeaning sympathy—sympathy which put forth no effort, made no sacrifices, endured no self-denial, braved no obloquy for the sake of advancing African interests." [128] Further, Lincoln's proclamation of January 1, 1863, ending slavery, and the use later in that year of Negro troops in the Union army, made American Negroes feel sure that a new day had dawned for them.

In this they were wrong, of course. Although Negroes were awarded political and civil rights during the period of Reconstruction (1867–1877), their hopes of full integration within American society were largely frustrated. This disappointment, continuing throughout the nineteenth century and into the twentieth, again resulted in a desire to leave for other parts of the Americas or for Africa. Many Negro leaders once more urged emigration to Africa: Henry M. Turner, bishop in the African Methodist Episcopal Church; Pap Singleton; R. H. Cain, like Turner an AME bishop; J. McCants Stewart, a lawyer; and J. Albert Thorne, a doctor from Barbados. Their activities are, however, beyond the scope of this article.[129]

Pan-Negro nationalists before 1862 did not succeed in creating and sustaining either a return to Africa on a large scale or any significant and persistent contact with African communities. The movement did not come to an end in 1862 and, in spite of the difficulties of the years following the

American civil war, it is hardly likely that everyone at the first Pan-African conference of 1900 had forgotten the personalities and events of fifty years earlier. The twentieth-century Pan-Africanists were concerned that Negroes should mobilize to defend and extend their rights wherever they lived. They held their first congress in London, the most imperial of capital cities, in the middle of the South African War, and increasingly they identified themselves with the larger movement against imperialism.

Nineteenth-century pan-Negro nationalism and Garveyism had much in common. They both owed their existence almost entirely to discrimination against Negroes in the New World, particularly in the United States. They shared a preoccupation with emigration, with a great African past, and with an equally great future, and both relied heavily on leaders from the West Indies, particularly those who had lived in the United States. Nineteenth-century pan-Negro nationalism produced no leader to match Marcus Garvey in the emotional quality of his oratory, the scale of organization and mobilization of resources he achieved, or, indeed, the bitter disillusionment that followed his failure. Though the nineteenth-century movement did achieve a sustained, if limited, emigration, both movements failed to achieve a massive emigration to Africa or its "regeneration."

In their frequent references to the need for action to save Africa, and to prove by deeds the fundamental equality of Africans with other peoples, these Negroes from the New World showed their indebtedness to the societies from which they came. References to the effects of "commerce and Christianity," "the mission of civilization," the great resources of Africa, and the racial bases of society are found as much in the writings of the pan-Negro nationalists as in the writings of missionary groups and subsequently among some believers in imperial rule. It is, however, in reference to "regeneration," with its implication of a great African past, and to the frontal attack on notions of white superiority that the pan-Negro nationalists of the nineteenth century were pioneers.

NOTES

1. This article on Pan-Africanism and pan-Negro nationalism is based on a paper given at the University of Massachusetts on December 13, 1962. I am grateful to Professor Gwendolen Carter for her assistance. Research was made possible by a travel grant from the Central Research Fund of the University of London, and by the British Commonwealth Scholarship Commission; to both of these bodies I am grateful.

2. *The Times*, July 24, 25, 26, 1900; also the account by an American delegate, Bishop Alexander Walters, *My Life and Work* (New York: Fleming H. Revell Co., 1917), p. xx.

3. See W.E.B. DuBois, *The World and Africa* (New York: International Publishers, 1947), pp. 7–12, 236–42; George Padmore, *Pan-Africanism or Communism?*

(London: D. Dobson, 1956), pp. 137–51; American Society of African Culture, ed., *Pan-Africanism Reconsidered* (Berkeley: University of California Press, 1962), pp. 37–52; and Vernon McKay, *Africa in World Politics* (New York: Viking Press, 1963), pp. 93–108.

4. For a list of the delegates of the 1945 Pan-African conference, see George Padmore, ed., *History of the Pan-African Congress* (Manchester: Pan-African Federation, 1947), pp. 71–73.

5. For Pan-Africanism since 1958, see Colin Legum, *Pan-Africanism* (London: Pall Mall, 1962); also McKay, *Africa*, pp. 109–33.

6. See Edmund David Cronon, *Black Moses* (Madison: University of Wisconsin Press, 1955).

7. See George Shepperson, "Notes on American Negro Influences on the Emergence of African Nationalism," *Journal of African History* 1 (1960): 299–312; Nnamdi Azikiwe, "The Future of Pan-Africanism," *Présence africaine* 12 (1962): 11.

8. James Redpath, ed., *A Guide to Hayti* (Boston, 1861), see preface and page 104.

9. See James G. Leyburn, *The Haitian People* (New Haven: Yale University Press, 1941), passim.

10. Some examples are: Prince Hall's African Lodge No. 1, the Free African Societies of Philadelphia and Newport, the African Institutions of New York and Philadelphia, various independent African Baptist churches, and the African Methodist Church. From about the third decade on, when American Negroes became convinced that the American Colonization Society (founded in 1817) wished forcibly to deport them to Africa, the title "African" became less popular among them and was replaced by "Colored."

11. See Ignatius Sancho, *Letters* (London, 1782); Ottobah Cugoano, *Thoughts and Sentiments on the Evil of Slavery* (London, 1787); and Gustavus Vassa, *The Interesting Narrative of the Life of Olaudah Equiano, or Gustavus Vassa, the African* (London, 1789).

12. R. R. Kuczynski, *Demographic Survey of the British Colonial Empire* (London: Oxford University Press, 1948), pp. 40–43; also Christopher Fyfe, *Short History of Sierra Leone* (London: Longman's, 1962), pp. 13–19.

13. Ibid., p. 112.

14. In 1800, there were 108,435 free Negroes in the United States. By 1830, this had risen mainly by natural increase, to 319,599, and to 488,070 by 1860. The free Negro population remained at roughly one tenth of the entire Negro population. See *Negro Population, 1790–1915* (Washington: Government Printing Office, 1918), p. 57.

15. For an elaboration of this thesis, see Leon F. Litwack, *North of Slavery: The Negro in the Free States* (Chicago: University of Chicago Press, 1962).

16. For the history of the society, see Early Lee Fox, *The American Colonization Society, 1817-1840* (Baltimore: Johns Hopkins University Press, 1919); and P. J. Staudenraus, *The African Colonization Movement, 1816–1865* (New York: Columbia University Press, 1961).

17. See Louis B. Mehlinger, "The Attitude of the Free Negro Toward Colonization," *Journal of Negro History* 1 (July 1916).

18. See John W. Cromwell, "The Early Negro Convention Movement," *Occasional Papers* [of the American Negro Academy] 9 (Washington, 1940); August Meier, "The Emergence of Negro Nationalism," *Midwest Journal* 4 (Winter 1951–52): 96–104; and Howard H. Bell, "A Survey of the Negro Convention Movement, 1830–1861" (unpublished dissertation, Northwestern University, 1953).

19. This is not, of course, meant to be an exhaustive list: these were chosen because they were articulate or outstanding men of action. For a discussion of American Negro procolonization views in this period, see Mehlinger, "Attitude." For an example of a project for colonization outside Africa, see the discussion of Delany and Holly that follows.

20. For Cuffee's biography, see Henry Noble Sherwood, "Paul Cuffee," *Journal of Negro History* 8 (April 1923): 153–229.

21. Ibid., p. 176.

22. Ibid., p. 206.

23. Ibid., p. 218.

24. Ibid., pp. 213–21; also Henry N. Sherwood, "Paul Cuffee and his Contribution to the American Colonization Society," *Proceedings of the Mississippi Valley Historical Association* 6 (1913): 370–402.

25. Daniel Coker, *A Dialogue Between a Virginian and an African Minister, Written by Daniel Coker, a Descendant of Africa, Minister of The African Methodist Episcopal Church in Baltimore* (Baltimore, 1810), p. 10.

26. Daniel A. Payne, *History of the African Methodist Episcopal Church* (Nashville, 1891), p. 89.

27. Daniel Coker, *The Journal of Daniel Coker, A Descendant of Africa . . . in the Ship Elizabeth, on a Voyage for Sherbro in Africa . . .* (Baltimore, 1820), pp. 15–16.

28. Harry Johnston, *Liberia* (London: Hutchinson & Co., 1906), I, p. 135; R. R. Gurley, *Life of Jehudi Ashmun* (Washington, 1835), pp. 147–60; William T. Alexander (comp.), *History of the Colored Race in America . . .* 3rd ed. (New Orleans: Palmetto Publishing Company, 1888), pp. 241–54.

29. Quoted in Alexander, *History*, p. 243.

30. See William M. Brewer, "John B. Russwurm," *Journal of Negro History* 13 (October 1928): 413–22.

31. See his editorials in *Freedom's Journal* 2 (February 14, 1829 et seq.).

32. For a history of the founding of the colony, see *Journal of Maryland Historical Society* 5 (February 1850): 129–52.

33. Russwurm's letters and reports as governor, not used in Brewer's "Russwurm," are in the archives of the Maryland Historical Society.

34. Carter G. Woodson, *The Mind of the Negro as Reflected in Letters Written during the Crisis, 1800–1860* (Washington: Association for the Study of Negro Life and History, 1926), passim.

35. See E. A. Payne, *Freedom in Jamaica* (London: Carey Kingsgate, 1946), pp. 73–74; C. P. Groves, *Planting of Christianity in Africa* (London: Lutterworth Press, 1954), II, p. 54; *A General Account of the West Indian Church Association for the Furtherance of the Gospel in West Africa* (London, 1855), pp. 5–7.

36. *Maryland Colonization Journal* 4 (1848): 213; also American Colonization Society, *Forty-Ninth Annual Report* (Washington, 1866), p. 7.

37. There is one exception to this. In 1865, 365 Negroes from Barbados emigrated to Liberia in an expedition sponsored by the Liberian government but financed mainly by the American Colonization Society. See American Colonization Society, *Fifty-Second Annual Report* (Washington, 1869), p. 53; and ch. 3 my book on Blyden cited below, footnote 38.

38. See discussion of Blyden below; also Hollis R. Lynch, *Edward Wilmont Blyden: Pan-Negro Patriot 1832–1912* (London: Oxford University Press, 1966).

39. See discussion of Blyden below; also Robert Campbell, *A Pilgrimage to my Motherland* (New York, 1861), p. 11.

40. A. Barrow, *Fifty Years in Western Africa: Being a Record of the West Indian Church on the Banks of the Rio Pongo* (London: 1900), passim.

41. In addition, many West Indian artisans and professionals were attracted to West Africa, particularly to Sierra Leone, but primarily because of the better economic opportunities there. See Abioseh Nicol, "West Indians in West Africa," *Sierra Leone Studies*, N.S., no. 13 (June 1960): 14–23. Also from about 1840, Brazilian and Cuban Negroes trickled back to Lagos and its hinterland where, as artisans, agriculturists, and traders, they formed an important section of the community.

42. For biographical details on these three missionaries, see Robert Glennie, *Joseph Jackson Fuller* (London: Carey Press, 1925); G. G. Findlay and W. W. Holdsworth, *History of the Wesleyan Methodist Missionary Society* (London: Epworth Press, 1922), II, p. 164; and Barrow, *Fifty Years*, passim.

43. The phrase is that of the American Negro leader, James McCune Smith. See his introduction to a *Memorial Discourse by Rev. Henry Highland Garnet, Delivered in the Hall of the House of Representatives* . . . (Washington, 1865), p. 56.

44. *Maryland Colonization Journal* 4 (1848): 213.

45. The American Colonization Society, *Thirty-Second Annual Report* (Washington, 1849), p. 8.

46. *African Repository* 24 (August 1848): 24.

47. American Colonization Society, *Fifty-Second Annual Report* (Washington, 1869), p. 53.

48. Up to 1850, 6,116 emigrants were sent out by the society: 2,315 were born free, 165 purchased their freedom, and 3,636 were emancipated for emigration.

49. Edward W. Blyden, *A Voice from Bleeding Africa* (Monrovia, 1856), p. 26.

50. For quotations from his poems extolling the Negro past and urging Liberia to "press towards the prize in glory's race," see Edward W. Blyden, *From West Africa to Palestine* (Freetown, Manchester, London, 1873), p. 104; also Frederick Alexander Durham, *The Lone-Star of Liberia* (London, 1892), p. 1.

51. Quoted in Wilson Armistead, *A Tribute to the Negro* (Manchester and New York, 1848), p. 532; also J.A.B. Horton, *West African Countries and Peoples* (London, 1868), p. 273.

52. Johnston, *Liberia*, pp. 149, 182–84.

53. Abayomi Karnga, *History of Liberia* (Liverpool: D. H. Tyte and Co., 1926), p. 45.

54. Johnston, *Liberia*, pp. 187–95.

55. The basic document was drafted by Simon Greenleaf, Professor of Law at Harvard University, but was somewhat revised at Liberia's constitutional convention; Liberians wrote the preamble.

56. See Lynch, *Edward W. Blyden*.

57. Slavery was not abolished in the Danish West Indies until 1848, but here, too, there was a small group of free Negroes before general emancipation.

58. *New York Colonization Journal* 1 (December 1850).

59. *African Repository* 27 (September 1851): 266.

60. The conference is discussed below. See also Martin R. Delaney, *Official Report of the Niger Valley Exploring Party* (New York, 1861), for a discussion of the conference.

61. *New York Colonization Journal* 4 (August 1854).

62. *African Repository* 31 (April 1855): 18.

63. Howard H. Bell, "The Negro Emigration Movement, 1849–54: A Phase of Negro Nationalism," *Phylon* 20 (November 1959): 136.

64. *Liberia Herald*, n.s. 3 (July 7, 1852); also *Maryland Colonization Society* 6 (November 1852): 277–80.

65. See Martin R. Delany, *The Condition, Elevation, and Destiny of the Colored People of the United States, Politically Considered* (Philadelphia, 1852).

66. Ibid., p. 27. Although Delany's statement was not strictly true, it is true that in Latin American countries Negroes were on the whole better treated than in Anglo-Saxon America. For a comparative study of the treatment of Negroes in Americas, see Frank Tannenbaum, *Slave and Citizen* (New York: A. A. Knopf, 1947); also Stanley M. Elkins, *Slavery* (Chicago: Chicago University Press, 1959).

76. Ibid., pp. 169–70.

68. *Liberia Herald*, n.s. 3 (October 6, 1852).

69. Cromwell, "Early Negro Convention," p. 16.

70. *Frederick Douglass' Paper* 6 (October 6, 1853) et seq.

71. Delany, *Official Report*, p. 6.

72. Martin R. Delany, "Political Destiny of the Colored Race of the American Continent," appendix no. 3, in *Report of the Select Committee on Emancipation and Colonization* (Washington, 1862), pp. 37–59.

73. Ibid., p. 43.

74. Delany, *Official Report*, pp. 8–9.

75. Ibid., p. 10.

76. James T. Holly, *A Vindication of the Capacity of the Negro Race for Self-Government, and Civilized Progress, as Demonstrated by Historical Events of the Haitian Revolution; and the Subsequent Act of the People since their National Independence* (New Haven, 1857), preface.

77. These were Thomas J. Bowen, *Central Africa: Adventures and Missionary Labors in the Interior of Africa, from 1849–1856* (Charleston, 1857), and Dr. Livingstone's *Seventeen Years' Explorations and Adventures in the Wilds of Africa*, John Hartley Coomb, ed. (Philadelphia, 1857).

78. Delany, *Official Report*, p. 10.

79. John W. Cromwell, *The Negro in American History* (Washington: American Negro Academy, 1916), p. 126; also William Wells Brown, *The Black Man: His Antecedents, His Genius, and His Achievements* (Boston: Wallcut, 1863), pp. 149–52.

80. *Weekly Anglo-African* 1 (September 3, 1859).

81. Ibid.

82. Ibid.

83. Ibid.; also Delany, *Official Report*, p. 14.

84. *Weekly Anglo-African* 1 (September 3, 1859).

85. Campbell, *Pilgrimage*, p. 11.

86. Ibid., p. 18. For the fullest treatment of this, see Jean F. Herskovits, "Liberated Africans and the History of Lagos Colony to 1886" (unpublished dissertation, Oxford University, 1960).

87. Campbell, *Pilgrimage*, p. 137.

88. *Weekly Anglo-African* 1 (October 1, 1859). Holly's *Vindication* was dedicated to Monroe.

89. *Weekly Anglo-African* 1 (October 1, 1859).

90. Delany, *Official Report*, p. 23.

91. *Weekly Anglo-African* 1 (September 24, 1859).

92. Ibid., 1 (October 15, 1859).

93. Ibid., 1 (September 24, 1859).

94. *New York Colonization Journal* 9 (October 1859).

95. Ibid.

96. *Weekly Anglo-African* 2 (January 1861).

97. Delany, *Official Report*, p. 27.

98. Ibid., p. 30.

99. *New York Times* (December 20, 1860).

100. Delany, *Official Report*, p. 64. Thomas Hodgkin was a prominent London physician and philanthropist; see *Dictionary of National Biography* 27: 63–64.

101. John Hope Franklin, *From Slavery to Freedom* (New York: A. A. Knopf, 1956), p. 264.

102. *Weekly Anglo-African* 1 (July 23, 1859).

103. Holly, *Vindication*, p. 7.

104. Ibid., p. 8.

105. *New York Colonization Journal* 10 (July 1860); Redpath, *Guide*, pp. 97–99.

106. Ibid., preface.

107. Ibid., p. 104.

108. *Weekly Anglo-African* 2 (February 16, 1861).

109. Ibid., 2 (January 26, 1861).

110. Howard H. Bell, "Negro Nationalism: A Factor in Emigration Projects, 1858–1861," *Journal of Negro History* 48 (January 1962): 43.

111. *Weekly Anglo-African* 2 (January 26, 1861).

112. *African Repository* 36 (January 1861): 87.

113. See, for example, Alexander Crummell, *The Duty of a Rising Christian State, Annual Oration Before the Common Council and Citizens of Monrovia, Liberia, July 26, 1855* (London, 1856).

114. Alexander Crummell, *The Relation and Duties of the Free Colored Men in America to Africa* (Hartford, 1861), p. 55.

115. Ibid., p. 45.

116. Ibid., p. 25.

117. Blyden to Gladstone, May 3, 1861, British Museum Add. Mss. 44396/63; Blyden to Lord Brougham, May 24, 1861, Brougham Papers, University College, London.

118. *Constitution of the African Civilization Society* (New Haven, 1861), p. 1.

119. *Weekly Anglo-African* 2 (March 16, 1861).

120. Delany, *Official Report*, and Campbell, *Pilgrimage*.

121. *Constitution of the African Civilization Society*, p. 4.

122. Blyden to Gladstone, June 16, 1862, British Museum Add. Mss. 44398/183.

123. Edward W. Blyden, *Hope for Africa, A Discourse* . . . (tract no. 8 from the *Colonization Journal*, 1861), p. 16.

124. *African Repository* 37 (September 1861): 279.

125. Cited in the American Colonization Society, *Forty-Sixth Annual Report* (Washington, 1863), p. 6.

126. Benjamin Quarles, *Lincoln and the Negro* (New York: Oxford University Press, 1962), p. 120.

127. Benjamin Quarles, *The Negro in the Civil War* (Boston: Little, Brown and Company, 1953), pp. 147–49.

128. Blyden, *Liberia's Offering*, p. 69.

129. See August Meier, *Negro Thought in America, 1880–1915* (Ann Arbor: University of Michigan Press, 1963).

III

Colonial Slavery and White Racism

One of the more neglected aspects of Afro-American history is the nature of slavery in colonial America. Because of the greater prevalence of source materials in the ante-bellum period as well as the romantic attraction of the nineteenth century prior to the Civil War, historians have written extensively about slavery in the Old South but have given limited attention to the equally important formative period.

In contrast to the nineteenth century, when slavery was confined to the South, involuntary servitude existed in all the original colonies of British North America. Within these possessions, however, the institution varied from colony to colony in terms of the number of slaves held, the degree of leniency practiced by masters, the level of skills possessed by the slaves, and the manner in which the system was first introduced.

Largely because of a general adversion to the admission of black people, the growth of slavery was slow, especially in the northern colonies. By the end of the seventeenth century, for example, fewer than 6,000 slaves were in Virginia while only about 500 resided in Massachusetts. During this same century, however, colonial governments under the encouragement of England molded legal systems of slavery that were strikingly similar in their provisions. Slavery came to be based upon race as the determining factor and upon the assumption that slaves were chattel property and not human beings entitled to civil protection or even to the most rudimentary rights of man.

The introduction of chattel slavery into the American colonies took several different forms. In Virginia, it developed from an indenture system, while slavery was brought into South Carolina by West Indian planters. The Dutch rather than the English were responsible for introducing slavery in New York. The situation was especially complicated in New England where religious predilections frequently clashed with economic interests and social attitudes. In Pennsylvania, Quaker sensibilities and white prejudices operated to discourage the growth of slavery.

Despite these diversities, black slavery became firmly rooted in the south-

103

ern colonies and fairly extensive in a few scattered northern colonies, especially New York and New Jersey. Certain geographical and economic factors were important in determining the direction slavery took. The need in the South for a ready supply of farm laborers encouraged white Southerners to follow the example of the West Indian planters in overcoming labor shortages by importing black Africans. The rapidity of southern economic development as well as the large profits of a few successful planters would have been impossible without the exploitation of black labor. The fostering in British North America of a system of chattel slavery when the number of slaves was still relatively small suggests that the existence of numerous black Africans was not essential to the development of harsh slave codes or to the rise of white prejudice. The fear of a black peril was enough to arouse animosity.

Yet the nature of the slave system cannot be understood apart from a consideration of cultural, ideological, and moral influences. Economic factors alone cannot account for the differences between slavery in Virginia and Massachusetts. There were always individuals, some prominent and others obscure, whose actions ran contrary to their economic interests. Furthermore, the black slave was not the only victim of the institution of slavery, for the white man—planter, yeoman, and lower class—was shaped and controlled by the system as well.

The following selections illustrate the diversity of slavery in seventeenth-century America. The authors attempt to deal meaningfully with the dynamics of a colonial society based, at least in part, upon slave labor. Jordan discusses the important question of the relationship between prejudice and slavery. Although McManus places more emphasis upon economic considerations, all of these writers demonstrate an awareness, not always present in the writings of earlier historians, that a multiplicity of factors was involved in the interplay between attitudes and institutions. There was greater unity to slavery in the nineteenth century partly because it was by law confined to the southern states and also because slave masters by then had time to devise a permanent form best designed to serve their economic interests as well as those of the society at large.

8. WINTHROP D. JORDAN, Modern Tensions and the Origins of American Slavery (1962)*

Winthrop Jordan, professor of history at the University of California at Berkeley, is one of the recognized authorities on the origin of racism in America. His detailed and perceptive study of the development

* Winthrop D. Jordan, "Modern Tensions and the Origins of American Slavery," *Journal of Southern History* 28 (February 1962): 18–30. Copyright © 1962 by the Southern Historical Association. Reprinted by permission of the Managing Editor and the author. A modified and much more complete description of the origin of American slavery is in Winthrop D. Jordan, *White Over Black: American Attitudes Toward the Negro, 1550–1812* (Chapel Hill: University of North Carolina Press, 1968).

of a racial ideology before 1815, *White Over Black,* has been received with critical acclaim by scholars. In this selection, Jordan reviews the older debate between Oscar Handlin who insisted that racism was a by-product of slavery and Carl Deglar who argued that racism preceded slavery and then dismisses it as irrelevant. Since both prejudice and involuntary servitude developed simultaneously in seventeenth-century Virginia each served to intensify the growth of the other. Jordan is more critical of Handlin's position in *White Over Black* where he demonstrates that racial prejudice against black Africans developed in Europe before it flourished in the American colonies.

Thanks to John Smith we know that Negroes first came to the British continental colonies in 1619.[1] What we do not know is exactly when Negroes were first enslaved there. This question has been debated by historians for the past seventy years, the critical point being whether Negroes were enslaved almost from their first importation or whether they were at first simply servants and only later reduced to the status of slaves. The long duration and vigor of the controversy suggest that more than a simple question of dating has been involved. In fact certain current tensions in American society have complicated the historical problem and greatly heightened its significance. Dating the origins of slavery has taken on a striking modern relevance.

During the nineteenth century historians assumed almost universally that the first Negroes came to Virginia as slaves. So close was their acquaintance with the problem of racial slavery that it did not occur to them that Negroes could ever have been anything but slaves. Philip A. Bruce, the first man to probe with some thoroughness into the early years of American slavery, adopted this view in 1896, although he emphasized that the original difference in treatment between white servants and Negroes was merely that Negroes served for life. Just six years later, however, came a challenge from a younger, professionally trained historian, James C. Ballagh. His *A History of Slavery in Virginia* appeared in the *Johns Hopkins University Studies in Historical and Political Science,* an aptly named series which was to usher in the new era of scholarly detachment in the writing of institutional history. Ballagh offered a new and different interpretation; he took the position that the first Negroes served merely as servants and that enslavement did not begin until around 1660, when statutes bearing on slavery were passed for the first time.[2]

There has since been agreement on dating the statutory establishment of slavery, and differences of opinion have centered on when enslavement began in actual practice. Fortunately there has also been general agreement on slavery's distinguishing characteristics: service for life and inheritance of like obligation by any offspring. Writing on the free Negro in Virginia for the Johns Hopkins series, John H. Russell in 1913 tackled the central question and showed that some Negroes were indeed servants but concluded that "between 1640 and 1660 slavery was fast becoming an established fact. In this twenty years the colored population was divided, part being servants and part being slaves, and some who were servants defended themselves with increasing difficulty from the encroachments of slavery." [3] Ulrich B. Phillips, though little interested in the matter, in 1918 accepted Russell's conclusion of early servitude and transition toward slavery after 1640. Helen T. Catterall took much the same position in 1926. On the other hand, in 1921 James M. Wright, discussing the free Negro in Maryland, implied that Negroes were slaves almost from the beginning, and in 1940 Susie M. Ames reviewed several cases in Virginia which seemed to indicate that genuine slavery had existed well before Ballagh's date of 1660.[4]

All this was a very small academic gale, well insulated from the outside world. Yet despite disagreement on dating enslavement, the earlier writers—Bruce, Ballagh, and Russell—shared a common assumption which, though at the time seemingly irrelevant to the main question, has since proved of considerable importance. They assumed that prejudice against the Negro was natural and almost innate in the white man. It would be surprising if they had felt otherwise in this period of segregation statutes, overseas imperialism, immigration restriction, and full-throated Anglo-Saxonism. By the 1920s, however, with the easing of these tensions, the assumption of natural prejudice was dropped unnoticed. Yet only one historian explicitly contradicted that assumption: Ulrich Phillips of Georgia, impressed with the geniality of both slavery and twentieth-century race relations, found no natural prejudice in the white man and expressed his "conviction that Southern racial asperities are mainly superficial, and that the two great elements are fundamentally in accord." [5]

Only when tensions over race relations intensified once more did the older assumption of natural prejudice crop up again. After World War II American Negroes found themselves beneficiaries of New Deal politics and reforms, wartime need for manpower, world-wide repulsion at racist excesses in Nazi Germany, and growingly successful colored anticolonialism. With new militancy Negroes mounted an attack on the citadel of separate but equal, and soon it became clear that America was in for a period of self-conscious reappraisal of its racial arrangements. Writing in this period of heightened tension (1949) a practiced and careful scholar, Wesley F. Craven, raised the old question of the Negro's original status, suggesting that Negroes had been enslaved at an early date. Craven also cautiously resuscitated the idea that white men may have had natural distaste for the Negro, an idea which fitted neatly with the suggestion of early enslavement. Original antipathy would mean rapid debasement.[6]

In the next year (1950) came a sophisticated counterstatement, which contradicted both Craven's dating and implicitly any suggestion of early prejudice. Oscar and Mary F. Handlin in "Origins of the Southern Labor System" offered a case for late enslavement, with servitude as the status of Negroes before about 1660. Originally the status of both Negroes and white servants was far short of freedom, the Handlins maintained, but Negroes failed to benefit from increased freedom for servants in mid-century and became less free rather than more.[7] Embedded in this description of diverging status were broader implications: Late and gradual enslavement undercut the possibility of natural, deep-seated antipathy toward Negroes. On the contrary, if whites and Negroes could share the same status of half freedom for forty years in the seventeenth century, why could they not share full freedom in the twentieth?

The same implications were rendered more explicit by Kenneth M. Stampp in a major reassessment of southern slavery published two years after the Supreme Court's 1954 school decision. Reading physiology with the eye of faith, Stampp frankly stated his assumption "that innately Negroes *are*, after all, only white men with black skins, nothing more, nothing less." [8] Closely following the Handlins' article on the origins of slavery itself, he almost directly denied any pattern of early and inherent racial antipathy: ". . . Negro and white servants of the seventeenth century seemed to be remarkably unconcerned about their visible physical differences." As for "the trend toward special treatment" of the Negro, "physical and cultural differences provided handy excuses to justify it." [9] Distaste for the Negro, then, was in the beginning scarcely more than an appurtenance of slavery.

These views squared nicely with the hopes of those even more directly concerned with the problem of contemporary race relations, sociologists and social psychologists. Liberal on the race question almost to a man, they tended to see slavery as the initial cause of the Negro's current degradation. The modern Negro was the unhappy victim of long association with base status. Sociologists, though uninterested in tired questions of historical evidence, could not easily assume a natural prejudice in the white man as the cause of slavery. Natural or innate prejudice would not only violate their basic assumptions concerning the dominance of culture but would undermine the power of their new Baconian science. For if prejudice was natural there would be little one could do to wipe it out. Prejudice must have followed enslavement, not vice versa, else any liberal program of action would be badly compromised. One prominent social scientist suggested in a UNESCO pamphlet that racial prejudice in the United States commenced with the cotton gin! [10]

Just how closely the question of dating had become tied to the practical matter of action against racial prejudice was made apparent by the suggestions of still another historian. Carl N. Degler grappled with the dating problem in an article frankly entitled "Slavery and the Genesis of American Race Prejudice." [11] The article appeared in 1959, a time when southern resistance to school desegregation seemed more adamant than ever and the North's hands none too clean, a period of discouragement for those hoping to end racial discrimination. Prejudice against the Negro now appeared firm and deep-seated, less easily eradicated than had been supposed in, say, 1954. It was Degler's view that enslavement began early, as a result of white settlers' prejudice or antipathy toward the first Negroes. Thus not only were the sociologists contradicted but the dating problem was now overtly and consciously tied to the broader question of whether slavery caused prejudice or prejudice caused slavery. A new self-consciousness over the American racial dilemma had snatched an arid historical controversy from the hands of an unsuspecting earlier generation and had tossed it into the arena of current debate.

Ironically there might have been no historical controversy at all if every historian dealing with the subject had exercised greater care with facts and greater restraint in interpretation. Too often the debate entered the realm of inference and assumption. For the crucial early years after 1619 there is simply not enough evidence to indicate with any certainty whether Negroes were treated like white servants or not. No historian has found anything resembling proof one way or the other. The first Negroes were sold to the English settlers, yet so were other Englishmen. It can be said, however, that Negroes were set apart from white men by the word *Negroes*, and a distinct name is not attached to a group unless it is seen as different. The earliest Virginia census reports plainly distinguished Negroes from white men, sometimes giving Negroes no personal name; and in 1629 every commander of the several plantations was ordered to "take a generall muster of all the inhabitants men woemen and Children as well *Englishe* as Negroes." [12] Difference, however, might or might not involve inferiority.

The first evidence as to the actual status of Negroes does not appear until about 1640. Then it becomes clear that *some* Negroes were serving for life and some children inheriting the same obligation. Here it is necessary to suggest with some candor that the Handlins' statement to the contrary rests on unsatisfactory documentation.[13] That some Negroes were held as slaves after about 1640 is no indication, however, that American slavery popped into the world fully developed at that time.

Many historians, most cogently the Handlins, have shown slavery to have been a gradual development, a process not completed until the eighteenth century. The complete deprivation of civil and personal rights, the legal conversion of the Negro into a chattel, in short slavery as Americans came to know it, was not accomplished overnight. Yet these developments practically and logically depended on the practice of hereditary lifetime service, and it is certainly possibly to find in the 1640s and 1650s traces of slavery's most essential feature.[14]

The first definite trace appears in 1640 when the Virginia General Court pronounced sentence on three servants who had been retaken after running away to Maryland. Two of them, a Dutchman and a Scot, were ordered to serve their masters for one additional year and then the colony for three more, but "the third being a negro named John Punch shall serve his said master or his assigns for the time of his natural life here or else where." No white servant in America, so far as is known, ever received a like sentence.[15] Later the same month a Negro was again singled out from a group of recaptured runaways; six of the seven were assigned additional time while the Negro was given none, presumably because he was already serving for life.[16] After 1640, too, county court records began to mention Negroes, in part because there were more of them than previously—about two percent of the Virginia population in 1649.[17] Sales for life, often including any future progeny, were recorded in unmistakable language. In 1646 Francis Pott sold a Negro woman and boy to Stephen Charlton "to the use of him . . . forever." Similarly, six years later William Whittington sold to John Pott "one Negro girle named Jowan; aged about Ten yeares and with her Issue and produce duringe her (or either of them) for their Life tyme. And their Successors forever"; and a Maryland man in 1649 deeded two Negro men and a woman "and all their issue both male and Female." The executors of a York County estate in 1647 disposed of eight Negroes—four men, two women, and two children—to Captain John Chisman "to have hold occupy posesse and inioy and every one of the afforementioned Negroes forever [.]"[18] The will of Rowland Burnham of "Rapahanocke," made in 1657, dispensed his considerable number of Negroes and white servants in language which clearly differentiated between the two by specifying that the whites were to serve for their "full terme of tyme" and the Negroes "for ever."[19] Nor did anything in the will indicate that this distinction was exceptional or novel.

In addition to these clear indications that some Negroes were owned for life, there were cases of Negroes held for terms far longer than the normal five or seven years.[20] On the other hand, some Negroes served only the term usual for white servants, and others were completely free.[21]

One Negro freeman, Anthony Johnson, himself owned a Negro.[22] Obviously the enslavement of some Negroes did not mean the immediate enslavement of all.

Further evidence of Negroes serving for life lies in the prices paid for them. In many instances the valuations placed on Negroes (in estate inventories and bills of sale) were far higher than for white servants, even those servants with full terms yet to serve. Since there was ordinarily no preference for Negroes as such, higher prices must have meant that Negroes were more highly valued because of their greater length of service. Negro women may have been especially prized, moreover, because their progeny could also be held perpetually. In 1645, for example, two Negro women and a boy were sold for 5,500 pounds of tobacco. Two years earlier William Burdett's inventory listed eight servants (with the time each had still to serve) at valuations ranging from 400 to 1,100 pounds, while a "very anntient" Negro was valued at 3,000 and an eight-year-old Negro girl at 2,000 pounds, with no time-remaining indicated for either. In the late 1650s an inventory of Thomas Ludlow's large estate evaluated a white servant with six years to serve at less than an elderly Negro man and only one half of a Negro woman.[23] The labor owned by James Stone in 1648 was evaluated as follows:

	lb tobo
Thomas Groves, 4 yeares to serve	1300
Francis Bomley for 6 yeares	1500
John Thackstone for 3 yeares	1300
Susan Davis for 3 yeares	1000
Emaniell a Negro man	2000
Roger Stone 3 yeares	1300
Mingo a Negro man	2000 [24]

Besides setting a higher value on the two Negroes, Stone's inventory, like Burdett's, failed to indicate the number of years they had still to serve. It would seem safe to assume that the time remaining was omitted in this and similar documents simply because the Negroes were regarded as serving for an unlimited time.

The situation in Maryland was apparently the same. In 1643 Governor Leonard Calvert agreed with John Skinner, "mariner," to exchange certain estates for seventeen sound Negro "slaves," fourteen men and three women between sixteen and twenty-six years old. The total value of these was placed at 24,000 pounds of tobacco, which would work out to 1,000 pounds for the women and 1,500 for the men, prices considerably higher than those paid for white servants at the time.[25]

Wherever Negro women were involved, however, higher valuations may have reflected the fact that they could be used for field work while white women generally were not. This discrimination between Negro and white women, of course, fell short of actual enslavement. It meant merely that Negroes were set apart in a way clearly not to their advantage. Yet this is not the only evidence that Negroes were subjected to degrading distinctions not directly related to slavery. In several ways Negroes were singled out for special treatment which suggested a generalized debasing of Negroes as a group. Significantly, the first indications of debasement appeared at about the same time as the first indications of actual enslavement.

The distinction concerning field work is a case in point. It first appeared on the written record in 1643, when Virginia pointedly recognized it in her taxation policy. Previously tithable persons had been defined (1629) as "all those that worke in the ground of what qualitie or condition soever." Now the law stated that all adult men and *Negro* women were to be tithable, and this distinction was made twice again before 1660. Maryland followed a similar course, beginning in 1654.[26] John Hammond, in a 1656 tract defending the tobacco colonies, wrote that servant women were not put to work in the fields but in domestic employments, "yet som wenches that are nasty, and beastly and not fit to be so imployed are put into the ground." [27] Since all Negro women were taxed as working in the fields, it would seem logical to conclude that Virginians found them "nasty" and "beastly." The essentially racial nature of this discrimination was bared by a 1668 law at the time slavery was crystallizing on the statute books:

Whereas some doubts, have arisen whether negro women set free were still to be accompted tithable according to a former act, *It is declared by this grand assembly* that negro women, though permitted to enjoy their ffreedome yet ought not in all respects to be admitted to a full fruition of the exemptions and impunities of the English, and are still lyable to payment of taxes.[28]

Virginia law set Negroes apart in a second way by denying them the important right and obligation to bear arms. Few restraints could indicate more clearly the denial to Negroes of membership in the white community. This action, in a sense the first foreshadowing of the slave codes, came in 1640, at just the time when other indications first appear that Negroes were subject to special treatment.[29]

Finally, an even more compelling sense of the separateness of Negroes was revealed in early distress concerning sexual union between the races. In 1630 a Virginia court pronounced a now famous sentence: "Hugh Davis to be soundly whipped, before an assembly of Negroes and others for abusing himself to the dishonor of God and shame of Christians, by defiling his body in lying with a negro." [30] While there were other instances of punishment for interracial union in the ensuing years, fornication rather than miscegenation may well have been the primary offense, though in 1651 a Maryland man sued someone who he claimed had said "that he had a black bastard in Virginia." [31] There may have been nothing racial about the 1640 case by which Robert Sweet was compelled "to do penance in church according to laws of England, for getting a negroe woman with child and the woman whipt." [32] About 1650 a white man and a Negro woman were required to stand clad in white sheets before a congregation in Lower Norfolk County for having had relations, but this punishment was sometimes used in ordinary cases of fornication between two whites.[33]

It is certain, however, that in the early 1660s when slavery was gaining statutory recognition, the colonial assemblies legislated with feeling against miscegenation. Nor was this merely a matter of avoiding confusion of status, as was suggested by the Handlins. In 1662 Virginia declared that "if any christian shall committ ffornication with a negro man or woman, hee or shee soe offending" should pay double the usual fine. Two years later Maryland prohibited interracial marriages:

forasmuch as divers freeborne English women forgettfull of their free Condicōn and to the disgrace of our Nation doe intermarry with Negro Slaves by which alsoe divers suites may arise touching the Issue of such woemen and a great damage doth befall the Masters of such Negros for prevention whereof for deterring such freeborne women from such shameful Matches . . . ,

strong language indeed if the problem had only been confusion of status. A Maryland act of 1681 described marriages of white women with Negroes as, among other things, "always to the Satisfaccōn of theire Lascivious & Lustfull desires, & to the disgrace not only of the English butt allso of many other Christian Nations." When Virginia finally prohibited all interracial liaisons in 1691, the assembly vigorously denounced miscegenation and its fruits as "that abominable mixture and spurious issue." [34]

One is confronted, then, with the fact that the first evidences of enslavement and of other forms of debasement appeared at about the same time. Such coincidence comports poorly with both views on the causation of prejudice and slavery. If slavery caused prejudice, then invidious distinctions concerning working in the fields, bearing arms, and sexual union should have appeared only after slavery's firm establishment. If prejudice caused slavery, then one would expect to find such lesser discriminations preceding the greater discrimination of outright enslavement.

Perhaps a third explanation of the relationship between slavery and prejudice may be offered, one that might fit the pattern of events as revealed by existing evidence. Both current views share a common starting point: They predicate two factors, prejudice and slavery, and demand a distinct order of causality. No matter how qualified by recognition that the effect may in turn react upon the cause, each approach inevitably tends to deny the validity of its opposite. But what if one were to regard both slavery and prejudice as species of a general debasement of the Negro? Both may have been equally cause and effect, constantly reacting upon each other, dynamically joining hands to hustle the Negro down the road to complete degradation. Mutual causation is, of course, a highly useful concept for describing social situations in the modern world.[35] Indeed it has been widely applied in only slightly altered fashion to the current racial situation: Racial prejudice and the Negro's lowly position are widely accepted as constantly reinforcing each other.

This way of looking at the facts might well fit better with what we know of slavery itself. Slavery was an organized pattern of human relationships. No matter what the law might say, it was of different character than cattle ownership. No matter how degrading, slavery involved human beings. No one seriously pretended otherwise. Slavery was not an isolated economic or institutional phenomenon; it was the practical facet of a general debasement without which slavery could have no rationality. (Prejudice, too, was a form of debasement, a kind of slavery in the mind.) Certainly the urgent need for labor in a virgin country guided the direction which debasement took, molded it, in fact, into an institutional framework. That economic practicalities shaped the external form of debasement should not tempt one to forget, however, that slavery was at bottom a social arrangement, a way of society's ordering its members in its own mind.

NOTES

1. "About the last of August came in a dutch man of warre that sold us twenty Negars." Smith was quoting John Rolfe's account. Edward Arber and A. G. Bradley, eds., *Travels and Works of Captain John Smith* . . . , 2 vols. (Edinburgh: J. Grant, 1910), II, p. 541.

2. Philip A. Bruce, *Economic History of Virginia in the Seventeenth Century*, 2 vols. (New York, 1896), II, pp. 57–130; James C. Ballagh, *A History of Slavery in Virginia* (Baltimore: Johns Hopkins Press, 1902), pp. 28–35.

3. John H. Russell, *The Free Negro in Virginia, 1619–1865* (Baltimore: Johns Hopkins Press, 1913), p. 29.

4. Ibid., pp. 23–39; Ulrich B. Phillips, *American Negro Slavery* (New York: D. Appleton and Company, 1918), pp. 75–77, and *Life and Labor in the Old South* (Boston: Little, Brown, and Company, 1929), p. 170; Helen T. Catterall, ed., *Judicial*

Cases Concerning American Slavery and the Negro, 5 vols. (Washington: Carnegie Institution of Washington, 1926–37), I, pp. 54–55, 57–63; James M. Wright, *The Free Negro in Maryland, 1634–1860* (New York: Columbia University Press, 1921), pp. 21–23; Susie M. Ames, *Studies of the Virginia Eastern Shore in the Seventeenth Century* (Richmond: Dietz Press, 1940), pp. 100–6. See also T.R. Davis, "Negro Servitude in the United States," *Journal of Negro History* 8 (July 1923): 247–83, and Edgar T. Thompson, "The Natural History of Agricultural Labor in the South," in David K. Jackson, ed., *American Studies in Honor of William Kenneth Boyd* (Durham, N. C.: Duke University Press, 1940), pp. 127–46.

5. Phillips, *American Negro Slavery*, p. viii.

6. Wesley F. Craven, *The Southern Colonies in the Seventeenth Century, 1607–1689* (Baton Rouge: Louisiana State University Press, 1949), pp. 217–19, 402–3.

7. *William and Mary Quarterly*, 3rd Ser., 7 (April 1950): 199–222.

8. Kenneth M. Stampp, *The Peculiar Institution: Slavery in the Ante-Bellum South* (New York: A. A. Knopf, 1956), pp. vii–viii, 3–33.

9. Ibid., pp. 21–22.

10. Arnold Rose, "The Roots of Prejudice," in UNESCO, *The Race Question in Modern Science* (New York: Whiteside, Inc., 1956), p. 244. For examples of the more general view see Frederick G. Detweiler, "The Rise of Modern Race Antagonisms," *American Journal of Sociology* 37 (March 1932): 743; M. F. Ashley Montagu, *Man's Most Dangerous Myth: The Fallacy of Race* (New York: Columbia University Press, 1945), pp. 10–11, 19–20; Gunnar Myrdal, *An American Dilemma: The Negro Problem and Modern Democracy* (New York: Harper & Brothers, 1944), pp. 83–89, 97; Paul Kecskemeti, "The Psychological Theory of Prejudice: Does it Underrate the Role of Social History?" *Commentary* 18 (October 1954): 364–66.

11. *Comparative Studies in Society and History* 2 (October 1959): 49–66. See also Degler, *Out of Our Past: The Forces that Shaped Modern America* (New York: Harper & Row, 1959), pp. 26–39.

12. H. R. McIlwaine, ed., *Minutes of the Council and General Court of Colonial Virginia, 1622–1632, 1670–1676* (Richmond: The Colonial Press, Everett Wadley Co., 1924), p. 196. See the lists and musters of 1624 and 1625 in John C. Hotten, ed., *The Original Lists of Persons of Quality . . .* (New York, 1880), pp. 169–265.

13. "The status of Negroes was that of servants; and so they were identified and treated down to the 1660's." ("Origins," p. 203). The footnote to this statement reads, "For disciplinary and revenue laws in Virginia that did not discriminate Negroes from other servants, see Hening, *Statutes*, I, pp. 174, 198, 200, 243, 306 (1631–1645)." But pp. 200 and 243 of William Waller Hening, ed., *The Statutes at Large; Being a Collection of All the Laws of Viriginia . . .* (2nd ed. of vols. 1–4, New York, 1823), I, in fact contain nothing about either servants or Negroes, while a tax provision on p. 242 specifically discriminates against Negro women. The revenue act on p. 306 lists the number of pounds of tobacco levied on land, cattle, sheep, horses, etc., and on tithable persons, and provides for collection of lists of the above so that the colony can compute its tax program; nothing else is said of servants and tithables. To say, as the Handlins did in the same note, that Negroes, English servants, and horses, etc., were listed all together in some early Virginia wills, with the implication that Negroes and English servants were regarded as alike in status, is hardly correct unless one is to assume that the horses were sharing this status as well. (For complete bibliographical information on Hening, ed., *Statutes*, see E. G. Swem, *Virginia Historical Index*, 2 vols. [Roanoke, Va.: Stone Printing and Manufacturing Co., 1934–36], I, pp. xv–xvi.)

14. Latin-American Negroes did not lose all civil and personal rights, did not

become mere chattels, yet we speak of "slavery" in Latin America without hesitation. See Frank Tannenbaum, *Slave and Citizen: The Negro in the Americas* (New York: A. A. Knopf, 1947), and Gilberto Freyre, *The Masters and the Slaves: A Study in the Development of Brazilian Civilization* (New York: A. A. Knopf, 1946).

15. "Decisions of the General Court," *Virginia Magazine of History and Biography* 5 (January 1898): 236. Abbot Emerson Smith in the standard work on servitude in America, *Colonists in Bondage: White Servitude and Convict Labor in America, 1607–1776* (Chapel Hill: University of North Carolina Press, 1947), p. 171, says that "there was never any such thing as perpetual slavery for any white man in any English colony." There were instances in the seventeenth century of white men sold into "slavery," but this was when the meaning of the term was still indefinite and often equated with servitude.

16. "Decisions of the General Court," pp. 236–37.

17. *A Perfect Description of Virginia* . . . (London, 1649), reprinted in Peter Force, ed., *Tracts* . . . 4 vols. (Washington, 1836–46), II.

18. These four cases may be found in Northampton County Deeds, Wills &c. (Virginia State Library, Richmond), No. 4 (1651–54), 28 (misnumbered 29), p. 124; *Archives of Maryland*, 69 vols. (Baltimore, 1883–1961) XLI, pp. 261–62; York County Records (Virginia State Library), No. 2 (transcribed Wills & Deeds, 1645–49), pp. 256–57.

19. Lancaster County Loose Papers (Virginia State Library), Box of Wills, 1650–1719, Folder 1656–59.

20. For examples running for as long as thirty-five years, see *William and Mary Quarterly*, 1st Ser., 20 (October 1911): 148; Russell, *Free Negro in Virginia*, pp. 26–27; Ames, *Eastern Shore*, p. 105. Compare the cases of a Negro and an Irish servant in *Calendar of Virginia State Papers* . . . 11 vols. (Richmond, 1875–93), I, pp. 9–10, and *Maryland Archives* XLI, pp. 476–78; XLIX, pp. 123–24.

21. Russell, *Free Negro in Virginia*, pp. 24–41. See especially the cases in *Virginia Magazine of History and Biography* 5 (July 1897): 40; York County Deeds, Wills, Orders, etc. (Virginia State Library), No. 1 (1633–57, 1691–94), pp. 338–39.

22. John H. Russell, "Colored Freemen as Slave Owners in Virginia," *Journal of Negro History* 1 (July 1916): 234–37.

23. York County Records, No. 2, p. 63; Northampton County Orders, Deeds, Wills, &c., No. 2 (1640–45), p. 224; York County Deeds, Orders, Wills, &c. (1657–62), pp. 108–9.

24. York County Records, No. 2, p. 390.

25. Apparently Calvert's deal with Skinner was never consummated. *Maryland Archives* IV, pp. vii, 189, 320–21. For prices of white servants see ibid., IV, pp. 31, 47–48, 74, 78–79, 81, 83, 92, 98, 108–9, 184, 200, 319.

26. Hening, *Statutes*, I, pp. 144, 242, 292, 454. The Handlins erroneously placed the "first sign of discrimination" in this matter at 1668 ("Origins," p. 217n). For Maryland, see *Maryland Archives* I, p. 342; II, pp. 136, 399, 538–39; XIII, pp. 538–39.

27. John Hammond, *Leah and Rachel, or, Two Fruitfull Sisters Virginia, and Mary-land: Their Present Condition, Impartially Stated and Related* . . . (London, 1656), reprinted in Force, ed., *Tracts*, II.

28. Hening, ed., *Statutes*, II, p. 267. The distinction between white and colored women was neatly described at the turn of the century by Robert Beverley, *The History and Present State of Virginia*, Louis B. Wright, ed. (Chapel Hill: University of North Carolina Press, 1947), pp. 271–72.

29. Hening, ed., *Statutes*, I, p. 226, and for the same act in more detail see *Wil-*

liam and Mary Quarterly, 2nd Ser., 4 (July 1924): 147. The Handlins discounted this law: "Until the 1660's the statutes on the Negroes were not at all unique. Nor did they add up to a decided trend." ("Origins," p. 209.) The note added to this statement reads, "That there was no trend is evident from the fluctuations in naming Negro slaves or servants and in their right to bear arms. See Hening, *Statutes*, I, pp. 226, 258, 292, 540; Bruce, *Institutional History*, II, pp. 5 ff., 199 ff. For similar fluctuations with regard to Indians, see Hening, *Statutes*, I, pp. 391, 518." But since the terms "servants" and "slaves" did not have precise meaning, as the Handlins themselves asserted, fluctuations in naming Negroes one or the other cannot be taken to mean that their status itself was fluctuating. Of the pages cited in Hening, p. 258 is an act encouraging Dutch traders and contains nothing about Negroes, servants, slaves, or arms. Page 292 is an act providing that fifteen tithable persons should support one soldier; Negroes were among those tithable, but nothing was said of allowing them to arm. Page 540 refers to "any negro slaves" and "said negro," but mentions nothing about servants or arms. In the pages dealing with Indians, p. 391 provides that no one is to employ Indian servants with guns, and p. 518 that Indians (not "Indian servants") are to be allowed to use their own guns; the two provisions are not contradictory. Philip A. Bruce, *Institutional History of Virginia in the Seventeenth Century*, 2 vols. (New York: G. P. Putnam's Sons, 1910), II, p. 5 ff., indicates that Negroes were barred from arming in 1639 and offers no suggestion that there was any later fluctuation in this practice.

    30. Hening, *Statutes*, I, p. 146. "Christianity" appears instead of "Christians" in McIlwaine, *Minutes of the Council*, p. 479.

    31. *Maryland Archives* X, pp. 114–15.

    32. Hening, *Statutes*, I, p. 552; McIllwaine, *Minutes of the Council*, p. 479.

    33. Bruce, *Economic History of Virginia*, II, p. 110.

    34. Hening, *Statutes*, II, p. 170; III, pp. 86–87; *Maryland Archives* I, pp. 533–34; VII, p. 204. Opinion on this matter apparently was not unanimous, for a petition of several citizens to the Council in 1699 asked repeal of the intermarriage prohibition. H. R. McIlwaine, ed., *Legislative Journals of the Council of Colonial Virginia*, 3 vols. (Richmond: The Colonial Press, Everett Wadley Co., 1918-1919), I, p. 262. The Handlins wrote ("Origins," p. 215), "Mixed marriages of free men and servants were particularly frowned upon as complicating status and therefore limited by law." Their citation for this, Hening, *Statutes*, II, p. 114 (1661-62), and Marcus W. Jernegan, *Laboring and Dependent Classes in Colonial America, 1607-1783* (Chicago: University of Chicago Press, 1931), pp. 55, 180, gives little backing to the statement. In Virginia secret marriage or bastardy between whites of different status got the same punishment as such between whites of the same status. A white servant might marry any white if his master consented. See Hening, *Statutes*, I, pp. 252–53, 438–39; II, pp. 114–15, 167; III, pp. 71–75, 137–40. See also James C. Ballagh, *White Servitude in the Colony of Virginia* (Baltimore, 1895), p. 50. For Maryland, see *Maryland Archives* I, pp. 73, 373–74, 441–42; II, pp. 396–97; XIII, pp. 501–2. The Handlins also suggested that in the 1691 Virginia law, "spurious" meant simply "illegitimate," and they cited Arthur W. Calhoun, *A Social History of the American Family from Colonial Times to the Present*, 3 vols. (Cleveland: The Arthur H. Clark Company, 1917-19), I, p. 42, which turns out to be one quotation from John Milton. However, "spurious" was used in colonial laws with reference only to unions between white and black, and never in bastardy laws involving whites only. Mulattoes were often labeled "spurious" offspring.

    35. For example, George C. Homans, *The Human Group* (New York: Harcourt, Brace & World, 1950).

9. ROBERT C. TWOMBLY AND ROBERT H. MOORE, Black Puritan: The Negro in Seventeenth-Century Massachusetts (1967)*

In this description of Afro-Americans in seventeenth-century Massachusetts, Robert C. Twombly and Robert H. Moore take issue with the older view that New England states were no different from southern states in their treatment of slaves. The authors find that Afro-Americans in the Bay Colony confronted few if any cases of discrimination in the administration of justice or in seeking economic opportunities during the seventeenth century. At the turn of the century, however, the situation for black citizens worsened, and the authors suggest some reasons for these changes.

Historians have assumed that seventeenth-century Massachusetts was no different from other American colonies in its treatment of Negroes.[1] It has been easy to overlook a colony where, as late as 1715, there were only 2,000 Negroes in a population of 96,000, and where whites seemed to hold racial views similar to those of other settlers. But an analysis of Negro life in the Puritan Commonwealth reveals the inaccuracy of this view.

Most authorities agree that Negroes first came to Massachusetts in 1638, but it seems clear to us that at least one Negro had arrived as early as 1633. Contemporaries estimated that there were between 100 and 200 in 1680 and 550 by 1708.[2] Although Negroes were numerous enough to be familiar in the everyday affairs of many communities by the 1660s, most Puritans regarded blacks as strange and exotic creatures. Despite the inconsistent terminology used to refer to Negroes,[3] Massachusetts whites held certain derogatory attitudes.

John Josselyn noted that some New Englanders thought Negro blackness resulted from the African climate, while others believed it came from Ham's curse. Blackness was commonly associated with evil. During the witchcraft hysteria many people claimed to have seen the Devil in the form of a "Blackman"; white women accused of having evil spirits were sometimes called "black witches." Blackness connoted ugliness as well as evil. "Sea-Devils," a fish found off the Maine coast, were popularly called "Negroes" because they were a very "ugly," "hideous" species, "having a black scale." [4]

* Robert C. Twombly and Robert H. Moore, "Black Puritan: The Negro in Seventeenth-Century Massachusetts," first appeared in *The William and Mary Quarterly* 24 (April 1967): 224–42. Reprinted by permission.

If some derogatory attitudes found expression in metaphor, others appeared in social relations. Whites were insulted when compared closely with a Negro. "A Lieutenant of a Man of War," the perturbed Cotton Mather wrote, "whom I am a Stranger to, designing to putt an Indignity upon me, has called his *Negro-Slave* by the Name of COTTON MATHER." Samuel Sewall recorded in his diary that "Mr Cotton Mather came to Mr. Wilkins's shop, and there talked very sharply against me as if I used his father worse than a Neger; spake so loud that the people in the street might hear him." Such opinions sometimes led to bizarre actions. Josselyn wrote that fish did not respond to herring as quickly as they did for a "waggish lad at Cape-porpus [Maine], who baited his hook with the drown'd Negro's buttocks." Puritan racial attitudes do not seem appreciably different from those held by other contemporary white men.[5]

One might expect the Puritans to have treated Negroes with an indignity matching their attitudes. But the real test of the colony's race relations must be based not on what whites thought and said but on what they did. How the Negro fared in day to day activity is the best indication of the nature of Negro life in the Puritan Commonwealth.

Central to the maintenance of order and stability in any society is the administration of justice. This was particularly true in Massachusetts where respect for the law was primary in the colonists' conception of a vigorous, stable, and godly society. A profound commitment to the law and the judicial process overpowered antipathetical racial views and assured fair and equal treatment, guaranteeing the basic legal rights of Englishmen to free, servant, and slave Negroes. These rights—including police protection, legal counsel, trial by jury, fair and considered hearings, and impartial justice—are very much expected in the twentieth century. In the seventeenth they were incipient concepts in much of the western world. But Massachusetts guarded these liberties jealously, applying them without regard for skin color. The Puritans did not hold advanced racial views but they did place a high priority on the universality of justice. Throughout the century Negroes and whites received essentially equal treatment before the law.

Important principles were observed even in minor offenses. In 1680, for example, Goodman Wolland accused Daniel King's Negro boy of insulting him on a Boston street. When the boy denied the allegation, Wolland brought him to court where the case was thrown out for lack of witnesses. That the case went to court at all indicates a predilection to seek legal redress rather than to initiate private action. When, in 1653, "a contravercy" developed between John Smith of Plymouth and John Barnes's "neager maide servant," the Plymouth court listened to "whatso-

ever could bee saide on either side." Both were cleared of any misdemeanor, but they were admonished for public quarreling.[6]

Like whites, Negroes received police protection and were shielded
from extralegal punitive action. When three Indians broke into the home
of Angola, a free Negro, in 1672, he prosecuted. All three were given
twenty stripes and ordered to remain in prison until they paid court costs.
In another case Pelatiah Glover brought suit against Betty Negro for
insulting his son and mother. Richard White and Tom, a Negro, testified
against her. She was found guilty of slander and given ten stripes but by
being taken to court Betty at least found a measure of protection. The
principle of using judicial means rather than resorting to personal retribu-
tion extended to the colony's Maine jurisdiction where in 1686 George
Norton prosecuted his own Negro for stealing his wool. Due process
and a willingness to use the courts minimized expeditious extralegal punishment. Even masters recognized this principle.[7]

Other incidents established that Negro testimony was admissible as
evidence against whites. In 1673 a defendant challenged a witness's legal
right to testify, but the plaintiff replied "that the negro was of such
carriage and knowledge that her testimony had been accepted several
times before this." Later, in 1679, Wonn Negro testified against Bridget
Oliver, who was suspected of witchcraft. In 1680 Mingo the Negro was
a witness in a suit involving warehouse arson. Instances of Negro testimony
for and against both races are numerous.[8]

It is also evident from the records that Negroes had access to legal
counsel. In 1679 Hannah, a Negro servant, was convicted for stealing a box
of "Chyrurgions Jnstrumts." From prison she persuaded three white men
to post forty pounds bond for her release and petitioned the Suffolk
County court for dismissal of her fines. Her appeal, a sophisticated legal
argument, cited page and section numbers of the laws governing burglary.
Although the jury dismissed it, Zachariah Chaffee, Jr., commenting on
Hannah's appeal, noted the "refined distinctions" that could only have
been "written by men accustomed to legal problems." [9]

An additional example of the many elements of justice accorded
Negroes stemmed from the Salem witch controversy. In 1692 a warrant
was issued for the arrest of Mary Black, a Negro owned by Lieutenant
Nathaniel Putnam of Salem Village. Although maintaining her innocence,
Mary was tried, convicted, and imprisoned for witchcraft. The next year,
however, cooler heads had apparently prevailed, and Mary was not forgotten. Upon petition she was released from prison by proclamation of
the Governor.[10]

These cases introduce important principles illustrating Negro legal
rights. A Negro's word was admissible as evidence and his testimony

could be as acceptable as that of whites. Charges against Negroes had to be documented and they received the thoughtful consideration of juries and magistrates. Negroes had police protection and were shielded from extralegal practices that would have denied them due process of law. They could appeal, use legal counsel, and receive gubernatorial pardons.

The principles operative in the cases described above were applicable when more abhorrent crimes were committed. Negroes were given the same judicial treatment as whites in all aspects of the case from indictment to punishment. Some crimes, like burglary, are impossible to analyze, for penalites were distributed on the basis of the kinds and amounts of items stolen; we were unable to find cases in which Negroes and whites appropriated exactly the same things. For this reason we have not attempted comparisons of thefts, but have analyzed arson, murder, manslaughter, and sexual offenses—the four main areas in which comparison between the races is possible.

Of the sexual crimes committed in Massachusetts, fornication, bastardy, and rape were most prevalent. According to the 1675 Laws and Ordinances of War—a compilation of previous statutes—rape, ravishment, and unnatural abuses were punishable by death. Fornication and other "dissolute lasciviousness" were penalized at the judge's discretion, taking into account the severity and circumstances of the case. Fornication, by both Negro and white, was a considerable problem in early Massachusetts, and the many recorded cases provide ample opportunity for comparative analysis.[11]

Essex County punished its Negro fornicators by whipping or fine, the choice sometimes being left to the offender. In 1660, Captain White's Negro Jugg was whipped; Grace and Juniper, convicted in 1674, were "to be fined or whipped." In 1678, two "neager" servants, David and Judith, chose to pay a fine rather than feel the lash ten and five times respectively. The whites in Essex County received similar treatment. Mary Dane, an indentured servant, was whipped. The same year, 1654, Elizabeth Osgood was given thirty stripes and her mate twenty-five. Most infringers, regardless of race, received from ten to twenty stripes or were ordered to pay from forty to fifty shillings.[12]

Representative of Suffolk County's treatment of fornicators was the case of Mary Plumb, a white, who was punished with fifteen stripes and court and prison fees for "Lascivious carriage by being seene in bed with a man." For the same offense, Phoebe Lovell received ten stripes or a forty shilling fine plus court costs. Negroes in Suffolk County got the same penalties. Joan and her partner, Jasper Indian, were given their choice of fifteen stripes or a forty shilling fine plus court costs. In a significant case, Robert Corbet, a white, and George, a Negro, both servants of

Stephen French, received identical sentences in 1679 for committing fornication with the Negro Maria: twenty sripes and court costs. Fornication between the races was not punished any more stringently than that between members of the same race. In Suffolk, as in Essex County, the most common penalty ranged from ten to twenty lashes or a forty to fifty shilling fine plus fees of court.[13]

Although there is no evidence that it was practiced, racial intermarriage was not illegal until 1705. Before then most miscegenation was illicit. If it led to bastardy, penalties for both races were generally the same as for simple fornication. In most cases the court sought to determine paternity in order to provide the child's support, and this led to additional costs for the father. Usually the woman was whipped from ten to twenty stripes or ordered to pay a forty to fifty shilling fine. The man was given a similar number of stripes and then bound to pay weekly support or a lump sum to be administered over the years. In 1682, for example, Richard Prior gave thirty pounds surety to save Ipswich from maintaining his illegitimate child. The same year John Tucker was fined six pounds and ordered to pay an undisclosed amount for birth and support. In 1679 the court ordered John Hunkins to give his partner's father one shilling per week. When the races mixed the penalties were about the same: William Rane, father of a child by the Indian servant Ann, paid three shillings a week. For "haveing a bastard," the white Hannah Bonny was "well whipt"; her mate, Nimrod Negro, was also whipped and made to turn over eighteen pence weekly for his offspring. Illegitimate Negro children were generally awarded financial support in amounts similar to those paid to white and mixed offspring. In 1673 the Negro Silvanus provided two shillings six pence per week for his son's upbringing.

A humorous episode took place in Maine in 1695. Alice Metherill, for being pregnant, was given a choice of ten stripes and fifteen shillings or five pounds and court costs; her alleged partner was ordered to pay eleven shillings six pence bond and two shillings six pence maintenance per week payable monthly. When the child was born, however, it was quite black. The "father," already punished by the court, quickly prosecuted Alice for falsely associating him with her "black bastard." Alice, by now known as a "whore" and a "witch," finally admitted that Black Will, a Negro slave, was her real consort. The province did not hold Black Will's past against him, however, for several years later when he was accused of fathering the baby of Elizabeth Brooks, a single white woman, he was acquitted.[14]

Rape, a more serious offense, could be punished by death. The two Negro cases in the published records reveal the severity dealt offenders. Basto Negro was convicted in 1676 of raping the three year old daughter of Robert Cox, his master. When Cox appealed Basto's death sentence, the jury substituted thirty-nine lashes and ordered him "allwayes to weare a roape about his neck, to hang doune two foot." If ever he was found without his rope Basto would feel an additional twenty lashes. Shortly thereafter John Negro confessed to "pulling Sarah Phillips of Salem off her horse and attempting to ravish her." John's penalty for attempted rape was a five pound payment to Miss Phillips, prosecution and court costs, and banishment from the colony.[15]

Whites also received stiff penalties. John Man, perhaps the Marquis de Sade of his time, for "wanton and lascivious carriages . . . and cruell beating" of his indentured servant, gave two hundred pounds sureties until the next court, paid prosecution costs and court fees, and terminated his girl's contract. John Kempe attempted rape on "3 yong girles [and] was censured to bee whiped both heare [Boston], at Roxberry and at Salem very severely and was Comitted for a slave to Lieft Davenport." Two other white rapists, William Cheny and Samuel Guile, were hanged until dead.[16]

Two rapes involving Indians demonstrate important aspects of Massachusetts jurisprudence. In 1674, Tom, indicted for raping another Indian, pleaded not guilty before a "Jury of twelve men six English and six Indians against none of which he Objected." Although he was found guilty, Tom held the right to challenge a jury containing six members of his own race. The second case, from Plymouth in 1682, dealing with "Sam, the Indian," reveals a paternalistic strain in legal approaches to non-whites. Sam was proven guilty: "although in an ordinary consideration hee deserved death, yett considering hee was but an Indian, and therefore in an incapasity [unable] to know the horibleness . . . of this abominable act . . . he was centanced . . . to be severely whipt att the post and sent out of the country." In spite of this decision, leniency for Indians and Negroes, who ordinarily met the same penalties as whites, does not appear the rule. Indeed, judges followed the argument presented by a defendant in a 1660 Essex County case, although his suggestion about Negroes was not considered valid: "the law is undeniable that the indian may have the same distribusion of Justice with our selves," John Hawthorne had argued. But "ther is as I humbly consieve not the same argument as amongst the negroes for the light of the gospell is [not] a begineing to appeare amongst them. . . ." The application of the law to Negroes followed the pattern of Tom's case and Hawthorne's suggestion for Indians—due process and equality in punishment. The courts did not consider Christianity a prerequisite for equality before the law; nor did they apply Plymouth's leniency for Sam Indian or Hawthorne's views on Negroes to the blacks in their midst.[17]

Equitable treatment for Negroes extended to other capital offenses

According to the law, murder was to be "expiated with the death of the murderer." A measure of Massachusett's concern for justice was the care with which she appraised murder cases, often meting out punishment for manslaughter instead. Thoughtful scrutiny reflected a recognition of extenuating circumstances. And this attitude did not exclude Negro assailants of whites.

The average penalty for manslaughter was a twenty pound fine and the costs of prosecution, court, and detention. Depending on the circumstances, part of the fine went to the colony and part to the deceased's relatives.[18] Both instances of Negro manslaughter, originally indictments for murder against whites, were handled equitably. A 1684 defendant, "Robert Trayes, negro," wounded the "legg of Daniell Standlake . . . , of which wound, and cutting the legg occationed therby, died. . . ." Since he had meant to fire at Standlake's door, the jury decided that Trayes was "an instrument of the death of Daniell Standlake by misadventure," and sentenced the defendant to pay the deceased's father five pounds or be whipped. The second case, in which the servant Robin was accused, is of particular note, not only for its dealing with manslaughter but also for its clear statement of Negro legal rights.[19]

Robin was guilty of giving John Cheeny of Cambridge "a mortall wound on the head with a stick" in 1689. His punishment was light: charges of prosecution, fees of court, and costs of prison where he was to remain until he paid. Robin had pled not guilty, but what extenuating circumstances had brought about the easy sentence are not recorded. More important, however, is that after the jury had been selected Robin was allowed to "make . . . challenge against any of them." In addition, one juror, feeling as Hawthorne had in 1660, that Negroes did not deserve "the same distribution of Justice with our selves," refused to appear. In reply the court fined him five shillings. Through this concrete act the court clearly stated that shirking jury duty was inexcusable and that due process extended to blacks as well as whites.

The only recorded case in which a white killed a Negro took place in Maine in 1694 when a master's continual mistreatment of his servant led to her death. In the South well before this time, as Carl Degler points out, masters were without "any fear of prosecution" if they killed slaves; the law "allowed punishment for refractory slaves up to and including accidental death. . . ." But the Puritans showed more restraint. Indicted by a grand jury on suspicion of murder, Nathaniel Cane was convicted of manslaughter for "Cruelty to his Negro woman by Cruell Beating and hard usage." His fine—ten pounds ten shillings—was light. Nonetheless, a master could not mistreat, abuse, or murder his Negro without threat of legal action.[20]

Arson, an infrequent but serious offense, brought harsh penalties. Severity was demonstrated early in the colony's history when in 1640 Henry Stevens fired his master's barn and had his indenture extended by twenty-one years. Throughout the century the penalties were stiff: Jack, a Negro arsonist, was hanged in 1681. Two Negroes implicated in the Maria arson case the same year were banished and Maria was burned alive, the only punishment of its kind in Massachusetts history.[21] Maria's fire had caused the death of a baby girl. She had deliberately destroyed her master's house and had not intended murder. But since she had caused a death by burning she in turn was burned. Her severe sentence may have been prompted by uneasiness over a rash of fires in the Boston vicinity. Social pressure may have induced the court to be unduly harsh in this affair but it was not stampeded. The strict sentence was a response to a specific situation and did not become a precedent for future dealings with either arsonists, murderers, or Negroes. But the case stands as an ugly blot on Puritan history.[22]

This review of legal cases indicates that throughout the seventeenth century the Negro received due process and only in isolated incidents, like the Maria case, was he given unusual treatment. But even on that occasion it is questionable to what extent skin color dictated severity. In general, the Negro held the rights of Englishmen before the courts. The legal apparatus did not undergo subtle shifts when Negroes came before it.

If the Negro's legal status was not circumscribed by pigmentation neither were his economic opportunities. Several black men, servant and free, accumulated real and other property; the color of their skin did not by definition render them ineligible for economic gain. Although most Negroes were members of the servant class and therefore at the bottom of the economic ladder, some were able to carve out an enviable niche in the white business world.

The story of Angola illustrates the possibilities. In 1653 he was owned by Captain Robert Keayne, who in his will in 1656 left Angola a two pound legacy. Then the free Negro Bostian Ken purchased Angola and set him free by bonding his property to Mrs. Keayne. In 1670 Governor Richard Bellingham sold a piece of land bordered "Upon the North East with the land of Angola, the Negro." Bellingham had given him this fifty-foot square piece in the late 1660s when Angola, paddling in a river, had rescued the Governor from his sinking boat. When he died in 1675 Angola's will confirmed his house, land, and other possessions upon his widow Elizabeth, her children, and her heirs forever. In the twenty years before his death Angola had paid his eighteen pound obligation to Ken and had moved from a servant with a two pound legacy to a free Negro of means.[23]

Bostian Ken, Angola's benefactor, was another prosperous Negro. In order to purchase his friend's freedom in 1656 Ken bonded his house and land in Dorchester plus four and one half acres of wheat. In 1662 he sold his one-third share of the fourteen-ton ship *Hopewell* to his "loving friend Francis Vernon" along with "one barrell of liquor one barr of Sugar one Barr mackerell and one Barr Codfish." From 1656 to 1662 Ken dealt in considerable amounts of property.[24]

Most of the other seventeenth-century Negro landowners received their holdings from their masters. In 1677 Increase Mather bought land bordered on the "Northwest by the land of Jethro the Negro." If Governor Bellingham and the Reverend Mr. Mather owned choice land, the bordering Negro holdings may have also been desirable.[25] Other Negroes held land, houses, and small businesses. When Thomas, owner of a chairmaking establishment, married Katherine in 1678, he drew up a lengthy document granting her his estate in case of his death and bound himself for one hundred pounds surety. Zippora Potter, daughter of one of Robert Keayne's Negroes, bought a twenty-eight by sixty-foot "parcell of land with a dwelling house thereupon" in 1670 for "forty Six pounds currant Mony of New England in hand paid." Although the number of successful Negroes was small, they came from a total Negro population in the colony that was at most only two hundred at this time.[26]

A few Negroes were property owners, but the majority were house servants living with white families. Many resided in Boston but those in the outlying areas and the Boston blacks who traveled about broadened interracial contact. Most Negroes lived in their masters' homes, were often left alone, and could come and go as they pleased when not working. They were not restricted to the towns in which they lived and in many cases moved freely about the countryside.[27]

Freedom of movement opened up certain options. One option, running away, may have been a product of working class discontent; but running away was also encouraged by alternatives that lack of repression offered.[28] Freedom of movement permitted a certain amount of fraternization between races in the lower classes; the derogatory views of most whites did not preclude informal relations. Occasionally mutual activities were forms of antisocial behavior. In 1673, for example, "John Burrington, Edward Fish, Richard Hollingsworths Negro Tom, Thomas [,] Clark Cliffords Servt," and a fifth man, stole saddles and bridles and "complotted to run away." About the same time "Gregory, Nath. Emerson, Arthur Abbot and a Negro" broke into a house, took wine, and improvised a drinking party. But not all interracial mingling was mischievous. For five years in the 1690s one of Boston's four chimney sweepers was "Jeremiah the Negro"; for one year, 1693, he was joined by "Negro Will," who along with Jeremiah brought token integration to Boston's public employ. During the smallpox epidemic in the 1680s Mary Heall, a seventy-four year old widow living alone, took the Negro Zanckey into her home to watch over his recovery. On another occasion, Jack, a runaway Negro, came to Anthony Dorchester's home. Jack was a stranger but Dorchester invited him in and made him welcome:

> . . . after asking for a Pipe of Tobacco which I told him there was some on the Table he tooke my knife and Cut some and then put it in his Pocket and after that tooke downe a Cutlass and offered to draw it but it Coming out stiff I closed in upon him . . .

Jack was overpowered and taken to prison, but Dorchester's initial hospitality is noteworthy.[29]

The colony's mechanisms of social control which permitted easy interracial contact did not make Negroes full fledged citizens or the social equals of whites, but neither were the blacks shunted to another realm of existence. The absence of rigid barriers in Massachusetts did not create a Negro utopia. But neither were Bay Colony blacks forced into a separate and demeaning world of their own. The Negro hovered on the fringes of full participation in social and economic life.

Overcoming the obstacles of nature was of immediate importance to the first generation of Puritans; in their attempt to construct a "city upon a hill" their first concerns were the problems of building communities, of keeping their children from barbarism, and of reproducing essential and familiar institutions. But as the generations passed, as trade increased, as the frontier receded, and as the complexities of a growing colony burgeoned, the Commonwealth's problems shifted. Social order and stability had been of major importance from the beginning but during the last two decades of the seventeenth century serious social introspection increased. Ministers warned that God was angry with the people; family structure, education, the churches, and other social institutions came under closer scrutiny. It was in this context that the colony passed her first laws to regulate the Negro's behavior.

Except for militia policy, no laws were passed applying only to Negroes until the 1680s.[30] Old and New England had fitted the black man into the social system without legally recognizing slavery or a slave caste. Within the broad guidelines of the Common Law and Puritan religious views Massachusetts had extended century-old rights of Englishmen to

Negroes. But in the 1680s the colony began to place restrictions upon them. The new Negro policies were responses to three social concerns: a widespread anathema for the slave trade, a pervasive uneasiness about the colony's economic future, and a growing anxiety about the Negro's behavior.

In spite of the unpopularity of slaving, several Massachusetts merchants were active traders in the 1680s, selling Negroes in Virginia for three to five thousand pounds of tobacco per head. Public pressure could not prohibit businessmen from dealing with Southerners but it could discourage the practice at home. Fear of public reprisal forced John Saffin, John Usher, James Wetcomb, and Andrew Belcher to import Negroes secretly in 1681. Fearing seizure, these merchants rerouted their Guinea trader from Swansea, Rhode Island, to Nantasket, Massachusetts, where, they wrote, "before you come in there take in such negroes . . . of ours and come up in the night with them, giveing us notice thereof wth what privacy you can. . . ." "Keepe your men Ignorant of your designe," the traders told their agent, and do nothing "prejudiciall to our mayne designe."[31]

Analyses of the economy seemed to demonstrate little benefit in the Negro's presence. In 1702 the General Court decided to promote "the bringing of White Servants and to put a period to Negroes being slaves." Beneath this admirable statement were more complex and mundane considerations. In 1708 Governor Joseph Dudley remarked that Negroes were costly to maintain during the winter months because they did little work and demanded great amounts of clothing. Negroes "are usually the worst servants," he noted. "The planters here do so much prefer white" laborers. The most complete statement of the economic disadvantages of Negroes appeared in an anonymous 1716 pamphlet. "Slaves . . . are a great hinderance to the Peopling and Improving the Country," the author began. If Negroes were excluded it "would greatly Encourage [white] Servants to come," and thereby aid the colony's growth. Since the land was "generally taken up," white servants could not acquire property and frequently became runaways and thieves. To avoid unruly indentured labor, a master could buy Negroes, and because of the tax structure, come off "cheaper than his poorer Neighbour that has an Apprentice." Apprentices cost more than slaves to maintain, were subject to regular militia training, and went to war. Slaves discouraged economic growth by draining their owners of wealth and by displacing laborers, apprentices, and craftsmen who used indenture as a stepping stone to greater things. To the author, the Negro posed a serious threat to indenture which, he felt, was the key to economic growth.[32]

The first regulations on Negroes were clauses inserted into general laws prohibiting Negroes, mulattoes, Indians, servants, and apprentices from buying or being served alcoholic beverages. Later in the 1680s the same groups were warned about stealing or giving away stolen goods and whites who induced thefts or received stolen merchandise were similarly promised punishment.[33]

No further legislation appeared until after the turn of the century. In 1703 Indian, Negro, and mulatto servants and slaves could be on the streets after nine in the evening only with masters' consent. After 1703 no Negro or mulatto could be manumitted unless his master gave fifty pounds surety for the servant's welfare. The first law was directed toward night time unrest, and the second prevented masters from throwing elderly, unemployable servants on the town charge. Both were concerned with specific and observable social problems.

The most stringent new measure, "An Act for the Better Preventing of a Spurious and Mixt Issue" of 1705, drove a deep wedge between the races. Sexual intercourse and racial intermarriage were now specifically prohibited. Fixed penalties were imposed on both races. Fornication was no longer left to judicial decision; Negro offenders were banished and the white consort, male or female, assumed responsibility for the offspring. The law reemphasized the desirability of Negro marriages, presumably a part of an effort to minimize mulatto births.

The 1705 law also placed a four pound duty on Negroes imported into the colony, and set heavy penalties on violators. The new duty aimed to discourage the slave trade. Some Puritans wished to rid the colony of Negroes or prevent any more from coming but restrictions on importation did not rest on this basis alone. Seven years later, in 1712, the General Court prohibited the trade in Indians. Revulsion for the slave trade and suspicion of outsiders worked to prevent nonwhites from coming to the Puritan Commonwealth.

A five-part law in 1707 prevented free Negroes from harboring or entertaining nonwhite servants in their homes without masters' approval and ordered them to repair highways, clean streets, or perform other tasks equal in time and amount to military duty. Since free Negroes had "a share in the benefit" of common defense, they would also go to the parade ground "in case of alarm" and "perform such tasks as the first commission of the company shall direct. . . ." The several laws were supplemented by town ordinances which, throughout the eighteenth century, further limited Negro freedom of movement.[34]

The new Massachusetts statutes dealing with Negroes were response to specific and observable colonial problems. The measures arose from what the Puritans thought were manifestations of social disorder. The legislation was not a premeditated program to debase the Negro, for the Puritans believed that their regulations were in the Negro's best interest. Some colonial leaders like Samuel Sewall and Cotton Mather wanted to incorporate Negroes more intimately into the colony's social and religious institutions; but men of narrower vision passed laws which overruled better intentions. The Bay Colony reluctantly accepted the black man's presence but believed by the 1700s that it precipitated social disorder. Legal restrictions on Massachusetts's Negroes neither followed from nor led to slavery. In the Bay Colony these restrictions were part of a hasty problem-solving endeavor that prevalent attitudes and predispositions made possible. The Negro felt the brunt of discriminatory laws but he was not without due process and never totally removed from participation in the white social and economic orbit. These advantages reflected an attitude that later enabled the Bay Colony to lead the way in constitutional prohibitions of slavery.

NOTES

1. Recent scholarship on early American slavery has ignored Massachusetts or assumed similarity with the South: Oscar and Mary Handlin, "Origins of the Southern Labor System," *The William and Mary Quarterly*, 3d Ser., 7 (1950): 199–222, and Oscar Handlin, "The Origins of Negro Slavery," *Race and Nationality in American Life* (New York: Doubleday & Co., 1957), pp. 3–29, argue that discrimination developed because of the institutionalization of slavery. Carl N. Degler, "Slavery and the Genesis of American Race Prejudice," *Comparative Studies in Society and History* 2 (1959): 49–66, reverses the Handlin thesis, attributing slavery to innate white discriminatory attitudes. Winthrop D. Jordan, "Modern Tensions and the Origin of American Slavery," *Journal of Southern History* 28 (1962): 18–30, sees both slavery and discrimination as part of a worldwide debasement of the Negro. Other relevant works are: Jordan, "The Influence of the West Indies on the Origins of New England Slavery," *William and Mary Quarterly*, 3d Ser., 18 (1961): 243–250; Lawrence W. Towner, " 'A Fondness for Freedom'; Servant Protest in Puritan Society," ibid., 19 (1962): 201–19; Towner, "The Sewall-Saffin Dialogue on Slavery," ibid., 21 (1964): 40–52; Jules Zanger, "Crime and Punishment in Early Massachusetts," ibid., 22 (1965): 471–77; Emory Washburn, "Slavery as it Once Prevailed in Massachusetts," in *Early History of Massachusetts: Lectures Delivered . . . Before the Lowell Institute, in Boston* (Boston, 1869), pp. 199–225; and Lorenzo J. Greene, *The Negro in Colonial New England, 1620–1776* (New York: Columbia University Press, 1942).

2. William Wood's 1634 *New-England's Prospect* . . . (1764 ed.), in *Publications of the Prince Society*, III (Boston, 1865), p. 86; and Deloraine P. Corey, *The History of Malden, Mass., 1633–1785* (Malden, Mass., 1899), p. 415, refer to a Negro living in Plymouth at least as early as 1633. Population estimates are taken from Simon Bradstreet to the Committee of Trade and Plantations, May 18, 1680, in Elizabeth Donnan, ed., *Documents Illustrative of the History of the Slave Trade to America* (Washington, D. C.: Carnegie Institution of Washington, 1930–35), III, pp. 14–15; Edward Randolph's Report to the Lords of the Committee of the Colonies, Aug., 1681, in Samuel G. Drake, *The History and Antiquities of Boston* . . . (Boston,

1856), p. 441; Joseph Dudley to the Council of Trade and Plantations, Oct. 1, 1708, in Cecil Headlam, ed., *Calendar of State Papers, Colonial Series, America and West Indies, June, 1708–1709* (London: Her Majesty's Stationery Office, 1922), p. 110; and Evarts B. Greene and Virginia D. Harrington, *American Population Before the Federal Census of 1790* (New York: Columbia University Press, 1932), p. 14.

3. "Slave" was not precisely defined in seventeenth-century Massachusetts; its flexible usage permitted several meanings. The conventional definition was "one who is the property of, and entirely subject to, another person, whether by capture, purchase, or birth; a servant completely divested of freedom and personal rights." See W. A. Cragie, ed., *A New English Dictionary on Historical Principles* (Oxford: Clarendon Press, 1919), X, pp. 182–184. The burden of this article is to demonstrate that Massachusetts never forced Negroes into this status. Puritans also used "slavery" to describe prisoners of war and criminals, and the term functioned as a rhetorical device to indicate dissatisfaction with government or authority. "Slave" and "servant" were used interchangeably in reference to Negroes: John Noble and John F. Cronin, eds., *Records of the Court of Assistants of . . . Massachusetts . . .* (Boston: Published by the County of Suffolk, 1901–28), I, p. 74; and John Josselyn, *An Account of Two Voyages to New England, Made during the Years 1638, 1663* (Boston, 1865), pp. 139–40.

4. The long history of black men in the European experience and the development of white racial opinion has been admirably treated in Winthrop D. Jordan, *White Over Black: American Attitudes Toward the Negro, 1550–1812* (Chapel Hill: University of North Carolina Press, 1968), ch. 1. Puritan racial attitudes are illustrated in Josselyn, *Two Voyages*, p. 143; George L. Burr, ed., *Narratives of the Witchcraft Cases, 1648–1706* (New York: C. Scribner's Sons, 1914), pp. 309–10, 312, 425; and William S. Southgate, "History of Scarborough, from 1633 to 1783," Maine Historical Society, *Collections*, III (1853), p. 92.

5. Dec. 10, 1721, in Worthington C. Ford, ed., *Diary of Cotton Mather* (New York: F. Unger Publishing Co., 1957), II, p. 663; Barrett Wendell, *Cotton Mather: The Puritan Priest* (New York, [1891]), p. 153, quoting Samuel Sewall, Oct. 20, 1701; Josselyn, *Two Voyages*, p. 159; Jordan, "White Over Black," ch. 1.

6. George F. Dow, ed., *Records and Files of the Quarterly Courts of Essex County* (Salem: Essex Institute, 1911–21), VII, p. 425; Nathaniel B. Shurtleff, ed., *Records of the Colony of New Plymouth in New England* (Boston, 1855–61), III, p. 39. To demonstrate racial equality before the law we shall compare the several kinds of criminal and civil offenses committed by Negroes to similar cases involving whites. We have appraised all the published records (falling between 1650 and 1690) in which Negroes appear; those presented here are not ayptical. We believe these cases accurately reflect the temper of the Negro's participation in the legal process.

7. The Angola case is in Samuel Eliot Morison, ed., *Records of the Suffolk County Court, 1671–1680*, 2 vols., in *Publications of the Colonial Society of Massachusetts, Collections*, 29–30 (Boston, 1933), I, p. 119. The Glover incident is listed in Joseph H. Smith, ed., *Colonial Justice in Western Massachusetts (1639–1702): The Pynchon Court Record . . .* (Cambridge, Mass.: Harvard University Press, 1961), p. 375. A comparable case involving a white woman brought a penalty of twenty stripes and the order to wear a paper "pinned upon her forehead with this inscription in capital letters: 'A SLANDERER OF MR. ZEROBABELL ENDICOTT,'" in Dow, ed., *Essex Court Records*, I, p. 380. Norton and Peter appear in Robert E. Moody, ed., *Province and Court Records of Maine* (Portland: Maine Historical Society,

1928–64), III, p. 226. Carl Degler, on the Southern administration of justice to Negroes, says: "As early as 1669 the Virginia law virtually washed its hands of protecting the Negro held as a slave. It allowed punishment of refractory slaves up to and including accidental death, relieving the master, explicitly, of any fear of prosecution. . . . ," in "Slavery and the Genesis of American Race Prejudice," p. 61. Compare this situation also with the 1694–95 Nathaniel Cane murder case cited in Moody, ed., *Maine Recs.*, IV, pp. 34–35.

8. See Dow, ed., *Essex Court Recs.*, V, p. 179; VI, p. 255; VII, pp. 329–30, 373, 410. For white testimony on behalf of Negroes see Noble and Cronin, eds., *Assistants Recs.*, III, p. 194.

9. Morrison, ed., *Suffolk Court Recs.*, II, pp. 1153–57. Chaffee's remarks are in the Intro., I, p. xxv.

10. Charles W. Upham, *Salem Witchcraft* . . . (Boston, 1867), II, pp. 128, 136–37.

11. The 1675 statutes are in Nathaniel B. Shurtleff, ed., *Records of the Governor and Company of the Massachusetts Bay in New England* (Boston, 1854), V, pp. 49–50, Sections 13 and 14. Also see Jordan, "White Over Black," p. 119. Fornication and adultery were usually treated as one crime in the seventeenth century. Married men, engaging in sexual activity with women other than their wives, were often tried for fornication.

12. For Essex County Negro fornication cases see Dow, ed., *Essex Court Recs.*, II, p. 247; V, p. 411; VI, pp. 73, 135; VII, pp. 141, 411; for whites see I, pp. 71, 80, 82, 337, 347, 404, 414, 420; III, pp. 17, 61, 198–99; VII, pp. 377–78, 398, 406, 410; VIII, pp. 375, 377, 424. This list is by no means exhaustive.

13. Because the published records are incomplete, the only Suffolk County cases are from the 1670's. For Negro offenders see Morison, ed., *Suffolk Court Recs.*, I, p. 233; II, p. 991; for whites see, for example, I, pp. 22, 80, 90–91, 114, 119, 185, 233–34; II, pp. 885, 1012–14, 1097–99, 1102, 1153. The Courts sometimes required a couple fornicating before marriage to make public confession before the church. See I, pp. 80, 90–91. In Maine fornicators usually received seven or more stripes or a fine ranging from fifteen to fifty shillings. See Moody, ed., *Maine Recs.*, IV, pp. 268–269, 293, 340, 344–45, 358, 360, and 371 for examples.

14. As with fornication interracial bastardy was not punished more severely than bastardy between two members of the same race. For examples of penalties accorded illegitimate white births see Morison, ed., *Suffolk Court Recs.*, II, 1097–99; Dow, ed., *Essex Court Recs.*, VII, pp. 97, 187; VIII, pp. 12–13, 279; Shurtleff, ed., *Plymouth Recs.*, I, p. 127. For illegitimate Negro births see Morison, ed., *Suffolk Court Recs.*, I, pp. 113, 259; II, pp. 809, 841, 1164; Dow, ed., *Essex Court Recs.*, I, pp. 196, 323; VI, p. 137. Interracial bastardy cases are: Dow, ed., *Essex Court Recs.*, V, p. 409; VI, p. 23; VII, p. 410; Morison, ed., *Suffolk Court Recs.*, I, pp. 185, 232; II, p. 809; Shurtleff, ed., *Plymouth Recs.*, VI, p. 177. Alice Metherill and Black Will are in Moody, ed., *Maine Recs.*, IV, pp. 47–49, 64–66; V, pp. 126, 169–71, 199–201; *York Deeds* (Portland, 1887–1910), VI, fol. 88.

15. Basto's case is in Noble and Cronin, eds., *Assistants Recs.*, I, p. 74, and Shurtleff, ed., *Mass. Recs.*, V, pp. 117–118. John Negro is in Morison, ed., *Suffolk Court Recs.*, II, p. 1067.

16. Ibid., II, p. 807; Noble and Cronin, eds., *Assistants Recs.*, I, pp. 50, 199; II, p. 86; innocent whites are *ibid.*, I, pp. 73, 158.

17. Ibid., I, 21–22; *Plymouth Recs.*, VI, p. 98; Hawthorne's argument is in Dow, ed., *Essex Court Recs.*, II, 240.

18. Shurtleff, ed., *Mass. Recs.*, V, p. 50, lists penalties for manslaughter and murder. White manslaughter cases are cited in Noble and Cronin, eds., *Assistants Recs.*, I, pp. 54, 114, 188, 358–359.

19. The Trayes case is in Shurtleff, eds., *Plymouth Recs.*, VI, pp. 141–142; Robin's is in Noble and Cronin, eds., *Assistants Recs.*, I, pp. 304–305, 321.

20. Moody, ed., *Maine Recs.*, IV, pp. 34–35. We saw no published court records convicting Negroes of murder. But note the equality of sentence in this extract from Samuel Sewall's diary, June 8, 1693: "Elisabeth Emerson of Havarill and a Negro Woman were executed after Lecture, for murdering their Infant Children." Massachusetts Historical Society, *Collections*, 5th Ser., V (1878), p. 379.

21. The Stevens case is in Noble and Cronin, eds., *Assistants Recs.*, II, p. 100. The documents relating to Maria, her accomplices, and Jack have been brought together by John Noble. See *Publications of the Colonial Society at Massachusetts, Transactions, 1899, 1900*, VIII (Boston: The Society, 1904), pp. 323–336.

22. Noble, ibid., argues that Maria was hanged before burning, dismissing both Cotton and Increase Mather's assertions that she was burned alive. But Noble overlooked evidence that substantiates the Mathers' contentions: a Milton minister who had witnessed Jack's and Maria's execution noted in his diary on Sept. 22, 1681: ". . . two negroes burnt, one of them was first hanged." "Rev. Peter Thacher's Journal" in Albert K. Teele, ed., *The History of Milton, Mass. 1640 to 1887* (Boston, 1887), p. 646. Increase Mather wrote: Maria was "burned to death,—the first that has suffered such a death in New England." Mass. Hist. Soc., *Proceedings*, III (1859), p. 320. Edgar Buckingham's allegation that in 1675 Phillis, a Negro slave, was burned alive in Cambridge, in "Morality, Learning, and Religion, in Massachusetts in Olden Times," *History and Proceedings of the Pocumtuck Valley Memorial Association, 1880–1889* (Deerfield, Mass., 1898), II, p. 20, seems unsupported.

23. *Suffolk Deeds* (Boston, 1880–1906), II, p. 297; III, p. 78; VII, pp. 22, 144; VIII, pp. 298–299; Morison, ed., *Suffolk Court Recs.*, II, p. 598; *Report of the Record Commissioners of the City of Boston Containing Miscellaneous Papers* (Boston, 1876–1909), X, p. 25.

24. Bostian Ken (Kine, Kajne), also known as Sebastian and Bus Bus, probably took his surname from the Keayne family. It was common for a Negro if he had a last name, to use his master's or former master's. *Suffolk Deeds*, II, p. 297; IV, pp. 111, 113.

25. Angola's land fronted on the main road between Boston and Roxbury and at least one man, James Pennyman, envied it. Ibid., VIII, p. 298.

26. Property owning Negroes and master's gifts are ibid., VII, p. 43; X, pp. 278, 295; Dow, ed., *Essex Court Recs.*, II, p. 183; VIII, p. 434; *York Deeds*, IV, fol. 52; Ford, ed., *Diary of Cotton Mather*, I, p. 278; Henry A. Hazen, *History of Billerica, Mass.* (Boston, 1883), pp. 170–71. Charles Taussig noted a Rhode Island Negro couple that had accumulated a 300 pound fortune and in 1735 sailed back to Guinea where they were independently wealthy; see *Rum, Romance and Rebellion* (New York: Minton, Balch & Company, 1928), p. 33.

27. Horizontal mobility and freedom of movement are illustrated by the Maria case, discussed above; Dow, ed., *Essex Court Recs.*, VI, p. 255; VIII, pp. 297–98; *Suffolk Deeds*, IV, p. x–xi; Ford, ed., *Diary of Cotton Mather*, II, p. 139; *Diary of Samuel Sewall*, Mass. Hist. Soc., *Collections*, 5th Ser., VI (1879), p. 5; the travel account of an unknown Frenchman, ca. 1687, in Nathaniel B. Shurtleff, *A Topographical and Historical Description of Boston* (Boston, 1871), p. 48; James R. Trumbull, *History of Northampton* (Northampton, 1898), I, pp. 376–77. Exemplifying freedom from

masters' supervision is the case of a servant who persisted in wooing a young lady although repeatedly warned by *her* master to keep away. Both were later convicted for fornication. Dow, ed., *Essex Court Recs.*, VII, p. 141.

28. Revolts were never a problem in Massachusetts but runaways were frequent. Closest to a slave revolt was an unsuccessful 1690 attempt by a New Jerseyite with abolitionist tendencies to induce Negroes, Indians, and Frenchmen to attack several Bay Colony towns. See Joshua Coffin, *A Sketch of the History of Newbury* . . . (Boston, 1845), pp. 153–54, and Sidney Perley, "Essex County in the Abolition of Slavery," *Essex-County Historical and Genealogical Register*, I (1894), p. 2.

29. On informal relations see Dow, ed., *Essex Court Recs.*, I, p. 287; V, p. 141; VII, pp. 394–95; VIII, p. 297; Morison, ed., *Suffolk Court Recs.*, I, p. 249; II, pp. 648–49; Robert F. Seybolt, *The Town Officials of Colonial Boston, 1634–1775* (Cambridge, Mass.: Harvard University Press, 1939), pp. 77, 79, 83, 85, 87; Joseph Dudley to Gabriel Bernon, May 20, 1707, in George F. Daniels, *History of the Town of Oxford Massachusetts* (Oxford, 1892), pp. 26–27. The quotation is from Smith, ed., *Colonial Justice in Western Massachusetts*, pp. 298–99.

30. Massachusetts never formally denied Negroes the right to bear personal arms and specifically included them in the militia in 1652. But in 1656, without explanation, she reversed her policy, excluding Indians and Negroes from training. Shurtleff, ed., *Mass. Records*, IV, Pt. i, pp. 86, 257.

31. William Fitzhugh, King George County Virginia, to Mr. Jackson of Piscataway, in New England, Feb. 11, 1683, in R. A. Brock, "New England and the Slave Trade," *William and Mary Quarterly*, 1st Ser., 2 (1894): 176–77; Saffin, Usher, Wetcomb, and Belcher to Welstead, June 12, 1681, in *New-England Historical and Genealogical Register* 31 (1877): 75–76.

32. Drake, *History and Antiquities*, p. 525, quotes the General Court, June, 1702; Dudley to Council, Oct. 1, 1708, in Headlam, ed., *California State Papers, Colonial Ser.*, June, 1708–9, p. 110; "Some Considerations Upon the several sorts of Banks Proposed as a Medium of Trade: And Some Improvements that might be made in this Province, hinted at" (Boston, 1716), in Andrew McFarland Davis, ed., *Colonial Currency Reprints, 1682–1751* (Boston: Prince Society, 1910–11), I, pp. 343, 346.

33. Acts regulating alcoholic consumption are in the Records of the Council of Massachusetts under the Administration of President Joseph Dudley, "Dudley Records," Mass. Hist. Soc., *Proceedings*, 2d Ser., XIII (Boston, 1899, 1900), p. 252; Ellis Ames and Abner C. Goodell, eds., *Acts and Resolves of the Province of Massachusetts Bay, 1692–1714* (Boston, 1869–1922), I, p. 154; Moody, ed., *Maine Recs.*, IV, p. 51; Edward W. Baker, "The 'Old Worcester Turnpike,'" *Proceedings of the Brookline Historical Society* (Jan. 23, 1907), p. 29. Laws governing stolen goods are in Ames and Goddell, eds., *Acts and Resolves*, I, pp. 156, 325; see also Greene, *The Negro in Colonial New England*, p. 130. The only other seventeenth-century statute aimed at Negroes was passed in 1680: that no ship of more than 12 tons should entertain any passenger, servant or Negro, without permit from the governor. *The Colonial Laws of Massachusetts. Reprinted from the Edition of 1672, With the Supplements through 1686* (Boston, 1887), p. 281.

34. The laws discussed in these paragraphs are in Ames and Goodell, eds., *Acts and Resolves*, I, pp. 535, 578–79, 606–607; John B. Dillon, ed., *Oddities of Colonial Legislation in America* . . . (Indianapolis, 1879), pp. 206–07, 211–12; *Report of the Record Commissioners of the City of Boston*, VIII, pp. 173–77.

10. EDGAR J. MCMANUS, The Negro Under Slavery (1966)*

In examining the nature of slavery in New York, Edgar J. Mc-
Manus, professor of history at Queens College of the City University of
New York, also discovers significant differences between slavery there
and in the Old South. The most important of these was the high level of
proficiency and skill exhibited by Afro-American slaves in New York.
McManus shows how they adroitly used these skills to win concessions
from their masters, thereby steadily loosening the bonds which tied them
to slavery. McManus sees economic factors as more important than humanitarian considerations in bringing an end to slavery in New York.

"ANOTHER INSTANCE IN WHICH I CONCEIVE I AND MY FELLOW SERVANTS
ARE MORE HARDLY DEALT WITH THAN THE NEGROES, IS THAT THEY UNIVER-
SALLY ALMOST HAVE ONE DAY IN SEVEN WHETHER TO REST OR TO GO TO CHURCH
OR SEE THEIR COUNTRY FOLKS—BUT WE ARE COMMONLY COMPELLED TO WORK
AS HARD EVERY SUNDAY."
                —*Richard Cain to William Kempe, October 23, 1754.*

Slave relations after the English occupation were not as good as under
the Dutch, for the rapid progress of the colony and the growth of the
slave population created regulatory problems which were unknown in
New Netherlands. Nevertheless, relations were generally good by the
standards of the times, and the government took measures to protect the
slaves as well as regulate them. A law enacted in 1686 made the willful killing of a slave a capital offense.[1] And in 1709 Governor Hunter was instructed by England to see to it that private slave discipline was not unduly
severe and that the physical needs of slaves were not neglected by masters.[2]
Owners were forbidden to allow their slaves to beg under penalty of a
fine of £10 for each offense.[3] Moreover, slaves were encouraged to report
abusive treatment to the provincial council.[4] All in all, the English authorities strove to keep the slave system as humane as possible.

The rationale of slavery of course was race, but the test of race really
applied only to the first slaves. With the passage of time and the growth
of a racially mixed population, the simple racial test became obsolete from
a legal standpoint. By the end of the seventeenth century slave status no
longer depended upon Negro blood but upon slave blood on the maternal
side. The offspring of a male slave and a free woman was free, and the offspring of a free man and a slave woman was a slave.[5] Thus slavery was not
confined exclusively to Negroes but included anyone with slave blood on

* Edgar J. McManus, *A History of Negro Slavery in New York*, chapter 4, "The
Negro Under Slavery," pp. 59–78. Copyright © 1966 by Syracuse University Press,
Syracuse, New York. Reprinted by permission of the publisher.

the maternal side. The slightest admixture of slave blood was legally sufficient to subject a person to slavery regardless of complexion or physical
appearance.[6] Persons of predominantly Negro ancestry were often free,
whereas persons visibly white were slaves. By the eighteenth century the
latter had become quite numerous. Advertisements for fugitive slaves
make it clear that some runaways gained freedom simply by passing over
into the white population.[7]

In cases where the status of racially mixed persons was in doubt, the
courts had to decide who were to be treated as Negroes and who were to
be treated as whites. The resolution of this question could be vitally important, for Negroes as a class were presumed to be slaves. A Negro claimed
as a slave had the burden of rebutting the claim, whereas a white had no
burden of proof because the law presumed him to be free. The test was
physical appearance, and persons visibly white or Negro were treated as
such for the purpose of allocating the burden of proof.[8] When Thomas
Thatcher, a resident of New York City, claimed a predominantly white
mulatto as a slave in 1677, the court gave him eight days to prove his claim;
in the meantime the mulatto was presumed to be free.[9] Although the visi-
bility test could and did result in injustice, it was the only practical test
available for a slave system based upon race. Moreover, it was not conclusive as to the ultimate question of status, for in every case the putative
slave had the right of rebuttal.

Although the formal structure of slavery was not unusual, its everyday operation was in some ways unique. For one thing, the efficiency of
the system required a high degree of collaboration between masters and
slaves. Since a large proportion of the bondsmen were highly skilled
workers who could not be managed efficiently through coercion alone,
concessions had to be made in order to obtain their cooperation. Masters
who owned such slaves were usually willing to close their eyes to minor
breaches of discipline and even to pay bribes in the form of clothing,
liquor, and small sums of money in order to obtain loyal service. There
were few concessions within reason that could not be extorted from the
masters. The most highly skilled slaves bargained for manumission and
were even able to prevent unwanted sales by indicating their reluctance
to work for a prospective buyer.[10] The value of skilled slaves of course
depended largely on their willingness to work. Threats which might be
sufficient to compel physical exertion could not on the other hand guarantee the quality of the performance. Such was their bargaining power
that skilled slaves were known to break up auctions merely by announcing
their unwillingness to work for any of the bidders.[11]

The concessions won by the skilled slaves set precedents which affected the entire slave system. Not every slave of course was able to bar-

gain effectively for freedom; only skilled slaves could do so, for without occupational skill a slave had nothing with which to bargain. The privileges enjoyed by the skilled bondsmen nevertheless brought a spirit of give and take to slave relations in general that made the system more humane in everyday operation. Slaves usually received adequate food, clothing, medical care, and time off for rest and relaxation.[12] With one day off in every seven, they often had more leisure time than white indentured servants, who were usually required to work a full seven-day week.[13] Nor is there any evidence that the mortality rate was higher among Negroes than among whites. Indeed, against the most dreaded epidemic disease of colonial times, smallpox, Negroes often fared better than whites.[14]

Perhaps the most unusual privilege enjoyed by the slaves was the privilege of owning private property. Slaves were allowed to accumulate property for their own purposes without fear that it might be taken from them by the masters. Although the privilege had no legal standing, in practice it was universally respected and protected. Evidence of this can be found in the numerous legacies given to slaves in the eighteenth century.[15] These legacies, made by persons with firsthand knowledge of slavery, could easily have been conditioned on the slave's right of enjoyment if there had been the slightest chance that the proceeds might be taken by the masters. The fact that testators did not make use of this obvious protective device is convincing evidence that they did not regard it as necessary. The property privilege was in fact so well established that the slaves themselves often drew up wills leaving their possessions to friends and relatives.[16]

What use they made of property that came their way depended on the character and outlook of the individual slave. Some bondsmen sedulously saved every penny in order to buy their freedom.[17] Others, however, sought immediate satisfactions and wasted whatever came into their possession on frivolous luxuries. A mania for fine clothing, for example, caused many slaves to squander the wages earned during their free time on the latest fashions. Tailors and bootmakers in New York City did a profitable business outfitting slaves with fancy shoes and fine clothing.[18] The desire to own such apparel was responsible for much petty crime, for slaves unable or unwilling to hire their free time often resorted to theft and burglary.[19] The sartorial mania inspired so much petty theft that some masters tried to protect themselves against pilferage by rewarding loyal slaves with special clothing.[20]

The exaggerated importance given to fine clothing was a natural reaction of the slaves to the general deprivations inherent in bondage. Slaves obtained in expensive attire an illusion of importance that their real condition denied them. Classed as property, it was difficult if not impossible for them to grasp normal social values. Marital and family ties, for example, meant little or nothing to most of the slaves. The average slave lived for satisfactions as ephemeral as the fine clothing which he yearned to own. Perhaps the greatest tragedy of slavery was the way it distorted the outlook of the Negro bondsman and imposed on him a mean and frivolous view of himself. In place of the stabilizing ties of family life, slavery conditioned the Negro to values which were petty and inferior by the standards of the whites.[21]

Not that every master was indifferent to the family ties of his slaves, for many of them were obviously troubled by the destructive effect of slavery on the slave family. Some tried to improve conditions by solemnizing slave marriages with civil or religious ceremonies calculated to upgrade the significance of the marital relationship.[22] Curfew regulations were frequently relaxed to permit married slaves to visit their spouses in the evening.[23] Men were often released from their regular duties to spend extra time with their wives and children.[24] It was not unusual, either, for a master to refuse to sell married slaves unless the buyer promised to keep the spouses together.[25]

But for most of the slaves family attachments were casual and impermanent. The slave system was simply not structured to support slave families and no amount of good will could surmount this fact or mitigate its effects. Slave families that were somehow kept together inevitably burdened slaveholders with costly and unmanageable numbers of slave children.[26] Another difficulty was that the typical slave family was divided among several owners. Although one of the owners might be willing, even eager, to protect family ties, he was powerless to do so without cooperation from the others. Since it was economically unfeasible for slaveholders as a class to subordinate their buying and selling to the stability of the slave family, it was inevitable that families should disintegrate.

Even when slave families were not physically disrupted, the absence of normal economic conditions weakened their stability. The men could not support their families, for they spent most of their time at tasks which benefited the masters. Most of them in fact had no desire or motivation to support their wives and children, for they understood this to be the responsibility of the masters. Whatever economic significance the slave family had involved the sort of responsibilities which fell entirely to the women. Men neither were the head of the family, nor did they have anything to do with the raising of children. It was the mother who provided the children with the essentials of life and with a symbol of authority and protection.[27] Indeed, newspaper advertisements of slaves for sale made it clear that women with dependent children were looked upon as complete family units without the father.[28]

Such conditions created a bad climate of sexual morality. Most slaves regarded monogamy as an aberration when they regarded it at all, for spouses who might be separated at any time by sale were not likely to develop deep emotional loyalties to one another.[29] And the example of the whites was certainly not a source of moral edification. Slavery bound whites and Negroes in a relationship debasing to the standards of both races. For one thing, the defenseless condition of the slave woman was a constant invitation to sexual exploitation. How much of this took place cannot be estimated with much precision, for disreputable practices of this sort were carefully kept out of sight. But evidence that such contacts were common can be found in the emergence of a mixed race with various degrees of white and Negro blood. By the middle of the eighteenth century large numbers of mulatttoes could be found in all parts of the province.[30]

How the slaveholders regarded their mixed progeny is also hard to determine, for such relationships were rarely acknowledged openly. There is nevertheless considerable indirect evidence that some among the master class treated their mulatto children with affection and compassion. The best evidence of this can be found in testamentary emancipations which hint at bonds of affection much stronger than usual master-slave relationship. Some of the masters who freed mulatto children by will set up generous trust funds to provide for their education and future well-being.[31] One master in Westchester County instructed his executors "to take charge of my little Negroes and bring them up to a good business." [32] One in New York City left his entire estate to three mulatto children in his household.[33] The generosity and affection evidenced by some of the bequests strongly suggest that the beneficiaries were offspring of the masters.

But the most important point of contact between the races after the English occupation was not blood but religion. Racial intermixture was always tainted with an element of sexual exploitation which disturbed the conscience of the community. This explains in part the reluctance of masters to legitimize offspring for whom they obviously felt deep affection. Religion, on the other hand, carried no illicit taint; rather, it was respectable and, superficially at least, provided a point of contact between the races not blighted by exploitation. It is not surprising therefore that attempts to indoctrinate the slaves in the religious beliefs of the whites not only had wide support but reassured the whites of their own moral superiority. And the colonial authorities were strongly in favor of proselytization, for they equated Christianity with civil stability.[34] As early as 1686 Governor Dongan was instructed by England "to find out the best means to facilitate and encourage the conversion of Negroes." [35] Many slaveholders proselytized their bondsmen, at least to the extent of bringing them to religious services and encouraging them to conform outwardly to Christianity.[36]

The masters, however, were generally unwilling to have their slaves indoctrinated by anyone but themselves. They did not want them to receive catechetical instruction from either clergy or lay preachers, for they were morbidly suspicious of activities affecting their slaves over which they did not have direct personal control.[37] Thus it is not surprising that the main impetus to organized proselytization came not from the slaveholders but from a missionary group in England known as the Society for the Propagation of the Gospel in Foreign Parts. This organization had the support of the highest civil and ecclesiastical officials in England and was probably the most powerful branch of organized philanthropy in the eighteenth century.[38] Founded to save souls, both white and black, the S.P.G. provided much of the drive and most of the money behind the missionary effort in New York.[39]

For its overseas missions the S.P.G. recruited catechists in the communities which they were to serve so that their activities would not arouse suspicion or hostility among the local inhabitants. The S.P.G. was convinced that catechists with personal contacts in the community would be in the best possible position to win the support and cooperation of the slaveholding class. This was the principal reason for the appointment of Elias Neau, a respected merchant and close friend of Governor Hunter, to serve as catechist to the slaves of New York City.[40] The policy of making local appointments whenever possible was followed throughout the province. The S.P.G. enlisted the Anglican pastors of Jamaica, Rye, and New Rochelle, as well as the schoolmasters of Albany, Hempstead, and Staten Island, to give religious instruction to the bondsmen.[41] Everything that could be done was done to make the missionary effort respectable and safe in the eyes of the masters.

The instruction provided by the S.P.G. was not limited to religious indoctrination. Besides catechetical instruction, the teachers employed by the S.P.G. ran day and evening courses for slaves in reading and writing.[42] The classes held by John Beasly, the catechist at Albany, were so popular that Beasly's home was crowded at all hours of the day with Negroes seeking instruction.[43] In 1760 the S.P.G. opened a school at New York City to provide Negro children with a rudimentary education. All the children attending were given instruction in reading, writing, and arithmetic; the girls were given additional lessons in sewing.[44] The costs of instruction and books were covered by the S.P.G., which requested the slaveholders only to provide wood to heat the building during the winter months.[45]

The S.P.G. nevertheless encountered stubborn resistance to its activities in all parts of the province. Most slaveholders were bitterly opposed to the indoctrination of their slaves by professional proselytizers. Many of them warned their slaves that they would be sold outside New York if they had anything to do with the missionaries.[46] They preferred instead to indoctrinate the slaves themselves in a safe version of Christianity with dangerous ideas carefully deleted. Slaveholders were well aware that some of the evangelical sects, particularly the Baptists and Quakers, preached an equalitarian gospel inimical to slaveholding. The hostility of these sects toward slavery compromised even the conservative denominations in the eyes of the slaveholding class. Clergymen and lay catechists who attempted to proselytize slaves invariably aroused suspicion regardless of religious affiliation or standing in the community.[47]

Another reason for resistance to the missionary effort was the fear that formal conversion to Christianity might give the slaves a legal claim to freedom.[48] This fear sprang mainly from the fact that in colonial times civil status was tied closely to religion. The right to vote, to hold public office, and to own real property were all subject to religious tests. Moreover, the legal basis of slavery was somewhat unclear, for even after legalization it rested exclusively on local municipal law. Since the English common law did not recognize chattel bondage, the legal premises of the slave system were in fact extremely shaky.[49] Indeed, on some points the system conflicted directly with the common law. For one thing, the rule that the status of a child followed the status of its mother was borrowed from the civil law, not from the common law, which fixed status by paternal descent.[50] The uncertainty surrounding the legal status of slavery made masters morbidly suspicious of attempts to change the status of the bondsmen in any respect.

Slaveholders were also worried by the judicial decisions in England which equated civil status with religion. In several cases the courts held that no Christian could be kept in slavery regardless of race or prior condition of servitude.[51] Although these decisions were not strictly binding outside of England, they were a source of great anxiety to the master class. This anxiety was especially acute in New York, where the bungling of local officials created the impression that the colonial government favored the English rule. Carelessly drafted statutes and slipshod census taking seemingly equated Christianity with freedom. A statute of 1686, for example, outlawed the enslavement of Christians "except such who shall be judged thereto by authority, or such as willingly have sold or sell themselves." [52] This was meant to apply only to indentured servants, but imprecise draftsmanship gave it a more sweeping meaning. Likewise the census of 1712 identified the free population as the "Christian" population.[53] Obviously not every non-Christian was a slave nor was every Christian free, but the careless overlapping of categories implied a relation between religion and freedom.

With so much to feed their suspicions—the English decisions, ambiguous statutes, and equivocal census returns—it is easy to understand why so many slaveholders were hostile to any attempt to proselytize the slaves. Nothing could dissuade them from believing that the missionary effort was basically inimical to their interests. Even assurances from the Solicitor and Attorney General of England that their legal rights would not be impaired in any way failed to move them, for their anxiety was not confined to legal consequences alone.[54] Many of them were convinced that any change brought about by the proselytizers—and this included the moral improvement of the slaves—would only work to undermine the slave system. One master in New York City pointed out that such improvement might fill the slaves with "dangerous conceits." [55] They might, for instance, be led to question the premises of a system which subjected them to morally inferior masters. Slaveholders did not forget for a moment that Christian slaves had played a leading role in the bloody insurrection of 1730 in Virginia. Many believed that proselytization had been responsible for the Virginia uprising, and even those who did not share this belief did not want to put the theory to a test in New York.[56]

In point of fact, however, the missionary effort was not nearly so dangerous as the slaveholders imagined. Most of the proselytizers employed by the S.P.G. were solid Anglicans with a stolid respect for things as they found them. Although they never apologized for slavery or acted as conscious lackeys of the master class, it is also true that they never questioned the premises of the system. Anglican missionaries were more concerned with liturgy and doctrine than with the secular implications of Christianity. They spent long hours drilling their Negro catechumens in religious orthodoxy. Slaves who underwent indoctrination by the S.P.G. were generally fed a bland diet of homiletics seasoned with occasional exhortations about the hereafter and the need for submission to lawful authority. The only remotely radical idea advanced by the missionaries was the brotherhood of all men under the Fatherhood of God. Certainly, however, none of the proselytizers ever attempted to equate Christianity with freedom or secular equality.[57]

There is no evidence which indicates that religious indoctrination caused discontent among the slaves. Indeed, all the evidence is to the contrary: that slaves who accepted Christianity were more submissive and adapted better to bondage than the non-Christians. The latter were responsible for numerous brawls, disorders, and even more serious threats to the public safety. The uprising of 1712, for instance, was organized and led by superstitious non-Christians who believed that heathen spells could make them invulnerable to the white man's bullets.[58] Christian slaves took no part at all in the conspiracy, a fact most gratifying to the missionaries.[59] One proselytizer seized upon the event to point out that all his converts had perfect records for orderly and sober living after conversion.[60] This does not mean that proselytization necessarily induced submissiveness, for it is possible that only the most docile slaves were attracted to Christianity in the first place. In either case the evidence is convincing that the proselytizers were not a threat to the slave system.

A difficult obstacle encountered by the S.P.G. was the extreme hostility of the dissenting denominations to any agency sponsored by the Church of England. Quakers would not permit their slaves to have any contact with S.P.G. proselytizers, and the Presbyterians, though they permitted instruction, would not allow their slaves to be baptized.[61] Anti-Anglican sentiment made it difficult for the S.P.G. to obtain financial support where it was most needed—at the local level.[62] Some proselytizers found that the hostility of the dissenters brought Anglicanism into disrepute among the slaves to such an extent that in some communities the missionary effort was foredoomed to failure.[63]

Another obstacle was the difficulty of reaching widely scattered slaves living on farms in the rural areas. One proselytizer found the slave population of Hempstead so widely dispersed that it was virtually impossible to bring more than a few Negroes together at the same time for instruction.[64] The same problem existed in Westchester and other country districts.[65] The Reverend Thomas Poyer reported to the S.P.G. that he could not even estimate the number of slaves living in his Jamaica parish.[66] Another proselytizer reported in 1729 that there were about one thousand slaves in Albany County with whom it was impossible to establish contact.[67] There can be no doubt that the difficulty of reaching slaves in the outlying areas seriously hampered the missionary effort.

What the slaves in turn thought of Christianity cannot be known directly, for they left no diaries or written records. Their attitude nevertheless can be inferred from their response to the missionaries, which by and large was negative. This apathy, rather than the opposition of the masters, was the main obstacle to the missionary effort. Even when the proselytizers somehow managed to win the confidence of individual slaveholders, they could not long hold the interest of the slaves.[68] A missionary working in Albany County ruefully informed the S.P.G. that the slaves there displayed no interest at all in the Christian religion.[69] Only one slave in every ten in New York City was a Christian after a decade of the most intense missionary activity.[70] Results were just as bad in other parts of the province. Only fifty-three slaves were baptized in Huntington over a period of fifty-six years, a conversion rate of somewhat less than one slave per year—clear proof that the slaves were not won over in significant numbers.[71] In the township of Rye only one slave in every hundred was a Christian after ten years of proselytization.[72] From a statistical standpoint at least, such results must spell failure for the missionary effort.

One of the reasons the slaves did not respond more favorably to proselytization was their dissatisfaction with the secular aspects of Christianity. Not only did conversion fail to improve their everyday lives, but it subjected them to a moral discipline utterly incompatible with slavery. Some proselytizers admitted as much in their reports to the S.P.G. One catechist decried the hypocrisy of expecting the slaves to practice monogamy when their marital ties might be broken at any moment by the vagaries of slavery.[73] Christian mores were too remote from real life for the slave to take them seriously. The New York bondsman was much more sophisticated in this regard than his counterpart in the southern colonies. His contempt for hypocrisy caused him to reject religious formulas which could not be put into actual practice. One proselytizer mistakenly complained to the S.P.G. that the slaves "lacked the facility of understanding." [74] The truth is they understood only too well the impossibility of reconciling preachment with reality.

The missionary effort, however, did have the positive effect of focusing attention on the slave's spiritual and moral equality with the whites. Although most of the proselytizers carefully skirted the social implications of Christianity, some of them were more daring, at least to the extent of warning masters that they had a religious duty to treat their slaves as fellow human beings.[75] In all meetings sponsored by the S.P.G., whites and Negroes came together on terms of complete equality. The proselytizers and schoolmasters employed by the Society held fully integrated meetings in all parts of the province.[76] Moreover, whatever the arrangements, Negroes were admitted to white churches everywhere.[77] Organized religion was in fact the only institution which even pretended to treat free whites and Negro slaves as equals. Although most of the proselytizers were conservative clerics, they made no attempt to justify slavery by giving it religious sanction. They treated it in the only way that was possible in a slaveholding society: they ignored it and left it to the masters to rationalize as best they could.

Taken together, the missionary effort caused slavery much indirect harm. By asserting the spiritual equality of the slaves with the masters, the proselytizers struck a hard blow at the principal ideological basis of the system—the idea that it was justified by an inferiority of race. The proselytizers failed in their attempts to extend Christianity, for they won relatively few converts among the slaves. But they made a deep impression on the white population by insisting that the ultimate worth of a man had nothing to do with race or status. The open hostility of slaveowners to the missionary effort was motivated in part by an awareness that it was basically incompatible with slavery. Although the proselytizers never attacked the institution directly, they boldly asserted the slave's spiritual equality with the rest of the population.[78] This assertion was ultimately of far greater importance than the failure of the proselytizers to win converts. It was, as many of the slaveholders had feared, an opening to freedom.

NOTES

1. E. B. O'Callaghan and Berthold Fernow, eds., *Documents Relative to the Colonial History of the State of New York*, 15 vols. (Albany: Weed, Parsons & Co., 1856–57), I, p. 374.

2. Ibid., V, p. 138.

3. Alexander C. Flick, ed., *History of the State of New York*, 10 vols. (New York: Columbia University Press, 1933–1937), II, p. 300.

4. E. B. O'Callaghan, ed., *Calendar of Historical Manuscripts* 2 (1866): 371.

5. Thomas R. R. Cobb, *An Inquiry into the Law of Slavery in the United States of America* (1858), p. 67.

6. A statute of 1706 provided that "all and every Negro, Mulatto, and mestee bastard child and children, who is, are, and shall be born of any Negro, Indian, or mestee, shall follow the state and condition of the mother." *Colonial Laws of New York from 1664 to the Revolution* (1894) I, pp. 597–98.

7. *New York Weekly Post-Boy*, August 27, 1759; June 18, 1768; March 18, 1771; *New York Mercury*, July 17, 1758; June 15, 1761; May 10, August 30, 1762; October 10, 1763; November 19, 1764; July 20, 1772; October 12, 1776.

8. Cobb, *Inquiry*, p. 67.

9. O'Callaghan, *Calendar*, II, p. 56.

10. Register of Manumissions, pp. 65–66, 73, MS collection Museum of the City of New York; *Letter Book of John Watts* in New York Historical Society, *Collections* 61 (1928): 151; Huntington Town Records, III, p. 142; *New York Weekly Post-Boy*, March 23, 1746/47; March 30, 1747; August 30, 1756; January 8, 1758; September 1, 1763; *New York Mercury*, September 5, 1763; May 27, 1765; February 26, June 1, 1772; January 18, April 26, 1773; March 4, November 10, 1777.

11. Schermerhorn to Clinton, January 13, 1788, in Beekman Papers, Box 32, MS collection of New York Historical Society.

12. Philip Evertse Wendell's Day Book (1754–60), p. 30, MS collection of the New York Historical Society; *Papers of the Lloyd Family of the Manor of Queens Village*, in 2 vols., in New York Historical Society, *Collections*, 59–60 (1926–27), I, pp. 341, 309–10; II, p. 719.

13. Richard Cain to William Kempe, October 23, 1754, in John Tabor Kempe Papers, Box 4, Folio A-C, MS collection of New York Historical Society. See Richard B. Morris, *Government and Labor in Early America* (New York: Columbia University Press, 1946), pp. 478–79.

14. During the New York City epidemic of 1730, only 71 of the 509 persons who died were Negroes. Although Negroes constituted at least 20 percent of the

population, their mortality rate was only 12 percent. John Duffy, *Epidemics in Colonial America* (Baton Rouge: Louisiana State University Press, 1953), pp. 78–80.

15. *Abstracts of Wills*, VII, pp. 129, 380–81, 407; IX, p. 72; XII, pp. 155–57; XIV, pp. 1–3; XV, pp. 112–13, 127–28.

16. Register of Manumissions, p. 87.

17. *Jamaica Town Records* (New York: Long Island Historical Society, 1914), III, pp. 346–47, 349–55; *Abstracts of Wills*, XV, pp. 114–16.

18. Charles Nicoll's Account Book (1753–58), January 27, October 24, 1756; October 2, 1760; March 21, 1761; Ledger (1759–65), pp. 4, 9, 11, 13–16, 33.

19. Joel Munsell, ed., *Collections on the History of Albany* (Albany: Joel Munsell, 1865), II, pp. 382–83; *New York Weekly Post-Boy*, April 15, 1762.

20. Hendrick Denker's Account Book (1747–58), *passim*, MS. collection New York Historical Society; Charles Nicoll's Ledger (1759–65), p. 11; *Lloyd Papers*, II, p. 725.

21. This frivolous attitude toward life in general and toward themselves in particular tends to support Stanley M. Elkins' thesis that slavery "infantilized" the values of many bondsmen. Elkins, *Slavery* (New York: Grosset & Dunlap, 1963), pp. 103–5.

22. Anne Grant, *Memoirs of an American Lady*, 2 vols. (New York: Dodd, Mead & Co., 1901), I, pp. 265-267.

23. William S. Pelletreau, ed., *Records of the Town of Smithtown* (Huntington, N.Y.: Long Islander Print, 1898), p. 170.

24. David Humphreys, *An Account of the Endeavours Used by the Society for the Propagation of the Gospel in Foreign Parts to Instruct the Negro Slaves in New York* (London, 1730), p. 7.

25. *New York Weekly Post-Boy*, March 23, 1746/47; March 21, November 28, 1765; *New York Mercury*, March 5, November 19, 1770; February 8, 1779; *Abstracts of Wills*, V, pp. 99–100; VI, pp. 97–98; XII, pp. 374–75.

26. *New York Weekly Post-Boy*, April 9, 1750; *Abstracts of Wills*, VI, pp. 459–62; Frederic Shonnard and W. W. Spooner, *History of Westchester County* (New York: The New York History Co., 1900), p. 153.

27. This was typical of Negro family life everywhere under the American slave system. See Kenneth Stampp, *The Peculiar Institution* (New York: Alfred A. Knopf, 1956), pp. 343–44.

28. *New York Weekly Post-Boy*, (1743–1773); *New York Mercury* (1752–83).

29. *Revolutionary and Miscellaneous Papers*, in New York Historical Society, *Collections* XI-XIII (1878–80), III, p. 355. Hereinafter cited as *Rev. and Misc. Papers*.

30. Grant, *Memoirs*, I, pp. 85–87.

31. *Abstracts of Wills*, V, pp. 61–62, 113–14, 165–66; VI, pp. 165–66, 275, 417; VII, pp. 34–36, 147–48, 266, 346–47; VIII, pp. 32, 243–45; IX, pp. 84, 118–19; X, pp. 92–93; XI, pp. 86–87; XII, pp. 147–48, 191–93, 241–42; XIII, pp. 304-6, 357–59; XIV, pp. 102–3, 136–38, 202–7, 210–11, 236, 316–17; XV, pp. 15, 32–35, 53–56, 96–97, 109–12, 128–30, 143–45, 220–23, 231–34.

32. Ibid., VII, pp. 178–89.

33. Ibid., XV, pp. 53–56.

34. Edward T. Corwin, ed., *Ecclesiastical Records of the State of New York*, 7 vols. (Albany: James B. Lyon Co., 1901–16) II, pp. 916, 954, 1034; W. Noel Sainsbury et al., eds., *Calendar of State Papers: Colonial Series, America and West Indies*, 42 vols. (London: H. M. S. O., 1860–1953), 17 (1699): 176.

35. *New York Colonial Documents*, III, p. 374.

36. *New York Ecclesiastical Records*, I, p. 489.

37. Humphreys, *Account*, pp. 9–10. See also Morgan Dix, *A History of the Parish of Trinity Church*, 5 vols. (New York: vols. I–IV, The Knickerbocker Press; vol. V, Columbia University Press, 1898–1950), I, pp. 349–50.

38. Humphreys, *Account*, p. 3.

39. *Rev. and Misc. Papers*, III, p. 357. See Humphreys, *Account*, p. 18.

40. *Rev. and Misc. Papers*, III, p. 349. See Dix, *History of Trinity Church*, I, p. 162.

41. Francis L. Hawks' Records of the General Convention of the Protestant Episcopal Church of New York, I, pp. 635–37, MS collection New York Historical Society; Ernest Hawkins, *Historical Notices of the Missions of the Church of England in the North American Colonies; Previous to the Independence of the United States: Chiefly from the MS Documents of the Society for the Propagation of the Gospel in Foreign Parts* (London: B. Fellowes, 1845), p. 273; Joseph Hooper, *A History of St. Peter's Church in the City of Albany* (Albany, N. Y.: Fort Orange Press, 1900), pp. 70–72. See C. E. Pierre, "The Work of the Society for the Propagation of the Gospel in Foreign Parts among the Negroes of the Colonies," *Journal of Negro History* 1 (1916): 358–59.

42. Hawks' Records, II, pp. 9–10. See Hawkins, *Historical Notices of the Church of England*, p. 273.

43. Hooper, *History of St. Peter's Church*, pp. 70–72.

44. Dix, *History of Trinity Church*, I, pp. 294–95.

45. *New York Mercury*, September 15, 1760.

46. Hawkins, *Historical Notices of the Church of England*, p. 271.

47. Ibid., pp. 50, 73.

48. *Calendar of State Papers: Colonial Series* 17 (1699): 176.

49. William Goodell, *The American Slave Code* (New York: The American and Foreign Anti-Slavery Society, 1853), pp. 260–61; John Codman Hurd, *The Law of Freedom and Bondage in the United States*, 2 vols. (Boston: Little Brown & Company, 1858–62), I, p. 278.

50. *Colonial Laws of New York*, I, pp. 597–98. See George M. Stroud, *A Sketch of the Laws in Relation to Slavery in the United States of America* (Philadelphia: Kimber & Sharpless, 1827), pp. 2–3, 10–11.

51. The English rule was that Negroes could be held as slaves "until they become Christians and thereby they are enfranchised." See *Butts v. Penny*, 3 Kemble's Reports 785, 1 Lord Raymond's Reports 147.

52. *Colonial Laws of New York*, I, p. 18.

53. *New York Colonial Documents*, V, pp. 339–40.

54. Cobb, *Inquiry*, pp. 153, 162. See *New York Packet*, April 25, 1788.

55. Hawks' Records, I, p. 639. See Dix, *History of Trinity Church*, I, pp. 185–86.

56. Hawks' Records, II, pp. 33–34.

57. Hawks' Records, I, pp. 133–35; Humphreys, *Account*, p. 5; *New York Ecclesiastical Records*, III, pp. 1559, 1609, 1613–14; Dix, *History of Trinity Church*, I, p. 162; Hawkins, *Historical Notices of the Church of England*, p. 272; *Rev. and Misc. Papers*, III, p. 348; William Berrian, *An Historical Sketch of Trinity Church* (New York: Stanford & Swords, 1847), pp. 35, 58–60.

58. Infra, pp. 122–23.

59. *Rev. and Misc. Papers*, III, p. 353.

60. Berrian, *Historical Sketch of Trinity Church*, pp. 59–60.

61. Charles W. Baird, *History of Rye* (1871), p. 185.'

62. Humphreys, *Account*, p. 18.

63. Hawks' Records, I, pp. 218–19.

64. Ibid., II, pp. 6–7, 9.

65. Ibid., I, pp. 693–94; II, pp. 33–34.

66. Ibid., I, p. 634.

67. Ibid., II, pp. 19–20.

68. Humphreys, *Account*, p. 7.

69. Hawks' Records, II, pp. 19–20.

70. *Rev. and Misc. Papers*, III, p. 356.

71. Ebenezer Prime, ed., *Records of the First Church of Huntington, Long Island, 1723–1779* (Huntington, N. Y.: Moses L. Scudder, 1899).

72. *New York Ecclesiastical Records*, III, p. 1695.

73. *Rev. and Misc. Papers*, III, pp. 350, 355.

74. Hawks' Records, I, p. 229; II, pp. 33–34; *Rev. and Misc. Papers*, III, p. 355.

75. Humphreys, *Account*, pp. 28–30.

76. *New York Ecclesiastical Records*, IV, p. 2357. See William T. Davis, C. Leng, and R. W. Vosburgh, *The Church of St. Andrew, Richmond, Staten Island* (New York: Staten Island Historical Society, 1925), pp. 29, 124.

77. *New York Ecclesiastical Records*, III, pp. 1613–14; Prime, ed., *Records of the First Church of Huntington*, passim. See Berrian, *Historical Sketch of Trinity Church*, pp. 117–18.

78. Humphreys, *Account*, pp. 28–30.

IV

Slavery in the Americas: A Comparison

Until recently, the institution of slavery was viewed almost exclusively in national settings. American historians rarely gave any consideration to systems other than that of the Old South. Typical of this approach was the first scholarly and comprehensive study done by Ulrich B. Phillips who in 1918 published his *American Negro Slavery*, followed several years later by *Life and Labor in the Old South*. These studies gained wide acceptance both because they appeared to be models of impeccable scholarship and because the author's own racial attitudes were compatible with those held by most white Americans. A Georgian by birth and rearing, Phillips absorbed the prevailing racial views of his native South. At Columbia University, where he received his graduate training, Phillips was taught the nineteenth-century pseudoscientific theories of race which further confirmed his belief in Anglo-Saxon superiority. Despite this obvious racial bias, Phillips was so competent as a historian that these studies are still extremely valuable, and no student should fail to consult them.

To Phillips, slavery was not only the proper solution to southern economic problems, but it also provided the South with a well-balanced social structure perfectly suited to the needs of "inert and backward" Negroes. While providing black people with the rudiments of civilization, slavery also so ordered southern life that it produced an unusual degree of harmony between a naturally inferior race of black people and a specially endowed race of white people. Under this arrangement, both races benefitted and the South achieved a level of grandeur which otherwise would have been unobtainable.

Utilizing almost the same sources but interpreting them from a liberal northern perspective rather than a conservative southern one, Kenneth Stampp, professor of history at the University of California at Berkeley, arrived at entirely different conclusions. Far from creating a harmonious, progressive society, slavery spawned a dissatisfied population of blacks who were always ready to defy the system by any means feasible, and a fearful, unproductive, and narrow-minded group of whites whose way of life was dependent upon perpetuating an anachronistic slave society. As a result, violent revolution was necessary to rid the nation of this intolerable moral evil.

Even before Stampp penned his revisionist study of the "peculiar institution," Frank Tannenbaum, a Latin-American specialist at Columbia University, attempted to place southern slavery in the context of other slave systems in the western hemisphere. Tannenbaum believed that the existence of better race relations in Latin America during the twentieth century, which he took for granted, could be explained by a thorough analysis of the historical variations in slave systems. To Tannenbaum, the fact that the slave was viewed as a legal person and guaranteed protection by Spanish-American law but not by Anglo-American law accounted largely for whatever differences in race relations existed during the mid-twentieth century. This comparative approach failed to attract much attention, however, until Stanley Elkins' *Slavery* appeared in 1959. In this study, Elkins not only accepted the tentative conclusions of Tannenbaum that North American slavery was the most brutal and the least "open" slave system in the Western Hemisphere, but he also enlarged upon this interpretation by analyzing the psychological shock which the slave system of the Old South had upon the southern slave.

In contrast to Tannenbaum's historical and legal essay, Elkins' more polemic study aroused instant controversy and rebuttal. If nothing else, Elkins redirected the attention of historians away from the moralistic debate between Phillips and Stampp to the more fruitful field of comparative analysis. While the influence of Elkins was especially significant upon popular writers, most scholars believed that he had either exaggerated the differences between slave systems or relied too heavily upon questionable studies to prove his thesis.

One of the most provocative critics of the Tannenbaum-Elkins interpretation has been David Brion Davis, a professor of history at Yale University. In his Pulitzer prize winning study, *The Problem of Slavery in Western Culture*, Davis questioned two assumptions accepted by this school of historians. He doubted if black slavery in the British colonies and in the southern United States was as uniformly severe as they had suggested or if the Spanish and Portuguese were that much more liberal in their treatment of slaves, not only in terms of providing for their physical well-being but also in terms of promoting manumission and freedom. Instead, Davis emphasized the great variations within slave systems of the New World rather than the differences in severity between North and South American slavery. For instance, Brazil by itself contained an area and variety comparable to all British North America. Among the privileged classes of artisans and domestic servants in colonial Brazilian cities were slaves whose conditions compared favorably with black slaves in colonial Philadelphia and New England. In contrast, the lot of slaves on the coffee plantations of southern Brazil was no better than that of slaves who labored in the cotton fields of ante-bellum Mississippi. Davis concluded that "the subject is too complex and the evidence too contradictory for us to assume that the treatment of slaves was substantially better in Latin America than in the British colonies, taken as a whole." *

* David Brion Davis, *The Problem of Slavery in Western Culture* (Ithaca, New York: Cornell University Press, 1966), p. 243.

The two selections included in this volume illustrate the poles of this historical controversy. The first is from Professor Frank Tannenbaum's seminal study, *Slave and Citizen*, where he summarizes the basic differences between Latin American and North American slavery and suggests some reasons for their development. In the second selection, Professor Carl Degler of Stanford University agrees with Tannenbaum that there were significant differences between the slave systems of Brazil and the United States. To Degler, however, these differences cannot be attributed to the influence of the Catholic Church or to the tradition of Roman law in Brazil as Tannenbaum contended. Instead these differences arise from Brazil's greater dependency upon the African slave trade for new laborers and the preponderance of male over female slaves in Brazil. Consequently Brazilian masters did not believe, as did the planter in the southern United States, that it was cheaper to raise their own slaves than purchase them from abroad. As a result Degler suggests that slavery in North America may have been more lenient than it was in Brazil.

11. FRANK TANNENBAUM, Slave and Citizen (1947)*

This selection, taken from Tannenbaum's classic, *Slave and Citizen*, contains the heart of his thesis that slavery in Latin America was more open than it was in the United States. Although highly regarded by Latin American specialists, Tannenbaum's seminal study in comparative history was practically ignored by United States historians until the appearance of Stanley Elkins' *Slavery*. Tannenbaum insists that Spanish and Portuguese laws and the Roman Catholic Church provided for the black slave in Latin America protection of the person and a recognition of humanity which was lacking in the slave codes of the Old South and in the activity of Protestant churches in North America.

But this adventure of the Negro in the New World has been structured differently in the United States than in the other parts of this hemisphere. In spite of his adaptability, his willingness, and his competence, in spite of his complete identification with the *mores* of the United States, he is excluded and denied. A barrier has been drawn against the Negro. This barrier has never been completely effective, but it has served to deny to him the very things that are of greatest value among us—equality of opportunity for growth and development as a man among men. The shadow of slavery is still cast ahead of us, and we behave toward the Negro as if the imputation of slavery had something of a slave by nature in it. The Emancipation may have legally freed the Negro, but it failed morally to free

* Frank Tannenbaum, *Slave and Citizen* (New York: Random House, Inc., 1946), pp. 42–82. Reprinted by permission.

the white man, and by that failure it denied to the Negro the moral status requisite for effective legal freedom.

But this did not occur in the other parts of this world we call new and free. It did not occur because the very nature of the institution of slavery was developed in a different moral and legal setting, and in turn shaped the political and ethical biases that have manifestly separated the United States from the other parts of the New World in this respect. The separation is a moral one. We have denied ourselves the acceptance of the Negro as a man because we have denied him the moral competence to become one, and in that have challenged the religious, political, and scientific bases upon which our civilization and our scheme of values rest. This separation has a historical basis, and in turn it has molded the varied historical outcome.

The Negro slave arriving in the Iberian Peninsula in the middle of the fifteenth century found a propitious environment.[1] The setting, legal as well as moral, that made this easy transition possible was due to the fact that the people of the Iberian Peninsula were not strangers to slavery. The institution of slavery, which had long since died out in the rest of Western Europe, had here survived for a number of reasons, especially because of the continuing wars with the Moors, which lasted until the very year of the discovery of America. At the end of the fifteenth century there were numerous slaves in Portugal and Spain, and especially in Andalusia, among them not only Negroes, but Moors, Jews, and apparently Spaniards as well.[2] For we have records of white slaves sent to America by special permission of the crown. We know that Rodrigo Contreras, the Governor of Nicaragua, was allowed by special *cedula*, of July 15, 1534, to import two white slaves; Fernando Pizarro in 1535 was permitted four white slaves; and there were a number of similar records.[3] There were large numbers of Negro slaves in both Portugal and Spain. By the middle of the sixteenth century Algarves was almost entirely populated by Negroes, and they outnumbered the whites in Lisbon.[4] In Spain, in 1474, Ferdinand and Isabella empowered the Negro Juan de Valladolid, known as the "Negro Count," as the "mayoral of the Negroes," to settle their quarrels and to enforce the King's justice among them.[5] But long after this date there were still Moorish and Jewish slaves in Spain. In 1500–01, Jewish slaves held by Spaniards were required to be baptized or to be sent out of the country within two months. Slaves were to be freed by baptism if their masters were Moors or Jews.[6] As late as 1616 the law speaks of baptized Moorish slaves.[7]

But the mere survival of slavery in itself is perhaps less important than the persistence of a long tradition of slave law that had come down through the Justinian Code. The great codification of Spanish traditional law, which in itself summarizes the Mediterranean legal *mores* of many centuries, was elaborated by Alfonso the Wise between the years 1263 and 1265. In this code there is inherent belief in the equality of men under the law of nature, and slavery therefore is something against both nature and reason.[8] But the doctrine of the equality of human nature had long before been asserted by Cicero. According to him, there is "no resemblance in nature so great as that between man and man, there is no equality so complete." [9] Reason is common to all men, and all are equal in their capacity for learning. Under guidance, every race of men is capable of attaining virtue. This doctrine of the equality of man is applied to the idea of slavery by Seneca with great vigor. Virtue is immune to misfortune. "A slave can be just, brave, magnanimous." Slavery is the result of misfortune, and hateful to all men. But, after all, slavery affects only the body, which may belong to the master; the mind "cannot be given into slavery." [10] The soul of the slave remains free.

The slave is a man and suffers from the same pains, and delights in the same joys, that all men do. The slave, as a human being, is derived from the same source, and will finally come to the same end, as other men. The distinction between slavery and freedom is a product of accident and misfortune, and the free man might have been a slave. These theories of the equality of man were in the background when the New Testament and the Christian fathers came upon the scene and proclaimed that all men are equal in the sight of God. The conception of the identity of human nature over all the world is like that in Cicero and Seneca.[11] And when St. Paul touches upon the subject of slavery, it is to the effect that in the sight of God "there is neither bond nor free." [12] That is, in their brotherhood as children of one God, the bondsman and the master are equal in his sight. This does not involve a repudiation of slavery, but rather an assertion that spiritually they are equal. And when St. Paul sends Onesimus, apparently an escaped slave, back to his master, it is with the admonition that he should be received as "a brother beloved." [13] There is no suggestion of freedom for the returning slave, but rather that he should be received "as myself." [14] Slavery is not formally opposed: "Let every man abide in the same calling wherein he was called"; [15] but there is also a favoring of freedom: "Art thou called being a bond servant? Care not for it; but if thou mayest be made free, use it rather." [16]

St. Paul further develops the theme of the equality of master and slave: "Servants, be obedient to them that are your masters according to the flesh with fear and trembling, in singleness of your heart, as unto Christ. . . . And, ye masters, do the same things unto them, forbearing threatening, knowing that your Master also is in heaven; neither is there respect of persons with him." [17] There is perhaps no great distinction to be drawn between St. Paul's attitude toward the equality of man and that of Cicero and Seneca, but clearly the doctrine that slavery merely affects the outer man and that spiritually master and slave are equal is here reaffirmed, and was to "dominate the thought and practical tendencies of the church." [18] These underlying doctrines become part of the theory of the later church fathers, and take the form of saying that God made not slaves and free men, but all men free.

This belief that equality among men is natural and reasonable is, therefore, both pagan and Christian, and stems from the Stoics and from the Christian fathers. The conception that man is free and equal, especially equal in the sight of God, made slavery as such a mundane and somewhat immaterial matter. The master had, in fact, no greater moral status than the slave, and spiritually the slave might be a better man than his master. *Las Siete Partidas* was framed within this Christian doctrine, and the slave had a body of law, protective of him as a human being, which was already there when the Negro arrived and had been elaborated long before he came upon the scene. And when he did come, the Spaniard may not have known him as a Negro, but the Spanish law and *mores* knew him as a slave and made him the beneficiary of the ancient legal heritage. This law provided, among other matters, for the following:

The slave might marry a free person if the slave status was known to the other party. Slaves could marry against the will of their master if they continued serving him as before. Once married, they could not be sold apart, except under conditions permitting them to live as man and wife. If the slave married a free person with the knowledge of his master, and the master did not announce the fact of the existing slave status, then the slave by that mere fact became free.[19] If married slaves owned by separate masters could not live together because of distance, the church should persuade one or the other to sell his slave. If neither of the masters could be persuaded, the church was to buy one of them so that the married slaves could live together.[20] The children followed the status of their mother, and the child of a free mother remained free even if she later became a slave.[21] In spite of his full powers over his slave, the master might neither kill nor injure him unless authorized by the judge, nor abuse him against reason or nature, nor starve him to death. But if the master did any of these things, the slave could complain to the judge, and if the complaint were verified, the judge must sell him, giving the price to the owner, and the slave might never be returned to the original master.[22] Any Jewish or Moorish slave became free upon turning Christian, and even if the master himself later became a Christian, he recovered no rights over his former slave.[23]

Las Siete Partidas goes into considerable detail in defining the conditions under which manumission could occur. A master might manumit his slave in the church or outside of it, before a judge or other person, by testament or by letter; but he must do this by himself, in person.[24] If one of the owners of a slave wished to free him, then the other must accept a just price fixed by the local judge.[25] A slave became free against his master's will by denouncing a forced rape against a virgin, by denouncing a maker of false money, by discovering disloyalty against the King, by denouncing the murderer of his master.[26] The slave could become free if he became a cleric with the consent of his master, or in certain cases without his consent, providing another slave in his place. And if the former slave became a bishop, he had to put up two slaves, each valued at the price that he himself was worth, while still a slave.[27] A Christian slave living among the Moors might return to live among the Christians as a free man.[28]

The slave could appeal to the courts (1) if he had been freed by will and testament, and the document maliciously hidden; under these circumstances he could appeal against anyone holding him; (2) if the slave had money from another and entrusted it to someone for the purpose of being bought from his master and given his liberty, and if then this person refused to carry out the trust, by refusing either to buy him or to free him if he had bought him; and (3) if he had been bought with the understanding that he would be freed on the receipt of the purchase price from the slave, and refused either to accept the money or to release him after accepting it.[29] He could appeal to the courts for defense of the property of his master in his master's absence, and the King's slaves could appeal to the courts in defense of the King's property, or of their own persons—a special privilege permitted the King's slaves in honor of their master.[30] A man considering himself free, but demanded for a slave, might have a representative to defend him; a man held a slave, but claiming to be free, might argue his own case, but not have a representative, and he must be permitted to argue and reason his case; the slave's relatives might plead for him, and even a stranger could do so, for "all the laws of the world aid toward freedom." [31] Slaves could be witnesses, even against their masters, in accusations for treason against the King; in cases of murder of either master or mistress by either spouse; or in cases against the mistress for adultery; when one of the two owners of a slave was accused of killing the other; or in case of suspicion that the prospective heirs have killed the master of another slave.[32] A slave who became the heir of his master, in part or in totality, automatically became free.[33] If a father appointed a slave as the guardian of his children, the slave by that fact became free; [34] and if he was the slave of more than one person and became an heir of one of his masters, the other must accept a price in reason for that part of the slave which belonged to him.[35] He who killed his slave intentionally must suffer the penalty for homicide, and if the slave died as a result of punishment without intention to kill, then the master must suffer five years' exile.[36]

Spanish law, custom, and tradition were transferred to America and came to govern the position of the Negro slave. It is interesting to note that a large body of new law was developed for the treatment of the Indians in America, whereas the Negro's position was covered by isolated *cedulas* dealing with special problems. It was not until 1789 that a formal code dealing with the Negro slave was promulgated.[37] But this new code, as recognized by the preamble itself, is merely a summary of the ancient and traditional law. Saco [38] says of it that it merely repeats in amplified form "our ancient laws," and the practice recommended is "very usual in our dominions of the Indies."

This body of law, containing the legal tradition of the Spanish people and also influenced by the Catholic doctrine of the equality of all men in the sight of God, was biased in favor of freedom and opened the gates to manumission when slavery was transferred to the New World. The law in Spanish and Portuguese America facilitated manumission, the tax-gatherer did not oppose it,[39] and the church ranked it among the works singularly agreeable to God. A hundred social devices narrowed the gap between bondage and liberty, encouraged the master to release his slave, and the bondsman to achieve freedom on his own account. From the sixteenth to the nineteenth century, slaves in Brazil, by reimbursing the original purchase price, could compel their masters to free them.[40] In Cuba and in Mexico the price might be fixed at the request of the Negro, and the slave was freed even if he cost "triple of the sum." [41] The right to have his price declared aided the Negro in seeking a new master, and the owner was required to transfer him to another.[42]

The law further permitted the slave to free himself by installments, and this became a widely spread custom, especially in Cuba.[43] A slave worth six hundred dollars could buy himself out in twenty-four installments of twenty-five dollars each, and with every payment he acquired one twenty-fourth of his own freedom. Thus, when he had paid fifty dollars, he owned one twelfth of himself.[44] On delivering his first installment, he could move from his master's house,[45] and thereafter pay interest on the remaining sum, thus acquiring a position not materially different in effect from that of a man in debt who had specific monetary obligations. There seem to have been many instances of slaves paying out all of the installments due on their purchase price except the last fifty or one hundred dollars, and on these paying one half a real per day for every fifty pesos. The advantage in this arrangement apparently lay in the fact that a Negro, thus partially a slave, could escape the payment of taxes on his property and be free from military service.[46]

In effect, slavery under both law and custom had, for all practical purposes, become a contractual arrangement between the master and his bondsman. There may have been no written contract between the two parties, but the state behaved, in effect, as if such a contract did exist, and used its power to enforce it. This presumed contract was of a strictly limited liability on the part of the slave, and the state, by employing the officially provided protector of slaves, could and did define the financial obligation of the slave to his master in each specific instance as it arose. Slavery had thus from a very early date, at least in so far as the practice was concerned, moved from a "status," or "caste," "by law of nature," or because of "innate inferiority," or because of the "just judgment and provision of holy script," to become a mere matter of an available sum of money for redemption. Slavery had become a matter of financial competence on the part of the slave, and by that fact lost a great part of the degrading imputation that attached to slavery where it was looked upon as evidence of moral or biological inferiority. Slavery could be wiped out by a fixed purchase price, and therefore the taint of slavery proved neither very deep nor indelible.

In addition to making freedom something obtainable for money, which the slave had the right to acquire and possess, the state made manumission possible for a number of other reasons. A Negro could be freed if unduly punished by his master.[47] He was at liberty to marry a free non-slave (and the master could not legally interfere), and as under the law the children followed the mother, a slave's children born of a free mother were also free.[48] Slaves in Brazil who joined the army to fight in the Paraguayan war were freed by decree on November 6, 1866, and some twenty thousand Negroes were thus liberated.[49]

In the wars of independence many thousands of slaves in Venezuela and Colombia were freed by Bolívar and enlisted in the army of liberation. In Argentina perhaps as many as a third of San Martín's host that crossed the Andes was composed of freed Negroes. And, finally, as early as 1733, by a special *cedula* repeated twice later, slaves escaping to Cuba from other West Indian islands because they wished to embrace the Catholic religion could be neither returned to their masters, nor sold, nor given in slavery to any other person.[50]

But significant and varied as were these provisions of the law in the Spanish and Portuguese colonies, they were less important in the long run than the social arrangements and expectancies that prevailed. It was permissible for a slave child in Brazil to be freed at the baptismal font by an offer of twenty milreis,[51] and in Cuba for twenty-five dollars.[52] A female slave could seek a godfather for her baby in some respectable person, hoping that the moral obligation imposed upon the godfather would lead to freeing the child. It was both a meritorious and a pious deed to accept such a responsibility and to fulfill its implicit commitments, and it bestowed distinction upon him who accepted them.[53] In the mining regions of Minas Geraes a slave who found a seventeen-and-a-half-carat diamond was crowned with a floral wreath, dressed in a white suit, carried on the shoulders of fellow slaves to the presence of his master, and freed and allowed to work for himself.[54] A parent having ten children could claim freedom, whether male or female.

The freeing of one's slaves was an honorific tradition, and men fulfilled it on numerous occasions. Favorite wet nurses were often freed; slaves were manumitted on happy occasions in the family—a birth of a first son, or the marriage of one of the master's children. In fact, the excuses and the occasions were numerous—the passing of an examination in school by the young master, a family festival, a national holiday, and, of course, by will upon the death of the master.[55] A cataloguing of the occasions for manumission in such a country as Brazil might almost lead to wonder at the persistence of slavery; but as I have pointed out above, the importations of slaves were large and continuous in Brazil all through the colonial period and late into the nineteenth century.

Opportunities for escape from slavery were further facilitated by the system of labor that prevailed in many places, particularly in cities. Slaves were often encouraged to hire themselves out and bring their masters a fixed part of their wages, keeping the rest. Skilled artisans, masons, carpenters, blacksmiths, wheelwrights, tailors, . and musicians were special gainers from the arrangement.[56] But even ordinary laborers were allowed to organize themselves in gangs, *gente de Ganho*, as they were called. Preceded by a leader, who would guide them in a rhythmic chant, they would offer their services as carriers on the wharves of the city or to do any heavy work that came to hand. The description of these chanting gangs of Negro slaves in the city of Rio, carrying bags of coffee on their heads, their sweating bodies stripped to the waist, marching in rhythm to their own song, is like nothing else in social history:

> . . . the rapid lope and monotonous grunt of the coffee-bag carriers, their naked bodes reeking with oily sweat; the jingling and drumming of the tin rattles or gourds borne by the leaders of gangs, transporting on their heads all manner of articles—chairs, tables, sofas, and bedsteads, the entire furniture of a household; the dull recitative, followed by the loud chorus, with which they move along; the laborious cry of others, tugging and hauling and pushing over the rough pavements heavily laden trucks and carts, an overload for an equal number of mules or horses, all crowd on the observation. Others, both male and

female, more favored in their occupation, are seen as peddlers, carrying in the same manner, trunks and boxes of tin, containing various merchandise; glass cases filled with fancy articles and jewelry; trays with cakes and confectionery; and baskets with fruit, flowers and birds. And yet again others of the same color and race, more fortunate still, in being free—the street vendor, the mechanic, the tradesman, the soldier; the merchant and the priest in his frock.[57]

But the slave in this procession had his wages for himself after paying the master his share. Individual persons in Rio, otherwise poor, would make their living from the owning of one or more of these male or female slaves, whom they permitted to hire themselves out.[58] Women often hired themselves out as wet nurses, and both male and female slaves peddled a thousand wares through the streets.

Slaves of both sexes cry wares through every street. Vegetables, flowers, fruits, edible roots, fowls, eggs, and every rural product, cakes, pies, rusks, doces, confectionery, "heavenly bacon," etc., pass your windows continually. Your cook wants a skillet, and, hark! the signal of a pedestrian copper-smith is heard; his bell is a stew-pan, and the clapper a hammer. A water-pot is shattered; in half an hour a meringue-merchant approaches. You wish to replenish your table-furniture with fresh sets of knives, new-fashioned tumblers, decanters, and plates, and, peradventure, a cruet, with a few articles of silver. Well, you need not want them long. If cases of cutlery, of glassware, china, and silver have not already passed the door, they will appear anon. So of every article of female apparel, from silk dress or shawl to a handkerchief and a paper of pins. Shoes, bonnets, ready trimmed, fancy jewelry, toy-books for children, novels for young folks, and works of devotion for the devout; "Art of Dancing" for the awkward; "School of Good Dress" for the young; "Manual of Politeness" for boors; "Young Ladies' Oracle"; "Language of Flowers"; "Holy Reliquaries"; "Miracles of Saints," and "A Sermon in Honor of Bacchus"—these things, and a thousand others, are hawked about daily.[59]

With all its cruelty, abuse, hardship, and inhumanity, the atmosphere in Brazil and in the Spanish-American countries made for manumission. Even in the rural regions individuals were allowed to sell the products from their own plots, given them to work for themselves, and to save their money toward the day of freedom. In Cuba, one writer notes, the raising of pigs by slaves provided a ready source of the sums accumulated for such a purpose.[60] It should be further noticed that, in addition to their Sundays, the Negroes in Brazil had many holidays, amounting all together to eighty-four days a year, which they could use for their own purposes, and for garnering such funds as their immediate skill and opportunities made possible. The purchase of one's freedom was so accepted a tradition among the Negroes that many a Negro bought the freedom of his wife and children while he himself continued laboring as a slave, and among the freed Negroes societies were organized for pooling resources and collecting funds for the freeing of their brethren still in bondage.[61]

These many provisions favoring manumission were strongly influenced by the church. Without interfering with the institution of slavery where the domestic law accepted it, the church early condemned the slave trade and prohibited Catholics from taking part in it. The prohibition was not effective, though it in some measure may have influenced the Spaniards to a rather limited participation in the trade as such. The slave trade had been condemned by Pius II on October 7, 1462, by Paul III on May 29, 1537, by Urban VIII on April 2, 1639, by Benedict XIV on December 20, 1741, and finally by Gregory XVI on December 3, 1839. The grounds of the condemnation were that innocent and free persons were illegally and by force captured and sold into slavery, that rapine, cruelty, and war were stimulated in the search for human beings to be sold at a profit.[62] The Franciscan Father Thomas Mercado had condemned the slave trade in the strongest terms in the year 1587, on the grounds that it fostered two thousand falsehoods, a thousand robberies, and a thousand deceptions. But the church did not interfere with the customary institution where it derived from known practices in a given community, such as born slaves, slaves taken in a just war, or those who had sold themselves or had been condemned by a legitimate court.

The presumption against the slave trade was that it forced people into slavery outside the law and against their will. More important in the long run than the condemnation of the slave trade proved the church's insistence that slave and master were equal in the sight of God. Whatever the formal relations between slave and master, they must both recognize their relationship to each other as moral human beings and as brothers in Christ. The master had an obligation to protect the spiritual integrity of the slave, to teach him the Christian religion, to help him achieve the privileges of the sacraments, to guide him into living a good life, and to protect him from mortal sin. The slave had a right to become a Christian, to be baptized, and to be considered a member of the Christian community. Baptism was considered his entrance into the community, and until he was sufficiently instructed to be able to receive it, he was looked upon as out of the community and as something less than human.[63]

From the very beginning the Catholic churches in America insisted that masters bring their slaves to church to learn the doctrine and participate in the communion. The assembled bishops in Mexico in the year 1555 urged all Spaniards to send the Indians, and especially the Negroes, to church;[64] similarly in Cuba in 1680.[65]

In fact, Negroes were baptized in Angola [66] before leaving for their Atlantic journey to Brazil. Upon arrival they were instructed in the doctrine, and as evidence of their baptism carried about their necks a mark of the royal crown. As a Catholic the slave was married in the church, and the banns were regularly published.[67] It gave the slave's family a moral and religious character unknown in other American slave systems. It became part of the ordinary routine on the slave plantations for the master and slaves to attend church on Sundays, and regularly before retiring at night the slaves gathered before the master's house to receive his blessings.[68] If married by the church, they could not be separated by the master. Religious fraternities sprang up among the slaves. These were often influential and honorific institutions, with regularly elected officers, and funds for the celebration of religious holidays subscribed to by the slaves out of their own meager savings. In Brazil the slaves adopted the Lady of the Rosary as their own special patroness, sometimes painting her black. In a measure these religious fraternities emulated those of the whites, if they did not compete with them, and the slaves found a source of pride in becoming members, and honor in serving one of these religious fraternities as an official.[69]

If the Latin American environment was favorable to freedom, the British and American were hostile.[70] Legal obstacles were placed in the way of manumission, and it was discouraged in every other manner. The presumption was in favor of slavery.[71] A Negro who could not prove that he was free was presumed to be a runaway slave and was advertised as such; if no claimant appeared, he was sold at public auction for the public benefit.[72] In Demerara no slave could be manumitted without the consent of the Governor and Council. In most of the British colonies heavy taxes had been imposed on manumission, and as late as 1802 a law was passed in the Northern Leeward Islands requiring the owner who would register his slave for manumission to pay five hundred pounds into the public treasury,[73] and this sum had to be provided in his will if it made provision for the liberation of the slave. The slave could not be freed without the master's consent, even if the full price of the slave was offered. In the fear of an increase of freemen, Barbados, in 1801, passed a law taxing the manumission of a female slave much more heavily than a male. St. Christopher, which taxed manumission for the first time in 1802, declared it to be a "great inconvenience . . . that [the number of] free Negroes and . . . free persons of color was augmented" by releasing slaves from bondage, and provided that a slave who had been released by his master, but not formally enfranchised, should be "publicly sold at vendue." [74]

In the southern part of the United States the position of the slave was closely similar to that in the British West Indies. What is important to note is the tendency to identify the Negro with the slave. The mere fact of being a Negro was presumptive of a slave status. South Carolina in 1740 (similarly Georgia and Mississippi) provided that "all negroes, Indians (those now free excepted) . . . mulattoes, or mestizos, who are or shall hereafter be in the province, and all their issue and offspring, born or to be born, shall be and they are hereby declared to be and remain forever hereafter absolute slaves and shall follow the condition of the mother." [75] Equally striking is an early law of Maryland, dating from 1663: "All negroes or other slaves within the province, all negroes to be hereafter imported, shall serve *durante vita*"; and their children were to follow the condition of the father. Significantly the same law said: "That whatsoever freeborn women (English) shall intermarry with any slave . . . shall serve the master of such slave during the life of her husband; all the issue of such freeborn women, so married, shall be slave as their fathers were." [76] A free Negro in South Carolina (1740) harboring a runaway slave, or charged "with any criminal matter," upon inability to pay the fine and court charges was to be sold "at public auction." [77] The same state provided that an emancipated Negro set free otherwise than according to the act of 1800 could be seized and kept as a slave by "any person whatsoever."

The Negro was a slave, and the pressure seemed, in a number of states, anyway, to keep him one, or to reduce him to slavery if free. In Virginia an emancipated slave who had not left the state in the twelve months after being manumitted could be sold by the overseer of the poor "for the benefit of the Literary Fund"; [78] similarly in North Carolina. In Florida a free mulatto or Negro could be made a slave for the smallest debt executed against him. In Mississippi any Negro or mulatto not being able to show himself a free man could be sold by the court as a slave. In Maryland (1717) any free Negro or mulatto, man or woman, intermarrying with a white person became a slave for life.[79] Because the Negroes were brought in as slaves, the black color raised the presumption of slavery, which was generally extended to mulattoes, and in many states this presumption was enunciated by statute, putting on them the onus of proving that they were free. In Virginia and Kentucky one-fourth Negro blood constituted a presumption of slavery, and all children born of slave mothers were slaves.[80]

Under the British West Indian and United States laws the Negro slave could not hope for self-redemption by purchase, and as slavery was assumed to be perpetual, there was only one route to freedom— manumission. But this route, if not entirely blocked, was made difficult by numerous impediments. The bias in favor of keeping the Negro in servitude contrasts with the other slave systems here under consideration, describes the explicit and the implicit test of the two systems, and foreshadows their ultimate outcome. For the attitude toward manumission is the crucial element in slavery; it implies the judgment of the moral status of the slave, and foreshadows his role in case of freedom.

Just as the favoring of manumission is perhaps the most characteristic and significant feature of the Latin American slave system, so opposition to manumission and denial of opportunities for it are the primary aspect of slavery in the British West Indies and in the United States. The frequency and ease of manumission, more than any other factor, influence the character and ultimate outcome of the two slave systems in this hemisphere. For the ease of manumission bespeaks, even if only implicitly, a friendly attitude toward the person whose freedom is thus made possible and encouraged, just as the systematic obstruction of manumission implies a complete, if unconscious, attitude of hostility to those whose freedom is opposed or denied. And these contrasting attitudes toward manumission work themselves out in a hundred small, perhaps unnoticed, but significant details in the treatment of the Negro, both as a slave and when freed. Either policy reveals the bent of the system, and casts ahead of itself the long-run consequence of immediate practice and attitude.

In the United States, "in every slaveholding state . . . restrictions . . . have been placed upon the manumission of Negro slaves. . . . In several of the states domestic manumission, that is, manumission to take effect within the state is prohibited." [81] In Mississippi, Alabama, and Maryland manumission by will was void. Manumission could not be effected to the prejudice of creditors, and if the estate proved insolvent, manumission by will was of no effect.[82] In states like Mississippi, Virginia, and Kentucky, where a widow was entitled to one third of her deceased husband's estate, slaves emancipated by will could be held for the satisfaction of the widow's rights.[83] In South Carolina, Georgia, Alabama, and Mississippi manumission was valid only with the consent of the state legislature. A fine of two hundred dollars was visited upon the master in Georgia (1801) for attempting to manumit a slave without previous consent of the legislature, and the slave continued in bondage as before. In 1818 this same state imposed a fine of one thousand dollars on anyone giving effect to a last will and testament freeing a slave or permitting him to work for himself beyond the control of a master. In North Carolina (1836–37) a surety of one thousand dollars was required before manumission for the guarantee of the freed slave's good behavior, and the freed slave had to leave the state within ninety days, never to return. Tennessee (1801) required a bond, the consent of the court, and immediate departure from the state; whereas in Mississippi (1822) there had to be an instrument in writing proving to the General Assembly that the slave had performed a meritorious deed, and then a special act sanctioning the manumission in question.[84] The laws of Virginia effecting emancipation had undergone many changes.

In Virginia, in 1691, it was provided that a Negro could not be set free unless "pay for the transportation of such negro" out of the "country" within six months be provided.[85] In 1723 an act provided that a Negro could be set free only by the action of the Governor and Council, and only for some "meritorious service." In 1805 Virginia prohibited emancipation unless the Negro left the state.[86] In 1824 the Virginia courts ruled that the freeing of a mother by will after she reached a certain age did not apply to her children born after the date of the will.[87] Many similar statutes were passed in other states.

The slave had no protector to appeal to, and the master had, in some instances, exceeding power over him. An early Jamaican statute provided: "If any slave by punishment from his owner for running away, or other offence, suffer in life or limb, none shall be liable to the law for the same; but whoever shall kill a slave out of willfullness, wantonness, or bloody-mindedness, shall suffer three months' imprisonment and pay £50 to the owner of the slave." [88] Thus willful murder had been reduced to a misdemeanor if committed on a slave. But it is more surprising that if the murder was committed by an indentured servant, he too could expiate the murder by thirty-nine lashes and four years' service.[89] Tennessee provided that the law defining the killing of a slave as murder should not apply "to any one person killing a slave . . . in the act of resistance . . . or dying under moderate correction." [90] The Georgia constitution safeguards against the charge of murder if the "death should happen by accident in giving such slave moderate correction." [91] In South Carolina the act of 1740 provided that willful murder of a slave should cost the perpetrator "seven hundred pounds current money," and this law, which remained on the statute books till 1821, further provided that if the murder occurred "on sudden heat and passion," it should cost him only £350.[92] But such minor punishments as willfully cutting out the tongue, putting out the eye, castrating, scalding, and similar offenses would, according to the above law, involve the culprit in a cost of merely "one hundred pounds of current money." [93]

Where laws existed protecting the slave against unusual punishment, they were difficult to enforce because he was denied the right to testify in the courts. In the United States, according to Cobb,[94] the rule that slaves could not testify for or against free white persons was enforced without exception; most of the state prohibited such testimony by express statute, others by custom and decision of the courts. In Illinois and Iowa this prohibition extended to free persons of color or emancipated slaves. The testimony of any Negro or mulatto, free or bond, was accepted in

Virginia only in cases where free Negroes and mulattoes were parties, and in no other case whatsoever.[95] Similar laws were enacted in most of the southern states.

The slave had no protector to appeal to, and he could not have his price specified for purposes of redemption and was not allowed to accumulate property to buy his freedom. The slave could acquire no property, and if any property came to him, it would belong to his master;[96] and, being incapable of acquiring property, he could not convey it or give it away. The laws on this point are numerous. In Louisiana, "all that a slave possesses belongs to his master,"[97] and he "cannot dispose or receive by donation." In South Carolina, "Slaves cannot take by descent or purchase"; in North Carolina, "Slaves cannot take by sale, or device, or descent." As one court put it, "Our slaves can do nothing in their own right, can hold no property, can neither buy, sell, barter, nor dispose of anything without express permission of master or overseer. . . ."[98] But other states went further—they denied the right of the slave to own property, even with the consent of the master. Under the act of 1740 South Carolina made it illegal for any slave to "raise and breed for the benefit of such slave, any horses, mares, cattle, sheep, or hogs under pain of forfeiture of all such goods, etc."[99] Georgia punished the master by a fine of thirty dollars "for every weekly offence" if he permitted his slave to hire himself out to another for his own benefit.[100] Similar laws were enacted in Kentucky, Tennessee, Virginia, and Missouri. In Mississippi a slave could not raise cotton for his own use, and the master permitting it was fined fifty dollars. The laws further restricted the hiring out of slaves to others; Virginia in 1819 made it permissible to sell a slave for hiring himself out.[101]

The marriage contract having no validity, none of its consequences followed. While in a state of slavery, marriage, even with the master's consent, produced no civil effect.[102] The question of marriage of the slave troubled the conscience of good people, and they attempted to meet the issue posed by the absolute power of separation by the master.

In 1835, the following query relating to slaves was propounded to the Savannah River Baptist Association of ministers: Whether, in case of involuntary separation of such a character as to preclude all further intercourse, the parties may be allowed to marry again?

ANSWER.—That such separation, among persons situated as our slaves are, is, civilly, a separation by death, and they believe that, in the sight of God, it would be so viewed. To forbid second marriage in such cases, would be to expose the parties not only to greater hardships and stronger temptations, but to *church censure* for acting in *obedience to their masters,* who cannot be expected to acquiesce in a regulation at variance with justice to the slaves, and to the spirit of that command which regulates marriage between Christians. *The slaves are not free agents*, and a dissolution by death is not more entirely without their consent and beyond their control than by such separation.[103]

In 1779 North Carolina prohibited the ownership of animals by slaves. Mississippi prohibited a master from allowing his slave to trade like a freeman, and Maryland from permitting him to keep "stock of any description," nor could he acquire money beyond his wages for the purchase of the freedom of his children.[104]

There was no custom of freeing the children at the baptismal font for a nominal price, there was nothing known of the moral role of the godfather for the slave child, and the slave family had no status either in law or in public recognition.

The law recognized no marriage relation between slaves.[105] There followed no inheritance of blood even after emancipation,[106] and spouses might be witnesses against each other. It was part of the record that "A slave never has maintained an action against the violator of his bed. A slave is not admonished for incontinence, or punished for fornication or adultery; never prosecuted for bigamy, or petty treason, for killing a husband being a slave, any more than admitted to an appeal for murder." [107]

Under the law of most of the southern states, there was no regard for the Negro family, no question of the right of the owner to sell his slaves separately, and no limitation upon separating husband and wife, or child from its mother. That this was so may be seen from the following advertisements.

NEGROES FOR SALE.—A negro woman, 24 years of age, and her two children, one eight and the other three years old. Said negroes will be sold SEPARATELY or together, *as desired*. The woman is a good seamstress. She will be sold low for cash, or EXCHANGED FOR GROCERIES.
For terms, apply to MATTHEW BLISS & Co., 1 Front Levee.

[New Orleans Bee]

I WILL GIVE THE HIGHEST CASH PRICE for likely Negroes, from 10 to 25 years of age.

GEORGE KEPHART
[Alexandria (D. C.) Gazette]

ONE HUNDRED AND TWENTY NEGROES FOR SALE.—The subscriber has *just arrived from Petersburg, Virginia*, with one hundred and twenty *likely young negroes* of both sexes and every description, which he offers for sale on the most reasonable terms. The lot now on hand consists of ploughboys, several likely and well-qualified house servants of both sexes, *several women with children, small girls* suitable for nurses, and SEVERAL SMALL BOYS WITHOUT THEIR

MOTHERS. Planters and *traders* are earnestly requested to give the subscriber a call previously to making purchases *elsewhere,* as he is enabled to sell as cheap or cheaper than can be sold by *any other person in the trade.*

BENJAMIN DAVIS

(Hamburg, S. C., September 28, 1838)[108]

But even more convincing than the advertisements is the following record compiled by Frederic C. Bancroft from four cargoes of Negroes shipped to New Orleans in 1834 and 1835:

Of the four cargoes making a total of 646 slaves, 396 were apparently owned by Franklin & Armfield. Among these there were only two full families: the fathers were 21 and 22 years of age, the mothers 19 and 20, and the children 1 and 1½. There were 20 husbandless mothers with 33 children, of whom one was 2 weeks old, 4 others were less than 1 year old, 19 were from 1 to 4 years old, and 9 were from 5 to 12 years of age. The remaining 337 were single and may be grouped thus:

```
  5 were from  6 to  9 years old, both inclusive
 68    "      "  10 " 15   "    "    "    "
145    "      "  16 " 21   "    "    "    "
101    "      "  22 " 30   "    "    "    "
  9    "      "  31 " 39   "    "    "    "
  8    "      "  40 " 50   "    "    "    "
  1 above      50,   a man of 60.
```

93 per cent of these 337 were from 10 to 30 years of age.[109]

Under the law a slave could not acquire property by earning it, by gift, or by inheritance. Not having any property, he could make no will, and could not take by descent, "there being in him no inheritable blood." [110] In South Carolina slaves were described as "chattels personal . . . to all intents, constructions and purposes whatsoever." [111] In Louisiana the slave ". . . can do nothing, possess nothing, nor acquire anything but what must belong to his master." [112] In 1806, slaves were defined as real estate. The same principle ruled in Kentucky, but except for purposes of sale and execution of debts they were considered chattel. Most of the states defined slaves as chattel, and the laws of Maryland (1791) declared that "In case the personal property of a ward shall consist of specific articles such as slaves, working beasts, animals of any kind, stock furniture, plate, books, and so forth, the court . . . may at any time pass an order for the sale thereof." [113]

In fact, the issue of female slaves in Maryland was considered part of the use, like that of other female animals. Court decisions are cited to the effect: "Suppose a brood mare is hired for five years, the foals belong to him who has a part of the use of the dam. The slave in Maryland, in this respect, is placed on no higher or different grounds." [114] In fact, the breeding of slaves for sale as if they were mere cattle came to be part of the recognized practice of slave and plantation-owners in some, perhaps most, of the slave states. The practice was of long standing, and seems to have antedated the abolition of the slave trade, for as far back as 1796 the following advertisement appeared in Charleston, South Carolina, offering fifty Negroes for sale:

. . . they are not Negroes selected out of a larger gang for the purpose of a sale, but are prime, their present Owner, with great trouble and expense, selected them out of many for several years past. They were purchased for stock and breeding Negroes, and to any Planter who particularly wanted them for that purpose, they are a very choice and desirable gang.[115]

In 1830 Virginia was credited with exporting 8,500 slaves annually. Thomas Jefferson Randolph said: "It is a practice, and an increasing practice in parts of Virginia, to rear slaves for market." [116] And the protagonist of slavery Thomas R. Dew, who became president of William and Mary College in 1836, said with pride that "Virginia is in fact a negro raising state for other states; she produces enough for her own supply, and six thousand for sale. . . . Virginians can raise [them] cheaper than they can buy; in fact, it [raising slaves] is one of their greatest sources of profit." [117]

This business had its implications and consequences. The Negro female was reduced to a breeding animal. "She [a girl about twenty years of age] . . . is very prolific in her generating qualities, and affords a rare opportunity for any person who wishes to raise a family of strong, healthy servants for . . . [his] own use. . . ." [118] The emphasis was upon raising children, for they could be sold at high prices. The records show that a child of four was worth $200, and another of six $150,[119] while there are indications of even higher prices. In 1857 children of four, five, and eight years were sold for $376, $400, and $785, respectively.[120] The thing to do was to breed the Negro girls young. "A girl of seventeen that had borne two children was called a 'rattlin' good breeder' and commanded an extraordinary price." [121] The demise of the sanctity of marriage had become absolute, and the Negro had lost his moral personality. Legally he was a chattel under the law, and in practice an animal to be bred for the market. The logic of the situation worked itself out in time, but in the process the moral personality of the slave as a human being became completely obscured. It is no wonder that the right of redemption was seemingly nonexistent and the opportunity for manumission greatly restricted.

NOTES

1. Elizabeth Donnan, ed., *Documents Illustrative of the History of the Slave Trade to America*, 4 vols. (Washington: Carnegie Institute of Washington, 1930–35), I ("1441–1700," 1930), p. 29: "For as our people did not find them hardened in the belief of the other Moors, and saw how they came in unto the law of Christ with a good will, they made no difference between them and their free servants, born in our own country. But those whom they saw fitted for managing property, they set free and married to women who were natives of the land, making with them a division of their property, as if they had been bestowed on those who married them by the will of their own fathers, and for the merits of their service they were bound to act in a like manner. Yea, and some widows of good family who bought some of these female slaves, either adopted them or left them a portion of their estate by will, so that in the future they married right well, treating them as entirely free. Suffice it that I never saw one of these slaves put in irons like other captives, and scarcely any one who did not turn Christian and was not very gently treated." Quoted from *The Chronicle of the Discovery and Conquest of Guinea*, by Gomes Eannes de Azurara.

2. Dieudonné P. Rinchon, *La Traité et L'esclavage des Congolais par les Européens* (Bruxelles: chez l'auteur, 1929), p. 44.

3. George Scelle, *La Traité négrière* (Paris: L. Lerose & L. Tenin, 1906), I, pp. 219–20.

4. H. Morse Stephens, *Portugal* (New York, 1891), p. 182.

5. Arthur Helps, *The Spanish Conquest in America*, 4 vols. (London, 1855), I, p. 32.

6. Henry Charles Lea, *A History of the Inquisition of Spain*, 4 vols. (New York: The Macmillan Co., 1906), I, pp. 142–45.

7. Ibid., III, p. 405.

8. "*Servidumbre es postura et establescimiento qui ficieron antiguamente las gentes, por la qual los homes, que eran naturalmiente libres, se facían siervos et se sometían a señorio de otri contra razon de natura.*" Ley I, título xxi, partida 4, *Las Siete Partidas del Rey Don Alfonso el Sabio, Cortejadas con Varios Códices Antiguos por la Real Academia de la Historia, y Glosadas por el Lic. Gregorio Lopez, del Consejo Real de Insias de S.M. Nueva Edición, precedida del Elogio del Rey Don Alfonso por D. J. de Vargas y Ponce, y Enriquecida con su Testamento Político*, 5 vols. (Paris, 1847).

9. R. W. Carlyle and A. J. Carlyle, *A History of Mediaeval Political Theory in the West*, 6 vols. (Edinburgh and London: W. Blackwood and Sons, 1903–1936), I, p. 8.

10. Ibid., p. 21.
11. Ibid., p. 84.
12. Galatians iii, 28.
13. Philemon, 16.
14. Ibid., 17.
15. Corinthians viii, 20.
16. Ibid., viii, 21.
17. Ephesians vi, 5, 9.
18. R. W. and A. J. Carlyle, *Medieval Political Theory*, I, pp. 88–89.
19. *Las Siete Partidas*, Ley I, tit. v, part 4.
20. Ibid., Ley II.
21. Ibid., Ley II, tit. xxi, part 4.

22. Ibid., Ley III.
23. Ibid., Ley VIII.
24. Ibid., Ley VI, tit. xxii, part 4.
25. Ibid., Ley II.
26. Ibid., Ley IV.
27. Ibid., Ley IV.
28. Ibid., Ley VII.
29. Ibid., Ley VII, tit. ii, part 3.
30. Ibid., Ley IX, tit. ii, part 3.
31. Ibid., Ley IV, tit. v, part 3.
32. Ibid., Ley XIII, tit. xvi, part 3.
33. Ibid., Ley XXI, tit. v, part 6.
34. Ibid., Ley VII, tit. xvi, part 6.
35. Ibid., Ley XXIII, tit. iii, part 6.
36. Ibid., Ley IX, tit. viii, part 7.
37. *Real Cédula de Su Magestad sobre la Educación, Trato, y Ocupaciones de los Esclavos, en Todos sus Dominios de Indias, e Islas Filipinas, Baxo las Reglas que Se Expresan.* This law has been reprinted several times, most recently in an article by Raúl Carrancá y Trujillo in *Revista de Historia de America* 3 (Mexico, September 1938): 50–59.
38. José Antonio Saco, *Historia de la Esclavitud de la Raza Africana en el Nuevo Mundo y en especial en los Países Américo-Hispanos* (Havana: Cultural, s.a., 1938), III, pp. 265–66.
39. "In the Cuban market freedom was the only commodity which could be bought untaxed; every negro against whom no one had proved a claim of servitude was deemed free. . . ." William Law Mathieson, *British Slavery and Its Abolition* (London: Longmans, Green & Co., 1926), pp. 37–38.
40. Sir Harry Johnston, *The Negro in the New World* (London: Methuen & Co., 1910), p. 89. D. P. Kidder and J. C. Fletcher, *Brazil and the Brazilians* (New York: Childs and Peterson, 1857), p. 133.
41. Alexander Humboldt, *Political Essay on the Kingdom of New Spain*, trans. John Black, 2 vols. (New York: John Riley, 1811), I, p. 181.
42. Richard Henry Dana, Jr., *To Cuba and Back* (Boston: Tichnor and Fields, 1859), p. 249.
43. Fernando Ortiz Fernandez, *Hampa Afro-cubana. Los Negros Esclavos* (Havana: Revista Bimestre Cubana, 1916), p. 313.
44. Alexander Humboldt, *The Island of Cuba* (New York, 1856), p. 211.
45. Ortiz, *Negros Esclavos*, p. 317.
46. Ibid., p. 315.
47. Humboldt, *Essay*, p. 181.
48. Henry Koster, *Travels in Brazil*, 2 vols. (Philadelphia: M. Carey & Son, 1817), II, p. 202. Ortiz, *Negros Esclavos*, p. 337.
49. Percy Alvin Martin, "Slavery and Abolition in Brazil" in *Hispanic American Historical Review* 13 (May 1933): 174.
50. Ortiz, *Negros Esclavos*, p. 351.
51. Robert Southey, *History of Brazil* (London, 1819), part III, p. 784.
52. Mathieson, *British Slavery*, p. 37.
53. Koster, *Travels*, p. 195.
54. John Mawe, *Travels in the Interior of Brazil* (London: Longman, Hurst, Orme & Brown, 1812), p. 318.

55. Martin, "Slavery," p. 170.

56. Ortiz, *Negros Esclavos*, p. 318.

57. C. S. Stewart, *Brazil and La Plata: The Personal Record of a Cruise* (New York: G. P. Putnam & Co., 1856), p. 20.

58. Rev. R. Walsh, *Notices of Brazil* (New York, 1831), II, p. 20.

59. Thomas Ewbank, *Life in Brazil, or the Land of the Cocoa and the Palm* (London, 1856), pp. 92–93.

60. Rev. Abiel Abbot, *Letters Written in the Interior of Cuba* (Boston: Bowles and Dearborn, 1829), p. 97.

61. Arthur Ramos, *The Negro in Brazil*, trans. Richard Pattee (Washington, D. C.: Associated Publishers, 1939), p. 70.

62. Saco, *Historia de la Esclavitud*, III, pp. 64–66.

63. Koster, *Travels*, p. 199.

64. *Concilios Provinciales, Primero y Segundo, Mexico, En los Años de 1555 y 1565* (Mexico, 1769), Concilio primero, Cap. III, p. 44.

65. Saco, *Historia de la Esclavitud*, I, pp. 165–167.

66. Koster, *Travels*, p. 198.

67. Ibid., p. 202.

68. Alfred R. Wallace, *A Narrative of Travels on the Amazon and Río Negro* (London: Reeve & Co., 1853), p. 92.

69. Southey, *History of Brazil*, p. 784.

70. There were, briefly speaking, three slave systems in the Western Hemisphere. The British, American, Dutch, and Danish were at one extreme, and the Spanish and Portuguese at the other. In between these two fell the French. The first of these groups is characterized by the fact that they had no effective slave tradition, no slave law, and that their religious institutions were little concerned about the Negro. At the other extreme there were both a slave law and a belief that the spiritual personality of the slave transcended his slave status. In between them the French suffered from the lack of a slave tradition and slave law, but did not have the same religious principles as the Spaniards and Portuguese. If one were forced to arrange these systems of slavery in order of severity, the Dutch would seem to stand as the hardest, the Portuguese as the mildest, and the French, in between, as having elements of both.

71. Mathieson, *British Slavery*, pp. 38–40.

72. Ibid., pp. 38–40.

73. Johnston, *Negro in the New World*, p. 231.

74. Mathieson, *British Slavery*, pp. 38–40.

75. George M. Stroud, *A Sketch of the Laws Relating to Slavery in the Several States of the United States of America*, 2nd edition (Philadelphia: H. Longstreth, 1856), pp. 60–61.

76. Ibid., p. 14.

77. Ibid., p. 24.

78. Quoted in ibid., p. 27.

79. Ibid., pp. 27–30.

80. Thomas R. R. Cobb, *An Inquiry into the Law of Negro Slavery in the United States of America* (Philadelphia and Savannah, 1858), p. 238.

81. Ibid., pp. 287, 290.

82. Ibid., pp. 296, 298.

83. Stroud, *Sketch of the Laws*, p. 231.

84. Ibid., pp. 219–36.

85. Helen Tunnicliff Catterall, *Judicial Cases Concerning American Slavery and*

the Negro, with additions by James J. Hayden, 5 vols. (Washington, D. C.: Carnegie Institution of Washington, 1926–37), I, p. 72.

86. Ibid., p. 73.

87. Ibid., p. 74.

88. Charles Leslie, *A New and Exact Account of Jamaica* (Edinburgh, 1739), p. 234. *The Laws of Jamaica, Passed by the Assembly and Confirmed by His Majesty, in Council, April 17, 1684* (London, 1684). In 1696 willful killing of a slave on the second offense was to be considered as murder and punishable as such without benefit of clergy. *Acts of Jamaica 1681–1737* (London, 1738), p. 8. In 1717 anyone ordering a slave dismembered was to pay £100 (ibid., p. 160).

89. Leslie, *Jamaica,* p. 234.

90. Stroud, *Sketch of the Laws,* pp. 60–61.

91. Ibid., Art. 4, par. 12, p. 61.

92. Ibid., p. 64.

93. Ibid., p. 66.

94. Cobb, *Inquiry,* p. 230.

95. "Revised Code 422," quoted in Stroud, *Sketch of the Laws,* p. 300.

96. Cobb, *Inquiry,* p. 238.

97. William Goodell, *The American Slave Code* (New York, 1853), p. 90.

98. Ibid., p. 52.

99. Ibid., pp. 97–100.

100. Ibid., p. 98.

101. Ibid., p. 101. The states having slaves were so numerous, the changes in the law so frequent, and their enforcement so uneven at different times that it is impossible to describe every detail in all its variations. A special treatise on the law and practice for every state would be required. But even if the details vary, in all the southern states the tendency to discourage manumission and to identify the freedman with the slave is clear.

102. Ibid., p. 107.

103. Quoted in Goodell, *American Slave Code,* p. 109.

104. Stroud, *Sketch of the Laws,* p. 81.

105. Cobb, *Inquiry,* p. 243.

106. Ibid., p. 245.

107. "Opinion of Daniel Dulany, Esq., Attorney General of Maryland," Maryland Reports, 561, 563; quoted in Stroud, *Sketch of the Laws,* p. 99.

108. Goodell, *American Slave Code,* pp. 54–55.

109. Frederic C. Bancroft, *Slave-Trading in the Old South* (Baltimore: J. H. Furst Co., 1931), p. 63.

110. Cobb, *Inquiry,* p. 238.

111. Goodell, *American Slave Code,* p. 23.

112. Ibid.

113. Ibid., p. 25, quoted from *A Practical Treatise of the Law of Slavery, being a Compilation of all the Decisions made on that subject, in the several Courts of the United States, and State Courts; with copious notes and references to the Statutes and other authorities, systemaically arranged,* by Jacob D. Wheeler, Esq., Counsellor at Law (New York: Allan Pollock, Jr., and New Orleans: Benjamin Levy, 1837).

114. Goodell, *American Slave Code,* p. 20.

115. Quoted in Bancroft, *Slave-Trading,* p. 68, from U. B. Phillips, ed., *Plantation and Frontier Documents: 1649–1863,* 2 vols. (Cleveland: A. H. Clark Company, 1902), II, p. 57.

116. Quoted in Bancroft, *Slave-Trading*, p. 69.
117. Quoted in Bancroft, *Slave-Trading*, p. 71, from Thomas R. Dew, *A Review of the Debate in the Virginia Legislature of 1831 and 1832* (Richmond, 1832).
118. Quoted by Bancroft, *Slave-Trading*, p. 74, from the *Charleston Mercury* of May 16, 1838.
119. Catterall, *Judicial Cases*, I, p. 186.
120. Quoted in Bancroft, *Slave-Trading*, p. 79, note, from George M. Weston, *The Progress of Slavery in the United States* (Washington: The Author, 1857), pp. 116–17.
121. Bancroft, *Slave-Trading*, p. 82.

12. CARL N. DEGLER, Slavery in Brazil and the United States: An Essay in Comparative History (1970)*

Carl N. Degler, who is a specialist in American social history, teaches at Stanford University. He has recently completed a comparative study of race relations and slavery in the United States and Brazil. In this selection, Degler discusses some of the similarities and differences between the slave systems of these two countries. In the process, Degler reveals several important differences other than those suggested by such earlier historians as Tannenbaum and Elkins. For example, Degler attributes the more rebellious nature of Brazilian blacks to their more intimate contact with Africa through a greater reliance on the African slave trade. Consequently Brazilian slaves were in continuous contact with new arrivals from Africa who were not conditioned to accept slavery as their assigned role in life. The fact that Brazil depended so heavily upon the African slave trade also accounts for the greater prevalence of African survivals.

Over twenty years ago Frank Tannenbaum made a comparison of slavery in the societies of the New World in which he argued that the differences in contemporary race relations between the United States and Latin America are to be traced to differences in the character of slavery in the two places. A decade later Stanley Elkins built a provocative book upon Tannenbaum's conclusions. More recently, Arnold Sio and David Brion Davis entered strong demurrers to the Tannenbaum-Elkins conclusions by arguing that slavery as an institution was more similar than different throughout the societies of the New World.[1]

These and a number of other writings on the comparative history of slavery in the Western Hemisphere attest to a burgeoning scholarly interest. But throughout the debate one of the prominent difficulties has been the great breadth and diversity of the areas being compared. To make convincing comparisons among some two dozen societies presents obvious

* From Carl N. Degler, "Slavery in Brazil and the United States," *The American Historical Review* 75 (April 1970): 1004–28. Reprinted by permission of the author.

problems and is open to the dangers of superficiality. It is the intention here, therefore, to draw a much more restricted comparison, not because the large problem that Tannenbaum raised will finally be resolved by such a limited approach, but simply because two countries are more manageable as variables than two continents. It is also worth noting that Brazil and the United States have the advantage of being the two most important slave societies in the New World. Both had a long history of slavery—only Cuba and Brazil retained slavery longer than the United States—and in both societies slavery occupied an important, if not actually a central, place in the economy.[2]

Essentially this essay seeks to answer two quite limited questions: First, in what respects were the systems of slavery in Brazil and the United States alike during their mature years—that is, during the nineteenth century—and in what ways did they differ? Second, to what extent are these differences related to the laws and practices of the state and the Church in Brazil, as both Tannenbaum and Elkins have contended? Even if these questions can be answered with some degree of certainty, it should be said that the large question that Tannenbaum raised and sought to answer in his book will not be settled. But I hope that the ground will be cleared for a new attack upon the problem.

How were the two systems of slavery alike? Tannenbaum and Elkins stress the different legal conceptions of the slave in the United States and in Latin America. Tannenbaum, for example, contrasts the definition of a slave as a chattel in the United States with the more ambiguous definition in Latin America.

In fact, *the element of human personality was not lost in the transition to slavery from Africa to the Spanish or Portuguese dominions*. He [the Negro] remained a person even while he was a slave. . . . He was never considered a mere chattel, never defined as unanimated property, and never under the law treated as such. His master never enjoyed the powers of life and death over his body, even though abuses existed and cruelties were performed.[3]

Yet an examination of Brazilian and United States law reveals striking similarities in the definition of a slave.

The law in both the United States and Brazil, for example, recognized that a slave was both a human being and a piece of property. As a Tennessee court in 1846 put it,

A slave is not in the condition of a horse, he is made after the image of the creator. He has mental capacities and an immortal principal in his nature, that constitute him equal to his owner but for the accidental position in which fortune has placed him . . . the laws . . . cannot extinguish his high born nature, nor deprive him of many rights which are inherent in man. . . .[4]

In 1818 a Mississippi court went so far as to observe that "Slavery is condemned by reason and the laws of nature. It exists and can only exist through municipal regulations, and in matters of doubt" the courts must lean in favor of freedom.[5] As late as 1861 an Alabama court concluded that because slaves "are rational beings, they are capable of committing crimes; and in reference to acts which are crimes, are regarded as persons. Because they are slaves, they are . . . incapable of performing civil acts, and, in reference to all such, they are things, not persons."[6]

That last statement is close, in phraseology as well as meaning, to that set forth in Brazilian slave law by its principal authority, Agostino Marques Perdigão Malheiro. "In regard to the penal code," he wrote, "the slave, as subject of the offense or agent of it, is not a *thing*, he is a *person* . . . he is a human entity." Hence he is held personally responsible for crimes. But when he is an "Object or sufferer *of* a crime" the matter is different. The slave is not indemnified for such injuries, though the master may be. "In the latter case the question is one of *property*, but in the other it is one of *personality*." Perdigão Malheiro makes clear, moreover, that the position of the slave in court was not much different from that of the slave in the United States. No slave in Brazil could enter a complaint himself; it had to be done by his master or by the public authority. Nor could a slave make an accusation against his master. In fact, a slave could not give sworn testimony, only information. Perdigão Malheiro writes that in only three circumstances did a slave have standing in court: in regard to spiritual matters, such as marriage; in regard to his liberty; and in matters of obvious public concern. Only in regard to the first did the legal position of the slave in the United States differ; slave marriages had no legal basis in the United States.[7]

If there was little difference in the conception of the slave in Brazilian and United States law, there was also little difference in the law's supposed protection of the slave's humanity. Despite the general statements of some scholars,[8] both societies had laws protecting the slave against murder, mistreatment, or overwork by his master.[9] The operative question is whether the law or the church in fact interceded between the master and the slave in behalf of the latter. Certainly for the United States the evidence is not convincing. And in Brazil, too, the power of the state or the church to affect the life of the slave seems to have been limited. As Henry Koster, an English planter in Brazil, pointed out early in the nineteenth century, the Brazilian government was a weak reed on which to lean for anything, much less for control over members of the ruling slaveholding class. He tells, for example, of an instance in which one of his own slaves injured the slave of another man, but says that nothing was done about the matter. The owner of the injured slave might have pressed charges, if he so chose, "but the law of itself seldom does anything. Even in the cases of murder the prose-cutor . . . has it at his option to bring the trial forward or not; if he can be bribed or otherwise persuaded to give up the accusation, the matter drops to the ground." It is not likely that the state, which was run by slaveholders, would be more energetic in protecting the slave's humanity. Koster writes that occasionally a cruel master was fined for maltreating his slaves, "but," he adds, "I never heard of punishment having been carried farther than this trifling manner of correction." [10] Later in the century an-other traveler, the German painter John Rugendas, put the matter even more directly. Although there were laws in Brazil limiting the use of the whip and fixing the number of lashes at one time, he wrote in 1835:

these laws have no force and probably may be unknown to the majority of the slaves and masters; on the other hand, the authorities are so removed that in actuality the punishment of the slave for a true or imaginary infraction or the bad treatment resulting from the caprice and the cruelty of the master, only encounters limits in the fear of losing the slave by death, by flight, or as a consequence of public opinion. But these considerations are never sufficient to impede the evil and it is inescapable that examples of cruelty are not lack-ing, which result in the mutilation and death of slaves.[11]

It is only toward the end of the era of slavery, when the abolitionists brought cases of mistreatment to court, that Brazilian laws in behalf of the slaves actually protected them.

Both Elkins and Tannenbaum emphasize the role of the Roman Catholic Church in giving the Negro slave in Latin America a higher "moral" position than in the United States.[12] If that means that the Church accepted Negro slaves as members, the churches of the United States did, too. If that means that the Church actively intervened between master and slave in behalf of the latter, then it must be said that in Brazil the interest of the Church in and its power to protect the slave's humanity were as lim-ited as those of the state. For one thing, few plantations had resident priests; most plantations saw a priest only once a year when he came to legalize unions and to baptize. There were not, in fact, enough priests in the coun-try to affect the daily life of the slave, even if they had the interest to do so. As Emilia Viotti da Costa points out, not until 1885 did the archbishop of Bahia rule that no master could prevent a slave from marrying or sell him away from his spouse. Yet even at that late date, a slave could marry against his master's will only if the slave could demonstrate that he knew Christian doctrine—the Lord's Prayer, the Ave Maria, the Creed, and the commandments—understood the obligations of holy matrimony, and was clear in his intention to remain married for life. Furthermore, as in the United States, religion in Brazil was used by churchmen to buttress slavery. One priest told a group of planters: "Confession is the antidote to insurrections, because the confessor makes the slave see that his master is in the place of his father to whom he owes love, respect, and obedience. . . ."[13]

In 1887, on the eve of abolition in Brazil, the abolitionist Anselmo Fonseca wrote a long book castigating the Brazilian Catholic clergy for its lack of interest in the then highly active abolitionist movement in his country. Caustically he observed that in 1871 when Rio Branco fought for the Law of the Free Womb of slave mothers, the Church was silent, for slavery "still had much vitality. . . . It was dangerous to take it on frontally. Why did not the Bishops then show the solidarity and courage and the energy with which in 1873-74 they combated Masonry and the government?" Fonseca draws the interesting contrast between the massive indifference to the plight of the slave on the part of the Brazilian Catholic Church throughout the history of slavery and the activities of Protestant clergymen like William Ellery Channing in behalf of the slave in the United States.[14]

Slave marriages were valid in the eyes of the Brazilian Church; marriages of slaves in Protestant churches in the United States also qualified as sacramental acts, though masters, it was understood, were not bound to honor such unions. Given the weakness of the Church's control over slave masters, it is not likely that marriages of slaves in Brazil were any more enduring or protected from disruption through sale than in the United States. In any event, in Brazil only a small proportion of slaves were married by the Church. Early in the nineteenth century the reformer José Bonifacio asked for laws to compel masters to permit slaves to marry freely and to require that at least two-thirds of a master's slaves be married. Yet, forty years later, travelers still reported that few Negros were married and that "rarely were [marriages] confirmed by a religious act." A traveler in 1841 found only 10 slaves married out of 2,500 on the Isle of Santa Catherina in southern Brazil. In northeastern Brazil, in Rio Grande do Norte, a local document listed only about 5 per cent of the 13,000 slaves in the province in 1874 as married or widowed, though 30 per cent of free persons were married. Of the 660,000 slaves in all of Brazil in 1875, who were 14 years or older, only about 1 out of 6 was recorded as married or widowed.[15]

In the United States the lack of protection for the informal slave family is acknowledged as a fact of slave life. Tannenbaum has summarized it well: "Under the law of most of the Southern states there was no regard for the Negro family, no question of the right of the owner to sell his slaves separately, and no limitation upon separating husband and wife, or child from its mother."[16]

Yet, for most of the nineteenth century, the same generalization is quite accurate for Brazil. Prior to 1869 there was no legal protection for the slave family, though, as was the case in the United States, a vigorous internal slave trade was a powerful cause for the breaking up of many families, whether their ties had been solemnized by the Church or not. The internal slave trade in Brazil was especially active in the middle years of the nineteenth century when the coffee areas in the South were expanding and thousands of slaves were brought down from the economically declining Northeast. One estimate in 1862 put at five thousand per year the number arriving from the North at Rio de Janeiro by coastal shipping alone. A modern authority has cited thirty thousand a year as the number that went from the North to the state of São Paulo between 1850 and 1870.[17]

There is little doubt that the disruption of the slave family was common in Brazil at least prior to 1869. Indeed, to take an extreme example, one of the great Brazilian abolitionists, Luis Gama, was sold into slavery by his own white father. Stanley Stein reports that in the 1870s it was not unknown in Vassouras for a planter to sell his mulatto offspring to a passing slave trader.[18] A law passed in 1875, prohibiting the sale of one's own children, suggests that such a practice was known even at that late date.[19] Another sign that the slave family was disintegrating throughout the nineteenth century, at least, is that antislavery reformers like Bonifacio in the early nineteenth century and others as late as 1862 were demanding that ways be found to protect the slave family.[20] In 1854 Baron Cotegipe, who was later to oppose abolition, argued for limitations on the internal slave trade because it disrupted families. "It is a horror, gentlemen," he told the Senate, "to see children ripped from their mothers, husbands separated from wives, parents from children! Go to Law Street . . . and be outraged and touched by the spectacle of such sufferings. . . ." In 1866 Perdigão Malheiro was still asking that the law prevent the separation of married slave couples and children of less than seven years of age. Without such legal protection, he contended, there was little reason to expect the slave family to exist at all.[21]

The fact is that in Brazil prior to 1869 there was no law preventing the disruption of slave families. And even the law passed in 1869 required some nine years of agitation before it was enacted.[22] Most slave states in the United States, as Tannenbaum has pointed out, never enacted such laws, but a few did. A law of 1829 in Louisiana prohibited the sale of children under ten; apparently it was adhered to by slave traders. Laws in Alabama and Georgia forbade the dissolution of inherited slave families, but not others. In practice, probably most planters in the United States tried to avoid breaking up slave families, though undoubtedly many were disrupted.[23]

Perhaps the most frequently stressed difference between slavery in

Latin America and the United States concerns manumission. Yet, even here, as Davis has pointed out, manumission in Brazil was not unlimited, and in the United States it was not absolutely denied.[24] The purchase of freedom by the slave himself, so much emphasized in discussions on Brazilian slavery, was, moreover, far from rare in the United States. Sumner Matison, for example, found several hundred examples of self-purchase. Luther Jackson, studying self-purchase in three cities of Virginia, found twenty examples even at the height of the sectional conflict of the 1850s and despite a law requiring removal of manumitted slaves out of the state.[25]

On the Brazilian side of the comparison it must be said that prior to 1871, despite tradition and the assertions of Tannenbaum and Elkins,[26] there was no law requiring a master to permit a slave to buy his freedom. One American historian of Brazil made a search for such a law, but found none before 1871, when emancipationists insisted upon it; this suggests that the practice of self-purchase was not as firmly protected as has been alleged.[27] It is true that in Brazilian law there were none of the limitations that became increasingly common in the southern United States after 1830. Under Brazilian law emancipation was legal in almost any form: by letter, by will, or by explicit statement at baptism.[28] In Brazil, moreover, there were no statutes requiring the removal of emancipated slaves to other states, though such laws were characteristic of the southern United States. But Brazilian law contained a curious qualification to its otherwise liberal policy on emancipation: freedom might be revoked by the master for ingratitude on the part of the freedman, even if that ingratitude was expressed only orally and outside of the presence of the former master. Perdigão Malheiro, who reports this provision of the law, doubted that it was still valid in 1866. In 1871 the power to revoke freedom was explicitly withdrawn in an antislavery law, suggesting that the old provision was not such a dead letter that opponents of slavery were willing to let it remain on the statute books.[29] The provision also raises a question as to whether the law in Brazil was in fact helping to preserve the Negro's moral personality as some modern historians have argued. At the very least it encouraged masters to think of their Negroes as minors or wards rather than as persons on an equal footing. At worst, it perpetuated in the Negro that sense of subordination and inferiority derived from the degraded status of slavery, thereby counteracting whatever elevating effects flow from the relative ease of manumission.

Some modern historians, like Tannenbaum and Elkins,[30] have emphasized the slave's right to hold property in Latin America and therefore to be in a position to buy his freedom, as contrasted with the lack of that right in the United States. In Brazil, however, the law did not permit slaves to possess property, or a peculium, until near the end of the era of slavery.

Perdigão Malheiro writes in his treatise on slave law that, as late as 1866, "Among us, no law guarantees to the slave his peculium; nor the disposition overall by the last will, nor the succession. . . ." However, he goes on, most masters tolerated the slave's holding property, generally permitting the slave to use it as he saw fit.[31] The same situation prevailed, by and large, in the United States, where slave property was neither recognized nor protected by law, but in practice was generally recognized by the master. Occasionally the courts would throw a protective arm around the peculium, as in a South Carolina case in 1792, when a slave was held capable of holding property separate from that of his master. On the basis of that case, a half century later, Judge J. B. O'Neall of South Carolina concluded that "by the law of this state a slave might acquire personal property." [32]

Yet, after all these qualifications have been made in the usually optimistic picture of manumission under Brazilian slavery, Brazil still appears to have been more liberal on manumission than was the United States. And the principal reason for this conclusion is the higher proportion of free Negroes in Brazil than in the United States. Because of the paucity of adequate figures for both countries, a quantitative comparison can be made only for the nineteenth century. In 1817–18 the number of slaves in Brazil was about three times that of free Negroes and mulattoes.[33] This ratio may be compared with that in the United States in 1860, when the number of free Negroes reached its maximum under slavery. At that date there were eight times as many slaves as free Negroes in the whole of the United States and sixteen times as many slaves if the comparison is made in the slave states only. As slavery came to an end in Brazil the number of free Negroes grew enormously, so that in 1872 the number of free Negroes and colored was more than double that of the slaves.[34]

Although it is not the intention of this essay to explain this difference in attitude toward manumission, if only because of the complexity of the issue, at least two suggestions are worth brief examination. One of these is that Brazilian masters were freeing the sick and the old in order to relieve themselves of responsibility and cost. Denunciations in newspapers and laws prohibiting such practices indicate that masters were indeed freeing their infirm, aged, and incurable slaves.[35] Yet it is difficult to believe that such practices, however widespread they appear to be, could have been the principal source of the relatively large free colored population. Infirm, aged, or sick slaves simply would not have been numerous enough or have been able to produce offspring in sufficient numbers to account for the great number of free colored.

Marvin Harris has advanced a more reasonable explanation, in which he emphasizes the differences in the processes of settlement and economic development in Brazil and the United States.[36] In Brazil a freed Negro or mulatto had a place in a society that was only sparsely populated and in a slave economy that was focused upon staple production. Free blacks and mulattoes were needed in the economy to produce food, to serve as slave catchers, militiamen, shopkeepers, craftsmen, artisans, and so forth. They filled the many petty jobs and performed the "interstitial" work of the economy that slave labor could not easily perform and that white labor was insufficient to man. Octavio Ianni, writing about slavery in southern Brazil, and Nelson de Senna, describing conditions in Minas Gerais, emphasize the great variety of occupations filled by free Negroes and mulattoes.[37]

In the southern United States many plantations also allocated their labor in this fashion, that is, by importing food rather than growing it. But the food was produced by a large number of nonslaveholding whites in the South and the Northwest. Virtually from the beginning of settlement in the South there had been more than enough whites to perform all the tasks of the society except that of compulsory labor. In fact, throughout the ante-bellum years, as later, the South exported whites to the rest of the nation. Hence, in the United States there was no compelling economic reason for emancipation; nor, more importantly, was there any economic place for those who were manumitted. But this demographic or materialist interpretation is not the complete explanation, suggestive as it is. As we shall see later, the relative ease of manumission in Brazil was part of a larger and deeper difference in attitudes between the two societies.

Comparisons between slavery in Brazil and the United States traditionally emphasize the greater rebelliousness of slaves in Brazil. But here, too, the distinction, when examined closely, is not as sharp as has frequently been alleged. The most often mentioned measure of the greater rebelliousness of Brazilian slaves is the large slave hideaway or *quilombo* of Palmares in northeastern Brazil, which, during the seventeenth century, resisted the attacks of government and other troops for more than fifty-years. Examples of other *quilombos*, less spectacular or famous than Palmares, are also well documented.[38] It is questionable, however, whether such groups of runaways, no matter how long lived or large scale, ought to be classed as slave rebellions. Generally the *quilombos* neither attempted to overthrow the slave system nor made war on it, except when whites sought to destroy them. Even Palmares would have been content to remain as an African state separate from white society if the government and the *paulistas* had left it alone.[39] Thus, if one is counting armed uprisings against slaveholders, such as took place under Nat Turner in Virginia in 1831, then the total number in Brazil is considerably smaller if one excludes the *quilombos*. For in Brazil, as in the United States, the most common expression of slave unrest was the runaway, not the insurrectionist.

Rumors of revolts were common in both countries, but, except during the last years of slavery and with the exception of a series of revolts in Bahia in the early nineteenth century, slave revolts in Brazil were scattered, and in some areas almost nonexistent. Koster, the English planter, wrote in the early nineteenth century that "Pernambuco has never experienced any serious revolt among the slaves." Modern historians of the coffee region point out that neither slave revolts nor *quilombos* were on anything but a small scale. Da Costa speaks of revolts as "rare in the coffee regions." F. H. Cardoso also found little opportunity for, or evidence of, slave revolts in Rio Grande do Sul. Girão writes that in Ceará Province in the early nineteenth century "fugitives were not common and rebellions very rare." Octavio Eduardo reports that "no series of revolts occurred in Maranhão as they did in Bahia, although the revolt of the Balaios from 1838 to 1841" attracted runaway slaves to the cause.[40]

On the other hand, general works on slave rebellions in Brazil as a whole emphasize their importance, and a recent study of the sugar areas in São Paulo Province refers to the large number of slave rebellions there.[41] In short, much work remains to be done on the extent and character of slave unrest in Brazil, and it seems safe to say that most of the writing on slave rebellions has not been careful to distinguish between military outbreaks and runaways or between those uprisings striking at the slave system directly and those simply fleeing from it, as for example, has been done for American slave revolts by Marion Kilson.[42]

In the broadest sense, of course, both slave rebellions and runaways threatened the slave system, for they constituted avenues by which some slaves could escape from the system and raised the expectations of those who remained behind. In this regard, Brazilian slaves had somewhat greater opportunities for escape than had slaves in the United States. Actual revolts may not have been much more numerous in Brazil, but the numbers of slaves involved in those that did take place were greater, just as the size of the *quilombos* were larger than those in the United States. Stein described a revolt in Vassouras, for example, that mobilized three hundred slaves and required federal troops to suppress it. At least two revolts involving several hundred slaves were reported in 1820 in Minas Gerais. In the first half of the nineteenth century in the province of Espírito Santo, uprisings of two hundred and four hundred slaves occurred, though it is not clear whether these were revolts or collective runaways.[43]

The really striking examples of undoubted slave insurrections are the half dozen that erupted in and around the city of Bahia between 1807 and 1835, several of which involved pitched battles between armed slaves and government troops. It is significant that these rebellions occurred in the city, not in the plantation region. They are, moreover, among the few that can be confidently classified as violent attacks upon whites and the slave system rather than as flights to a *quilombo*.[44] But, in the history of Brazilian slavery, the Bahian revolts were unusual and, as we shall see, the consequence of special circumstances.

There were true slave revolts in the United States, too, though they were fewer and generally much smaller in number of participants than in Brazil. Of the three biggest and best-known uprisings, those at Stono, South Carolina, in 1739, New Orleans in 1811, and Southampton, Virginia, in 1831, only the second involved more than one hundred slaves. The *quilombos* in the United States were considerably fewer and smaller in size than those in Brazil.[45] The climate in the United States was largely responsible for the smaller number of maroons, or *quilombos*. In most of the United States the winter is simply too harsh for a *quilombo* to survive for very long, whereas the greater part of Brazil lies in the tropics. The frontier area in the United States was, moreover, too well settled and, accordingly, too well policed, especially after the seventeenth century, to provide many opportunities for colonies of runaways. The only example of a *quilombo* approaching the size and endurance of Palmares was the Second Seminole War, during which Indians and runaway blacks held out against the United States Army for seven years.[46] It is significant that the struggle took place in the warmest part of the United States and in an area unsettled by whites.

Another difference between the two slave societies was the dependence of the Brazilians upon the African slave trade. Although the foreign slave trade in Brazil was supposedly ended in 1831 by treaty with Great Britain, all authorities agree that importations of slaves continued at high annual rates for another twenty years. Over 300,000 slaves entered Brazil between 1842 and 1851 alone, bringing the total number of slaves in the country to 2,500,000 in 1850, probably the highest figure ever reached.[47] There is also general agreement that the importation of large numbers of slaves into the United States ceased in 1807, with the federal prohibition of the foreign trade. Actually, every one of the slave states themselves had prohibited importation prior to 1800. Only South Carolina reopened the trade before the federal government finally closed it. Thus even before 1807 the influx of native Africans had decreased considerably.

The larger number of recently imported Africans in Brazil all through the history of slavery probably accounts for the greater number of revolts there.[48] Revolts were hard enough to organize and carry out under any circumstances, but they were especially difficult under a slave system like that in the United States where the slaves were principally native and almost entirely shorn of their African culture or identity. In Brazil the presence of thousands of newly arrived Africans, alienated from their new masters and society while often united by their common African tribal culture, was undoubtedly a source of slave rebellion. Stein calls attention to a rash of attempted uprisings in Vassouras in the 1840s just as the number of imported Africans reached its peak. Particularly in the cities were the slaves able to retain their African languages, dances, religious rites, and other customs, even though the authorities, aware of the nucleus such African traits provided for discontent and revolt, attempted to suppress them.[49] It is certainly not accidental that the greatest revolts in Brazil were in the city of Bahia and that they were generally led by Hausa and Yoruba Negroes, who were Muslims. A common African tribal culture, language, and religion provided the necessary cement of organization and the incentives to resistance, which were almost wholly lacking among the slaves in the United States. It is significant that the documents captured from the Bahian rebels in 1835 were written in Arabic script, and, though there is some doubt as to the extent of the religious basis for the revolt, a number of the leaders were clearly Muslims.[50] In the nineteenth century, coffee planters in the southern part of Brazil were so conscious of the dangers of newly arrived slaves from the same African tribal background that they limited their purchases of such slaves to small numbers in order to minimize revolts. C. R. Boxer writes that the diversity of African nations among the slaves in eighteenth-century Minas Gerais was the chief safeguard against the outbreak of revolts.[51]

The connections between Brazil and Africa were so close in the nineteenth century that some slaves, after they earned their freedom or otherwise gained manumission, elected to return to Africa. One historian, for example, has reported on a number of leaders of nineteenth-century Nigerian society who had been slaves in Brazil, but who after manumission returned to Africa to make a living in the slave trade. So intimate was the connection between Brazil and Africa that until 1905 at least—almost twenty years after abolition—ships plied between Bahia and Lagos, "repatriating nostalgic, emancipated Negroes and returning with West Coast products much prized by Africans and their descendants in Brazil." [52] In striking contrast is the well-known reluctance of Negroes in the United States during the ante-bellum years to have anything to do with removal to Africa. That contrast emphasizes once again the overwhelmingly native character of slavery in the United States and the dearth of African survivals.

The persistence, and even expansion, of the slave system of the United States without any substantial additions from importations is unique in history. Neither in antiquity nor in Latin America was a slave system sustained principally by reproduction. Even if one accepts the highest figure for smuggling into the United States—270,000 in the fifty years prior to 1860, or about 5,000 a year—the figure can hardly account for the steady and large increase in the slave population recorded by the decennial censuses. For example, in the 1790s, prior to the federal closing of the slave trade, the increase was 30 percent; in the 1840s the increase was still 28 percent, while the absolute average annual figures were 20,000 and 70,000, respectively. In short, it seems clear that reproduction was the principal source of slaves for the United States, at least since the first census.[53] One consequence was that the ratio between the sexes was virtually equal, a fact that was conducive to holding slaves in so-called family units as well as to breeding. (It was also conducive to greater control over the slaves.) Thus the ratio between the sexes in Mississippi counties according to the census of 1860 was about the same as among the whites. In 1860 in all of the southern slave states the numerical difference between the sexes was 3 percent or less of the total, except in Louisiana where the surplus of males was 3.6 percent. This ratio among the slaves was closer to an absolute balance between the sexes than obtained among the whites themselves in five southern states, where the surplus of males ran between 4 and 8 percent of the white population. Thus in both the so-called breeding and consuming regions of the South the sexes were remarkably well balanced.

Although Gilberto Freyre writes of the Brazilian master's interest in the "generative belly" of the female slave, other writers make clear that slave breeding was not important to Brazilian slaveholders. Stein, for example, found a genuine reluctance among slaveholders to breed and rear slaves; the very hours during which male and female slaves could be together were deliberately limited. Lynn Smith cites a number of sources to show that masters consciously restricted slave reproduction by locking up the sexes separately at night.[54]

Undoubtedly the availability of slaves from Africa accounts for some of the lack of interest in slave breeding in Brazil prior to 1851. For within five years after the closing of the slave trade, books began to appear in Brazil advising planters to follow the example of Virginians, who were alleged to be such efficient breeders of slaves that the infants were bought while still in the mother's womb.[55] These exhortations do not seem to have had much effect, however, for twenty years after the end of the African slave trade the slaveholder's customary rationale for not raising slaves was still being advanced:

One buys a Negro for 300 milreis, who harvests in the course of the year 100 arobas of coffee, which produces a net profit at least equal to the cost of the slave; thereafter everything is profit. It is not worth the trouble to raise children, who, only after sixteen years, will give equal service. Furthermore, the pregnant Negroes and those nursing are not available to use the hoe; heavy fatigue prevents the regular development of the fetus in some; in others the diminution of the flow of milk, and in almost all, sloppiness in the treatment of the children occurs, from which sickness and death of the children result. So why raise them? [56]

And apparently infant mortality among slaves was amazingly high, even after the foreign slave trade had ended. One authority on the coffee region has placed it as high as 88 percent. The census of 1870 revealed that in the city of Rio de Janeiro the mortality of slave children exceeded births by 1.8 percent; even this shocking figure must have been a minimum since most slaves in Rio were domestic and presumably better cared for than agricultural slaves. Rio Branco, the Brazilian statesman who gave his name to an important emancipationist law, calculated that on the basis of the excess of slave deaths over births alone slavery would die out within seventy-five years. And although the British minister at Rio, W. D. Christie, was highly incensed at Brazilian complacency over the persistence of slavery, he had to admit in 1863 in a report to his home government that

the slave population is decreasing, though not considerably. . . . The mortality among the children of slaves is very great; and Brazilian proprietors do not appear to have given nearly so much attention as might have been expected, from obvious motives of self-interest, to marriages among slaves, or the care of mothers or children.[57]

One undoubted consequence of the continuance of the foreign slave trade was that Brazilian planters made no effort to balance the sexes among the slaves. Since male slaves were stronger and more serviceable, they apparently constituted the overwhelming majority of the importations throughout the history of Brazilian slavery. According to one authority, on some plantations there were no female slaves. For Brazil as a whole he estimates that one Negro woman was imported for each three or four males. The statistics compiled by Stein for Vassouras support that estimate, for he found that between 1820 and 1880 70 percent or more of the African-born slaves were males. Robert Conrad, quoting from the records of captured slave ships in the 1830s and 1840s, found ratios of one to four and one to five in favor of males.[58] The heavy imbalance between the sexes meant that once the slave trade was stopped, Brazilian slavery began to decline, for the paucity of women, not to mention the masters' lack of interest in breeding, ensured that the reduction in the foreign supply of slaves would not be easily or quickly made up.

The imbalance between the sexes in Brazil may help also to explain the somewhat greater number of rebellions and runaways in that country as compared with the United States. In the United States, with slaves more or less divided into family units, for a male slave to rebel or to run away meant serious personal loss, since he probably would have to leave women and children behind. Such a consequence was much less likely in Brazil.

One indication that the pairing of the sexes in the United States reduced rebelliousness is provided by a report from São Paulo toward the last years of slavery when masters were quoted as saying about a restless or rebellious slave: "It is necessary to give the Negro in marriage and give him a piece of land in order to calm him down and cultivate responsibility in him." [59]

Although it is often said or implied that slavery in Latin America in general was milder than in the United States,[60] there are several reasons for believing that in a comparison between Brazil and the United States the relationship is just the reverse. Admittedly such comparisons are difficult to make since the evidence that might be mustered on either side is open to serious doubts as to its representativeness. But this problem can be circumvented in part, at least, if general classes of evidence are used. There are at least three general reasons, aside from any discrete examples of treatment of slaves, suggesting that slavery was harsher in Brazil than in the United States. First, the very fact that slavery in the United States was able to endure and expand on the basis of reproduction alone is itself strong testimony to a better standard of physical care. It is true that the imbalance of the sexes in Brazil played a part in keeping down reproduction, but the high mortality of slave children and the care and expense involved probably account for the reluctance to rear slaves in the first place. Moreover, as we have seen, even after the slave trade was closed, the rearing of slave children was still resisted in Brazil. Masters said that it was easier to raise three or four white children than one black child, the difference being attributed to the "greater fragility of the black race." In 1862 a French visitor reported that "the most simple hygienic measures are almost always neglected by the owners of slaves, and the mortality of '*negrillons*' is very considerable, especially on the plantations of the interior." [61] Brazilians, in short, simply did not take sufficient care of their slaves for them to reproduce.

Second, there are kinds of severe and cruel treatment of slaves in Brazil that rarely occurred in the United States. A number of Brazilian sources, both during the colonial period and under the Empire in the nineteenth century, speak of the use of female slaves as prostitutes.[62] So far as I know, this source of income from slaves was unknown or very rare in the United States. Brazilian sources also contain numerous references to the use of iron or tin masks on slaves, usually to prevent them from eating dirt or drinking liquor. Indeed, the practice of using masks was sufficiently common that pictures of slaves wearing them appear in books on slavery. I have yet to see such a picture in the literature of slavery in the United States, and references to the use of the mask are rare, though not unknown.[63] As already noted, Brazilian sources call attention to another practice that also suggests severe treatment: the freeing of ill, old, or crippled slaves in order to escape the obligation of caring for them. The several efforts to legislate against this practice, much less to put a stop to it, were fruitless until just before the abolition of slavery.[64] Finally, because of the imbalance of the sexes, most slaves in Brazil had no sexual outlets at all.

Though making comparisons of physical treatment may have pitfalls, the effort has value because such comparisons give some insight into the nature of the slave systems in the two countries. Some authorities, like Elkins, for example,[65] argue that a comparative analysis of treatment is not germane to a comparison of the impact of slavery on the Negro, for "in one case [Latin America] we would be dealing with cruelty of man to men, and in the other [the United States], with the care, maintenance, and indulgence of men toward creatures who were legally and morally *not* men. . . ." But this argument collapses, as Davis has pointed out,[66] when it can be shown that the law in Brazil and the United States defined the slave as both a man and a thing. Under such circumstances, treatment can no longer be confidently separated from attitudes. Instead, the way a master treats a slave, particularly *when the slave is a member of a physically identifiable class*, becomes a part of the historian's evidence for ascertaining the attitude of white men toward black men who are slaves, and of the way in which blacks are conditioned to think of themselves. When a master muzzles a slave, for example, he is literally treating him like a dog. The master's behavior, at the very least, is evidence for concluding that he considered his slave on the level with a dog; at the most, his behavior suggests that its source was the belief that the slave was from the beginning no better than a dog. In either case, the master's treatment of the slave is part of the evidence to be evaluated in ascertaining white men's attitudes toward black slaves. Perhaps even more important is the real possibility that a slave who is muzzled or who sees other black men muzzled may well be led to think of himself as a dog, worthy of being muzzled. In short, the treatment accorded black slaves in both societies is relevant to the question of how white men think about black men.

A second reason for making a comparison of physical treatment is to call attention to the importance of the slave trade in accounting for some of the differences between slavery in Brazil and the United States. Brazilians simply did not have to treat their slaves with care or concern when new slaves were obtainable from outside the system. That the slave trade played this role was recognized by Perdigão Malheiro in 1866, after the trade had been stopped for fifteen years. He asserted that since the closing of the traffic from abroad the treatment of slaves in Brazil had improved. No longer, he wrote, did one "meet in the streets, as in other not remote times, slaves with their faces covered by a wire mask or a great weight on the foot. . . ." Slaves were so well dressed and shod, he continued, "that no one would know who they are," that is, they could not be distinguished from free blacks. Two visiting Americans noticed the same change even earlier:

Until 1850, when the slave-trade was effectually put down, it was considered cheaper, on the country plantations to use up a slave in five or seven years, and purchase another, than to take care of him. This I had, in the interior, from intelligent native Brazilians, and my own observation has confirmed it. But, since the inhuman traffic has ceased, the price of slaves has been enhanced, and the selfish motives for taking greater care of them have been increased.[67]

But it needs to be added that the closing of the foreign slave trade in Brazil had at least one worsening effect upon the lot of the slave. It undoubtedly increased the internal slave trade, thereby enhancing the likelihood of the dissolution of slave families. Prior to 1850 the foreign slave trade probably kept to a minimum the movement of established slaves from one part of the country to another. In the United States, on the other hand, slaves prior to 1850 probably experienced more disruption of families, simply because the foreign slave trade was closed and the opening of new areas in the Southwest provided a growing market for slaves, who had to be drawn from the older regions, especially the upper South.

One of the earliest signs of discrimination against Negroes in seventeenth-century Virginia, Maryland, and even New England was the legal denial of arms to blacks, free or slave, but not to white indentured servants.[68] This discrimination constitutes perhaps the sharpest difference between the slave systems of the United States and Brazil. Almost from the beginning of settlement, the Portuguese and then the Brazilians permitted not only Negroes, but slaves themselves, to be armed. Arthur Ramos has eves suggested that whites encouraged the slaves to arm themselves.[69] During the wars against the French and the Dutch invaders in the sixteenth and seventeenth centuries, large numbers of slaves and free Negroes fought on the side of the Brazilians. The Dutch occupation of northeastern Brazil, which entailed almost continuous warfare, lasted for a quarter of a century. Negroes, slave and free, also fought in the War of the Farrapos in southern Brazil against the Empire in the late 1830s. Indeed, as Roger Bastide has written, "the Negro appears in all the civil revolts, the war of the *paulistas* against the Emboabos, the wars of national independence, and one even sees them in the party struggles under the Empire, between royalists and republicans or in the rivalries of political leaders among themselves." Slaves served in the Paraguayan War of 1865–70, often being sent by masters to fight in their places or to win favor with the Emperor. Fugitive slaves also served in the Brazilian army in the nineteenth century. At the end of the Paraguayan War some twenty thousand slaves who had served in the army were given their freedom.[70]

When comparable occasions arose in the United States the results were quite different. During the American Revolution, for example, Henry and John Laurens, leading figures in South Carolina, proposed in 1779 that slaves be enlisted to help counter the military successes of the British in the southern colonies. It was understood that the survivors would be freed. Although the Laurenses were joined by a few other South Carolinians and the Continental Congress approved of the plan, the South Carolina legislature overwhelmingly rejected it. The Laurenses raised the issue again in 1781, but once more the proposal was rejected by both the South Carolina and Georgia legislatures. When the slave South was faced with a struggle for survival during the Civil War it again steadfastly refused to use slave soldiers until the very last month of the war; indeed, the Confederacy rejected even free Negroes when they offered their services at the beginning of the war.[71]

That slaves in Brazil were often armed and that they rarely were in the United States is obviously a significant difference between the practices of slavery in the two places. To arm Negro slaves surely affects how one feels about Negroes, whether slave or free. As Octavio Ianni has observed, concerning the use of Negro slaves in the Paraguayan War, Brazilian whites could not help but obtain a new and larger view of Negro capabilities when blacks served as defenders of the nation.[72] How can this difference in practice be explained?

A part of the explanation is undoubtedly related to the quite dissimilar colonial histories of the two countries. Sixteenth-century Brazil was a tiny, sparsely settled colony, desperately clinging to the coast, yet attractive to foreign powers because of its wealth, actual and potential. At different times during the sixteenth and seventeenth centuries the French and Dutch attempted to wrest the colony from Portugal by actual invasion. Since the mother country was too weak to offer much help, all the resources of the colony had to be mobilized for defense, which included every scrap of manpower, including slaves. The recourse to armed slaves, it is worth noticing, was undertaken reluctantly. For as Ramos writes, Negroes were first used only as a kind of advanced guard, being denied a place in the regular army during the sixteenth and seventeenth centuries. But as the need for soldiers continued and a new generation of Brazilian-born Negroes entered the scene, the whites came to demand that they serve in the armed forces. That the acceptance of Negro troops was the result of circumstances rather than ideology is shown by the fact that the Negroes were usually segregated until the years of the Empire, and even when they were no longer set apart, "whites tended to occupy the military posts of major responsibility."[73] Use of Negroes in the colonial period was, therefore, not the result of the prior acceptance of the colored man as an equal, but of the need of him as a fighter. Throughout the eighteenth century, as before, the law *denied* Negroes and mulattoes the right to carry arms.[74]

In striking contrast is the history of the Negro in the British colonies of North America, where conditions and circumstances of settlement and development differed. In the first fifty years of settlement, when the necessities of defense might have encouraged the arming of slaves, there were very few blacks available. As is well known, in the South white indentured servants made up the great preponderance of the unfree labor supply until the end of the seventeenth century. Even at that time, in both Maryland and Virginia, Negroes constituted considerably less than one-fifth of the population. Meanwhile, the white population, servant and free, had long been more than adequate for purposes of defense. Unlike the situation in Brazil, moreover, colonial Englishmen experienced no foreign invasions and only an occasional foreign threat. In short, neither at the beginning nor at the close of the formative seventeenth century were English colonists under any pressure to use Negroes or slaves as defensive troops. As a consequence they could indulge their acute awareness of their difference in appearance, religion, and culture from Africans by permitting their social institutions to reflect this awareness. Thus in both the southern and northern colonies Negroes were resolutely kept from bearing arms. At one time, in 1652, Massachusetts had enlisted Indians and Negroes in the militia, but in 1656 this policy was reversed by the statement that "henceforth no negroes or Indians, altho servants of the English, shalbe armed or permitted to trayne." In 1660 Connecticut also excluded Indians and "negar servants" from the militia.[75]

There is one exception to the English colonists' attitudes toward the arming of slaves, but it is an exception that proves the rule. Early in the eighteenth century, when South Carolina was weak and threatened by Spanish invasion, slaves were required to be trained in the use of arms and included in an auxiliary militia.[76] The policy, however, was only temporary, since the colony was soon able to protect itself by dependence upon whites alone and the feared invasions did not materialize.

Further differences in attitudes toward Negroes and slaves in the United States and in Brazil are the responses that the two societies made to the threat of slave insurrections. In both societies, it should be said, fear of slave revolts was widespread. One of the several measures that whites in the southern United States took to forestall slave insurrections was to place restrictions upon free Negroes, who were widely believed to be fomenters of slave conspiracies and revolts. Thus the uncovering in 1822 of a plot allegedly organized by the free Negro Denmark Vesey moved South Carolina and other southern states to enact new and stricter limitations on the free movement of Negroes. Fear of the free Negro as a potential instigator of slave revolts was also the principal reason for the many restrictions placed upon manumission in the southern states during the nineteenth century. The most common limitation was the requirement that all newly manumitted Negroes must leave the state. At the end of the antebellum era several southern states so feared the influence of the free Negro that they enacted laws prohibiting manumission; at least one state passed a law requiring the enslavement of all free Negroes found within the state after a certain date.[77] White society obviously saw a connection between the Negro slave and the free Negro; the important thing was not that one was free and the other a slave, but that both belonged to the same race.

In one sense, of course, Brazilian slavery was also racially based. Only Negroes, and, for a while, Indians, were slaves, though in Brazil, as in the United States, there was an occasional slave who was fair-skinned and with blue eyes, so that he was a white in everything but status.[78] But in Brazil the connection between the inferior status of slavery and race did not persist into freedom to the same extent that it did in the United States. If slaveholders in the United States viewed the free Negro as a potential threat to the slave system, their counterparts in Brazil saw him as a veritable prop to the system of slavery. Many, if not most of the *capitães de mato* (bush captains or slave catchers), for example, were mulattoes or Negroes. One nineteenth-century Brazilian asserted that two-thirds of the overseers, slave catchers, and slave dealers in Bahia were either mulattoes or blacks. Moreover, many free blacks and mulattoes showed little if any interest in abolition, and some, evidently, actively opposed the end of slavery.[79] In Brazil, in other words, more important than race in differentiating between men was legal status. The mere fact that a man was a Negro or a mulatto offered no presumption that he would identify with slaves.

The refusal of Brazilians to lump together free Negroes and slaves is reflected also in their failure to justify slavery on grounds of race. For, contrary to the prevailing situation in the southern United States, in Brazil there was no important proslavery argument based upon the biological inferiority of the Negro. It is true that a racist conception of the black man existed in nineteenth-century Brazil,[80] but defenders of slavery on clearly racist grounds were rare among public supporters of the institution. A Brazilian historian has written that in the debates in the Brazilian legislature concerning the treaty with Britain in 1827 that closed the international slave trade, only one member of that body clearly asserted the racial inferiority of Negroes, though other kinds of defenses of slavery were made.[81] A French commentator in 1862 noted that in Brazil slaveholders "do not believe themselves obliged, like their American colleagues, to invent for the Negro a new original sin, nor to erect a system of absolute distinction between the races, nor to place an insurmountable barrier between the offspring of descendants of slaves and of those of free men." [82] The most common defenses of the system were the argument in behalf of property and the assertion that the prosperity of the country depended on slave labor. Some defenders of the institution, even late in the nineteenth century, spoke of it as a "necessary evil," as North Americans had done in the early years of the century. In 1886, as slavery in Brazil was coming under increasing attack from abolitionists, a member of the Brazilian Congress from the coffee district asserted that the planters in his area would have no objection to emancipation if they could be assured of a new, adequate supply of labor, presumably immigrants.[83] Even more dramatic is the fact that some of the principal leaders of the abolition movement who held elective office came from the slaveholding provinces of Brazil. No such willingness to contemplate the wholesale increase in the number of free blacks was thinkable in the slaveholding regions of the United States. Even defenders of slavery in nineteenth-century Brazil spoke of the absence of color prejudice in their country and noted with apparent approval the high position achieved by some Negroes and mulattoes.[84] Leaving aside the assertion that there was no prejudice in Brazil, one would find it difficult indeed to point to a slaveholder in the United States in the middle of the nineteenth century who would utter publicly a similar statement of praise for free Negroes as a class.

What may be concluded from this examination of slavery in Brazil and the United States? That there were in fact differences in the practices of slavery in the two countries there can be no doubt. The explanation for those differences, however, as I have tried to show, is to be sought neither in the laws of the Crown nor in the attitude and practices of the Roman Catholic Church in Brazil. The behavior of neither state nor Church displayed any deep concern about the humanity of the slave, and, in any event, neither used its authority to affect significantly the life of the slave. Certainly demographic, economic, and geographic factors account for some of the differences between the two slave systems that have been explored in this essay. But these materialist explanations do not help us to understand the more interesting and profound difference that emerges from the comparison.

This difference becomes evident only as one contemplates the various specific differences in conjunction with one another. In Brazil the slave was feared, but the black man was not, while in the United States the black man as well as the slave was feared. Once this difference in attitude is recognized, certain differences between the two systems are recognized as stemming from a common source. Thus the willingness of Brazilians to manumit slaves much more freely than North Americans is clearly a result of their not fearing free blacks in great numbers. (Indeed, in Brazil today, a common explanation for the obviously greater acceptance of blacks in northeastern Brazil than in the southern part of the country is that in the North there is a greater proportion of Negroes than in the South. Just the opposite explanation, of course, is current in the United States, where it is said that when Negroes constitute a large proportion of the population they are more likely to be tightly controlled or restricted.) Brazilians, therefore, did not restrict manumission in anything like the degree practiced in the slave states of the United States. This same difference in attitude toward the Negro is also evident in the willingness of Brazilian slaveholders to use blacks as slave catchers and overseers, while in the United States slaveholders in particular and white men in general could scarcely entertain the idea. Finally, this difference emerges when one asks why the slave trade remained open in Brazil to 1851, but was closed in most of the United States before the end of the eighteenth century. Even before the Revolution, in fact, Englishmen in North America had been seeking ways to limit the number of blacks in their midst, free or slave. In 1772, for example, the Virginia legislature asked the Crown to permit it to check the slave traffic since "The importation of slaves into the colonies from the coast of Africa hath long been considered as a trade of great inhumanity, and under its *present encouragement,* we have too much reason to fear, *will endanger the very* existence of your Majesty's American dominions. . . ." This fear that an unimpeded slave trade was dangerous ran through the history of all the English colonies, especially that of South Carolina. One of colonial South Carolina's several laws calling for limitation on the slave trade advocated encouragement to white immigration as "the best way to prevent the mischiefs that may be attended by the great importation of negroes into the province. . . ." In 1786 North Carolina placed a tax on slaves on the ground that "the importation of slaves into this state is productive of evil consequences, and highly impolitic." [85] The widespread fear of Negroes also explains why all but one of the states prohibited the importation of slaves years before the federal prohibition in 1808. Certainly there was a humanitarian motive behind the movement to stop the African slave trade, but also of great importance was the fear that if the importations were not limited or stopped white men would be overwhelmed by black. For as the founding and the work of the American Colonization Society in the nineteenth century reveal, even those people in the slave states who conscientiously opposed slavery did not want the Negro as a free man in the United States.

In Brazil, on the other hand, the slave trade came to an end principally because of pressures from *outside* the society. For a quarter of a century before 1851 the British government badgered the Brazilians to put an end to the trade. It is easy to believe that without the pressure from the British and the humiliating infringements of Brazilian sovereignty by ships of the Royal Navy the Brazilians would have kept the slave trade open even longer. Apparently Brazilians rarely worried, as did the North Americans, that they would be overwhelmed by blacks.

This article opened with the observation that Tannenbaum's work began a long and continuing scholarly debate over the role that slavery in North and South America had played in bringing about a different place for the Negro in the societies of the Western Hemisphere. If the evidence and argument of this essay are sound, then the explanations of the differences offered by Tannenbaum and Elkins, at least as far as Brazil is concerned, are not supported by the evidence. But if Tannenbaum's explanation has to be abandoned, his belief that there was a strikingly different attitude toward blacks in Brazil from that in the United States has not been challenged at all. Rather it has been reinforced. For if factors like demography, geography, and the continuance of the international slave trade in Brazil help to account for some of the differences in the practices of slavery in the two societies, those same factors do not really aid us in explaining why Brazilians feared slaves but not blacks, while North Americans feared both. What is now needed is a more searching and fundamental explanation than can be derived from these factors alone or found in the practices or laws of state and church regarding the slave. Clearly that explanation will have to be sought in more subtle and elusive places, such as among the inherited cultural patterns and social structures and values of the two countries. For it is the argument of this article that the differences between Brazilian and United States slavery, rather than being the sources of the different patterns of race relations in the two countries are, in fact, merely the consequence themselves of deeper divergences in the culture and history of the two peoples.

NOTES

1. The books and articles referred to are: Frank Tannenbaum, *Slave and Citizen: The Negro in the Americas* (New York: A. A. Knopf, 1947); Stanley Elkins, *Slavery: A Problem in American Institutional and Intellectual Life* (Chicago: University of Chicago Press, 1969), the text of which is identical with the first edition of 1959 except for an added appendix; Arnold Sio, "Interpretations of Slavery: The Slave States in the Americas," *Comparative Studies in Society and History* 7 (April 1965): 289–308; and David Brion Davis, *The Problem of Slavery in Western Culture* (Ithaca: Cornell University Press, 1966).

2. It has sometimes been said that the diversity of the crops and topography of

Brazil resulted in a diversity of slavery that makes it difficult if not impossible to generalize about the institution in that country. It is true that slavery in the northeastern sugar regions was different in style from that practiced in Maranhão on the cotton and rice plantations. Writers on Brazilian history have noted, furthermore, that slavery was much harsher in a newly opened province like Maranhão than in the old and declining sugar areas in the northeast. (See Gilberto Freyre, *Nordeste* [Rio de Janeiro: J. Olympio, 1937], p. 219; and Henry Koster, *Travels in Brazil*, 2 vols., 2d ed. [London, 1817], II, p. 292.) But the diversity of crops and terrain and the differences in "styles" of slavery that resulted are well recognized in the United States; the slavery on tobacco farms in Virginia, for example, is often contrasted with the kind of slavery on sugar or cotton plantations in Louisiana. In the United States, moreover, the threat to sell a slave "down the river" reflected a recognition that planters in the newer areas of the Deep South tended to work slaves harder than in the older regions where slavery was more firmly established. Despite their recognitions of regional diversity, however, historians of slavery in the United States have not been prevented from generalizing about the institution; hence, it would seem to be equally legitimate to ignore the regional differences in Brazilian slavery so long as an effort is made to draw evidence from most of the principal slave areas of the country. The regional differences are certainly there in both societies, but they are refinements rather than essentials. One further statement on the problems of comparison: although the literature on slavery in the United States is voluminous, there being a monograph for virtually every southern slave state, the literature on Brazilian slavery is uneven. For some important slave regions like Maranhão and Minas Gerais, for example, there are no monographic studies on slavery at all; scattered references in travel accounts and general histories must be relied upon. On the other hand, for other areas, like the coffee country to the south, two excellent, recently written monographs are available: Stanley Stein, *Vassouras: A Brazilian Coffee County, 1850-1900* (Cambridge, Mass.: Harvard University Press, 1957); and Emilia Viotti da Costa, *Da Senzala à Colônia* (São Paulo: Difusão Européia do Livro, 1966). Of immense importance for its historiographical impact, if nothing else, is the impressionistic, virtuoso performance of Gilberto Freyre, *The Masters and the Slaves* (New York: A. A. Knopf, 1946), which deals primarily with domestic slavery in northeastern Brazil though it purports to speak of slavery in general.

3. Tannenbaum, *Slave and Citizen*, pp. 97–98, 103.

4. Helen T. Catterall, ed., *Judicial Cases Concerning American Slavery and the Negro*, 5 vols. (Washington, D. C.: Carnegie Institution of Washington, 1926), II, p. 530.

5. Charles Sackett Sydnor, *Slavery in Mississippi* (New York: D. Appleton-Century Co., 1933), p. 239.

6. Catterall, *Judicial Cases*, III, p. 247.

7. Agostino Marques Perdigão Malheiro, *A Escravidão no Brasil: Ensaio Historico-Juridico-Social* (reprint of 1867 ed., 2 vols. São Paulo: Edisões Cultura, 1944), I, pp. 39–40, 44–45, 67.

8. See, e.g., Tannenbaum, *Slave and Citizen*, p. 93.

9. Kenneth M. Stampp, *The Peculiar Institution: Slavery in the Ante-Bellum South* (New York: A. A. Knopf, 1956), p. 192, summarizes the situation in the United States as follows: "The law required that masters be humane to their slaves, furnish them adequate food and clothing, and provide care for them during sickness and old age. In short, the law endowed masters with obligations as well as rights and assumed some responsibility for the welfare of the bondsmen." For elaboration of the obligations laid down by law, see ibid., pp. 218–24.

10. Koster, *Travels in Brazil*, I, pp. 375–76; II, p. 237; Da Costa, *Da Senzala*, pp. 295–96. Charles Expilly, a French traveler in Brazil in the 1860s, conceded that in the big cities like Rio a slave might occasionally be able to get to the police to complain of bad treatment, but, away from the cities, it was quite different. There, Expilly wrote, the power of the master was like that of "a feudal baron, who exercises in his dominion the highest and the lowest justice." There were no appeals from his sentences. "No guarantee is conceded to the slave." (Charles Expilly, *Mulheres e costumes do Brasil*, tr. Gastao Penalva [São Paulo: Companhia Editoria Nacional, 1935], p. 361.)

11. João Mauricio Rugendas, *Viagem pitoresca através do Brasil*, tr. Sergio Milliet, 3rd ed. (São Paulo: Livaria Martins, 1941), p. 185.

12. Tannenbaum, *Slave and Citizen*, pp. 62–64, 98; Elkins, *Slavery*, pp. 73, 76–77.

13. Da Costa, *Da Senzala*, pp. 250, 271, 249.

14. Luis Anselmo Fonseca, *A Escravidão, O clero e O abolicionismo* (Bahia, 1887), pp. 440–41, 1–27. The references to Channing are on pages 12–15.

15. Ibid., p. 268; Fernando Henrique Cardoso and Octávio Ianni, *Côr e mobilidade social em Florianapolis* (São Paulo: Companhia Editoria Nacional, 1960), pp. 128–29; Robert Edgar Conrad, "The Struggle for the Abolition of the Brazilian Slave Trade, 1808–53," doctoral dissertation, Columbia University, 1967, pp. 55–56.

16. Tannenbaum, *Slave and Citizen*, p. 77.

17. W. D. Christie, *Notes on Brazilian Questions* (London, 1865), p. 93; Pedro Calmon, *História Social do Brasil*, 3 vols. (São Paulo: Companhia Editoria Nacional, 1937–39), I, p. 151. Roberto Simonsen, "As Consequências economica da abolição," *Revista do Arquivo Municipal de São Paulo* 47 (May 1938): 261, says that in 1888 over two-thirds of the slaves in the Empire were in the provinces of Rio, Minas Gerais, São Paulo, and those to the south. I am indebted to Professor Richard Graham of the University of Utah for this reference.

18. Stein, *Vassouras*, p. 159.

19. Richard M. Morse, *From Community to Metropolis: A Biography of São Paulo, Brazil* (Gainesville, Fla.: University of Florida Press, 1958), p. 146; Magnus Mörner, *Race Mixture in the History of Latin America* (Boston: Little, Brown & Company, 1967), p. 117.

20. Arthur Ramos, *The Negro in Brazil*, tr. Richard Pattee (Washington, D. C.: The Associated Publishers, 1939), pp. 58–59.

21. Maurilio de Gouveia, *História da escravidão* (Rio de Janeiro: publisher unknown, 1955), p. 134; Perdigão Malheiro, *A Escravidão no Brasil*, II, p. 223.

22. Da Costa, *Da Senzala*, pp. 271, 385. The law prohibited selling children under fifteen away from their parents. The so-called Law of the Free Womb of 1871, however, lowered the age to twelve.

23. Joe Gray Taylor, *Negro Slavery in Louisiana* (Baton Rouge, La.: Louisiana Historical Association, 1963), pp. 40–41; Stampp, *Peculiar Institution*, pp. 252, 239–41; Edward W. Phifer, "Slavery in Microcosm: Burke County, North Carolina," *Journal of Southern History* 28 (May 1962): 48.

24. Davis, *Problem of Slavery*, pp. 262–64.

25. Sumner E. Matison, "Manumission by Purchase," *Journal of Negro History* 33 (April 1948): 165; Luther P. Jackson, "Manumission in Certain Virginia Cities," ibid., 15 (July 1930), 306.

26. Tannenbaum, *Slave and Citizen*, p. 54; Elkins, *Slavery*, p. 75.

27. Mary Wilhelmine Williams, "The Treatment of Negro Slaves in the Brazilian Empire: A Comparison with the United States of America," *Journal of Negro History* 15 (July 1930): 331.

28. Perdigão Malheiro, *A Escravidão no Brasil*, I, p. 95.

29. Ibid., pp. 167–68; Gouveia, *História de escravidão*, p. 396. The Code Noir of Louisiana, which also had liberal provisions for manumission, contained the following restrictions: "We command all manumitted slaves to show the profoundest respect to their former masters, to their widows and children, and any injury or insult offered by said manumitted slaves to their former master, their widows or children, shall be punished with more severity than if it had been offered by any other person." (Quoted in Taylor, *Negro Slavery in Louisiana*, p. 16.)

30. Tannenbaum, *Slave and Citizen*, p. 54; Elkins, *Slavery*, p. 246.

31. Perdigão Malheiro, *A Escravidão no Brasil*, I, p. 60.

32. Catterall, *Judicial Cases*, II, pp. 267, 275, n.

33. Agostino Marques Perdigão Malheiro, *A Escravidão no Brasil: ensaio historico-juridico-social* (Rio de Janeiro, 1866), Pt. 3, pp. 13–14.

34. Raymond Sayers, *Negro in Brazilian Literature* (New York: Hispanic Institute in the United States, 1956), p. 7.

35. Da Costa, *Da Senzala*, pp. 262–63; Stein, *Vassouras*, p. 79, n; see also the report of the British minister, August 1852, quoting the effort by the president of the province of Bahia to have the practice stopped by law. The report is given in Christie, *Notes on Brazilian Questions*, pp. 218–19.

36. Marvin Harris, *Patterns of Race in the Americas* (New York: Walker, 1964), pp. 84–89.

37. Octávio Ianni, *As Metamorfoses do escravo* (São Paulo: Difusão Européia do Livro, 1962), p. 175; Nelson de Senna, *Africanos no Brasil* (Bello Horizonte, Brazil: officinas Graphicas Queiroz Breyner Limitada, 1938), p. 62. Caio Prado Junior, *História economica do Brasil* (São Paulo: Editória Brasiliense, 1962), p. 45, asserts that cattle raising in the *sertão* of the northeast required free men rather than slaves.

38. The fullest and most recent account of Palmares in English is R. K. Kent, "Palmares: An African State in Brazil," *Journal of African History* 6 (No. 2, 1965): 161–75. As his title suggests, Kent argues (pp. 163–64) against depicting Palmares as merely a *quilombo*, but that issue is not important in this discussion. Clovis Moura, *Rebeliões da senzala* (São Paulo: Edisóes Zumbí, 1959), contains a number of accounts of *quilombos* aside from Palmares.

39. See Edison Carneiro, *Ladinos e Crioulos (Estudos sôbre o negro no Brasil)* (Rio de Janeiro: Editoria Civiliçào Brasileira, 1964), pp. 30–32, for a statement on this point by an authority on Palmares and *quilombos* in general.

40. Koster, *Travels in Brazil*, II, p. 258; *Relações raciais entre negros e brancos em São Paulo*, ed. Roger Bastide (São Paulo: Editória Anhembi, 1955), p. 199; Da Costa, *Da Senzala*, pp. 300-301, 315; Fernando Henrique Cardoso, *Capitalismo e escravidão no Brasil meridional* (São Paulo: Difusão Européia do Livro, 1962), pp. 159–60; Raimundo Girão, *A Abolição no Ceará* (Forteleza, Ceara: Editoria A. Batista Fontelle, 1956), p. 42; Aderbal Jurema, *Insurreições negras no Brasil* (Recife, Brazil: Casa Mozart, 1935), pp. 53–55; Maura, *Rebeliões de senzala*, pp. 65–66; Octavio da Costa Eduardo, *The Negro in Northern Brazil* (New York: J. J. Augustin, 1948), p. 18.

41. See, e.g., Jurema, *Insurreições negras no Brasil;* Maura, *Rebeliões da senzala;* and Maria Theresa Schorer Petrone, *A Lavoura canaviera em São Paulo* (São Paulo: Difusão Européia do Livro, 1968), pp. 121–25. Professor Graham brought the last reference to my attention.

42. Marion D. de B. Kilson, "Towards Freedom: An Analysis of Slave Revolts in the United States," *Phylon* 25 (2d Quarter, 1964): 175–87.

43. Da Costa, *Da Senzala*, p. 304; Maria Stella de Novaes, *A Escravidão e abolição no Espirito Sante* (Vitória, Brazil: n.p., 1963), p. 77.

44. Ramos, *Negro in Brazil*, pp. 34–37. The basic source for the revolts in Bahia is Raymundo Nina Rodrigues, *Os Africanos no Brasil* (2d ed., São Paulo: Companhia Editoria Nacional, 1935), Chap. II, but Raymond Kent will soon publish a thorough examination of the revolt of 1835, a copy of which he has kindly permitted me to read in typescript.

45. Herbert Aptheker, *American Negro Slave Revolts* (New York: Columbia University Press, 1943), *passim*, and Herbert Aptheker, "Maroons Within the Present Limits of the United States," *Journal of Negro History* 24 (April 1939): 167–84.

46. See Kenneth W. Porter, "Negroes and the Seminole War, 1835–1842," *Journal of Southern History* 30 (November 1964): 427–40.

47. Mauricio Goulart, *Escravidão africana no Brasil* (2d ed., São Paulo: Livraria Martins, 1950), pp. 249–63; the total figure for slaves is given in Stein, *Vassouras*, p. 294. Christie (*Notes on Brazilian Questions*, pp. 69–70) insists that when he was writing, in 1865, slaves numbered three million. The lack of a census makes it impossible to arrive at anything more accurate than estimates.

48. Mörner (*Race Mixture in the History of Latin America*, p. 76) suggests that most slave revolts were led by African-born slaves.

49. Stein, *Vassouras*, p. 145; Da Costa, *Da Senzala*, p. 232; Cardoso and Ianni, *Côr e mobilidade*, pp. 126–27.

50. Ramos, *Negro in Brazil*, pp. 30–31, 36–37; Donald Pierson, *Negroes in Brazil* (Chicago: University of Chicago Press, 1942), pp. 39–40; E. Franklin Frazier, "Some Aspects of Race Relations in Brazil," *Phylon* 3 (Third Quarter, 1942): 290. Kent, in the unpublished article referred to in note 44, above, strongly questions the religious basis for the 1835 revolt in Bahia, which heretofore has been the standard interpretation. (See e.g., Roger Bastide, *Les religions africaines au Brésil* [Paris: Presses Universitaires de France, 1960], p. 146.)

51. Da Costa, *Da Senzala*, pp. 235, 252; Charles Ralph Boxer, *The Golden Age of Brazil, 1695–1750* (Berkeley, Calif.: University of California Press, 1962), pp. 176–77.

52. David A. Ross, "The Career of Domingo Martinez in the Bight of Benin," *Journal of African History* 6, no. 1 (1965): 83. Freyre (*Nordeste*, pp. 130–31) and Da Costa (*De Senzala*, pp. 56–57, n.) also report blacks returning to Africa and acting as slave traders. See also Donald Pierson, "The Educational Process and the Brazilian Negro," *American Journal of Sociology* 48 (May 1943): 695, n.; and Gilberto Freyre, *Ordem e Progresso*, 2d ed. (Rio de Janeiro: J. Olympio, 1962), pp. 572, n. 33. The close connection between Africa and Brazil is forcefully demonstrated in José Honório Rodrigues, *Brazil and Africa* (Berkeley, Calif.: University of California Press, 1965).

53. The above was written before the publication of Philip D. Curtin, *The Atlantic Slave Trade. A Census* (Madison, Wis.: University of Wisconsin Press, 1969). Curtin, p. 234, estimates that after 1808 the total number of slaves entering the United States directly from Africa was fewer than 55,000.

54. Stein, *Vassouras*, p. 155; T. Lynn Smith, *Brazil, People and Institutions* (Baton Rouge, La.: Louisiana State University Press, 1963), p. 130.

55. Da Costa, *Da Senzala*, p. 130.

56. Quoted in Joaquim Nabuco, *O Abolicionismo*, in *Obras completas*, 14 vols. (São Paulo: Instituto Progresso Editorial, 1944–49), VII, pp. 89–90. The book from which Nabuco quoted was published in 1872.

57. Da Costa, *Da Senzala*, p. 256; Gouveia, *História da escravidão*, p. 208; Christie, *Notes on Brazilian Questions*, p. 102, n.

58. Rodrigues, *Brazil and Africa*, p. 159; Stein, *Vassouras*, p. 155; Conrad, "Struggle for Abolition of the Brazilian Slave Trade," p. 55.

59. *Relações raciais entre negros e brancos em São Paulo*, ed. Bastide, p. 81.

60. See, e.g., Elkins, *Slavery*, pp. 77–78.

61. Da Costa, *Da Senzala*, pp. 257–58; Élisée Reclus, "Le Brésil et la Colonisation. II," *Revue des deux mondes*, 40 (July–August 1862): 391.

62. Boxer, *Golden Age of Brazil*, pp. 138, 165; Gilberto Freyre, *Masters and the Slaves*, p. 455.

63. See the picture, e.g., in Da Costa, *Da Senzala*, facing p. 240; Gilberto Freyre, *O Escravo nos anúncios de jornais brasilieros do seculo* xix (Recife, Brazil: Imprênsa Universitária, 1963), p. 100, discusses the use of the mask; Thomas Ewbank, *Life in Brazil* (New York, 1856), pp. 437–38, describes the masks he saw worn on the street. Stampp (*Peculiar Institution*, p. 304) notes that masks were sometimes used in the United States to prevent eating clay. There is a least one reference to masks in that compendium of horrors by Theodore Weld, *American Slavery as It Is* (New York, 1839), p. 76.

64. References to the practice are common. See, e.g., Gouveia, *História da escrividão*, p. 179; Perdigão Malheiro, *A Escravidão no Brasil*, II, pp. 220, 348; Da Costa, *Da Senzala*, p. 263.

65. Elkins, *Slavery*, p. 78, n.

66. Davis, *Problem of Slavery in Western Culture*, p. 229, n.

67. Perdigão Malheiro, *A Escravidão no Brasil*, II, pp. 114–15; D. P. Kidder and J. C. Fletcher, *Brazil and the Brazilians* (Philadelphia, 1857), p. 132.

68. Carl N. Degler, "Slavery and the Genesis of American Race Prejudice," *Comparative Studies in Society and History* 2 (Oct. 1959): 57, 64; see also Winthrop D. Jordan, *White Over Black: American Attitudes toward the Negro, 1550–1812* (Chapel Hill, N. C.: University of North Carolina Press, 1968), pp. 71, 125–26. Jordan notes that free Negroes served in all the wars of colonial New England, but that few slaves served in any colonial militias.

69. Ramos, *Negro in Brazil*, p. 157.

70. Charles R. Boxer, *The Dutch in Brazil, 1624–1654* (Oxford, Eng.: Clarendon Press, 1957), pp. 166–69; Cardoso, *Capitalismo e escravidão*, pp. 153–54, n; Bastide, *Religions africaines au Brésil*, p. 109; Da Costa, *Da Senzala*, p. 401. Ianni (*Metamorfoses*, pp. 175–76) cites an example of a slave being sent by his master to serve in place of a white man; after service, he was freed. Rodrigues (*Brazil and Africa*, pp. 45–52) is one of several sources for the figure of twenty thousand slaves freed after the Paraguayan War.

71. John Alden, *The First South* (Baton Rouge, La.: Louisiana State University Press, 1961), pp. 37–40; Benjamin Quarles, *The Negro in the American Revolution* (Chapel Hill, N. C.: University of North Carolina Press, 1961), pp. 60–67. Some slaves, however, were enlisted by their masters in the northern states, usually as substitutes. On the offer of blacks to support the Confederacy, see D. E. Everett, "Ben Butler and the Louisiana Native Guards, 1861–1862," *Journal of Southern History* 24 (May 1958): 202–4.

72. Ianni, *Metamorfoses*, p. 217.

73. Ramos, *Negro in Brazil*, pp. 151–54.

74. Mörner, *Race Mixture in the History of Latin America*, p. 52.

75. *Records of the Governor and Company of the Massachusetts Bay in New*

England, ed. N. F. Shurteff, 5 vols. (Boston, 1853–54), III, pp. 268, 397; *Public Records of the Colony of Connecticut [1636–1766]*; 15 vols. (Hartford, Conn., 1850–90), I, p. 349. See Jordan, *White over Black*, pp. 122–28, for a survey of legal discrimination against free blacks in the English colonies of North America.

76. Ulrich B. Phillips, *American Negro Slavery* (New York: D. Appleton and Company, 1928), p. 87.

77. Stampp, *Peculiar Institution*, pp. 232–35; John Hope Franklin, *From Slavery to Freedom* (New York: A. A. Knopf, 1947), pp. 218–19.

78. Freyre (*O Escravo nos anúncios de jornais brasilieros do seculo* xix, p. 195) cites examples of light-colored slaves in the advertisements for runaways and refers to a royal order of 1773 in which it was said that, much to the shame of humanity and religion, there were slaves who were lighter than their owners, but who were called "Pretos e . . . negras." Freyre also cites an advertisement in a newspaper in 1865 in which the fugitive was described as having blond hair and blue eyes. Stampp (*Peculiar Institution*, p. 194) refers to blond, blue-eyed runaways in newspaper advertisements in the U. S.

79. Williams, "Treatment of Negro Slaves in the Brazilian Empire," p. 327; Da Costa, *Da Senzala*, p. 29; Pierson, *Negroes in Brazil*, p. 47, n.

80. See Stein, *Vassouras*, pp. 133–34; Da Costa, *Da Senzala*, pp. 354–55. Expilly provides probably the most explicit examples of racial arguments in defense of slavery. He quotes one slaveholder as saying that one could free slaves "today, and tomorrow, instead of using this freedom, they will rob and kill in order to satisfy their needs. Only by terror do they perform services. . . . I believe, gentlemen, Negroes would be baffled by freedom. God created them to be slaves." A little later, Expilly quotes the planter as saying, "The Africans represent an intermediate race between the gorilla and man. They are improved monkeys, not men." A priest is also cited as justifying slavery on the grounds that St. Thomas Aquinas claimed "that nature intended certain creatures for physical and moral reasons to be slaves." (Expilly, *Mulheres e costumes do Brasil*, pp. 381–83.)

81. Rodrigues, *Brazil and Africa*, p. 151.

82. Reclus, "Brésil et la Colonisation," p. 386.

83. Da Costa, *Da Senzala*, pp. 354–56; Cardoso, *Capitalismo e escravidão*, p. 280; Florestan Fernandes, *A Integração do negro no Sociedade de classes* (2 vols., São Paulo: Dominus Editoria, 1965), I, p. 200, n.

84. Da Costa, *Da Senzala*, p. 358.

85. W. E. Burghardt DuBois, *The Suppression of the African Slave-Trade to the United States of America, 1638–1870* (New York, 1896), pp. 221, 215, 229. The appendix to this work contains a number of other excerpts from colonial statues to the same effect. Don B. Kates, Jr., "Abolition, Deportation, Integration: Attitudes toward Slavery in the Early Republic," *Journal of Negro History* 53 (Jan. 1968): 33–47, contains a number of expressions by white Americans of their opposition to freed Negroes remaining in the United States.

V

The Afro-American and the Slave System

Few recent historians, either black or white, still accept uncritically U. B. Phillips' interpretation of southern slavery as a benign institution, and a well structured social system in which each class and race contributed the maximum of its capabilities and in turn received in proportion to its contribution a fair return. To Phillips the absence of insurrections supported his contentions that white masters were lenient and considerate as well as that black slaves were happy and satisfied with their assigned role in southern society. While most historians recognize that there were fewer slave rebellions in the ante-bellum South than in other comparable slave systems, they also acknowledge that bloody revolution was not the only means of demonstrating discontent. Perhaps as effective if less sensational than bloody insurrection were such forms of protest as sabotage, guerilla warfare, work slow downs and even suicide. The amount of unrest and discontent can hardly be measured strictly in terms of the number of attempted or successful insurrections.

Furthermore, there has been little agreement over what constituted a slave revolt. Few historians agree with the findings of Herbert Aptheker who recorded a minimum of two hundred and fifty revolts in North America before the Civil War. Most critics recognize only three serious attempts to overthrow the southern slave system—the abortive rebellion of Gabriel Prosser in 1800, the plot of Denmark Vesey in 1822, and the Nat Turner insurrection of 1831.

Related to the issue of contentment among southern slaves was the degree of docility among blacks. Most historians who insist that the southern slave system was benevolent attribute its tranquility to the fact that blacks by nature were docile and slothful. While disagreeing that blacks naturally possessed the characteristics of the "Sambo" stereotype, Stanley Elkins in his *Slavery* insisted that the harsh slave system of British North America produced slaves with these behavioral traits. By attempting to demonstrate how successful Nazi Germany was in molding Jewish inmates of concentration camps into obedient servants, Elkins argued that a brutal system could actually

reduce black slaves, many of whom came from highly developed and sophisticated cultures, into a state of childishness and dependency which closely resembled the "Sambo" personality of white mythology. In addition, Elkins noted
that Afro-American slaves, like Jewish inmates, tended to adjust to the degradation of life by identifying with and accepting the values of their oppressors.
Only those willing to adjust in this manner to the cruelties and barbarities imposed upon them managed to survive. In the end, the type of personality produced by the system was the one which was thought would best perpetuate
the status quo. Sambo existed not as a natural racial characteristic but as the
dehumanized product of the most brutal slave system devised by man.

Many historians welcomed Elkins' interpretation both as relief from the
moralistic views of earlier historians, and as a more realistic picture of the deep-
seated racism of white America. Its immediate influence was widespread. Such
varied authors as the journalist Charles B. Silberman in his *Crisis in Black and
White* and the novelist William Styron in his Pulitzer prize winning *Confessions of Nat Turner* made use of one or more of his conclusions.

The reaction to Elkins was not all favorable. In addition to scholars who
criticized his methodology as well as his reliance on older and questionable
monographs, several historians objected that Elkins had also demeaned the
black man even while condemning white planters. In order to accomplish
this feat, they argued, Elkins had played fast and loose with historical data.
By erroneously assuming that an absence of slave rebellions proved docility,
he overlooked completely the evidence of previous historians who had documented the presence of other forms of discontent and opposition. In addition,
as Eugene Genovese implied, Elkins' treatment was too simple. The Elkins
thesis carried out to its logical conclusion meant that all slaves who refrained
from asserting any aspect of manhood and who submitted quietly to the humiliation of slavery were reduced to a state of infantilism. If, on the other
hand, they rebelled against this system of conditioning, they were sooner or
later annihilated by masters who could ill afford to tolerate any lasting disobedience to their authority. Naturally, then, all those left were stereotype
Sambos. The actions of man are hardly that easily resolved. Unquestionably
the slave experience left lasting psychological scars on the black man's psyche,
but all slaves did not react in the same way nor did all masters treat their
slaves alike. While monolithic interpretations such as the one proposed by
Elkins are always open to serious criticism, he at least treated the important
question of what effect slavery had upon the personality of Afro-Americans.

The following selections are divided into white and black views of the
slave experience. The first three are the work of white historians while the last
two were written by black authors. Among white historians the debate has
centered on the question of just how content the slaves really were. U. B. Phillips assumed, as many whites still do, that the absence of militant protest from
the black community implied satisfaction with the existing system, but the
Bauers disagree. They suggest that whites have consistently misinterpreted
black behavior. The frequency with which slaves broke hoes may be seen as
an act of defiance rather than as proof of black clumsiness or stupidity, espe-

cially since black Africans had demonstrated considerable adroitness with the use of this implement in West Africa. It is possible that the Sambo personality was a cleverly developed role played by black slaves in order to provide some protection from white exploitation. If whites thought of black slaves as naturally stupid and lazy, they were likely to make fewer demands than if they considered these slaves as highly intelligent and industrious. Furthermore, there was little incentive in a slave economy for drive and ambition since the more you produced the more the master expected.

In contrast black writers are more concerned with the questions of manhood and humanity as well as with the tendency of white writers, either consciously or unconsciously, to treat black people as something less than men. Both Elkins' *Slavery* and Styron's *Confessions* are recent examples of this subtle tendency. The selection by Mike Thelwell is typical of the angry reaction of many black authors to Styron's fictionalized study of Nat Turner. In attacking Styron's interpretation, the author reveals his own understanding of what the militant black slave was like and what motivated his extreme behavior.

The essay by Sterling Stuckey is a good example of the black response to the Elkins thesis. Although he does not take issue with Elkins' view that southern slavery was the harshest system in the New World, he does criticize Elkins for suggesting that black slaves who survived the brutality of slavery were transformed from adult personalities into child-like Sambos. On the other hand, two black psychiatrists, William H. Grier and Price M. Cobbs, indicated in *Black Rage* how the slave mentality described by Elkins still lingers among black Americans. This study, however, has aroused almost as much controversy among black writers as Elkins' *Slavery* did originally.

13. STANLEY M. ELKINS, Slavery (1959)*

This selection from Stanley Elkins' *Slavery: A Problem in American Institutional and Intellectual Life* is perhaps the most controversial portion of his widely discussed book. In writing history from the viewpoint of the slaves, the historian immediately confronts a hiatus of source material. Elkins, who is currently professor of history at Smith College, tries to overcome this handicap by using evidence gained from the experiences of Jewish inmates in Nazi concentration camps to demonstrate that persons with a highly developed culture can be reduced by brutal treatment to a state of complete dependency.

* From Stanley M. Elkins, *Slavery: A Problem in American Institutional and Intellectual Life* (Chicago: University of Chicago Press, 1959), pp. 103–15. Copyright © 1959 by University of Chicago Press. Reprinted by permission of the author and publisher.

Adjustment to Absolute Power
in the Concentration Camp

A certain amount of the mellowness in Ulrich Phillips' picture of ante-bellum plantation life has of necessity been discredited by recent efforts not only to refocus attention upon the brutalities of the slave system but also to dispose once and for all of Phillips' assumptions about the slave as a racially inferior being. And yet it is important—particularly in view of the analogy about to be presented—to keep in mind that for all the system's cruelties there were still clear standards of patriarchal benevolence inherent in its human side, and that such standards were recognized as those of the best southern families. This aspect, despite the most drastic changes of emphasis, should continue to guarantee for Phillips' view more than just a modicum of legitimacy; the patriarchal quality, whatever measure of benevolence or lack of it one wants to impute to the regime, still holds a major key to its nature as a social system.

Introducing, therefore, certain elements of the German concentration-camp experience involves the risky business of trying to balance two necessities—emphasizing both the vast dissimilarities of the two regimes and the essentially limited purpose for which they are being brought together, and at the same time justifying the use of the analogy in the first place. The point is perhaps best made by insisting on an order of classification. The American plantation was not even in the metaphorical sense a "concentration camp"; nor was it even "like" a concentration camp, to the extent that any standards comparable to those governing the camps might be imputed to any sector of American society, at any time; but it should at least be permissible to turn the thing around—to speak of the concentration camp as a special and highly preverted instance of human slavery. Doing so, moreover, should actually be of some assistance in the strategy, now universally sanctioned, of demonstrating how little the products and consequences of slavery ever had to do with race. The only mass experience that Western people have had within recorded history comparable in any way with Negro slavery was undergone in the nether world of Nazism. The concentration camp was not only a perverted slave system; it was also—what is less obvious but even more to the point—a perverted patriarchy.

The system of the concentration camps was expressly devised in the 1930s by high officials of the German government to function as an instrument of terror. The first groups detained in the camps consisted of prominent enemies of the Nazi regime; later, when these had mostly been eliminated, it was still felt necessary that the system be institutionalized and made into a standing weapon of intimidation—which required a continuing flow of incoming prisoners. The categories of eligible persons were greatly widened to include all real, fancied, or "potential" opposition to the state. They were often selected on capricious and random grounds, and together they formed a cross-section of society which was virtually complete: criminals, workers, businessmen, professional people, middle-class Jews, even members of the aristocracy. The teeming camps thus held all kinds—not only the scum of the underworld but also countless men and women of culture and refinement. During the war a specialized objective was added, that of exterminating the Jewish populations of subject countries, which required special mass-production methods of which the gas chambers and crematories of Auschwitz-Birkenau were outstanding examples. Yet the basic technique was everywhere and at all times the same: the deliberate infliction of various forms of torture upon the incoming prisoners in such a way as to break their resistance and make way for their degradation as individuals. These brutalities were not merely "permitted" or "encouraged"; they were prescribed. Duty in the camps was a mandatory phase in the training of SS guards, and it was here that particular efforts were made to overcome their scruples and to develop in them a capacity for relishing spectacles of pain and anguish.

The concentration camps and everything that took place in them were veiled in the utmost isolation and secrecy. Of course complete secrecy was impossible, and a continuing stream of rumors circulated among the population. At the same time so repellent was the nature of these stories that in their enormity they transcended the experience of nearly everyone who heard them; in self-protection it was somehow necessary to persuade oneself that they could not really be true. The results, therefore, contained elements of the diabolical. The undenied existence of the camps cast a shadow of nameless dread over the entire population; on the other hand the *individual* who actually became a prisoner in one of them was in most cases devastated with fright and utterly demoralized to discover that what was happening to *him* was not less, but rather far more terrible than anything he had imagined. The shock sequence of "procurement," therefore, together with the initial phases of the prisoner's introduction to camp life, is not without significance in assessing some of the psychic effects upon those who survived as long-term inmates.

The arrest was typically made at night, preferably late; this was standing Gestapo policy, designed to heighten the element of shock, terror, and unreality surrounding the arrest. After a day or so in the police jail came the next major shock, that of being transported to the camp itself. "This transportation into the camp, and the 'initiation' into it," writes Bruno Bettelheim (an ex-inmate of Dachau and Buchenwald), "is often the first torture which the prisoner has ever experienced and is, as a rule, physically and psychologically the worst torture to which he will ever be exposed." [1] It involved a planned series of brutalities inflicted by guards making repeated rounds through the train over a twelve- to thirty-six-hour period during which the prisoner was prevented from resting. If transported in cattle cars instead of passenger cars, the prisoners were sealed in, under conditions not dissimilar to those of the Middle Passage. [2] Upon their arrival—if the camp was one in which mass exterminations were carried out—there might be sham ceremonies designed to reassure temporarily the exhausted prisoners, which meant that the fresh terrors in the offing would then strike them with redoubled impact. An SS officer might deliver an address, or a band might be playing popular tunes, and it would be in such a setting that the initial "selection" was made. The newcomers would file past an SS doctor who indicated, with a motion of the forefinger, whether they were to go to the left or to the right. To one side went those considered capable of heavy labor; to the other would go wide categories of "undesirables"; those in the latter group were being condemned to the gas chambers. [3] Those who remained would undergo the formalities of "registration," full of indignities, which culminated in the marking of each prisoner with a number. [4]

There were certain physical and psychological strains of camp life, especially debilitating in the early stages, which should be classed with the introductory shock sequence. There was a state of chronic hunger whose pressures were unusually effective in detaching prior scruples of all kinds; even the sexual instincts no longer functioned in the face of the drive for food. [5] The man who at his pleasure could bestow or withhold food thus wielded, for that reason alone, abnormal power. Another strain at first was the demand for absolute obedience, the slightest deviation from which brought savage punishments. [6] The prisoner had to ask permission—by no means granted as a matter of course—even to defecate. [7] The power of the SS guard, as the prisoner was hourly reminded, was that of life and death over his body. A more exquisite form of pressure lay in the fact that the prisoner had never a moment of solitude: he no longer had a private existence; it was no longer possible, in any imaginable sense, for him to be an "individual." [8]

Another factor having deep disintegrative effects upon the prisoner was the prospect of a limitless future in the camp. In the immediate sense this meant that he could no longer make plans for the future. But there would eventually be a subtler meaning: it made the break with the outside world a *real* break; in time the "real" life would become the life of the camp, the outside world an abstraction. Had it been a limited detention, whose end could be calculated, one's outside relationships—one's roles, one's very "personality"—might temporarily have been laid aside, to be reclaimed more or less intact at the end of the term. Here, however, the prisoner was faced with the apparent impossibility of his old roles or even his old personality ever having any future at all; it became more and more difficult to imagine himself resuming them.[9] It was this that underlay the "egalitarianism" of the camps; old statuses had lost their meaning.[10] A final strain, which must have been particularly acute for the newcomer, was the omnipresent threat of death and the very unpredictable sudden-ness with which death might strike. Quite aside from the periodic gas-chamber selections, the guards in their sports and caprices were at liberty to kill any prisoner at any time.[11]

In the face of all this, one might suppose that the very notion of an "adjustment" would be grotesque. The majority of those who entered the camps never came out again, but our concern here has to be with those who survived—an estimated 700,000 out of nearly eight million.[12] For them, the regime must be considered not as a system of death but as a way of life. These survivors did make an adjustment of some sort to the system; it is they themselves who report it. After the initial shocks, what was the nature of the "normality" that emerged?

A dramatic species of psychic displacement seems to have occurred at the very outset. This experience, described as a kind of "splitting of personality," has been noted by most of the inmates who later wrote of their imprisonment. The very extremity of the initial tortures produced in the prisoner what actually amounted to a sense of detachment; these brutalities went so beyond his own experience that they became somehow incredible—they seemed to be happening no longer to him but almost to someone else. "[The author] has no doubt," writes Bruno Bettelheim, "that he was able to endure the transportation, and all that followed, because right from the beginning he became convinced that these hor-rible and degrading experiences somehow did not happen to 'him' as a subject, but only to 'him' as an object." [13] This subject-object "split" ap-pears to have served a double function: not only was it an immediate psychic defense mechanism against shock,[14] but it also acted as the first thrust toward a new adjustment. This splitting-off of a special "self"—a self which endured the tortures but which was not the "real" self—also provided the first glimpse of a new personality, which, being not "real," would not need to feel bound by the values which guided the individual in his former life. "The prisoners' feelings," according to Mr. Bettelheim, "could be summed up by the following sentence: 'What I am doing here, or what is happening to me, does not count at all; here everything is permissible as long and insofar as it contributes to helping me survive in the camp.' " [15]

One part of the prisoner's being was thus, under sharp stress, brought to the crude realization that he must thenceforth be governed by an entire new set of standards in order to live. Mrs. Lingens-Reiner puts it bluntly: "Will you survive, or shall I? As soon as one sensed that this was at stake everyone turned egotist." [16] ". . . I think it of primary importance," writes Dr. Cohen, "to take into account that the superego acquired new values in a concentration camp, so much at variance with those which the prisoner bore with him into camp that the latter faded." [17] But then this acquisition of "new values" did not all take place immediately; it was not until some time after the most acute period of stress was over that the new, "unreal" self would become at last the "real" one.

"If you survive the first three months you will survive the next three years." Such was the formula transmitted from the old prisoners to the new ones,[18] and its meaning lay in the fact that the first three months would generally determine a prisoner's capacity for survival and adaptation. "Be inconspicuous": this was the golden rule.[19] The prisoner who called attention to himself, even in such trivial matters as the wearing of glasses, risked doom. Any show of bravado, any heroics, any kind of resistance condemned a man instantly. There were no rewards for martyrdom: not only did the martyr himself suffer, but mass punishments were wreaked upon his fellow inmates. To "be inconspicuous" required a special kind of alertness—almost an animal instinct [20]—against the apathy which tended to follow the initial shocks.[21] To give up the struggle for survival was to commit "passive suicide"; a careless mistake meant death. There were those, however, who did come through this phase and who managed an adjustment to the life of the camp. It was the striking contrasts between this group of two- and three-year veterans and the perpetual stream of newcomers which made it possible for men like Bettelheim and Cohen to speak of the "old prisoner" as a specific type.

The most immediate aspect of the old inmates' behavior which struck these observers was its *childlike* quality. "The prisoners developed types of behavior which are characteristic of infancy or early youth. Some of these behaviors developed slowly, others were immediately imposed on the prisoners and developed only in intensity as time went on." [22] Such infantile behavior took innumerable forms. The inmates' sexual impotence brought about a disappearance of sexuality in their talk; [23] instead, excretory functions occupied them endlessly. They lost many of the customary inhibitions as to soiling their beds and their persons.[24] Their humor was shot with silliness and they giggled like children when one of them would expel wind. Their relationships were highly unstable. "Prisoners would, like early adolescents, fight one another tooth and nail

. . . only to become close friends within a few minutes." [25] Dishonesty became chronic. "Now they suddenly appeared to be pathological liars, to be unable to restrain themselves, to be unable to make objective evaluation, etc." [26] "In hundreds of ways," writes Colaço Belmonte, "the soldier, and to an even greater extent the prisoner of war, is given to understand that he is a child. . . . Then dishonesty, mendacity, egotistic actions in order to obtain more food or to get out of scrapes reach full development, and theft becomes a veritable affliction of camp life." [27] This was all true, according to Elie Cohen, in the concentration camp as well.[28] Benedikt Kautsky observed such things in his own behavior: "I myself can declare that often I saw myself as I used to be in my school days, when by sly dodges and clever pretexts we avoided being found out, or could 'organize' something." [29] Bruno Bettelheim remarks on the extravagance of the stories told by the prisoners to one another. "They were boastful, telling tales about what they had accomplished in their former lives, or how they succeeded in cheating foremen or guards, and how they sabotaged the work. Like children they felt not at all set back or ashamed when it became known that they had lied about their prowess." [30]

This development of childlike behavior in the old inmates was the counterpart of something even more striking that was happening to them: *"Only very few of the prisoners escaped a more or less intensive identification with the SS."* [31] As Mr. Bettelheim puts it: "A prisoner had reached the final stage of adjustment to the camp situation when he had changed his personality so as to accept as his own the values of the Gestapo." [32] The Bettelheim study furnishes a catalogue of examples. The old prisoners came to share the attitude of the SS toward the "unfit" prisoners; newcomers who behaved badly in the labor groups or who could not withstand the strain became a liability for the others, who were often instrumental in getting rid of them. Many old prisoners actually imitated the SS; they would sew and mend their uniforms in such a way as to make them look more like those of the SS—even though they risked punishment for it. "When asked why they did it, they admitted that they loved to look like . . . the guards." Some took great enjoyment in the fact that during roll call "they really had stood well at attention." There were cases of nonsensical rules, made by the guards, which the older prisoners would continue to observe and try to force on the others long after the SS had forgotten them.[33] Even the most abstract ideals of the SS, such as their intense German nationalism and anti-Semitism, were often absorbed by the old inmates—a phenomenon observed among the politically well-educated and even among the Jews themselves.[34] The final quintessence of all this was seen in the "Kapo"—the prisoner who had been placed in a supervisory position over his fellow inmates. These creatures, many of them professional criminals, not only behaved with slavish servility to the SS, but the way in which they often outdid the SS in sheer brutality became one of the most durable features of the concentration-camp legend.

To all these men, reduced to complete and childish dependence upon their masters, the SS had actually become a father-symbol. "The SS man was all-powerful in the camp, he was the lord and master of the prisoner's life. As a cruel father he could, without fear of punishment, even kill the prisoner and as a gentle father he could scatter largesse and afford the prisoner his protection.[35] The result, admits Dr. Cohen, was that "for all of us the SS was a father image. . . ."[36] The closed system, in short, had become a kind of grotesque patriarchy.

The literature provides us with three remarkable tests of the profundity of the experience which these prisoners had undergone and the thoroughness of the changes which had been brought about in them. One is the fact that few cases of real resistance were ever recorded, even among prisoners going to their death.

> With a few altogether insignificant exceptions, the prisoners, no matter in what form they were led to execution, whether singly, in groups, or in masses, never fought back! . . . there were thousands who had by no means relapsed into fatal apathy. Nevertheless, in mass liquidations they went to their death with open eyes, without assaulting the enemy in a final paroxysm, without a sign of fight. Is this not in conflict with human nature, as we know it? [37]

Even upon liberation, when revenge against their tormentors at last became possible, mass uprisings very rarely occurred. "Even when the whole system was overthrown by the Allies," says David Rousset writing of Buchenwald, "nothing happened. . . . The American officer appointed to command of the camp was never called upon to cope with any inclination toward a popular movement. No such disposition existed." [38]

A second test of the system's effectiveness was the relative scarcity of suicides in the camps.[39] Though there were suicides, they tended to occur during the first days of internment, and only one mass suicide is known; it took place among a group of Jews at Mauthausen who leaped into a rock pit three days after their arrival.[40] For the majority of prisoners the simplicity of the urge to survive made suicide, a complex matter of personal initiative and decision, out of the question. Yet they could, when commanded by their masters, go to their death without resistance.

The third test lies in the very absence, among the prisoners, of hatred toward the SS. This is probably the hardest of all to understand. Yet the burning spirit of rebellion which many of their liberators expected to find would have had to be supported by fierce and smoldering emotions; such emotions were not there. "It is remarkable," one observer notes, "how little hatred of their wardens is revealed in their stories." [41]

NOTES

1. Bruno Bettelheim, "Individual and Mass Behavior in Extreme Situations," *Journal of Abnormal Psychology* 38 (October 1943): 424.

2. A description of such a trip may be found in Olga Lengyel, *Five Chimneys: The Story of Auschwitz* (Chicago: University of Chicago Press, 1947), pp. 7–10. See also Eugen Kogon, *The Theory and Practice of Hell* (New York: Farrar, Straus, 1946), p. 67.

3. Elie Cohen, *Human Behavior in the Concentration Camp* (New York: Norton, 1953), pp. 118–22; Kogon, *Theory and Practice*, pp. 66–76; Lengyel, *Five Chimneys*, pp. 12–22.

4. One aspect of this registration ceremony involved a sham "inspection" of the body, whose effect on the women prisoners in particular was apparently very profound. See Lengyel, *Five Chimneys*, p. 19; Ella Lingens-Reiner, *Prisoners of Fear* (London: Victor Gollancz, 1948), p. 26. This may be compared with Degrandpré's description of a similar "inspection" on the African slave coast in the 1780s; see his *Voyage*, II, pp. 55–56. "Apart from the fact that for every newcomer his transformation into a 'prisoner' meant a degradation," writes an ex-prisoner of Auschwitz and Mauthausen, "there was also the *loss of his name*. That this was no trifling circumstance should be apparent from the great importance which, according to Freud, a man attaches to his name. This is, in Freud's view, sufficiently proven by 'the fact that savages regard a name as an essential part of a man's personality. . . .' Anyhow, whether one agrees with Freud or not, the loss of one's name is not without significance, for the name is a personal attribute. Because he no longer had a name, but had become a number, the prisoner belonged to the huge army of the nameless who peopled the concentration camp." Cohen, *Human Behavior*, pp. 145–46.

5. Ibid., pp. 134–35, 140–43.

6. These punishments are discussed most vividly in Kogon, *Theory and Practice*, pp. 102–8, 207–11.

7. Bettelheim, "Individual and Mass Behavior," p. 445.

8. The effects of never being alone are noted in Cohen, *Human Behavior*, pp. 130–31, and David Rousset, *The Other Kingdom* (New York: Reynal & Hitchcock, 1947), p. 133.

9. "When the author [Bettelheim] expressed to some of the old prisoners his astonishment that they seemed not interested in discussing their future life outside the camp, they frequently admitted that they could no longer visualize themselves living outside the camp, making free decisions, taking care of themselves and their families." Bettelheim, "Individual and Mass Behavior," p. 439.

10. M. Rousset tells of how, on one of the death marches, a prisoner came to him bringing a French compatriot and begging his protection for the wretched man. "He told me that he was a lawyer from Toulouse, and it was only with the greatest difficulty that I kept from laughing aloud. For this social designation, *lawyer*, no longer fitted the poor wretch in the slightest. The incongruity of the thought was irresistibly comic. And it was the same with all of us." Rousset, *Other Kingdom*, p. 77.

11. Kogon, *Theory and Practice*, p. 274; Cohen, *Human Behavior*, p. 155; Hilde O. Bluhm, "How Did They Survive?" *American Journal of Psychotherapy* 2 (January 1948): 5.

12. Kogon, *Theory and Practice*, p. 277.

13. Bettelheim, "Individual and Mass Behavior," p. 431. See also Cohen, *Human Behavior*, pp. 116–17, 172.

14. "Many kept their bearings only by a kind of split personality. They surrendered their bodies resistlessly to the terror, while their inner being withdrew and held aloof." Kogon, *Theory and Practice*, p. 71. "I arrived at that state of numbness where I was no longer sensitive to either club or whip. I lived through the rest of that scene almost as a spectator." Lengyel, *Five Chimneys*, p. 20.

15. Bettelheim, "Individual and Mass Behavior," p. 432. "We camp prisoners," writes Mrs. Lingens-Reiner, "had only one yardstick: whatever helped our survival was good, and whatever threatened our survival was bad, and to be avoided." *Prisoners of Fear*, p. 142.

16. Lingens-Reiner, *Prisoners of Fear*, p. 23.

17. *Human Behavior*, p. 136.

18. Bettelheim, "Individual and Mass Behavior," p. 438.

19. Cohen, *Human Behavior*, p. 169.

20. This should in no sense be considered as a calculating, "rational" alertness, but rather as something quite primitive. "Of myself," writes Dr. Cohen, "I know that I was not continuously occupied by the reflection: I am going to win through. The actions which contributed to my survival were performed instinctively rather than consciously. . . . Like animals warned by their instinct that danger is imminent, we would act instinctively at critical moments. These instinctive acts must, I think, be considered as manifestations of the life instinct. If the life instinct is not strong enough, the instinct will desert the individual, and instead of rising to the emergency, the individual will succumb, whereas a stronger life instinct would have seen him through." *Human Behavior*, p. 163.

21. Those who had in fact succumbed to this apathy—who had given up the struggle, and for whom death would be a mere matter of time—were known as "Moslems."

22. Bettelheim, "Individual and Mass Behavior," p. 141.

23. Says Dr. Cohen, "I am not asserting that sex was never discussed; it was, though not often. Frankl also states 'that in contrast to mass existence in other military communities . . . here (in the concentration camp) there is *no smut talk.*'" *Human Behavior*, p. 141.

24. "With reference to this phenomenon Miss Bluhm has pointed out that it is not at all unusual that people in extraordinary circumstances, for example soldiers in wartime, 'are able to give up their habitual standards of cleanliness without deeper disturbance; yet only up to certain limits.' The rules of anal cleanliness, she adds, are not disregarded. 'Their neglect means return to instinctual behavior of childhood.'" Ibid., p. 175.

25. Bettelheim, "Individual and Mass Behavior," p. 445.

26. Ibid., p. 421.

27. Quoted in Cohen, *Human Behavior*, p. 176.

28. Ibid.

29. Ibid., p. 174.

30. Bettelheim, "Individual and Mass Behavior," pp. 445–46. This same phenomenon is noted by Curt Bondy: "They tell great stories about what they have

been before and what they have performed." "Problems of Internment Camps," *Journal of Abnormal and Social Psychology* 38 (October 1943): 453–75.

31. Cohen, *Human Behavior,* p. 177. Italics in original.

32. Bettelheim, "Individual and Mass Behavior," p. 447.

33. Ibid., pp. 448–50. "Once, for instance, a guard on inspecting the prisoners' apparel found that the shoes of some of them were dirty on the inside. He ordered all prisoners to wash their shoes inside and out with water and soap. The heavy shoes treated this way became hard as stone. The order was never repeated, and many prisoners did not execute it when given. Nevertheless there were some old prisoners who not only continued to wash the inside of their shoes every day but cursed all others who did not do so as negligent and dirty. These prisoners firmly believed that the rules set down by the Gestapo were desirable standards of human behavior, at least in the camp situation." Ibid., p. 450.

34. Ibid. See also Cohen, *Human Behavior,* pp. 189–93, for a discussion of anti-Semitism among the Jews.

35. Cohen, *Human Behavior,* pp. 176–77.

36. Ibid., p. 179. On this and other points I must also acknowledge my indebtedness to Mr. Ies Spetter, a former Dutch journalist now living in this country, who was imprisoned for a time at Auschwitz during World War II. Mr. Spetter permitted me to see an unpublished paper, "Some Thoughts on Victims and Criminals in the German Concentration Camps," which he wrote in 1954 at the New School for Social Research; and this, together with a number of conversations I had with him, added much to my understanding of concentration-camp psychology.

37. Kogon, *Theory and Practice,* p. 284.

38. *The Other Kingdom,* p. 137.

39. "In the preference camp Bergen Belsen, only four cases of attempted suicide were witnessed by Tas, three of which were saved with great effort, while in the Stammlager Auschwitz only one successful attempt came to my knowledge. This does not mean that there were not more, but their number was certainly small. Kaas, on the other hand, witnessed several attempted suicides in Buchenwald. He has remembered three that were successful (two by hanging, one by rushing into the electric fence). He also knows of prisoners who were known to be depressive cases, and who were shot down when during the night they had deliberately gone out of bounds. As compared with the large number of prisoners, the number of suicides, however, was very small." Cohen, *Human Behavior,* p. 158.

40. Kogon, *Theory and Practice,* pp. 166–67. This occurred during fearful tortures at the quarry, where the Jews knew they were about to be killed anyway.

41. A. Hottinger, *Hungerkrankheit, Hungerödem, Hungertuberkulose,* p. 32, quoted in Cohen, *Human Behavior,* p. 197. "After the liberation many writers were struck by the callousness of the onetime prisoners, and particularly by their apathy when relating their experiences, even the most horrible." Ibid., p. 144.

14. EUGENE D. GENOVESE, Rebelliousness and Docility in the Negro Slave: A Critique of the Elkins Thesis (1967)*

Among the critics of Elkins' "Sambo" thesis, none is more provocative than Professor Eugene D. Genovese who is presently chairman of the history department at the University of Rochester. A member of the "New Left School" of historians and an admirer of the Marxian interpretation of history, Genovese praises Elkins for his originality but concludes that his thesis lacks validity. There were too many differences between the slave system of the Old South and the Nazi concentration camp to allow the historian to draw definite conclusions. In addition, Genovese believes that a "Sambo" personality can be found wherever slavery existed. By disregarding the principle of contradiction in human personality, Elkins is unable to explain the behavior of an obedient house slave who suddenly participates in violent rebellion.

Despite the hostile reception given by historians to Stanley M. Elkins' *Slavery: A Problem in American Institutional and Intellectual Life*,[1] it has established itself as one of the most influential historical essays of our generation. Although Elkins ranges widely, we may restrict ourselves to his most important contribution, the theory of slave personality, and bypass other questions, such as his dubious theory of uncontrolled capitalism in the South. His psychological model would fit comfortably into other social theories and may, up to a point, be analytically isolated.

Elkins asserts that the Sambo stereotype arose only in the United States. He attempts to explain this allegedly unique personality type by constructing a social analysis that contrasts a totalitarian plantation South with a feudal Latin America in which church, state, and plantation balanced one another. To relate this ostensible difference in social structure to the formation of slave personality he invokes an analogy to Nazi concentration camps to demonstrate the possibility of mass infantilization and proceeds to apply three theories of personality: (1) the Freudian, which relates the growth of a personality to the existence of a father figure and which accounts for the identification of a tyrannized child with a tyrannical father; (2) Sullivan's theory of "significant others," which relates the growth of a personality to its interaction with individuals who hold or seem to hold power over its fortunes; and (3) role theory, which relates the growth of a personality to the number and kinds of roles it can play.[2] Elkins assumes that Sambo existed only in the United States and that our task is to explain his unique appearance in the Old South. I propose to show, on the contrary, that Sambo existed wherever slavery

* From Eugene D. Genovese, "Rebelliousness and Docility in the Negro Slave," *Civil War History* 13 (1967): 293–314. Reprinted by permission.

existed, that he nonetheless could turn into a rebel, and that our main task is to discover the conditions under which the personality pattern could become inverted and a seemingly docile slave could suddenly turn fierce.

Elkins asserts that the United States alone produced the Sambo stereotype—"the perpetual child incapable of maturity." He does not, as so many of his critics insist, equate childishness with docility, although he carelessly gives such an impression. Rather, he equates it with dependence and, with a subtlety that seems to elude his detractors, skillfully accounts for most forms of day-to-day resistance. His thesis, as will be shown later, is objectionable not because it fails to account for hostile behavior, but because it proves too much and encompasses more forms of behavior than can usefully be managed under a single rubric.

Elkins' assumption that the existence of a stereotype proves the reality behind it will not stand critical examination either as psychological theory or as historical fact. As psychological theory, it is at least open to question. John Harding and his collaborators have argued that stereotypes, under certain conditions, may in fact be without foundation; [3] this side of the problem may be left to specialists and need not alter the main lines of the argument. Historically, Sambo was emerging in the United States at the same time he was emerging in the French colonies. Negroes, if we would believe the French planters, were childlike, docile, helpless creatures up until the very moment they rose and slaughtered the whites. Accordingly, I have a sporting proposition for Elkins. Let us substitute French Saint-Domingue for the United States and apply his logic. We find a Sambo stereotype and a weak tradition of rebellion. True, there was a century of maroon activity, but only the efforts of Mackandal constituted a genuine revolt. Those efforts were, in the words of C. L. R. James, "the only hint of an organized attempt at revolt during the hundred years preceding the French Revolution." [4] Boukman's revolt ought properly to be regarded as the first phase of the great revolution of 1791 rather than a separate action. In short, when the island suddenly exploded in the greatest slave revolution in history, nothing lay behind it but Sambo and a few hints. Now, let us rewrite history by having the French Jacobins take power and abolish slavery in 1790, instead of 1794. With the aid of that accident the slaves would have been freed as the result of the vicissitudes of Jacobin-Girondist factionalism and not by their own efforts. We would then today be reading a Haitian Elkins whose task would be to explain the extraordinary docility of the country's blacks. As the rewriting of history goes, this excursion requires little effort and ought to make us aware of how suddenly a seemingly docile, or at least adjusted, people can rise in violence. It would be much safer to assume that dangerous and strong currents run beneath that docility and adjustment.

Reaching further back into history, we find an identification of Negroes, including Africans, with a Sambo-like figure. As early as the fourteenth century—and there is no reason to believe that it began that late—so learned and sophisticated a scholar as Ibn Khaldun could write:

Negroes are in general characterized by levity, excitability, and great emotionalism. They are found eager to dance whenever they hear a melody. They are everywhere described as stupid. . . . The Negro nations are, as a rule, submissive to slavery, because (Negroes) have little (that is essentially) human and have attributes that are quite similar to those of dumb animals.[5]

In 1764, in Portugal, a pamphlet on the slavery question in the form of a dialogue has a Brazilian slaveowning mine operator say: "I have always observed that in Brazil the Negroes are treated worse than animals. . . . Yet, withal the blacks endure this." The conclusion drawn was that this submissiveness proved inferiority.[6]

Sambo appears throughout Brazilian history, especially during the nineteenth century. In the 1830s the idealogues of Brazilian slavery, significantly under strong French influence, assured planters that the black was a "man-child" with a maximum mental development equivalent to that of a white adolescent. This and similar views were widespread among planters, particularly in the highly commercialized southern coffee region.[7] Brazilian sociologists and historians accepted this stereotype well into the twentieth century. Euclides da Cunha, in his masterpiece, *Rebellion in the Backlands*, described the Negro as "a powerful organism, given to an extreme humility, without the Indian's rebelliousness." [8] Oliveira Lima, in his pioneering comparative history of Brazil and Spanish and Anglo-Saxon America, described the Negro as an especially subservient element.[9] Joao Pandía Calógeras, in his long standard *History of Brazil*, wrote:

The Negro element in general revealed a perpetual good humor, a childish and expansive joy, a delight in the slightest incidentals of life. . . . Filled with the joy of youth, a ray of sunshine illumined his childlike soul. Sensitive, worthy of confidence, devoted to those who treated him well, capable of being led in any direction by affection and kind words, the Negro helped to temper the primitive harshness of the Portuguese colonists.[10]

One of the leading interpretations in Brazil today regards the blacks as having been subjected to a regime designed to produce alienation and the destruction of the personality by means of the exercise of the arbitrary power of the master. The account given in Kenneth M. Stampp's *The Peculiar Institution* of the efforts to produce a perfect slave has a close parallel in Octavio Ianni's *As Metamorfoses do Escravo*, which analyzes southern Brazil during the nineteenth century.[11]

Nor did Sambo absent himself from Spanish America. The traditional advocacy of Indian freedom often went together with a defense of Negro slavery based on an alleged inferiority that suggests a Sambo stereotype.[12] In 1816, Simón Bolívar wrote to General Jean Marión of Haiti:

I have proclaimed the absolute emancipation of the slaves. The tyranny of the Spaniards has reduced them to such a state of stupidity and instilled in their souls such a great sense of terror that they have lost even the desire to be free!! Many of them would have followed the Spaniards or have embarked on British vessels [whose owners] have sold them in neighboring colonies.[13]

Elkins cites evidence that the Spanish regarded the Indians as docile and the Negroes as difficult to control, but evidence also exists that shows the reverse. The view of the Indian or Negro as docile or rebellious varied greatly with time, place, and circumstance.[14] Sidney Mintz, with one eye on Cuba and Puerto Rico and the other eye on Brazil, has suggested that, regardless of institutional safeguards, the more commercialized the slave system the more it tended to produce dehumanization. This thesis needs considerable refinement but is at least as suggestive as Elkins' attempt to construct a purely institutional interpretation.[15]

On close inspection the Sambo personality turns out to be neither more nor less than the slavish personality; wherever slavery has existed, Sambo has also.[16] "Throughout history," David Brion Davis has written, "it has been said that slaves, though occasionally as loyal and faithful as good dogs, were for the most part lazy, irresponsible, cunning, rebellious, untrustworthy, and sexually promiscuous." [17] Only the element of rebelliousness does not seem to fit Sambo, but on reflection, even that does. Sambo, being a child, could be easily controlled but if not handled properly, would revert to barbarous ways. Davis demonstrates that by the fifth century B.C. many Greeks had come to regard the submission of barbarians to despotic and absolute rulers as proof of inferiority.[18] By the end of the eighteenth century, America and Europe widely accepted the image of the dehumanized black slave, and even Reynal believed that crime and indolence would inevitably follow emancipation.[19]

Sambo has a much longer pedigree and a much wider range than Elkins appreciates. Audrey I. Richards, in 1939, noted the widespread existence of "fatal resignation" among primitive peoples in Africa and suggested that their psychological and physical sluggishness might be attributable in a large part to poor diet and severe malnutrition.[20] Josué de Castro, former head of the United Nations Food and Agriculture Organization, has made the same point about Brazilian slaves and about people in underdeveloped countries in general.[21] As Jean-Paul Sartre has suggested, "Beaten, under-nourished, ill, terrified—but only up to a certain point—he has, whether he's black, yellow, or white, always the same traits of character: he's a sly-boots, a lazy-bones, and a thief, who lives on nothing and who understands only violence." [22] By constructing a single-factor analysis and erroneously isolating the personality structure of the southern slave, Elkins has obscured many other possible lines of inquiry. We do not as yet have a comparative analysis of slave diets in the United States, Brazil, and the West Indies, although it might tell us a great deal about personality patterns.

It is generally believed that Elkins merely repeated Tannenbaum when he declared Sambo to be a native of the Old South; in fact, the assertion is, for better or worse, entirely his own. I would not dwell on this point were it not that I cannot imagine Tannenbaum's taking so one-sided a view. I intend no disrespect to Elkins by this observation, for, as a matter of fact, his single-mindedness, even when misguided, has helped him to expose problems others have missed entirely. Elkins' greatest weakness, nonetheless, is his inability to accept the principle of contradiction, to realize that all historical phenomena must be regarded as constituting a process of becoming, and that, therefore, the other-sidedness of the most totalitarian conditions may in fact represent the unfolding of their negation. If Sambo were merely Sambo, then Elkins must explain how an overseer could publicly defend his class, without challenge, for having "to punish and keep in order the negroes, at the risk of his life." [23]

Elkins recognizes a wide range of institutional factors as having contributed to the contrast between the Latin and Anglo-Saxon slave systems, but he places special emphasis on the system of law in relation to the structure and policies of Church and Crown.[24] Although in this way Elkins follows Tannenbaum, he necessarily must go well beyond him, and therein lies his greatest difficulty. Tannenbaum's well-known thesis need not be reviewed here, but we might profitably recall his suggestive comment on *Las Siete Partidas:*

Las Siete Partidas was formed within the Christian doctrine, and the slave had a body of law, protective of him as a human being, which was already there when the Negro arrived and had been elaborated long before he came upon the scene.[25]

The essential point of Tannenbaum's contrast between this legal tradition and that of the Anglo-Saxon lies in its bearing on the problem of emancipation. Whereas the Hispanic tradition favored and encouraged it, the Anglo-Saxon blocked it.[26] So long as a general contrast can be demonstrated, Tannenbaum's thesis obtains, for he is primarily concerned with the social setting into which the Negro plunged upon emancipation. His thesis, therefore, can absorb criticism such as that of Arnold A. Sio, who argues that the Romans assimilated the rights of their slaves to property despite a legal code which respected the moral personality of the slave. Sio finds evidence of a similar tendency in Latin as well as Anglo-Saxon America.[27] Tannenbaum's thesis would fall only if the tendency were equally strong everywhere; but obviously it was not.[28] Elkins, however, cannot absorb such qualifications, for he necessarily must demonstrate the uniqueness of the southern pattern as well as the absoluteness of the contrast with Latin America. If the contrast could be reduced to a matter of degree, then we should be left with more American than Latin American Sambos, but Elkins' notion of a special American personality pattern and problem would fall.

Elkins, like Tannenbaum, ignores the French slave colonies, but nowhere was the gap between law and practice so startling. The *Code Noir* of 1685 set a high standard of humanity and attempted to guarantee the slaves certain minimal rights and protection. It was treated with contempt in the French West Indies, especially when the islands began to ride the sugar boom. It is enough to quote a governor of Martinique, one of the men charged with the enforcement of these laws: "I have reached the stage of believing firmly that one must treat the Negroes as one treats beasts." [29] On the eve of the Haitian Revolution probably not one of the protective articles of the *Code Noir* was being enforced.[30]

Elkins offers Brazil as a counterpoint to the Old South and invokes the Iberian legal tradition, together with the power of Church and Crown. Yet, even Gilberto Freyre, on whom Elkins relies so heavily, writes of the widespread murders of slaves by enraged masters.[31] As late as the nineteenth century, slaves were being whipped to death in the presence of all hands. The law might say what it would, but the *fazendeiros* controlled the police apparatus and supported the doctors who falsified the death certificates.[32] The measures designed to prevent wanton killing of slaves do not seem to have been better in Latin American than in Anglo-Saxon America.[33] If Brazilian slaves went to the police to complain about unjust or illegally excessive punishment, the police would, in Freyre's words, give them a double dose.[34] If the law mattered much, we need to know the reason for the repeated reenactment of legislation to protect slaves. The famous Rio Branco Law of 1871, for example, granted slaves rights they were supposed to have enjoyed for centuries, and these too remained largely unrespected.

The Portuguese Crown could legislate in any manner it wished, and so later could the Emperor of Brazil; local power resided with the *fazendeiros*, as the emissaries of the Crown learned soon enough. We may imagine conditions in the first three centuries of colonization from Freyre's succinct comment on conditions in the middle of the nineteenth century: "The power of the great planters was indeed feudalistic, their patriarchal-

ism being hardly restricted by civil laws." [35] Not until that time did a
strong central government arise to challenge effectively the great
planters.[36] That the contrast with the Old South might have been the
reverse of what Elkins thinks is suggested by the diary of an ex-Con-
federate who fled to Brazil after the war. George S. Barnsley, formerly a
Georgia planter and Confederate army surgeon, complained as late as 1904
of the lack of government and the prevalence of virtually feudal conditions.[37]

Las Siete Partidas constituted a theoretical work and standard of
values, the importance of which ought not to be minimized, but it had
little to do with the actual practice on which Elkins' thesis depends.[38]
The kind of protection that transcended the theoretical and might have
conditioned decisively the personality development of the slave population as a whole probably did not appear until the *Real Cédula* of 1789. As
Davis suggests, "There are many indications, moreover, that Spanish
planters paid little attention to the law." [39]

Elkins assumes that the strongly centralized Spanish state could and
did prevail over the planters. No doubt it did in matters of prime importance to its survival and income. In most matters, notwithstanding its
best efforts at institutional control, the planters continued to have their
way on their own estates. The Spanish court promulgated humane legislation to protect the natives of the Canary Islands, but attempts at enforcement so far from home proved futile. The problem swelled enormously
when transferred to the West Indies, not to mention to the mainland.[40]
The fate of the protective features of the Laws of Burgos (1512) and of
similar legislation is well known.[41] The British and other foreigners who
did business in Spanish America ridiculed the mass of laws and the
clumsy administrative apparatus designed to enforce them. As the agent
of the South Sea Company at Jamaica noted in 1736, he who wants to
deal illegally with the Spanish officials needs only the cash necessary to
bribe them.[42] The lot of the slaves could, under such conditions, hardly
reflect other than the disposition of the masters. A case study by Jaime
Jaramillo Uribe of the judicial system of New Grenada shows that even
the reform laws of the eighteenth century could not reach down into
the plantations to protect the slaves.[43]

Much of Elkins' treatment of Spanish law deals with Cuba and flows
from the work of Herbert Klein.[44] Without attempting a close examination of the intricacies of the Cuban case, we ought to note that it
presents a striking picture of a bitter struggle between planters and state
officials. The planters, there too, usually won the day. The liberal Governor Concha finally admitted that the resistance of the slaveowners to
government intervention was justified by the necessity for controlling

the blacks and avoiding any ambiguity in authority. In 1845 the government did seriously challenge the masters' power, but the uproar proved so great that the militant officials had to be removed.[45]

The fate of the law during the sugar boom requires more attention than Elkins and Klein have given it. In its earlier phases Cuban slavery was exceptionally mild and fit much of Elkins' schema. When the Haitian Revolution removed the Caribbean's leading sugar producer from the world market, Cuba entered into a period of wild expansion and prosperity. The status of the slave declined accordingly. The old institutional arrangements did not disappear, but their bearing on the life of the great mass of slaves became minimal or nonexistent.[46]

The legal and political structure of Spanish America in general and of Cuba in particular helped ease the way to freedom by providing a setting in which the slave might be abused brutally but retained a significant degree of manhood in the eyes of society. For Tannenbaum's purpose, this distinction establishes the argument: the slave was abused as a slave but only incidentally as a Negro. The master might rule with absolute authority, but only because he could get away with it, not because it was, by the standards of his own class, church, and society, just and proper. Tannenbaum and Freyre do make too much of this argument. The persistence and depth of racial discrimination and prejudice in twentieth-century Brazil and Cuba ought to remind us that the enslavement of one race by another must generate racist doctrines among all social classes as well as the intelligentsia. Qualitative and quantitative distinctions nonetheless obtain, and Tannenbaum's argument requires correction and greater specificity, not rejection. For Elkins, Tannenbaum's distinction, however qualified, is not enough. If, as seems likely, the great majority of the slaves labored under such absolutism, theoretical or not, their personalities would have been shaped in response to conditions equivalent to those he describes for the United States.

In the United States, as in the British West Indies and everywhere else, custom and conventional moral standards had greater force than the law, as Ulrich B. Phillips long ago argued. Just as the vast range of rights granted the slaves in Latin America usually proved unenforceable in a society in which power was largely concentrated in local planter oligarchies, so in Anglo-Saxon America the quasi-absolute power of the master was tempered by the prevailing ethos. Tannenbaum, and especially Elkins, go much too far in denying that English and American law recognized the moral personality of the slave. As Davis has demonstrated, the double nature of the slave as thing and man had to be, and in one way or another was, recognized in law and custom by every slave society since ancient times. As a result, every southern planter knew intuitively the limits of his power, as imposed by the prevailing standards of decency. If he exceeded those limits, he might not suffer punishment at law and might even be strong enough to prevent his being ostracized by disapproving neighbors. For these reasons historians have dismissed community pressure as a factor. In doing so, they err badly, for the point is not at all what happened to a violator of convention but the extent to which the overwhelming majority of slaveholders internalized conventional values. In this respect the legal structures of Brazil and the United States were important in conditioning those conventional values. Once again, the difference between the two cases suffices for Tannenbaum's thesis but not for Elkins'—which depends entirely on the experience of absolute power by the slave.

Elkins follows Tannenbaum in ascribing a special role to the Catholic Church in the development of Ibero-American slave societies. The Church defended the moral personality of the slave from a position of independent institutional strength, whereas in the Anglo-Saxon world the separation of church and state, the bourgeois notion of property rights, and the divisions within the religious community largely excluded the churches from the field of master-slave relations. The religious as well as the legal structure helped generate a particular climate of moral opinion into which the Negro could fit as a free man. The difference in structure and result satisfies Tannenbaum's argument; it does not satisfy Elkins' argument, which turns on the specific role played by the priesthood in the life of the slave.

Since Brazil, as the largest Catholic slaveholding country, ought properly to serve as a test case, we might profitably begin with a consideration of developments in Angola, which supplied a large part of its slaves. The clergy, including Jesuits and Dominicans, participated in every horror associated with the slave trade; there is little evidence of its having played a mediating role.[47] By the middle of the seventeenth century Catholic proselytism in the Congo and Angola had spent its force. Contemporary Catholic sources admitted that much of the failure was due to the greed of the clergy in pursuing slave-trade profits and to the generally venal character of priests, secular officials, and laymen.[48] The governor of Angola, the troops, the bishop, and the entire staff of civil and ecclesiastical officials drew their salaries from the direct and indirect proceeds of the slave trade. The Holy House of Mercy [*Misericordia*] at Luanda, as well as the Municipal Council [*Camara*] lived off the trade. Since the *Junta das missoēs*, the chief missionary agency, was supported by these proceeds we need not be surprised that it accomplished little.[49]

In Brazil itself the decisive questions concern the number, character, and relative independence of the priests.[50] We have little data on numbers, but in the mid-twentieth century, Brazil, with a population of fifty million, of whom 95 percent were nominal Catholics, had, according to Vianna Moog, only six thousand priests.[51] We may, nonetheless, assume for a moment that a high ratio of priests to slaves existed. There is good reason to believe that a significant percentage of the priests who ventured to the colonies had questionable characters and that many of good character succumbed to the indolence, violence, and corruption that marked their isolated, quasi-frontier environment. It is no insult to the Church to affirm this state of affairs, for the Church has had to struggle for centuries to raise the quality of its priests and to maintain high standards of performance. Like other institutions of this world it has consisted of men with all the weaknesses of men, and in the difficult circumstances of colonial life the adherence of its men to the high standards of the Church Militant proved erratic and uncertain.

Even if we grant the Brazilian clergy a higher quality than it probably deserved, we confront the question of its relationship to the master class. The local chaplain depended on and deferred to the planter he served more than he depended on his bishop. The Brazilian Church never achieved the strength and cohesion of the Church in Spanish America. The typical sugar planter, in Freyre's words, "though a devout Catholic, was a sort of Philip II in regard to the Church: he considered himself more powerful than the bishops or abbots." Under these conditions the interposition of priest between master and slave was probably little more significant than the interposition of the mistress on a plantation in Mississippi. The analogy assumes particular force when we consider that, increasingly, the Brazilian priesthood was recruited from the local aristocracy.[52] In coffee-growing southern Brazil, in which slavery centered during the nineteenth century, few priests resided on plantations at all and visits were possibly less common than in the United States. The large number of Africans imported during 1830–1850 received little attention from the Church.[53]

The situation in Spanish America worked out more favorably for Elkins' argument because the Church there came much closer to that independence and crusading spirit which has been attributed to it. Even so, the ruthless exploitation of Indians and Negroes by large sections of the clergy is well documented. The position of the Church as a whole, taken over centuries, demonstrates its growing subservience to state and secular power in respects that were decisive for Elkins' purposes. The bulls of Popes and the decrees of kings proved inadequate to temper the rule of the great planters of the New World, although they did play a role in shaping their moral consciousness.[54] In Cuba the clergy acted more boldly and, according to Klein, had a numerical strength adequate to its tasks. However, the effective interposition of even the Cuban clergy during the sugar boom of the nineteenth century has yet to be demonstrated, and if it were to be, Cuba would stand as an exception to the rule.

That more Brazilian and Cuban slaves attended religious services than did southern is by no means certain, the law to the contrary notwithstanding. That the Catholic clergy of Latin America interposed itself more often and more effectively than the Protestant clergy of the South cannot be denied. On balance, Tannenbaum's case is proven by the ability of the Catholic Church to help shape the ethos of slave society and the relative inability of the Protestant to do the same. But Elkins' case falls, for the difference in the potentialities for and especially the realities of personal interposition remained a matter of degree.

Despite the efforts of law and Church in Latin America it is quite possible that as high or higher a percentage of southern slaves lived in stable family units than did Latin American. The force of custom and sentiment generally prevailed over the force of law or institutional interference. In Brazil, as in the Caribbean, male slaves greatly outnumbered female; in the United States the sexes were numerically equal. This factor alone, which derived primarily from economic and technological conditions, encouraged greater family stability in the United States and therefore casts great doubt on Elkins' thesis. To the extent that participation in a stable family life encouraged the development of a mature personality, the slaves of the South probably fared no worse than others. Elkins argues that the Latin American families could not be broken up because of Church and state restrictions. In fact, they often were broken up in open defiance of both. The greatest guarantee against sale existed not where the law forbade it, but where economic conditions reduced the necessity.

The attendant argument that Latin American slaves could function in the roles of fathers and mothers, whereas southern slaves could not, is altogether arbitrary. The feeling of security within the family depended on custom and circumstance, not law, and a great number of southern slaves worked for masters whose economic position and paternalistic attitudes provided a reasonable guarantee against separate sales. In any case, all slaves in all societies faced similar problems. When a slaveowner beat or raped a slave woman in Brazil or Cuba, her husband was quite as helpless as any black man in Mississippi. The duties, responsibilities, and privileges of fatherhood were, in practice, little different from one place to another.

The point of Elkins' controversial concentration camp analogy is not altogether clear. Sometimes he seems to wish to demonstrate only the possibility of mass infantilization, but if this were all he intended, he could have done so briefly and without risking the hostile reaction he brought down on himself. At other times he seems to intend the analogy as a direct device. Although he denies saying that slavery was a concentration camp or even "like" a concentration camp, he does refer to concentration camps as perverted patriarchies and extreme forms of slavery; he finds in them the same total power he believes to have existed on the southern plantations. In the first, restricted, sense the analogy, used suggestively, has its point, for it suggests the ultimate limits of the slave experience. In the second, and broader, sense it offers little and is generally misleading. Unfortunately, Elkins sometimes exaggerates and confuses his device, which only demonstrates the limiting case, with the historical reality of slavery. His elaborate discussion of detachment offers clues but is dangerously misleading. The process did not differ for slaves bound for different parts of the New World; only the post-shock experience of the slave regimes differed, so that we are led right back to those regimes. No doubt Elkins makes a good point when he cites concentration camp and slave trade evidence to show that many participants were spiritually broken by the process, but he overlooks the contribution of newly imported Africans to slave disorders. Everywhere in the Americas a correlation existed between concentrations of African-born slaves and the outbreak of revolts. The evidence indicates that creole slaves were generally more adjusted to enslavement than those who had undergone the shock and detachment processes from Africa to America.[55]

The fundamental differences between the concentration camp and plantation experience may be gleaned from a brief consideration of some of the points made in Bruno Bettelheim's study, on which Elkins relies heavily.[56] Prisoners received inadequate clothing and food in order to test their reaction to extremities of inclement weather and their ability to work while acutely hungry. Slaves received clothing and food designed to provide at least minimum comfort. Slaves suffered from dietary deficiencies and hidden hungers, but rarely from outright malnutrition. In direct contrast to prisoners, slaves normally did not work outdoors in the rain or extreme cold; usually, they were deliberately ordered to stay indoors. Pneumonia and other diseases killed too many slaves every winter for planters not to take every precaution to guard their health. Therein lay the crucial differences: prisoners might be kept alive for experimental purposes, but slaves received treatment designed to grant them long life. Prisoners often did useless work as part of a deliberate program to destroy their personality; slaves did, and knew they did, the productive work necessary for their own sustenance. Prisoners were forbidden to talk to each other much of the day and had virtually no privacy and no social life. Slaves maintained a many-sided social life, which received considerable encouragement from their masters. The Gestapo deliberately set out to deny the individuality of prisoners or to distinguish among them. Planters and overseers made every effort to take full account of slave individuality and even to encourage it up to a point. Prisoners were deliberately subjected to torture and arbitrary punishment; those who followed orders endured the same indignities and blows as those who did not. Slaves, despite considerable arbitrariness in the system, generally had the option of currying favor and avoiding punishment. As Hannah Arendt has so perceptively observed: "Under conditions of total terror not even fear can any longer serve as an advisor of how to behave, because terror chooses its victims without reference to individual actions or thoughts, exclusively in accordance with the objective necessity of the natural or historical process." [57] Concentration camp prisoners changed work groups and barracks regularly and could not develop attachments. Slaves had families and friends, often for a lifetime. The Gestapo had no interest in indoctrinating prisoners. They demanded obedience, not loyalty. Masters wanted and took great pains to secure the loyalty and ideological adherence of their slaves. In general, the slave plantation was a social system, full of joys and sorrows and a fair degree of security, notwithstanding great harshness and even brutality, whereas the concentration camp was a particularly vicious death-cell. They shared a strong degree of authoritarianism, but so does the army or a revolutionary party, or even a family unit.

With these criticisms of data we may turn to Elkins' discussion of personality theory. His use of Sullivan's theory of "significant others" breaks down because of his erroneous notion of the absolute power of the master. In theory the master's power over the slave in the United States was close to absolute; so in theory was the power of Louis XIV over the French. In practice, the plantation represented a series of compromises between whites and blacks. Elkins' inability to see the slaves as active forces capable of tempering the authority of the master leads him into a one-sided appraisal.[58]

According to Elkins, the Latin American slave could relate meaningfully to the friar on the slave ship; the confessor who made the plantation rounds; the zealous Jesuit who especially defended the sanctity of the family; the local magistrate who had to contend with the Crown's official protector of the slaves; and any informer who could expect to collect one-third of the fines. In general, it would not be unfair to say that, notwithstanding all these institutional niceties, the Latin American slave-owners, especially the Brazilian, ruled their plantations as despotically as any southerner. Priest, magistrate, and anyone careless enough to risk his life to play the informer came under the iron grip of the plantation owners' enormous local power.

Various other persons did affect meaningfully the lives of slaves in all systems. The plantation mistress often acted to soften her husband's rule. The overseer did not always precisely reflect the master's temperament and wishes, and slaves demonstrated great skill in playing the one against the other. The Negro driver often affected their lives more directly than anyone else and had considerable authority to make their lives easy or miserable. Slaves who found it difficult to adjust to a master's whims or who feared punishment often ran to some other planter in the neighborhood to ask for his intercession, which they received more often than not. Elkins ignores these and other people because they had no lawful right to intervene; but they did have the power of persuasion in a world of human beings with human reactions. To the vast majority of slaves in all systems, the power of the master approached the absolute and yet was tempered by many human relationships and sensibilities. To the extent that slavery, in all societies, restricted the number of "significant others," it may well have contributed toward the formation of a slavish personality, but Latin America differed from the South only in permitting a somewhat larger minority to transcend that effect.

Similar objections may be made with reference to the application of role theory. The Latin American slave could ordinarily no more act the part of a husband or father than could the southern. The typical field hand had roughly the same degree of prestige and authority in his own cabin in all societies. Legal right to property did not make most Latin American slaves property owners in any meaningful sense, and many southern slaves were de facto property owners of the same kind. The theoretical right of the one and the mere privilege of the other did not present a great practical difference, for the attitude of the master was decisive in both cases. For Tannenbaum's social analysis the significance of the difference stands; for Elkins' psychological analysis it does not.

The theory of personality that Elkins seems to slight, but uses to greatest advantage, is the Freudian, perhaps because it offers a simple direct insight quite apart from its more technical formulations. We do not need an elaborate psychological theory to help us understand the emergence of the slaveowner as a father figure. As the source of all privileges, gifts, and necessaries, he loomed as a great benefactor, even when he simultaneously functioned as a great oppressor. Slaves, forced into dependence on their master, viewed him with awe and identified their interests and even their wills with his. Elkins' analogy with concentration camp prisoners who began to imitate their SS guards indicates the extreme case of this tendency. All exploited classes manifest something of this tendency—the more servile the class the stronger the tendency. It is what many contemporary observers, including runaway slaves and abolitionists, meant when they spoke of the reduction of the slave to a groveling creature without initiative and a sense of self-reliance. Elkins, using Freudian insight, has transformed this observation into the politically relevant suggestion that the slave actually learned to see himself through his master's eyes.

Elkins has often been criticized for failing to realize that slaves usually acted as expected while they retained inner reservations, but he did recognize this possibility in his discussion of a "broad belt of in-determinacy" between playing a role and becoming the role you always play. The criticism seems to me to miss the point. The existence of such reservations might weaken the notion of total infantilization but would not touch the less extreme notion of a dependent, emasculated personality. The clever slave outwitted his master at least partly because he was sup-posed to. Masters enjoyed the game: it strengthened their sense of superiority, confirmed the slaves' dependence, and provided a sense of pride in having so clever a man-child. On the slave's side it made him a devilishly delightful fellow but hardly a man. The main point against Elkins here is the same as elsewhere—when he is sound he describes not a southern slave but a slave; not a distinctly southern Sambo personality but a slavish personality.[59]

Elkins' general argument contains a fundamental flaw, which, when uncovered, exposes all the empirical difficulties under review. In his model a regime of total power produces a Sambo personality. Confronted by the undeniable existence of exceptions, he pleads first things first and waives them aside as statistically insignificant. Even if we were to agree that they were statistically insignificant, we are left with a serious problem. Elkins did not construct a model to determine probabilities; he constructed a deterministic model, which he cannot drop suddenly to suit his con-venience. The notion of "total power" loses force and usefulness and in-deed approaches absurdity in a world of probabilities and alternatives. If Elkins were to retreat from this notion and consequently from his de-terminism, he could not simply make an adjustment in his model; he would have to begin, as we must, from different premises, although with-out necessarily sacrificing his remarkable insights and suggestions. If the basic personality pattern arose from the nature of the regime, so did the deviant patterns. It would be absurd to argue that a regime could be suf-ficiently complex to generate two or more such patterns and yet sufficiently simple to generate them in mutual isolation. The regime threw up all the patterns at once, whatever the proportions, and the root of every deviation lay in the same social structure that gave us Sambo.

This range of patterns arose from the disparity between the planta-tions and farms, between resident owners and absentees, and above all between the foibles and sensibilities of one master and another. They arose, too, within every slaveholding unit from the impossibility of absolute power—from the qualities, perhaps inherited, of the particular personalities of slaves as individuals; from the inconsistencies in the human behavior of the severest masters; from the room that even a slave plantation provides for breathing, laughing, crying, and combining acquiescence and protest in a single thought, expression, and action. Even modern totalitarian regimes, self-consciously armed with unprecedented weapons of terror, must face that opposition inherent in the human spirit to which Miss Arendt draws attention. The freedom of man cannot be denied even by totalitarian rulers, "for this freedom—irrelevant and arbitrary as they may deem it—is identical with the fact that men are being born and that therefore each of them *is* a new beginning, begins, in a sense, the world anew." [60] We need not pretend to understand adequately that remarkable process of spiritual regeneration which repeatedly unfolds before our eyes. The evidence extends throughout history, including the history of our own day; its special forms and content, not its existence, constitute our problem. Miss Arendt therefore concludes her analysis of terror wisely: "Every end in history necessarily contains a new beginning. . . . Beginning, before it becomes a historical event, is the supreme capacity of man; politically, it is identical with man's freedom. . . . This beginning is guaranteed by each new birth; it is indeed every man." [61]

Sambo himself had to be a product of a contradictory environment, all sides of which he necessarily internalized. Sambo, in short, was Sambo only up to the moment that the psychological balance was jarred from within or without; he might then well have become Nat Turner, for every element antithetical to his being a Sambo resided in his nature. "Total power" and "Sambo" may serve a useful purpose in a theoretical model as a rough approximation to a complex reality, provided that we do not confuse the model with the reality itself. Neither slavery nor slaves can be treated as pure categories, free of the contradictions, tensions, and potentialities that characterize all human experience.

Elkins, in committing himself to these absolutist notions, overlooks the evidence from his own concentration camp analogy. Bettelheim notes that even the most accommodating, servile, and broken-spirited prisoners sometimes suddenly defied the Gestapo with great courage. Eugen Kogon devotes considerable space in his *Theory and Practice of Hell* to the development and maintenance of resistance within the camps.[62] In a similar way the most docile field slaves or the most trusted house slaves might, and often did, suddenly rise up in some act of unprecedented violence. This transformation will surprise us only if we confuse our theoretical model with the reality it ought to help us to understand.

Elkins has not described to us the personality of the southern slave, nor, by contrast, of the Latin American slave; he has instead demonstrated the limiting case of the slavish personality. Every slave system contained a powerful tendency to generate Sambos, but every system generated countervailing forces. Elkins, following Tannenbaum, might properly argue that differences in tradition, religion, and law guaranteed differences in the strength of those countervailing forces; he cannot prove and dare not assume that any system lacked them.

Elkins accounts for such forms of deviant behavior as lying, stealing, and shirking by absorbing them within the general framework of childish response. He is by no means completely wrong in doing so, for very often the form of a particular act of hostility degraded the slave as much as it irritated the master. Elkins' approach is not so much wrong as it is of limited usefulness. Once we pass beyond the insight that the form of rebelliousness might itself reveal accommodation, we cannot go much further. If all behavior short of armed revolt can be subsumed within the framework of childishness and dependence, then that formulation clearly embraces too much. Our historical problem is to explain how and under what conditions accommodation yields to resistance, and we therefore need a framework sufficiently flexible to permit distinction between accommodating behavior that, however slightly, suggests a process of transformation into opposite qualities; such a framework must, moreover, be able to account for both tendencies within a single human being and even within a single act.

It has become something of a fashion in the adolescent recesses of our profession to bury troublesome authors and their work under a heap of carping general and specific complaints; it is no part of my purpose to join in the fun. Elkins' book has raised the study of southern slavery to a far higher level than ever before, and it has done so at a moment when the subject seemed about to be drowned in a sea of moral indignation. It has demonstrated forcefully the remarkable uses to which psychology can be put in historical inquiry. It has brought to the surface the relationship between the slave past and a wide range of current problems flowing from that past. These are extraordinary achievements. To advance in the direction Elkins has pointed out, however, we shall first have to abandon most of his ground. We cannot simply replace his psychological model with a better one; we must recognize that all psychological models may only be used suggestively for flashes of insight or as aids in forming hypotheses and that they cannot substitute for empirical investigation. As the distinguished anthropologist, Max Gluckman, has observed, respect for psychology as a discipline requiring a high degree of training in the acquisition and interpretation of data forces us to bypass psychological analyses whenever possible.[63] Or, to put it another way, if we are to profit fully from Elkins' boldness, we shall have to retreat from it and try to solve the problems he raises by the more orthodox procedures of historical research.

NOTES

1. Stanley M. Elkins, *Slavery: A Problem in American Institutional and Intellectual Life* (Chicago: University of Chicago Press, 1959). For a brief critique of the book as a whole see Genovese, "Problems in Nineteenth-Century American History," *Science & Society* 25 (1961). This present paper shall, so far as possible, be limited to questions of method and assumption. A much shorter version was read to the Association for the Study of Negro Life and History, Baltimore, Maryland, Oct., 1966, where it was incisively criticized by Professor Willie Lee Rose of the University of Virginia. Mrs. Rose was also kind enough to read and criticize the first draft of this longer version. I do not know whether or not my revisions will satisfy her, but I am certain that the paper is much better as a result of her efforts.

2. Elkins, *Slavery*, pp. 115–33 and the literature cited therein.

3. John Harding, *et al.*, "Prejudice and Ethnic Relations," *Handbook of Social Psychology*, Gardner Lindzey (ed.) (Cambridge: Addison-Wesley Publishing Co., 1954), II, pp. 1021–62, esp. 1024.

4. C. L. R. James, *The Black Jacobins: Toussaint L'Ouverture and the San Domingo Revolution* (New York: Vintage Books, 1963), p. 21.

5. Ibn Khaldun, *The Muqaddimah* (tr. Franz Rosenthal; New York: Pantheon Books, 1958), I, pp. 174, 301; the parentheses were inserted by the translator for technical reasons. David Brion Davis maintains that as Muslims extended their hegemony over Africa, they came to regard black Africans as fit only for slavery: *The Problem of Slavery in Western Culture* (Ithaca: Cornell University Press, 1966), p. 50. Cf. Basil Davidson, *Black Mother* (Boston: Little, Brown & Co., 1961), pp. xvii, 7, 45, 92–93 for Sambo's appearance in Africa.

6. C. R. Boxer, ed., "Negro Slavery in Brazil" [trans. of *Nova e Curiosa Relacao* (*1764*)], *Race* 5 (1964): 43.

7. Stanley J. Stein, *Vassouras: A Brazilian Coffee County, 1850–1900* (Cambridge, Mass.: Harvard University Press, 1957), p. 133.

8. Euclides da Cunha, *Rebellion in the Backlands* (*Os Sertoes*) (trans. Samuel Putnam; Chicago: University of Chicago Press, 1944), p. 71; for a critical review of some of this literature see Arthur Ramos, *The Negro in Brazil* (Washington: The Associated Publishers, 1939), pp. 22–24.

9. Manoel de Oliveira Lima, *The Evolution of Brazil Compared with That of Spanish and Anglo-Saxon America* (Stanford: Stanford University Press, 1914), p. 122.

10. Joao Pandía Calógeras, *A History of Brazil* (Chapel Hill: University of North Carolina Press, 1939), p. 29. Even today, when Negroes face discrimination in Brazil, whites insist that it is a result of their own incapacities and sense of inferiority. See Fernando Henrique Cardoso and Octavio Ianni, *Côr a mobilidade em Florianópolis* (São Paulo: Difusão Européia do Livro, 1964), p. 231.

11. Kenneth M. Stampp, *The Peculiar Institution* (New York: Vintage Books, 1956), p. 148: "Here, then, was the way to produce the perfect slave: accustom him to rigid discipline, demand from him unconditional submission, impress upon him his innate inferiority, develop in him a paralyzing fear of white men, train him to

adopt the master's code of good behavior, and instill in him a sense of complete dependence. This at least was the goal."

Octavio Ianni, *As Metamorfoses do Escravo* (São Paulo: Difusão Européia do Livro, 1962), pp. 134–35: "Essential to the full functioning of the regime [was] a rigorous, drastic system of control over the social behavior of the enslaved laborer; . . . mechanisms of socialization appropriate to the dominant social strata . . . ; the impossibility of vertical social mobility; . . . rules of conduct ordered according to a standard of rigid obedience of the Negroes in front of white men, whether masters or not."

See also Fernando Henrique Cardoso, *Capitalismo e Escravidao no Brasil Meridional* (São Paulo: Difusão Européia do Livro, 1962), pp. 312–13. Davis follows Ianni and others and speaks of Brazilian slaves as having been reduced "to a state of psychic shock, of flat apathy and depression, which was common enough in Brazil to acquire the special name of *banzo.*" *Problem of Slavery*, p. 238; cf. Ramos, *Negro in Brazil*, pp. 22, 135–36.

12. Davis, *Problem of Slavery*, p. 171.

13. *Selected Writings of Bolívar*, 2 vols. (New York: Colonial Press, 1951), I, p. 131.

14. For an interpretation of the Spanish slave law as holding Negroes to be an especially revolutionary people see Augustín Alcalá y Henke, *Esclavitud de los negros en la América espanola* (Madrid: Impr. d. J. Pueyo, 1919), p. 51. For a view of Brazilian Indians that sounds much like Sambo see the comments of the famous Dutch sea captain, Dierck de Ruiter, as reported in C. R. Boxer, *Salvador de Sá and the Struggle for Brazil and Angola* (London: University of London, 1952), p. 20.

15. Sidney Mintz, review of Elkins' *Slavery*, *American Anthropologist* 63 (1961): 585.

16. "Slavery is determined 'pas par l'obeissance, ni par rudesse des labeurs, mais par le statu d'instrument et la réduction de l'homme a l'etat de chose.'" François Perroux, *La Coexistence pacifique*, as quoted by Herbert Marcuse, *One-Dimensional Man: Studies in the Ideology of Advanced Industrial Society* (Boston: Beacon Press, 1964), pp. 32–33.

17. Davis, *Problem of Slavery*, pp. 59–60.

18. Ibid., pp. 66–67.

19. Ibid., p. 420.

20. Audrey I. Richards, *Land, Labour and Diet in Northern Rhodesia: An Economic Study of the Bemba Tribe* (London: Oxford University Press, 1939), p. 400.

21. Josué de Castro, *The Geography of Hunger* (Boston: Little, Brown, 1952), passim.

22. Jean-Paul Sartre, preface to Frantz Fanon, *The Wretched of the Earth* (New York: Grove Press, 1965), p. 14.

23. Quoted from the *Southern Cultivator* 7 (Sept. 1849): 140, by William K. Scarborough, "The Southern Plantation Overseer: A Re-evaluation," *Agricultural History* 38 (1964): 16.

24. See his explicit summary statement, "Culture Contacts and Negro Slavery," *Proceedings of the American Philosophical Society* 107 (1963): 107–10, esp. p. 107.

25. Frank Tannenbaum, *Slave & Citizen: The Negro in the Americas* (New York: A. A. Knopf, 1946), p. 48.

26. Ibid., pp. 65, 69, and passim.

27. Arnold A. Sio, "Interpretations of Slavery: The Slave Status in the

THE AFRO-AMERICAN AND THE SLAVE SYSTEM 233

Americas," *Comparative Studies in Society and History* 7 (1965): 303, 308. For a fresh consideration of the problem of slave law in the islands see Elsa V. Goveia, "The West Indian Slave Laws in the Eighteenth Century," *Revista de Ciencias Sociales* 4 (1960): 75–105.

28. Marvin Harris has counterposed an economic viewpoint to Tannenbaum's. Despite considerable exaggeration and one-sidedness, he does demonstrate the partial applicability of an institutional approach. For a critical analysis of Harris' polemic and the literature it touches see Genovese, "Materialism and Idealism in the History of Negro Slavery in the Americas," *Journal of Social History* 7 (Summer 1968): 374–94.

The experience of the Dutch demonstrates how much religious and national attitudes gave way before the necessities of colonial life. The Dutch experience in Surinan, New Netherland, Brazil, etc. varied enormously. See, e.g., C. R. Boxer, *The Dutch in Brazil* (Oxford: Clarendon Press, 1957), esp. p. 75; Edgar J. McManus, *A History of Negro Slavery in New York* (Syracuse, New York: Syracuse University Press, 1966), ch. 1.

29. Quoted by James, *Black Jacobins*, p. 17.

30. Ibid., p. 56; Davis, *Problem of Slavery*, p. 254 and the literature cited therein.

31. Gilberto Freyre, *The Masters and the Slaves: A Study in the Development of Brazilian Civilization* (2nd English Language ed., rev.; New York: A. A. Knopf, 1956), p. xxxix.

32. Stein, *Vassouras*, p. 136.

33. See, e.g., the discussion of the law of 1797 in Antigua in Elsa V. Goveia, *Slave Society in the British Leeward Islands at the End of the Eighteenth Century* (New Haven: Yale University Press, 1966), p. 191.

34. Gilberto Freyre, *The Mansions and the Shanties: The Making of Modern Brazil* (New York: A. A. Knopf, 1963), p. 226.

35. Gilberto Freyre, "Social Life in Brazil in the Middle of the Nineteenth Century," *Hispanic American Historical Review* 5 (1922): 597–628; see also, Freyre, *Masters*, pp. xxxiii, 24, 42; *New World in the Tropics: The Culture of Modern Brazil* (New York: Vintage Books, 1963), p. 69.

36. Alan A. Manchester describes 1848 as the turning point. See *British Pre-Eminence in Brazil* (Chapel Hill: University of North Carolina Press, 1933), pp. 261–62.

37. George S. Barnsley MS Notebook in the Southern Historical Collection, University of North Carolina, Chapel Hill.

38. For a penetrating discussion of these two sides of *Las Siete Partidas* see Davis, *Problem of Slavery*, pp. 102–5.

39. Ibid., p. 240.

40. Arthur Percival Newton, *The European Nations in the West Indies, 1493–1689* (London: A. and C. Black, Ltd., 1933), p. 3.

41. For a useful recent summary discussion of the literature see Harris, *Patterns of Race*, pp. 18–20.

42. Cf., Arthur S. Aiton, "The Asiento Treaty as Reflected in the Papers of Lord Shelburne," *Hispanic American Historical Review* 8 (1928): 167–77, esp. p. 167.

43. Jaime Jaramillo Uribe, "Esclavos y Senores en la sociedad colombiana del siglo XVIII," *Anuario colombiano de historia social y de cultura* 1 (1963): 1–22.

44. Herbert Klein, "Anglicanism, Catholicism and the Negro," *Comparative Studies in Society and History* 8 (1966): 295–327; *Slavery in the Americas: A Com-*

parative Study of Cuba and Virginia (Chicago: University of Chicago Press, 1967).

45. See H. H. S. Aimes, *A History of Slavery in Cuba, 1511 to 1868* (New York: G. P. Putnam's Sons, 1907), pp. 150–51, 175–77.

46. On this point see Sidney Mintz, foreword to Ramiro Guerra y Sánchez, *Sugar and Society in the Caribbean* (New Haven: Yale University Press, 1964), and his review of Elkins' book in the *American Anthropologist* 63 (1961): 579–87. Klein, Tannenbaum and Elkins make much of the practice of *coartación*. For a critical assessment see Davis, *Problem of Slavery*, pp. 266–67.

47. Boxer, *Salvador de Sá*, p. 279.

48. C. R. Boxer, *Race Relations in the Portuguese Colonial Empire, 1415–1825* (Oxford: Clarendon Press, 1963), pp. 7–8, 11–12, 21.

49. C. R. Boxer, *Portuguese Society in the Tropics: The Municipal Councils of Goa, Macao, Bahia, and Luanda, 1510–1800* (Madison: University of Wisconsin Press, 1965), pp. 131–32, Basil Davidson, *Black Mother* (Boston: Little, Brown & Co., 1961), p. 158.

50. Elkins certainly errs in ascribing a protective role to the Jesuits, whose efforts on behalf of the Indians were not repeated with the Negroes. Jesuit treatment of those Negroes within their reach does not constitute one of the more glorious chapters in the history of the order. The literature is extensive; for a good, brief discussion see Joao Dornas Filho, *A Escravidao no Brasil* (Rio de Janeiro: Civilização Brasileira, 1939), p. 105.

51. Vianna Moog, *Bandeirantes and Pioneers* (New York: G. Graziller, 1964), p. 209. Cf., Percy Alvin Martin, "Slavery and Abolition in Brazil," *Hispanic American Historical Review* 13 (1933): 168: "On most plantations the spiritual life of the slaves received scant attention. Priests were found only on the larger estates."

52. Freyre, *New World in the Tropics*, pp. 70–71, 87–88; *Mansions*, p. 244.

53. Stein, *Vassouras*, pp. 196–99.

54. Cf., René Maunier, *The Sociology of Colonies*, 2 vols. (London: Routledge & Kegan Paul, 1949), I, pp. 293–94.

55. Elkins seems troubled by this—see p. 102—but he does not pursue it. K. Onwuka Dike points out that Guineans brought to the trading depots of the Niger Delta had already been prepared psychologically for slavery by the religious indoctrination accompanying the cult of the Aro oracle. See "The Question of Sambo: A Report of the Ninth Newberry Library Conference on American Studies," *Newberry Library Bulletin* 5 (1958): 27 and K. Onwuka Dike, *Trade and Politics in the Niger Delta, 1830–1885* (Oxford: Clarendon Press, 1956), ch. 2.

56. Bruno Bettelheim, "Individual and Mass Behavior in Extreme Situations," *Journal of Abnormal and Social Psychology* 38 (1943): 417–52. On the general problem of the concentration camp analogy see the remarks of Daniel Boorstin as reported in the *Newberry Library Bulletin* 5 (1958): 14–40 and Earle E. Thorpe, "Chattel Slavery & Concentration Camps," *Negro History Bulletin* 25 (1962): 171–76. Unfortunately, Mr. Thorpe's thoughtful piece is marred by a clumsy discussion of the problem of wearing a mask before white men.

57. Hannah Arendt, "Ideology and Terror: A Novel Form of Government," *Review of Politics* 15 (1953): 314. I am indebted to Professor Daniel Walden of the Pennsylvania State University for calling this illuminating article to my attention and for suggesting its relevance to the subject at hand.

58. For a perceptive and well-balanced discussion of this side of plantation life see Clement Eaton, *The Growth of Southern Civilization* (New York: Harper & Row, 1961), p. 74 and passim.

59. Brazilian slaves saw their masters as patriarchs and, in Freyre's words, "almighty figures." Freyre, *Mansions*, p. 234. See also Celso Furtado, *The Economic Growth of Brazil* (Berkeley: University of California Press, 1963), pp. 153–54.

60. Arendt, *Review of Politics* 15 (1953): 312.

61. Ibid., p. 327.

62. Bettelheim, *Journal of Abnormal and Social Psychology* 38 (1943): 451; Eugen Kogon, *The Theory and Practice of Hell* (New York: Farrar, Straus, 1950), esp. chs. 20, 31.

63. Max Gluckman, *Order and Rebellion in Tribal Africa* (New York: Free Press, 1963), pp. 2–3.

15. RAYMOND A. AND ALICE H. BAUER, Day to Day Resistance to Slavery (1942)*

In this selection, the Bauers, who were then two young anthropologists at Northwestern University, also attacked the myth that "slaves were docile, well adapted to slavery, and reasonably content in their lot." They were among the first scholars to broaden the definition of slave discontent to include more than armed rebellion. The Bauers catalogue the many subtle but effective forms of resistance prevalent among Afro-American slaves in the Old South. Raymond A. Bauer is currently a member of the faculty of the Graduate School of Business Administration of Harvard University.

The tradition that has grown up about Negro slavery is that the slaves were docile, well adapted to slavery, and reasonably content with their lot.[1] A standard work on the Negro problem in the United States says:

"The Negroes brought into the New World situation and presently reduced to a perpetual servitude became very rapidly accommodated to the environment and status. The explanation of the comparative ease with which this was brought about doubtless lies in the peculiar racial traits of the Negro peoples themselves. They are strong and robust in physique and so everywhere sought after as laborers. In disposition they are cheerful, kindly and sociable: in character they are characteristically extrovert, so readily obedient and easily contented. More than most other social groups they are patiently tolerant under abuse and and oppression and little inclined to struggle against difficulties. These facts of racial temperament and disposition make the Negroes more amenable to the condition of slavery than perhaps any other racial group."[2]

* From Raymond A. and Alice H. Bauer, "Day to Day Resistance to Slavery," *Journal of Negro History* 27 (October 1942): 388–419. Copyright © by The Association for the Study of Negro Life and History, Inc. Reprinted by permission.

This concept is gradually being changed as the study of slave revolts, and of the social tension caused by the constant threat of revolt progresses.[3] In answer to the question, " 'Are the masters afraid of insurrection?' (a slave) says, 'They live in constant fear upon this subject. The least unusual noise at night alarms them greatly. They cry out, 'What is that?' 'Are the boys all in'?" [4]

The purpose of this paper is to study a less spectacular aspect of slavery—the day to day resistance to slavery, since it is felt that such a study will throw some further light on the nature of the Negro's reaction to slavery. Our investigation has made it apparent that the Negroes not only were very discontented, but that they developed effective protest techniques in the form of indirect retaliation for their enslavement. Since this conclusion differs sharply from commonly accepted belief, it would perhaps be of value if a brief preliminary statement were made of how belief so at variance with the available documentary materials could gain such acceptance.

The picture of the docile, contented Negro slave grew out of two lines of argument used in ante-bellum times. The pro-slavery faction contended that the slaves came of an inferior race, and that they were happy and contented in their subordinate position, and that the dancing and singing Negro exemplified their assumption. Abolitionists, on the other hand, tended to depict the Negro slave as a passive instrument, a good and faithful worker exploited and beaten by a cruel master. As one reads the controversial literature on the slavery question, it soon becomes apparent that both sides presented the Negro as a docile creature; one side because it wished to prove that he was contented, the other because it wished to prove that he was grossly mistreated. Both conceptions have persisted to the present time. Writers who romanticize the "Old South" idealize the condition of the slaves, and make of them happy, willing servitors, while those who are concerned with furthering the interests of the Negroes are careful to avoid mention of any aggressive tendencies which might be used as a pretext for further suppressing the Negroes.

Many travelers in the South have accepted the overt behavior of the slaves at its face value. The "yas suh, Cap'n," the smiling, bowing, and scraping of the Negroes have been taken as tokens of contentment. Redpath's conversations with slaves indicated how deep seated this behavior was.[5] This point of view, however, neglects the fact that the whites have always insisted on certain forms of behavior as a token of acceptance of inferior status by the Negro. The following quotation from Dollard is pertinent:

"An informant already cited has referred to the Negro as a 'Dr. Jekyll and Mr. Hyde.' He was making an observation that is well understood among

Negroes—that he has a kind of dual personality, two roles, one that he is forced to play with white people and one the 'real Negro' as he appears in his dealings with his own people. What the white southern people see who 'know their Negroes' is the role that they have forced the Negro to accept, his caste role." [6]

The conceptual framework within which this paper is written is that the Negro slaves were forced into certain outward forms of compliance to slavery; that, except for the few who were able to escape to the North, the Negroes had to accept the institution of slavery and make their adjustments to that institution. The patterns of adjustment which we have found operative are: slowing up of work, destruction of property, malingering and self-mutilation.

The sources of our material are: (1) general works on slavery, labor, and the Negro; (2) the journals and the travel accounts of southerners and of visitors to the slave territory; and (3) the biographies and autobiographies of slaves. Most of the secondary sources take some cognizance of the fact that slaves slowed up their work, feigned illness, and the like, but this behavior is regarded as a curiosity. There has been no attempt by those writers who set down such facts to understand their social and economic significance. The journals and travel-books vary greatly in the amount of information they contain. This, of course, is due to the authors' variations in interest and acuteness. Olmsted's *Seaboard Slave States*, for instance, abounds in anecdotes, and in expressions of opinion as to the extent of loafing and malingering. Susan Smedes' *Memorials of a Southern Planter*, on the other hand, contains just one footnoted reference to any such behavior. Life stories of ex-slaves emphasize running away, forms of punishment, and other aspects of slavery that would make interesting reading. Yet while references to slowing up work, or feigning illness, are thus few in number, where they are made they are stated in such a way that they leave no doubt that there was a persistent pattern of such behavior.

"Slaveholders ever underrate the intelligence with which they have to grapple. I really understood the old man's mutterings, attitudes and gestures, about as well as he did himself. But slaveholders never encourage that kind of communication, with the slaves, by which they might learn to measure the depths of his knowledge. Ignorance is a high virtue in a human chattel; and as the master studies to keep the slave ignorant, the slave is cunning enough to make the master think he succeeds. The slave fully appreciates the saying, 'where ignorance is bliss 'tis folly to be wise'." [7]

We have felt it wise to quote extensively. Much of the meaning of incidents and interpretations lies in the phrasing of the author—in sensing his own emphasis on what he says. Methodologically, in attempting to analyze an existing stereotype, as we are trying to do here, it would seem wisest to present the picture as it appeared to contemporaries, and thus as given in their own words.

The Negroes were well aware that the work they did benefited only the master. "The slaves work and the planter gets the benefit of it." [8] "The conversation among the slaves was that they worked hard and got no benefit, that the masters got it all." [9] It is thus not surprising that one finds many recurring comments that a slave did not do half a good day's work in a day. A northerner whom Lyell met in the South said: "Half the population of the South is employed in seeing that the other half do their work, and they who do work, accomplish half what they might do under a better system." [10] An English visitor, with a very strong pro-slavery bias corroborates this: "The amount of work expected of the field hand will not be more than one half of what would be demanded of a white man; and even that will not be properly done unless he be constantly over-looked." [11] Statements of other writers are to the same effect:

"It is a common remark of those persons acquainted with slave-labor, that their proportion is as one to two. This is not too great an estimate in favor or the free-laborer; and the circumstances of their situation produce a still greater disparity." [12]

"A capitalist was having a building erected in Petersburg, and his slaves were employed in carrying up the brick and mortar for the masons on their heads: a Northerner, standing near, remarked to him that they moved so indolently that it seemed as if they were trying to see how long they could be in mounting the ladder without actually stopping. The builder started to re-prove them, but after moving a step turned back and said: 'It would only make them move more slowly still when I am not looking at them, if I should hurry now. *And what motive have they to do better?* It's no concern of theirs how long the masons wait. I am sure if I was in their place, I shouldn't move as fast as they do.'" [13]

A well-informed capitalist and slave-holder remarked,

"In working niggers, we always calculate that they will not labor at all except to avoid punishment, and they will never do more than just enough to save themselves from being punished, and no amount of punishment will prevent their working carelessly or indifferently. It always seems on the plan-tations as if they took pains to break all the tools and spoil all the cattle that they possibly can, even when they know they'll be directly punished for it." [14]

Just how much of this was due to indifference and how much due to deliberate slowing up is hard to determine. Both factors most probably entered. A worker who had to devote himself to a dull task from which he can hope to gain nothing by exercising initiative soon slips into such a frame of mind that he does nothing more than go through the motions. His chief concern is to escape from the realities of his task and put it in the back of his mind as much as possible.

There is, indeed, a strong possibility that this behavior was a form of indirect aggression. While such an hypothesis cannot be demonstrated on the basis of the available contemporary data, it is supported by Dollard's interpretation of similar behavior which he found in southern towns.

"If the reader has ever seen Stepin Fetchit in the movies, he can picture this type of character. Fetchit always plays the part of a well-accommodated lower-class Negro, whining, vacillating, shambling, stupid, and moved by very simple cravings. There is probably an element of resistance to white society in the shambling, sullenly slow pace of the Negro; it is the gesture of a man who is forced to work for ends not his own and who expresses his reluctance to perform under these circumstances." [15]

Certainly description after description emphasizes the mechanical plodding of the slave workers:

"John Lamar wrote, 'My man Ned the carpenter is idle or nearly so at the plantation. He is fixing gates and, like the idle groom in Pickwick, trying to fool himself into the belief that he is doing something—He is an eye servant.'" [16]

"Those I saw at work appeared to me to move very slowly and awkwardly, as did those engaged in the stables. These also were very stupid and dilatory in executing any orders given them, so that Mr. C. would frequently take the duty off their hands into his own, rather than wait for them, or make them correct their blunders; they were much, in these respects, what our farmers call *dumb Paddees*—that is, Irishmen who do not readily understand the English language, and who are still weak and stiff from the effects of the emigrating voyage. At the entrance gate was a porter's lodge, and, as I approached I saw a black face peeping at me from it, but both when I entered and left, I was obliged to dismount and open the gate myself.

"Altogether, it struck me—slaves coming here as they naturally did in comparison with free laborers, as commonly employed on my own and my neighbors' farms, in exactly similar duties—that they must have been difficult to direct efficiently, and that it must be irksome and trying to one's patience, to have to superintend their labor." [17]

To what extent this reluctant labor was the rule may be appreciated when it is pointed out that a southern doctor classified it under the name *Dysaesthesia Aethiopica* as a mental disease peculiar to Negroes. Olmsted quotes this Dr. Cartwright as follows:

"'From the careless movements of the individual affected with this complaint, they are apt to do much mischief, which appears as if intentional, but it is mostly owing to the stupidity of mind and insensibility of the nerves induced by the disease. Thus, they break, waste, and destroy everything they handle—abuse horses and cattle—tear, burn, or rend their own clothing, and, paying no attention to the rights of property, steal others to replace what they have destroyed. They wander about at night, and keep in a half nodding state by day. They slight their work—cut up corn, cotton and tobacco, when hoeing it, as if for pure mischief. They raise disturbances with their overseers, and among their fellow servants, without cause or motive, and seem to be insensible to pain when subjected to punishment.

"'. . . The term "rascality" given to this disease by overseers, is founded on an erroneous hypothesis, and leads to an incorrect empirical treatment, which seldom or never cures it.'" [18]

There are only two possible interpretations of the doctor's statement. Either the slaves were so extraordinarily lazy that they gave the appearance of being mentally diseased, or the doctor was describing cases of hebephrenic schizophrenia. Either situation is startling. The phenomenon was obviously widespread, and if it was actually a mental disease it certainly would indicate that Negroes did not become "easily adjusted to slavery."

Whatever the case, it is certain that the slaves consciously saved their energy. Olmsted, who always had his eye open for such incidents, reported: "The overseer rode among them, on a horse, carrying in his hand a raw-hide whip, constantly directing and encouraging them; but, as my companion and I, both, several times noticed, as often as he visited one line of the operations, the hands at the other end would discontinue their labor, until he turned to ride toward them again." [19]

The few statements on this point we have by ex-slaves seem to indicate that the slaves as a group made a general policy of not letting the master get the upper hand.

"I had become large and strong; and had begun to take pride in the fact that I could do as much hard work as some of the older men. There is much rivalry among slaves, at times, as to which can do the most work, and masters generally seek to promote such rivalry. But some of us were too wise to race with each other very long. Such racing, we had the sagacity to see, was not likely to pay. We had times out for measuring each other's strength, but we knew too much to keep up the competition so long as to produce an extraordinary day's work. We knew that if, by extraordinary exertion, a large quantity of work was done in one day, the fact, becoming known to the master, might lead him to require the same amount every day. This thought was enough to bring us to a dead halt whenever so much excited for the race." [20]

Writer after writer, describing incidents in which slaves were compelled to assist in punishing other slaves, states that they did so with the greatest of reluctance.

"The hands stood still;—they knew Randall—and they knew him also to be a powerful man, and were afraid to grapple with him. As soon as Cook had ordered the men to seize him, Randall turned to them, and said—'Boys, you all know me; you know that I can handle any three of you, and the man that lays hands on me shall die. This white man can't whip me himself, and therefore he has called you to help him.' The overseer was unable to prevail upon them to seize and secure Randall, and finally ordered them all to go to their work together." [21]

In some cases it was noted that the slave resisting punishment took pains not to treat his fellows with any more than the absolute minimum of violence.

With such demonstrations of solidarity among the slaves it is not surprising to find a slave telling of how he and his fellows "captured" the institution of the driver. The slave Solomon Northrup was such a driver. His task was to whip the other slaves in order to make them work.

" 'Practice makes perfect,' truly; and during eight years' experience as a driver I learned to handle the whip with marvelous dexterity and precision, throwing the lash within a hair's breadth of the back, the ear, the nose without, however, touching either of them. If Epps was observed at a distance, or we had reason to apprehend he was sneaking somewhere in the vicinity, I would commence plying the lash vigorously, when, according to arrangement, they would squirm and screech as if in agony, although not one of them had in fact been grazed. Patsey would take occasion, if he made his appearance presently, to mumble in his hearing some complaints that Platt was whipping them the whole time, and Uncle Abram, with an appearance of honesty peculiar to himself would declare roundly I had just whipped them worse than General Jackson whipped the enemy at New Orleans." [22]

Williams, another slave whose task was to drive his fellows, said: "He was at these periods terribly severe to his hands, and would order me to use up the cracker of my whip every day upon the poor creatures who were toiling in the field; and in order to satisfy him, I used to tear it off when returning home at night. He would then praise me for a good fellow and invite me to drink with him." [23]

The amount of slowing up of labor by the slaves must, in the aggregate, have caused a tremendous financial loss to plantation owners. The only way we have of estimating it quantitatively is through comparison of the work done in different plantations and under different systems of labor. The statement is frequently made that production on a plantation varied more than 100 percent from time to time. Comparison in the output of slaves in different parts of the South also showed variations of over 100 percent. Most significant is the improvement in output obtained under the task, whereby the slaves were given a specific task to fulfill for their day's work, any time left over being their own. Olmsted gives us our best information on this point:

"These tasks certainly would not be considered excessively hard by a northern laborer; and, in point of fact, the more industrious and active hands finished them often by two o'clock. I saw one or two leaving the field soon after one o'clock, several about two; and between three and four, I met a dozen women and several men coming home to their cabins, having finished their day's work.

"Under this 'Organization of Labor' most of the slaves work rapidly and well. In nearly all ordinary work, custom has settled the extent of the task, and it is difficult to increase it. The driver who marks it out, has to remain on the ground until it is finished, and has no interest in overmeasuring it; and if it should be systematically increased very much, there is danger of a general stampede to the swamp, a danger the slave can always hold before his master's cupidity." [24]

"It is the custom of tobacco manufacturers to hire slaves and free negroes at a certain rate of wages each year. A task of 45 pounds per day is given them to work up, and all they choose to do more than this, they are paid for—payment being made once a fortnight; and invariably this over-wages is used by the slave for himself, and is usually spent in drinking, licentiousness, and gambling. The man was grumbling that he had saved but $20 to spend at the holidays. One of the manufacturers offered to show me by his books, that nearly all gained by over-work $5 a month, many $20 and some as much as $28.[25]

"He (the speaker) was executor of an estate in which, among other negroes, there was one very smart man, who, he knew perfectly well, ought to be earning for the estate $150 a year, and who could if he chose, yet whose wages for a year being let out by the day or job, had amounted to but $18, while he had paid for medical attendance upon him $45." [26]

The executor of the estate finally arranged for this man to work out his freedom, which he readily accomplished.

A quantitative estimate can be made from another situation which Olmsted observed. Rain during a previous day had made certain parts of the work more difficult than others. The slaves were therefore put on day work, since it would not be possible to lay out equitable tasks.

"Ordinarily it is done by tasks—a certain number of the small divisions of the field being given to each hand to burn in a day; but owing to a more than usual amount of rain having fallen lately, and some other causes, making the work harder in some places than in others, the women were now working by the day, under the direction of a 'driver,' a negro man, who walked about among them, taking care they had left nothing unburned. Mr. X inspected the ground they had gone over, to see whether the driver had done his duty. It had been sufficiently well burned, but not more than a quarter as much ground had been gone over, he said, as was usually burned in tasked work,—and he thought they had been very lazy, and reprimanded them for it." [27]

Most revealing of all is this statement:

> "'Well, now, old man,' said I, 'you go and cut me two cords today!' 'Oh, massa! two cords! Nobody could do dat. Oh! massa, dat is too hard! Neber heard o' nobody's cuttin' more 'n a cord o' wood in a day, round heah. No nigger couldn't do it.' 'Well, old man, you have two cords of wood cut to-night or to-morrow morning you shall get two hundred lashes—that's all there is about it. So look sharp.' And he did it and ever since no negro ever cut less than two cords a day for me, though my neighbors never get but one cord. It was just so with a great many other things—mauling rails—I always have two hundred rails mauled in a day; just twice what it is the custom of the country to expect of a negro, and just twice as many as my negroes had been made to do before I managed them myself.
>
> "These estimates, let it be recollected in conclusion, are all deliberately and carefully made by gentlemen of liberal education, who have had unusual facilities of observing both at the North and the South." [28]

The slaves were well aware of their economic value, and used it to good advantage. The skilled laborers among the slaves knew their worth, and frequently rebelled against unsatisfactory work situations. Slaves who were hired out would run away from the masters who had hired them, and then either return home, or remain in hiding until they felt like returning to work.

> "The slave, if he is indisposed to work, and especially if he is not treated well, or does not like the master who has hired him, will sham sickness—even make himself sick or lame—that he need not work. But a more serious loss frequently arises, when the slave, thinking he is worked too hard, or being angered by punishment or unkind treatment, 'getting the sulks,' takes to 'the swamp,' and comes back when he has a mind to. Often this will not be till the year is up for which he is engaged, when he will return to his owner, who, glad to find his property safe, and that it has not died in the swamp, or gone to Canada, forgets to punish him, and immediately sends him for another year to a new master.
>
> "'But, meanwhile, how does the negro support life in the swamp?' I asked.
>
> "'Oh, he gets sheep and pigs and calves, and fowls and turkey; sometimes they will kill a small cow. We have often seen the fires, where they were cooking them, through the woods in the swamp yonder. If it is cold, he will crawl under a fodder stack, or go into the cabins with some of the other negroes, and in the same way, you see, he can get all the corn, or almost anything else he wants.
>
> "'He steals them from his master?'

" 'From anyone: frequently from me. I have had many a sheep taken by them.' [29]

" 'It is a common thing, then?'

" 'Certainly it is, very common, and the loss is sometimes exceedingly provoking. One of my neighbors here was going to build, and hired two mechanics for a year. Just as he was ready to put his house up, the two men, taking offense at something, both ran away, and did not come back at all, till their year was out, and then their owner immediately hired them out again to another man.' " [30]

One plantation overseer wrote to the plantation owner concerning a carpenter he had hired out to one G. Moore: "Not long before Jim run away G More (sic.) wanted him to make some gates and I sent him theireselves (sic.) and he run away from him and cum home and then he left me withow (sic.) a cause." [31]

Even the threat of a whipping did not deter such slaves from running off for a time when they were displeased. The quotation from Olmsted below is typical of a constantly recurring pattern of statements: "The manager told me that the people often ran away after they have been whipped or something else had happened to make them angry. They hide in the swamp and come into the cabins at night to get food. They seldom remain away more than a fortnight and when they come in they are whipped." [32] Some of the resistance took on the aspects of organized strikes:

"Occasionally, however, a squad would strike in a body as a protest against severities. An episode of this sort was recounted in a letter of a Georgia overseer to his absent employer: 'Sir: I write you a few lines in order to let you know that six of your hands has left the plantation—every man but Jack. They displeased me with their work and I give some of them a few lashes, Tom with the rest. On Wednesday morning they were missing. I think they are lying out until they can see you or your Uncle Jack.' The slaves could not negotiate directly at such a time, but while they lay in the woods they might make overtures to the overseer through slaves on a neighboring plantation as to terms upon which they would return to work, or they might await their master's posthaste arrival and appeal to him for a redress of grievances. Humble as their demeanor might be, their power of renewing the pressure by repeating their act could not be ignored." [33]

John Holmes, an escaped slave, told how he ran off and hid in the swamp after an overseer attempted to whip him. "At last they told all the neighbors if I would come home, they wouldn't whip me. I was a great hand to work and made a great deal of money for our folks." [34] The same overseer had further trouble with the slaves.

"She (a slave) was better with her fists, and beat him, but he was better at wrestling and threw her down. He then called the men to help him, but all hid from him in the brush where we were working. . . . Then (later) the calculation was to whip us every one, because we did not help the overseer. . . . That night every one of us went away into the woods. . . . We went back, but after a while (the overseer) came back too, and stayed the year out. He whipped the women but he did not whip the men, of fear they would run away." [35]

The indifference of the slaves to the welfare of the masters extended itself to a complete contempt for property values. The slaves were so careless with tools that they were equipped with special tools, and more clumsy than ordinary ones:

"The 'nigger hoe' was first introduced into Virginia as a substitute for the plow, in breaking up the soil. The law fixes its weight at four pounds,—as heavy as the woodman's axe. It is still used, not only in Virginia, but in Georgia and the Carolinas. The planters tell us, as the reason for its use, that the negroes would break a Yankee hoe in pieces on the first root, or stone that might be in their way. An instructive commentary on the difference between free and slave labor!" [36]

"The absence of motive, and the consequent want of mental energy to give vigor to the arm of the slave is the source of another great drawback upon the usefulness of his labor. His implements or tools are at least one-third (in some instances more than twofold) heavier and stronger than the northern man's to counteract his want of skill and interest in his work. A Negro hoe or scythe would be a curiosity to a New England farmer." [37]

Not only tools but livestock suffered from the mistreatment by the slaves. Olmsted found not only the "nigger hoe" but even discovered that mules were substituted for horses because horses could not stand up under the treatment of the slaves.

. . . . "I am shown tools that no man in his senses, with us, would allow a laborer, to whom he was paying wages, to be encumbered with; and the excessive weight and clumsiness of which, I would judge, would make work at least ten percent greater than those ordinarily used with us. And I am assured that, in the careless and clumsy way they must be used by the slaves, anything lighter or less crude could not be furnished them with good economy, and that such tools as we constantly give our laborers and find profit in giving them, would not last out a day in a Virginia corn-field—much lighter and more free from stones though it be than ours.

"So, too, when I ask why mules are so universally substituted for horses on the farm, the first reason given, and confessedly the most conclusive one, is, that horses cannot bear the treatment they always must get from negroes; horses are always soon foundered or crippled by them but mules will bear cudgeling, and lose a meal or two now and then, and not be materially injured, and they do not take cold or get sick if neglected or overworked. But I do not need to go further than to the window of the room in which I am writing, to see, at almost any time, treatment of cattle that would insure the immediate discharge of the driver, by almost any farmer owning them in the North." [38]

Redpath verifies Olmsted's statement—by telling how he saw slaves treat stock. It is important to note that Redpath was a strong abolitionist and most sympathetic toward the slaves.

"He rode the near horse, and held a heavy cowhide in his hand, with which from time to time he lashed the leaders, as barbarous drivers lash oxen when at work. Whenever we came to a hill, especially if it was very steep, he dismounted, lashed the horses with all his strength, varying his performances by picking up stones, none of them smaller than half a brick, and throwing them with all his force, at the horses' legs. He seldom missed.
"The wagon was laden with two tons of plaster in sacks.
"This is a fair specimen of the style in which Negroes treat stock." [39]

The indifference to livestock is well illustrated by an incident which Olmsted recounts:

"I came, one afternoon, upon a herd of uncommonly fine cattle as they were being turned out of a field by a negro woman. She had given herself the trouble to let down but two of the seven bars of the fence, and they were obliged to leap over a barrier at least four feet high. Last of all came, very unwillingly, a handsome heifer, heavy with calf; the woman urged her with a cudgel and she jumped, but lodging on her belly, as I came up she lay bent, and, as it seemed, helplessly hung upon the top bar. . . . The woman struck her severely and with a painful effort she boggled over." [40]

In the Sea Islands off the coast of Georgia, Kemble reported that the slaves started immense fires, destroying large sections of woods through carelessness or maliciousness.

"The 'field hands' make fires to cook their midday food wherever they happen to be working, and sometimes through their careless neglect, but sometimes, too, undoubtedly on purpose, the woods are set fire to by these means. One benefit they consider . . . is the destruction of the dreaded rattlesnakes." [41]

The slaves on Lewis' West Indies plantation let cattle get into one of his best canepieces because they neglected to guard them, being more interested in a dance which was going on. They were fully aware that the cattle were ruining the sugar cane, but kept right on singing and dancing. Lewis was able to get only a handful of house servants to drive the cattle out of the cane, and that not until the canepiece was ruined. [42]

One tobacco planter complained that his slaves would cut the young plants indiscriminately unless they were watched. When it became late in the season and there was need of haste to avoid frost they would work only the thickest leaving the sparser ones untouched.[43] Another planter said that he could cultivate only the poorer grades of tobacco because the slaves would not give necessary attention to the finer sort of plants.[44] An English visitor said: "The kitchens and out-offices are always at the distance of several yards from the principal dwelling. This is done as well to guard against the house-Negroes through carelessness setting the houses on fire, for they generally sit over it half the night, as to keep out their noise." [45]

The full import of these practices strikes home fully only when they are read in the words of the original observers. Olmsted's comments, and the ease with which he found incidents to illustrate them, are most valuable. So important is his testimony that we must once more quote him at some length.

"Incidents, trifling in themselves, constantly betray to a stranger the bad economy of using enslaved servants. The catastrophe of one such occurred since I began to write this letter. I ordered a fire to be made in my room, as I was going out this morning. On my return, I found a grand fire—the room door having been closed and locked upon it 'out of order.' Just now, while I was writing, down tumbled upon the floor, and rolled away close to the valance of the bed, half a hod-full of ignited coal, which had been so piled upon the diminutive grate, and left without a fender or any guard, that this result was almost inevitable. If I had not returned at the time I did, the house would have been fired." [46]

"On the rice plantation which I have particularly described, the slaves were, I judge, treated with at least as much discretion and judicious consideration of economy, consistently with humane regard to their health, comfort, and morals, as on any other in all the Slave States; yet I could not avoid observing—and I certainly took no pains to do so, nor were any special facilities offered me for it—repeated instances of that waste and misapplication of labor which it can never be possible to guard against, when the agents of industry are slaves. Many such evidences of waste it would not be easy to specify; and others, which remain in my memory after some weeks, do not adequately account for the general impression that all I saw gave me; but there were, for instance, under my observation gates left open and bars left down, against standing orders; rails removed from fences by the negroes (as was conjectured, to kindle their fires with), mules lamed, and implements broken, by careless usage; a flat boat, carelessly secured, going adrift on the river; men ordered to cart rails for a new fence depositing them so that a double expense of labor would be required to lay them, more than would have needed if they had been placed, as they might have almost as easily been, by a slight exercise of forethought . . . making statements which their owner was obliged to receive as sufficient excuse, though, he told me, he reit assured they were false—all going to show habitual carelessness, indolence, and mere eye-service." [47]

But not only did the Negro slaves refuse to work, and not only did they destroy property, but they even made it impossible for planters to introduce new work techniques by feigning clumsiness. They prevented the introduction of the plow in this way on many plantations.[48] Olmsted here cites many instances. Lewis, quoted in *Plantation Documents*, found the same thing to be true in Jamaica.

"It appears to me that nothing could afford so much relief to the negroes, under the existing system of Jamaica, as the substituting of labor of animals for that of slaves in agriculture wherever such a measure is practicable. On leaving the island, I impressed this wish of mine upon the mind of my agents with all my power; but the only result has been the creating a very considerable expense in the purchase of ploughs, oxen and farming implements; the awkwardness and still more the obstinacy of the few negroes, whose services were indispensable, was not to be overcome: they broke plough after plough, and ruined beast after beast, till the attempt was abandoned in despair." [49]

Malingering was a well-known phenomenon throughout the slave states.[50] The purpose of feigning illness was generally to avoid work, although occasionally a slave who was being sold would feign a disability either to avoid being sold to an undesirable master, or to lower his purchase price so as to obtain revenge on a former master. The women occasionally pretended to be pregnant, because pregnant women were given lighter work assignments and were allowed extra rations of food.

In a situation such as this in which physical disability was an advantage, one would expect much malingering. One might also expect to find functional mental disorders, hysterical disorders which would get one out of work. There is some evidence that many had such functional disorders.

"There are many complaints described in Dr. Cartwright's treatise, to which the Negroes, in slavery, seem to be peculiarly subject.

" 'Negro-consumption,' a disease almost unknown to medical men of the Northern States and of Europe, is also sometimes fearfully prevalent among the slaves. 'It is of importance,' says the Doctor, to know the pathognomic signs in its early stages, not only in regard to its treatment but to detect impositions, as negroes, afflicted with this complaint are often for sale; the acceleration of the pulse, on exercise, incapacitates them for labor, as they quickly give out, and have to leave their work. This induces their owners to sell them, although they may not know the cause of their inability to labor. Many of the negroes brought South, for sale, are in the incipient stages of this disease; they are found to be inefficient laborers, and sold in consequence thereof. The effect of superstition—a firm belief that he is poisoned or con- jured—upon the patient's mind, already in a morbid state (dysaesthesia), and his health affected from hard usage, overtasking or exposure, want of wholesome food, good clothing, warm, comfortable lodging, with the distressing idea (sometimes) that he is an object of hatred or dislike, both to his master or fellow-servants, and has no one to befriend him, tends directly to generate the erythism of mind which is the essential cause of negro consumption. . . . 'Remedies should be assisted by removing the *original cause* [51] of the dis- satisfaction or trouble of mind, and by using every means to make the patient comfortable, satisfied and happy.' " [52]

Of course it is impossible to determine the extent of these disorders. Assuming that Dr. Cartwright's assumption was correct, very few ob- servers would be qualified to make an adequate diagnosis, and a very small proportion of these would be inclined to accept his interpretation. After all, functional disorders are in many cases almost impossible to tell from real disorders or from feigning, and since the behavior which Cartwright describes could very easily be interpreted on another, and easier, level by a less acute observer.

Of the extent to which illness was feigned there can, however, be little doubt. Some of the feigning was quite obvious, and one might wonder why such flagrant abuses were tolerated. The important thing to remember is that a slave was an important economic investment. Most slave owners sooner or later found out that it was more profitable to give the slave the benefit of the doubt. A sick slave driven to work might very well die.

"But the same gentleman admitted that he had sometimes been mistaken and had made men go to work when they afterwards proved to be really ill; therefore, when one of his people told him he was not able to work, he usually thought, 'very likely he'll be all the better for a day's rest, whether he's really ill or not,' and would let him off without being very particular in his examina- tion. Lately he had been getting a new overseer, and when he was engaging him he told him that this was his way. The observer replied, 'It's my way too, now; it didn't used to be, but I had a lesson. There was a nigger one day at Mr. ——'s who was sulky and complaining; he said he couldn't work. I looked at his tongue, and it was right clean, and I thought it was nothing but damned sulki- ness so I paddled him, and made him go to work; but, two days after, he was under ground. He was a good eight hundred dollar nigger, and it was a lesson to me about taming possums, that I ain't going to forget in a hurry.' " [53]

So one might find situations like this: "At one, which was evidently the 'sick house' or hospital, there were several negroes, of both sexes, wrapped in blankets, and reclining on the door steps or on the ground, basking in sunshine. Some of them looked ill, but all were chatting and laughing as I rode up to make inquiry." [54]

The situation turned in on itself. The masters were always suspicious of the sick slaves, so that slaves who were moderately sick accentuated their symptoms in order to make out a convincing case.

"It is said to be nearly as difficult to form a satisfactory diagnosis of ne-groes' disorders, as it is of infants', because their imagination of symptoms is so vivid, and because not the smallest reliance is to be placed on their accounts of what they have felt or done. If a man is really ill, he fears lest he should be thought to be simulating, and therefore exaggerates all his pains, and locates them in whatever he supposes to be the most vital parts of his system.

"Frequently the invalid slaves will neglect or refuse to use the remedies prescribed for their recovery. They will conceal pills, for instance, under their tongue, and declare they have swallowed them, when, from their producing no effect, it will be afterwards evident that they have not. This general custom I heard ascribed to habit acquired when they were not very disagreeably ill and were loth to be made quite well enough to have to go to work again." [55]

Fortunately in this field we have some quantitative estimates which enable us to appreciate fully the extent of these practices. Sydnor has digested the records of sickness on various plantations. From the Wheeles plantation records he found that of 1,429 working days 179 were lost on account of sickness, a ratio of almost one to seven. On the Bowles' planta-tion, in one year 159½ days were missed on account of sickness but only five days were on Sundays. This is a recurrent pattern, everybody sick on Saturday, and scarcely anybody sick on Sunday. On the Leigh plantation, where thirty persons were working there were 398 days of sick-ness. In examining this recording Sydnor discovered that the rate of sick-ness was greatest at the times of the year when there was the most work to be done.[56] Olmsted says that he never visited a plantation on which twenty Negroes were employed where he did not find one or more not at work on some trivial pretext.[57]

Lewis' anecdote is typical:

"On Saturday morning there were no fewer than forty-five persons (not in-cluding children) in the hospital; which makes nearly a fifth of my whole gang. Of these the medical people assured me that not above seven had anything whatever the matter with them. . . . And sure enough on Sunday morning they all walked away from the hospital to amuse themselves, except about seven or eight." [58]

Sometimes the feigning did not work, as is shown by two incidents that Olmsted relates:

A Mr. X asked if there were any sick people.

" 'Nobody, oney dat boy Sam, sar.'

" 'What Sam is that?'

" 'Dat little Sam, sar; Tom's Sue's Sam, sar.'

" 'What's the matter with him?'

" 'Don' spec der's nothing much de matter wid him nof, sar. He came in Sa'dy, complaining he had de stomach-ache, an' I give him some ile, sar, 'spec he mu' be well dis time, but he din go out dis mornin'.'

" 'Well, I see to him.'

"Mr. X went to Tom's Sue's cabin, looked at the boy and concluded that he was well, though he lay abed, and pretended to cry with pain, ordered him to go out to work." [59]

A planter asked the nurse if anyone else was sick.

" 'Oney dat woman Caroline.'

" 'What do you think is the matter with her?'

" 'Well, I don't think there is anything de matter wid her, masser; I mus' answer you for true, I don't tink anything de matter wid her, oney she's a little sore from dat whipping she got.' "

The manager found the woman groaning on a dirty bed and after examing her, scolded her and sent her to work.[60]

The prevalence of malingering may be better appreciated when one realizes that despite the fact that Olmsted refers to it throughout four volumes of his works, in one place he has five whole pages of anecdotes concerning it.[61]

Pretending to be pregnant was a type of escape in a class by itself, since the fraud must inevitably have been discovered. This in itself may give us some insight into the Negroes' attitude toward the relative advantages of escaping work and of escaping punishment. Just as the slave who ran off into the woods for a temporary relief from work, the pseudo-pregnant woman must have realized in advance that she would inevitably be punished.

"I will tell you of a most comical account Mr. ——— has given me of the prolonged and still protracted pseudo-pregnancy of a woman called Markie, who for many more months than are generally required for the process of continuing the human species, pretended to be what the Germans pathetically and poetically call 'in good hope' and continued to reap increased rations as the reward of her expectation, till she finally had to disappoint the estate and receive a flogging." [62]

One woman sought to escape from the consequences of her fraud. The results were quite tragic:

"A young slave woman, Becky by name, had given pregnancy as the reason for a continued slackness in her work. Her master became skeptical and gave notice that she was to be examined and might expect the whip in case her excuse were not substantiated. Two days afterwards a Negro midwife announced that Becky's baby had been born; but at the same time a neighboring planter began search for a child nine months old which was missing from his quarter. This child was found in Becky's cabin, with its two teeth pulled and the tip of its navel cut off. It died; and Becky was convicted only of manslaughter." [63]

An outstanding example of malingering is given by Smedes, a writer who insisted so emphatically on the devotion of the slaves to their masters.

"The cook's husband, who for years had looked on himself as nearly blind, and therefore unable to do more than work about her, and put her wood on the fire, sometimes cutting a stick or two, made no less than eighteen good crops for himself when the war was over. He was one of the best farmers in the country." [64]

The most effective means of retaliation against an unpopular master which the slave had at his command was by feigning disability on the auction block. How often this was done we do not know, but Phillips accepts it as a recognized pattern.

"Those on the block often times praised their own strength and talents, for it was a matter of pride to fetch high prices. On the other hand if a slave should bear a grudge against his seller, or should hope to be bought only by someone who would expect but light service he might pretend a disability though he had it not." [65]

Coleman offers the same opinion:

"Similar actions were not unknown in slave sales. Frequently on such occasions there is a strong indisposition in such creatures to be sold, and that by stratagem to avoid sale, they may frequently feign sickness, or magnify any particular complaint with which they are affected.[66]

"As was customary at a public auction of slaves, the auctioneer announced that Mr. Anderson, the master, would give a bill of sale for his slave with the usual guarantee—'sound of mind and body and a slave for life.' While there began a lively bidding among the Negro traders, George suddenly assumed a strange appearance—his head was thrown back, his eyes rolled wildly, his body and limbs began to twitch and jerk in an unheard of manner.

" 'What's the matter with your boy, Mr. Anderson?' one of the traders asked the owner, who, astonished and puzzled, drew nearer the block. But Mr. Anderson did not answer the question. George was now foaming at the mouth, and the violent twitching and jerking increased precipitously.

" 'What's the matter with you, boy?' gruffly demanded the trader. 'O, I 'es fits I has!' exclaimed George, whereupon his body doubled up and rolled off the block.

"Of course the auction was hastily terminated. George was hustled off to jail, and a doctor sent for; but, after a careful examination, the medical man was somewhat mystified as to the slave's actual condition. He advised the master to leave George in the jailer's custody for a while, promising to look in on him the next morning. Under his master's instruction, the wily slave was put to bed in the debtor's room, where he soon sank, apparently, into a sound sleep.

"Next morning when the jailer brought in breakfast, he found the bed empty. George was gone and nothing was heard of him again until word came, several weeks later, that he was safe in Canada." [67]

Or, again, we read:

"A young girl, of twenty years or thereabouts, was the next commodity put up. Her right hand was entirely useless—'dead,' as she aptly called it. One finger had been cut off by a doctor, and the auctioneer stated that she herself chopped off the other finger—her forefinger—because it hurt her, and she thought that to cut it off would cure it.

" 'Didn't you cut your finger off?' asked a man, 'kase you was mad?'

"She looked at him quietly, but with a glance of contempt, and said:

" 'No, you see it was a sort o' sore, and I thought it would be better to cut it off than be plagued with it.'

"Several persons around me expressed the opinion that she had done it willfully, to spite her master or mistress, or to keep her from being sold down South." [68]

Another instance is described as follows:

"As I came up, a second-rate plantation hand of the name of Noah, but whom the crier persisted in calling 'Noey,' was being offered, it being an administrator's sale. Noey, on mounting the steps, had assumed a most drooping aspect, hanging his head and affecting the feebleness of old age. He had probably hoped to have avoided sale by a dodge, which is very common in such cases. But the first bid—$1,000—startled him, and he looked eagerly to the quarter whence it proceeded. 'Never mind who he is, he has got the money. Now, gentlemen, just go on; who will say fifty.' And so the crier proceeds with his monotonous calling. 'I ain't worth all that, mass'r; I ain't much count no how,' cried Noey energetically to the first bidder. 'Yes you are, Noey—ah, $1,000, thank you, sir,' replies the crier." [69]

The strength of Negro resistance to slavery becomes apparent in the extent to which the slaves mutilated themselves in their efforts to escape work. A girl on Lewis' plantation who had been injured tied pack thread around her wounds when they started to heal and then rubbed dirt in them. In her anxiety to avoid work she gave herself a very serious infection.[70] But this action was mild compared to that of others.

"General Leslie Coombs, of Lexington, owned a man named Ennis, a house carpenter. He had bargained with a slave-trader to take him and carry him down the river. Ennis was determined not to go. He took a broadaxe and cut one hand off; then contrived to lift the axe, with an arm pressing it to his body, and let it fall upon the other, cutting off the ends of the fingers." [71]

   "*'But some on 'em would rather be shot then be took, sir,'* he added simply.

   "A farmer living near a swamp confirmed this account, and said he knew of three or four being shot on one day." [72]

   Planters had much trouble with slaves fresh from Africa, the new slaves committing suicide in great numbers. Ebo landing in the Sea Islands was the site of the mass suicide of Ebo slaves who simply walked in a body into the ocean and drowned themselves. A planter writing on the handling of slaves mentions the difficulty of adjusting the Africans to slavery. He advocates mixing them in with seasoned slaves. "It too often happens that poor masters, who have no other slaves or are too greedy, require hard labor of these fresh negroes, exhaust them quickly, lose them by sickness and more often by grief. Often they hasten their own death; some wound themselves, others stifle themselves by drawing in the tongue so as to close the breathing passage, others take poison, or flee and perish of misery and hunger." [73]

   The one problem of Negro resistance to slavery which is most enticing is that of the attitude of slave mothers toward their children. There are frequent references in the literature to Negro women who boasted about the number of "niggers they hade for the massah," but breeding was probably quite secondary to sex activity. It would be interesting to discover the motives behind this apparent pleasure in presenting babies to the master. Some of the women may have been sincere in their pride. What makes this problem peculiarly important is the presence of much indirect evidence that the Negro mothers either had no affection for their children, or did not want them to be raised as slaves.

   We know quite well that African Negroes are (at least reasonably) able to take care of their children, and that the slave women efficiently tended the children of the plantation mistress. Yet one runs across comment after comment that the Negro mothers were ignorant, and careless, and did not know how to care for their own offspring. Typical of such statements is this: "The Negro mothers are often so ignorant and idolent, that they cannot be trusted to keep awake and administer medicine to their own children; so that the mistress has often to sit up all night with a sick Negro child." [74] Guion Johnson states that plantation owners in the Sea Islands offered the mothers rewards to take good care of their children. They were paid for those who survived the first year! This at least would indicate that there was something to be desired in their attitude toward their children.

Occasionally one runs across a reference to a slave mother killing her child, but the statements are almost invariably incomplete. For instance, Catterall [75] has a record of a trial, the details of which are: "The prisoner was indicted for murder of her own child," no more. Or a plantation overseer writes, "Elizabeth's child died last night. She smothered it somehow." [76] There is no indication as to whether or not the smothering was deliberate.

Several cases, where it was certain that parents killed their children to keep them from slavery, have been described. They are important enough to be given in detail.

"Of all the cases of slave rendition, the saddest and probably the most circulated at the time was that of Margaret Garner. Winter was the best time for flight across the Ohio River, for when it was frozen over the difficulties of crossing were fewer. Simeon Garner, with his wife Margaret and two children, fled from slavery in Kentucky during the cold winter of 1856 and, after crossing the frozen stream at night, made their ways to the house of a free Negro in Cincinnati.

"Quickly tracing the fugitive Negroes to their hideout in Cincinnati, the armed pursuers, after some resistance, broke down the door and entered the house. There they found Margaret, the mother, who, preferring death to slavery for her children, had striven to take their lives, and one child lay dead on the floor. The case was immediately brought into court, where despite the efforts made by sympathetic whites, rendition was ordered. On their return to slavery, Margaret in despair attempted to drown herself and child by jumping into the river but even the deliverance of death was denied her, for she was recovered and soon thereafter sold to a trader who took her to the cotton fields of the Far South." [77]

"Not only were slaves known to take the lives of their masters or overseers, but they were now and then charged with the murder of their own children, sometimes to prevent them from growing up in bondage. In Covington a father and mother, shut up in a slave baracoon and doomed to the southern market, 'when there was no eye to pity them and no arm to save,' did by mutual agreement 'send the souls of their children to Heaven rather than have them descend to the hell of slavery,' and then both parents committed suicide." [78]

" 'Take off your shoes, Sylva,' said Mrs. A., 'and let this gentleman see your feet.'
" 'I don't want to,' said Sylva.
" 'But I want you to,' said her mistress.
" 'I don't care if you do,' replied Sylva sullenly.
" 'You must,' said the mistress firmly.
"The fear of punishment impelled her to remove the shoes. Four toes on one foot, and two on the other were wanting! 'There!' said the mistress, 'my

husband, who learned the blacksmith's trade for the purpose of teaching it to the slaves, to increase their market value, has, with his own hands, pounded off and wrung off all those toes, when insane with passion. And it was only last week that he thought Sylva was saucy to me, and he gave her thirty lashes with the horse whip. She was so old that I could not bear to see it, and I left the house.

" 'Sylva says,' Mrs. A. continued, 'that she has been the mother of thirteen children, every one of whom she has destroyed with her own hands, in their infancy, rather than have them suffer slavery'!" [79]

The patterns of resistance to slavery studied in this paper are: (1) deliberate slowing up of work; (2) destruction of property, and indifferent work; (3) feigning illness and pregnancy; (4) injuring one's self; (5) suicide; (6) a possibility that a significant number of slave mothers killed their children.

The motivation behind these acts was undoubtedly complex. The most obvious of the motives was a desire to avoid work. It has been demonstrated that the slaves were acutely conscious of the fact that they had nothing to gain by hard work except in those instances where they were working under the task system. The destruction of property and the poor quality of the slaves' work was mainly due to their indifference to their tasks. There is enough evidence that they could, and did, work hard and well when sufficiently motivated to refute any contention that the Negro slaves were congenitally poor workers.

Many of the slaves reacted to the institution of slavery in a far more drastic fashion than could be manifested by a mere desire to avoid work. Some of these slaves committed suicide; others killed members of their families, usually their children, in order that they might not grow up as slaves.

Possibly the most significant aspect of these patterns of resistance is the aggression against the white masters they imply. Unfortunately, however, though this aspect may be the most significant, it is the least subject to proof. On the plane of logic, there is every reason to believe that a people held in bondage would devise techniques such as have been described above as an indirect means of retaliation. The statement of Dollard, previously quoted,[80] indicates that such techniques (slowness, inefficiency, etc.) are used at the present time as a means of indirect aggression.

The material presented here suggests the need for a reconsideration of the concept of the Negro's easy adjustment to slavery. He was not a cheerful, efficient worker, as has been assumed. Rather, he was frequently rebellious, and almost always sullen, as any person faced with a disagreeable situation from which he cannot escape will normally be. Nor, can the belief that racial inferiority is responsible for inefficient workmanship on his part be supported. For such deficiencies of his workmanship as he manifested, or, indeed, may still be manifested, are seen to be explainable in terms that are in no sense to be couched in the conventional mold of inherent racial differences.

NOTES

1. We wish to express our appreciation to Professor M. J. Herskovits, under whose direction this research has been carried on.

2. E. B. Reuter, *The American Race Problem* (New York: Thomas Y. Crowell, 1927), p. 7.

3. Cf. Herbert Aptheker, "American Negro Slave Revolts," *Science and Society* 1 (1937): 512–38; Harvey Wish, "American Slave Insurrections before 1861," *Journal of Negro History* 23 (1928): 435–50; Harvey Wish, "The Slave Insurrection Panic of 1856," *Journal of Southern History* 5 (1939): 206–22; see also M. J. Herskovits, *The Myth of the Negro Past* (New York: Harper & Brothers, 1941), pp. 99–105.

4. Lewis Clarke, *Narratives of the Sufferings of Lewis and Milton Clarke* (Boston, 1846), p. 123.

5. James Redpath, *The Roving Editor: or, Talks with Slaves in the Southern States* (New York, 1859).

6. John Dollard, *Caste and Class in a Southern Town* (New Haven: Yale University Press, 1937), pp. 255, 256.

7. Frederick Douglass, *Life and Times of Frederick Douglass* (New York: Pathway Press, 1941), p. 8.

8. Wm. Brown, an escaped slave, in: Benjamin Drew, *The Refugee* (Boston, 1856), p. 281.

9. Thomas Hedgebeth, a free Negro, in: Benjamin Drew, *The Refugee* (Boston, 1856), p. 276.

10. Sir Charles Lyell, *A Second Visit to the United States of America*, 2 vols. (New York, 1849), II, p. 72.

11. T. D. Ozanne, *The South as It Is* (London, 1863), pp. 165, 166.

12. Anon., *An Inquiry Into the Condition and Prospects of the African Race* (Philadelphia, 1839), p. 83.

13. F. L. Olmsted, *A Journey in the Seaboard Slave States* (New York, 1863), p. 210.

14. Ibid., p. 104.

15. Dollard, *Caste and Class*, p. 257.

16. U. B. Phillips, *American Negro Slavery* (New York: D. Appleton and Company, 1918), p. 192.

17. Olmsted, *Journey*, p. 11.

18.. Olmsted, *Journey*, pp. 192, 193.

19. Ibid., p. 388.

20. Douglass, *Life and Times*, p. 261.

21. W. W. Brown, *Life of Williams Wells Brown, A Fugitive Slave* (Boston, 1848), p. 18. See also James Williams, *Narratives of James Williams* (Boston, 1838), pp. 56, 62, 65.

22. Solomon Northrup, *Twelves Years a Slave* (New York, 1853), pp. 226, 227.

23. James Williams, *Narratives*, p. 43.

24. Olmsted, *Journey*, pp. 435, 436.

25. Ibid., p. 103.

26. Ibid.

27. Ibid., p. 430.

28. Ibid., p. 207.

29. The speaker had freed his slaves.

30. Olmsted, *Journey*, pp. 100, 101.

31. J. S. Bassett, *The Southern Plantation Overseer as Revealed in His Letters* (Northampton, Mass.: Smith College, 1925), p. 66.

32. F. L. Olmsted, *A Journey in the Back Country* (New York, 1863), p. 79.

33. U. B. Phillips, *American Negro Slavery*, pp. 303, 304.

34. B. Drew, *The Refugee*, p. 164.

35. Ibid., p. 167.

36. C. G. Parson, *Inside View of Slavery* (Boston, 1853), p. 94.

37. Anon., *An Inquiry Into the Condition and Prospects of the African Race*, p. 83.

38. F. L. Olmsted, *A Journey in the Seaboard Slave States*, pp. 46, 47.

39. Redpath, *Roving Editor*, p. 241.

40. F. L. Olmsted, *A Journey in the Back Country*, p. 227.

41. F. A. Kemble, *Journal of a Residence on a Georgian Plantation in 1838–1839* (New York, 1863), p. 242.

42. M. G. Lewis, *Journal of a West Indian Proprietor, 1815–1817* (London, 1929), p. 267.

43. U. B. Phillips, *Plantation and Frontier Documents, 1649–1863* (Cleveland, 1909), p. 34.

44. F. L. Olmsted, *A Journey in the Seaboard Slave States*, p. 91.

45. C. W. Hanson, *The Stranger in America* (London, 1807), p. 357.

46. F. L. Olmsted, *A Journey in the Seaboard Slave States*, p. 145.

47. Ibid., p. 480.

48. Ibid., pp. 481–84.

49. U. B. Phillips, *Plantation and Frontier Documents, 1694–1863*, p. 137.

50. Since this paper was written a significant contribution has appeared which throws a new light on the subject of slave illness. (Felice Swados, "Negro Health on the Ante Bellum Plantations," *Bulletin of the History of Medicine* 10 [October, 1941].) Though Swados demonstrated that the rate of actual sickness among the Negroes was very high, she leaves some doubt as to what proportion of sickness was feigned. For instance, in a footnote (p. 472) she refers to Sydnor's compilations of the records of sickness on several plantations as indications of the extent of actual sickness, even going so far as to note that on one plantation most of the sickness occurred during the picking season. Sydnor, himself, indicates that he believes that these records demonstrate that a great deal of the sickness was feigned.

51. Cartwright's italics.

52. F. L. Olmsted, *A Journey in the Seaboard Slave States*, p. 193.

53. Ibid., p. 189.

54. Ibid., pp. 416, 417.

55. Ibid., p. 187.

56. C. S. Sydnor, *Slavery in Mississippi* (New York: D. Appleton·Century Co., 1933), pp. 45ff.

57. F. L. Olmsted, *A Journey in the Seaboard Slave States*, p. 187.

58. M. G. Lewis, *Journal of a West Indian Proprietor, 1815–1817* (London: G. Routledge & Sons, 1929), p. 168.

59. F. L. Olmsted, *A Journey in the Seaboard Slave States*, pp. 423, 424.

60. F. L. Olmsted, *A Journey in the Back Country*, p. 77.

61. F. L. Olmsted, *A Journey in the Seaboard Slave States*, pp. 187–91.

62. F. A. Kemble, *Journal*, p. 235.

63. U. B. Phillips, *American Negro Slavery*, p. 436.

64. S. Smedes, *Memorials of a Southern Planter* (Baltimore, 1887), p. 80.

65. U. B. Phillips, *American Negro Slavery*, p. 199.

66. J. W. Coleman, *Slavery Times in Kentucky* (Chapel Hill: University of North Carolina Press, 1940), p. 130.

67. Ibid., pp. 129–30.

68. Redpath, *Roving Editor*, pp. 253–54.

69. E. A. Pollard, *The Southern Spy* (Washington, 1859), pp. 13–14.

70. Lewis, *Journal*, p. 168.

71. Clarke, *Narratives*, p. 125.

72. F. L. Olmsted, *A Journey in the Seaboard Slave States*, p. 160.

73. U. B. Phillips, *Plantation and Frontier Documents*, II, p. 31.

74. Lyell, *Second Visit*, p. 264.

75. H. H. Catterall, ed., *Judicial Cases Concerning American Slavery and the Negro*, 5 vols. (Washington, D.C.: Carnegie Institution, 1926–37), II, p. 59.

76. Bassett, *Southern Plantation Overseer*, p. 59.

77. J. W. Coleman, *Slavery Times*, p. 208.

78. Ibid., p. 269.

79. C. G. Parson, *Inside View*, p. 212.

80. Dollard, *Caste and Class*, p. 120.

16. STERLING STUCKEY, Through the Prism of Folklore: The Black Ethos in Slavery (1968)*

In this essay, Sterling Stuckey of Northwestern University utilizes black spirituals and folk tales, sources long neglected by the historian, in order to gain a deeper insight into the personality of the black slave. After studying their songs and tales, Stuckey concluded that the development of a black ethos enabled Afro-Americans to resist the dehumanization of chattel slavery. This ethos consisted of a "life style and set of values . . . which prevented them from being imprisoned altogether by the definitions which the larger society sought to impose." In this way, "a very large number of slaves . . . were able to maintain their essential humanity."

It is not excessive to advance the view that some historians, because they have been so preoccupied with demonstrating the absence of signif-

* From Sterling Stuckey, "Through the Prism of Folklore," *The Massachusetts Review* 9 (1968): 417–37. Copyright © 1968, The Massachusetts Review, Inc. Reprinted by permission.

icant slave revolts, conspiracies, and "day to day" resistance among slaves, have presented information on slave behavior and thought which is incomplete indeed. They have, in short, devoted very little attention to trying to get "inside" slaves to discover what bondsmen thought about their condition. Small wonder we have been saddled with so many stereotypical treatments of slave thought and behavior.[1]

Though we do not know enough about the institution of slavery or the slave experience to state with great precision how slaves felt about their condition, it is reasonably clear that slavery, however draconic and well supervised, was not the hermetically sealed monolith—destructive to the majority of slave personalities—that some historians would have us believe. The works of Herbert Aptheker, Kenneth Stampp, Richard Wade, and the Bauers, allowing for differences in approach and purpose, indicate that slavery, despite its brutality, was not so "closed" that it robbed most of the slaves of their humanity.[2]

It should, nevertheless, be asserted at the outset that blacks could not have survived the grim experience of slavery unscathed. Those historians who, for example, point to the dependency complex which slavery engendered in many Afro-Americans, offer us an important insight into one of the most harmful effects of that institution upon its victims. That slavery caused not a few bondsmen to question their worth as human beings—this much, I believe, we can posit with certitude. We can also safely assume that such self-doubt would rend one's sense of humanity, establishing an uneasy balance between affirming and negating aspects of one's being. What is at issue is not whether American slavery was harmful to slaves but whether, in their struggle to control self-lacerating tendencies, the scales were tipped toward a despair so consuming that most slaves, in time, became reduced to the level of "Sambos." [3]

My thesis, which rests on an examination of folk songs and tales, is that slaves were able to fashion a life style and set of values—an ethos—which prevented them from being imprisoned altogether by the definitions which the larger society sought to impose. This ethos was an amalgam of Africanisms and New World elements which helped slaves, in Guy Johnson's words, "feel their way along the course of American slavery, enabling them to endure. . . ." [4] As Sterling Brown, that wise student of Afro-American culture, has remarked, the values expressed in folklore acted as a "wellspring to which slaves" trapped in the wasteland of American slavery "could return in times of doubt to be refreshed." [5] In short, I shall contend that the process of dehumanization was not nearly as pervasive as Stanley Elkins would have us believe; that a very large number of slaves, guided by this ethos, were able to maintain their essential humanity. I make this contention because folklore, in its natural setting, is of, by and for those who create and respond to it, depending for its survival upon the accuracy with which it speaks to needs and reflects sentiments. I therefore consider it safe to assume that the attitudes of a very large number of slaves are represented by the themes of folklore.[6]

Frederick Douglass, commenting on slave songs, remarked his utter astonishment, on coming to the North, "to find persons who could speak of the singing among slaves as evidence of their contentment and happiness." [7] The young DuBois, among the first knowledgeable critics of the spirituals, found white Americans as late as 1903 still telling Afro-Americans that "life was joyous to the black slave, careless and happy." "I can easily believe this of some," he wrote, "of many. But not all the past South, though it rose from the dead, can gainsay the heart-touching witness of these songs. They are the music of a unhappy people, of the children of disappointment; they tell of death and suffering and unvoiced longing toward a truer world, of misty wanderings and hidden ways." [8]

Though few historians have been interested in such wanderings and ways, Frederick Douglass, probably referring to the spirituals, said the songs of slaves represented the sorrows of the slave's heart, serving to relieve the slave "only as an aching heart is relieved by its tears." "I have often sung," he continued, "to drown my sorrow, but seldom to express my happiness. Crying for joy, and singing for joy, were alike uncommon to me while in the jaws of slavery." [9]

Sterling Brown, who has much to tell us about the poetry and meaning of these songs, has observed: "As the best expression of the slave's deepest thoughts and yearnings, they (the spirituals) speak with convincing finality against the legend of contented slavery." [10] Rejecting the formulation that the spirituals are mainly otherworldly, Brown states that though the creators of the spirituals looked toward heaven and "found their triumphs there, they did not blink their eyes to trouble here." The spirituals, in his view, "never tell of joy in the 'good old days'. . . . The only joy in the spirituals is in dreams of escape." [11]

Rather than being essentially otherworldly, these songs, in Brown's opinion, "tell of this life, of 'rollin' through an unfriendly world!" To substantiate this view, he points to numerous lines from spirituals: "Oh, bye and bye, bye and bye, I'm going to lay down this heavy load"; "My way is cloudy"; "Oh, stand the storm, it won't be long, we'll anchor by and by"; "Lord help me from sinking down"; and "Don't know what my mother wants to stay here fuh, Dis ole world ain't been no friend to huh." [12] To those scholars who "would have us believe that when the Negro sang of freedom, he meant only what the whites meant, namely freedom from sin," Brown rejoins:

Free individualistic whites on the make in a prospering civilization, nursing the American dream, could well have felt their only bondage to be that of sin, and freedom to be religious salvation. But with the drudgery, the hardships, the auction block, the slave-mart, the shackles, and the lash so literally present in the Negro's experience, it is hard to imagine why for the Negro they would remain figurative. The scholars certainly did not make this clear, but rather take refuge in such dicta as: "the slave never contemplated his low condition." [13]

"Are we to believe," asks Brown, "that the slave singing 'I been rebuked, I been scorned, done had a hard time sho's you bawn,' referred to his being outside the true religion?" A reading of additional spirituals indicates that they contained distinctions in meaning which placed them outside the confines of the "true religion." Sometimes, in these songs, we hear slaves relating to divinities on terms more West African than American. The easy intimacy and argumentation, which come out of a West African frame of reference, can be heard in "Hold the Wind." [14]

> When I get to heaven, gwine be at ease,
> Me and my God *gonna do as we please.*
>
> Gonna chatter with the Father, argue with the Son,
> *Tell um 'bout the world I just come from.*[15] (Italics added.)

If there is a tie with heaven in those lines from "Hold the Wind," there is also a clear indication of dislike for the restrictions imposed by slavery. And at least one high heavenly authority might have a few questions to answer. *Tell um 'bout the world I just come from* makes it abundantly clear that some slaves—even when released from the burdens of the world—would keep alive painful memories of their oppression.

If slaves could argue with the son of God, then surely, when on their knees in prayer, they would not hesitate to speak to God of the treatment being received at the hands of their oppressors.

> Talk about me much as you please,
> Chillun, talk about me much as you please,
> Gonna talk about you when I get on my knees.[16]

That slaves could spend time complaining about treatment received from other slaves is conceivable, but that this was their only complaint, or even the principal one, is hardly conceivable. To be sure, there is a certain ambiguity in the use of the word "chillun" in this context. The reference appears to apply to slaveholders.

The spiritual, *Samson*, as Vincent Harding has pointed out, probably contained much more (for some slaves) than mere biblical implications. Some who sang these lines from *Samson*, Harding suggests, might well have meant tearing down the edifice of slavery. If so, it was the ante-bellum equivalent of today's "burn baby burn."

> He said, 'An' if I had-'n my way,'
> He said, 'An' if I had-'n my way,'
> He said, 'An' if I had-'n my way,
> I'd tear the build-in' down!'
>
> He said, 'And now I got my way,
> And I'll tear this buildin' down.' [17]

Both Harriet Tubman and Frederick Douglass have reported that some of the spirituals carried double meanings. Whether most of the slaves who sang those spirituals could decode them is another matter. Harold Courlander has made a persuasive case against widespread understanding of any given "loaded" song,[18] but it seems to me that he fails to recognize sufficiently a further aspect of the subject: slaves, as their folktales make eminently clear, used irony repeatedly, especially with animal stories. Their symbolic world was rich. Indeed, the various masks which many put on were not unrelated to this symbolic process. It seems logical to infer that it would occur to more than a few to seize upon some songs, even though created originally for religious purposes, assign another meaning to certain words, and use these songs for a variety of purposes and situations.

At times slave bards created great poetry as well as great music. One genius among the slaves couched his (and their) desire for freedom in a magnificent line of verse. After God's powerful voice had "Rung through Heaven and down in Hell," he sang, "My dungeon shook and my chains, they fell." [19]

In some spirituals, Alan Lomax has written, Afro-Americans turned sharp irony and "healing laughter" toward heaven, again like their West African ancestors, relating on terms of intimacy with God. In one, the slaves have God engaged in a dialogue with Adam:

> 'Stole my apples, I believe.'
> 'No, marse Lord, I spec it was Eve.'
>
> Of this tale there is no mo'
> Eve et the apple and Adam de co'.[20]

Douglass informs us that slaves also sang ironic seculars about the institution of slavery. He reports having heard them sing: "We raise de wheat, dey gib us de corn; We sift de meal, dey gib us de huss; We peel de meat, dey gib us de skin; An dat's de way dey take us in." [21] Slaves would often stand back and see the tragicomic aspects of their situation, sometimes admiring the swiftness of blacks:

> Run, nigger, run, de patrollers will ketch you,
> Run, nigger run, its almost day.
> Dat nigger run, dat nigger flew;
> Dat nigger tore his shirt in two.[22]

And there is:

> My ole mistiss promise me
> W'en she died, she'd set me free,
> She lived so long dat 'er head got bal'
> An' she give out'n de notion a-dyin' at all.[23]

In the ante-bellum days, work songs were of crucial import to slaves. As they cleared and cultivated land, piled levees along rivers, piled loads on steamboats, screwed cotton bales into the holds of ships, and cut roads and railroads through forest, mountain and flat, slaves sang while the white man, armed and standing in the shade, shouted his orders.[24] Through the sense of timing and coordination which characterized work songs well sung, especially by the leaders, slaves sometimes quite literally created works of art. These songs not only militated against injuries but enabled the bondsmen to get difficult jobs done more easily by not having to concentrate on the dead level of their work. "In a very real sense the chants of Negro labor," writes Alan Lomax, "may be considered the most profoundly American of all our folk songs, for they were created by our people as they tore at American rock and earth and reshaped it with their bare hands, while rivers of sweat ran down and darkened the dust."

> Long summer day makes a white man lazy,
>   Long summer day.
> Long summer day makes a nigger run away, sir,
>   Long summer day.[25]

Other slaves sang lines indicating their distate for slave labor:

> Ol' massa an' ol' missis,
> Sittin' in the parlour,
> Jus' fig'in' an' a-plannin'
> How to work a nigger harder.[26]

And there are these bitter lines, the meaning of which is clear:

> Missus in the big house,
> Mammy in the yard,
> Missus holdin' her white hands,
> Mammy workin' hard
> Missus holdin' her white hands,
> Mammy workin' hard.

> Old Marse ridin' all time,
> Niggers workin' round,
> Marse sleepin' day time,
> Niggers diggin' in the ground,
> Marse sleepin' day time,
> Niggers diggin' in the ground.[27]

Courlander tells us that the substance of the work songs "ranges from the humorous to the sad, from the gentle to the biting, and from the tolerant to the unforgiving." The statement in a given song can be metaphoric, tangent or direct, the meaning personal or impersonal. "As throughout Negro singing generally, there is an incidence of social criticism, ridicule, gossip, and protest." [28] Pride in their strength rang with the downward thrust of axe—

> When I was young and in my prime, (hah!)
> Sunk my axe deep every time, (hah!)

Blacks later found their greatest symbol of manhood in John Henry, descendant of Trickster John of slave folk tales:

> A man ain't nothing but a man,
> But before I'll let that steam driver beat me down
> I'll die with my hammer in my hand.[29]

Though Frances Kemble, an appreciative and sensitive listener to work songs, felt that "one or two barbaric chants would make the fortune of an opera," she was on one occasion "displeased not a little" by a self-deprecating song, one which "embodied the opinion that 'twenty-six black girls not make mulatto yellow girl,' and as I told them I did not like it, they have since omitted it." [30] What is pivotal here is not the presence of self-laceration in folklore, but its extent and meaning. While folklore contained some self-hatred, on balance it gives no indication whatever that blacks, as a group, liked or were indifferent to slavery, which is the issue.[31]

To be sure, only the most fugitive of songs sung by slaves contained direct attacks upon the system. Two of these were associated with slave rebellions. The first, possibly written by ex-slave Denmark Vesey himself, was sung by slaves on at least one island off the coast of Charleston, S. C., and at meetings convened by Vesey in Charleston. Though obviously not a folksong, it was sung by the folk.

> Hail! all hail! ye Afric clan,
> Hail! ye oppressed, ye Afric band,
> Who toil and sweat in slavery bound
> And when your health and strength are gone

> Are left to hunger and to mourn,
> Let independence be your aim,
> Ever mindful what 'tis worth.
> Pledge your bodies for the prize,
> Pile them even to the skies! [32]

The second, a popular song derived from a concrete reality, bears the marks of a conscious authority:

> You mought be rich as cream
> And drive you coach and four-horse team,
> But you can't keep de world from moverin' round
> Nor Nat Turner from gainin' ground.
>
> And your name it mought be Caesar sure,
> And got you cannon can shoot a mile or more,
> But you can't keep de world from moverin' round
> Nor Nat Turner from gainin' ground. [33]

The introduction of Denmark Vesey, class leader in the A.M.E. Church, and Nat Turner, slave preacher, serves to remind us that some slaves and ex-slaves were violent as well as humble, impatient as well as patient.

It is also well to recall that the religious David Walker, who had lived close to slavery in North Carolina, and Henry Highland Garnett, ex-slave and Presbyterian minister, produced two of the most inflammatory, vitriolic and doom-bespeaking polemics America has yet seen. [34] There was theological tension here, loudly proclaimed, a tension which emanated from and was perpetuated by American slavery and race prejudice. This dimension of ambiguity must be kept in mind, if for no other reason than to place in bolder relief the possibility that a great many slaves and free Afro-Americans could have interpreted Christianity in a way quite different from white Christians.

Even those songs which seemed most otherworldly, those which expressed profound weariness of spirit and even faith in death, through their unmistakable sadness, were accusatory, and God was not their object. If one accepts as a given that some of these appear to be almost wholly escapist, the indictment is no less real. Thomas Wentworth Higginson came across one—". . . a flower of poetry in that dark soil," he called it. [35]

> I'll walk in de graveyard, I'll walk through de graveyard,
>   To lay dis body down.
> I'll lie in de grave and stretch out my arms,
>   Lay dis body down.

Reflecting on "I'll lie in de grave and stretch out my arms," Higginson said that "Never, it seems to me, since man first lived and suffered, was his infinite longing for peace uttered more plaintively than in that line." [36]

There seems to be small doubt that Christianity contributed in large measure to a spirit of patience which militated against open rebellion among the bondsmen. Yet to overemphasize this point leads one to obscure a no less important reality: Christianity, after being reinterpreted and recast by slave bards, also contributed to that spirit of endurance which powered generations of bondsmen, bringing them to that decisive moment when for the first time a real choice was available to scores of thousands of them.

When that moment came, some slaves who were in a position to decide for themselves did so. W. E. B. DuBois re-created their mood and the atmosphere in which they lived.

> There came the slow looming of emancipation.
> Crowds and armies of the unknown, inscrutable,
> unfathomable Yankees; cruelty behind and before;
> rumors of a new slave trade, but slowly,
> continuously, the wild truth, the bitter truth,
> the magic truth, came surging through. There
> was to be a new freedom! And a black nation
> went tramping after the armies no matter what
> it suffered; no matter how it was treated, no
> matter how it died.[37]

The gifted bards, by creating songs with an unmistakable freedom ring, songs which would have been met with swift, brutal repression in the ante-bellum days, probably voiced the sentiments of all but the most degraded and dehumanized. Perhaps not even the incredulous slavemaster could deny the intent of the new lyrics. "In the wake of the Union Army and in the contraband camps," remarked Sterling Brown, "spirituals of freedom sprang up suddenly. . . . Some celebrated the days of Jubilo: 'O Freedom; O Freedom!' and 'Before I'll be a slave, I'll be buried in my grave!' and 'Go home to my lord and be free.' " And there was: "No more driver's lash for me. . . . Many thousand go.' " [38]

DuBois brought together the insights of the poet and historian to get inside the slaves: "There was joy in the South. It rose like perfume—like a prayer. Men stood quivering. Slim dark girls, wild and beautiful with wrinkled hair, wept silently; young women, black, tawny, white and golden, lifted shivering hands, and old and broken mothers, black and gray, raised great voices and shouted to God across the fields, and up to the rocks and the mountains." [39]

Some sang:

> Slavery chain done broke at last, broke at last, broke at last,
> Slavery chain done broke at last,
> Going to praise God till I die.
>
> I did tell him how I suffer,
> In de dungeon and de chain,
> *And de days I went with head bowed down,*
> And my broken flesh and pain,
> Slavery chain done broke at last, broke at last, broke at last.[40]

Whatever the nature of the shocks generated by the war, among those vibrations felt were some that had come from Afro-American singing ever since the first Africans were forcibly brought to these shores. DuBois was correct when he said that the new freedom song had not come from Africa, but that "the dark throb and beat of that Ancient of Days was in and through it." [41] Thus, the psyches of those who gave rise to and provided widespread support for folk songs had not been reduced to *tabula rasas* on which a slave-holding society could at pleasure sketch out its wish fulfillment fantasies.

We have already seen the acute degree to which some slaves realized they were being exploited. Their sense of the injustice of slavery made it so much easier for them to act out their aggression against whites (by engaging in various forms of "day to day" resistance) without being overcome by a sense of guilt, or a feeling of being ill-mannered. To call this nihilistic thrashing about would be as erroneous as to refer to their use of folklore as esthetic thrashing about.[42] For if they did not regard themselves as the equals of whites in many ways, their folklore indicates that the generality of slaves must have at least felt superior to whites morally. And that, in the context of oppression, could make the difference between a viable human spirit and one crippled by the belief that the interests of the master are those of the slave.

When it is borne in mind that slaves created a large number of extraordinary songs and greatly improved a considerable proportion of the songs of others, it is not at all difficult to believe that they were conscious of the fact that they were leaders in the vital area of art—giving protagonists rather than receiving pawns. And there is some evidence that slaves were aware of the special talent which they brought to music. Higginson has described how reluctantly they sang from hymnals—"even on Sunday" —and how "gladly" they yielded "to the more potent excitement of their own 'spirituals.' " [43] It is highly unlikely that the slaves' preference for their own music went unremarked among them, or that this preference did not affect their estimate of themselves. "They soon found," commented Alan Lomax, "that when they sang, the whites recognized their superiority as singers, and listened with respect." [44] He might have added that those ante-bellum whites who listened probably seldom understood.

What is of pivotal import, however, is that the esthetic realm was the one area in which slaves knew they were not inferior to whites. Small wonder that they borrowed many songs from the larger community, then quickly invested them with their own economy of statement and power of imagery rather than yield to the temptation of merely repeating what they had heard. Since they were essentially group rather than solo performances, the values inherent in and given affirmation by the music served to strengthen bondsmen in a way that solo music could not have done.[45] In a word, slave singing often provided a form of group therapy, a way in which a slave, in concert with others, could fend off some of the debilitating effects of slavery.

The field of inquiry would hardly be complete without some mention of slave tales. Rich in quantity and often subtle in conception, these tales further illumine the inner world of the bondsmen, disclosing moods and interests almost as various as those found in folksongs. That folk tales, like the songs, indicate an African presence, should not astonish; for the telling of tales, closely related to the African griot's vocation of providing oral histories of families and dynasties, was deeply rooted in West African tradition. Hughes and Bontemps have written that the slaves brought to America the "habit of story-telling as pastime, together with a rich bestiary." Moreover, they point out that the folk tales of slaves "were actually projections of personal experiences and hopes and defeats, in terms of symbols," and that this important dimension of the tales "appears to have gone unnoticed." [46]

Possessing a repertoire which ranged over a great many areas, perhaps the most memorable tales are those of Brer Rabbit and John.[47] Brer Rabbit, now trickster, ladies' man and braggart, now wit, joker and glutton, possessed the resourcefulness, despite his size and lack of strength, to outsmart stronger, larger animals. "To the slave in his condition," according to Hughes and Bontemps, "the theme of weakness overcoming strength through cunning proved endlessly fascinating." [48] John, characterized by a spiritual resilience born of an ironic sense of life, was a secular high priest of mischief and guile who delighted in matching wits with Ole Marster, the "patterollers," Ole Missy, and the devil himself. He was clever enough to sense the absurdity of his predicament and that of white people, smart enough to know the limits of his powers and the boundaries of those of the master class. While not always victorious, even on the spacious plane of the imagination, he could hardly be described as

a slave with an inferiority complex. And in this regard it is important to
to note that his varieties of triumphs, though they sometimes included
winning freedom, often realistically cluster about ways of coping with
everyday negatives of the system.[49]

Slaves were adept in the art of storytelling, as at home in this area
as they were in the field of music. But further discussion of the scope
of folklore would be uneconomical, for we have already seen a depth and
variety of thought among bondsmen which embarrasses stereotypical
theories of slave personality. Moreover, it should be clear by now that
there are no secure grounds on which to erect the old, painfully con-
stricted "Sambo" structure.[50] For the personalities which lay beneath the
plastic exteriors which slaves turned on and off for white people were
too manifold to be contained by cheerful, childlike images. When it is
argued, then, that "too much of the Negro's own lore" has gone into
the making of the Sambo picture "to entitle one in good conscience to
condemn it as 'conspiracy'," [51] one must rejoin: Only if you strip the
masks from black faces while refusing to read the irony and ambiguity
and cunning which called the masks into existence. Slave folklore, on
balance, decisively repudiates the thesis that Negroes *as a group* had
internalized "Sambo" traits, committing them, as it were, to psychological
marriage.

It is one of the curiosities of American historiography that a people
who were as productive esthetically as American slaves could be studied
as if they had moved in a cultural cyclotron, continually bombarded by
devastating, atomizing forces which denuded them of meaningful Africanisms while destroying any and all impulses toward creativity. One historian, for example, has been tempted to wonder how it was ever possible that "*all* this (West African) native resourcefulness and vitality have
been brought to such a point of *utter* stultification in America." [52] (Italics
added.) This sadly misguided view is, of course, not grounded in any
recognition or understanding of the Afro-American dimension of American
culture. In any event, there is a great need for students of American slavery
to attempt what Gilberto Freyre tried to do for Brazilian civilization—an
effort at discovering the contributions of slaves toward the shaping of
the Brazilian national character.[53] When such a study has been made of
the American slave we shall probably discover that, though he did not rival
his Brazilian brother in staging bloody revolutions, the quality and place
of art in his life compared favorably. Now this suggests that the humanity
of people can be asserted through means other than open and widespread
rebellion, a consideration that has not been appreciated in violence-prone
America. We would do well to recall the words of F. S. C. Northrop

who has observed: "During the pre-Civil War period shipowners and southern landowners brought to the United States a considerable body of people with a color of skin and cultural values different from those of its other inhabitants. . . . Their values are more emotive, esthetic and intuitive. . . . (These) characteristics can become an asset for our culture. For these are values with respect to which Anglo-American culture is weak." [54]

These values were expressed on the highest level in the folklore of slaves. Through their folklore black slaves affirmed their humanity and left a lasting imprint on American culture. No study of the institutional aspects of American slavery can be complete, nor can the larger dimensions of slave personality and style be adequately explored, as long as historians continue to avoid that realm in which, as DuBois has said, "the soul of the black slave spoke to man." [55]

In its nearly two and one-half centuries of existence, the grim system of American slavery doubtless broke the spirits of uncounted numbers of slaves. Nevertheless, if we look through the prism of folklore, we can see others transcending their plight, appreciating the tragic irony of their condition, then seizing upon and putting to use those aspects of their experience which sustain in the present and renew in the future. We can see them opposing their own angle of vision to that of their oppressor, fashioning their own techniques of defense and aggression in accordance with their own reading of reality and doing those things well enough to avoid having their sense of humanity destroyed.

Slave folklore, then, affirms the existence of a large number of vital, tough-minded human beings who, though severely limited and abused by slavery, had found a way both to endure and preserve their humanity in the face of insuperable odds. What they learned about handling misfortune was not only a major factor in their survival as a people, but many of the lessons learned and esthetic standards established would be used by future generations of Afro-Americans in coping with a hostile world. What a splendid affirmation of the hopes and dreams of their slave ancestors that some of the songs being sung in ante-bellum days are the ones Afro-Americans are singing in the freedom movement today: "Michael, row the boat ashore"; "Just like a tree planted by the water, I shall not be moved."

NOTES

1. Historians who have provided stereotypical treatments of slave thought and personality are Ulrich B. Phillips, *American Negro Slavery* (New York: D. Appleton and Company, 1918); Samuel Eliot Morrison and Henry Steele Commager, *The Growth of the American Republic* (New York: Oxford University Press, 1950); and

Stanley Elkins, *Slavery: A Problem in American Institutional and Intellectual Life* (Chicago: University of Chicago Press, 1959).

2. See Herbert Aptheker, *American Negro Slave Revolts* (New York: International Publishers, 1963); Kenneth M. Stampp, *The Peculiar Institution* (New York: A. A. Knopf, 1956); Richard Wade, *Slavery in the Cities* (New York: Oxford University Press, 1964); and Alice and Raymond Bauer, "Day to Day Resistance to Slavery," *Journal of Negro History* 27 (October 1942): 388–419.

3. I am here concerned with the Stanley Elkins' version of "Sambo," that is, the inference that the overwhelming majority of slaves, as a result of their struggle to survive under the brutal system of American slavery, became so callous and indifferent to their status that they gave survival primacy over all other considerations. See chapters 3 through 6 of *Slavery* for a discussion of the process by which blacks allegedly were reduced to the "good humor of everlasting childhood."

4. I am indebted to Guy Johnson of the University of North Carolina for suggesting the use of the term "ethos" in this piece, and for helpful commentary on the original paper which was read before the Association for the Study of Negro Life and History at Greensboro, North Carolina, on October 13, 1967.

5. Professor Brown made this remark in a paper delivered before The Amistad Society in Chicago, Spring, 1964. Distinguished poet, literary critic, folklorist, and teacher, Brown has long contended that an awareness of Negro folklore is essential to an understanding of slave personality and thought.

6. I subscribe to Alan Lomax's observation that folk songs "can be taken as the signposts of persistent patterns of community feeling and can throw light into many dark corners of our past and our present." His view that Afro-American music, despite its regional peculiarities, "expresses the same feelings and speaks the same basic language everywhere" is also accepted as a working principle in this paper. For an extended treatment of these points of view, see Alan Lomax, *Folk Songs of North America* (New York: Cassell, 1960), Introduction, p. xx.

7. Frederick Douglass, *Narrative of the Life of Frederick Douglass* (Cambridge, Massachusetts: The Belknap Press, 1960), p. 38. Originally published in 1845.

8. W. E. B. DuBois, *Souls of Black Folk* in John Hope Franklin, ed., *Three Negro Classics* (New York: Avon Books, 1965), p. 380. Originally published in 1903.

9. Douglass, *Narrative*, p. 38. Douglass' view adumbrated John and Alan Lomax's theory that the songs of the folk singer are deeply rooted "in his life and have functioned there as enzymes to assist in the digestion of hardship, solitude, violence (and) hunger." John A. and Alan Lomax, *Our Singing Country* (New York: The Macmillan Co., 1941), Preface, p. xiii.

10. Sterling Brown, "Negro Folk Expression," *Phylon* 14 (October 1953): 47.

11. Ibid., p. 48.

12. Ibid., p. 47.

13. Ibid., p. 48.

14. Addressing himself to the slave's posture toward God, and the attitudes toward the gods which the slave's African ancestors had, Lomax has written: "The West African lives with his gods on terms of intimacy. He appeals to them, reviles them, tricks them, laughs at their follies. In this spirit the Negro slave humanized the stern religion of his masters by adopting the figures of the Bible as his intimates." Lomax, *Folk Songs of North America*, p. 463.

15. Quoted from Lomax, *Folk Songs of North America*, p. 475.

16. Quoted from Sterling A. Brown, Arthur P. Davis, and Ulysses Lee, *The Negro Caravan* (New York: The Dryden Press, 1941), p. 436.

17. Vincent Harding, *Black Radicalism in America*. An unpublished work which Dr. Harding recently completed.

18. See Harold Courlander, *Negro Folk Music, U.S.A.* (New York: Columbia University Press, 1963), pp. 42, 43. If a great many slaves did not consider Harriet Tubman the "Moses" of her people, it is unlikely that most failed to grasp the relationship between themselves and the Israelites, Egypt and the South, and Pharaoh and slavemasters in such lines as: "Didn't my Lord deliver Daniel / And why not every man"; "Oh Mary don't you weep, don't you moan / Pharoah's army got drowned / Oh Mary don't you weep"; and "Go down Moses / Way down in Egypt-land / Tell old Pharaoh / To let my people go."

19. Quoted from Lomax, *Folk Songs of North America*, p. 471.

20. Ibid., p. 476.

21. Frederick Douglass, *The Life and Times of Frederick Douglass* (New York: Collier Books, 1962), p. 146.

22. Brown, "Folk Expression," p. 51.

23. Brown, *Caravan*, p. 447.

24. Lomax, *Folk Songs of North America*, p. 514.

25. Ibid., p. 515.

26. Ibid., p. 527.

27. Courlander, *Negro Folk Music*, p. 117.

28. Ibid., p. 89.

29. Brown, "Folk Expression," p. 54. Steel-driving John Henry is obviously in the tradition of the axe-wielding blacks of the ante-bellum period. The ballad of John Henry helped spawn John Henry work songs:

> Dis ole hammer—hunh
> Ring like silver—hunh
> Shine like gold, baby—hunh
> Shine like gold—hunh
>
> Dis ole hammer—hunh
> Kilt John Henry—hunh
> Twont kill me baby, hunh
> Twon't kill me.

(Quoted from Brown, "Folk Expression," p. 57.)

30. Frances Anne Kemble, *Journal of a Residence on a Georgia Plantation, 1838–1839* (New York: Alfred A. Knopf, 1961), pp. 260–61. Miss Kemble heard slaves use the epithet "nigger": "And I assure you no contemptuous intonation ever equalled the prepotenza (arrogance) of the despotic insolence of this address of these poor wretches to each other." Kemble, *Journal*, p. 281. Here she is on solid ground, but the slaves also used the word with glowing affection, as seen in the "Run, Nigger, Run" secular. At other times they leaned toward self-laceration but refused to go the whole route: "My name's Ran, I wuks in de sand, I'd rather be a nigger dan a po' white man." Brown, "Folk Expression," p. 51. Some blacks also sang, "It takes a long, lean, black-skinned gal, to make a preacher lay his Bible down." Newman I. White, *American Negro Folk Songs* (Cambridge: Harvard University Press, 1928), p. 411.

31. Elkins, who believes southern white lore on slavery should be taken seriously, does not subject it to serious scrutiny. For a penetrating—and devastating—analysis of "the richest layers of Southern lore" which, according to Elkins, resulted from "an exquisitely rounded collective creativity," see Sterling A. Brown, "A Century of

Negro Portraiture in American Literature," *The Massachusetts Review* 7 (Winter 1966): 73–96.

32. Quoted from Archie Epps, "A Negro Separatist Movement," *The Harvard Review* 4 (Summer–Fall 1956): 75.

33. Quoted in William Styron, "This Quiet Dust," *Harpers*, April 1965, p. 135.

34. For excerpts from David Walker's *Appeal* and Henry H. Garnett's *Call to Rebellion*, see Herbert Aptheker, ed., *A Documentary History of the Negro People in the United States*, 2 vols. (New York: Citadel Press, 1965). Originally published in 1951.

35. Thomas Wentworth Higginson, *Army Life in a Black Regiment* (New York: Collier, 1962), p. 199.

36. Ibid.

37. W. E. B. DuBois, *Black Reconstruction* (Philadelphia: Harcourt, Brace & Co., 1935), p. 122.

38. Brown, "Folk Expression," p. 49.

39. DuBois, *Reconstruction*, p. 124.

40. Quoted in Brown, *Caravan*, pp. 440–41. One of the most tragic scenes of the Civil War period occurred when a group of Sea Island freedmen, told by a brigadier-general that they would not receive land from the government, sang, "Nobody knows the trouble I've seen," DuBois, *Souls*, p. 381.

41. DuBois, *Reconstruction*, p. 124.

42. If some slavemasters encouraged slaves to steal or simply winked at thefts, then slaves who obliged them were most assuredly *not acting against their own interests*, whatever the motivation of the masters. Had more fruitful options been available to them, then and only then could we say that slaves were playing into the hands of their masters. Whatever the masters thought of slaves who stole from them—and there is little reason to doubt that most slaves considered it almost obligatory to steal from white people—the slaves, it is reasonable to assume, were aware of the unparalleled looting in which masters themselves were engaged. To speak therefore of slaves undermining their sense of self-respect as a result of stealing from whites—and this argument has been advanced by Eugene Genovese—is wide of the mark. Indeed, it appears more likely that those who engaged in stealing were, in the context of an oppressor-oppressed situation, on the way to realizing a larger measure of self-respect. Moreover, Genovese, in charging that certain forms of "day to day" resistance, in the absence of general conditions of rebellion, "amounted to individual and essentially nihilistic thrashing about," fails to recognize that that which was possible, that which conditions permitted, was pursued by slaves in preference to the path which led to passivity or annihilation. Those engaging in "day to day" resistance were moving along meaningful rather than nihilistic lines, for their activities were designed to frustrate the demands of the authority-system. For a very suggestive discussion of the dependency complex engendered by slavery and highly provocative views on the significance of "day to day" resistance among slaves, see Eugene Genovese, "The Legacy of Slavery and the Roots of Black Nationalism," *Studies on the Left* 6 (Nov.–Dec. 1966), especially p. 8.

43. Higginson, *Black Regiment*, p. 212. Alan Lomax reminds us that the slaves sang "in leader-chorus style, with a more relaxed throat than the whites, and in deeper-pitched, mellower voices, which blended richly." "A strong, surging beat underlay most of their American creations . . . words and tunes were intimately and playfully united, and 'sense' was often subordinated to the demands of rhythm and melody." Lomax, *Folk Songs of North America*, Introduction, p. xx.

44. Lomax, *Folk Songs*, p. 460.

45. Commenting on the group nature of much of slave singing, Alan Lomax points out that the majority of the bondsmen "came from West Africa, where music-making was largely a group activity, the creation of a many-voiced, dancing throng. . . . Community songs of labor and worship (in America) and dance songs far outnumbered narrative pieces, and the emotion of the songs was, on the whole, joyfully erotic, deeply tragic, allusive, playful, or ironic rather than nostalgic, withdrawn, factual, or aggressively comic—as among white folk singers." Lomax, *Folk Songs*, pp. xix and xx of Introduction. For treatments of the more technical aspects of Afro-American music, see Courlander, *Negro Folk Music*, especially ch. 2; and Richard A. Waterman, "African Influences on the Music of the Americas," in *Acculturation in the Americas*, edited by Sol Tax.

46. Arna Bontemps and Langston Hughes, ed., *The Book of Negro Folklore* (New York: Dodd, Mead & Company, 1965), Introduction, p. viii. Of course if one regards each humorous thrust of the bondsmen as so much comic nonsense, then there is no basis for understanding, to use Sterling Brown's phrase, the slave's "laughter out of hell." Without understanding what humor meant to slaves themselves, one is not likely to rise above the superficiality of a Stephen Foster or a Joel Chandler Harris. But once an effort has been made to see the world from the slave's point of view, then perhaps one can understand Ralph Ellison's reference to Afro-Americans, in their folklore, "backing away from the chaos of experience and from ourselves," in order to "depict the humor as well as the horror of our living." Ralph Ellison, "A Very Stern Discipline," *Harpers*, March, 1967, p. 80.

47. For additional discussions of folk tales, see Zora Neale Hurston, *Mules and Men* (Philadelphia: J. B. Lippincott, 1935); Richard Dorson, *American Negro Folktales* (Greenwich, Connecticut: Fawcett, 1967); and B. A. Botkin, *Lay My Burden Down* (Chicago: University of Chicago Press, 1945).

48. Bontemps and Hughes, *Negro Folklore*, Introduction, p. ix.

49. The fact that slaveowners sometimes took pleasure in being outwitted by slaves in no way diminishes from the importance of the trickster tales, for what is essential here is how these tales affected the slave's attitude toward himself, not whether his thinking or behavior would impress a society which considered black people little better than animals. DuBois' words in this regard should never be forgotten: "Everything Negroes did was wrong. If they fought for freedom, they were beasts; if they did not fight, they were born slaves. If they cowered on the plantation, they loved slavery; if they ran away, they were lazy loafers. If they sang, they were silly; if they scowled, they were impudent. . . . And they were funny, funny—ridiculous baboons, aping men." DuBois, *Reconstruction*, p. 125.

50. Ralph Ellison offers illuminating insight into the group experience of the slave: "Any people who could endure all of that brutalization and keep together, who could undergo such dismemberment and resuscitate itself, and endure until it could take the initiative in achieving its own freedom is obviously more than the sum of its brutalization. Seen in this perspective, theirs has been one of the great human experiences and one of the great triumphs of the human spirit in modern times, in fact, in the history of the world." Ellison, "A Very Stern Discipline," p. 84.

51. Elkins sets forth this argument in *Slavery*, p. 84.

52. Ibid., p. 93.

53. Gilberto Freyre, *The Masters and the Slaves* (New York: Alfred A. Knopf, 1956). Originally published by Jose Olympio, Rio de Janeiro, Brazil.

54. F. S. C. Northrop, *The Meeting of East and West* (New York: The Macmillan Co., 1952), pp. 159–60.

55. DuBois, *Souls*, p. 378. Kenneth M. Stampp in his *The Peculiar Institution* (New York: Alfred A. Knopf, 1956), employs to a limited extent some of the materials of slave folklore. Willie Lee Rose, in *Rehearsal for Reconstruction* (New York: The Bobbs-Merrill Company, 1964), makes brief but highly informed use of folk material.

17. MIKE THELWELL, Back with the Wind: Mr. Styron and the Reverend Turner *

No publication has stirred the black intellectuals more than William Styron's *The Confessions of Nat Turner*. The best summary of their reaction is contained in *William Styron's Nat Turner: Ten Black Writers Respond*, from which the following selection is taken. Mike Thelwell, who teaches at the University of Massachusetts, explains why he feels that a white writer cannot comprehend "the impulses, beliefs, emotions, and thought patterns of a black slave."

When a work of fiction is cast in the form of a novel, utilizing techniques of narrative, situation, and structure that we associate with that form, and is about an important historical event, but is defined for us as "a meditation on history" rather than a "conventional" historical novel, certain questions are forced upon us.

William Styron's *Confessions* is such a work. It straddles two genres; claims, in a sense, to transcend both; and manages to combine the problems of the two while reaping dual dividends as a "novel" which is also "history." Because the book is both "history" and a novel the public mind seems to have invested it with qualities it does not necessarily possess. The events and situations are assumed to be accurate because by being "historical" they must of necessity be "true." And as the "facts" of history are true, so, in a different sense, are the insights (read "symbolic truths") of the novel.

There can be no question that this is happening. This novel has been hailed by the white literary establishment as "revealing the agonizing essence of Negro slavery," as "a book that will make history," and one which "shows us our American past, our present, ourselves in a dazzling shaft of light." Clearly, we are in the presence of no mere "fiction" but a cultural and social document which is both "illuminating" and potentially definitive of contemporary attitudes.

* Mike Thelwell, "Back with the Wind: Mr. Styron and the Reverend Turner," in *William Styron's Nat Turner: Ten Black Writers Respond*, edited by John Henrik Clarke (Boston: Beacon Press, 1968). Reprinted by permission of Mike Thelwell's literary representative, The Roslyn Targ Literary Agency, Inc.

In these terms certain extra-literary questions become important. Is it possible, for example, for a white southern gentleman to tune in on the impulses, beliefs, emotions, and thought-patterns of a black slave? This miracle of empathy entails an imaginative leap not only into history, but across cultures. It necessitates that writer divorcing himself from that vast mythic tradition about slavery, black people, and history which is so integral a part of his background. Then he has to devise a literary idiom through which to record his insights, since the gentleman and the slave lack common language or experience.

When black people were brought to America they were deprived of their language and of the underpinnings in cultural experience out of which a language comes. It is clear that they developed two languages, one for themselves and another for the white masters. The latter has been preserved ("parodied" is a better word) as the "Sambo" dialect in the works of southern dialect humorists—and even in Samuel Clemens at times—to whom it was often simply quaint and humorous. The only vestiges we can find of the real language of the slaves are in the few spirituals which have come down to us, which give a clue to its true tenor. It is a language produced by oppression, but one whose central impulse is survival and resistance. And it is undoubtedly the language in which Turner's rebellion and the countless other plots for insurrection were formulated. Anyone who has been privileged to catch the performance of a good black preacher in the rural South (or has heard Martin Luther King talking to a black audience) understands something of the range and flexibility of this language. Lacking complicated syntactical structure and vast vocabulary, it depends on what linguists call paralanguage; that is, gesture, physical expression, and modulation of cadences and intonation which serve to change the meaning—in incredibly subtle ways—of the same collection of words. It is intensely poetic and expressive, since vivid simile, creative and effective juxtaposition of images, and metaphor must serve in the absence of a large vocabulary to cause the audience to see and feel. It is undoubtedly a language of action rather than a language of reflection, and thus more available to the dramatist than the novelist.

But the characterization of Nat Turner requires some literary approximation of this language. Yet Mr. Styron's Nat speaks, or rather meditates in no language at all. His creator places in his mouth a sterile and leaden prose that not even massive transfusions of Old Testament rhetoric can vitalize, a strange fusion of Latinate classicism, a kind of New England Episcopalian prissiness. At times it would seem that Mr. Styron was trying, for whatever reason, to imitate the stodgy "official" prose of the nineteenth-century lawyer who recorded the original confessions, at other times Nat sounds like nothing so much as a conscious parody of the prose voice of James Baldwin, the Negro Mr. Styron knows best, or Faulkner at his least inspired. This is not to say that the prose is not clear, even elegant in a baroque Victorian way, especially in the functionally inexplicable passages of nature writing that continuously interrupt the narrative. But, finally, it is the language of the essay, heavy and declarative.

The language combines with the structure of the novel to disastrous effect. Since the story begins after the fact, with Nat already in prison reflecting on his life, much of the book is in the form of long, unbroken monologues. Even the most violent action or intensely felt experience seems distanced and without immediacy, strangely lumpen.

Nat Turner operates in this novel with a "white" language and a white consciousness. (The voice that we hear in this novel as Turner's is that of a nineteenth-century plantation owner. The terms in which the owner of that voice perceives experience, and the assumptions he accepts about blacks are colored by the racism of that class.) Since he lacks the idiom in which Nat might communicate intimately with his peers, Styron simply avoids the problem by having Nat spend most of his life in that paradoxical, typically southern situation, close to but isolated from whites. This isolation in proximity becomes his obsession. And as his language is "white," so are his values and desires. Styron's Nat Turner, the house nigger, is certainly not the emotional or psychological prototype of the rebellious slave: he is the spiritual ancestor of the contemporary middle-class Negro, that is to say the Negro type with whom whites including Mr. Styron feel most comfortable.

Conspicuously intelligent—in their terms—Nat aspires hopelessly to the culture and stature of his white masters. Naturally (in his master's terms), he holds in contempt the society of his own people whom he considers dumb, mindless, unsalvageable brutes unfitted either for freedom or salvation. Hating the blackness which limits the possibilities which he feels should be his by right of intelligence and accomplishment, he becomes a schizoid nigger-baiter. What this Nat Turner really wants is to become white, and, failing that, to integrate. As a type this Nat certainly exists *today;* 1831 is a different question. There is nothing in the historical record to justify such a characterization of Turner.

The primary historical source, Gray's *Confessionas of Nat Turner*, is extremely brief, about 4,000 words. What emerges there is that Nat's character and attitudes in his formative years were influenced by his family (his father, mother, and grandmother, with whom he was very close) and the slave society. He becomes a leader and a plotter very early, and organizes his black brothers in the clandestine resistance of slavery symbolized by stealing. Later he becomes a preacher, that is a leader and a minister among the slaves. When he stops fraternizing with his peers it is not out of any disdain or contempt, but for the very good political reason that "Having soon discovered to be great, I must appear so, and therefore studiously avoided mixing in society, and wrapped myself in mystery, . . ."

In Mr. Styron's novel Nat's formative years are somewhat different. He has no knowledge of his father. His grandmother, a mute, catatonic, culturally shocked Coromantee wench, barely survives to give birth to his mother after disembarking from the slave ship. But Nat's master, who is mentioned only once in the Gray text, and then it is stated only that he was "religious," is elevated by Styron to be the major influence on Nat's early life. Discovering Nat with a book stolen from his library (an occasion of great surprise since no nigger ever expressed interest in literacy) he has Nat tutored by his own daughter. Nat becomes a favorite, does light work around the great house, and observes the elegance, enlightenment, and moral superiority of his owners and strives to emulate and impress them. He feels superior to all other "niggers." Of his kindly and benevolent master Nat reports: ". . . I hold him in such awe, that I am forced to regard him, physically as well as spiritually, in terms of the same patriarchal and venerable grandeur that glows forth from . . . Moses on the mount, . . ." Such "awe" indeed that, in his own rather than Styron's version, he is leading his fellows in raids on the venerable patriarch's property!

Marse Samuel does in due course reveal to Nat that having educated him, he intends to free him. This contingency terrifies Styron's Nat who knows only one free black man. The wise and kindly master has however anticipated his insecurity and reassures Nat that he has devised a method to give him his freedom gradually. Nat is satisfied. (No explanation is given in the novel of the process by which Nat moves from this abject dependence to the self-confidence that allows him to accept responsibility for a colony of free rebels that it was his intention to found in the Dismal Swamp.)

This response (Please, good Massa, dis yer Darkie ain't studyin' no freedom) is, of course, one of the favorite clichés of a certain school of plantation melodrama. Its inclusion here violates the historical evidence. This is not to say that it had no basis in reality, but that there were other realities which are not shown. In order to make Nat's response credible (remember he is the most intelligent and enlightened of any slave shown) Styron includes an image of "The Freed Slave," who is starving, confused, and totally incapable of surviving. This is misleading, since the fact is that there were free blacks in every southern community, at times whole colonies of them, who worked in many instances as skilled artisans, and some of whom, to their discredit, even owned slaves. In 1831 there were in Southampton County 1,746 free blacks many of whom owned land. What is important here is that both slave masters and slaves knew this, and, for the slaves, these free Negroes represented a constant inspiration.

The figure of Marse Samuel is familiar: a landed Virginia gentleman, for whom slavery is not a financial operation, but the exercise of a moral obligation. His home, to which the First Families of Virginia, "with names like Byrd and Clark" traveled gathered in elaborate carriages, rivals Tara in its gentility, charm, and benevolence. This is the golden age of southern chivalry, and what is being reconstructed for us is the enlightened benevolence of the "Old Dominion" version of slavery, surely the least oppressive serfdom in mankind's history. It applies only, as Mr. Styron is careful to indicate, to slaves fortunate enough to be owned by the enlightened gentry; it is the poor white overseers and small landholders who made the lot of slaves unendurable. But we do know that it is precisely on these large Virginia plantations that the most degrading and debasing form of slavery was developed. Even as early as the 1830s, the Virginia land being increasingly exhausted by tobacco, these enlightened aristocrats had begun converting their plantations to breeding farms—that is to say, to breeding black men and women like animals for the purpose of supplying the labor markets of the Deep South. That's one reality which is only fleetingly mentioned in this novel.[1]

But in the great house Nat becomes "a pet, . . . the little black jewel of Turner's Mill. Pampered, fondled, nudged, pinched, I was the household's spoiled child, . . ." Enjoying great leisure he can lurk around for "a rare glimpse, face to face, of the pure, proud, astonishing, smooth-skinned beauty . . ." of Miss Emmaline, she who moved with ". . . a proud serenity . . . which was pure and good in itself, like the disembodied, transparent beauty of an imagined angel," worshiping her with a "virginal" passion. Imagine then, his trauma when he finds her rutting with her cousin on the lawn and, in her passion, blaspheming God's name.

For Nat, the experience, shattering as we are asked to believe it is, constitutes a form of emancipation. He had long rejected as too common the idea of sex with black wenches and substituted for it onanistic fantasies with faceless white women. After his "angel's" fall from grace, he says, ". . . in my fantasies she began to replace the innocent, imaginary girl with the golden curls as the object of my craving, . . . and . . . allowed me to partake of the wicked and godless yet unutterable joys of defilement." Nat becomes an inverted, frustrated, onanistic, emotionally short-circuited lecher after white women. Presumably, if he had given way to his secret lust and raped the white girl he is later to murder, the rebellion would never have occurred. This Freud, moonlight, and magnolia view of history is presented as the basic motivation for the rebellion. Even if it did not come dangerously close to reiterating the infuriating sexual slander of the Negro male that is the stock-in-trade of the American racist, desire turned malignant in frustration would be as unacceptable as a theory of Turner's motives, since this kind of neurotic frustration finds expression in solitary, suicidal acts of violence, not in planned, public, political acts of rebellion.

In Gray's *Confessions* Nat Turner tells us that as he grew to young manhood the memory of what had been said about him as a child by "white and black" that he was too spirited to be a tractable slave began to obsess him, "finding I had arrived to man's estate and was a slave." But he says he is consoled by the spirit of prophecy which indicates to him that there is a preordained role for him in that position. He begins his ministry and continually exhorts his people who "believed and said my wisdom came from God." That he is a man of charisma and magnetism is evident. He seems totally preoccupied with his God and his people and the only mention of any white person at this time is of an overseer from whom he runs away. Nat is at large for thirty days, and then returns voluntarily because the Spirit orders him to return to his "mission," the exact nature of which he does not yet know. Upon his return the Negroes were astonished —"and murmured against me, saying that if they had my sense they would not serve any master in the world." This is, significantly, one of the few cases on record of any slave returning voluntarily to slavery. What did it mean?

Nat's stated reason for returning must stand as a masterpiece of irony. He simply quotes one of the Biblical texts best loved by slave owners, "he who knoweth his Master's will, and doeth it not, shall be beaten with many stripes, and thus have I chastened you." To the slave master this must have been gratifying indeed, evidence further of the faithful darky, well-steeped in the acceptable slave morality. To Nat, knowing that his master is God, a terrible, vengeful God, who has selected him for a "mission," it meant quite something else. He may even have undertaken the escape simply to establish his trustworthiness, thereby getting the mobility necessary to organize.

Let us examine how Styron's omission of this incident serves the "interpretation" presented in his novel. While the historical Turner is trying to regain the confidence of his fellows, who are angry, incredulous, and suspicious at the idea of a man returning voluntarily to slavery, Styron's Nat Turner is fuming and fulminating endlessly at the spiritless servility of his fellow slaves, who are presented as totally lacking in the will or imagination to change their condition. There can be no question that "Uncle Toms" existed, but it is also equally clear that they and the attitudes they represented were seized upon by slavery's apologists and publicized and exaggerated out of all proportion, while militance and rebelliousness were played down. Who can doubt this after hearing any contemporary southern sheriff mouthing his eternal platitude, "our niggers are happy."

The reality of slavery [2] was that the slaves were constantly resisting and rebelling, whether by sabotage, malingering, escape to the North, physical retaliation to attack, plotting insurrection (with a frequency that caused the masters to live in a state of constant apprehension and under conditions of continual vigilance and security), running off to join Indian tribes, or forming small bands of armed guerillas operating out of swamps and remote areas. It is difficult to imagine why, if the majority of slaves were inert "Sambos," broken in mind and spirit, as Styron's Nat suggests, southern governors have filled the official record with so many requests for federal troops to guard against insurrection.

Two further examples of incidents reported in the original *Confessions* and transformed by Mr. Styron's imagination are indicative of the pattern of interpretation throughout the book. Turner tells of converting and baptizing a white man, an event unprecedented in Tidewater Virginia of the time, and one which would probably cause an equally great furor were it to happen today. The two men are refused access to the church and repair to the river for the ceremony, where they are mocked and threatened by a white crowd.

In Styron's version, the white convert is a drunken, degenerate, child-molesting pederast, and is shown as a type—the subhuman, white trash "cracker"—that one finds in the works of writers like Erskine Caldwell. As in the omission of Nat's voluntary return, the logic dictating such an interpretation is not clear, but this is how the only white who is shown associating with slaves on anything that looks like simple human terms is presented.

Another instance of arbitrary and derogatory "interpretation" concerns a slave called Will, who invited himself to join the insurrection. He is different from the other conspirators in that he does not have to be recruited, he volunteers. In the original *Confessions*, Turner reports finding Will among his men when he joins them on the day of the insurrection: "I . . . asked Will how came he there, he answered, his life was worth no more than others, and his liberty as dear [to him.] I asked him if he thought to obtain it? He said he would, or lose his life. This was enough to put him in full confidence." In the subsequent violence Will is identified specifically as "dispatching" a number of people, while most of the other murders are not attributed to members of the band. The most that can be said of Turner's references to Will is that they show him operating with a single-minded efficiency in carrying out the work at hand. In the context of Turner's narrative there is no suggestion of dementia or frenzy in Will's actions. Like Joshua he is simply engaged in the destruction of the Lord's enemies.

In the novel, Styron's Nat sees "the demented, . . . hate-ravished, mashed-in face . . ." of Will, whose "woolly head was filled with cockleburs. A scar glistened on his black cheek, shiny as as eel cast up on a mud bank. I felt that if I reached out I could almost touch with my fingertips the madness stirring within him, feel a shaggy brute heaving beneath the carapace of a black skin." Will is "streaked with mud, stinking, fangs bared beneath a nose stepped upon and bent like a flattened spoon, . . ." His eyes shine with a "malign fire" and he bears a hatred toward "all mankind, all creation." We learn that Will has been reduced to this condition of bestiality by the unendurable cruelties of a sadistic master so that his is not the "natural depravity" that another generation of southern writers would have evoked. But even so, this portrait of an evolutionary marvel, half-nigger, half-beast, is surely familiar to anyone who knows such classics of southern literature as Dixon's *The Klansman*. His has been a long history and I had hoped that having served his time on the pages of southern fiction this particular stereotype could now be laid to rest. It is saddening to see the poor fellow resurrected by a writer of Mr. Styron's unquestioned sophistication. As he sidles into the scene, stinking and licking his fangs, we recognize his function: he will rape a white woman. And thirty pages later, despite Nat's injunctions against rape (no sexual incidents are mentioned in the record of the trial), an injunction all the nobler in light of his own perennial, frustrated cravings, we find this scene:

There deserted of all save those two acting out their final tableau—the tar-black man and the woman, bone-white, bone-rigid with fear beyond telling, pressed urgently together against the door in a simulacrum of shattered oneness and heartsick farewell . . .

and it looks as if nigger-beast has struck again.[3]

There is, finally, the major invention that gives color to the entire novel. Mr. Styron, contrary to any historical evidence, has Turner's ultimate defeat coming as a result of the actions of loyal slaves who fought in defense of their beloved masters. That these slaves are identified as "owned by the gentry" further underlines the book's emphasis on the benign nature of "aristocratic slavery," which was able to command the loyalty of these slaves who were, in one white character's words, "living too well."

This thing which did not happen is made into one of the central motifs of the book. Turner broods on the memory of "Negroes in great numbers . . . firing back at us with as much passion and fury and *even* skill as their white owners . . ." When his lieutenant, Hark, falls, Turner recalls "three bare-chested Negroes . . . in the pantaloons of *coachmen*

. . . kick him back to earth with booted feet. Hark flopped around in desperation, but they kicked him again, kicked him with an exuberance not caused by any white man's urging or threat or exhortation but with rackety glee, . . ." [Emphasis added]. And so, dispirited and broken, Nat sits in his cell feeling himself betrayed by his people and his God: "It seemed . . . that my black shit-eating people were surely like flies, God's mindless outcasts, lacking even that will to destroy by their own hand their unending anguish . . ." [4]

In the original *Confessions* he shows no such uncertainty or bitterness. When asked if he could not see that the entire undertaking was a mistake, he answers simply, "Was not Christ crucified?" Gray's final description of him is significant. ". . . clothed with rags and covered with chains: yet daring to raise his manacled hands to heaven, with a spirit soaring above the attributes of man; I looked on him and my blood curdled in my veins."

If this book is important, it is so not because it tells much about Negro experience during slavery but because of the manner in which it demonstrates the persistence of white southern myths, racial stereotypes, and literary clichés even in the best intentioned and most enlightened minds. Their largely uncritical acceptance in literary circles shows us how far we still have to go. The real "history" of Nat Turner, and indeed of black people, remains to be written.

NOTES

1. In 1837 the Old Dominion exported to the death camps of the Deep South 40,000 black bodies for a net income of twenty-four million dollars.

2. By testimony of the slaves themselves. See Benjamin A. Botkin, ed., *Lay My Burden Down: A Folk History of Slavery* (Chicago: University of Chicago Press, 1945).

3. William Wells Brown, a Negro, whose book on the Negro in the American Revolution appeared in 1867, mentions the Nat Turner rebellion. His version does not in any way contradict the meager court record that is the original *Confessions*, but it adds information not included. One may speculate as to the source of this information—possibly newspaper accounts of the time, or the testimony of black survivors of the incident—but the account is of interest, representing, as it does, an early account of the insurrection, by a black man. About Will, Brown has this to say:

> Among those who joined the conspirators was Will, a slave who scorned the idea of taking his master's name. Though his soul longed to be free, he evidently became one of the party as much to satisfy revenge as for the liberty he saw in the dim future . . . His own back was covered with scars from his shoulders to his feet. A large scar running from his right eye down to his chin showed that he had lived with a cruel master. Nearly six feet in height and one of the strongest and most athletic of his race, he proved to be one of the most

unfeeling of the insurrectionists. His only weapon was a broad axe, sharp and heavy.

Brown then quotes, from the original *Confessions*, Will's path of carnage, and next describes his death in the final skirmish.

> In this battle there were many slain on both sides. Will, the blood-thirsty and revengeful slave, fell with his broad axe uplifted, after having laid three of the whites dead at his feet with his own strong arm and terrible weapon. His last words were, "Bury my axe with me." For he religiously believed, that, in the next world, the blacks would have a contest with the whites, and he would need his axe.

No sociological comment is necessary. But from a purely literary standpoint, it should be clear that Will, lifelong rebel and archetypal destroyer, presents possibilities which Mr. Styron simply ignored in favor of the "ravening, incoherent black beast" stereotype.

4. Brown's version makes it clear, as do the court records, that Turner's defeat came at the hands of whites. No black loyalist mercenaries are mentioned, but he does give an instance of a master's life being saved by a slave. That, too, is instructive:

> On the fatal night, when Nat and his companions were dealing death to all they found, Capt. Harris, a wealthy planter, had his life saved by the devotion and timely warning of his slave Jim, said to have been half brother to his master. After the revolt had been put down, and parties of whites were out hunting the suspected blacks, Capt. Harris with his faithful slave went into the woods in search of the Negroes. In saving his master's life Jim felt he had done his duty, and could not consent to become a betrayer of his race; and, on reaching the woods, he handed his pistol to his master, and said, "I cannot help you hunt down these men: they, like myself, want to be free. Sir, I am tired of the life of a slave: please give me my freedom or shoot me on the spot." Capt. Harris took the weapon, and pointed at the slave . . . The Capt. fired and the slave fell dead at his feet.

I do not claim that this incident necessarily took place in exactly the way that Brown relates it. But it also seems too specific to be pure invention on the part of Mr. Brown, who was, after all, writing history and not fiction. It seems most probable that this was one of those minor incidents which become part of the folk lore surrounding any major event; it is discussed, passed on, almost certainly distorted in the telling, but for some reason not included in "official" records. In this case, moreover, the nature of the incident suggests a reason for its exclusion.

VI

Black Protest Leaders

During the period between the emergence of the cotton kingdom in the South and the outbreak of the Civil War, several prominent black activists arose to express either by word or deed the sentiments and grievances held, but suppressed by the mass of inarticulate Afro-Americans. Essentially these figures can be divided into leaders of slave revolts in the South and champions of black rights in the North. Among the former, the most prominent were Gabriel Prosser, Denmark Vesey, and Nat Turner. These men concluded that black slaves could secure their freedom only by armed revolt against the plantation system. Consequently, they and their necessarily small band of followers took it upon themselves to plot and to engage in insurrections aimed at dismantling this system. In the cases of Prosser and Vesey, their plans were revealed by insiders who either lost their nerve or desired favor from their white masters more than freedom for their black brothers.

Of the three black rebels, Denmark Vesey developed the most sophisticated and elaborate if not the most effective conspiracy to revolt. In 1800, the same year that Turner was born and the abortive revolt of Gabriel Prosser occurred, Vesey purchased his freedom and settled in Charleston, South Carolina where he practiced his trade of carpentry. Although Vesey enjoyed a rather favored existence by comparison to the lot of most black Southerners, he gained no satisfaction from that fact. Instead it made him more sensitive to the pitiful lot of his black brothers and eventually drove him to draw up an elaborate scheme—first to seize the city of Charleston and later to transport all black participants to freedom beyond the borders of the United States. Despite careful precautions, Vesey's plans were revealed to local authorities by two black informers. The results were mass arrests of blacks, both free and bond, and the subsequent conviction of forty-seven persons, most of whom were condemned either to death or to be transported to the West Indies and sold.

In contrast to southern slaves who were forced to depend strictly upon the collaboration of a small group of co-conspirators, northern blacks frequently sought the assistance of white patrons whose wealth and positions could be utilized to overcome their own inaccessibility to the principal organs of public opinion—the printed word and the lecture platform. The scarcity of financial resources, the limited number of potential subscribers, and the lack of publishing facilities hampered most efforts by Afro-Americans to get their message across through newspapers and pamphlets. In 1829, a group of blacks in New York founded *The Freedom's Journal*, which two years later folded because of inadequate financial backing. In 1829, David Walker of Boston published his incendiary but powerful *Walker's Appeal* which white America largely succeeded in suppressing. Black Americans were not much more effective in getting their message across in public speeches. Dependent upon white assistance in procuring meeting halls and large audiences, black Americans were forced into accepting ceremonial roles by white abolitionists. Even Frederick Douglass, a star performer, was advised by his white patrons that unless he gave the people a little "plantation talk" they would never believe he had been a slave. In addition black speakers were frequently made to moderate their positions lest they lose white sympathy. The limited results of these early efforts illustrated the serious handicaps under which black Americans operated in proclaiming their own ideologies and in counteracting the propaganda of white Americans.

The abolitionist crusade of the 1830s nevertheless provided Afro-Americans with additional resources even if only a tiny percentage of white Americans were sympathetic to the movement. With the assistance of William L. Garrison, the fiery white abolitionist of Boston, Frederick Douglass rose to a position of leadership among free blacks of the North and became a symbol of black success for a few white Americans.

Although Douglass' life was obviously more exceptional than typical, the publication of his autobiography provided readers with some understanding of the horrors of the slave experience. Like many men of character and intelligence, Douglass was more effective as a public speaker. Douglass spoke before many northern audiences through the auspices of the American Anti-Slavery Society. Tiring of white pressure, he later declared himself independent of Garrison and began publishing his own newspaper, *The North Star*. In the process of these activities Douglass became the best known if not always the most popular of the several prominent black leaders in the North before 1860.

For the most part, Douglass was a spokesman for the integration of Afro-Americans into the mainstream of American life. Consequently he stressed the similarity of interests and capabilities between black and white Americans. More race conscious was another prominent black leader, the Reverend Henry Highland Garnet. Although generally more neglected by historians than Douglass, Garnet was a more militant defender of black rights. Frustrated and despondent over the future of Afro-Americans to obtain justice in the United States, Garnet in the 1843 meeting of the Negro Convention Movement, endorsed Walker's call for militant action and urged slaves to kill any master who refused to free them. A resolution supporting Garnet's position and declaring that "a righteous govenment" would abolish slavery failed of passage by a single vote. Leading the opposition to this resolution was Frederick Douglass.

Another vehicle for black protest was the famous "underground railroad." Contrary to popular impression, it was neither a well-organized conspiracy nor was it operated primarily by white conductors. Although there were a few important white participants like Levi Coffin of Cincinnati, almost all of the dangerous work in the South was done by black agents and most of the northern stations were run by blacks. Since the underground railroad was a secret and highly unstructured institution, black fugitives could hardly afford to run the risk of seeking white assistance; instead they looked to their own people whom they could more readily trust for assistance in escaping into northern cities or into Canada. Prominent northern blacks who were active in this movement included David Ruggles and Charles Ray of New York City, J. W. Loguen of Syracuse, Douglass of Rochester, and Robert Purvis and William Still of Philadelphia.

The following essays focus on four of these principal leaders. In the first selection, Thomas Wentworth Higginson, a prominent white abolitionist who commanded a regiment of black soldiers during the Civil War, discusses the exploits of Denmark Vesey and describes the details of his efforts to lead an insurrection in 1822. August Meier discusses the integrationist ideology and modern-like protests of Frederick Douglass. In another essay, William M. Brewer describes the more militant position of Henry Highland Garnet. In the final selection, Larry Gara illustrates his contention that black abolitionist activities have been unfairly downgraded by white historians as he describes the courageous work of William Still in Philadelphia.

18. THOMAS WENTWORTH HIGGINSON, Black Rebellion (1889)*

Unlike the other authors included in this book, Thomas W. Higginson was not a trained scholar but a talented essayist of the nineteenth century. In addition, Higginson was a militant white abolitionist who commanded the first regiment of freedmen to fight in the Civil War. While his sympathies were clearly with the slaves, Higginson's account of the Vesey Plot is more descriptive than interpretative. The selection is from Higginson's widely praised and recently reprinted monograph in which he describes the revolts of Prosser, Vesey, and Turner and the Maroons of Jamaica and Surinam.

Denmark Vesey

On Saturday afternoon, May 25, 1822, a slave named Devany, belonging to Col. Prioleau of Charleston, S.C., was sent to market by his mistress, —the colonel being absent in the country. After doing his errands, he strolled down upon the wharves in the enjoyment of that magnificent

* From Thomas Wentworth Higginson, *Black Rebellion* (New York: Arno Press, 1969), pp. 103–63. Reprinted by permission.

wealth of leisure which usually characterized the former "house-servant" of the South, when beyond hail of the street-door. He presently noticed a small vessel lying in the stream, with a peculiar flag flying; and while looking at it, he was accosted by a slave named William, belonging to Mr. John Paul, who remarked to him, "I have often seen a flag with the number 76, but never one with the number 96 upon it before." After some further conversation on this trifling point, William suddenly inquired, "Do you know that something serious is about to take place?" Devany disclaiming the knowledge of any graver impending crisis than the family dinner, the other went on to inform him that many of the slaves were "determined to right themselves." "We are determined," he added, "to shake off our bondage, and for that purpose we stand on a good foundation; many have joined, and if you will go with me, I will show you the man who has the list of names, and who will take yours down."

This startling disclosure was quite too much for Devany: he was made of the wrong material for so daring a project; his genius was culinary, not revolutionary. Giving some excuse for breaking off the conversation, he went forthwith to consult a free colored man, named Pensil or Pencell, who advised him to warn his master instantly. So he lost no time in telling the secret to his mistress and her young son; and on the return of Col. Prioleau from the country, five days afterward, it was at once revealed to him. Within an hour or two he stated the facts to Mr. Hamilton, the intendant, or, as he would now be called, mayor; Mr. Hamilton at once summoned the corporation, and by five o'clock Devany and William were under examination.

This was the first warning of a plot which ultimately filled Charleston with terror. And yet so thorough and so secret was the organization of the Negroes, that a fortnight passed without yielding the slightest information beyond the very little which was obtained from these two. William Paul was, indeed, put in confinement, and soon gave evidence inculpating two slaves as his employers,—Mingo Harth and Peter Poyas. But these men, when arrested, behaved with such perfect coolness, and treated the charge with such entire levity;—their trunks and premises, when searched, were so innocent of all alarming contents;—that they were soon discharged by the wardens. William Paul at length became alarmed for his own safety, and began to let out further facts piecemeal, and to inculpate other men. But some of those very men came voluntarily to the intendant, on hearing that they were suspected, and indignantly offered themselves for examination. Puzzled and bewildered, the municipal government kept the thing as secret as possible, placed the city guard in an efficient condition, provided sixteen hundred rounds of ball cartridges, and ordered the sentinels and patrols to be armed with loaded muskets.

"Such had been our fancied security, that the guard had previously gone on duty without muskets, and with only sheathed bayonets and bludgeons."

It has since been asserted, though perhaps on questionable authority, that the Secretary of War was informed of the plot, even including some details of the plan and the leader's name, before it was known in Charleston. If so, he utterly disregarded it; and, indeed, so well did the Negroes play their part, that the whole report was eventually disbelieved, while—as was afterwards proved—they went on to complete their secret organization, and hastened by a fortnight the appointed day of attack. Unfortunately for their plans, however, another betrayal took place at the very last moment, from a different direction. A class-leader in a Methodist church had been persuaded or bribed by his master to procure further disclosures. He at length came and stated, that, about three months before, a man named Rolla, slave of Gov. Bennett, had communicated to a friend of his the fact of an intended insurrection, and had said that the time fixed for the outbreak was the following Sunday night, June 16. As this conversation took place on Friday, it gave but a very short time for the city authorities to act, especially as they wished neither to endanger the city nor to alarm it.

Yet so cautiously was the game played on both sides that the whole thing was still kept a secret from the Charleston public; and some members of the city government did not fully appreciate their danger till they had passed it. "The whole was concealed," wrote the governor afterwards, "until the time came; but secret preparations were made. Saturday night and Sunday morning passed without demonstrations; doubts were excited, and counter orders issued for diminishing the guard." It afterwards proved that these preparations showed to the slaves that their plot was betrayed, and so saved the city without public alarm. Newspaper correspondence soon was full of the story, each informant of course hinting plainly that he had been behind the scenes all along, and had withheld it only to gratify the authorities in their policy of silence. It was "now no longer a secret," they wrote; adding, that, for five or six weeks, but little attention had been paid by the community to these rumors, the city council having kept it carefully to themselves until a number of suspicious slaves had been arrested. This refers to ten prisoners who were seized on June 18, an arrest which killed the plot, and left only the terrors of what might have been. The investigation, thus publicly commenced, soon revealed a free colored man named Denmark Vesey as the leader of the enterprise,—among his chief coadjutors being that innocent Peter and that unsuspecting Mingo who had been examined and discharged nearly three weeks before.

It is matter of demonstration, that, but for the military preparations on the appointed Sunday night, the attempt would have been made. The ringleaders had actually met for their final arrangements, when, by comparing notes, they found themselves foiled; and within another week they were prisoners on trial. Nevertheless, the plot which they had laid was the most elaborate insurrectionary project ever formed by American slaves, and came the nearest to a terrible success. In boldness of conception and thoroughness of organization there has been nothing to compare with it; and it is worth while to dwell somewhat upon its details, first introducing the *dramatis personae*.

Denmark Vesey had come very near figuring as a revolutionist in Haiti, instead of South Carolina. Capt. Vesey, an old resident of Charleston, commanded a ship that traded between St. Thomas and Cape Français, during our Revolutionary War, in the slave-transportation line. In the year 1781 he took on board a cargo of three hundred and ninety slaves, and sailed for the Cape. On the passage, he and his officers were much attracted by the beauty and intelligence of a boy of fourteen, whom they unanimously adopted into the cabin as a pet. They gave him new clothes, and a new name, Télémaque, which was afterwards gradually corrupted into Telmak and Denmark. They amused themselves with him until their arrival at Cape Français, and then, "having no use for the boy," sold their pet as if he had been a macaw or a monkey. Capt. Vesey sailed for St. Thomas; and, presently making another trip to Cape Français, was surprised to hear from his consignee that Télémaque would be returned on his hands as being "unsound,"—not in theology nor in morals, but in body,—subject to epileptic fits, in fact. According to the custom of that place, the boy was examined by the city physician, who required Capt. Vesey to take him back; and Denmark served him faithfully, with no trouble from epilepsy, for twenty years, travelling all over the world with him, and learning to speak various languages. In 1800 he drew a prize of fifteen hundred dollars in the East Bay-street Lottery, with which he bought his freedom from his master for six hundred dollars,—much less than his market value. From that time, the official report says, he worked as a carpenter in Charleston, distinguished for physical strength and energy. "Among those of his color he was looked up to with awe and respect. His temper was impetuous and domineering in the extreme, qualifying him for the despotic rule of which he was ambitious. All his passions were ungovernable and savage; and to his numerous wives and children he displayed the haughty and capricious cruelty of an Eastern bashaw."

"For several years before he disclosed his intentions to any one, he appears to have been constantly and assiduously engaged in endeavoring to imbitter the minds of the colored population against the white. He rendered himself perfectly familiar with all those parts of the Scriptures which he thought he could pervert to his purpose, and he would readily quote them to prove that slavery was contrary to the laws of God; that slaves were bound to attempt their emancipation, however shocking and bloody might be the consequences; and that such efforts would not only be pleasing to the Almighty, but were absolutely enjoined, and their success predicted, in the Scriptures. His favorite texts when he addressed those of his own color were Zech. xiv. 1–3, and Josh. vi. 21; and in all his conversations he identified their situation with that of the Israelites. The number of inflammatory pamphlets on slavery brought into Charleston from some of our sister States within the last four years (and once from Sierra Leone), and distributed amongst the colored population of the city, for which there was a great facility, in consequence of the unrestricted intercourse allowed to persons of color between the different States in the Union, and the speeches in Congress of those opposed to the admission of Missouri into the Union, perhaps garbled and misrepresented, furnished him with ample means for inflaming the minds of the colored population of the State; and by distorting certain parts of those speeches, or selecting from them particular passages, he persuaded but too many that Congress had actually declared them free, and that they were held in bondage contrary to the laws of the land. Even whilst walking through the streets in company with another, he was not idle; for if his companion bowed to a white person, he would rebuke him, and observe that all men were born equal, and that he was surprised that any one would degrade himself by such conduct; that he would never cringe to the whites, nor ought any one who had the feelings of a man. When answered, 'We are slaves,' he would sarcastically and indignantly reply, 'You deserve to remain slaves;' and if he were further asked, 'What can we do?' he would remark, 'Go and buy a spelling-book, and read the fable of Hercules and the Wagoner,' which he would then repeat, and apply it to their situation. He also sought every opportunity of entering into conversation with white persons, when they could be overheard by negroes near by, especially in grog-shops,—during which conversation he would artfully introduce some bold remark on slavery; and sometimes, when, from the character he was conversing with, he found he might still be bolder, he would go so far, that, had not his declarations in such situations been clearly proved, they would scarcely have been credited. He continued this course until some time after the commencement of the last winter; by which time he had not only obtained incredible influence amongst persons of color, but many feared him more than their owners, and, one of them declared, even more than his God."

It was proved against him, that his house had been the principal place of meeting for the conspirators, that all the others habitually referred to him as the leader, and that he had shown great address in dealing with different temperaments and overcoming a variety of scruples. One witness testified that Vesey had read to him from the Bible about the deliverance of the children of Israel; another, that he had read to him a speech which had been delivered "in Congress by a Mr. King" on the subject of slavery, and Vesey had said that "this Mr. King was the black man's friend; that he, Mr. King, had declared he would continue to speak, write, and publish pamphlets against slavery the longest day he lived, until the Southern States consented to emancipate their slaves, for that slavery was a great disgrace to the country." But among all the reports there are only two sentences which really reveal the secret soul of Denmark Vesey, and show his impulses and motives. "He said he did not go with Creighton to Africa, because he had not a will; he wanted to stay and see what he could do for his fellow-creatures." The other takes us still nearer home. Monday Gell stated in his confession, that Vesey, on first broaching the plan to him, said "he was satisfied with his own condition, being free; but, as all his children were slaves, he wished to see what could be done for them."

It is strange to turn from this simple statement of a perhaps intelligent preference, on the part of a parent, for seeing his offspring in a condition of freedom, to the *naïve* astonishment of his judges. "It is difficult to imagine," says the sentence finally passed on Denmark Vesey, "what infatuation could have prompted you to attempt an enterprise so wild and visionary. You were a free man, comparatively wealthy, and enjoyed every comfort compatible with your situation. You had, therefore, much to risk and little to gain." Yet one witness testified: "Vesey said the negroes were living such an abominable life, they ought to rise. I said, I was living well; he said, though I was, others were not, and that 'twas such fools as I that were in the way and would not help them, and that after all things were well he would mark me." "His general conversation," said another witness, a white boy, "was about religion, which he would apply to slavery; as, for instance, he would speak of the creation of the world, in which he would say all men had equal rights, blacks as well as whites, etc.; all his religious remarks were mingled with slavery." And the firmness of this purpose did not leave him, even after the betrayal of his cherished plans. "After the plot was discovered," said Monday Gell, in his confession, "Vesey said it was all over, unless an attempt were made to rescue those who might be condemned, by rushing on the people and saving the prisoners, or all dying together."

The only person to divide with Vesey the claim of leadership was Peter Poyas. Vesey was the missionary of the cause, but Peter was the organizing mind. He kept the register of "candidates," and decided who should or should not be enrolled. "We can't live so," he often reminded his confederates; "we must break the yoke." "God has a hand in it; we have been meeting for four years, and are not yet betrayed." Peter was a ship-carpenter, and a slave of great value. He was to be the military leader. His plans showed some natural generalship: he arranged the night-attack; he planned the enrollment of a mounted troop to scour the streets; and he had a list of all the shops where arms and ammunition were kept for sale. He voluntarily undertook the management of the most difficult part of the enterprise,—the capture of the main guard-house,—and had pledged himself to advance alone and surprise the sentinel. He was said to have a magnetism in his eyes, of which his confederates stood in great awe; if he once got his eye upon a man, there was no resisting it. A white witness has since narrated, that, after his arrest, he was chained to the floor in a cell, with another of the conspirators. Men in authority came, and sought by promises, threats, and even tortures, to ascertain the names of other accomplices. His companion, wearied out with pain and suffering, and stimulated by the hope of saving his own life, at last began to yield. Peter raised himself, leaned upon his elbow, looked at the poor fellow, saying quietly, "Die like a man," and instantly lay down again. It was enough; not another word was extorted.

One of the most notable individuals in the plot was a certain Jack Purcell, commonly called Gullah Jack,—Gullah signifying Angola, the place of his origin. A conjurer by profession and by lineal heritage in his own country, he had resumed the practice of his vocation on this side the Atlantic. For fifteen years he had wielded in secret an immense influence among a sable constituency in Charleston; and as he had the reputation of being invulnerable, and of teaching invulnerability as an art, he was very good at beating up recruits for insurrection. Over those of Angolese descent, especially, he was a perfect king, and made them join in the revolt as one man. They met him monthly at a place called Bulkley's Farm, selected because the black overseer on that plantation was one of the initiated, and because the farm was accessible by water, thus enabling them to elude the patrol. There they prepared cartridges and pikes, and had primitive banquets, which assumed a melodramatic character under the inspiriting guidance of Jack. If a fowl was privately roasted, that mystic individual muttered incantations over it; and then they all grasped at it, exclaiming, "Thus we pull Buckra to pieces!" He gave them parched corn and groundnuts to be eaten as internal safeguards on the day before the outbreak, and a consecrated *cullah*, or crab's claw, to be carried in the mouth by each, as an amulet. These rather questionable means secured him a power which was very unquestionable; the witnesses examined in his presence all showed dread of his conjurations, and referred to him indirectly, with a kind of awe, as "the little man who can't be shot."

When Gullah Jack was otherwise engaged, there seems to have been a sort of deputy seer employed in the enterprise, a blind man named Philip. He was a preacher; was said to have been born with a caul on his head, and so claimed the gift of second-sight. Timid adherents were brought to his house for ghostly counsel. "Why do you look so timorous?" he said to William Garner, and then quoted Scripture, "Let not your heart be troubled." That a blind man should know how he looked, was beyond the philosophy of the visitor; and this piece of rather cheap ingenuity carried the day.

Other leaders were appointed also. Monday Gell was the scribe of the enterprise; he was a native African, who had learned to read and write. He was by trade a harness-maker, working chiefly on his own account. He confessed that he had written a letter to President Boyer of the new black republic; "the letter was about the sufferings of the blacks, and to know if the people of St. Domingo would help them if they made an effort to free themselves." This epistle was sent by the black cook of a northern schooner, and the envelope was addressed to a relative of the bearer.

Tom Russell was the armorer, and made pikes "on a very improved model," the official report admits. Polydore Faber fitted the weapons with handles. Bacchus Hammett had charge of the fire-arms and ammunition, not as yet a laborious duty. William Garner and Mingo Harth were to lead the horse-company. Lot Forrester was the courier, and had done, no one ever knew how much, in the way of enlisting country Negroes, of whom Ned Bennett was to take command when enlisted. Being the governor's servant, Ned was probably credited with some official experience. These were the officers: now for the plan of attack.

It was the custom then, as later, for the country Negroes to flock largely into Charleston on Sunday. More than a thousand came, on ordinary occasions, and a far larger number might at any time make their appearance without exciting any suspicion. They gathered in, especially by water, from the opposite sides of Ashley and Cooper Rivers, and from the neighboring islands; and they came in a great number of canoes of various sizes,—many of which could carry a hundred men,—which were ordinarily employed in bringing agricultural products to the Charleston market. To get an approximate knowledge of the number, the city government once ordered the persons thus arriving to be counted,—and that during the progress of the trials, at a time when the Negroes were rather fearful of coming into town; and it was found, that, even then, there were more than five hundred visitors on a single Sunday. This fact, then, was the essential point in the plan of insurrection. Whole plantations were found to have been enlisted among the "candidates," as they were termed; and it was proved that the city Negroes, who lived nearest the place of meeting, had agreed to conceal these confederates in their houses to a large extent, on the night of the proposed outbreak.

The details of the plan, however, were not rashly committed to the mass of the confederates; they were known only to a few, and were finally to be announced only after the evening prayer-meetings on the appointed Sunday. But each leader had his own company enlisted, and his own work marked out. When the clock struck twelve, all were to move. Peter Poyas was to lead a party ordered to assemble at South Bay, and to be joined by a force from James's Island; he was then to march up and seize the arsenal and guard-house opposite St. Michael's Church, and detach a sufficient number to cut off all white citizens who should appear at the alarm-posts. A second body of Negroes, from the country and the Neck, headed by Ned Bennett, was to assemble on the Neck, and seize the arsenal there. A third was to meet at Gov. Bennett's Mills, under command of Rolla, and, after putting the governor and intendant to death, to march through the city, or be posted at Cannon's Bridge, thus preventing the inhabitants of Cannonsborough from entering the city. A fourth, partly from the country, and partly from the neighboring localities in the city, was to rendezvous on Gadsden's Wharf, and attack the upper guard-house. A fifth, composed of country and Neck Negroes, was to assemble at Bulkley's Farm, two miles and a half from the city, seize the upper powder-magazine, and then march down; and a sixth was to assemble at Denmark Vesey's, and obey his orders. A seventh detachment, under Gullah Jack, was to assemble in Boundary Street, at the head of King Street, to capture the arms of the Neck company of militia, and to take an additional supply from Mr. Duquercron's shop. The naval stores on Mey's Wharf were also to be attacked. Meanwhile, a horse-company, consisting of many draymen, hostlers, and butcher-boys, was to meet at Lightwood's Alley, and then scour the streets to prevent the whites from assembling. Every white man coming out of his own door was to be killed; and, if necessary, the city was to be fired in several places,—slow-match for this purpose having been purloined from the public arsenal, and placed in an accessible position.

Beyond this, the plan of action was either unformed or undiscovered; some slight reliance seems to have been placed on English aid,—more on assistance from St. Domingo. At any rate, all the ships in the harbor were to be seized; and in these, if the worst came to the worst, those most deeply inculpated could set sail, bearing with them, perhaps, the spoils of shops and of banks. It seems to be admitted by the official narrative, that they might have been able, at that season of the year, and with the aid of the fortifications on the Neck and around the harbor, to retain possession of the city for some time.

So unsuspicious were the authorities, so unprepared the citizens, so open to attack lay the city, that nothing seemed necessary to the success of the insurgents except organization and arms. Indeed, the plan of organization easily covered a supply of arms. By their own contributions they had secured enough to strike the first blow,—a few hundred pikes and daggers, together with swords and guns for the leaders. But they had carefully marked every place in the city where weapons were to be obtained. On King-street Road, beyond the municipal limits, in a common wooden shop, were left unguarded the arms of the Neck company of militia, to the number of several hundred stand; and these were to be secured by Bacchus Hammett, whose master kept the establishment. In Mr. Duquercron's shop there were deposited for sale as many more weapons; and they had noted Mr. Schirer's shop in Queen Street, and other gunsmiths' establishments. Finally, the state arsenal in Meeting Street, a building with no defenses except ordinary wooden doors, was to be seized early in the outbreak. Provided, therefore, that the first moves proved successful, all the rest appeared sure.

Very little seems to have been said among the conspirators in regard to any plans of riot or debauchery, subsequent to the capture of the city. Either their imaginations did not dwell on them, or the witnesses did not dare to give testimony, or the authorities to print it. Death was to be dealt out, comprehensive and terrible; but nothing more is mentioned. One prisoner, Rolla, is reported in the evidence to have dropped hints in regard to the destiny of the women; and there was a rumor in the newspapers of the time, that he or some other of Gov. Bennett's slaves was to have taken the governor's daughter, a young girl of sixteen, for his wife, in the event of success; but this is all. On the other hand, Denmark Vesey was known to be for a war of immediate and total extermination; and when some of the company opposed killing "the ministers and the women and children," Vesey read from the Scriptures that all should be cut off, and said that "it was for their safety not to leave one white skin alive, for this was the plan they pursued at St. Domingo." And all this was not a mere dream of one lonely enthusiast, but a measure which had been maturing for four full years among several confederates, and had been under discussion for five months among multitudes of initiated "candidates."

As usual with slave-insurrections, the best men and those most trusted were deepest in the plot. Rolla was the only prominent conspirator who was not an active church-member. "Most of the ringleaders," says a Charleston letter-writer of that day, "were the rulers or class-leaders in what is called the African Society, and were considered faithful, honest fellows. Indeed, many of the owners could not be convinced, till the fellows confessed themselves, that they were concerned, and that the first object of all was to kill their masters." And the first official report declares that it would not be difficult to assign a motive for the insurrectionists, "if it had not been distinctly proved, that, with scarcely an exception, they had no individual hardship to complain of, and were among the most humanely treated negroes in the city. The facilities for combining and confederating in such a scheme were amply afforded by the extreme indulgence and kindness which characterize the domestic treatment of our slaves. Many slave-owners among us, not satisfied with ministering to the wants of their domestics by all the comforts of abundant food and excellent clothing, with a misguided benevolence have not only permitted their instruction, but lent to such efforts their approbation and applause."

"I sympathize most sincerely," says the anonymous author of a pamphlet of the period, "with the very respectable and pious clergyman whose heart must still bleed at the recollection that his confidential class-leader, but a week or two before his just conviction, had received the communion of the Lord's Supper from his hand. This wretch had been brought up in his pastor's family, and was treated with the same Christian attention as was shown to their own children." "To us who are accustomed to the base and proverbial ingratitude of these people, this ill return of kindness and confidence is not surprising; but they who are ignorant of their real character will read and wonder."

One demonstration of this "Christian attention" had lately been the closing of the African Church,—of which, as has been stated, most of the leading revolutionists were members,—on the ground that it tended to spread the dangerous infection of the alphabet. On January 15, 1821, the city marshal, John J. Lafar, had notified "ministers of the gospel and others who keep night- and Sunday-schools for slaves, that the education of such persons is forbidden by law, and that the city government feel imperiously bound to enforce the penalty." So that there were some special as well as general grounds for disaffection among these ungrateful favorites of fortune, the slaves. Then there were fancied dangers. An absurd report had somehow arisen,—since you cannot keep men ignorant without making them unreasonable also,—that on the ensuing Fourth of July the whites were to create a false alarm, and that every black man coming out was to be killed, "in order to thin them"; this being done to prevent their joining an imaginary army supposed to be on its way from Haiti. Others were led to suppose that Congress had ended the Missouri Compromise discussion by making them all free, and that the law would protect their liberty if they could only secure it. Others, again, were threatened with the vengeance of the conspirators, unless they also joined; on the night of attack, it was said, the initiated would have a countersign, and all who did not know it would share the fate of the whites. Add to this the reading of Congressional speeches, and of the copious magazine of revolution to be found in the Bible,—and it was no wonder, if they for the first time were roused, under the energetic leadership of Vesey, to a full consciousness of their own condition.

"Not only were the leaders of good character, and very much indulged by their owners; but this was very generally the case with all who were convicted,—many of them possessing the highest confidence of their owners, and not one of bad character." In one case it was proved that Vesey had forbidden his followers to trust a certain man, because he had once been seen intoxicated. In another case it was shown that a slave named George had made every effort to obtain their confidence, but was constantly excluded from their meetings as a talkative fellow who could not be trusted,—a policy which his levity of manner, when examined in court, fully justified. They took no women into counsel,—not from any distrust apparently, but in order that their children might not be left uncared-for in case of defeat and destruction. House-servants were rarely trusted, or only when they had been carefully sounded by the chief leaders. Peter Poyas, in commissioning an agent to enlist men, gave him excellent cautions: "Don't mention it to those waiting-men who receive presents of old coats, etc., from their masters, or they'll betray us; I will speak to them." When he did speak, if he did not convince them, he at least frightened them. But the chief reliance was on those slaves who were hired out, and therefore more uncontrolled,—and also upon the country Negroes.

The same far-sighted policy directed the conspirators to disarm suspicion by peculiarly obedient and orderly conduct. And it shows the precaution with which the thing was carried on, that, although Peter Poyas was proved to have had a list of some six hundred persons, yet not one of his particular company was ever brought to trial. As each leader kept to himself the names of his proselytes, and as Monday Gell was the only one of these leaders who turned traitor, any opinion as to the numbers actually engaged must be altogether conjectural. One witness said nine thousand; another, six thousand six hundred. These statements were probably extravagant, though not more so than Gov. Bennett's assertion, on the other side, that "all who were actually concerned had been brought to justice,"—unless by this phrase he designates only the ringleaders. The avowed aim of the governor's letter, indeed, is to smooth the thing over, for the credit and safety of the city; and its evasive tone contrasts strongly with the more frank and thorough statements of the judges, made after the thing could no longer be hushed up. These high authorities explicitly acknowledge that they had failed to detect more than a small minority of those concerned in the project, and seem to admit, that, if it had once been brought to a head, the slaves generally would have joined in.

"We cannot venture to say," says the intendant's pamphlet, "to how many the knowledge of the intended effort was communicated, who without signifying their assent, or attending any of the meetings, were yet prepared to profit by events. That there are many who would not have permitted the enterprise to have failed at a critical moment, for the want of their cooperation, we have the best reason for believing." So believed the community at large; and the panic was in proportion, when the whole danger was finally made public. "The scenes I witnessed," says one who has since narrated the circumstances, "and the declaration of the impending danger that met us at all times and on all occasions, forced the conviction that never were an entire people more thoroughly alarmed than were the people of Charleston at that time. . . . During the excitement, and the trial of the supposed conspirators, rumor proclaimed all, and doubtless more than all, the horrors of the plot. The city was to be fired in every quarter; the arsenal in the immediate vicinity was to be broken open, and the arms distributed to the insurgents, and a universal massacre of the white inhabitants to take place. Nor did there seem to be any doubt in the mind of the people that such would actually have been the result had not the plot fortunately been detected before the time appointed for the outbreak. It was believed, as a matter of course, that every black in the city would join in the insurrection, and that if the original design had been attempted, and the city taken by surprise, the negroes would have achieved a complete and easy victory. Nor does it seem at all impossible that such might have been, or yet may be, the case, if any well-arranged and resolute rising should take place."

Indeed, this universal admission, that all the slaves were ready to take part in any desperate enterprise, was one of the most startling aspects of the affair. The authorities say that the two principal state's evidence declared that "they never spoke to any person of color on the subject, or knew of any one who had been spoken to by the other leaders, who had withheld his assent." And the conspirators seem to have been perfectly satisfied that all the remaining slaves would enter their ranks upon the slightest success. "Let us assemble a sufficient number to commence the work with spirit, and we'll not want men; they'll fall in behind us fast enough." And as an illustration of this readiness, the official report mentions a slave who had belonged to one master for sixteen years, sustaining a high character for fidelity and affection, who had twice travelled with him through the Northern States, resisting every solicitation to escape, and who yet was very deeply concerned in the insurrection, though knowing it to involve the probable destruction of the whole family with whom he lived.

One singular circumstance followed the first rumors of the plot.

Several white men, said to be of low and unprincipled character, at once began to make interest with the supposed leaders among the slaves, either from genuine sympathy, or with the intention of betraying them for money, or by profiting by the insurrection, should it succeed. Four of these were brought to trial; but the official report expresses the opinion that many more might have been discovered but for the inadmissibility of slave testimony against whites. Indeed, the evidence against even these four was insufficient for a capital conviction, although one was overheard, through stratagem, by the intendant himself, and arrested on the spot. This man was a Scotchman, another a Spaniard, a third a German, and the fourth a Carolinian. The last had for thirty years kept a shop in the neighborhood of Charleston; he was proved to have asserted that "the negroes had as much right to fight for their liberty as the white people," had offered to head them in the enterprise, and had said that in three weeks he would have two thousand men. But in no case, it appears, did these men obtain the confidence of the slaves; and the whole plot was conceived and organized, so far as appears, without the slightest cooperation from any white man.

The trial of the conspirators began on Wednesday, June 19. At the request of the intendant, Justices Kennedy and Parker summoned five freeholders (Messrs. Drayton, Heyward, Pringle, Legaré, and Turnbull) to constitute a court, under the provisions of the Act "for the better ordering and governing negroes and other slaves." The intendant laid the case before them, with a list of prisoners and witnesses. By a vote of the court, all spectators were excluded, except the owners and counsel of the slaves concerned. No other colored person was allowed to enter the jail, and a strong guard of soldiers was kept always on duty around the building. Under these general arrangements the trials proceeded with elaborate formality, though with some variations from ordinary usage,— as was, indeed, required by the statute.

For instance, the law provided that the testimony of any Indian or slave could be received, without oath, against a slave or free colored person, although it was not valid, even under oath, against a white. But it is best to quote the official language in respect to the rules adopted: "As the court had been organized under a statute of a peculiar and local character, and intended for the government of a distinct class of persons in the community, they were bound to conform their proceedings to its provisions, which depart in many essential features from the principles of the common law and some of the settled rules of evidence. The court, however, determined to adopt those rules, whenever they were not repugnant to nor expressly excepted by that statute, nor inconsistent with the local situation and policy of the State; and laid down for their own government the following regulations: First, that no slave should be tried except in the presence of his owner or his counsel, and that notice should be given in every case at least one day before the trial; second, that the testimony of one witness, unsupported by additional evidence or by circumstances, should lead to no conviction of a *capital* nature; third, that the witnesses should be confronted with the accused and with each other in every case, except where testimony was given under a solemn pledge that the names of the witnesses should not be divulged,—as they declared, in some instances, that they apprehended being murdered by the blacks, if it was known that they had volunteered their evidence; fourth, that the prisoners might be represented by counsel, whenever this was requested by the owners of the slaves, or by the prisoners themselves if free; fifth, that the statements or defences of the accused should be heard in every case, and they be permitted themselves to examine any witness they thought proper."

It is singular to observe how entirely these rules seem to concede that a slave's life has no sort of value to himself, but only to his master. His master, not he himself, must choose whether it be worth while to employ counsel. His master, not his mother or his wife, must be present at the trial. So far is this carried, that the provision to exclude "persons who had no particular interest in the slaves accused" seems to have excluded every acknowledged relative they had in the world, and admitted only those who had invested in them so many dollars. And yet the very first section of that part of the statute under which they were tried lays down an explicit recognition of their humanity: "And whereas natural justice forbids that any *person*, of what condition soever, should be condemned unheard." So thoroughly, in the whole report, are the ideas of person and chattel intermingled, that when Gov. Bennett petitions for mitigation of sentence in the case of his slave Batteau, and closes, "I ask this, gentlemen, as an individual incurring a severe and distressing loss," it is really impossible to decide whether the predominant emotion be affectional or financial.

It is matter of painful necessity to acknowledge that the proceedings of most slave-tribunals have justified the honest admission of Gov. Adams of South Carolina, in his legislative message of 1855: "The administration of our laws, in relation to our colored population, by our courts of magistrates and freeholders, as these courts are at present constituted, calls loudly for reform. Their decisions are rarely in conformity with justice or humanity." This trial, as reported by the justices themselves, seems to have been no worse than the average,—perhaps better. In all, thirty-five were sentenced to death, thirty-four to transportation, twenty-seven acquitted by the court, and twenty-five discharged without trial, by the Committee of Vigilance,—making in all one hundred and twenty-one.

The sentences pronounced by Judge Kennedy upon the leading rebels, while paying a high tribute to their previous character, of course bring all law and all Scripture to prove the magnitude of their crime. "It is a melancholy fact," he says, "that those servants in whom we reposed the most unlimited confidence have been the principal actors in this wicked scheme." Then he rises into earnest appeals. "Are you incapable of the heavenly influence of that gospel, all whose paths are peace? It was to reconcile us to our destiny on earth, and to enable us to discharge with fidelity all our duties, whether as master or servant, that those inspired precepts were imparted by Heaven to fallen man."

To these reasonings the prisoners had, of course, nothing to say; but the official reports bear the strongest testimony to their fortitude. "Rolla, when arraigned, affected not to understand the charge against him, and, when it was at his request further explained to him, assumed, with wonderful adroitness, astonishment and surprise. He was remarkable, throughout his trial, for great presence and composure of mind. When he was informed he was convicted, and was advised to prepare for death, though he had previously (but after his trial) confessed his guilt, he appeared perfectly confounded, but exhibited no signs of fear. In Ned's behavior there was nothing remarkable; but his countenance was stern and immovable, even whilst he was receiving the sentence of death: from his looks it was impossible to discover or conjecture what were his feelings. Not so with Peter: for in his countenance were strongly marked disappointed ambition, revenge, indignation, and an anxiety to know how far the discoveries had extended; and the same emotions were exhibited in his conduct. He did not appear to fear personal consequences, for his whole behavior indicated the reverse; but exhibited an evident anxiety for the success of their plan, in which his whole soul was embarked. His countenance and behavior were the same when he received his sentence; and his only words were, on retiring, 'I suppose you'll let me see my wife and family before I die?' and that not in a supplicating tone. When he was asked, a day or two after, if it was possible he could wish to see his master and family murdered, who had treated him so kindly, he only replied to the question by a smile. Monday's behavior was not peculiar. When he was before the court, his arms were folded; he heard the testimony given against him, and received his sentence, with the utmost firmness and composure. But no description can accurately convey to others the impression which the trial, defense, and appearance of Gullah Jack made on those who witnessed the workings of his cunning and rude address. When arrested and brought before the court, in company with another

African named Jack, the property of the estate of Pritchard, he assumed so much ignorance, and looked and acted the fool so well, that some of the court could not believe that this was the necromancer who was sought after. This conduct he continued when on his trial, until he saw the witnesses and heard the testimony as it progressed against him; when, in an instant, his countenance was lighted up as if by lightning, and his wildness and vehemence of gesture, and the malignant glance with which he eyed the witnesses who appeared against him, all indicated the savage, who indeed had been *caught*, but not *tamed*. His courage, however, soon forsook him. When he received sentence of death, he earnestly implored that a fortnight longer might be allowed him, and then a week longer, which he continued earnestly to solicit until he was taken from the courtroom to his cell; and when he was carried to execution, he gave up his spirit without firmness or composure."

Not so with Denmark Vesey. The plans of years were frustrated; his own life and liberty were thrown away; many others were sacrificed through his leadership; and one more was added to the list of unsuccessful insurrections. All these disastrous certainties he faced calmly, and gave his whole mind composedly to the conducting of his defense. With his arms tightly folded, and his eyes fixed on the floor, he attentively followed every item of the testimony. He heard the witnesses examined by the court, and cross-examined by his own counsel; and it is evident from the narrative of the presiding judge, that he showed no small skill and policy in the searching cross-examination which he then applied. The fears, the feelings, the consciences, of those who had betrayed him, all were in turn appealed to; but the facts were quite overpowering, and it was too late to aid his comrades or himself. Then turning to the court, he skillfully availed himself of the point which had so much impressed the community: the intrinsic improbability that a man in his position of freedom and prosperity should sacrifice every thing to free other people. If they thought it so incredible, why not give him the benefit of the incredibility? The act being, as they stated, one of infatuation, why convict him of it on the bare word of men who, by their own showing, had not only shared the infatuation, but proved traitors to it? An ingenious defense,—indeed, the only one which could by any possibility be suggested, anterior to the days of Choate and somnambulism; but in vain. He was sentenced; and it was not, apparently, till the judge reproached him for the destruction he had brought on his followers, that he showed any sign of emotion. Then the tears came into his eyes. But he said not another word.

The executions took place on five different days; and, bad as they were, they might have been worse. After the imaginary Negro Plot of

New York, in 1741, thirteen Negroes had been judicially burned alive; two had suffered the same sentence at Charleston in 1808; and it was undoubtedly some mark of progress, that in this case the gallows took the place of the flames. Six were hanged on July 2, upon Blake's lands, near Charleston,—Denmark Vesey, Peter Poyas, Jesse, Ned, Rolla, and Batteau, —the last three being slaves of the governor himself. Gullah Jack and John were executed "on the Lines," near Charleston, on July 12; and twenty-two more on July 26. Four others suffered their fate on July 30; and one more, William Garner, effected a temporary escape, was captured, and tried by a different court, and was finally executed August 9.

The self-control of these men did not desert them at their execution. When the six leaders suffered death, the report says, Peter Poyas repeated his charge of secrecy: "Do not open your lips; die silent, as you shall see me do"; and all obeyed. And though afterwards, as the particulars of the plot became better known, there was less inducement to conceal, yet every one of the thirty-five seems to have met his fate bravely, except the conjurer. Gov. Bennett, in his letter, expresses much dissatisfaction at the small amount learned from the participators. "To the last hour of the existence of several who appeared to be conspicuous actors in the drama, they were pressingly importuned to make further confessions,"— this "importuning" being more clearly defined in a letter of Mr. Ferguson, owner of two of the slaves, as "having them severely corrected." Yet so little was obtained, that the governor was compelled to admit at last that the really essential features of the plot were not known to any of the informers.

It is to be remembered, that the plot failed because a man unauthorized and incompetent, William Paul, undertook to make enlistments on his own account. He happened on one of precisely that class of men,— favored house-servants,—whom his leaders had expressly reserved for more skillful manipulations. He being thus detected, one would have supposed that the discovery of many accomplices would at once have followed. The number enlisted was counted by thousands; yet for twenty-nine days after the first treachery, and during twenty days of official examination, only fifteen of the conspirators were ferreted out. Meanwhile the informers' names had to be concealed with the utmost secrecy; they were in peril of their lives from the slaves,—William Paul scarcely dared to go beyond the doorstep,—and the names of important witnesses examined in June were still suppressed in the official report published in October. That a conspiracy on so large a scale should have existed in embryo during four years, and in an active form for several months, and yet have been so well managed, that, after actual betrayal, the authorities were again thrown off their guard, and the plot nearly brought to a head again,—

this certainly shows extraordinary ability in the leaders, and a talent for concerted action on the part of slaves generally, with which they have hardly been credited.

And it is also to be noted, that the range of the conspiracy extended far beyond Charleston. It was proved that Frank, slave of Mr. Ferguson, living nearly forty miles from the city, had boasted of having enlisted four plantations in his immediate neighborhood. It was in evidence that the insurgents "were trying all round the country, from Georgetown and Santee round about to Combahee, to get people"; and, after the trials, it was satisfactorily established that Vesey "had been in the country as far north as South Santee, and southwardly as far as the Euhaws, which is between seventy and eighty miles from the city." Mr. Ferguson himself testified that the good order of any gang was no evidence of their ignorance of the plot, since the behavior of his own initiated slaves had been unexceptionable, in accordance with Vesey's directions.

With such an organization and such materials, there was nothing in the plan which could be pronounced incredible or impracticable. There is no reason why they should not have taken the city. After all the governor's entreaties as to moderate language, the authorities were obliged to admit that South Carolina had been saved from a "horrible catastrophe." "For, although success could not possibly have attended the conspirators, yet, before their suppression, Charleston would probably have been wrapped in flames, many valuable lives would have been sacrificed, and an immense loss of property sustained by the citizens, even though no other distressing occurrences were experienced by them; while the plantations in the lower country would have been disorganized, and the agricultural interests have sustained an enormous loss." The northern journals had already expressed still greater anxieties. "It appears," said the New York *Commercial Advertiser*, "that, but for the timely disclosure, the whole of that State would in a few days have witnessed the horrid spectacle once witnessed in St. Domingo."

My friend, David Lee Child, has kindly communicated to me a few memoranda of a conversation held long since with a free colored man who had worked in Vesey's shop during the time of the insurrection; and these generally confirm the official narratives. "I was a young man then," he said; "and, owing to the policy of preventing communication between free colored people and slaves, I had little opportunity of ascertaining how the slaves felt about it. I know that several of them were abused in the street, and some put in prison, for appearing in sackcloth. There was an ordinance of the city, that any slave who wore a badge of mourning should be imprisoned and flogged. They generally got the law, which is thirty-nine lashes; but sometimes it was according to the decision of the court." "I heard, at the time, of arms being buried in coffins at Sullivan's Island." "In the time of the insurrection, the slaves were tried in a small room in the jail where they were confined. No colored person was allowed to go within two squares of the prison. Those two squares were filled with troops, five thousand of whom were on duty day and night. I was told, Vesey said to those that tried him, that the work of insurrection would go on; but as none but white persons were permitted to be present, I cannot tell whether he said it."

During all this time there was naturally a silence in the Charleston journals, which strongly contrasts with the extreme publicity at last given to the testimony. Even the *National Intelligencer*, at Washington, passed lightly over the affair, and deprecated the publication of particulars. The northern editors, on the other hand, eager for items, were constantly complaining of this reserve, and calling for further intelligence. "The Charleston papers," said the Hartford *Courant* of July 16, "have been silent on the subject of the insurrection; but letters from this city state that it has created much alarm, and that two brigades of troops were under arms for some time to suppress any risings that might have taken place." "You will doubtless hear," wrote a Charleston correspondent of the same paper, just before, "many reports, and some exaggerated ones." "There was certainly a disposition to revolt, and some preparations made, principally by the plantation negroes, to take the city." "We hoped they would progress so far as to enable us to ascertain and punish the ringleaders." "Assure my friends that we feel in perfect security, although the number of nightly guards, and other demonstrations, may induce a belief among strangers to the contrary."

The strangers would have been very blind strangers, if they had not been more influenced by the actions of the Charleston citizens than by their words. The original information was given on May 25, 1822. The time passed, and the plot failed on June 16. A plan for its revival on July 2 proved abortive. Yet a letter from Charleston, in the Hartford *Courant* of August 6, represented the panic as unabated: "Great preparations are making, and all the military are put in preparation to guard against any attempt of the same kind again; but we have no apprehension of its being repeated." On August 10, Gov. Bennett wrote the letter already mentioned, which was printed and distributed as a circular, its object being to deprecate undue alarm. "Every individual in the State is interested, whether in regard to his own property, or the reputation of the State, in giving no more importance to the transaction than it justly merits." Yet, five days after this,—two months after the first danger had passed,—a reinforcement of United States troops arrived at Fort Moultrie; and, during the same month, several different attempts were made by small parties of armed Negroes to capture the mails between Charleston and Savannah, and a reward of two hundred dollars was offered for their detection.

The first official report of the trials was prepared by the intendant, by request of the city council. It passed through four editions in a few months,—the first and fourth being published in Charleston, and the second and third in Boston. Being, however, but a brief pamphlet, it did not satisfy the public curiosity; and in October of the same year (1822), a larger volume appeared at Charleston, edited by the magistrates who presided at the trials,—Lionel H. Kennedy and Thomas Parker. It contains the evidence in full, and a separate narrative of the whole affair, more candid and lucid than any other which I have found in the newspapers or pamphlets of the day. It exhibits that rarest of all qualities in a slave-community, a willingness to look facts in the face. This narrative has been faithfully followed, with the aid of such cross-lights as could be secured from many other quarters, in preparing the present history.

The editor of the first official report racked his brains to discover the special causes of the revolt, and never trusted himself to allude to the general one. The Negroes rebelled because they were deluded by Congressional eloquence; or because they were excited by a church squabble; or because they had been spoilt by mistaken indulgences, such as being allowed to learn to read,—"a misguided benevolence," as he pronounces it. So the Baptist Convention seems to have thought it was because they were not Baptists; and an Episcopal pamphleteer, because they were not Episcopalians. It never seems to occur to any of these spectators, that these people rebelled simply because they were slaves, and wished to be free.

No doubt, there were enough special torches with which a man so skillful as Denmark Vesey could kindle up these dusky powder-magazines; but, after all, the permanent peril lay in the powder. So long as that existed, every thing was incendiary. Any torn scrap in the street might contain a Missouri-Compromise speech; or a report of the last battle in St. Domingo, or one of those able letters of Boyer's which were winning the praise of all, or one of John Randolph's stirring speeches in England against the slave-trade. The very newspapers which reported the happy extinction of the insurrection by the hanging of the last conspirator, William Garner, reported also, with enthusiastic indignation, the massacre of the Greeks at Constantinople and at Scio; and then the northern editors, breaking from their usual reticence, pointed out the inconsistency of southern journals in printing, side by side, denunciations of Mohammedan slave-sales, and advertisements of those of Christians.

Of course the insurrection threw the whole slavery question open to the public. "We are sorry to see," said the *National Intelligencer* of August 31, "that a discussion of the hateful Missouri question is likely to be revived, in consequence of the allusions to its supposed effect in producing the late servile insurrection in South Carolina." A member of the Board of Public Works of South Carolina published in the Baltimore *American Farmer* an essay urging the encouragement of white laborers, and hinting at the ultimate abolition of slavery "if it should ever be thought desirable." More boldly still, a pamphlet appeared in Charleston, under the signature of "Achates," arguing with remarkable sagacity and force against the whole system of slave-labor *in towns;* and proposing that all slaves in Charleston should be sold or transferred to the plantations, and their places supplied by white labor. It is interesting to find many of the facts and arguments of Helper's "Impending Crisis" anticipated in this courageous tract, written under the pressure of a crisis which had just been so narrowly evaded. The author is described in the preface as "a soldier and patriot of the Revolution, whose name, did we feel ourselves at liberty to use it, would stamp a peculiar weight and value on his opinions." It was commonly attributed to Gen. Thomas Pinckney.

Another pamphlet of the period, also published in Charleston, recommended as a practical cure for insurrection the copious administration of Episcopal Church services, and the prohibition of Negroes from attending Fourth of July celebrations. On this last point it is more consistent than most pro-slavery arguments. "The celebration of the Fourth of July belongs *exclusively* to the white population of the United States. The American Revolution was *a family quarrel among equals.* In this the negroes had no concern; their condition remained, and must remain, unchanged. They have no more to do with the celebration of that day than with the landing of the Pilgrims on the rock at Plymouth. It therefore seems to me improper to allow these people to be present on these occasions. In our speeches and orations, much, and sometimes more than is politically necessary, is said about personal liberty, which negro auditors know not how to apply except by running the parallel with their own condition. They therefore imbibe false notions of their own personal rights, and give reality in their minds to what has no real existence. The peculiar state of our community must be steadily kept in view. This, I am gratified to learn, will in some measure be promoted by the institution of the South Carolina Association."

On the other hand, more stringent laws became obviously necessary to keep down the advancing intelligence of the Charleston slaves. Dangerous knowledge must be excluded from without and from within. For the first purpose the South Carolina Legislature passed, in December, 1822, the Act for the imprisonment of northern colored seamen, which afterwards produced so much excitement. For the second object, the Grand Jury, about the same time, presented as a grievance "the number of schools which are kept within the city by persons of color," and proposed their prohibition. This was the encouragement given to the intellectual progress of the slaves; while, as a reward for betraying them, Pensil, the free colored man who advised with Devany, received a present of one thousand dollars; and Devany himself had what was rightly judged to be the higher gift of freedom, and was established in business, with liberal means, as a drayman. He lived long in Charleston, thriving greatly in his vocation, and, according to the newspapers, enjoyed the privilege of being the only man of property in the State whom a special statute exempted from taxation.

More than half a century has passed since the incidents of this true story closed. It has not vanished from the memories of South Carolinians, though the printed pages which once told it have gradually disappeared from sight. The intense avidity which at first grasped at every incident of the great insurrectionary plot was succeeded by a prolonged distaste for the memory of the tale; and the official reports which told what slaves had once planned and dared have now come to be among the rarest of American historical documents. In 1841, a friend of the writer, then visiting South Carolina, heard from her hostess, for the first time, the events which are recounted here. On asking to see the report of the trials, she was cautiously told that the only copy in the house, after being carefully kept for years under lock and key, had been burnt at last, lest it should reach the dangerous eyes of the slaves. The same thing had happened, it was added, in many other families. This partially accounts for the great difficulty now to be found in obtaining a single copy of either publication; and this is why, to the readers of American history, Denmark Vesey and Peter Poyas have commonly been but the shadows of names.

19. AUGUST MEIER, Frederick Douglass' Vision for America: A Case Study in Nineteenth-Century Negro Protest (1967)*

August Meier of Kent State University is one of the most productive scholars in the field of Black History. Author of the widely praised *American Negro Thought, 1890–1914,* Meier in this essay assesses the importance of Frederick Douglass as the race leader of the nineteenth cen-

* From "Frederick Douglass' Vision for America: A Case Study in Nineteenth-Century Negro Protest" by August Meier in *Freedom and Reform, Essays in Honor of Henry Steele Commager,* Edited by Harold M. Hyman and Leonard W. Levy. Copyright © 1967 by Harold M. Hyman and Leonard W. Levy. Reprinted by permission of Harper & Row, Publishers, Inc.

tury. Meier contrasts the strategy employed by Douglass to obtain full racial equality with the later tactics of Booker T. Washington. While consistently working for the goals of integration, equality, and assimilation into American society, Douglass frequently varied his methods and program to meet changing conditions in the United States.

The most distinguished Negro in nineteenth-century America was Frederick Douglass. His fame rest chiefly upon his work as a brilliant antislavery orator and newspaper editor. Yet Douglass was also deeply concerned with developing a program to secure full citizenship rights and acceptance in American society for the free Negroes—both for the minority who were free before the Civil War and for the great masses after emancipation. With his thinking rooted in the principles of American democracy and Christianity—in the Declaration of Independence and the Sermon on the Mount—Douglass' life was a moral crusade for the abolition of slavery and racial distinction, the attainment of civil and political rights and equality before the law, and the assimilation of Negroes into American society. However his specific tactics and programs for racial elevation might vary—and they did undergo significant changes over the years—Douglass was ever the militant agitator, ever the forthright editor and orator, who consistently worked toward these goals through his half-century (1841–1895) of leadership.

Douglass' antislavery career has received detailed treatment at the hands of other scholars,[1] but his ideologies concerning the advancement of free Negroes have not yet been the subject of systematic analysis. This paper, therefore, is limited to a discussion of the programs he advocated for the achievement of full racial equality, and the relationship of these programs to the dominant patterns in nineteenth-century Negro thought.

Today Negro protest is expressed in the form of demands rather than appeals, in terms of power as well as justice, and is identified with a strategy of direct action rather than one of oratory and propaganda. The character of modern Negro protest is founded on the international pressures raised in behalf of American Negroes, the growing support for civil rights in the white population, and the increasing power of the Negro vote, which now acts as a balance of power in national elections. Throughout the nineteenth century, however, Negroes lacked leverage of this sort. They utilized the written and spoken word as their major vehicle of protest, combining denunciation of the undemocratic and un-Christian oppression under which they lived, with pleas directed at awakening the conscience of white Americans in order to secure redress of these grievances and recognition of their constitutional rights. Instances of what we would today call direct action did occur, but they were rare. Where conditions warranted it—as in those states where the ante-bellum

Negroes could vote, and especially during Reconstruction—advocacy of political activity, in itself the central constitutional right which Negroes asked, was a leading theme, supplementing and lending weight to written and oral agitation, to conventions and meetings, to petitions and resolutions.

On the other hand articulate Negroes in that era ordinarily gave nearly equal emphasis to urging Negroes to cultivate good character, to be thrifty and industrious, and to acquire as much property as possible. It was believed that by thus achieving middle-class moral and economic respectability, Negroes would earn the respect of the whites, counteract prejudice, and ease the way toward recognition of their manhood and their citizenship.

Many nineteenth-century advocates of thrift, industry, and economic accumulation placed special emphasis on the value of industrial education or training in mechanical trades. Most prominently associated with the accommodating ideology of Booker T. Washington at the end of the century, industrial education had been seriously advocated by prominent Negroes as early as the 1830s. Many Negro and white abolitionists viewed manual-labor schools, where the students earned their way through the productive work they performed while learning a useful trade, as an instrument for uplifting the lowly of both races and assimilating them into the mainstream of American middle-class society. Such schools, it was believed, would inculcate the values of thrift and industry at the same time that they provided the students with the means of making a living. At mid-century, the economic crisis facing unskilled Negro workers fostered a resurgence of interest in industrial training.

Underlying the moral and economic program was a theme of individual and racial self-help that in turn overlapped with an ideology of racial solidarity—of racial cooperation and racial unity. This ideology of racial solidarity was one that caused considerable division and argument among articulate nineteenth-century Negroes. While a few went so far as to question the advisability of Negro churches and social organizations, the debate raged chiefly over whether or not Negroes should form their own protest organizations, and establish and support their own protest publications, rather than rely solely upon cooperation with sympathetic whites. This division of opinion was due to more than the attitudes and policies of the many white abolitionists who failed to concern themselves with the Negroes' citizenship rights, who objected to employing Negroes in other than menial positions, and who even refused to allow Negroes to participate fully in the decision-making process of the antislavery societies. It was more than an argument over the question of whether or not it was consistent for Negroes to ask for integration and for acceptance into the mainstream of white society, and at the same time segregate themselves into separate organizations. Beyond these matters the debate was rooted in a fundamental ethnic dualism—an identification with both American society on the one hand, and the persecuted Negro group on the other. This dualism arose out of the contradiction in American culture as Negroes experienced it: the contradiction between the American dream of equality for all and the reality of American race prejudice and discrimination.

Racial solidarity and self-help were always most characteristically associated with the advocacy of morality and economic accumulation, and like these doctrines tended to be especially popular in periods of greatest discouragement, particularly during the 1850s and again at the end of the century. During the decade before the Civil War, the passage of the Fugitive Slave Law of 1850, the decline of the antislavery societies, the increasing competition for menial and laboring jobs offered by Irish immigrants, the southern ascendancy in the national government which culminated in the Dred Scott Decision, all made the outlook appear increasingly hopeless. Later, after the overthrow of Reconstruction, the increasing disfranchisement, segregation, and mob violence in the South and, by the 1890s, the growing evidence of prejudice and discrimination in the North, again "forced the Negro back upon himself," as contemporaries expressed it. In the latter period, protest efforts declined sharply, and the advocacy of racial solidarity, self-help, and economic and moral uplift tended to be most often coupled with an ideology of accommodation, especially in the South. This combination of ideas received its most notable expression in the philosophy of Booker T. Washington.

Proposals for racial union, self-help, and solidarity are generally recognized as a variety of Negro "nationalism." It was a form of nationalism which insisted upon the Negro's American citizenship, and viewed the cultivation of race pride and unity as a prerequisite for Negroes organizing themselves for the struggle to obtain equality and integration in American society. Related to this kind of ideology, though eschewing ethnic dualism and the notion that Negroes could ever hope to achieve freedom and equal rights in the United States, was the philosophy of emigration or colonization. Its advocates held that the only solution to the problems facing American Negroes was to emigrate and create a national state of their own, either in the Caribbean area or in Africa. Such proposals, especially popular during the 1850s, cropped up with varying intensity throughout the century. Actually the function of colonization as an ideology is ambiguous. While its advocates protested vigorously against race discrimination in America, they nevertheless favored a form of withdrawal that was in effect an escapist accommodation to the American race system, rather than an assault upon it.

Except for colonization, Douglass enunciated all of these ideologies—agitation, political action, the practice of morality and economy, the acquisition of property, self-help, and racial cooperation. Like other Negroes he shifted his emphasis as the changing situation seemed to warrant. Yet Douglass' views are not simply a reflection of what Negroes generally were saying. Ever the independent thinker, he was willing at times to diverge widely from the patterns of thought ascendant among his friends and contemporaries.[2]

The Ante-Bellum Era

While in the latter part of the century Douglass was a symbol rather than a man of broad influence, during the years prior to the Civil War he was undoubtedly the most powerful leader in the northern Negro community, and his views roughly paralleled the ascendant ideologies among the ante-bellum free people of color.

Because there was an interrelationship between his program for securing the emancipation of the slaves and his proposals for advancing the status of free Negroes, a brief recapitulation of his antislavery career is in order. Born a slave on the Eastern Shore of Maryland, Douglass succeeded in escaping from his Baltimore master in 1838. By 1841 he had entered the ranks of Massachusetts abolitionist orators. His public career during the abolitionist period may be fairly neatly divided into two parts: the 1840s when he followed the moral suasion tactics of the Garrisonians, and the 1850s when he espoused the cause of political abolition. The four years following the establishment of his weekly newspaper, *North Star*, in Rochester, were a period of transition during which, influenced by western abolitionists like Gerrit Smith, he reexamined his views and finally came to support political abolition, openly breaking with Garrison in 1851.[3] From then on, agitation for political rights and stress upon the value of political activity became one of the most important themes in his thinking, and one which he articulated consistently for the rest of his life. Moreover, it was probably from his abolitionist role that Douglass derived a belief in the value of verbal agitation, and a social philosophy which saw the world in essential moral terms, explaining social institutions and social change as based on the good and evil propensities in human nature. To Douglass the solution of America's race problem lay not in any fundamental institutional changes, beyond the destruction of slavery. Rather, the solution lay in a sincere effort to apply the moral principles upon which the Republic was founded. How to activate these moral principles was his major lifelong concern.

In the years from the founding of *North Star* to the election of Lincoln, Douglass' program for the advancement of free Negroes consisted of three principal elements: a major emphasis on protest and citizenship rights, and secondary emphases on self-help, race pride, and racial solidarity on the one hand, and economic development on the other. First and foremost, he regarded Negroes as Americans: "By birth, we are American citizens; by the principles of the Declaration of Independence, we are American citizens; within the meaning of the United States Constitution, we are American citizens; by the facts of history . . . by the hardships and trials endured, by the courage and fidelity displayed by our ancestors in defending the liberties and in achieving the independence of our land, we are American citizens." [4] Only on the rarest of occasions did his alienation and anger lead him to declare that "I have no love for America," that he could feel no patriotism for a country like the United States,[5] or to warn that the oppressed black men might some day rise up and "become the instruments of spreading desolation, devastation, and death throughout our borders." [6]

Douglass constantly condemned the prejudice and discrimination which Negroes met daily: the segregation, the lack of economic opportunity, the exclusion from churches and schools, from juries and armed forces, and above all the disfranchisement. He denounced the "shameful" and "diabolical" Black Laws of Ohio as "the servile work of pandering politicians." He called upon the white people of Ohio to repeal the Black Laws and enfranchise the Negro, thus wiping out "a most foul imputation" upon their character and making Ohio "the paragon of all the free States." [7] In 1860, in the midst of a campaign to abolish the discriminatory franchise qualifications of the New York State Constitution, he declared:

It is a mockery to talk about protection in a government like ours to a class in it denied the elective franchise. The very denial of that right strips them of "protection," and leaves them at the mercy of all that is low, vulgar, cruel, and base in the community. The ballot box and the jury box both stand closed against the man of color. . . . The white people of this country would wade knee-deep in blood before they would be deprived of either of these means of protection against power and oppression.[8]

Not satisfied with mere resolves and declarations, Douglass was constantly in active rebellion against segregation and discrimination in all its forms, and was one of the few men of his time who engaged in what today would be regarded as nonviolent direct action. While residing in Massachusetts in the early 1840s he refused to ride on the Jim Crow railroad car, and was forcibly removed from the white coach.[9] He withdrew his daughter from school rather than permit her to attend segregated schools in Rochester, and agitated for their elimination until he was successful.[10] As his biographer says, "He made it a point to go into hotels, sit down at tables in restaurants, and enter public carriers." [11] A well-known incident was his insistence upon being admitted to the reception President Lincoln held on the eve of his second inauguration, even though the guards tried to keep him out.[12]

Douglass was interested in more than protesting against discrimination and agitating for citizenship rights. Firmly in the American middle-class tradition he also campaigned for "education, that grand lever of improvement," and for moral elevation and economic independence.[13] While "not insensible" to the "withering prejudice" and "malignant and active hate" that placed obstacles in the Negro's pathway to respectability "even in the best parts of the country," he nevertheless believed: "The fact that we are limited and circumscribed ought rather to incite us to a more vigorous and persevering use of the elevating means within our reach, than to dishearten us." What Negroes needed, he went on, was character, and this they could only obtain for themselves through hard toil. "A change in our political condition would do very little for us without this. . . . Industry, sobriety, honesty, combined with intelligence and a due self-respect, find them where you will, among black or white, *must be looked up to.*" With character would come power, in the sense that with it "we may appeal to the sense of justice alive in the public mind, and by an honest, upright life, we may at least wring from a reluctant public the all-important confession that we are men, worthy men, good citizens, good Christians, and ought to be treated as such." [14] True, hostility was directed not at the lower-class Negroes whom whites found acceptable in their subordinate status, but against respectable Negroes; but this, he asserted, was only because color had for so long been associated in the public mind with the degradation of slavery. If Negroes generally acquired middle-class ways, whites would cease to couple undesirable qualities with a black skin.[15]

Along with this emphasis on Negroes helping themselves through moral elevation and the cultivation of good character went a decided interest in economic matters—an interest greatly intensified by the growing competition from immigrants who threatened the Negroes' hold upon even the unskilled and service occupations. Accordingly, Douglass emphatically urged the acquisition of skilled trades to stave off impending disaster. Dramatically he called upon Negroes to "Learn Trades or Starve." In phraseology that was remarkably similar to that which Washington employed a half-century later, Douglass insisted:

We must become valuable to society in other departments of industry than those service ones from which we are rapidly being excluded. We must show that we can *do* as well as *be;* and to this end we must learn trades. When we can build as well as live in houses; when we can *make* as well as *wear* shoes; when we can produce as well as consume *wheat,* corn and rye—then we shall become valuable to society. Society is a hard-hearted affair. With it the helpless may expect no higher dignity than that of paupers. The individual must lay society under obligation to him, or society will harbor him only as a stranger. . . . *How* shall this be done? In this manner: Use every means, strain every nerve to master some important mechanic art.[16]

Neither classical education, nor "holding conventions and passing strong resolutions" could prevent the "degradation of Negroes. . . . The fact is . . . the education of the hand must precede that of the head. We can never have an educated class until we have more men of means amongst us." [17] Negroes could not become merchants or professional men "in a single leap," but only "when we have patiently and laboriously . . . passed though the intermediate gradations of agriculture and mechanic arts." [18] Backed by an offer of financial assistance (later withdrawn) from Harriet Beecher Stowe, Douglass presented a proposal for a manual-labor school to the National Convention of Negro leaders which met at Rochester in 1853. The conferees, convinced that a strong emphasis on racial solidarity and economic accumulation was essential to the securing of citizenship rights, enthusiastically endorsed Douglass' plan.[19]

The hopes of the Rochester Convention proved illusory. Nevertheless, it is significant that over a generation before industrial education became a major plank in Booker T. Washington's platform of accommodation, arguments almost identical to those later employed by the Tuskegeean had been utilized by the noted protest leader, Frederick Douglass, to justify emphasis on training for the trades over education for the learned professions.

For Douglass, of course, the advocacy of character development and economic accumulation was no substitute for agitation for citizenship rights. When Horace Greeley in 1855 urged Negroes to stop agitating for the vote and instead direct their energies toward achieving the economic standing necessary for them to meet the discriminatory franchise qualifications of New York State, Douglass replied:

Why should we be told to break up our Conventions, cease "jawing" and "clamoring," when others equally *"indolent, improvident, servile and licentious"* (all of which adjectives we reject as untruthful . . .) are suffered to indulge . . . in similar demonstrations? In a word, why should we be sent to hoeing, and planting corn, to digging potatoes, and raising cabbages, as the *"preferable and more effective"* method of abrogating the unjust, anti-Republican and disgraceful race restrictions imposed upon us, in the property qualification?[20]

Thus, for Douglass the acquisition of morality and property was a supplemental instrument in the struggle for equal rights. Character and wealth certainly did not take precedence over protest and agitation, or an appeal to the conscience of white America, based upon its democratic and egalitarian values.

Deteriorating conditions also led Douglass to place considerable emphasis on self-help and racial solidarity. *North Star* in fact was founded in a period when the advocacy both of these ideas and of colonization was on the rise. In fact, in the very first issue Douglass urged his "oppressed countrymen" to "remember that we are one, that our cause is one, and that we must help each other, if we would succeed. . . . We are indissolubly united, and must fall or flourish together." [21] He criticized Negroes for depending too much on whites to better their condition. True, he counselled Negroes to "Never refuse to act with a white society or institution because it is white, or a black one, because it is black. But act with all men without distinction of color. . . . We say avail yourselves of *white* institutions, not because they are white, but because they afford a more convenient means of improvement." [22] Nevertheless, he maintained that "the main work must be commenced, carried on, and concluded by ourselves. . . . Our destiny, for good or evil . . . is, by an all-wise God, committed to us. . . . It is evident that we can be improved and elevated only just so fast and far as we shall improve and elevate ourselves." [23]

Douglass perceived that race prejudice produced among Negroes what in today's terms would be called an awareness of a separate identity. He held that while all men were brothers, and were "naturally and self-evidently entitled to all the rights, privileges and immunities common to every member of that family," nevertheless "the force of potent circumstance" made it proper for him to address Negroes as "our own people." [24] Indeed, he referred to Negroes as an oppressed "nation within a nation," slave and free alike united in a "destiny [that] seems one and the same." [25] He proposed a "Union of the Oppressed for the Sake of Freedom," to organize Negroes in order to obtain their rights and elevate themselves through collective effort.[26] His propaganda bore fruit when the Rochester Convention of 1853, which marked the high tide of enthusiasm for racial solidarity among the ante-bellum Negro conventions, organized an abortive Protective Union to coordinate race interests and efforts.

Douglass defended his plans for racial union against charges that such a segregated organization would create a "complexional issue." It was not the colored men but whites who, by their policy of discrimination, had created a "complexional issue." As he put it in 1855, in roundly criticizing that class of abolitionists who kept Negroes subservient to whites in the movement: "Every day brings with it renewed evidence of the truthfulness of the sentiment, now. . . . gaining the confidence and sympathy of our oppressed People, THAT OUR ELEVATION AS A RACE, IS ALMOST WHOLLY DEPENDENT UPON OUR OWN EXERTIONS. . . . The history of other oppressed nations will confirm us in this assertion . . . the oppressed nation itself, has always taken a prominent part in the conflict." [27]

Douglass, with his feeling that prejudice and discrimination made Negroes a "nation within a nation," resembled many other articulate Negroes of this period in exhibiting strong ethnocentric tendencies. Yet he never went as far as did a number of others who completely rejected American society and advocated colonization. It is not unlikely that a majority of Negro leaders at one time or another in the 1850s espoused emigration,[28] but Douglass consistently affirmed that

Nothing seems more evident to us, than that our destiny is sealed up with that of the white people of this country, and we believe that we must fall or flourish with them. We must banish all thought of emigration from our minds, and resolve to stay just where we are . . . among white people, and avail ourselves of the civilization of America.[29]

Born in America, Negroes had fought and bled for the country: "We are here; . . . this is *our* country; . . . The white man's happiness cannot be purchased by the black man's misery. . . ." [30] Even during the fifties, when colonization sentiments were making strong inroads into the thinking of articulate Negroes, he opposed them. Writing to Henry Highland Garnet, the eminent Presbyterian minister and abolitionist who had become an emigrationist, Douglass maintained that the emigrationists actually weakened the efforts to elevate Negroes in this country, since they channeled their energies, which might have helped Negroes in the United States, into visionary colonization schemes.[31]

Yet the pressure for expatriation was exceedingly strong. As the fifties drew to a close, conditions seemed to grow worse. Lincoln's policy after his inauguration appeared to Douglass to be one of appeasing the slaveholders, and he was bitterly disappointed.[32] Discouraged, he finally lent an open ear and eye toward emigration, and agreed to undertake a trip to Haiti; not with the intention of settling there himself, but to obtain information that might be useful to those who, alarmed at the persecution and hardships that were becoming "more and more rigorous and grievous with every year," were "looking out into the world for a place of retreat," and were "already resolved to look for homes beyond the boundaries of the United States." [33]

Even before this editorial appeared in print the attack on Fort Sumter occurred. To Douglass this was a welcome event and one which completely changed his plans. To him the war presaged both the emancipation of the slaves and the attainment of racial equality. As he said in a speech in Philadelphia in 1863, "The Mission of the War" was twofold: "the utter extirpation of slavery from every facet of American soil, and the complete enfranchisement of the entire colored people of this country." [34]

Reconstruction and After

Douglass' wartime efforts to secure the emancipation of the slaves, and the admission of Negro soldiers to the Union armies, have been amply described by other scholars. [35] Both of these activities were, in his view, but a prelude to the larger task of securing full citizenship rights and ending all forms of race discrimination. Speaking at the thirtieth anniversary meeting of the American Anti-Slavery Society in December, 1863, Douglass warned that the struggle was not over; "that our work will not be done until the colored man is admitted a full member in good and regular standing in the American body politic." [36] Merely to abolish slavery was no solution to the race problem. Rather, "the question is: Can the white and colored peoples of this country be blended into a common nationality . . . and enjoy together in the same country, under the same flag, the inestimable blessings of life, liberty, and the pursuit of happiness, as neighborly citizens of a common country." [37]

Over the course of the next two decades, during Reconstruction and the years immediately following, Douglass' philosophy retained the broad scope of the pre-Civil War decade, but with some differences in emphasis. Basically, Douglass demanded the immediate and complete integration of Negroes into American society. He held to a vision of the United States as a "composite nation," in which all races of men participated without discrimination. "In whatever else other nations may have been great and grand," Douglass explained, "our greatness and grandeur will be found in the faithful application of the principle of perfect civil equality to the people of all races and creeds." [38] Addressing the Massachusetts Anti-Slavery Society in the spring of 1865, he called for the " 'immediate, unconditional and universal' enfranchisement of the black man." He pointed out that Negroes wanted the suffrage

because it is our right, first of all. No class of men can, without insulting their own nature, be content with any deprivation of their rights. . . . Again, I want the elective franchise . . . because ours is a peculiar government, based upon a peculiar idea, and that idea is universal suffrage. If I were in a monarchical government, or an aristocratic government, where the few ruled and the many were subject, there would be no special stigma resting upon me because I did not exercise the elective franchise. . . . But here, where universal suffrage

. . . is the fundamental idea of the Government, to rule us out is to make us an exception, to brand us with the stigma of inferiority, and to invite to our heads the missiles of those about us.

Later, when men hitherto friendly toward the Negroes became critical of their stress on political rights, alleging that their interest in politics was "far more lively than is consistent" with their welfare, he conceded that no intelligent person could want to see the Negroes "look to politics as their proper vocation, or to government as their only means of advancement." But he also insisted that "scarcely less deplorable would be the condition of this people, if among them there should be found no disposition . . . for political activity. That man who would advise the black man to make no effort to distinguish himself in politics will advise him to omit one of the most important levers that can be employed to elevate his race." [39]

Meanwhile, Douglass placed greater emphasis on the gospel of wealth and racial cooperation than did most of his articulate contemporaries, though these ideas were less prominent in his ideology than formerly. As president of the national conventions held by Negro leaders at Syracuse in 1864 and at Louisville in 1883 (Douglass presiding over both of them), he replied to critics of the idea of holding a race convention by calling attention to the prejudice and discrimination which Negroes still encountered, in spite of the Emancipation Proclamation and in spite of the legislation and constitutional amendments enacted during Reconstruction.[40] When he and others established a newspaper known as *The New Era* in 1870, he appealed for Negro support for a race journal on the basis of self-help and racial solidarity: "Our friends," he declared, "can do much for us, but there are some things which colored men can and must do for themselves." Later he grew irate when Negroes failed to support the publication, and he criticized them because were "not conscious of any associated existence or a common cause." [41]

On economic matters his thought remained unchanged. In 1864 he advised the freedmen "to shape their course toward frugality, the accumulation of property, and above all, to leave untried no amount of effort and self-denial to acquire knowledge, and to secure a vigorous moral and religious growth." Sixteen years later, in a rhetoric typical of the age, and in words that Booker T. Washington would have fully approved, he was still uttering the standard pieties of middle-class Americans:

Neither we, nor any other people, will ever be respected till we respect ourselves, and we will never respect ourselves till we have the means to live respectably. . . . A race which cannot save its earnings, which spends all it makes . . . can never rise in the scale of civilization. . . .

. . . This part of our destiny is in our own hands. . . . If the time shall ever come when we shall possess in the colored people of the United States, a class of men noted for enterprise, industry, economy and success, we shall no longer have any trouble in the matter of civil and political rights. The battle against popular prejudice will have been fought and won. . . . The laws which determine the destinies of individuals and nations are impartial and eternal. We shall reap as we shall sow. There is no escape. The conditions of success are universal and unchangeable. The nation or people which shall comply with them will rise, and those which violate them will fall.[42]

Douglass' basically middle-class orientation toward the solution of the problems facing American Negroes is revealed in the way in which he expressed his very genuine concern with the problems of the Negro working classes. Basically he believed that the ordinary person, of whatever race, should strive to become an entrepreneur. He admitted that "the disproportionate distribution of wealth certainly is one of the evils which puzzle the greatest national economists," but thought that attacking capital was to attack a "symptom" rather than a cause. "Real pauperism," he continued, existed only in those states "where liberty and equality have been mere mockeries until lately." Workers had the right to strike, but Douglass thought it "tyranny" when they tried to prevent others from working in their places.[43] Douglass' attitudes were perceptibly reinforced by a personal experience—the exclusion of his son from the typographical society of Washington.[44] Yet on occasion he could express a vague consciousness of the identity of interest between white and black workers, as when he argued in 1883 that the white labor unions should not isolate themselves and "throw away this colored element of strength." Labor everywhere, regardless of race, wanted the same thing: "an honest day's pay for an honest day's work." Unity among black and white workers was desirable, he concluded, because "Experience demonstrates that there may be a slavery of wages only a little less galling and crushing in its effects than chattel slavery, and this slavery of wages must go down with the other." [45]

After the failure of Radical Reconstruction and the restoration of white supremacy in the South, Douglass' philosophy did not change; if anything, he became more vigorous in his denunciations of caste and oppression and proscription. Writing in the *North American Review* in 1881, he denounced the growing repression in the South in scathing terms:

Of all the varieties of men who have suffered from this feeling [of race prejudice] the colored people of this country have endured most. . . . The workshop denies him work, and the inn denies him shelter; the ballot-box a fair vote, and the jury-box a fair trial. He has ceased to be the slave of an individual, but has in some sense become the slave of society. . . .

Ridiculing the inconsistencies of the color line, he pointed out that the Chinese were hated because they were industrious, the Negroes because they were thought to be lazy. Southerners thought the Negro so deficient in "intellect and . . . manhood, that he is but the echo of the designing white man," and yet so strong and clearheaded "that he cannot be persuaded by arguments or intimidated by threats, and that nothing but the shotgun can restrain him from voting. . . . They shrink back in horror from contact with the Negro as a man and a gentleman, but like him very well as a barber, waiter, coachman or cook." Two years later, when the Supreme Court declared the Civil Rights Act of 1875 unconstitutional, Douglass, speaking at an indignation meeting in Washington, called the decision a "shocking" sign of "moral weakness in high places," a "calamity" resulting from the "autocratic" powers of the court that embarrassed the country before the world. If the Civil Rights Act was "a bill for social equality, so is the Declaration of Independence, which declares that all men have equal rights; so is the Sermon on the Mount, so is the Golden Rule . . . ; so is the Apostolic teaching that of one blood, God has made all nations . . . ; so is the Constitution. . . ." Douglass became so bitter that in 1884 he suggested that Negroes might resort to retaliatory violence. Unfortunately the "safety valves" provided by American institutions for the peaceful expression and redress of grievances—free speech, a free press, the right of assembly, and the ballot box—did not exist in the South. Only such institutions made violence and insurrection, daggers and dynamite, unnecessary for an oppressed people; and he warned the South that ideas were contagious, and that the black man was aware of the example set by revolutionists in European countries. Such statements were extremely rare in Douglass' speeches; that he made them at this juncture reveals the depth of his disillusionment and anger as he observed the worsening situation of southern Negroes.[46]

Meanwhile, Douglass had developed misgivings about the compromising course of the Republican party in regard to protecting the rights of southern Negroes, even though Presidents Hayes, Garfield, Arthur, and Harrison appointed him to political office.[47] Sharply criticized for his supposed support of the Compromise of 1877, Douglass, at the Louisville Convention in 1883, felt it necessary to defend himself from charges of indifference to the Compromise. He described himself as "an uneasy Republican," who had opposed Hayes' policy. He was quoted as saying that "Parties are made for men and not men for parties. . . . Follow no party blindly. If the Republican Party cannot stand a demand for justice and fairplay it ought to go down. . . ." Six years later, in a widely circulated address delivered before the Bethel Literary and Historical Society of Washington, the most celebrated forum in the American Negro community, Douglass defended the favorable comments he had made about Cleveland in 1885, and argued that even though the Republican party had recently returned to power in Washington, "past experience makes us doubtful" that anything would be done for Negro rights. To Douglass the question was purely a moral one: the Republican defeat in the Congressional elections of 1890, like Blaine's defeat in 1884, was due to the fact that the party had deserted the Negro's cause. "The success of the Republican Party," he averred, "does not depend mainly upon its economic theories. . . . Its appeal is to the conscience of the Nation, and its success is to be sought and found in firm adhesion to the humane and progressive ideas of liberty and humanity which called it into being." [48]

Douglass had traveled a long road indeed from 1872 when he had uttered his famous phrase, "The Republican Party is the deck, all else is the sea." [49] Yet he never deserted the party, and during the eighties campaigned vigorously on its behalf. "I am sometimes reproached," he once wrote, "[for] being too much addicted to the Republican Party. I am not ashamed of that reproach." Negroes, he continued, owed a great deal to the party, and to desert it would be to ignore both this debt and the atrocities suffered at the hands of southern Democrats.[50] Indeed, in the final analysis the situation in the South, where the Democrats dominated, demanded loyalty to the Republicans,[51] and at election time he expressed nothing but contempt for those Negroes who were Democrats—men whose talks were "rank with treason to the highest and best interest of the Negro race." [52] Yet continued loyalty was not rewarded, and by 1892 Douglass confessed that he was only lukewarm in his support of the party.[53]

The Final Decade

It is a noteworthy fact that during the 1880s and 1890s, as conditions grew worse, as Negro thought veered from emphasis on political activity and immediate attainment of equal rights to doctrines of self-help, racial solidarity, and economic advancement, Douglass' thought moved in an opposite direction to a position more consistently assimilationist than at any time since the founding of *North Star* in 1847. More than ever he stressed assimilation and amalgamation as the solution to the race problem, and he constantly asserted that it was not a Negro problem, to be solved largely by the Negro's efforts to acquire morality and wealth, but the problem of the nation and the whites who had created the situation. It should be stressed that these ideas were not new in Douglass' philosophy; what is notable is the shift in emphasis, for in the last years of his life he discarded almost completely the idea of self-help, ignored the theme of race solidarity, declaimed against race pride, and said little of the gospel of wealth.

One may surmise that this shift came about as a result of one or both of two factors. Undoubtedly he was deeply concerned about the rising ascendancy of an accommodating ideology which accepted white stereotypes of Negroes as ignorant, immoral, lazy, and thriftless; blamed Negroes themselves for this state of affairs and for the white prejudice they suffered; placed the principal burden of Negro advancement upon Negroes themselves; accepted segregation; depreciated agitation and politics; and stressed self-help, character-building, the frugal virtues, and the acquisition of wealth as a program for achieving the respect of the white man and thus ultimately, it was implied, "earning" the "privilege" of enjoying citizenship rights. Accordingly Douglass may well have decided to cease stressing those aspects of his philosophy which had been appropriated by the accommodators.

More likely his ideological change was due largely to the influence of his second wife, a white woman, Helen Pitts, whom he married in January 1884. Douglass had earlier expressed the view that race intermixture would increase,[54] and the year preceding his second marriage he had declared: "There is but one destiny, it seems to me, left for us, and that is to make ourselves and be made by others a part of the American people in every sense of the word. Assimilation and not isolation is our true policy and our national destiny." [55] The marriage caused quite an uproar among many Negroes, who accused Douglass of lacking race pride. As he wrote to his friend and supporter, George L. Ruffin: "What business has any man to trouble himself about the color of another man's wife? Does it not appear violently impertinent—this intermeddling? Every man ought to try to be content with the form and color of his own wife and stop at that." [56] Two years later he explicitly predicted that amalgamation of the races would be the "inevitable" solution of the race problem.[57]

In a widely reprinted address, originally delivered before the Bethel Literary Association in 1889, Douglass summarized the views he held during the last decade of his life. In the first place, he said, the problem was not one for Negroes to solve themselves: "It is not what we shall do but what the nation shall do and be, that is to settle this great national problem." Admittedly Negroes could in part combat discrimination "by lives and acquirements which counteract and put to shame this narrow and malignant" prejudice. Indeed, "we have errors of our own to abandon, habits to reform, manners to improve, ignorance to dispel, and character to build up."

Douglass then went on to specify, even though he ran "the risk of

incurring displeasure," other errors committed by Negroes which contemporaries usually listed as virtues—race pride, race solidarity, and
economic nationalism (or the advocacy of Negro support of Negro business). First among them was the "greater prominence of late" being
given to the "stimulation of a sentiment we are pleased to call race pride,"
to which Negroes were "inclining most persistently and mischievously.
. . . I find it in all our books, papers and speeches." Douglass could see
nothing to be either proud or ashamed of in a "gift from the Almighty,"
and perceived "no benefit to be derived from this everlasting exhortation
to the cultivation of race pride. On the contrary, I see in it a positive evil.
It is building on a false foundation. Besides, what is the thing we are
fighting against . . . but race pride . . . ? Let us away with this supercilious nonsense."

A second error was the doctrine "that union among ourselves is an
essential element of success in our relations with the white race." Douglass
held that "our union is our weakness," that the trouble was that when
assembled together "in numerous numbers" rather than scattered among
whites, "we are apt to form communities by ourselves." This, in turn,
"brings us into separate schools, separate churches, separate benevolent
and literary societies, and the result is the adoption of a scale of manners,
morals and customs peculiar to our condition . . . as an oppressed people."
Moreover, "a nation within a nation is an anomaly. There can be but one
American nation . . . and we are Americans." Negroes should yield as
little as humanly possible to the circumstances that compelled them to
maintain separate neighborhoods and institutions. "We cannot afford to
draw the line in politics, trade, education, manner, religion, or civilization."
Douglass then went on to ridicule as "another popular error flaunted in our
faces at every turn, and for the most part by very weak and impossible
editors, the alleged duty of the colored man to patronize colored newspapers . . . because they happen to be edited and published by colored
men." Though he continued to believe that an "able" Negro paper was
"a powerful lever for the elevation and advancement of the race," colored
journals like colored artisans should be supported only on the basis of the
"character of the man and the quality of his work." [58]

In short, during his last years, Douglass was the protest and assimilationist leader epitomized.

Yet interestingly enough he was on friendly terms with Booker T.
Washington. In 1892 he gave the Commencement Address at Tuskegee
Institute, and two years later obtained a substantial gift for the school
from an English friend.[59] At the same time he proudly recalled his
earlier advocacy of industrial education.[60]

There is no reason to believe that Douglass would have favored

Washington's ascendancy as a race leader, which began a few months after Douglass' death with Washington's famous address at the Atlanta Exposition in September 1895. It is true that during the 1850s, and even for some years after the Civil War, Douglass had frequently expressed himself in terms that were remarkably similar to those that Washington enunciated at the end of the century. Like Washington, and using the same arguments and clichés, Douglass had stressed the middle-class virtues and middle-class respectability; the importance of trades and industrial education; the necessity for self-help and racial solidarity. But unlike Washington, Douglass was always clear and explicit about his desire for full equality. In fact he always subordinated these aspects of his philosophy to his advocacy of agitation and political activity. He never employed the flattering and conciliatory phraseology of the Tuskegeean; he never put the principal blame on Negro shoulders, nor did he make Negro self-improvement a panacea for the solution of the race problem. Finally, unlike Washington, he never permitted his ends to be obscured by his emphasis on the means.

We have pointed out that as the constellation of ideas which Washington epitomized was achieving ascendancy in Negro thought during the years after Reconstruction, Douglass' writings and speeches moved in an opposite direction. Integration, assimilation, protest against segregation and all other forms of oppression, and spirited advocacy of political rights and political activity were the hallmarks of his creed. Washington's ascendancy symbolized Negro acquiescence in segregation and disfranchisement and a soft-pedaling of political activity. And if there was one thing which Douglass had emphasized consistently, from mid-century on, it was the importance of political rights and political activity as essential for protecting Negroes and advancing their status in American society.

To raise Negroes to the highest status in American society, to secure their inclusion in the "body politic," to make them integrally a part of the American community, had been Douglass' aim, his vision, his dream. In constructing his program he naturally stressed and utilized the basic values and ideologies of American culture. If whites treasured political and civil rights, Negroes as a minority group treasured them even more. If white Americans valued self-help, independence, virtuous character, and the accumulation of property, these things would also be of inestimable aid to Negroes in their struggle for advancement. If white Americans were proud of their nationality and what they had achieved by the collective effort of the nation, Negroes also needed to be proud of themselves and cooperate with each other in order to advance and progress. Douglass, like his friends and associates, thus fashioned the basic ideologies of

American civilization into a program for the elevation of a minority group that would secure its acceptance into the larger society. Beyond all else Douglass was the moralist, constantly appealing to the democratic and Christian values of brotherhood, equality and justice—values which Americans cherished but which, for Negroes, remained unfulfilled. As Douglass put it in 1889: "The real question is whether American justice, American liberty, American civilization, American law and American Christianity can be made to include and protect alike and forever all American citizens. . . . It is whether this great nation shall conquer its prejudices, rise to the dignity of its professions and proceed in the sublime course of truth and liberty [which Providence] has marked out for it." [61]

NOTES

1. See the two biographies, Philip S. Foner, *Frederick Douglass: A Biography* (New York: Citadel Press, 1964), and especially Benjamin Quarles, *Frederick Douglass* (Washington: Associated Publishers, 1948).

2. On Negro thought in the nineteenth century see especially Carter G. Woodson, ed., *The Mind of the Negro as Reflected in Letters Written During the Crisis, 1800–1860* (Washington: Association for the Study of Negro Life and History, 1926); Howard H. Bell, "A Survey of the Negro Convention Movement, 1830–1861" (Unpublished doctoral dissertation, Northwestern University, 1953); August Meier, *Negro Thought in America, 1880–1915* (Ann Arbor: University of Michigan Press, 1963), chs. 1 to 7.

3. Quarles, *Frederick Douglass*, chs. 1–5, 7–9; Foner, *Frederick Douglass*, Parts I and II; Quarles, "Abolition's Different Drummer: Frederick Douglass," in Martin Duberman, ed., *The Antislavery Vanguard: New Essays on the Abolitionists* (Princeton: Princeton University Press, 1965), pp. 123–34.

4. Douglass, "The Claims of Our Common Cause," Address to the 1853 Colored National Convention, in *Proceedings of the Colored National Convention . . . 1853* (Rochester, 1853), p. 19.

5. Douglass, "The Right to Criticize American Institutions," Speech before the American Anti-Slavery Society, May 11, 1847, reprinted in Foner, ed., *The Life and Writings of Frederick Douglass*, 4 vols. (New York: International Publishers, 1950–55), I, p. 236.

6. *North Star*, Nov. 9, 1849.

7. Douglass to Sidney Howard Gay, Sept. 17, 1847, in Foner, *Life and Writings*, I, p. 265.

8. *Douglass' Monthly*, October, 1860.

9. Douglass, *Life and Times of Frederick Douglass* (Hartford, 1882), pp. 250–51.

10. Ibid., pp. 298–99; Quarles, *Frederick Douglass*, p. 108.

11. Quarles, *Frederick Douglass*, pp. 101–2.

12. Ibid., p. 219; Foner, *Frederick Douglass*, pp. 231–32; Douglass, *Life and Times*, pp. 402–4.

13. *North Star*, January 19, 1849.

14. Ibid., July 14, 1848.

15. Ibid., June 13, 1850.

16. *Frederick Douglass' Paper*, March 4, 1853. See also Douglass and others, Address to the Colored People of the United States of the Colored National Convention of 1848, *North Star*, September 29, 1848; and *Proceedings of the National Convention of Colored People . . . 1847* (Troy, N.Y., 1847), pp. 37–38.

17. *Frederick Douglass' Paper*, March 11, 1853.

18. Douglass to Harriet Beecher Stowe, March 8, 1853, in *Proceedings of the Colored National Convention, 1853*, pp. 33–38.

19. Ibid., pp. 22–40. On the 1853–55 movement for industrial educational generally, see Bell, "Survey of the Negro Convention Movement," pp. 171–75.

20. *Frederick Douglass' Paper*, October 5, 1855.

21. *North Star*, December 3, 1847.

22. Address to the Colored People of the United States, 1848 national convention, in *North Star*, September 29, 1848.

23. Ibid., July 14, 1848.

24. Ibid., January 19, 1849.

25. Douglass, "The Present Condition and Future Prospects of the Negro People," Speech at annual meeting of the American and Foreign Anti-Slavery Society, New York, May, 1853, reprinted in Foner, *Life and Writings*, II, pp. 243, 246.

26. *North Star*, August 10 and October 29, 1849.

27. Ibid., December 14, 1849; *Frederick Douglass' Paper*, April 13, 1855.

28. Bell, "Survey of the Negro Convention Movement," passim.

29. *North Star*, January 19, 1848.

30. Ibid., November 16, 1849.

31. *Douglass' Monthly*, February, 1859.

32. Ibid., April, 1861.

33. Ibid., May, 1861.

34. Douglass, "The Mission of the War," 1863, MS, Frederick Douglass Papers at the Frederick Douglass Home, Washington, D.C.; available on microfilm at the Schomburg Collection, New York Public Library, Reel 13.

35. Quarles, *Frederick Douglass*, chs. 11 and 12; Foner, *Frederick Douglass*, Part III; James M. McPherson, *The Negro's Civil War* (New York: Pantheon Books, 1965), pp. 17–18, 37–40, 161–63.

36. Douglass, "Our Work is Not Done," Speech delivered at the Annual Meeting the American Anti-Slavery Society, Philadelphia, December 3–4, 1863, reprinted in Foner, *Life and Writings*, III, p. 381. See also Quarles, *Frederick Douglass*, pp. 214–15; Douglass, *Life and Times*, p. 418.

37. *Douglass' Monthly*, June, 1863.

38. Douglass, "A Composite Nation," Lecture, 1867, MS, Douglass Papers, Microfilm Reel 13.

39. Douglass, "What the Black Man Wants," in William D. Kelley, Wendell Phillips, and Frederick Douglass, *The Equality of All Men Before the Law* (Boston, 1865), pp. 36–37; *New National Era*, August 24, 1871.

40. *Proceedings of the National Convention of Colored Men . . . 1864* (Boston, 1864), pp. 13–14; Douglass, "Address to the People of the United States," Delivered at National Convention of Colored Men, Louisville, 1883, in *Three Addresses on the Relations Subsisting Between the White and Colored People of the United States* (Washington, 1886), pp. 4–6.

41. *The New Era*, January 27, 1870; Douglass to Gerrit Smith, September 26, 1873, cited in Quarles, *Frederick Douglass*, p. 110.

42. *Proceedings of the National Convention of Colored Men, 1864,* p. 5; Appendix to Douglass, *Life and Times,* pp. 561–62.

43. *New National Era,* April 20, 1871.

44. Ibid., February 2, 1871.

45. Douglass, "Address to the People of the United States," Louisville Convention, 1883, in *Three Addresses,* pp. 12–13.

46. Douglass, "The Color Line," *North American Review* 132 (June, 1881): 568–75; *Proceedings of the Civil Rights Mass-Meeting . . . Washington, October 22, 1883* (Washington, 1883), pp. 5, 7, 8, 14; Douglass, "Address on American Civilization" (1884), MS, Douglass Papers, Microfilm Reel 13.

47. Hayes made Douglass Marshal of the District of Columbia; Garfield and Arthur appointed him Recorder of the Deeds of the District of Columbia; and Harrison made him minister to Haiti.

48. Alexandria, Va. *People's Advocate,* October 6, 1883; New York *Globe,* Sept. 29, 1883; Douglass, "The Future of the Race," *African Methodist Episcopal Church Review,* 6 (October 1889): 232–33; Douglass, *Life and Times* (Hartford, 1891 ed.), pp. 559; Douglass, "The Cause of Republican Defeat" (1890), MS, Douglass Papers, Microfilm Reel 12.

49. Quarles, *Frederick Douglass,* p. 260.

50. Douglass to C. N. Bliss, October 5, 1887, MS, Douglass Papers, Microfilm Reel 1.

51. Cleveland *Gazette,* October 30, 1886.

52. Douglass to D. A. Straker, August 2, 1888, MS, Douglass Papers, Microfilm Reel 1.

53. Quarles, *Frederick Douglass,* p. 354.

54. For example, *New National Era,* September 27, 1870.

55. Douglass, *Address . . . on the Twenty-First Anniversary of Emancipation in the District of Columbia* (Washington, 1883), p. 16.

56. Francis J. Grimké, "The Second Marriage of Frederick Douglass," *Journal of Negro History* 19 (July 1934): 324–29; Douglass to George L. Ruffin, January 28 [1884], photostatic copy, Ruffin Papers, Howard University Library. Ruffin, a Massachusetts lawyer, was the first Negro appointed to a judgeship in the North.

57. Douglass, "The Future of the Colored Race," *North American Review* 142 (May 1886): 438–39.

58. Douglass, "The Future of the Race," pp. 225–36.

59. Samuel R. Spencer, Jr., *Booker T. Washington and the Negro's Place in American Life* (Boston: Little, Brown & Co., 1955), p. 108; Washington to Douglass, April 2, 1894, MS, Douglass Papers, Microfilm Reel 7.

60. Douglass, "Oration" delivered at Manassas Industrial School, Virginia, September 3, 1894, MS, Douglass Papers, Microfilm Reel 13.

61. Douglass, "The Future of the Race," pp. 225–26.

20. WILLIAM M. BREWER, Henry Highland Garnet (1928)*

Henry Highland Garnet was one of the most important as well as the most neglected black protestor of the nineteenth century. William M. Brewer, who has been associated with the *Journal of Negro History* since 1923 and its editor since 1951, provides one of the few descriptions of the activities and ideology of this talented Afro-American. In this essay, Brewer denotes the differences as well as the more important similarities between Douglass and Garnet.

Henry Highland Garnet represents a type of Negro leadership during the antislavery and Reconstruction periods that has not received due consideration. Volumes have been written on these stormy days, but little attention has been given to the role of Garnet who deserves front rank as the radical forerunner of Frederick Douglass, the advocate of moral suasion rather than resistance. Beginning in the late thirties, Garnet truly blazed the way for the Negro abolitionists and kept the flame of freedom burning while the nation was absorbed with the problems of expansion and the contest over the extension of slavery in the Trans-Mississippi territories. On the platform and through the press Garnet's message was delivered in the defense of his oppressed fellow sufferers in bondage. With them he was able fully to sympathize in that he had escaped from that estate and knew the bitterness of slave life. Such experiences burned into his soul an ambition and determination to lead the way in protest and action for the liberation of his people. Like one crying in the wilderness, Garnet pointed out a way which was modified and finally adopted.

For the peculiar task of leading the slaves to freedom Garnet was especially fitted. There was something about his personality which few leaders possess—the commanding presence which inspires courage and the will to fight through difficulties. In his personality were reflected the fire and genius of African chieftains who had defied [1] the slave catchers and later had rankled in southern bondage. No disappointment could crush such a spirit as that which Garnet manifested in behalf of his people. His personality and his method of attack heartened alike the escaped fugitive and the abolitionist leader. In 1843 when weaker minds vacillated and quailed at the suggestion of using physical force to promote

* From William M. Brewer, "Henry Highland Garnet," *Journal of Negro History* 13 (January 1928): 36–52. Copyright © by The Association for the Study of Negro Life and History, Inc. Published in said *Journal of Negro History* (January 1928). Reprinted by permission.

liberation, and Negro leaders branded his advice to the slaves as dangerous and incendiary, Garnet insisted that this was the only remedy.

Henry Highland Garnet was born December 23, 1815, at New Market, Kent County, Maryland.[2] He was the descendant of a kidnapped African chief from the Mandingo tribe.[3] In a tribal fight his grandfather had been captured and sold to the slave traders who brought him to America where he was resold in Virginia.[4] Landing on the James River, this ancestor of Garnet was transferred to Colonel William Spencer in Maryland.[5] The fact that he survived the horrors of the Middle Passage is evidence of the physical strength and endurance which were the inheritance of Henry Highland Garnet. The desire for liberty surged, therefore, in the blood which young Garnet inherited from his royal grandfather who, because of his moral and religious power [6] and his absolute integrity of character, had been made a trusty on the plantation at New Market, Maryland. There is serious doubt whether such blood could be successfully enslaved. Its superior quality would inevitably rise, at least, to a position of command. Such is the chief characteristic of innate leadership though it may happen to be in bondage for a time. Thus Henry Highland Garnet received from his African ancestry the qualities which were to distinguish him through a long career of leadership and usefulness.

From his father, George Garnet, Henry not only inherited the sterling traits and bearing which were so dominant in the celebrated grandfather, but he owed much to his mother,[7] a woman of extraordinary energy and industry. She was "tall and finely moulded with bright intellectual face, lighted up with lustrous, twinkling, laughing, eyes." [8] Henry's eyes were bright and unclouded; above them was a massive forehead of "a finely shaped head which might have been taken as a model for an artist." [9] To this priceless gift may be added a disposition which was fascinating to all who came into contact with him. Garnet possessed the capacity to ingratiate himself into the esteem of hundreds whom he unconsciously influenced.

Garnet's escape from bondage is unique; doubtless it had much to do with the attitude toward slavery which he maintained in later years. He knew what oppression meant and his escape from it reflects ingenuity and courage. Late in 1824 his parents had secured permission to attend a funeral of a relative in Maryland, some distance from New Market. "Henry's father, mother, sister, and seven others, including himself, composed the company. . . . For several days they slept in the woods and swamps,[10] traveling all night long. Henry now nine years old, kept up with the fugitives until his little limbs gave out." Relatives carried him on their backs until the party reached the home of Thomas Garrett, a Quaker and sponsor of the underground railway, who lived at Wilmington, Delaware. At this station the party separated and Henry's family went to New Hope, Bucks County,[11] Pennsylvania, where he first entered a school house. From this point the pilgrims continued their journey to New York City, where some of the happiest and some of the bitterest experiences of Garnet's life were ahead.

The next step in the escape from slavery was to give thanks, which the father, George Garnet, did by calling the family together. This, however, was not sufficient cause for reassurance in those days. Foresight prompted the band to change their names in order to avoid capture and persecution by the slave hunters who were always busy on the trails of fleeing fugitives. The boy was told that his name was Henry. Thus, in the prime of youth, Garnet learned the difficulties surrounding flight from bondage and oppression. In later years he was to speak out of this trying experience in appeal to the slaves and the abolitionists against the institution which had been responsible for his sufferings. It is not easy to visualize one hundred years later the conditions and circumstances which faced this future leader of the ante-bellum period. These circumstances, however, were the fiery crucible in which the metal of Garnet and other brave and courageous leaders was refined.

Garnet had endured quite enough in the subtle flight from Maryland, but this was not the end of his pilgrimage from the land of oppression. All had gone very well thus far. A sudden turn brought slave hunters, the nemesis of all fugitives. In 1829, while Henry was away cooking on a schooner which plied between New York City and [12] Washington, D. C., the slave catchers invaded the Garnet home. On his return he learned that "his father in escaping had leaped from the roof of a two-story house; his mother had barely eluded their grasp; his sister had been arrested and tried as a fugitive from labor before Richard Riker, Recorder of the City of New York." [13] This incident caused Henry's blood to surge for revenge upon those who had mistreated his relatives. With the meager money which he had he purchased a [14] large clasp knife and boldly walked up Broadway in the hope that some slave hunter would approach him. Nothing could have possibly stung Garnet worse than an injury to his mother. He adored her with the most tender love and devotion and for her he would gladly have died. Realizing his danger, friends lured him away to the home of Thomas Willis,[15] in Jericho, Long Island. Here Henry Highland Garnet enjoyed himself much before departing for permanent employment, which was his next experience on Long Island.

Garnet was given to "the care and keeping of Epenetus Smith under a certain form of indenture." [16] In this service Garnet remained two years before he returned to New York City and joined his family. During his indentured service, one of his legs was injured permanently. The revelations [17] of the cowardly attack upon his family had made an enduring impression upon Garnet's mind. This was a constant physical reminder of the slough of despond from which he had escaped. Slavery had produced in him one of the greatest foes which the crisis from 1830 to 1860 would ever face. To the liberation of fellow slaves Garnet's life was now firmly dedicated. Douglass and others had escaped from bondage, but few if any of them suffered in mind and body the agony of Henry Highland Garnet. Naturally he placed responsibility for his condition at the door of slavery, to the destruction of which he was resolved to lend his utmost of intellect and character. To this tremendous task he brought strength and courage which the stormiest difficulties of the conflict never daunted.

Garnet's school days began in 1826, when he was sent to the African Free School No. 1 [18] in Mulberry Street, New York City. He continued his education in School No. 2 in the same city. The curriculum in the latter included spelling, penmanship, grammar, geography, and astronomy. Mr. Charles C. Andrews, an Englishman, was the director. He held constantly before his students the highest ideals. In order to inspire [19] the pupils, Mr. Andrews inaugurated fairs for the exhibition of special talents and at his own expense hired additional instructors for the work.[20] Garnet remained in this school until 1828, when he made two trips to Cuba as a cabin attendant. On returning to America he resumed his studies with Mr. Andrews for a year, at the end of which the latter had to give up his work on account of his colonization views. He had kindled in the mind of Garnet, however, a desire for learning which would never be extinguished.

In 1831 Garnet continued his studies in the High School for Colored Youth which was organized in New York by Curtis and Leiboldt.[21] Having a background in the common branches, Garnet began the study of Latin and Greek in which he became an excellent student. While engaged in the study of the classics young Garnet met the Rev. Theodore S. Wright who, in 1833, was pastor of the first Negro Presbyterian Church in New York City. This acquaintance was far-reaching in its influence upon Garnet's life in that it was responsible for his choice of the ministry as his life work. Rev. Mr. Wright, an abolitionist, saw Garnet's fine possibilities for training not only for the ministry but for the cause of abolition.

The next step in Garnet's education was at Canaan, New Hampshire, where the Rev. William Scales was conducting a school. Garnet matriculated in 1835 [22] and, with Alexander Crummell, a lifelong friend, and others, entered joyously upon his studies.[23] There was in this rural community, however, a race prejudice which was even more discomforting than that in the cities. The inhabitants, who loathed the idea of having Negroes educated in their community, began to lay sinister designs upon the institution to which Garnet and his fellow pilgrims had journeyed. The feeling of hatred soon crystallized into mob action in August of 1835.[24] Ninety-five yoke of oxen were assembled for the purpose of moving the academy. The task, being difficult, required two days, after which the building was destroyed by fire. The mob further attacked Garnet in the home of one Mr. Kimball with whom Garnet was boarding. In this incident Henry showed the bravery and courage which were characteristic of his life. Although lame, suffering with a fever, and using a crutch, he fired at the mob which had shot up the house. The remainder of the time he spent molding bullets for the double-barrelled [25] shot gun which he used in defending himself against the further attacks of the rioters.

From Canaan, New Hampshire, Garnet went by stage and other means of travel across Vermont to Whitesboro, New York. There his study was to be resumed under the inspiration and encouragement of the Rev. Beriah Green,[26] President of Oneida Institute. This period of study is significant in that it supplied the finishing touches of Garnet's training. The rising tide of reform, based upon the principles of morality and religion as taught in the Institute, attracted Garnet to the life which he was to lead.[27] In 1840 he completed his course with honor at Oneida Institute and entered immediately upon a career of leadership. "In his school life he always led his mates, and through life he always desired to be in advance, notwithstanding the hindrances his feeble health caused, for he was a cripple at the age of fifteen as a result of white swelling." [28]

That Garnet should enter the gospel ministry was logical and inevitable after the tutelage which he had received chiefly from clergymen. Those who were interested in the elevation of Negroes thought first of their spiritual welfare. As long as slaves were singing, praying, and shouting they would think less of their degraded estate. The point of emphasis was essentially similar to that of the missionary teachers who founded numerous schools for the freedmen in the South after 1865. Until quite recently the attack on Negro education has been chiefly through religion. This explains the dominance of the minister in Negro leadership. They were the first leaders of the headless host in pointing the way of the spiritual life. The history and traditions of the Bible are reflected in the subtle arguments of Garnet who based his appeals upon the rights of man as set forth in Holy Writ.

Garnet was first urged by the Rev. Theodore Wright of New York City to enter the ministry. By this minister Garnet was baptized and received into the Presbyterian Church. Upon graduation from Oneida Institute in 1840, however, Garnet began a school for Negro youth at Troy, New York, in the lecture room of the First Presbyterian Church.[29]

Two years later he was ordained and installed as the first pastor of the Liberty Street Negro Presbyterian Church of Troy. There he remained until 1843.

This was a remarkable period in Garnet's life in that he was actively identified with the wave of self-assertion which was spreading among northern Negroes during the forties. The fact that many of the conventions met at Troy, New York,[30] is further testimony of Garnet's leadership in these movements. Not only was he prominent in the affairs of his own race, but he took an active part as a member of the Young Men's Literary Society of the city, in discussions of such topics of the day as temperance and abolition. On both questions Garnet was eminently prepared to speak with power and conviction. It was a time when oratory was in great demand [31] as a means of arousing public opinion for or against a cause.

Henry Highland Garnet's leadership in the antislavery crusade from 1840 to 1860 is a span of his life which is outstanding in spite of the fact that it has generally been overlooked except by those who have examined his address to the slaves of America in 1843. It is scarcely known that Garnet was the forerunner of Frederick Douglass who assumed, eventually, the leadership of the movement for which Garnet deserves credit. The beacon light held out by Garnet at Troy, New York, deserves more attention than students of the ante-bellum leadership have given it. The problem of seizing an issue which another has created is much less difficult than that of choosing a path which can be blazed only by the prophet or pioneer, though he is often looked upon as a dreamer or fanatic.

The address to the slaves at the Convention of Colored Citizens at Buffalo, New York, in 1843, was unquestionably a milestone in the abolition movement. Garrison and other abolitionists had previously spoken frankly and fearlessly concerning the institution of slavery. Certain Negroes had voiced such sentiments. Before this time, however, no Negro had dared express himself in the language which Garnet used in this appeal: [32]

Brethren, arise, arise! Strike for your lives and liberties. Now is the day and the hour. Let every slave throughout the land do this, and the days of slavery are numbered. You can not be more oppressed than you have been—you cannot suffer greater cruelties than you have already. Rather die freemen than live to be slaves. Remember that you are four millions.

It is in your power so to torment the God-cursed slaveholders that they will be glad to let you go free. If the scale were turned, and black men were the masters and white men the slaves, every destructive agent and element would be employed to lay the oppressor low. Danger and death would hang over their heads day and night. . . . In the name of God, we ask, are you men?

Where is the blood of your fathers? Has it run out of your veins? Awake, awake; millions of voices are calling you! Your dead fathers speak to you from their graves. Heaven, as with a voice of thunder, calls on you to arise from the dust.

Let your motto be resistance! resistance! resistance! No oppressed people have ever secured their liberty without resistance. What kind of resistance you had better make you must decide by the circumstances that surround you, and according to the suggestion of expediency. Brethren, adieu! Trust in the living God. Labor for the peace of the human race, and remember that you are four millions!

These citations are from the address which attracted more attention than any other appeal ever presented to the Negroes of America. It is probable that John Brown was inspired by this appeal to force; at least he was so much pleased with the sentiment that Garnet had expressed that he had the speech published at his own expense. The raid at Harpers Ferry, Virginia, sixteen years later was a concrete attempt to test the possibilities of liberating the slaves.

The effect of Garnet's address upon the Buffalo Convention was like that of a thunderbolt. Free Negroes of the North stood aghast at the thought of action and force suggested by the speaker.[33] Frederick Douglass, not concurring with certain points in the address nor with the sentiments of Garnet, arose to advocate its reference to a committee and to reply. Garnet had aroused the fears of the delegates lest they should incur the disfavor of the northern communities to which they had fled from southern bondage.

The contrast between Frederick Douglass and Henry Highland Garnet here is so outstanding that it merits more than passing notice. The sources previously used do not fully reveal the impassable gulf of difference between the philosophy of these two distinguished leaders. Douglass remarked that "there was too much physical force both in the address and remarks of Garnet; that the address, could it reach the slaves, and the advice, either of (Garnet) or the address be followed, while it might not lead the slaves to rise in insurrection for liberty, would nevertheless, and necessarily be the occasion for insurrection, and that was what he wished in no way to have any agency in hurrying about and what we were called upon to avoid." [34]

Then followed a debate which occupied the convention for several days. A. M. Sumner of Cincinnati, Ohio, supporting the position taken by Douglass, asserted that approval by the convention would be fatal to the safety of free people of color who lived on the borders of the slave states. He thought that he was fully prepared to anticipate very properly what might be the results thereabouts and he felt bound on behalf of himself and his constituents to oppose the passage.[35] The resulting vote showed 18 in favor of the measure and 19 against it.

Later in the convention, Douglass read a report on abolition in which he used the phrase "moral suasion," to which Garnet took keen exception. The time having expired, the convention voted an extension in which Garnet asked that the report containing "moral suasion" be amended and stricken out. The effect of his appeal was to divide the convention. Douglass resumed the floor at the final count and won a majority.

This episode represents the parting of ways between the radical course approved by Garnet and the more diplomatic or palliative policy of Douglass.[36] The fear of the conservatives won and Douglass ever afterwards assumed a more conspicuous role [37] in the abolition movement than Henry Highland Garnet, his forerunner. It required fifty years to convince the American Negroes that there was a place for radical thinking among them. Gradually they came to agree with the more conciliatory and compromising attitude of Douglass who feared, with the masses, that resistance was fatal. They probably recalled the fate of Denmark Vesey and Nat Turner, whom Garnet lauded as worthy of emulation. The slave mind of the Negro in 1843 could not visualize the wisdom of such a course of action. While he yearned for freedom, physical resistance as a means towards its achievement was inconceivable then as now.

Some leaders of the abolition movement however were attracted to this daring new reformer who had appeared on the horizon. He was in great demand as a promoter of antislavery movements after 1843. The definite organization of the people of New York State owes much to this fearless and [38] courageous leader. From the time that he made his first appearance in New York City in 1837 he secured standing among first class orators. Requests came from all parts of New York, Pennsylvania and sections farther west, where audiences were eager to hear the cause of abolition presented.[39] His voice was to be heard in Faneuil Hall and beyond the Atlantic in behalf of his people. During the subsequent forty years Garnet maintained the attitude of 1843 in presenting and championing the cause of the Negro.

To many Henry Highland Garnet appears as a statesman rather than as a minister. It is very probable that he possessed the ability which would have achieved distinction in politics if he had been given the opportunity. "He had great consciousness of power and love of authority which made him in all conditions and at every period of his life a leader of men." [40] He believed in the power of the press and recommended it as a means of promoting the cause of abolition when Frederick Douglass opposed such procedure. Garnet advocated, as early as 1847, the establishment of a national printing press which "would send terror into the ranks of our enemies and encourage all of our friends, whose friendship is greater than selfishness." [41] To this Frederick Douglass gave no encouragement, as he believed in 1847 that a press would develop cliques. He realized later, as the publisher of the *North Star,* the power of the press and the importance of the pen in the struggle for the freedom of the American slaves.

News of Garnet's prominence as an antislavery speaker reached England by 1850. There the friends of Free Labor and Mrs. H. Richardson invited him to speak on the abolition movement. For more than three years Garnet remained in England, presenting his cause constantly before gatherings [42] of people who were desirous of aiding the movement. Continuing his journey into Europe, Garnet represented the cause at the World's Peace Congress held at Frankfort. There he was one of the most forceful and acceptable speakers. This occasion gave him the greatest opportunity of his life as he spoke from famous pulpits and, by his personality and the brilliancy of his intellect, discredited the alleged inferiority of the pure-blooded Negro.[43] While in London he served as the American delegate to the World's Anti-Slavery Convention. He spent three years in England, France, and Germany. His ability to converse in the native tongue of each country proved of value to him and his cause.

In 1852 Garnet joined the United Presbyterian Church of Scotland and accepted the call as a missionary to Jamaica, West Indies. In this field of service he gave his very best until he was attacked by a fever from which he recovered very slowly. His [44] physicians advised that he return North, which he did in 1855. On arriving at New York, he found that his former friend and adviser, the Rev. Theodore S. Wright, had deceased, and the Shiloh Church pulpit which he had filled was vacant. Garnet thereupon assumed the pastorate of this church. It had deteriorated, but he soon restored it to its former prosperity as a center of light and hope for the Negroes of New York City.[45] It was chiefly in this line of service that the remainder of his life was to be spent. He was, however, more than a minister. There was much of the vision of the statesman in his make-up and outlook. This may be said of many prominent Negro churchmen who have had to advise in things political as well as spiritual.

Garnet's efforts in the Civil War reveal the same distinguished traits as those characteristic of him in the antislavery crusade. While the riots were raging in New York City in 1863, Garnet's daughter removed the sign from his door—a precaution which possibly saved him from attack. He was, however, brave and fearless during this trying crisis of the rebellion when Lee [46] was invading the North to strike terror and bring the war to a successful conclusion. Throughout this time Garnet saw service in various forms of uplift work. The relief of the Negro sufferers placed upon him a task which he gladly assumed and performed creditably. Negro soldiers and other people of African blood were sorely in need of comfort, in the winter of 1863–1864. Relief committees were organized among the Negroes of New York City and much constructive work under Garnet's direction was done for the soldiers.

It deserves to be said that Garnet was a staunch advocate of the employment of Negro soldiers at a time when enlistment was bitterly opposed by the Union authorities.[47] Subsequently he served as a chaplain among the Negro troops. In this he was applying his principles of resistance which he urged so strenuously in the Buffalo Convention in 1843. Such action required courage during this period when Negroes were being pursued through the streets of New York City. Seeing that the Negro must have a part in the achievement of his freedom, Garnet devoted himself to the promotion of the scheme.

Garnet had a deep and abiding love for America, in spite of its record in the toleration and support of slavery. "I love every inch of soil which my feet pressed in my youth," said he, "and I mourn because the accursed shade of slavery rests upon it. I love my country's flag and hope that soon it will be cleansed of its stains, and be hailed by all nations as the emblem of freedom and independence."[48] It was such a spirit as this, after the dreadful riots of 1863, which inspired Garnet to throw his powerful influence into the recruiting of Negro troops. His was genuine patriotism which rose above personal ambition and refused to let discrimination and oppression dissuade him from his ideals. Then, as now, it required courage for Negroes to be patriotic There are thousands who have never felt the love of one's country revealed by Garnet.

On March 2, 1864, before the Civil War was over, Garnet was called to the pastorate of the Fifteenth Street Presbyterian Church of Washington, D. C. He accepted the call and assumed his duties in July of 1864 and continued in charge of the church over two years. He was at the height of his fame as a pulpit [49] orator and antislavery lecturer. His ministry attracted, therefore, many of both races to hear him. While Garnet was in Washington he became acquainted with President Lincoln and frequently advised him concerning the welfare of Negroes.

The visits of notables in public life to hear Garnet preach at the Fifteenth Street Presbyterian Church recommended him to President Lincoln as an appropriate speaker for the Emancipation Proclamation Anniversary in the House of Representatives, 1865. His performance on this occasion won the admiration of all and the astonishment of many of the foreign ministers who said that "if that is a specimen of the African race in this country it is time that they were free."[50] This eloquent address was so highly appreciated that a request for its publication with a sketch of

Garnet's life has left the chief account of the career of this splendid leader, who represents so peculiarly a voice crying alone in the darkness of bondage.

Leaving the pastorate at Washington, D. C., Garnet resumed his former charge at the Shiloh Church in New York City. His work there was a center of influence and inspiration to many young men who came to know him. Literary societies in which debating was prominent attracted many ambitious young men to the Shiloh Church. Dr. F. J. Grimké, while a student at Princeton, visited this church occasionally. Professor George W. Cook was a member of the Sunday School.

As Garnet approached the evening of life his attention was drawn to the land of his fathers. He longed to visit its shores and to see something of the empires and the type of leaders who, in Africa, were proving their metal. This feeling was, no doubt, due in part to a failure of the Negro American to recognize and fully appreciate the sterling worth of this man who had given forty years of his life to their uplift and advancement. His decision to visit Africa was directly opposed, however, to the resolution of his young manhood. "We are planted here," said he, "and we can not as a whole be recolonized back to the fatherland. It is too late to make a successful attempt to separate the white and black people of the New World. They love one another too much to endure a separation." [51] This shows that he had not believed in the idea of colonization for the entire group. No doubt his motives were due to the deep love which he had for his race. At the last dinner which he attended in Washington, D. C., Garnet remarked: "If I can just reach the land of my forefathers and with my feet press her soil I shall be content to die." [52]

The opportunity came in 1881 for the realization of Garnet's last ambition. He was at that time appointed minister to Liberia. He journeyed by way of England and thence to Monrovia where he arrived in December of 1881. There he became ill and died the following February. The Presbytery of New York said of him: "His long service in the church, his ability and fidelity as a preacher and pastor, the dignity, purity, and usefulness of his life and courage with which he maintained the honor of his high calling in the church and community commanded our esteem and respect and render his departure a real loss to the Presbytery." [53]

The life of this distinguished herald of freedom in America has not yet appeared. His work can never be fully appreciated except through an understanding of the mind of the American Negro slave during the crisis from 1820 to 1860. It is obvious that such a spirit of self-assertion as that which Garnet announced in his message to the slaves in 1843 deserves more than passing notice. The extent to which it inspired Douglass, Remond, and other Negroes of less courage than Garnet, will never be known. It is enough to say that Henry Highland Garnet created the idea which Frederick Douglass tempered and presented to the world in a more palliative and acceptable form. The truth of Garnet's message, however, was vindicated in the Civil War which emancipated the American Negro slaves to whom Garnet recommended force in 1843.

Frequently the prophet lives before his time. This may be said of Garnet, prior to 1850, when he was displaced by leaders who emphasized moral suasion. The possibilities of the latter course seem very dubious to the student of the ante-bellum period. The philosophy of Dew, Fitzhugh, Harper, and Calhoun had won the South to a moral justification of slavery. In such a slough of despond it took nothing less than the radical recommendation of a Garnet to shock the national consciousness with the wrongs of Negro slavery. It remained for John Brown, in 1859, to attempt to translate into action some of the suggestions which he undoubtedly received from Garnet.[54] While Negroes quailed at the idea of force and violence, the martyr of Harpers Ferry adopted it as a part of his mighty plan to lead slaves through the Appalachian ways to freedom. Slavery had destroyed the ancient semblance of African bravery; the masses to whom Garnet appealed could not see the achievements of their ancestors. Here we must keep in mind that very few of Garnet's type of African were ever enslaved. Only the weaker and more passive natives were captured for American slavery. The royal and warlike Comanches would fight until death rather than submit to capture. The degrading system of subserviency and brutality in this country left little of the erstwhile self-assertion in those who were brought here as slaves.

NOTES

1. Henry Highland Garnet, *A Memorial Discourse; . . . delivered in the Hall of the House of Representatives, Washington City, D. C., on Sabbath, February 12, 1865. With an Introduction by James McCune Smith, M. D.* (Philadelphia, J. M. Wilson, 1865) p. 33. (Hereafter cited as J. M. Smith, *Sketch of H. H. Garnet's Life*.)

2. Ibid., p. 17.

3. C. G. Woodson, *The History of the Negro Church* (Washington, D. C.: Associated Publishers, 1921), p. 275.

4. A. Crummell, *Africa and America* (Springfield, Mass., 1891), p. 273.

5. J. M. Smith, *Sketch of H. H. Garnet's Life*, p. 17.

6. Ibid., pp. 18 and 43.

7. Ibid., p. 18.

8. Samuel Smith, *A Letter Written in 1883*.

9. A. Crummell, *Africa and America*, p. 274.

10. J. M. Smith, *Sketch of H. H. Garnet's Life*, p. 19

11. W. J. Simmons, *Men of Mark* (Cleveland, 1897), p. 656.

12. J. M. Smith, *Sketch of H. H. Garnet's Life*, p. 25.

13. Ibid.

14. Ibid., p. 26.
15. Ibid.
16. Samuel A. Smith, *Letter Written 1883.*
17. J. M. Smith, *Sketch of H. H. Garnet's Life*, p. 26.
18. Ibid., p. 21.
19. Ibid., p. 23.
20. Ibid., p. 21.
21. Ibid., p. 27.
22. Ibid., pp. 29 and 30.
23. Wilson Armistead, *Tribute for the Negro* (Manchester, 1848), p. 511.
24. A. Crummell, *Africa and America*, p. 299.
25. J. M. Smith, *Sketch of H. H. Garnet's Life*, p. 30.
26. A. Crummell, *Africa and America*, p. 281.
27. Ibid., p. 280.
28. W. J. Simmons, *Men of Mark*, p. 658.
29. J. M. Smith, *Sketch of H. H. Garnet's Life*, p. 33.
30. Ibid., p. 36.
31. Wilson Armistead, *Tribute for the Negro*, p. 512.
32. C. G. Woodson, *Negro Orators and Their Orations* (Washington, D. C.: Associated Publishers, 1925), p. 157.
33. *Minutes of National Convention of Colored Citizens, Buffalo, New York, August, 1843*, p. 13.
34. Ibid.
35. *Minutes of National Convention of Colored People and Friends, Troy, New York, 1847*, p. 14.
36. Ibid., p. 18.
37. Ibid., p. 24.
38. Alexander Crummell, *Africa and America*, p. 292.
39. J. M. Smith, *Sketch of H. H. Garnet's Life*, pp. 47–54.
40. A. Crummell, *Africa and America*, p. 300.
41. *National Convention of Colored People, Troy, New York, 1847*, pp. 6 and 7.
42. C. G. Woodson, *Negro in Our History* (Washington, D. C.: Associated Publishers, 1922), p. 276.
43. Samuel Smith, *Letter 1883.*
44. A. Crummell, *Africa and America*, p. 296.
45. J. M. Smith, *Sketch of H. H. Garnet's Life*, p. 55.
46. A. Crummell, *Africa and America*, p. 299.
47. J. M. Smith, *Sketch of H. H. Garnet's Life*, p. 57.
48. H. H. Garnet, *Address Past, Present and Future of Colored People in America, Troy, New York, 1848*, p. 29.
49. F. J. Grimké, *Sermon in 1910* (Washington, D. C.: n.p., 1916), p. 12.
50. Samuel Smith, *Letter 1883.*
51. H. H. Garnet, Speech at Troy, New York, February 14, 1848, p. 25.
52. J. W. Cromwell, *Negro in American History* (Washington, D. C.: American Negro Academy, 1914), p. 129.
53. A. Crummell, *Africa and America*, p. 298.
54. J. M. Smith, *Sketch of H. H. Garnet's Life*, p. 52.

21. LARRY GARA, William Still and the Underground Railroad (1961)*

In his revisionist study of the underground railroad, *The Liberty Line*, Professor Larry Gara of Wilmington College emphasized the work of Afro-Americans in assisting slaves to escape. One of the important black conductors was William Still, secretary of the Philadelphia Vigilance Committee. In this essay, Gara describes the courage and cunning of this important black abettor of fugitive slaves in Philadelphia. Not only was William Still typical of black Northerners who sought to abolish slavery, but also the Philadelphia Vigilance Committee illustrated the organized work of a few undercover agents who assisted fugitives in avoiding recapture.

The writer of a popular account of the underground railroad in Pennsylvania stated in his preface that "it required the manhood of a man and the unflinching fortitude of a woman, . . . to be an abolitionist in those days, and especially an Underground Railroad agent." [1] He was referring to the noble minority who stood firm when the abolitionists were being "reviled and persecuted" in both the North and the South. Other underground railroad books—some of them written by elderly abolitionists—put similar emphasis on the heroic conductors of the mysterious organization. They reflected the history of the underground railroad from the vantage point of the abolitionist conductor. They also contributed to the growth of a favorite American legend, which is as much a part of folklore as of history. Two of the forgotten characters in the popular legend are the Negro members of various vigilance committees and the fugitives themselves. If it required strong character to be an abolitionist, it took even more courage to become a hunted fugitive or one of his colored abettors. William Still's work with the Philadelphia vigilance committee called attention to both of these neglected groups.

William Still's parents were both born slaves, and they left slavery at considerable personal sacrifice: his father purchased his freedom, and his mother, after one unsuccessful attempt to escape, finally ran away with two of her four children. They later farmed a forty-acre plot in the New Jersey pines near Medford. William was born there on October 7, 1821, the youngest of eighteen children. With a bare minimum of formal schooling he continued his own education by extensive reading. When he was twenty he left home, and three years later he moved to Philadelphia. He

* From Larry Gara, "William Still and the Underground Railroad," *Pennsylvania History* 28 (January 1961): 33–44. Reprinted by permission of the author and publisher.

held a number of jobs before joining the staff of the Pennsylvania Society for Promoting the Abolition of Slavery in the fall of 1847.[2]

Still began working with the abolition society as a combination janitor and mail clerk. After several years, both his duties and his salary were increased. He took a special interest in the society's efforts to assist slaves who had run away from the South. They were often boarded at his home before resuming their journey towards Canada. For fourteen years Still served the society. During that time he worked with such well known anti-slavery advocates as Robert Purvis, who was also colored, Lucretia and James Mott, Sarah Pugh, Thomas Garrett, and J. Miller McKim, who was the agent in charge of the Philadelphia office.[3]

In 1838 Philadelphia abolitionists had organized a vigilance committee to assist fugitives coming into the city. There was some underground railroad activity in the area. Thomas Garrett of Wilmington, the more militant anti-slavery Quakers of Philadelphia and the neighboring counties, and the vigilance committee were primarily responsible for the work. Although there was a semblance of organization to these efforts, much of the aid given the fugitive slaves was on a haphazard basis. By 1852 even the vigilance committee had disintegrated. In December of that year a group of abolitionists reported that the old committee "had become disorganized and scattered" and that for several years its duties "had been performed by individuals on their own responsibility, and sometimes in a very irregular manner," causing "much dissatisfaction and complaint." The group decided to organize a new vigilance committee, with an acting committee of four members, which should have the authority to attend "to every case that might require aid," to raise necessary funds, and "to keep a record of all their doings," and especially of their receipts and expenditures. They appointed William Still chairman of the acting committee.[4]

One of the principal activities of the new Philadelphia vigilance committee was to extend financial aid to fugitives. The committee provided money to board fugitives with families of free Negroes, sometimes for as long as thirteen days but usually for only a few days. As a Negro, William Still easily gained the confidence of the new arrivals and knew where to find them board and lodging among the colored population of Philadelphia. The committee also purchased clothing, medicine, and the fugitives' railroad fares to Canada. It advertised anti-slavery meetings in the newspapers and on one occasion spent twenty dollars for handbills and other expenses of a meeting. Mostly, the committee spent money in small amounts; very few items in its financial reports involved more than five dollars.[5]

At times William Still and other members of the acting vigilance committee were very busy with their labor on behalf of the fugitives.

Late in 1857 J. Miller McKim wrote another abolitionist, "Other rail-roads are in a declining condition and have stopped their semi annual dividends, but the Underground has never before done so flourishing a business." He further reported, "Exactly fifty—men, women and children—have passed though the hands of our Vigilance Committee in the last fortnight." [6] It was a dramatic time and a most unusual amount of work for the vigilance committee. According to the committee's journal it assisted approximately 495 fugitives between December, 1852, and February, 1857. In his later published account, covering eight years of vigilance committee activity, Still listed approximately eight hundred fugitives, including sixty children, who had received aid from the committee. [7]

Although a great deal of William Still's work was of such a routine nature as answering correspondence or meeting new arrivals at the rail-road station, he had some moments of high adventure too. One arrival from the South, who had purchased his freedom, contacted Still for information about his family. Upon investigation he proved to be Still's own brother, left in slavery forty years earlier when his mother fled to the North. Still also witnessed the arrival of the famous Henry "Box" Brown, who had literally had himself crated and sent north via the Adams' Express Company, and of the clever William and Ellen Craft. The Crafts had traveled all the way from Georgia with the nearly-white Ellen disguised as an ailing planter and William playing the part of the faithful servant. Still observed a number of other unusual and interesting cases, though none got the public attention given to Henry "Box" Brown and the Crafts. [8]

One of William Still's duties was to ask the newly arrived slaves their names, the names of their masters and where they had come from, and to question them about their escape experiences and the severity of their servitude. In part the interrogation was meant to protect the vigilance committee from the imposters who not infrequently found the abolitionists easy prey for a handout. Still not only recorded the data but carefully preserved the records. In his book he wrote that he had kept the documents for possible use in helping to reunite relatives and friends. [9] In 1884 he told a meeting of aged abolitionists that he had kept them because they were interesting, and because his family had been connected with the underground railroad. [10] Possibly, too, the records were a protection for him in case any of the Philadelphia abolitionists had requested a detailed accounting of Still's work for the anti-slavery society. To Still the vigilance committee was synonymous with the underground railroad. In 1893 he informed historian Wilbur H. Siebert that his "were the only records that were kept of the U.G.R.R.," and that when he collected them he had never dreamed that they could be published in his lifetime. [11]

Still's voluminous record books were a rich source of indisputable evidence had the government been inclined to invoke the Fugitive Slave Law against him or the vigilance committee. He hid the records after the Harpers Ferry fiasco and for a while they were stored in the loft of the Lebanon Cemetery building.[12] In a number of instances he faced possible prosecution. It was Still and others at the anti-slavery office who had warned the Negroes of Christiana that warrants were out for two slaves hiding there. The slave hunt resulted in a mob scene in which the slaves' master was murdered and his nephew seriously wounded. Several abolitionists and thirty-four Negroes were indicted for treason but none was convicted.[13] Still was not indicted with the Christiana rioters but the government brought charges against him for helping to entice Jane Johnson away from her master, Colonel John H. Wheeler, the American minister to Nicaragua. Still was acquitted, but two of five other Negroes indicted were sentenced to a week in jail on a charge of assault and battery, and Passmore Williamson, a Philadelphia Quaker, spent three months in jail for contempt of court.[14] John Brown had confided his plans to William Still six months before his raid on Harpers Ferry and a memorandum found among the papers of Brown's lieutenant, John Henry Kagi, seemed to implicate Still in the scheme.[15] In all these cases Still avoided punishment, but when a woman sued him for libel in 1860 he was not so fortunate.

The woman, a Mrs. Ellen Wells, who was a former slave from St. Louis, was traveling throughout the country raising money to purchase her mother, her children, and several other relatives from slavery. She stayed at William Still's rooming house in Philadelphia, but he did not encourage her project. When a Boston abolitionist wrote for information about Ellen Wells, Still answered that she was an imposter and a prostitute. The letter fell into Mrs. Wells' hands and she sued Still for scandalous and malicious libel. He pleaded guilty to having written the letter and the court sentenced him to ten days in jail and fined him a hundred dollars. Boston abolitionists supported Still and paid the fine from the treasury of the Massachusetts Anti-Slavery Society.[16]

A year later, with the Civil War in progress, Still resigned his position with the Pennsylvania Anti-Slavery Society.[17] He had already ventured into some real estate transactions, and he then bought and managed first a store and later a very successful retail coal business. In 1872 he published *The Underground Rail Road*. The book was another of William Still's contributions to the progress of his race. His work with the fugitive slaves had impressed upon him the need for Negroes to take the initiative to improve their condition. In August of 1860 he told a Negro audience at Kennett Square celebrating the anniversary of West Indian emancipation,

"The hundreds of heroic fugitives who yearly throw off their yokes, . . . seem to cry aloud in our ears—'Hereditary bondmen! know ye not who would be free themselves must strike the blow?' " [18]

In 1855 William Still had visited the former slaves who had settled in Canada, and he later wrote a strong defense of their conduct and achievements, answering those who maintained that slaves could not meet the responsibilities of free citizens. In 1859 he initiated a successful eight-year campaign to secure equal service for Negroes in the Philadelphia streetcars. In 1861 he helped organize an association for the purpose of collecting and disseminating accurate information about the American Negro population in order to improve its position.[19] These and many other activities stemmed from Still's determination to help improve the status of the colored people.[20] So did his book. He wanted to make the underground railroad "a monument to the heroism of the bondmen under the yoke." Their "heroism and desperate struggles," said Still, as well as "the terrible oppression that they were under, should be kept green in the memory of this and coming generations." He also believed that books written by Negroes would prove their mental ability and provide an effective answer to those who argued that the colored people were inferior. "We very much need works on various topics from the pens of colored men to represent the race intellectually," he wrote.[21]

He received added encouragement from the Philadelphia abolitionists. At a meeting in May, 1871, the Pennsylvania Anti-Slavery Society passed a resolution requesting Still to publish his reminiscences relating to the underground railroad. That same year there was a seven-months coal strike in Pennsylvania which made his business very dull but gave him the leisure he needed to prepare his material for publication. Still worked diligently in the preparation of his book, a task whch was made more difficult by the bitter division in the anti-slavery movement. He corresponded with old acquaintances, put his own records in order and collected material from others. The Philadelphia abolitionists with whom he had worked were all Garrisonians, but he included the political abolitionist Lewis Tappan among those whom he asked for information. One of the difficult tasks was to write a sketch of J. Miller McKim, his superior in the anti-slavery office. When McKim asked Still to outline the material concerning him, Still tactfully replied that "it would not be just to confine [McKim] to any special department of the work but to represent [him] as a general laborer," with many services in the anti-slavery cause.[22] Frederick Douglass, however, got no mention in Still's book, except in material reprinted from a British pamphlet. In 1893 Douglass boasted of his long service in the underground railroad and claimed that Still had omitted him because he had criticized Still's conduct toward the fugitives.[23]

William Still's book on the underground railroad is unique in that it emphasized the courage and ingenuity of the fugitives. White conductors are the heroes in the accounts which the abolitionists recorded for posterity; in Still's account, the daring fugitives are the heroes. Scattered throughout the volume are legal documents, letters, and newspaper items, but the focus of the narrative is always on the slaves themselves. Still placed his sketches of the abolitionist conductors at the end of the book, after the great bulk of material on the passengers. The book's numerous illustrations also focus the spotlight on the absconding slaves and on their heroic struggle for freedom.

In Still's book the vast majority of the fugitive slaves came from the neighboring border states. Most of them were young men, of more than average intelligence, though there were some women and children too. Although they were all considered underground railroad passengers, many of them had received little or no assistance before they contacted the vigilance committee. Some passed as white or as free Negroes, some traveled on foot at night, some adopted clever disguises, and more than a few hid or were hidden on steamers running from southern ports. Much of the escape drama was a self-help affair.

Although never a slave himself, Wiliam Still hated the South's peculiar institution. Not only did he have the zeal of the abolitionists, but as a Negro he was able to identify himself emotionally with the bondsmen. "The half will never be told of the barbarism of Slavery," he wrote. He described one fugitive as a "decided opponent to the no-pay system, to flogging, and selling likewise." Still said he had taken care "to furnish artless stories, [and] simple facts," and had restored "to no coloring to make the book seem romantic." He took great care to be factual but his bias was apparent throughout the book. In his preface Still commented that those who sought information regarding "the existence, atrocity, struggles and destruction of Slavery" would have no trouble finding the "hydra-headed monster ruling and tyrannizing over Church and State, North and South, white and black, without let or hindrance for at least several generations." [24]

The fugitives whom Still and the vigilance committee interviewed had confirmed his prejudice against the slave system. Although a few maintained that they had been treated well, the great majority testified to many hardships. Some were probably aware of the committee's preference for cruel and libertine masters. One slave from Maryland said that he had been "treated as bad as a man could be," another had been "allowed no privileges of any kind, Sunday or Monday," and a woman had "endured all outraged nature could endure and survive." The fugitives described their former owners with an abundance of such terms as "always a big devil—ill-grained," and "ill-natured man," and "a notorious frolicker." One described a cruel master who "made a common practice of flogging females when stripped naked." Still and the other committee members were also temperance advocates and duly noted in their records when a master was described as "given to 'intemperance' " and to "gross 'profanity,' " "a gambler and spree'r," and a man "devoted to card playing, rum-drinking and fox-hunting." [25]

Occasionally the committee sharply questioned fugitives whose stories did not seem plausible, but they sometimes took obviously exaggerated statements at face value. After trying to dispute her testimony, the committee gave "the benefit of the doubt" to Amarian, a good-looking girl of twenty-one who said she had always been treated very well. Similarly, they doubted Washington Somlor's description of inhuman treatment at the hands of a master who "believed in selling, flogging, cobbing, paddling, and all other kinds of torture. . . ." Yet they accepted the statements of William Jordon who said that he had lived three months in a cave "surrounded with bears, wild cats, rattle-snakes and the like." Theophilus Collins testified that he was brutally punished for attending a Sunday night religious meeting. His master called him in for a whipping and when he refused to remove his shirt, gave him twenty blows on the head with the butt of a cowhide, struck him on the head with fire-tongs, beat him with a parlor shovel until the handle broke, jabbed the shovel blade at his head with all his might, and, when the slave tried to make for the door, stabbed him in the head and stomach with a pocket knife. Nevertheless, Theophilus escaped and ran sixteen miles carrying a part of his entrails in his hands for the whole journey. [26]

William Still believed that a book containing such thrilling tales as the one Theophilus told to the vigilance committee should certainly sell many copies. His previous business experience enabled him to plan and promote the sale of his book to good advantage. He decided to sell it only by subscription and carefully supervised his sales campaign. [27]

Prospective agents for a particular territory had to apply personally to Still. If no suitable person applied, Still preferred to leave the area temporarily unsolicited. He had two editions, one in plain English cloth which sold for five dollars, and a sheepskin edition priced at five-fifty. Still prepared a full set of instructions for his agents and sold each of them a kit with sample copies. He gave them forty or fifty percent of the purchase price as commission, but they had to adhere strictly to his terms. During the financial panic of 1873 he permitted them to sell on the installment plan, but they were not to deliver the book until the last payment had been made. All of his agents had to submit weekly reports.[28]

Still preferred to hire colored men to sell his book, but he realized that few of his race had the necessary experience. He was confident it would be well received among the Negroes and among the Republicans, if the agents did their part well. "The book only needs to be presented by a man who appreciates and comprehends the value and importance of having our heroes and Martyrs under Slavery well represented in the history of our times—to make the work take exceedingly well," he wrote a representative in Kansas in 1873.[29] And the work took well indeed. A salesman in Pittsburgh cleared about a hundred dollars a week for six weeks. His best agent followed five others who had sold only a few copies in Baltimore, and at the end of six weeks he had more than three hundred subscriptions. In 1873 Still reported, "Agents are doing well with the U.G.R.R. this summer. East, West, North and South, wherever competent persons are presenting it." He first printed ten thousand copies but hoped to sell a hundred thousand before the demand ceased.[30] The first edition sold out completely, as did a second edition in 1879. In 1883 Still published a third edition with a new title, *Still's Underground Rail Road Records*, and with a sketch of the author written by James P. Boyd.

William Still's book undoubtedly circulated more widely than any other firsthand account of the underground railroad. In writing and distributing it Still proved that a Negro author could produce a creditable book and sell it on a large scale. He proudly exhibited it at the Philadelphia Centennial Exposition in 1876. It was a fitting tribute to his race. He hoped it would inspire other Negroes to greater efforts until they could exhibit such fruits "of their newly gained privileges" as "well-conducted shops and stores; lands acquired and good farms" well-managed, and "valuable books produced and published on interesting and important subjects." [31] It is not possible to evaluate the book's effect on American Negroes, but in one respect it failed to make its mark. William Still put the courageous fugitive slaves at the center of his stage. His book provided an excellent corrective for the many abolitionist-centered accounts. Yet in the popular mind, the white conductor of the underground railroad remains the leading figure in the drama. Despite Still's financial success, his message has been hidden under a mass of literature written by the abolitionists, their descendants, and admirers.

NOTES

1. Robert C. Smedley, *History of the Underground Railroad in Chester and the Neighboring Counties of Pennsylvania* (Lancaster, Pa., 1883), preface, p. xv.

2. James P. Boyd, "William Still: His Life and Work to This Time," in

William Still, *Still's Underground Rail Road Records* 3rd ed. (Philadelphia, 1883), pp. iii–xvii. The title page varied somewhat in each edition of Still's book, but the pagination of the text remained the same.

3. Ibid., p. xviii.

4. Still, *Underground Rail Road*, pp. 611–12.

5. Journal of the Philadelphia Vigilance Committee, 1852–57, in the Historical Society of Pennsylvania.

6. J. Miller McKim to Mrs. M. W. Chapman, November 19, 1857, in the Weston Papers in the Boston Public Library. McKim's letter was published in the 1858 edition of the *Liberty Bell*.

7. Journal of the Philadelphia Vigilance Committee; Still, *Underground Rail Road*, passim.

8. Lucretia Mott to Joseph and Ruth Dugdale, March 28, 1849, in the Lucretia Mott MSS in the Friends Historical Library of Swarthmore College; Still, *Underground Rail Road*, pp. 81–86, 368–77.

9. Still, *Underground Rail Road*, preface; Boyd, "Still," in Still, *Underground Rail Road*, p. xxxiv.

10. *Commemoration of the Fiftieth Anniversary of the Organization of the American Anti-Slavery Society, in Philadelphia* (Philadelphia, 1884), pp. 39–40.

11. William Still to Wilbur H. Siebert, November 18, 1893, in scrapbook "The Underground Railroad in Pennsylvania, vol. 3," in the Wilbur H. Siebert Papers in the Ohio Historical Society.

12. Boyd, "Still," in Still, *Underground Rail Road*, pp. xxiii, xxxiv.

13. Still, *Underground Rail Road*, pp. 348–68.

14. Ibid., pp. 86–95.

15. Boyd, "Still," in Still, *Underground Rail Road*, pp. xxii–xxiv.

16. J. Miller McKim to R. S. Webb, June 23, 1860, and Samuel May, Jr. to McKim, May 23, 1860, in the Garrison Papers in the Boston Public Library; New York *National Anti-Slavery Standard*, April 28, May 5, 1860.

17. Boyd, "Still," in Still, *Underground Rail Road*, p. xxx.

18. New York *National Anti-Slavery Standard*, August 18, 1860.

19. Boyd, "Still," in Still, *Underground Rail Road*, pp. xxv–xxviii, li–lvii; Harrod G. Villard, "William Still," in the *Dictionary of American Biography*, 18:23.

20. For Still's other activities see Alberta S. Norwood, "Negro Welfare Work in Philadelphia, Especially as Illustrated by the Career of William Still, 1775–1930," unpublished thesis in the Library of the University of Pennsylvania (1931).

21. William Still to Dr. Henry Charles, June 6, 1873, to J. W. Jones, November 4, 1873, and to J. C. Price, June 3, 1873, in the William Still Papers in the Historical Society of Pennsylvania.

22. Boyd, "Still," in Still, *Underground Rail Road*, p. xxxv; William Still to J. Miller McKim, November 10, 1871, in the J. Miller McKim Papers in the New York Public Library.

23. Frederick Douglass to Wilbur H. Siebert, March 27, 1893, in scrapbook, "The Underground Railroad in New York, vol. 2," in the Siebert Papers in the Ohio Historical Society.

24. William Still, *The Underground Rail Road* (Philadelphia, 1872), pp. 144, 290, preface, 3, 5. This preface appears only in the first edition.

25. Still, *Underground Rail Road*, pp. 185, 260, 307, 383, 388, 416, 480, 519, 533, 754.

26. Ibid., pp. 130, 304, 435, 495–96.

27. Boyd, "Still," in Still, *Underground Rail Road*, pp. xlvi–xlix, lxi–lxii.

28. Still to T. L. W. Titus, January 7, 1874, to W. D. Teister, June 10, 1873, to Robert Furnas, June 18, 1873, to James E. Thompson, July 9, 1873, and to J. C. Price, June 23, 1873, all in the Still Papers.

29. Still to Thomas E. Franklin, April 9, 1874, and the Rev. J. C. Embry, October 14, 1873, in the Still Papers.

30. Still to W. H. Jones, June 3, 1873, the Rev. Jones, November 12, 1873, and to E. Sanborn, June 11, 1873, in the Still Papers.

31. William Still, *The Underground Rail Road* (Philadelphia and Cincinnati, 1879), preface. This preface appears in the second and third editions.

VII

White Northerners and Black Americans

From the Civil War through the Civil Rights Movement of the twentieth century, a myth persisted that racism was much more pronounced in the South than in the North. The fact that southern Congressmen consistently opposed all civil rights legislation, that all southern states enacted rigid segregation laws, and that southern politicians openly espoused the concepts of white supremacy all served to confirm this view. So long as most Americans held to this belief, resolution of the race question seemed to rest almost entirely with the South. Either southern states must be compelled by legislation to respect the rights of Afro-Americans or white Southerners must be converted through education into recognizing the dignity and worth of all men. Recognizing the challenge implicit in these attitudes, social scientists and historians produced numerous studies on race relations in the United States aimed at convincing northern politicians and moderate Southerners of the need for extending greater justice to Afro-Americans. Gunnar Myrdal's *An American Dilemma* and C. Vann Woodward's *Strange Career of Jim Crow* were two influential publications growing out of these efforts.

Although after World War II there was an increased skepticism about the validity of this belief, it was not until the 1960s that it was fully exposed. The outbreak of racial violence in northern cities, the racial hatred encountered by Dr. Martin Luther King, Jr. when he extended his movement into the North, and the rise of such groups as the Black Muslims and Black Panthers gave meaning to Malcolm X's contention that the Mason-Dixon line was really the Canadian border. No longer would the American people accept the naive assumption that white racism was restricted to or even most prevalent in the states of the Old Confederacy.

Responding to the implications of these contemporary events, historians began increasingly to investigate the racial attitudes of white Northerners from abolitionists to urban workers during the decades preceding the Civil War. The findings of these studies indicated that the myth of sectional racism had never been valid.

354

In a study that broke new ground, Leon Litwack discovered that segregation was not an innovation of white Southerners. Before the Civil War, most northern states were just as adroit as later southern ones in maintaining separation of the races in public schools and in places of public accommodation from hotels to omnibuses. The establishment of separate black religious denominations and fraternal orders in the North was the direct result of the northern custom of exclusion. As immigrants from Europe flooded into northern states and took over skilled trades previously monopolized by Afro-Americans, blacks became increasingly relegated to the more menial jobs at the lower end of the economic order.

Ironically the economic positions of free black Northerners deteriorated during the period of Jacksonian Democracy as well as during the years of controversy over slavery. In fact a parallel seems to exist between the prevalence of serious racial disturbances and the rise of democratic aspirations among the masses. For instance, increases in racial violence characterized the 1830s, the 1890s and the 1960s.

In contrast to the 1960s, the earlier forms of mass violence were characterized by mobs of rampaging whites who invaded black neighborhoods inflicting heavy damages in property and human life. Linda Kerber provides an analysis of one of these disturbances, the New York City Riot of 1834. Others occurred in Cincinnati in 1829, Philadelphia in 1834, and Pittsburgh in 1839, as well as in such smaller communities as Utica, New York, New Haven, Connecticut and Palmyra, New York.

Following in the path of Litwack's pioneering study, other historians have examined critically the racial attitudes of white abolitionists and other anti-slavery adherents. Like their contemporary ultra-liberal counterparts, abolitionists were less prejudiced than the majority of the white population; but, as the Peases demonstrate, they were far from devoid of racial bias. On the other hand, the attitudes of most white Northerners were less a revulsion against the institution of slavery than a dislike for Negroes. Except for a few minor exceptions, the black population was concentrated in those areas where slavery either was still legal or had once existed but rarely were blacks found in areas where slavery had never been legal. Therefore, the best way of preventing Afro-Americans from settling in an area was to make certain that slavery never entered it. By strongly opposing the enslavement of black people, anti-slavery advocates left the impression of great sympathy for Afro-Americans. Although there were certainly many anti-slavery people who were motivated by humanitarian feelings, others were clearly Negrophobes.

These recent studies indicate that white northern opinion was more complex than previously believed. The need for more in depth studies and more sophisticated analyses of attitudes and behavior patterns is obvious. These historians have at least laid bare the fact that white prejudice has a continuous and universal history among white Americans. More study of southern attitudes is also needed. Although there was more insistence upon uniformity of thought in the South, there were a few critics and even more emigrants who left the South for freer areas in the North and West.

22. LINDA K. KERBER, Abolitionists and Amalgamators: The New York City Race Riots of 1834 (1967)*

In this selection, Linda K. Kerber discusses the similarity of race relations in New York during the 1830s and those in the South at the end of the nineteenth century. Racial segregation was the northern way of life, fear of black economic competition was prevalent among the lower white classes, and a general distrust of white sympathizers of Afro-Americans existed. New York City in 1834 was ripe for a racial disturbance which broke out in July in the midst of a serious economic depression. Disregarding conditions which created race tension in the city, the general public blamed the white abolitionists for causing the New York City riot of 1834.

The image of the southern white mob, howling for Negro blood, is a familiar one in American historiography. The image of a northern white mob, howling for the same commodity, is not, but it well might be. Violence exercised on the racial issue before the Civil War was not confined to the South, nor is it fully described by the soft tomatoes and heavier projectiles that northern audiences habitually flung at anti-slavery lecturers. In 1819, a Negro woman was stoned to death in Philadelphia; in 1829 over a thousand free Negroes were forced to flee Cincinnati; three years later local hostility made it impossible for John Randolph's manumitted slaves to settle in the free state of Ohio. One of the most virulent of these episodes occurred in the summer of 1834, when a choleric mob held New York City at bay for three full days.[1]

If the event, at first glance, seems more properly to belong to the South of the Gilded Age, so too does its environment, a New York as firmly Jim Crow as if the term had already been invented. The free Negro in ante-bellum New York lived in a world segregated by both law and custom. There were Negro pews in the churches, Negro seats in the courtrooms, Negro balconies in the theaters. Negroes were barred from the ballot box by custom if they held more than $250 worth of personal property; by law if they held less. Their presence was unwelcome in public schools, in the seats of public omnibuses (they might, however, stand) and in the cabins of Hudson River steamers (though they were permitted to travel on the exposed deck). The American belief that "God himself separated the white from the black" was to be found everywhere,

* From Linda K. Kerber, "Abolitionists and Amalgamators: The New York City Race Riots of 1834," *New York History* 48 (January 1967): 28–39. Reprinted courtesy of the New York State Historical Association, Cooperstown, New York.

"in the hospitals where humans suffer, in the churches where they pray, in the prisons where they repent, in the cemeteries where they sleep the eternal sleep." [2]

For all this, New York was a city that flattered itself that it had no racial problems. The activity of the New York Manumission Society, which had counted on its rosters some of the most esteemed names of the early republic, diminished after statewide abolition was achieved in 1817. The New York Colonization Society remained vigorous, but by the early 1830s the expense of its schemes and the failures of its colonial ventures gave ground for the suspicion that its real motive was to expel the Negro from white society, rather than to free the slave. William Lloyd Garrison forced the issue, as he would so many others, by publishing in 1832 a pamphlet called *Thoughts on Colonization;* and by partially subsidizing its circulation a New York merchant named Arthur Tappan set his foot on the path that was to make his home the target of a violent mob two years later.[3]

By October, 1833 Tappan was serving as first president of The New York Antislavery Society; the end of that year found him president of a similar national society. The platforms of these organizations were mild enough, demanding abolition in the District of Columbia and the territories where Congress had jurisdiction, and explicitly denying an intention to meddle in the states, where Congress did not. Even this was enough to earn anti-slavery a host of antagonists from both side of the political fence, but they had little immediate impact on its fortunes. The abolitionist movement in 1833 was invigorated by the example of the British Emancipation Act passed that year, by *The Liberator,* a going concern of two years standing, and by the wide circulation enjoyed by Lydia Maria Child's *Appeal in Behalf of that Class of Americans called Africans.* It even had a poet laureate of stature in the person of John Greenleaf Whittier.[4]

Thus when the new year (fated to be known in New York annals as "the year of the riots,") dawned, the abolitionist movement was in a position constantly to remind New Yorkers—by pamphlets, by speeches, and by its own exemplary integration—that the city *did* have a racial problem, and was not going to be allowed to ignore it. But it would not be the existence of an abolitionist movement alone that would pull the mob out into the streets during what one historian has called the "July Days" of 1834. New Yorkers were agitated over a wide variety of causes during the first half of that year: fraudulent elections, labor troubles, incipient Irish-nativist rivalries, and their own health, as newspaper reports warned that cholera was drifting inexorably toward the city. All these tensions would contribute to the explosion that was the July Riot;

hatred of abolitionists would become a password covering a multitude of political sins.[5]

Arthur Tappan and his brother Lewis always believed that they had James Watson Webb to thank for the attack on their homes, and perhaps they were right. The "abos" had few friends among New York's journalists, who had long been in the habit of using "fanatic" as a synonym for "abolitionist," and the Whig editor of the *Courier and Enquirer* was the most vitriolic of the lot. He lost no chance to accuse the abolitionists of functioning as a front for all sorts of radical doctrines, including interracial marriage, or, as these pre-Victorians put it, "amalgamation." It was a generation that found it difficult to sit through a performance of *Othello*. When Garrison criticized a Massachusetts law levying a fifty dollar fine on the minister who should officiate at an interracial marriage, and other abolitionists let drop hints that they saw nothing improper in such liaisons, Webb exploded. "The avowal of such feelings is disgustful in our society," he proclaimed in the fall of 1833, "and he, who does avow them, should be spurned from it." Thereafter Webb added "amalgamist" to his arsenal of epithets. He would find frequent occasion to use it in reporting the events of the week of July fourth, beginning with his inclusion, in a long list of parades and other activities scheduled for Independence Day, of the following description: "At eleven, the Fanatics meet at Chatham-street Chapel, to have their zeal inflamed by the doctrines of abolition and amalgamation." [6]

The abolitionists' troubles began when hecklers disrupted their integrated celebration. Rescheduled for the evening of July seventh, it was again disrupted, this time by members of the Chapel's Sacred Music Society, who insisted that the hall had been reserved for them and were furious at the sight of a Negro choir in *their* stalls. The clash, the *Courier and Enquirer* explained, "was a riot commenced and carried on by the negroes themselves. The white people present were there with no disposition to disturb the blacks . . . but were beaten—yes, beaten, fellow citizens, by the bludgeons of an infuriated and *encouraged* negro mob! How much longer are we to submit?" [7]

Newspapers spread the rumor that yet another session was planned for the evening of July 9, foreseeing "most serious" consequences if the Negroes "continue to allow themselves to be made the tools of a few blind zealots." To the Chapel that evening, one of the hottest of the year, drifted large, hostile crowds. Perhaps the *Courier and Enquirer* was right when it asserted the next day that what had been held the night of July 9 was a sort of test case, to see whether the good citizens of New York would permit the meetings which abolitionists called "by way of bravado" in order to flaunt their unpopular doctrines. The *Mercantile Advertiser* was sure that it was the very "bone and sinew of our city, very *cross*, at the attempts . . . by certain men to *cross* them with the blacks," that broke into the Chapel that hot July night, and withdrew only when the mayor himself gave the order.[8]

The mob withdrew, but it did not disperse. The rumor spread that William Farren, the English stage manager of the nearby Bowery Theater, had made disparaging remarks about the American people; the cry was raised, "To the Bowery!" and the crowd, shifting its hostility from Negroes to foreigners, went off to disrupt a performance of *Metamora* until the great matinee idol, Edwin Forrest, had to be called to quiet them down. Finding themselves not far from Arthur Tappan's home on Rose Street near St. John's Park, the crowd remembered its original target and flooded on. Discovering no one at home it broke in, and fending off police "with brickbats and other missiles" dragged furniture and bedding out as contribution to a bonfire. The work of destruction continued until the hour had reached 2 A.M. and the bill for the mob's services had reached five hundred dollars.[9]

The crowds were back at St. John's Park the next night. This time their hostility was directed at Tappan's neighbor and close friend, the Presbyterian minister Dr. Samuel H. Cox, who defended abolitionist doctrine from his pulpit as well as at Antislavery Society meetings. The brickbats flew at the windows of Dr. Cox's church and of his nearby home, while the police were resisted from behind improvised barricades until midnight. "It is time," pontificated the *Courier and Enquirer* the next morning, ". . . that these abolitionists and amalgamators should know the ground on which they stand. They are . . . always clamourous with the police for protection and demand it as a right inherent to their character of American citizens. Now we tell them, that when they openly and publicly promulgate doctrines which outrage public feeling, they have no right to demand protection from the people they thus insult." [10]

Not everyone was quite as complacent as James Watson Webb. Lewis Tappan sensed that by Friday, "The 'respectable' portion of the community, that had, thus far, looked on with indifference, or a willingness to see the hated band of abolitionists punished to a certain extent by popular violence, began to be alarmed for the safety of their own property." It was on Friday that Mayor Cornelius Lawrence first took official notice of the disturbances, by issuing a proclamation which agreed that the abolitionists' program was "repugnant" but directed "all good citizens to refrain from mingling with any crowd which may assemble." But the riots that began at 9:30 that evening proved uncontrollable. The 27th National Guard, which had readily quelled election rioters the previous

April, had more trouble with these throngs, and it was not sent at all to the Five Points neighborhood, where rioting was worst. Once again Arthur Tappan's store was damaged; once again Dr. Cox's church and home were threatened; and the Presbyterian church on Spring Street, whose minister was also suspected of abolitionist proclivities, became the new center of the rioters' enthusiasm and provided the setting for "a serious engagement between the people and the militia." [11]

The ugliest violence of the evening, however, was directed not at white friends of the Negro, but at the Negroes themselves. The pitched battle on Spring Street was only a sideshow; the main event was taking place well to the south, in the Sixth Ward, against its large Negro population. Following a rumor that the Reverend Peter Williams, the widely respected and first Negro priest in the Episcopal Church, had officiated at an interracial marriage, his church (the St. Phillip's African Episcopal Church on Center Street) was invaded, its furniture destroyed, and its organ demolished. The crowd spilled over into the narrow streets of the Five Points, its hostility redirected from abolitionist ministers to Negro ministers, from Negro ministers to Negroes. In a weird parody of the Book of Exodus, the mob demanded that white families illuminate their windows so that their race might be identified and their homes passed over; the mob would attack homes with darkened windows only.[12]

By this point even the "respectable" *Mercantile Advertiser* had had enough. "We have now reached a state of things which must be put a stop to," it fulminated, with more indignation than grammar. The same newspapers which had heard the death knell of the Republic in the election of Cornelius Lawrence the previous April now hailed him as a hero for his second proclamation, posted Saturday afternoon, calling out the militia. Clear orders were finally given that the troops were to fire on any reappearing insurgents, companies were stationed in the Five Points as well as St. John's Park, the Arsenal was guarded against attempted invasion, and a cavalry regiment clip-clopped through the streets all night. There was one last threat: a suspicious group appeared in the vicinity of the Chatham Street Chapel but was easily dispersed. "Torrents of rain" helped the militia keep the streets clear on Sunday; guards stayed on duty through Monday night, and were no longer needed by Tuesday.[13]

The July Riots, the worst New York suffered until the Civil War, found their way into fiction. They receive only brief mention in Richard Hildreth's *Archy Moore* as an episode witnessed by the protagonist on a trip through the North, but they became the pivotal episode in *Marie*, written by Alexis de Tocqueville's less renowned but only slightly less astute travelling companion, Gustave de Beaumont. *Marie* has received short shrift in the historical press. Perhaps this is because it is written in the tradition of the romantic novel, and includes rather more than its share of undulating grasses and tranquil lakes, to say nothing of a cabin built "only of a few logs . . . placed symmetrically in such a fashion as to outline a number of Gothic arches." But it also includes social analysis as astute as anything Tocqueville wrote, and Beaumont's appendix on the July Riots is probably the best account of them ever written. *Marie* is the story of a travelling Frenchman who seeks to marry a mulatto girl. Their wedding ceremony is disrupted by a riot modelled on New York's of 1834, and, fleeing to the West, they find no peace or sanction for their love until Marie dies of a fever in the Illinois forests. The novel's motto might well be the cryptic question her father asks in its opening chapter: "Are you sure that in this land of liberty there is no tyranny?"; the book itself is a long and bitter footnote to Tocqueville's famous passage on the tyranny of the majority. "Public opinion," Beaumont reflected, "so charitable when it protects, is the cruelest of tyrants when it persecutes. Public opinion, all-powerful in the United States, desires the oppression of a detested race, and nothing can thwart its hatred. . . . Everywhere, I found this tyranny of the people's will." [14]

Why did the people will the riot? 1834 was a recession year. What New Yorkers may have sensed hidden behind abolitionist egalitarianism was an economic challenge quite as much as a social one; though they claimed the riot was caused by outraged sensibilities, the outrage may well have been to pocketbooks. This alarm was verbalized by the interpretation of the July Riot offered by a Washington, D. C. newspaper:

It is impossible to conceal the fact, that in consequence of the competition between the free white labor and the black labor of the North, there is a feeling of bitter hatred already existing, which every collision will increase, until it becomes the means of rallying the entire mass against the South. It will then be a question of slave and free labor, and the influence of the section will be made to bear on our peculiar interests. [15]

Other sources of competition with free, white, skilled labor were given cause for uneasiness by the July Days: there were rumors of attacks against men who held contracts for the products of prison labor, and the unskilled Irish workers, who could usually be counted on to join in when there was rioting to be done, were noticeably absent from this affray. That the Irishman's rival for jobs in New York City in 1834 was not so much the free Negro as it was the white immigrant of older stock may have been reflected in their behavior. At any rate, it is certain that only a very few of the names of those brought to trial are Irish, and that a large number of Irishmen volunteered to help put down the Negroes' enemies. The draft riots of 1864 were a long way off.[16]

From the first, the leading abolitionists tried to dissociate their movement from the riot. The most important of their efforts were the handbills, headed "American Anti-Slavery Society—Disclaimer" circulated on the uneasy Saturday following the riot, which reiterated the principle that "even hard laws are to be submitted to by all men until they can by peaceable means be altered," and that no attack on the Union or the Constitution was intended. But the very first clause in the handbill had nothing to do with politics; the first accusation from which the abolitionists wanted to be cleared was "any desire to promote or encourage intermarriages between white and colored persons." The letter they and other officers of the society sent to the mayor a few days later began the same way: "We disclaim . . . any desire to promote or encourage intermarriages. . . ." The perceptive English visitor to the United States, Edward Abdy, was furious that they should have stooped to recognize the "amalgamation" complaint as valid enough to disavow; Beaumont saw in their groveling yet more evidence for his colleague's strictures on the tyranny of the majority. But the abolitionists were, and long would be, ambivalent on the subject of integration: far ahead of their generation in willingness to integrate, they shared its "sensibilities." The impact of the riot was to make them even more sensitive and increase their willingness to allow their enemies to set the terms of the post-riot dialogue. The cause of the riot was unclear, and remains so to this day, but the contemporary consensus was that anti-slavery agitators had invited it. Instead, for their part, of demanding an explanation of why the Mayor and Common Council had not moved sooner, the abolitionist response was purely defensive. "We have done nothing to excite resistance to the laws." A decade later they would be more sure of themselves.[17]

But if their words were mincing, they had learned how to make meaningful gestures, and in politics it is often the gestures that make the difference. The fact that a Negro minister's name was among the signatures on the letter was probably enough to ensure its frosty reception. Mayor Lawrence tossed the letter to the Board of Aldermen, which gave it to their clerk with instructions to send it right back where it came from with no reply. This resolution passed unanimously; banks and tariffs might be party issues, but abolitionists most assuredly were not. When William Leggett's *Evening Post* criticized the Board for its contemptuous attitude it called forth only a series of snide remarks for its pains, whose burden was that the only possible reason for the *Post's* stand was the hope of arousing a party fight. Soon, of course, the anti-slavery crusade *would* become a party issue, and eventually create its own party—and its own war—but in 1834, in New York City, abolitionists had no welcome from either party, and only a firebrand Democrat dared defend them. Which is perhaps only to suggest that though the Whigs had found their name (in the April elections) they were still National Republicans; and that not until the equal rights energies of Antimasonry had fused with anti-Jacksonism could a new party be said to exist. It was fusing, upstate, in the person of William H. Seward, but Seward made no comment on the riot that summer.[18]

Undoubtedly the riot frightened away some supporters of the abolitionist cause: the most prominent was the Negro minister Peter Williams, who resigned from the society "by the advice" of the Episcopal Bishop Onderdonk. But the balance sheet was not all loss. Theodore Dwight Weld was merely confirmed in his belief that "Truth has always been the gainer where men resort to bludgeons." Lewis Tappan left his house on Rose Street unrepaired, "a silent Anti-Slavery preacher," and among those who came to see it was a young boy named Schuyler Colfax, who would grow up to be a Radical Republican and Grant's Vice President. "I remember . . . that it made me prejudiced, even then, against the institution of slavery," Colfax told Tappan more than forty years later. "I have no doubt that that early adverse impression caused me to range myself with the anti-slavery wing of the Whig party. . . ." From Europe William Ellery Channing wrote to urge the abolitionists not "to recant anything"; Theodore Weld reported that "almost daily letters" informed him that the riots had helped, rather than hurt the cause. The most important single recruit, however, was the erudite William Jay, who had long sympathized and advised the abolitionists in private but who had doubted the usefulness of organized societies. Jay is undeservedly ignored by most histories of the movement, but as one of the few early leaders who could speak the language of the law as well as the language of the Bible his was an important voice, and one frequently raised in the interest of legality and moderation, with an eye always on efficiency rather than rhetoric.[19]

Recruits were the exception, however, not the rule. Perhaps the most disturbing feature of the riot was the near-unanimity of the community's response. Far from displaying remorse for the nights of violence and destruction, New Yorkers united in blaming the abolitionists for instigating them and in non-partisan praise for the mayor who had allowed the mob to wreak its will. The Democratic *Albany Argus* regretted that the abolitionists could not be banished "upon the same principle that dogs are muzzled in hot weather"; the Whig *Courier and Enquirer* denied the abolitionist right to police protection. "When they endeavor to disseminate opinions, which if generally imbibed, must infallibly destroy our

National Union, and produce scenes of blood and carnage . . . the egis (sic) of the law indignantly withdraws its shelter from them . . . when they debase the noble race from which we spring,—that race which called civilization into existence, and from which have proceeded all the great, the brave, and good, that have ever lived—and place it in the same scale as the most stupid, ferocious and cowardly of the divisions into which the creator has divided mankind, then they place themselves beyond the pale of the law, for they violate every law divine and human." [20]

It is common for contemporaries, reporting on the riot, to attribute the delay in calling out the militia to public and official sympathy with the rioters' ends. "These mobs," wrote William Ellery Channing, "have been too much the expression of public sentiment . . . because there was a willingness that the anti-slavery movement should be put down by force." Noting that the riots arose "from the determination . . . to prevent free discussion on the subject of slavery," the *Boston Commercial Gazette* made what was perhaps the central point. "Aye, as Petruchio says, 'there's the villany.' . . . A free discussion on that subject leads at once to abolition, amalgamation and immediate emancipation." In short, the right of free speech, a legacy of the same founding fathers whom this generation honored with a passion which verged on nativism, was to be tossed out with the bath water of emancipation and—horrors of horrors— amalgamation.[21]

The New York riots took place over a hundred and thirty years ago, but our newspapers daily offer fresh proof of the continued usefulness of the amalgamation battle-cry to opponents of integration. It is an irrelevant battle-cry, certainly, but the explicit egalitarianism of American political rhetoric has always made it embarrassing to voice outright demands that the Negro be "kept in his place." Opposition to miscegenation is still the single banner to which individuals opposed to equal rights for a wide variety of reasons find it most comfortable to repair; nor is the rationalization inappropriate, for, as Gunnar Myrdal suggested in his classic study *An American Dilemma*, "the supreme indication of social equality" is intermarriage.[22]

NOTES

1. John Hope Franklin, *From Slavery to Freedom* (New York: A. A. Knopf, 1956), pp. 231–32.

2. Lewis Tappan, *The Life of Arthur Tappan* (New York, 1870), pp. 191–92; Leo H. Hirsch, Jr., "The Negro and New York, 1783–1865," *Journal of Negro History* 16 (1931): 426–3, 441–4; Leo Hershkowitz, "New York City, 1834–1840: A Study in Local Politics" (Unpublished New York University Ph.D. thesis, 1960), p. 65; Gustave de Beaumont, *Marie, or Slavery in the United States*, trans. Barbara Chapman (Stanford, California: Stanford University Press, 1958), p. 66.

3. Hirsch, *The Negro and New York*, pp. 394–97; Wendell Phillips Garrison and Francis Jackson Garrison, *William Lloyd Garrison 1805–1879: The Story of his Life* (New York, 1885), I, pp. 299–300.

4. Phyllis Mary Bannan, "Arthur and Lewis Tappan: A Study in New York Religious and Reform Movements" (Unpublished Columbia University Ph.D. thesis, 1950), pp. 85, 88–89; Bayard Tuckerman, *William Jay and the Constitutional Movement for the Abolition of Slavery* (New York, 1894), pp. 46–48.

5. Bannan, "Arthur and Lewis Tappan," p. 98.

6. Tappan, *Arthur Tappan*, pp. 203–4; *Courier & Enquirer*, July 8, 18, 12, 1834; Francis J. Grund, *Aristocracy in America* (New York: Harper & Row, 1959), p. 79; *Liberator*, Jan. 8, 1831, Jan. 28, 1832. Webb is quoted in E. S. Abdy, *Journal of a Residence and Tour in the United States of North America, From April, 1833, to October, 1834* (London, 1835), I, p. 347; his views on slavery and abolition summarized in James L. Crouthamel, "James Watson Webb and the New York *Courier & Enquirer*" (Unpublished University of Rochester Ph.D. thesis, 1958), pp. 319, 255–57. *Courier & Enquirer*, July 4, 1834.

7. *Courier & Enquirer*, July 4, 8, 1834.

8. *Courier & Enquirer*, July 9, 10, 1834; *Mercantile Advertiser*, July 10, 1834.

9. Beaumont, *Marie*, p. 246; *Albany Argus*, July 12, 1834.

10. Tappan, *Arthur Tappan*, p. 67; Beaumont, *Marie*, p. 247; *Courier & Enquirer*, July 11, 1834.

11. Tappan, *Arthur Tappan*, p. 212; *Mercantile Adevrtiser*, July 11, 12, 1834; James Grant Wilson, ed., *The Memorial History of the City of New York* (New York, 1893), III, p. 342; Beaumont, *Marie*, p. 248.

12. *Albany Argus*, July 14, 1834; Beaumont, *Marie*, pp. 248–49.

13. *Mercantile Advertiser*, July 12, 14, 15, 1834. By the end of the month, most of the men arrested for rioting had been tried in the Court of General Sessions; penalties tended to be heavy (six months to one year imprisonment at hard labor) and were made more galling by a supercilious homily from the court recorder. *Journal of Commerce*, July 23, 1834.

14. Richard Hildreth, *The White Slave: Another Picture of Slave Life in America* (London, 1836), pp. 217–18; Beaumont, *Marie*, pp. 12, 13, 77.

15. *U. S. Telegraph*, quoted in *Albany Argus*, August 21, 1834.

16. Milo Osborne to Cornelius Lawrence, no date (but received during the riots), New York City Miscellaneous MSS., New-York Historical Society; *Courier & Enquirer*, July 12, 14, 1834; *Mercantile Advertiser*, July 18, 23, 1834.

17. Abdy, *Journal*, III, p. 124; Beaumont, *Marie*, p. 251. The Disclaimer is published in full in Tappan, *Arthur Tappan*, pp. 215–16; see also pp. 201–2.

18. *Evening Post*, July 22, 1834 (reprinted in Theodore Sedgwick, Jr., ed., *A Collection of the Political Writings of William Leggett* (New York, 1840), I, pp. 37–38); *Mercantile Advertiser*, July 18, 22, 24, 1834; New York City Board of Aldermen, *Proceedings* (New York, 1835), VII, p. 130.

19. *Mercantile Advertiser*, July 16, 1834; Theodore Dwight Weld to James G. Birney, August 7, 1834, in Dwight L. Dumond, ed., *The Letters of James G. Birney, 1831–1857* (New York: D. Appleton-Century Co., 1938), I, p. 128; Lewis Tappan to T. D. Weld, July 10, 1834, in Gilbert H. Barnes and Dwight L. Dumond, eds., *The Letters of Theodore Dwight Weld, Angelina Grimké Weld and Sarah Grimké, 1822–1844* (New York: D. Appleton-Century Co., 1934), I, p. 153; Tappan, *Arthur Tappan*, p. 420; Channing is quoted in Arthur W. Brown, *Always Young for Liberty* (Syracuse: Syracuse University Press, 1956), p. 227; Tuckerman, *William Jay*, p. 57.

20. Abdy, *Journal*, III, pp. 117–18; *Courier & Enquirer*, July 11, 1834.

21. Channing is quoted in Tuckerman, *William Jay*, p. 56; see also W. E. Channing to Jonathan Phillips, July 24, 1834, Phillips Papers, Massachusetts Historical Society; Michel Chevalier, *Lettres sur l'Amerique du Nord* (Paris, 1837), I, pp. 231–37. *Albany Argus*, August 26, 1834; *Hartford Courant*, July 21, 1834. *Boston Commercial Gazette* editorial is reprinted in *Courier & Enquirer*, July 18, 1834.

22. Gunnar Myrdal, *An American Dilemma: The Negro Problem and Modern Democracy* (New York: Harper & Brothers, 1944), I, p. 591. See also I, pp. 55–59, 587–90.

23. WILLIAM H. AND JANE H. PEASE, Antislavery Ambivalence: Immediatism, Expediency, Race (1965)*

> Although abolitionists were unanimous in labelling slavery a sin, they frequently showed a marked ambivalence in their attitudes about the Afro-American himself. In this essay, William H. and Jane H. Pease of the University of Maine suggest that such ambivalence was characteristic of the antislavery movement as a whole. More often than not, abolitionists treated Afro-Americans as if they were children rather than men. They also relegated blacks to menial positions in their organizations and in a few cases barred them from membership altogether.

Of constant distress to students of the American antislavery movement has been its ambivalence, especially its ambivalence over the term Immediatism. The term had originally defined a means to end British colonial slavery, but it failed to be similarly applicable to emancipation in the American South. Therefore the antislavery movement strained to give new meaning to emancipation *"instant and universal."* Did it not really mean gradual emancipation immediately begun or, perhaps, immediate emancipation gradually achieved? But no less than over immediatism, antislavery crusaders were beset by a fundamental ambivalence in their attitude toward the Negro himself. At the simplest level there was no issue. Slavery was sin; and the crusaders were moved to free the slave by a humanitarianism too genuine to be doubted.[1] Yet, sympathetic as they might appear and believe themselves to be toward the Negro, the abolitionists were, as Leon Litwack and others have shown, in part at least prejudiced against him.[2] And the variety of their response toward him demonstrates the ambivalence so characteristic of the antislavery movement as a whole.

Endemic was the abolitionists' tendency toward abstraction. Fre-

* From William H. and Jane H. Pease, "Antislavery Ambivalence: Immediatism, Expediency, Race," *American Quarterly* 17 (Winter 1965): 682–95. Copyright, 1965, Trustees of the University of Pennsylvania. Reprinted by permission.

quently they so abstracted both the "Negro" and the "Crusade" that they dealt not with people in a situation but only with intellectualizations in a vacuum. John Thomas has recently noted that William Lloyd Garrison failed "to understand people, black or white" and used them simply "as counters in the grim business of reform." [3] His analysis echoes publisher James Gordon Bennett's conclusion made one hundred years earlier that to Garrison "nothing [was] sacred . . . but the ideal intellect of the negro race." [4]

This preoccupation with the ideal is reflected by the American Anti-Slavery Society, which, at its inception in 1833, resolved that to guarantee education to the Negro was more important than to end "corporeal slavery itself, inasmuch as ignorance enslaves the mind and tends to the ruin of the immortal soul." [5] And, on the very eve of Emancipation, Philadelphia antislavery leader James Miller McKim, although emphasizing the importance of slave rehabilitation and active in prosecuting it, thought that it was "not the place . . . of [the] abolitionists to descend to the details of th[e] work, teaching, and the like; let this," he added, "be attended to by the neophytes and others. We are to continue to be what we always have been," he concluded, "a wheel within a wheel; an original motive power." [6] Thus for thirty years abolitionists, to a greater or lesser extent, heeded the kind of exhortation which Henry C. Wright enunciated so forcefully:

Watch, Sister, & pray that you enter not into temptation. *Watch, not* . . . for Abolition as an Organization, not even for our millions of crushed & bleeding slaves . . . , but watch *for* the eternal, immutable Principles of Justice & Right—watch for *Humanity*. . . . We are seeking an object that must command the respect of the world—i.e., *the redemption of man from the dominion of man*. This is Abolition.[7]

The abolitionists did, of course, at least partly understand their own position. They may not have realized just how fully they were depersonalizing the Negroes; but they were quite aware that they had difficulties in matching their protestations to their actions. "We are," said the Connecticut crusader Samuel J. May with a Zolaesque directness, "culpably ignorant of, or shamefully indifferent to the wrongs which are inflicted upon our colored brethren. . . . We are prejudiced against the blacks; and our prejudices are indurated . . . by the secret, vague consciousness of the wrong we are doing them. Men are apt to dislike those most, whom they have injured most." [8] And despite the teaching of the antislavery periodical, the *Abolitionist*, that the antislavery enthusiast ought "to banish from his own mind the unworthy feelings which would lead him to regard any human being with contempt merely on account of his color," New York abolitionist Lewis Tappan admitted "that when the subject of acting out our profound principles in treating men irrespective of color is discussed heat is always produced." [9]

This much, then, the abolitionists themselves perceived. But for the student of the antislavery movement it is also imperative to recognize that prejudice and abstraction were but the obvious symptoms of an ambivalence which gives to the antislavery crusade in the expediency and temporizing of its actions and in the complexity of its thought an architecture baroque in the richness of its variations.[10]

It was, for example, relatively simple to accept the humanity of the Negro; but then how did one account for his patently submerged position vis-à-vis the whites? Abolitionists like Lydia Maria Child of Northampton, Massachusetts, tried to link the two elements by admitting that, while all Negroes were not "Scotts or Miltons," they were "*men,* capable of producing their proportion of Scotts and Miltons, if they could be allowed to live in a state of physical and intellectual freedom." [11] At the other extreme the New York Whig politician, William Henry Seward, defending the mentally deranged William Freeman in 1846, tried to subordinate intellectual lack to simple humanity and to separate it from race. He pleaded with the jury that

the color of the prisoner's skin, and the form of his features, are not impressed upon the spiritual, immortal mind which works beneath. In spite of human pride, he is still your brother, and mine, in form and color accepted and approved by his Father, and yours, and mine, and bears equally with us the proudest inheritance of our race—the image of our Maker. Hold him then to be a MAN.[12]

In denying, furthermore, that the apparent differences between Negroes and whites were inherent the abolitionists became environmentalists. John Rankin, ex-slaveholder from Virginia and an ardent abolitionist, asserted with good will but dubious logic that, if racial inferiority were a valid criterion, then all Negroes would be inferior to all whites if but one was. Clearly this was not so. Therefore existing inferiority was explainable only in environmental terms.[13] Slavery it was, asserted German refugee Charles Follen of Boston, that debased and degraded the Negroes and generated among whites an "absurd and cruel prejudice against color." [14] The antislavery solution to prejudice was clear once the cause was thus linked to slavery. Charles Calistus Burleigh of Connecticut optimistically exhorted his fellow whites to "give [the Negro] his liberty, and as strong a motive to exertion as you have;—a prospect of reward as sure and ample; not only wages for his toil, but respect and honor and social standing according to his worth, and see what he can then become." [15]

Yet, for all their exuberance, for all their belief in equality, for all their efforts to raise the Negro above the debilitating influences of adverse environment, the abolitionists were never wholly convincing. Much of what they said betrayed an implicit and at times explicit belief in racial inferiority. Here again ambivalence emerged. That the abolitionists themselves were usually unconscious of their expression of prejudice and that they denied it when challenged should surprise no one. Nor, indeed, is the thoughtful student surprised to learn that such prejudice did in fact exist. Occasionally crude, more often hidden in underlying assumptions or in appeals to science, prejudice played a more pervasive role than the logic of consistency would admit.

Exasperated by poor printing, inferior paper and numerous misprints, and spurred on by his own literary pride, Edmund Quincy lashed out in a letter to Caroline Weston in 1846 at "Wendell's nigger," whom he held responsible for botching an Antislavery Report. Never, he urged, let the printing out to "*Smart people*"; they get things up so poorly.[16] Here clearly was not only a rather vulgar display of prejudice but also of a value structure in which the typography of a convention's report weighed more heavily than economic opportunity for the free Negro.

The acerbity of these outbursts may be attributed to Quincy alone. The subterranean import, however, was common property among antislavery people. As late as 1860 Theodore Parker, a backer of John Brown, observed that "the Anglo-Saxon with common sense does not like this Africanization of America; he wishes the superior race to multiply rather than the inferior."[17] His neighbor, Samuel Gridley Howe, known for his multiple reform interests, accepted Parker's assumptions but rejected his predictions by observing that, particularly among young Canadian refugee Negroes, many succumbed to "mesenteric and other glandular diseases" and suffered from "phthisical diseases" and a "softening of tubercles." "Many intelligent physicians," he stated, "who have practiced among both [white and Negro] classes, say that the colored people are feebly organized; that the scrofulous temperament prevails among them; that the climate tends to development of tuberculous diseases; that they are unprolific and short-lived."[18]

Whether feebly organized in physique or not, the Negroes were certainly docile in temperament. "It is paying a very poor compliment, indeed, to the courage and superiority of us whites," Richard Hildreth said through the sympathetically portrayed Mr. Mason in *Archy Moore*, "to doubt whether we, superior as well in numbers as in every thing else, could not inspire awe enough to maintain our natural position at the head of the community, and to keep these poor people in order without making slaves of them."[19] But, if Hildreth's Mason was fictional, the Lane Rebels were not. They had concluded, in their famous debates on slavery, that *"the blacks are abundantly able to take care of and provide for them-selves";* but had added immediately that they *"would be kind and docile if immediately emancipated."* [20] This emphasis on docility is important, for quite openly it reduced the status of the Negro below that of the white man. J. Miller McKim, for example, negated American standards of self-reliance and manly independence when he praised Negroes for "their susceptibility to control." [21]

Not unreasonably, many Negroes actively resented this abolitionist presumption about their "susceptibility to control." During the 1850s, in fact, this resentment was in large part responsible for the growth and activity of the Negro Convention movement, whose purpose it was to do for the Negroes themselves what they feared the whites, at last, would not accomplish for them. Frederick Douglass and Henry Highland Garnet, two Negro leaders of marked undocility, both took umbrage at Maria Weston Chapman for her paternal concern about their appropriate be-havior; and Douglass, disillusioned with radical abolitionism in the face of growing political antislavery activity and ambitious himself to assert his independence from white abolitionist domination, defied the Boston hier-archy by establishing his own newspaper in Rochester, New York. Like-wise, Martin Delany, a successful Negro doctor, resented the Negroes' exclusion from antislavery leadership and was highly dubious about the abolitionists' touted support of economic opportunity for free Negroes. Delany's disillusionment led him to abandon America as a viable home for the Negro and in the late 1850s to sponsor projects for African colonization.[22]

Despite concepts of racial inferiority, further borne out by an almost universal preference for the lighter-skinned over the darker-skinned Negro,[23] abolitionists in fact did demand just and equitable civil liberties for colored persons. "The oppressive civil disabilities laid upon them in the non-slaveholding States, and the settled opposition to their education and elevation . . . ," said the Andover Theological Seminary antislavery society,

are but glaring indications of the prevalent spirit of slavery. The same con-tempt of the black man—the same disposition to trample on his rights and to lord it over his person, follows him, whatever *degree* of emancipation he may have obtained, and in whatever part of the nation he takes his refuge. Though we had in view only the wrongs of the colored people in New-England, we should feel ourselves compelled to take our present stand, and vindicate their rights as brethren, as men, and as Americans.[24]

Abolitionists everywhere asserted that Negroes and whites should be judged and treated according to the same standards in the apportioning not only of civil rights but also of economic and educational opportunities. In its Declaration of Sentiments the American Anti-Slavery Society announced in 1833 that

all persons of color who possess the qualifications which are demanded of others, ought to be admitted forthwith to the enjoyment of the same privileges, and the exercise of the same prerogatives, as others; and . . . the paths of preferment, of wealth, and of intelligence, should be opened as widely to them as to persons of a white complexion.[25]

Schools, like Oberlin College and the Noyes Academy in New Hampshire, which admitted Negroes on equal terms with whites,[26] bore out these principles, as did Charles Sumner's argument in the Roberts Case in 1849 that separate schools were unequal and threatened cleavages in society.[27] And Samuel J. May, summing up the concept in a statement which avoided many of the pitfalls of prejudice into which his colleagues fell, averred that "all we demand for them is that negroes shall be permitted, encouraged, assisted to become as wise, as virtuous, and as rich as they can, and be acknowedged to be just what they have become, and be treated accordingly." [28]

Yet these appeals to the efficacy of education and economic betterment reveal the middle-class values to which almost all abolitionists subscribed and which both compound and explain much of the ambivalence in the antislavery movement. As middle-class Americans, abolitionists, naturally enough, measured the Negroes against middle-class standards, and to those standards they expected the Negroes to conform—Negroes who were generally ex-slaves from the lowest and most abject class in America. Assuredly the American Anti-Slavery Society was eager to uplift them to "an equality with the whites" but only after carefully disclaiming that it approved any such non-middle-class shenanigans as adopting colored children, encouraging interracial marriages or "exciting the people of color to assume airs." [29]

It was expected, then, that the Negroes should adapt themselves to the values of the white community, should, as one abolitionist advised, submit to prejudice "with the true dignity of meekness" so that their critics might be stilled. Thus was fulfilled the stereotype of the malleable, willing and docile colored man. Still, on limited occasions, the same writer observed, the Negroes should take a positive stand. They should demand admission to the public schools, they should organize or join lyceum groups, they should acquire knowledge and education. And, he said in a condensed version of a middle-class *Poor Richard's*, they should organize uplifting visits to their poor and degraded brethren and teach them "temperance . . . cleanliness, neatness, strict honesty, and all that belong to good morality." [30] In addition to these virtues, the American Anti-Slavery Society agents were admonished to instill in the free people of color

the importance of domestic order, and the performance of relative duties in families; of correct habits; command of temper and courteous manners. Also the duty and advantages of industry and economy; promptness and fidelity in the fulfillment of contracts or obligations, whether written or verbal; and encourage them in the acquisition of property, especially of real estate in fee simple, particularly dwellings for their own families. Present their duties and privileges as citizens, and encourage them to become voters, and to secure equal privileges with other citizens. . . .[31]

Others, varying little from the standard reforming attitudes of the day but less optimistic about raising the Negro to the middle class, urged him to adopt their own conception of lower-class standards. He should learn a trade and become a mechanic. Since these abolitionists categorized the social strata in such a way that the hardy mechanic always fell comfortably below the solid middle class, the Negro was bracketed, at worst, with the Irish hod carrier, and at best only identified with the honest toiler.[32]

Sometimes in the abolitionists' arguments one discovers strong overtones of ordinary self-interest. The *Anti-Slavery Almanac* assured its readers, for example, that emancipated Negroes would not flock to the North. Let no one be perturbed, the *Almanac* urged in unctuous tone. "If the slaves are gradually set free, they must leave the place where they are, (and will be likely to go to the North,) that they may not interfere with the slavery which remains. But if they are all set free at once, they may continue where they are." Putting the argument in other terms, emancipated Negroes would be a great boon to the economy not only in the South but in the North as well.[33] "The southern laborers, when free and paid," C. C. Burleigh had said, "would buy of us many comforts and conveniences not allowed them now . . . which would give new activity to our shops and mills and shipping, and steadier employment, and, most likely, higher wages, to all kinds of labor here." [34] Thus emancipation would not inconvenience the North with a mass of freed slaves; it would rather prove quite profitable.

Still, there was the thorny issue of defining the social position of the Negro in a predominantly white society. Many of the same abolitionists who demanded so unfalteringly no association with slaveholders found it ticklishly difficult to espouse social intercourse with Negroes and almost impossible to champion holy wedlock with those of black skin. In theory and in conscience, of course, they deplored the bans on interracial marriage; yet in practice they as often betrayed an opposite sentiment.[35] For his own part, Garrison defended the ideal goal but reconciled it with practical reality. "At the present time," he said expediently, "mixed marriages would be in bad taste. . . ."[36] Elizur Wright, however, scornfully ridiculed such temporizing over prejudice. "Pray, what is the matter? we ask of a generous and enlightened public," he snapped viciously.

The reply is couched with quaking apprehension, in the appalling interrogatory; *would you have your daughter marry a negro?* And the utter slavery to which this tyrant prejudice has reduced everything that is noble and good in the land, is evinced by nothing more clearly than by the pains taking of even abolitionists to show that colored men *may be* enfranchised and elevated without bringing on the dreaded consequence.[37]

It seemed necessary, in the end, to plaster over the tissue and to allay white fears. Mrs. Child, echoing the frequent antislavery assertion that there were scarcely enough abolitionists in the South to account for the evidences of miscegenation there, insisted that to say that abolitionists wished amalgamation was "a false charge, got up by the enemies of the cause, and used as a bugbear to increase the prejudices of the community." In fact, she added, "by universal emancipation we want to *stop* amalgamation."[38] More reassuring to those who hoped that the issues raised by by social equality would fail to materialize was Samuel G. Howe's commentary made after a close study of Canadian Negroes. "Upon the whole," he observed,

. . . the experience of the Canadian refugees goes to show that there need be no anxiety upon the score of amalgamation of races in the United States. With freedom, and protection of their legal rights; with an open field for industry, and opportunities for mental and moral culture, colored people will not seek relationship with whites, but will follow their natural affinities, and marry among themselves.[39]

The social distance decreed by class identification provided perhaps the most common and satisfactory framework for abolitionists' contacts with free Negroes. Thus, steeped in middle-class values and having identified the Negroes with the laboring classes, the antislavery band frequently assumed the patronizing air of the uplifter and the saved toward the downtrodden and unwashed. James G. Birney, speaking from a slaveholding background, observed that without question emancipation would, "where the superior intelligence of the master was acknowledged, produce on the part of the beneficiaries, the most entire and cordial reliance on his counsel and friendship."[40] And Sumner, in the Roberts Case, urged that "the vaunted superiority of the white race imposes corresponding duties. The faculties with which they are endowed, and the advantages they possess, must be exercised for the good of all. If the colored people are ignorant, degraded, and unhappy," he asserted with a fine sense of noblesse oblige, "then should they be especial objects of care." [41]

Such paternalism was, to be sure, most benign. At times, however, it was most insufferable. "The more I mingle with your people," Angelina Grimké wrote to Sarah Douglass in a display of tactlessness as gargantuan as it was overbearing,

the more I feel for their oppressions and desire to sympathize in their sorrows. Joshua Leavitt threw out a new and delightful idea on this subject on our way to Bloomfield. He said he believed the Lord had a great work for the colored people to do, and that your long continued afflictions and humiliations was the furnace in which He was purifying you from the dross[,] the tin[,] and the reprobate silver, that you might come out like gold seven times refined. I Hav[e] thought of this and fully believ[e] you will after all get up abov[e] us and be the favored instruments [to?] carry pure and undefiled Religion to the Heathen World. May the Lord lift you from the dung hill and set you among princes. . . .[42]

Helping the Lord hoist the poor Negroes off the dung hill was, as it often turned out, an arduous and dangerous chore, but one which gave the abolitionists a chance many of them coveted to become martyrs in the cause. To defend the Negro in court, to speak on his behalf before hostile audiences, to be harried from town after town by the frenzied mob was the stuff of which martyrdom was made. And the genuine joy in the experience of such martyrdom only enhanced the rewards of protective guardianship, as those who braved the mob when Pennsylvania Hall was burned well knew. Confronting the hostile elements, the stalwart women of the Female Anti-Slavery Convention "maintain[ed] the perilled cause to the last." As they adjourned "the colored members of the convention were protected by their white sisters, and Oh! Shame to say," one of the white sisters wrote, "at both were thrown a shower of stones." [43] And then, Oh! Shame to say, the brand new hall was set ablaze and totally destroyed.

In their enthusiasm to elevate the Negro, the abolitionists frequently carried on their shoulders an early version of the White Man's Burden. They taught their children in heavily freighted moral tales that "Negroes, even poor, degraded, despised slaves, are not without reason and understanding. [And that] many of them have a large share of sagacity." Go forth, they directed even the toddlers, instruct the poor and ignorant; become teachers, and help train the Negroes themselves to become missionaries that they may enlighten "their countrymen who are in ignorance and darkness." [44] The adults themselves set the initial example. When Helen Benson, daughter of Rhode Island abolitionist George Benson, was married to Garrison, she refused to allow cake at her wedding or to wear fancy clothes lest she be a poor model for the Negroes to follow.[45] Theodore Weld also cast himself as an exemplar of the good. "I attend Church with our colored friends," he wrote; "but," he honestly admitted, "I do it to cast my lot with them; and," he contentedly concluded, "tho not spiritually edified, I find joy and peace in it." [46]

It was, however, a far more difficult thing for the same abolitionists to follow through, unhestitatingly and courageously, the implications of their theories, to work unfalteringly and without equivocation, straight on to free the slave and obtain equality for the free Negro. Certainly the abolitionists were almost universally too forthright and too dedicated to be faithless to their ideals; certainly they did not knowingly forsake their plighted word. Still it was a constant fact of the antislavery crusade that it was clearly marked by the constant temporizing of its participants.[47] In Ohio, some Lane students objected when one of their number took up residence with Cincinnati Negro families while he was working among them because they thought it would be harmful to their project.[48] Throughout the North antislavery societies debated the questions "Ought abolitionists to encourage colored persons in joining Anti-Slavery Societies?" or "Is it expedient for Abolitionists to encourage social intercourse between white and colored families?" And their composite response was at best an equivocal "perhaps." [49]

This political temporizing was not, of course, without its reasons, particularly in the light of mobs and physical violence provoked by extremists. Some abolitionists, of course, merely thought of public relations and how best to draw support to the cause. Birney, for his part, thought it enough to strive for equal civil rights without, at the same time, trying for social equality. Too much too soon, he argued, would mean a denial of all rights to the Negro.[50] So too the American Anti-Slavery Society, after the serious antiabolitionist riots in New York in 1834, rejected charges that they supported amalgamation or attacked the Constitution. "We disclaim, and entirely disapprove," they asserted, "the language of a hand-bill recently circulated in this City the tendency of which is thought to be to excite resistance to the Laws. Our principle is, that even hard laws are to be submitted to by all men, until they can by peaceable means be altered." [51]

The abolitionists were painfully aware of their actions, yet in good conscience they believed that their course was the better part of wisdom and thus did not compromise their valor. Arthur Tappan for one was so fearful lest his earlier activities be misconstrued that he assured A. F. Stoddard of Glasgow in 1863 that "if . . . you should know of any one's charging me with any gross assault on the fastidiousness of the age, when

I became the avowed friend of the colored man, you may set it down to the score of ignorance or malignant falsehood." [52] But Sarah Forten, member of the actively antislavery Negro family of Philadelphia, understood. "How much of this leaven still lingers in the hearts of our white brethren and sisters is oftentimes made manifest to us," she wrote, referring specifically to an abolitionist who was comfortable with Negroes only under cover of night; "but when we recollect what great sacrifices to public sentiment they are called upon to make," she generously added, "we cannot wholly blame them." [53]

Briefly, then, the antislavery movement was beset, throughout its history, by a fundamental ambivalence. Never could the abolitionists decide collectively, and infrequently individually, whether the Negro was equal or inferior to the white; whether social equality for the Negro should be stressed or whether it should be damped; whether civil and social rights should be granted him at once or only in the indefinite and provisional future; whether, in fact, social and civil rights should be granted or whether only civil rights should be given him. The abolitionists, furthermore, were torn between a genuine concern for the welfare and uplift of the Negro and a paternalism which was too often merely the patronizing of a superior class. And their forthright concern for the Negro was still more qualified by an unhappy degree of temporizing.

These are the hallmarks of a critical and fundamental ambivalence. When such a quandary existed over the position and treatment of the free Negro and over the very nature of the beings to be freed, abolitionist temporizing becomes understandable. When immediate emancipation as a plan of abolition was translated to mean only immediate repentance of the sin of slavery, the needs of the human beings who were slaves were ignored. The abolitionists had sought solace in abstractions about humanity. And their hesitancy and confusion about the question of race illuminate much of the contention and indecision within the antislavery movement— a movement baffled and torn by ambivalence.

NOTES

1. The abolitionists were defined and set off from their contemporaries by their opposition to slavery and their concern for the welfare of the slaves, a concern which usually embraced the free Negroes as well. This article is not, however, designed to compare abolitionists as a group with nonabolitionists but rather to explore the variations within the group.

2. See, for example, Leon Litwack, "The Abolitionist Dilemma: The Antislavery Movement and the Northern Negro," *New England Quarterly* 34 (1961): 50–73; and his *North of Slavery: The Negro in the Free States, 1790–1860* (Chicago: University of Chicago Press, 1961). See also Larry Gara, Louis Filler, Gerda Lerner,

Stanley Elkins for considerations of prejudice. For psychological probing see David Donald, Hazel Wolf, Clifford Griffin, Martin Duberman.

3. John L. Thomas, *The Liberator, William Lloyd Garrison, A Biography* (Boston: Little, Brown & Co., 1963), p. 153.

4. Quoted in Wendell Phillips Garrison and Francis Jackson Garrison, *William Lloyd Garrison, 1805–1879; The Story of His Life as Told by His Children*, 4 vols. (New York, 1885–89), III, p. 283.

5. American Anti-Slavery Society, *Proceedings of the Anti-Slavery Convention, Assembled at Philadelphia, December 4, 5, and 6, 1833* (New York, 1833), p. 19.

6. James Miller McKim to Samuel J. May, May 20 [1862], in Samuel J. May Papers, Cornell University.

7. Henry C. Wright to Maria Weston Chapman, May 2, 1839, in Weston Papers, Antislavery Collection, Boston Public Library.

8. Samuel J. May, Sermon delivered May 29, 1831, in Boston, as reported in *Liberator*, July 23, 1831.

9. *Abolitionist*, I (Jan. 1833), as quoted in Merton L. Dillon, "The Failure of the American Abolitionists," *Journal of Southern History* 25 (1959): 167. Lewis Tappan, Diary entry [Apr. 1836], as quoted in Litwack, *North of Slavery*, p. 218. See also Garrison's July 4, 1829 oration in *Garrison*, I, pp. 133–34; Susan Cabot, *What Have We, as Individuals, To Do With Slavery* (American Anti-Slavery Society, *Anti-Slavery Tract No. 15.* New York, 1855), pp. 3–4; Beriah Green, *American Anti-Slavery Reporter*, I (June 1834), p. 88; and Birney to William Wright, June 20, 1845, in *Letters of James Gillespie Birney, 1831–1857*, ed. Dwight L. Dumond, 2 vols. (New York: D. Appleton-Century Co., 1938), II, p. 947.

10. This ideological ambivalence is reflected in the cleavages within the antislavery movement over the appropriate courses of action to be pursued. These cleavages have already been well examined in a variety of studies on antislavery published since 1935. Whether to take political action or to regard it as damaging to the requisite moral fervor, whether to expend time and funds on schools, give aid to fugitives and buy freedom for individual slaves or to work exclusively to propagate the antislavery faith are debates not only about means but also about the basic concepts of antislavery.

11. Lydia Maria Child, *An Appeal in Favor of that Class of Americans Called Africans*, orig. ed. 1833 (New York, 1836), p. 171.

12. William Henry Seward, *Argument in Defense of William Freeman on his Trial for Murder . . .* 4th ed. (Auburn, N. Y., 1846), pp. 8–9. See also C. T. C. Follen, *Works with a Memoir of His Life* [by Mrs. E. L. Follen], 5 vols. (Boston, 1841), I, pp. 627–28.

13. John Rankin, *Letters on American Slavery Addressed to Mr. Thomas Rankin . . .* 5th ed. (Boston, 1838), pp. 10–11. See also Lewis Tappan, *The Life of Arthur Tappan* (New York, 1870), p. 131; James A. Thome and J. Horace Kimball, *Emancipation in the West Indies. A Six Months Tour in Antigua, Barbados, and Jamaica in the Year 1837* (American Anti-Slavery Society, *Anti-Slavery Examiner No. 7.* New York, 1838), p. 75; and Sallie Holley to Gerrit Smith, Nov. 17, 1865, in the Smith Miller Papers, Syracuse University.

14. Charles Follen, "The Cause of Freedom in Our Country," *Quarterly Anti-Slavery Magazine* 2 (Oct. 1836): 65.

15. Charles Calistus Burleigh, *Slavery and the North* (New York [1855]), p. 4. Rankin essentially held the same view, but thought that it would take a long time to raise the Negro; see *Letters on American Slavery*, pp. 10–11.

16. Edmund Quincy to Caroline Weston, Feb. 1, 1846, in Weston Papers. A

year later Quincy complained about Frederick Douglass' independence (what he thought was Douglass' overcharging the *American Anti-Slavery Standard* for copy supplied) by observing that "These niggers, like Kings, are kittle cattle to shoe behind." Quincy to Caroline Weston, July 2, 1847, in Weston Papers.

17. Theodore Parker, *John Brown's Expedition Reviewed in a Letter from Theodore Parker, at Rome, to Francis Jackson, Boston* (Boston, 1860), p. 14.

18. Samuel Gridley Howe, *The Refugees from Slavery in Canada West. Report to the Freedmen's Inquiry Commission* (Boston, 1864), pp. 21–22.

19. Richard Hildreth, *Archy Moore: The White Slave*, 1st ed.; 1836 (New York, 1856), p. 264.

20. As reported in Henry B. Stanton to Joshua Leavitt, Mar. 10, 1834, in *American Anti-Slavery Reporter*, I (April 1834), p. 54.

21. James Miller McKim, *The Freedman of South Carolina* . . . (Philadelphia, 1862), p. 9. See also *Letters from Port Royal. Written at the Time of the Civil War*, ed. Elizabeth Ware Pearson (Boston: W. B. Clarke Co., 1906), pp. 102–3, 315–16; The *Anti-Slavery Record* 3 (Feb. 1837): 15; *Letters of Theodore Dwight Weld, Angelina Grimké Weld and Sarah Grimké, 1822–1844*, eds. Gilbert H. Barnes and Dwight L. Dumond 2 vols. (New York: D. Appleton-Century Co., 1934), II, p. 524; and Leon Litwack, *North of Slavery*, p. 223.

22. In the Western Papers one may find numerous examples of the patronizing antislavery atittude and of Negro response to it. See also Filler, *Crusade Against Slavery*, p. 143. In particular note Frederick Douglass to Maria Weston Chapman, Mar. 29, 1846, Western Papers; and Martin Robinson Delany, *The Condition, Elevation, Emigration, and Destiny of the Colored People of the United States Politically Considered* (Philadelphia, 1852), pp. 25–29.

23. Antislavery literature contains many illustrations of the preference for lighter-skinned Negroes. See Samuel May Jr., *The Fugitive Slave Law and Its Victims* (American Anti-Slavery Society, *Anti-Slavery Tract No. 18* [New York, 1855]); George Bourne, *Slavery Illustrated in its Effects Upon Woman and Domestic Society* (Boston, 1837); Hildreth's *Archy Moore;* and William I. Bowditch, *White Slavery in the United States* (American Anti-Slavery Society, *Anti-Slavery Tract No. 2* [New York, 1855]); see also in this connection Theodore Dwight Weld, *American Slavery as it is: Testimony of a Thousand Witnesses* (New York, 1839); and the juvenile [Jonathan Walker], *A Picture of Slavery, for Youth. By the Author of "The Branded Hand" and "Chattelized Humanity"* (Boston, n.d.).

24. This is a summary given by D. T. Kimball and F. Laine to *Genius of Temperance*, Aug. 22, 1833, as reported in *Liberator*, Sept. 28, 1833. Similar demands for equality of treatment can be found in Child, *Appeal*, pp. 195–208.

25. American Anti-Slavery Society, *Proceedings of the Anti-Slavery Convention, Assembled at Philadelphia*, contains the Declaration of Sentiments.

26. See *Liberator*, Oct. 25, 1834, for information about the Noyes Academy.

27. Charles Sumner, "Equality before the Law: Unconstitutionality of Separate Colored Schools in Massachusetts. Argument before the Supreme Court of Massachusetts, in the Case of Sarah C. Roberts *v.* The City of Boston . . .," in *The Works of Charles Sumner* (Boston, 1872), II, pp. 327–76.

28. Samuel Joseph May, *Some Recollections of Our Anti-Slavery Conflict* (Boston, 1869), p. 29. See also Birney, *Letters*, II, p. 945; and Garrison, *Garrison*, I, p. 148.

29. Executive Committee of the American Anti-Slavery Society to Mayor Cornelius Lawrence of New York, July 16, 1834, included in the microfilm printing of *Liberator*, between 1833 and 1834, reel 1.

30. This entire argument appeared in a series of articles, signed "S. T. U.," which

appeared in *Liberator*, Feb. 11, 18, 25, and Mar. 3, 1832. The quotations are from the first and last issues, respectively.

31. Executive Committee of the American Anti-Slavery Society to its agents, n.d. [1834–35?], included in the microfilm printing of *Liberator*, between 1833 and 1834, reel 1.

32. See, for example, the *Anti-Slavery Record*, 1 (June 1835): 68, urging that Negroes be apprenticed at good trades. And see also the commentary reprinted by *Liberator*, Mar. 31, 1837, from the Bangor *Mechanic*, in which it is made quite clear that the laborer is quite aware that the middle class looks down on the working class. See also, for comparisons with the Irish, Hildreth, *Archy Moore*, p. 264; Sarah Grimké to Elizabeth Pease [May 20? 1838], in *Weld-Grimké Letters*, II, p. 679; William Allen Diary, Nov. 10, 1863, State Historical Society of Wisconsin.

33. The *Anti-Slavery Almanac* (1837 and 1839). The quotation is from the earlier volume, p. 44. The self-interest showed in other ways as well. Defending what later became Radical Republican doctrine, Maria Weston Chapman wrote to Lizzy (Chapman) Laugel (Sept. 24, 1862) that "black *soldiers* would save our Armies, & black *citizens* our *republican institutions*." Weston Papers. And Wendell Phillips also unconsciously suggested the same prior self-concern when he spoke at the *Liberator's* 20th anniversary celebration: "My friends, if we never free a slave, we have at least freed ourselves in the effort to emancipate our brother man." Quoted in Garrison, *Garrison*, III, p. 320.

34. Burleigh, *Slavery and the North*, pp. 8–9.

35. See Birney, *Letters*, I, p. 397; Garrison, *Garrison*, II, p. 356; *Anti-Slavery Record*, 1 (June 1835): 71; and Gilbert H. Barnes, *The Antislavery Impulse, 1830–1844* (New York: D. Appleton-Century Co., 1933), p. 274, note 20. See also Louis Ruchames, "Race, Marriage and Abolition in Massachusetts," *Journal of Negro History* 40 (1955): 250–73, on the fight for repeal of discriminatory marriage laws.

36. *Liberator*, Aug. 13, 1831.

37. [Elizur Wright Jr.], "Caste in the United States: A Review," *Quarterly Anti-Slavery Magazine* 2 (Jan. 1837): 177.

38. Lydia Maria Child, *Anti-Slavery Catechism* (Newburyport, 1836), pp. 31–32.

39. Howe, *Refugees from Slavery*, p. 33.

40. Quoted in *The Legion of Liberty and Force of Truth, Containing the Thoughts, Words, and Deeds, of Some Prominent Apostles, Champions and Martyrs* (New York, 1843), n.p.

41. Sumner, "Equality before the Law," II, p. 376.

42. In Angelina and Sarah Grimké to Sarah Douglass, Feb. 22, 1837, *Weld-Grimké Letters*, I, pp. 364–65. Gerda Lerner contends that the Grimké sisters were almost if not totally above prejudice in "The Grimké Sisters and the Struggle against Race Prejudice," *Journal of Negro History* 48 (1963): 277–91.

43. Letter from a New York woman, May 18, 1838, in *Liberator*, May 25, 1838.

44. From a story in the Juvenile Department, signed "H. Sabbath School Treasury," *Liberator*, Jan. 14, 1832. The Juvenile column was a regular feature in the early years of the *Liberator*. Henry C. Wright was designated American Anti-Slavery Society agent to children.

45. Garrison, *Garrison*, I, p. 427.

46. Weld to Sarah and Angelina Grimké, Dec. 15 [1837], in *Weld-Grimké Letters*, I, p. 496. A similar viewpoint turns up in Unitarian observations quite frequently as a rejection of emotional-evangelical enthusiasms.

47. In a letter to Lewis Tappan, Weld, for example, wrote concerning a slave case in Connecticut that "not one of the Abolitionists here [in Hartford] was willing

to appear *openly* in the matter as the friend of the compla[i]nant. Brother Tyler and myself who are the only persons known publickly in the case as friends of the compla[i]nant, have been and are still plentifully threatened with mob vengeance." June 8, 1837, *Weld-Grimké Letters*, I, p. 399.

48. *Liberator*, Jan. 10, 1835.

49. From Litwack, *North of Slavery*, p. 218.

50. Birney to Weld, July 26, 1834, *Weld-Grimké Letters*, I, p. 163.

51. *Liberator*, July 19, 1834.

52. Arthur Tappan to A. F. Stoddard, Aug. 27, 1863, in Tappan, *Tappan*, pp. 201–2.

53. Sarah Forten to Angelina Grimké, Apr. 15, 1837, *Weld-Grimké Letters*, I, p. 380.

24. LEON LITWACK, North of Slavery (1961)*

The most thorough account of race relations in the North during the ante-bellum period is Leon Litwack's *North of Slavery*. In this important study, Professor Litwack of the University of California at Berkeley proved that segregation of the races was as pronounced in the pre-Civil War North as it was in the post-Civil War South. In this selection, Litwack discusses the frequently strained relations between black and white abolitionists and describes the different approaches adopted by each racial group in the anti-slavery crusade.

The widely publicized activities of white antislavery workers and the commanding figures of William Lloyd Garrison, Wendell Phillips, and Theodore Weld have tended to obscure the important and active role of the Negro abolitionist. The antislavery movement was not solely a white man's movement. Through their own newspapers, conventions, tracts, orations, and legislative petitions, Negroes agitated for an end to southern bondage and northern repression. The white abolitionist encountered strong and often violent public opposition, but the Negro abolitionist risked even greater hostility, for his very presence on the antislavery platform challenged those popular notions which had stereotyped his people as passive, meek, and docile. As a common laborer, the Negro might be tolerated, even valued, for his services; as an antislavery agitator, he was frequently mobbed.

Negro abolitionism preceded by several years the appearance of Garrison and *The Liberator*. Encouraged by the post-Revolutionary emancipation movement, Negroes worked with sympathetic whites to remove the last traces of slavery in the North and to call for its abolition

* From Leon Litwack, *North of Slavery* (Chicago: University of Chicago Press, 1961), pp. 230–46. Copyright © 1961 by The University of Chicago Press. Reprinted by permission.

in the South. As early as 1797, four illegally manumitted North Carolina Negroes, who had fled to the North to escape re-enslavement, petitioned Congress to consider "our relief as a people." Three years later, a group of Philadelphia free Negroes appealed directly to Congress to revise the federal laws concerning the African trade and fugitive slaves and to adopt "such measures as shall in due course emancipate the whole of their brethren from their present situation." [1] In addition to legislative petitions, meetings commemorating the abolition of the African slave trade or the end of slavery in a particular state afforded opportunities for such prominent Negro leaders as Peter Williams, Nathaniel Paul, William Hamilton, and Joseph Sidney to voice their sentiments on public issues.[2] The organization of independent churches, Free African societies, Masonic lodges, and anti-colonization meetings further intensified a growing race consciousness and helped to arouse the Negro community in several areas to a more vigorous defense of its civil rights.

Four years before the publication of the first issue of *The Liberator*, two Negro leaders, John Russwurm and Samuel E. Cornish, launched the first Negro newspaper—*Freedom's Journal*—in an effort to disseminate useful ideas and information and to attract public attention to the plight of those still in bondage. In the first issue, the editors announced that Negroes had to plead their own cause: "Too long have others spoken for us. Too long has the publick been deceived by misrepresentations." [3] During its two years of publication, *Freedom's Journal* featured articles on the evils of slavery and intemperance, the importance of education and the progress of Negro schools, literary and historical selections, moral lessons, information on the various Afro-American benevolent societies, and a discussion of colonization. Cornish subsequently withdrew from the partnership and established a short-lived newspaper, *The Rights of All*, and Russwurm abandoned his editorial duties to join the colonizationists.[4]

Negro antislavery agitation took on a more aggressive tone in 1829 as David Walker, a Boston clothing dealer and local agent for *Freedom's Journal*, contributed a powerful tract to abolitionist literature—*Walker's Appeal, in Four Articles*. Addressing his sentiments to the "coloured citizens" of the world, but particularly to those of the United States, Walker described American Negroes as "the most degraded, wretched, and abject set of beings that ever lived since the world began." Indeed, he asked, "Can our condition be any worse?—Can it be more mean and abject? If there are any changes, will they not be for the better, though they may appear for the worst at first? Can they get us any lower? Where can they get us? They are afraid to treat us worse, for they know well, the day they do it they are gone."

In Walker's estimation, four major factors accounted for this wretched state of affairs: slavery, ignorance, "the preachers of Jesus

Christ," and the African colonization movement. Consequently, Negroes had to strive for economic and educational improvement and resist the encroachments of the colonizationists. ("America is as much our country, as it is yours.") The southern Negro, on the other hand, faced an even greater challenge, for he had to strike directly and perhaps violently for his freedom as a natural right. Once that thrust for liberty had been made, Walker advised, "make sure work—do not trifle, for they will not trifle with you—they want us for their slaves, and think nothing of murdering us in order to subject us to that wretched condition—therefore, if there is an *attempt* made by us, kill or be killed." To prevent the outbreak of racial war, Walker warned the white man, recognize the legal rights of Negroes. There can be no mistaking the alternative. "Remember, Americans, that we must and shall be free and enlightened as you are, will you wait until we shall, under God, obtain our liberty by the crushing arm of power? Will it not be dreadful for you? I speak Americans for your good. We must and shall be free I say, in spite of you. . . . And wo, wo, will be to you if we have to obtain our freedom by fighting." [5]

Within a year after its publication, the apparent popularity—or notoriety—of Walker's pamphlet warranted a third edition. The often violent reaction to its contents and the mysterious death of the author in 1830 undoubtedly assisted its circulation.[6] Indeed, it had already caused some consternation in the North, and it understandably created outright alarm in portions of the South. Already beset by a growing fear of slave uprisings, the South could not afford to tolerate the potentially explosive appeal of a Boston clothing dealer. The governor of North Carolina denounced it as "an open appeal to their [the slaves'] natural love of liberty . . . and throughout expressing sentiments totally subversive of all subordination in our slaves"; the mayor of Savannah wrote to the mayor of Boston requesting that Walker be arrested and punished, and Richmond's mayor reported that several copies of *Walker's Appeal* had been found in the possession of local free Negroes; the governors of Georgia and North Carolina submitted the pamphlet to their state legislatures for appropriate action; and the Virginia legislature held secret sessions to consider proper measures to prevent the pamphlet's circulation. Finally, four southern states—Georgia, North Carolina, Mississippi, and Louisiana—seized upon the pamphlet to enact severe restrictions to cope with such "seditious" propaganda.[7]

The South was not alone in its critical reaction. Walker's medicine for the ills of American Negroes was too strong for many white abolitionists. "A more bold, daring, inflammatory publication, perhaps, never issued from the press of any country," antislavery publisher Benjamin Lundy declared. "I can do no less than set the broadest seal of condemnation on it." [8] Lundy's disciple, William Lloyd Garrison, had just launched his own career as an aggressive antislavery publicist and was more equivocal in his reaction. The editor of *The Liberator* found it difficult to reconcile his belief in nonresistance with his unconcealed admiration of Walker's courage and forthrightness. While deploring the circulation of this "most injudicious publication" and "its general spirit," Garrison admitted that it contained "many valuable truths and seasonable warnings." [9]

The appearance of *The Liberator* in 1831 and the formation of the American Anti-Slavery Society two years later thus found northern Negroes already engaged in a variety of abolitionist activities. In addition to publishing a newspaper and several antislavery tracts, Negroes had taken steps to coordinate their actions through annual national conventions. On September 15, 1830, delegates gathered in Philadelphia's Bethel Church to launch the first in a series of such conventions. Against a background of increasing repressive legislation in the North, the delegates adopted an address to the free Negro population, pointing out that their present "forlorn and deplorable situation" demanded immediate action. Where Negroes were subjected to constant harassment and denied even the right of residence, the most recent and blatant case being Ohio, such action would have to take the form of emigration to Canada. There, the convention advised, Negroes could establish themselves "in a land where the laws and prejudices of society will have no effect in retarding their advancement to the summit of civil and religious improvement." Meanwhile, those Negroes who chose to remain in the United States would have to utilize every legal means to improve their political and economic position. Before adjourning, the delegates called upon Negroes to establish auxiliary societies and send delegates to the next annual convention. [10]

Convening annually up to 1835 and periodically thereafter, the national Negro conventions regularly condemned the American Colonization Society, deprecated segregation and "oppressive, unjust and unconstitutional" legislation, stressed the importance of organization, education, temperance, and economy, and set aside the Fourth of July as a day of "humiliation, fasting and prayer" when Negroes would ask for divine intervention to break "the shackles of slavery." [11] Meanwhile, the formation of auxiliary state organizations, temperance groups, moral-reform societies, and educational associations created an unprecedented amount of unity and activity among northern Negroes, developed new leadership, and contributed mightily to the strength of the newly formed white antislavery societies.

While engaged in these independent activities, Negro abolitionists also hailed the appearance of a new militancy among their white supporters; they not only welcomed the publication of *The Liberator* but actually outnumbered white subscribers in the early years. "It is a remarkable fact," William Lloyd Garrison wrote in 1834, "that, of the whole number of subscribers to the *Liberator*, only about one-fourth are white. The paper, then, belongs emphatically to the people of color—it is their organ." [12] In addition to contributing articles and letters to the antislavery press, Negroes also attended and addressed abolitionist conventions and, notwithstanding some opposition, served as members of the executive committee and board of managers of both the American Anti-Slavery Society and its later rival, the American and Foreign Anti-Slavery Society. [13]

Negro abolitionists did not confine their activities to the United States. In the 1840s and 1850s, several of them toured the British Isles to promote antislavery sentiment and raise money for abolitionist enterprises. Englishmen crowded into meeting halls to see and hear leading American Negroes tell of the plight of their people and their own experiences as slaves or freemen. Frederick Douglass, for example, described his years of bondage in the South; William G. Allen told of his narrow escape from an enraged northern mob after proposing to marry a white girl; William and Ellen Craft related their flight to freedom and their subsequent exile to avoid prosecution under the Fugitive Slave Act; and Henry Highland Garnet undoubtedly mentioned the mob that ejected him from a Connecticut boys' academy. [14] While arousing their foreign audiences with these tales of slavery and racial violence, Negroes also found much to amaze them. "Here the colored man feels himself among friends, and not among enemies," one Negro "exile" wrote from England, "among a people who, when they treat him well, do it not in the patronizing (and, of course insulting) spirit, even of hundreds of the American abolitionists, but in a spirit rightly appreciative of the doctrine of human equality." [15] For some of these Negro abolitionists, returning home must have been difficult. After extensive travels in England and Europe, for example, William Wells Brown came back to Philadelphia, only to find himself proscribed from the Chestnut Street omnibus on his first day home. "The omnibuses of Paris, Edinburgh, Glasgow, and Liverpool, had stopped to take me up," he recollected, "but what mattered that? My face was not white, my hair was not straight; and, therefore, I must be excluded from a seat in a third-rate American omnibus." [16]

Both Negro and white abolitionists suffered from internal dissension over fundamental questions of policy and ideology. While the white antislavery societies split over the issues of political action, nonresistance, women's rights, disunion, and the nature of the Constitution, Negroes argued the merits of moral suasion and separate conventions. By 1835, the American Moral Reform Society, dominated largely by Philadelphia Negroes, replaced the regular convention movement. Dedicated to "improving the condition of mankind," the new organization urged Negroes to abandon the use of the terms "colored" and "African," to refrain from holding separate colored conventions, to integrate as fully as possible into white society, to support the equality of women, and to adopt the principles of peace, temperance, brotherly love, and nonresistance "under all circumstances." In adopting such a program, the moral reformers obviously allied themselves with the Garrisonians in the growing factional struggle within the antislavery movement.[17]

The American Moral Reform Society found little support outside the Garrisonian strongholds of Philadelphia and Boston. Meanwhile, New York Negro leaders launched a new weekly newspaper, the *Colored American*, which expressed dismay over the growing split in abolitionist ranks and the activities of the moral reformers. Editor Samuel Cornish noted that the delegates to a recent moral-reform convention had impressed him as "vague, wild, indefinite and confused in their views." Only drastic reorganization and the adoption of a more vigorous program of action could possibly salvage the society. As for their efforts to substitute the term "oppressed Americans" for "colored people," Cornish called this sheer nonsense. "Oppressed Americans! *who are they?*" he asked. "Nonsense brethren!! You are COLORED AMERICANS. The indians are RED AMERICANS, and the white people are WHITE AMERICANS and *you are good as they, and they are no better than you.*" [18]

While scolding the moral reformers, the *Colored American* also engaged in a controversy with the pro-Garrison *National Anti-Slavery Standard* over the advisability of colored conventions. "We oppose all exclusive action on the part of the colored people," the *Standard* announced in June, 1840, "except where the clearest necessity demands it." As long as Negroes contented themselves with separate churches, schools, and conventions, public sentiment would remain unaltered. Instead, Negroes should join with their white friends to demand equal rights as men, not as colored persons, and thus confirm the abolitionists' contention that racial distinctions had no place in American society. The moral reformers enthusiastically indorsed the position of the *Standard*. Other Negro leaders, however, immediately condemned it and upheld the need for independent action. The abolitionists had done much for the Negro, Samuel R. Ward wrote to the editor of the *Standard*, but too many of them "best love the colored man at a distance" and refuse to admit or eradicate their own prejudices. In the meantime, Negroes had to meet and act for themselves.[19]

Although the American Moral Reform Society had a short life, the split in white abolitionist ranks continued to undermine Negro unity. By 1840, Garrisonians shared the field of agitation with the American and Foreign Anti-Slavery Society and the Liberty party. New England and

Philadelphia Negroes generally supported the American Anti-Slavery Society and condemned the critics of Garrison as unworthy of confidence or support. New York Negroes, on the other hand, not only dissociated themselves from the moral reformers but generally indorsed direct political action and contributed to the leadership and campaigns of the Liberty party. At one point, the *Colored American* attempted to restore some semblance of sanity and unity to abolitionists by urging them to avoid peripheral issues and petty bickering and get back to opposing slavery. "Why . . . make governments or anti-governments—resistance or non-resistance—women's rights or men's rights—Sabbaths or anti-Sabbaths, a bone of contention?" The Negro newspaper asked. "None of these should have any thing to do with our Anti-Slavery efforts. *They are neither parts nor parcels of that great and holy cause,* nor should they be intruded into its measures." Rather than promote abolitionist harmony, however, such sentiments, coupled with the editors' indorsement of political action and their refusal to censure Garrison's critics, induced some severe attacks and threats to cut off financial support from the paper. Defending their right to differ with Garrison on any issue and to adopt an independent editorial policy, the editors of the *Colored American* warned Negroes that as long as they permitted white abolitionists to act and think for them, "so long they will outwardly treat us as men, while in their hearts they still hold us as slaves." [20]

In a desperate effort to retain their hold on the antislavery movement, Garrison and his associates made every effort to secure Negro support. In Boston and New Bedford, Negro meetings acclaimed Garrison as a "friend and benefactor" and indorsed his antislavery position.[21] Already abandoned by many of his white followers, Garrison expressed gratification over such reactions. The opposition knew, he wrote, "that, so long as I retain the confidence of my colored friends, all of their machinations against me will prove abortive." [22] Had Garrison known that his most important Negro ally, Frederick Douglass, was about to desert him, he would have had much less cause for optimism.

As late as September 4, 1849, Douglass had insisted that he was a loyal Garrisonian abolitionist, and there was little reason to doubt him. According to the tenets of that faith, he had excoriated the Constitution as "a most foul and bloody conspiracy" against the rights of three million slaves, had supported disunion as the most effective means to remove federal protection from the "peculiar institution," had belittled political action as futile and necessarily compromising, and had advocated moral persuasion rather than violence in attacking slavery.[23] Nevertheless, signs of revolt became increasingly apparent. After founding the *North Star* in 1847 against the advice of his Boston friends and moving from New England to Rochester, Douglass carefully re-evaluated his position and listened to the arguments of various New York abolitionists who had already broken with Garrison. Before long, the Negro leader reached the conclusion that disunion would only place the slaves at the complete mercy of the South, that political action constituted "a legitimate and powerful means for abolishing slavery," that southern bondage would probably have to expire in violence, and that the Constitution made no guarantees to slavery but in fact implied its eventual extinction.[24] In May, 1851, Douglass utilized the annual convention of the American Anti-Slavery Society to proclaim his heresy publicly. "There is roguery somewhere," Garrison reputedly declared as he moved to strike the *North Star* from the list of approved abolitionist publications.[25] Douglass had gone over to the enemy.

Although he voiced his new position on the lecture platform and in the *North Star*, Douglass hoped to avert a complete break with Garrison. "I stand in relation to him something like that of a child to a parent," he wrote to Charles Sumner.[26] Nevertheless, Garrisonian anxiety and alarm soon changed to vigorous denunciation and even personal defamation. *The Liberator* now placed Douglass' editorials in the section usually reserved for proslavery sentiments, and it charged that the Negro leader had betrayed his former friends for the sake of financial gain, that he possessed ambitions to become the spokesman of the colored race, and that he had lost much of his moral fervor and influence.[27] When Douglass reduced the size of his newspaper, one Garrisonian gleefully wrote to an English friend that the Negro editor "has the confidence of very few, the respect . . . of none. Do what he may, we shall take no notice of him, and I think his career—on professedly anti-slavery grounds—will soon come to an end." Although Garrison generally allowed his followers to deal editorially with the Negro upstart, he confided to friends that he regarded Douglass as a malignant enemy, "thoroughly base and selfish," "destitute of every principle of honor, ungrateful to the last degree, and malevolent in spirit," and unworthy of "respect, confidence, or countenance." Such was the thoroughness of the Garrison indictment.[28]

Replying to his critics with equal bitterness, Douglass called them "vigilant enemies" and labeled their Negro followers as "practical enemies of the colored people" and contemptible tools. The Garrisonians had first attempted to silence his newspaper, he charged, and now they sought to expel him from the antislavery fold as a dangerous heretic. "They talk down there [Boston] just as if the Anti-Slavery Cause belonged to them— and as if all Anti-Slavery ideas originated with them and that no man has a right to 'peep or mutter' on the subject, who does not hold letters patent from them." [29] Douglass also sought to clarify his differences with

Garrison, but these appeared to be lost in the bitter editorial war. Before long, Negroes in various parts of the country were meeting to discuss the conflict and to choose sides. Chicago Negroes condemned Garrison's "vile crusade" against "the voice of the colored people"; a Rhode Island convention hailed Douglass as "our acknowledged leader"; and an Ohio gathering decisively defeated a proposal calling on Negroes to abstain from voting in those areas where they enjoyed the franchise. Meanwhile, Garrisonian Negro leaders reiterated the charges of *The Liberator* and claimed to speak for "all the true colored men in the country." [30]

Efforts to reconcile the two antislavery leaders met with no success—only time could heal the deep wounds left by this useless and wasteful struggle. To many Negro and white abolitionists, the entire affair presented a rather sordid and dreary spectacle. "Where is this work of excommunication to end?" Harriet Beecher Stowe wrote Garrison. "Is there but one true anti-slavery church and all others infidels?—Who shall declare which it is." [31] While the dispute helped to reduce the effectiveness of the antislavery movement, it also clearly demonstrated some of the weaknesses in Garrison's ideological and tactical position. Nonresistance, the rejection of political action, disunion, and a proslavery interpretation of the Constitution did not strike many abolitionists in the 1840s and 1850s as being either suitable or realistic weapons with which to abolish southern bondage or northern proscription. Indeed, the final triumph of Garrisonian objectives resulted almost entirely from the employment of strictly non-Garrisonian methods—political agitation and armed force.

Internal dissension hampered but did not stifle the independent activities of Negro abolitionists. Despite the Garrisonian antipathy to "complexional conventions," local and state organizations continued to meet in the 1840s, and several national conventions revived interstate cooperation. On August 15, 1843, Negroes from various states met in Buffalo to consider "their moral and political condition as American citizens." After several heated debates—which partly reflected the growing split in abolitionist ranks—the convention adopted a series of resolutions which denounced the American Colonization Society and the proslavery churches, indorsed the Liberty party, stressed the value of temperance, education, the mechanical arts, and agriculture, and attributed the plight of free Negroes—North and South—to the evils of slavery.[32]

Henry Highland Garnet, a New York Negro leader, hoped to secure from the Buffalo delegates a more aggressive stand against slavery. Indicting the cruelties of southern bondage and praising as martyrs those Negroes who had led revolts for freedom, Garnet delivered a powerful plea to the slave population in tones reminiscent of David Walker's *Appeal*. "Brethren arise, arise!" he declared. "Strike for your lives and liberties. Now is the day and the hour. Let every slave throughout the land do this, and the days of slavery are numbered. You cannot be more oppressed than you have been—you cannot suffer greater cruelties than you have already. *Rather die freemen than live to be slaves.* Remember that you are FOUR MILLIONS! . . . Let your motto be resistance! resistance! RESISTANCE!" Although the Garrisonians had suffered a defeat on the issue of political action, they managed to steer the convention away from such a commitment to physical violence in overthrowing slavery. By a vote of nineteen to eighteen, the delegates refused to indorse Garnet's address. Instead, the convention affirmed its faith in the ultimate righteousness of human government and the abolition of slavery through its instrumentality.[33] Relieved at this outcome, one Garrisonian intimated that Garnet, who had also been one of the first Negroes to indorse the Liberty party, had fallen under the influence of bad advisers. "If it has come to this," Garnet replied, "that I must think as you do, because you are an abolitionist, or be exterminated by your thunder, then I do not hesitate to say that your abolitionism is abject slavery." [34]

Although the Buffalo delegates refused to indorse Garnet's address, its contents and the closeness of the convention vote indicated the emergence of a new militancy among Negro abolitionists. Six years later, Garnet's address and Walker's appeal appeared together in a published pamphlet—reportedly at the expense of an obscure New York farmer, John Brown.[35] An Ohio Negro convention immediately ordered five hundred copies to be "gratuitously" circulated.[36] That same year, a New York Negro editor reminded the governor and legislature of Louisiana that their recent expressions of sympathy for Hungarian rebels might be equally applicable to their own bondsmen. "Strike for your freedom now, at the suggestion of your enslavers," the editor wrote. "Make up your minds to die, rather than bequeath a state of slavery to your posterity." [37]

By the end of the 1840s, the appeals of Garnet and Walker—once deemed too radical—received growing support in Negro conventions, newspapers, and antislavery tracts. Even Frederick Douglass, who had bitterly opposed Garnet's address, abandoned his previous conviction that moral persuasion and nonresistance alone could abolish slavery. While still a loyal Garrisonian, he created a "marked sensation" in 1849 when he told a Faneuil Hall audience that he would "welcome the intelligence tomorrow, should it come, that the slaves had risen in the South, and that the sable arms which had been engaged in beautifying and adorning the South were engaged in spreading death and devastation there." Three years later, Douglass told the national Free Soil party convention that the slaveholders had forfeited their right to live. The potential horrors of a slave insurrection should no longer be allowed to obstruct the path to freedom.

"The slaveholder has been tried and sentenced," he declared in 1857. "He is training his own executioners." The following year, John Brown visited the Douglass home and remained there for several weeks, devoting most of his time to writing financial appeals for a yet unrevealed plan.[38]

NOTES

1. Herbert Aptheker, ed., *A Documentary History of the Negro People in the United States* (New York: Citadel Press, 1951), pp. 39–44.

2. For a convenient guide to the published addresses of these early Negro leaders, see Dorothy P. Porter, "Early American Negro Writings: A Bibliographical Study," *Papers of the Bibliographical Society of America* 39 (1945): 192-268. Especially valuable for an early Negro's views on national affairs is Joseph Sidney, *An Oration, Commemorative of the Abolition of the Slave Trade in the United States; Delivered before the Wilberforce Philanthropic Association, in the City of New York, on the second of January, 1809* (New York, 1809). Copy in Schomburg Collection, New York Public Library.

3. *Freedom's Journal*, March 16, 1827.

4. For some bitter criticism of Russwurm after his conversion to colonization, see Carter Godwin Woodson, ed., *The Mind of the Negro as Reflected in Letters Written During the Crisis, 1800–1860* (Washington, D. C.: The Association for the Study of Negro Life and History, Inc., 1926), pp. 160–63.

5. David Walker, *Walker's Appeal, in Four Articles; together with a Preamble, to the Coloured Citizens of the World, but in particular, and very expressly to those of the United States of America, written in Boston, State of Massachusetts, September 28, 1829.*, 3d ed. (Boston, 1830).

6. See Vernon Loggins, *The Negro Author* (New York: Columbia University Press, 1931), p. 86; Woodson, ed., *Mind of the Negro*, p. 222.

7. Clement Eaton, "A Dangerous Pamphlet in the Old South," *Journal of Southern History* 2 (1936): 323–34.

8. *Genius of Universal Emancipation*, April, 1830; *The Liberator*, January 29, 1831.

9. *The Liberator*, January 29, 1831.

10. "The First Colored Convention," *Anglo-African Magazine* 1 (October 1859): 305–10; Aptheker, *Documentary History*, pp. 102–7.

11. Selected proceedings of several of the national Negro conventions may be found in Aptheker, *Documentary History*, pp. 114–19, 133–37, 141–46, 154–57, 159, 226–33, and 341–57.

12. Francis and Wendell P. Garrison, *William Lloyd Garrison*, 4 vols. (Boston, 1894), I, p. 432.

13. Herbert Aptheker, "The Negro in the Abolitionist Movement," *Essays in the History of the American Negro* (New York: International Publishers, 1945), pp. 154–55; Philip S. Foner, ed., *The Life and Writings of Frederick Douglass*, 4 vols. (New York: International Publishers, 1950–55), I, pp. 33, 426.

14. Benjamin Quarles, "Ministers Without Portfolio," *Journal of Negro History* 39 (1954): 27–42.

15. *The Liberator*, July 22, 1853.

16. Williams Wells Brown, *The American Fugitive in Europe* (Boston, 1855), pp. 312–14.

17. *Minutes of the Fifth Annual Convention for the Improvement of the Free People of Colour in the United States* (Philadelphia, 1835), pp. 4–5, 9, 14–15, 31–32; *The Emancipator*, September 22, 1836; *The Minutes and Proceedings of the First Annual Meeting of the American Moral Reform Society* (Philadelphia, 1837); *Minutes of Proceedings at the Council of the Philadelphia Association for the Moral and Mental Improvement of the People of Color* (Philadelphia, 1837); *National Anti-Slavery Standard*, October 1, 1840.

18. *Colored American*, August 26, September 2, 9, 16, 1837.

19. *National Anti-Slavery Standard*, June 18, July 2, August 20, September 10, October 1, 1840.

20. *Colored American*, October 7, 14, 1837, May 11, August 17, October 5, 19, November 2, 1839.

21. *The Liberator*, June 7, 21, 1839. See also *Eighth Annual Report of the Board of Managers of the Massachusetts Anti-Slavery Society* (Boston, 1840), pp. 36–37; *The Liberator*, October 6, 1837, April 3, 1840; Dwight L. Dumond, ed., *Letters of James Gillespie Birney, 1831–57*, 2 vols. (New York: D. Appleton-Century Co., 1938), I, pp. 575–79.

22. William Lloyd Garrison to Elizabeth Pease, September 1, 1840, Garrison Papers.

23. Foner, *Life and Writings of Frederick Douglass*, II, pp. 49–52.

24. Frederick Douglass, *Life and Times of Frederick Douglass* (Hartford, Conn., 1884), pp. 322–24; Foner, *Life and Writings of Frederick Douglass*, II, pp. 52–53, 149–50, 152–53, 155–57.

25. Foner, *Life and Writings of Frederick Douglass*, II, pp. 53–54, 155–56.

26. Ibid., II, pp. 201–11.

27. *The Liberator*, September 16, 23, 30, December 16, 30, 1853.

28. Samuel May, Jr. to Richard Davis Webb, February 8, 1857, May Papers; William Lloyd Garrison to Samuel J. May, September 5, 1857, September 28, 1860, Garrison Papers.

29. *Frederick Douglass' Paper*, December 9, 1853; Foner, *Life and Writings of Frederick Douglass*, II, p. 270.

30. Foner, *Life and Writings of Frederick Douglass*, II, pp. 61–62; *Minutes of the State Convention of the Colored Citizens of Ohio* (Columbus, 1851), pp. 11–12.

31. Foner, *Life and Writings of Frederick Douglass*, II, p. 64.

32. *National Colored Convention, Buffalo, 1843*, pp. 11, 14–16, 19–22, 25, 27, 31–36.

33. Carter Godwin Woodson, ed., *Negro Orators and their Orations* (Washington, D. C.: The Associated Publishers, Inc., 1925), pp. 150–57; William M. Brewer, "Henry Highland Garnet," *Journal of Negro History* 13 (January, 1928): 46; *National Colored Convention, Buffalo, 1843*, p. 16.

34. *The Liberator*, December 3, 1843.

35. Loggins, *The Negro Author*, p. 192; Woodson, *Negro Orators and Their Orations*, p. 150.

36. *Ohio Colored Convention of 1849*, p. 18.

37. Aptheker, *Documentary History*, pp. 290–91.

38. *North Star*, June 15, 1849; *Frederick Douglass' Paper*, August 20, 1852; William Chambers, *American Slavery and Colour* (London: W. & R. Chambers, 1857), p. 174 n.; Foner, *Life and Writings of Frederick Douglass*, II, p. 88.

VIII

Black Resistance
in the North

While historians have endlessly debated the question of black docility under slavery, no such controversy has developed about the response of northern free blacks. Instead these Afro-Americans have until recently remained almost invisible to scholars and non-scholars alike. Only with the new interest in black history have the writings, speeches, and activities of northern Afro-Americans begun to receive the attention they have always deserved.

The racial ideologies of free blacks during the ante-bellum era spanned the spectrum from assimilation to nationalism. Their method of demonstrating displeasure ranged from indignant protest against discrimination in order to secure a proper share of their rights, to rejection of American society by advocating emigration abroad or separation at home. But then as now, there were no black conservatives in the sense that all Afro-Americans preferred change to preservation of the status quo. Except for a demand that slavery be abolished, however, they favored reform and not revolution. They sought to widen the distribution of rights and benefits under American democracy so that black Americans as well as Anglo-Americans would be included. Believing themselves entitled to the same privileges as other native-born Americans, they wanted the same opportunities for success in the society. Since they represented a tiny minority in an overwhelmingly white society, northern blacks were more likely to adopt the values of middle-class America than were black slaves of the South, many of whom had little contact with white society. Therefore, they found assimilation into American culture more attractive than separation, and protest more feasible than accommodation in any of its numerous forms.

While agreeing on the goals to be sought, Afro-Americans were never in complete agreement over how best to secure these rights, or over whether they were even obtainable. Those who thought it was futile to expect that white Americans would respect black people urged emigration as the only realistic objective. Their ranks increased as the level of despair among black Americans rose. Since emigration was in reality a form of accommodation or even surrender to white racism, most Afro-Americans viewed it as a measure of last resort. During the critical decade of the 1850s when Congressional laws and court decisions appeared to them unusually repressive, the number of Afro-Americans willing to consider this option definitely increased. More might have joined the ranks of the emigrationists had not the outbreak of the Civil War in 1861 bolstered their faith in the efficacy of the democratic process. But most Afro-Americans had no intention of sacrificing their hard labor to the white man without a struggle.

Instead, they preferred to protest against the immediate grievances which they faced in the North and to seek removal of the shackles of slavery for their brothers in the South. The blacks of New England were especially vigorous in protesting against efforts to exclude them from various places of public accommodation, to segregate them in public schools, and to provide separate transportation facilities. Their methods of protest were just as imaginative as those of any twentieth-century civil rights workers. They employed kneel-ins, sit-ins, and pray-ins. They also penned remonstrances to legislatures and organized mass meetings and national conferences to draw up lists of grievances and statements of principle.

Because Afro-Americans were unique in being the only people to have kinsman in slavery, their efforts went beyond those of securing their own personal rights. They advocated the immediate end of all forms of slavery in the United States. Although white abolitionists have received more attention from historians, black abolitionists accomplished most of the dangerous work at the time. Few if any whites were willing to risk everything (as was Harriet Tubman) by going into southern states to whisk slaves away. While a small number of Anglo-Americans lent valuable service in aiding fugitives to escape, most of the rescue work was in the hands of vigilance committees, composed entirely of Afro-Americans, since few if any blacks would trust white people with their lives. Only where fugitive slaves were certain of assistance would they turn to white persons. Despite all efforts of northern abolitionists, the vast majority of runaway slaves escaped with little or no help from Northerners. If one of these fugitives sought aid, naturally it would not be from a white person.

The essays included in this section reveal some of the different ideologies present in the black community from 1830 to 1860. As the essay by Howard Bell indicates, some Afro-Americans found the doctrine of Black Nationalism attractive in the nineteenth century. Since the vast majority of blacks in the United States were still in slavery, advocates of Black Nationalism naturally turned to the African homeland in search for a place to begin the long process of nation building. The appeal to black consciousness and black unity was not only present in the work of black separatists like Martin R. Delany but also in the efforts of black abolitionists. Professor Benjamin Quarles provides a good summary of their efforts. Unwilling to turn their back upon Afro-Americans in slavery, these men risked their lives and fortunes in aiding black fugitives to escape and in finding them a permanent home. By describing the indignant protests of Afro-Americans in Massachusetts, Louis Ruchames shows that blacks saw the need for coalition politics in the 1840s and 1850s. That efforts of blacks and whites to correct injustices against Negroes were most successful in Massachusetts is not surprising since it was also the first northern state to send a black person to the United States Senate.

25. LOUIS RUCHAMES, Jim Crow Railroads in Massachusetts (1956)*

In contrast to many historians, Louis Ruchames, professor of history at the University of Massachusetts, has nothing but praise for the protest activity of abolitionists. Although most of the protests grew out of the refusal of Afro-Americans to acquiesce in the Jim Crow laws in Massachusetts, white abolitionists worked with their black friends in seeking repeal of discriminatory legislation and practices. Ruchames believes that the progressive aspect of contemporary race relations in the Bay State can be traced to the work of this nineteenth-century coalition.

Massachusetts is today in the forefront of those states that have sought to achieve equality of status and opportunity for all racial groups. Its fair employment and fair educational practice laws are among the finest in the country and have achieved notable successes in opening up new opportunities for racial and religious groups within the state. Segregation of Negroes and whites, although it still exists to some extent, is a steadily shrinking element in the social structure of Massachusetts.

How different is this situation from what obtained a century or more ago. In the 1830s and 1840s segregation was the dominant pattern in the state. As late as 1843 Negroes were forbidden to marry whites; they were segregated in the churches, where they occupied the "Negro pew"; they were confined to the most menial occupations; they could not attend the same schools as white children—in Boston this situation continued to 1855; they were segregated on stagecoaches, railroads and steamboats. Writing in 1836, Lydia Maria Child, a prominent author and Abolitionist, charged that "our prejudice against colored people is even more inveterate than it is at the South. The planter is often attached to his Negroes, and lavishes caresses and kind words upon them, as he would on a favorite hound: but our coldhearted, ignoble prejudice admits of no exception—no intermission." [1]

The basic causes of this change are well known. The expansion of

* From Louis Ruchames, "Jim Crow Railroads in Massachusetts," *American Quarterly* 8 (Spring 1956): 61–75. Copyright, 1956, Trustees of the University of Pennsylvania. Reprinted by permission.

industry and the rise of large urban centers seriously weakened the system of caste. The growth of a large middle class whose interests and ideals favored individual freedom and equality before the law was a no less significant factor. Less well known, however, is the day to day activity of a large body of men and women, enrolled in the Abolitionist movement under the leadership of William Lloyd Garrison, whose self-sacrificing efforts on behalf of racial equality in the North, in addition to their efforts against slavery in the South, provided the motive power for the changes that did take place. It was they who exposed segregation and discrimination to the public eye, condemned them unreservedly and organized the campaigns which helped to diminish or eliminate such practices from significant areas of public life.

The first important Abolitionist campaign against segregation began with the appearance of the *Liberator*, edited and published by Garrison, in 1831. In its third issue it called attention to the existing law prohibiting the marriage of Negroes and whites, and demanded its repeal. The movement for repeal reached its peak in the 1840s, and success was finally achieved in 1843. It was in the midst of this campaign that the question of "Jim Crow" cars on certain of the railways of Massachusetts came to the fore.

Railroads had first come into public use in Massachusetts in 1836. Following existing customs on many stagecoaches and passenger vessels, several railroads instituted the practice of segregating Negroes in a separate car. These were the Eastern Railroad, extending at first from Boston to Salem and later reaching the New Hampshire border; the New Bedford and Taunton trunk line; and the Boston and Providence Railroad.

At first, the car for Negroes had no definite name. A letter to the *Massachusetts Spy* of Worcester in 1838, referred to it as a "dirt car." [2] In 1841, however, it came to be referred to quite widely as the "Jim Crow" car. The name was taken from a song and dance routine popularized during the 1830s by Thomas D. Rice, "the father of American Minstrelsy." The routine was called "jumping Jim Crow" and was an imitation, by a white, of a Negro referred to as Jim Crow, doing a song and dance. Reflecting prevailing white prejudices, it caricatured the Negro as an inferior and ignorant creature. Thus, the application of "Jim Crow" to the cars for Negroes on the railroads of Massachusetts was a natural development, and Massachusetts has come to have the dubious distinction of first using the term with reference to a segregated Negro car.

Before 1841 there were occasional references in the press of the Commonwealth to instances of enforced segregation on the railroads. There was no discernible public agitation on the subject, however, until the early part of 1841, when the issue came to a head through a series of incidents involving Negro and white leaders of the Abolitionist movement.

David Ruggles, a Negro Abolitionist of New York, who had played a prominent part in the underground railway and had helped more than five hundred Negro slaves to escape to the North, was ordered by a conductor, while going from New Bedford to Boston on the New Bedford and Taunton branch railroad on July 6, to leave the car in which he was seated and to move to another set aside for Negroes. On refusing, he was dragged out by the railroad superintendent and several others employed by the company, his clothing torn in the process, and thrown off the train. Ruggles brought suit for assault and battery against those who were involved in removing him.

The trial took place in New Bedford before Justice Henry A. Crapo on July 19 and 20. The company based its eviction of Ruggles on a regulation issued by its agent, William A. Crocker, on January 1, 1841, which read: "Passengers who go in the cars of the Taunton and New Bedford branch railroad, will take such seats as may be assigned them by the conductor." The company contended that a copy of the regulation had been pointed out to Ruggles when he had been asked to move to the Negro car. He had refused, and was then ejected. In delivering his opinion, Justice Crapo suggested that two issues were involved: (1) the right of the company to issue the regulation in question; and (2) whether or not undue force had been used to put the regulation into effect. On the first issue, he ruled that the railroad was the private property of the company, which therefore had the right to issue such regulations ensuring the welfare and comfort of its passengers as were not forbidden by the existing law of the state. The regulation in question, he ruled, was not contrary to the law of the state. As to the question of undue force, he ruled that such had not been proven. The charges brought by Ruggles were thereupon dismissed and the defendants adjudged not guilty.[3]

A few weeks later, on September 8, Frederick Douglass, the Negro Abolitionist, and J. A. Collins, the General Agent of the Massachusetts Anti-Slavery Society, a white man, were the center of another violent fracas. They had purchased tickets in Newburyport and were on their way, together, to the annual meeting of the Strafford County Anti-Slavery Society. On taking seats side by side in a car of the Eastern Railroad, they were approached by the conductor, who ordered Douglass to move into the Jim Crow car. Collins and several of the other passengers objected to the conductor's demand. Collins was ordered to leave his seat, the better to enable the conductor to drag or "snake" Douglass out of the car. He refused, remarking, "If you haul him out, it will be over my person, as I do not intend to leave this seat." The conductor left and returned with four or five men who seized Douglass and carried him into the Jim Crow car. In the process, Collins was injured and Douglass had his clothing torn.

About three weeks later, Collins, Douglass, J. M. Buffum, a white Abolitionist, and an unidentified woman were travelling on the Eastern Railroad to Newburyport. Collins and Douglass occupied one seat, with Buffum sitting behind them and the woman in front. In Lynn the conductor approached Douglass and ordered him out. The following colloquy, reported in detail in the *Liberator*, then took place:

> Buffum: Can't I ride with him, if he goes into the forward car! I want to have some conversation with him, and I fear I shall not have another opportunity so favorable.
> The Conductor: No! I'd as soon haul you out of his car, as I'd haul him from this.
> Douglass: There are but very few in this car, and why, since no objection has been made, do you order me out?
> A Passenger: I've no objection to riding with him—let's take a vote on the question.
> Buffum: That's just what I want—let us have a vote on the question.
> A Second Passenger: I've no objection to that step.

> The conductor remained adamant.

> Douglass: If you will give me any good reason why I should leave this car, I'll go willing; but, without such reason, I do not feel at liberty to leave; though, you can do with me as you please, I shall not resist.
> The Conductor: You have asked that question before.
> Douglass: I mean to continue asking the question over and over again, as long as you continue to assault me in this manner.

> Others took up the cry and called out: "Give him one good reason." Finally, forced to speak, the conductor muttered, "Because you are black."

Finding himself unequal to the task of dragging Douglass out, the conductor secured the help of eight or ten toughs. What happened next is vividly described by Collins:

> "Snake out the d - - - - d nigger," cries one. "Out with him," responded another guardian of the "peculiar institution" of the South. The gang of men stood in a leaping posture, with their hands extended and fingers half bent, ready for the going forth of the command of the captain to seize him. The word was given—"Take him out!" Five or six, like so many tigers, laid hold of Douglass, but he happened to be exceedingly heavy, as the laws of gravity were in full force. His attachment to his seat was so great, that these half dozen bullies found it no easy task to snake him out over me. "Damn that Collins," cried out one of them, "out with him, out with him." Whereupon five or six laid violent hands upon me. One gave me a severe blow upon the back part

of my head, and another hit me in my face, cutting my lip considerably. Like my friend Douglass, I did not feel inclined to part with my seat at the command of these ruffians, if I may be allowed the use of such an expression; in consequence of which, our seat gave way, and we, with five or six of these villains laying hold of our head, arms and legs, were dragged out head foremost, and deposited upon the ground in no very gentle manner. One of the gang gave me a very severe kick in my back, in consequence of which, I am lame at the present time. I was so badly bruised that my person, in various parts, is now black and blue. Buffum remained behind with Douglass, whose baggage was thrown out after him. I was allowed to pass on in the same train. Soon after the cars started, the conductor approached me, and made use of the most abusive language. I asked him if he was employed by the company to insult passengers; and, if so, I considered him the most faithful servant I ever met with; and then turned myself around, and began to read. He shook his little fist about my head a few times, and was greatly enraged because I would hold no conversation with him. I was now left to myself until we arrived at Salem.[4]

On arriving in Salem, Collins was accosted by the conductor and other officials of the railroad, including its president, Mr. Neal, and was ordered to leave the train because of its earlier defense of Douglass. After some remonstrance and only when it became clear that he would be dragged out if he failed to leave peacefully, he walked out of the train and took a private conveyance to Newburyport.

In the ensuing months, there occurred numerous other incidents. One morning, at the end of September, Mrs. Mary Newhall Green, the secretary of the Lynn Anti-Slavery Society, a light-complexioned Negro, who had previously without incident used the Eastern Railroad for trips from Lynn to Boston, was dragged out of the white car, with a baby in her arms. In the process, the baby was injured, and Mrs. Green's husband, who had sought to defend her, was badly beaten.

On the evening of that day, some three or four white men, who had boarded a train of the Eastern Railroad in East Boston, were dragged out of their car, together with a Negro whose ejection they had protested.[5] One of the whites, Dr. Daniel Mann, a dentist of Boston, brought charges of assault and battery against George Harrington, the conductor, who had led the assault. The trial took place in the Boston Police Court before a Justice Simmons. The lawyer for the defense was a Mr. Lord of Salem; Dr. Mann's counsel was Samuel E. Sewall, a well-known Abolitionist who was a descendant of Massachusetts Chief Justice Samuel Sewall, an outspoken opponent of Negro slavery in Colonial days.[6]

Lord argued that "all corporations in the Commonwealth have power to make such reasonable and proper by-laws for the management of their business as their own interests and the public good may require; that the established usage and the public sentiment of this community authorise a separation of the blacks from the whites in public places; that the regulation adopted by the Eastern Railroad Corporation was reasonable and proper, and such as they had a perfect right to adopt; that if the rule was unreasonable, neither Dr. Mann nor any other person had power to take the law into their own hands, and to right the wrong; and that he and his friends formed a conspiracy to prevent the execution of this rule; and in this they were trespassers." [7]

On the other hand, Sewall argued that the directors of the railroad did not have the legal right to authorize a conductor to separate passengers on the basis of color; that a rule of that kind was arbitrary and unlawful, as was the attempt to enforce it; that the conductor had no right to evict any person by force without first notifying him of the company's regulation—which had not been done in this case; and that the conductor had no right to evict passengers who had merely expressed their objections to his action.

Justice Simmons decided, however, "that the conductor was justified by the disorderly and unlawful conduct of Dr. Mann and his friends in ejecting them from the cars—and ordered that the defendant be discharged." [8]

Toward the end of the year, there occured an incident that had a strong impact upon public opinion. It involved Charles Lenox Remond, a Negro Abolitionist who had been chosen one of the American delegates to the World Anti-Slavery Convention held in London in June, 1840. Endowed with an attractive personality and eloquence of speech, Remond had been warmly received by the foremost leaders of English society. He returned to America in December, 1841, carrying with him the signatures of 60,000 Irishmen urging their countrymen in America to oppose slavery. On his arrival in Boston, Remond boarded a train of the Eastern Railroad to visit his parents, who were living in Salem. The conductor ordered him into the "Jim Crow" car. When several white friends, who had just welcomed him in Boston and were eager to hear the story of his visit abroad, moved to the "Jim Crow" car with him, they were ordered by the conductor to leave immediately or be dragged out.

In describing the incident, the Abolitionists were not slow to point out the difference between Remond's insulting reception in his own country and the love and respect accorded him in Europe. "In England, Scotland, and Ireland, Mr. Remond was received into the best circles, and treated with the utmost courtesy and respect. In Exeter Hall, London, with a royal duke in the chair, and succeeding Daniel O'Connell as one of the speakers on that occasion, he was listened to with admiration, and elicited thunders of applause. . . . But, in his own land, as soon as he steps his foot on the shore, he is treated more vilely than a dog, and prohibited from enjoying the society even of those who have crucified their own prejudices, and whose hearts are touched with sympathy for his lot! And America is the land of liberty and equality—the land which cannot tolerate a nobility—the land which scoffs at monarchy!" [9]

As these incidents came to their notice, the Abolitionists expressed their indignation and took steps to combat the policy of the railroads.[10] A speech in the state legislature, in March, 1841, by Representative George Bradburn, who had been leading the campaign for repeal of the marriage law, helped bring the problem to public attention.[11] Speaking on a bill to authorize the owners of the Eastern Railroad to extend their wharves, Bradburn surprised the House when he announced that, despite his interest in railroad expansion, he would vote against the bill because of the Eastern Railroad's policy of segregation. It was not until the attack upon David Ruggles, however, that public opinion was really aroused. On July 12, a mass meeting of protest, attended by prominent residents of the city, was held in New Bedford. Ruggles presented his version of the attack upon him and was followed by several other speakers. The meeting adjourned and reconvened the following day to hear the report of an investigating committee appointed to look into the incident. After hearing the report, those assembled resolved "that as citizens of a free and enlightened community, and descendants of those Revolutionary worthies who poured out their hearts' blood in the cause of our civil liberty, we do remonstrate in the most solemn manner against those inhuman proceedings as took place at the railroad depot, in this town on the 6th of the present month, in expelling David Ruggles of New York, from the car, for the unworthy cause of his having a color which the God of Nature was pleased to give him." [12]

The failure of Ruggles' suit against the New Bedford and Taunton Railroad outraged the Abolitionists and stimulated their campaign for further action. Soon after the trial, the *Liberator* printed a letter from Ruggles, dated July 24, giving his version of the proceedings before Justice Crapo. He charged that, "It was hardly to be supposed that his honor could give an equitable decision in this case—himself being a stockholder in said company, and therefore lawfully rendered incapable of occupying the bench of justice under such circumstances. In relation to Justice Crapo's court, I must confess, he rendered it the greatest farce I ever witnessed. In giving his opinion, he declared his ignorance of the law in the case, and, of course, adhered to the authority of Judge Lynch." Entitling the letter "Lynching in New Bedford, Justice Henry A. Crapo and Lynch Law," the *Liberator* commented: "The conduct of Justice Crapo, in giving his legal sanction to the dastardly assault and battery upon the person of Mr. Ruggles at the New Bedford depot by the conductors of the railroad train, is in our view, unspeakably atrocious." [13]

As the attacks upon Negroes and their white sympathizers in the railroad cars continued, other newspapers besides the *Liberator* condemned them, and public demand for action began to intensify. The Boston *Daily Times*, the Lynn *Record*, the Dover *Morning Star*, the Quincy *Patriot* and the *Massachusetts Spy* printed reports of incidents and letters from readers, and forcefully denounced the conduct of the railroad companies and the courts. The Dover *Morning Star* actually called for a boycott of the Eastern Railroad.[14] The *Liberator* emphasized that Stephen Chase, the superintendent of the Eastern Railroad, was a member in good standing of the Society of Friends, and called upon the Society to "disown" him or "be willing to lie under the imputation of conniving at the sanctioning of high-handed villainy and brutal ruffianism." [15]

The Abolitionists of Massachusetts initiated a concerted campaign against the railroads at a meeting of the Massachusetts Anti-Slavery Society on August 17, 1841. It was decided that in addition to the petitions for repeal of the marriage law, which they were circulating, they would also distribute petitions "for a law declaring equal rights of persons in the use of the means of conveyance furnished under charters from the State." [16] In September, three large public meetings were held in Lynn, with people of all shades of political opinion attending. At one of the meetings, in the First Universalist meeting house, resolutions were unanimously adopted condemning the attack upon Collins and Douglass as "a gross violation of our State constitution as well as of all law and decency," "the substitution of Lynch law and mobocracy for order and decorum," and asserting that those present would "use all the means in their power, consistent with their views of law and christianity, to defend the colored people who may see fit to take their seats in the long cars, in the enjoyment of their rights." [17]

At a meeting on September 30, it was further resolved that the attacks "demand the interference of Legislative authority," and that petitions to that effect be presented to the legislature. In order to secure the widest public support, another resolution affirmed that the Eastern Railroad's practices "be viewed not as a question between Abolitionists and Anti-Abolitionists, but as a matter connected with the freedom of every citizen." [18]

The campaign for legislative action quickly gathered momentum. On October 15, the *Liberator* printed a copy of a petition that was being circulated by the Board of Managers of the Massachusetts Anti-Slavery Society. The petition requested the legislature "to pass a law declaring and defining the rights of the people of this Commonwealth in the use of the means of conveyance furnished by the Railroad companies therein, in order that the officers of said companies may no longer claim the right of depriving any class of persons of the use of any of their cars, on the sole ground of color, and of insulting, assaulting and ejecting white passengers, merely for claiming the equal means of conveyance for persons of color." [19] Anti-Slavery societies throughout the state quickly swung into action and tied this campaign in with the already powerful one against the marriage law. Thus, the Norfolk County Anti-Slavery Society, at its quarterly meeting, resolved to "recommend to the Abolitionists of the several towns in this county, to interrogate the candidates of the whig and the democratic parties, of their respective towns, for the State Legislature, as to their view for the repeal of the marriage law, and for defining the powers of Rail-Road Corporations." [20] The quarterly meeting of the Worcester North Division Anti-Slavery Society passed a similar resolution and added the recommendation "to those who may be travelling to New York or Portland, to patronize the Boston and Norwich in preference to the Providence and Stonington Railroad, the Boston and Exeter in preference to the Boston and Newburyport Railroad, inasmuch as colored people are, by these companies respected and treated as equal human beings." [21]

In their public pronouncements, the Abolitionists kept repeating a number of points which proved to be extremely effective in swinging public opinion to their side. They emphasized, for instance, that the railroads which forcefully prevented whites and Negroes from sitting together were most solicitous in permitting southern slaveholders to keep their Negro slaves by their side when travelling in those very same cars. It was only the free Negro who was segregated, not the slave. Thus, the author of a letter to the *Massachusetts Spy* of Worcester, wrote: "That Corporation [the Eastern Railroad] consider this 'Jim Crow' car good enough for a 'Nigger,' if said 'Nigger' be a *free* man or woman. Let a southern slaveholder, however, get into one of their first class cars, accompanied by his 'chattels personal,' and no matter how black those 'chattels' may be, not a word will be uttered against the arrangement. After all, then, it is *not* color alone which excludes a man from the best car. The colored person to be excluded must also be *free!!* I ask every man or woman who may see these lines, if this be consistent? If it be right? I ask them if they are willing such an insult should be offered to freedom in Massachusetts? Ay, and in sight of Bunker Hill?" [22]

Another point stressed by the Abolitionists was the repression of freedom of speech by the railroad corporations, whose procedure it was to attack all those who protested the forcible evictions of Negroes from white cars. Dr. Daniel Mann, the white dentist who had been assaulted, emphasized this when he asked, in a letter to the *Liberator:* "But, *reader* are *you* willing to ride in the cars under the cringing sense that a padlock is on your lips, and that a power as despotic as that of the Turk, wielded by hands far less responsible and far more degraded, is ready to insult and trample upon your rights, and can do so with impunity, if by any censure of their abuse, you should provoke their rage?" [23]

A third argument, no less important than the others, concerned the wealth and power of the railroads, which had enabled them to flout public opinion and to secure the sympathetic decisions of those court justices before whom suits had been brought. The spectacle of judges justifying the evictions of Negroes and the attacks upon their white sympathizers strengthened the conviction that only through the power of popular protest, directed into legislative action, could the railroads' arrogance be curbed. As Dr. Daniel Mann emphasized in his letter to the *Liberator*, after Judge Simmons had dismissed his suit against the Eastern Railroad, "Justice was foiled and overcome in her own temple by the power and management of wealth, vested in a corporation which the people have established. The serpent hatched by their kindness has become a boa constrictor, to crush them in its folds. No court can guard the rights of the people against such a power. The people alone who created the power can prescribe its limits, and defend themselves from its encroachments. The need of their action is now demonstrated. . . . It is the contest of the unguarded rights of American citizenship with an overgrown, overbearing and unprincipled monopoly of wealth and power and wrong. . . . In short, let all the ready means by which a wealthy corporation can socially violate private rights with impunity, by force of arms, and force of falsehood, purchased by the form of wealth, be guarded against by law; and let every man feel that he is a member of a republic in which an injury offered to the meanest citizen is an insult to the whole community." [24]

The effect of Judge Simmons' decision upon the people and press of Massachusetts is illustrated by the reaction of the Lynn *Record*, which urged that "if the 'Great and General Court of Massachusetts' is not disfranchised, but has yet the power of *making laws* in favor of *the people*, without regard to the color of the skin, the color of the hair, the *breadth of the shoulders*, or the quality of the clothes, we trust, in the name of liberty, (if it is yet lawful to speak that word) that the independent voters at the coming election will see to it that men are chosen who will define the powers of corporations somewhat differently from the New Bedford Justice (Judge Crapo) or the Boston Justice." [25]

The movement against the "Jim Crow" car reached its peak at the beginning of 1842. As petitions demanding legislative action poured into the legislature, a joint legislative committee of both houses under the chairmanship of Seth Sprague, Jr., of Boston, was appointed to study the problem and bring in a report. It held a public meeting in February;

those who appeared before it were Remond and two of the most prominent white anti-slavery lawyers of Massachusetts, Wendell Phillips and Ellis Gray Loring. The *Bay State Democrat*, reporting that the State House, the scene of the meeting, "was crowded with a large audience, consisting of the members of the two houses, and ladies and gentlemen generally," noted that Remond's speech, "coming as it did from one of the proscribed race, and delivered in a manner at once graceful and pointed, seemed to produce much effect upon the assembly." [26]

Phillips, in his testimony, affirmed the right of the legislature to end segregation on the railroads. The railroad corporations, he argued, were created and protected by the legislature "in the exercise of special privileges and franchises. The legislature creates—of course, it can control them. They are bound to make reports, from time to time, of their proceedings to it. That fact presupposes the right to regulate their proceedings, if need be." The railroad corporations were in duty bound to observe the laws and constitution of the Commonwealth, and to do nothing to contravene "the equal rights of all the people which that Constitution was framed to secure." Declaring that it was "a right, not a privilege to be transported in the cars of the corporations, upon payment of a certain sum," he affirmed that such payment "and conformity to the usual and decent rules of society, *entitle* a man to the use of this conveyance." As a right, therefore, "it surely ought to be an equal right." But forcing a colored man to ride in a "Jim Crow" car constitutes "an injury to his rights, and insult to his person," and should therefore not be permitted by the legislature. Noting that segregation was confined to three roads and that "on the largest and most frequented of the railroads, no such regulation has obtained"—an indication that there was no general public opinion demanding such regulation—he emphasized that "we ask not for the *writing* of law;—we ask the Legislature to say *what is law*." By affirming that the railroads were acting contrary to the constitution and the law of Massachusetts, the legislature would not only acknowledge the equal rights of all citizens of the Commonwealth but would also end the violence prevailing on those roads. "A most definite action in the case is required," he continued. "If the Legislature be not ready to affirm and defend the rights of all, let them make it law that color is an important particular in the tenure of rights. Let that be clearly known, and it may be submitted to—till such a demonstration of the sense of the people as no Legislature can mistake, shall procure its repeal. But while uncertainty prevails, there will be continued brawls and breaches of the peace. What the petitioners do claim is action,—on one side or on the other." [27]

Remond argued that complexion could not "be rightfully made the criterion of rights"; he would oppose such a criterion, he said, even if the

Negro were in the majority. What he was asking for was justice "and not favor for either complexion"; the regulations in question "do not end with the termination of the route, but, in effect, tend to discourage, disparage and depress this class of citizens"; it means treating all Negroes as though they are one uniform mass. "No distinction is made by the community in which we live. The most vicious is treated as well as the most respectable, both in public and private . . . and I submit, whether this unkind and unchristian policy is not well calculated to make every man disregardful of his conduct, and every woman unmindful of her reputation"; the degrading treatment of the Negro in America, "finds a counterpart in no other"; the Negro does not deny to any man the social right of selecting his "society and associates, but he does demand equality of civil rights—such as on the railroads—where one man has not the prerogative to define rights for another. For instance, sir, in public conveyances, for the rich man to usurp the privileges to himself, to the injury of the poor man, would be submitted to in no well regulated society. And such is the position suffered by persons of color." [28]

Loring pointed out, in words that have a contemporary ring as we think of the recent Supreme Court decision in the education cases, that although the accommodations given the Negro were inferior, it was immaterial whether they were not. "To give inferior accommodations might be an injury; but to make any distinction whatever *is an insult;* one which men of color will suffer more from, than from an injury, if their feelings are what they ought to be. . . . Distinctions made between parties that are socially held to be unequal, are always an insult to the reputedly inferior party. If the peer's daughter be forbidden to marry the peasant's son, common sense tells us that the peasant is the insulted party, however plausibly it may be argued that the prohibition touches both alike." As common carriers the railroad corporations "have the right to make any regulations for the management of their business, which are not inconsistent with the public good." The regulations in question, however, are not consistent with the public good. Even if public opinion of the majority of the people of the state approved of the regulations, they would still not have the right to make them. "Are all our rights then at the mercy of a majority? Our Constitution and our laws are framed mainly to protect the rights of the *minority*, and to say to the majority, 'Thus far shalt thou go, and no further.' " [29]

Following the hearing, the joint legislative committee submitted a report which condemned the policy of segregation on the railroads, affirmed the need of remedial action through legislation and the right of the legislature to take such action, and presented a bill which declared that "no railroad corporation shall . . . make or establish any by-law or regulation which shall make any distinction, or give a preference in accommodation to any one or more persons over others on account of descent, sect, or color." Moreover, "Any officer or servant of any rail-road corporation, who shall assault any person for the purpose of depriving him of his right or privilege in any car or other rail-road accommodation, on account of descent, sect, or color, or shall aid or abet any other person in committing such assault, shall be punished by imprisonment in the county jail not less than six days, or by fine not less than ten dollars; and shall also be answerable to the person assaulted, to the full amount of his damage in an action of trespass." [30]

However, notwithstanding strong public sentiment and a unanimous committee recommendation, the bill was defeated in the Senate.[31] Despite this setback, the demands for legislative action continued. Petitions were again circulated and presented to the legislature at the beginning of the next session in January, 1843, and a bill similar to that of the previous year was reintroduced. It passed the Senate but was victimized by a maneuver in the House by Representative Park of Boston. Park moved the deletion of the words "rail-road," so that the bill applied to all corporations—he indicated that he planned to vote against the bill after his amendment was accepted, thus admitting that the purpose of the amendment was to increase opposition to the bill—the amendment was passed by a vote of 164 to 67, and the bill itself indefinitely postponed by a vote of 171 to 61.[32]

The vote was not taken by yeas and nays, which meant that the vote of each legislator was not made public. Apparently, public opinion was too strongly opposed to the policy of the railroads to be openly defied. The *Liberator* was undoubtedly correct in its observation, after characterizing the result as "inexcusable and dastardly," that the legislators "refused to allow the vote to be taken by yeas and nays, in order that they might not be identified." [33]

But the bill's defeat in the legislature actually marked the final stages in the resistance of the railroads to public pressure. During the debate, Representative Adams of Boston, a member of the committee submitting the bill, had observed that he preferred a voluntary abandonment by the railroads of their policy, rather than the passage of legislation. With public pressure rising all about them, and faced with the certainty that the legislation would be enacted the following year if segregation continued, the railroads accepted Representative Adams' advice and abolished segregation during the ensuing weeks. Although Remond did write, in a letter to the *Liberator* dated April 25, 1843, that on boarding a train in Salem for Boston he had been ordered by the conductor into a separate car, he did admit that for the past three weeks he had had no difficulty at any other point.[34] Thereafter, all discrimination and segregation on the railroads of Massachusetts ended and no further incidents were reported. The *Twelfth Annual Report* of the Massachusetts Anti-Slavery Society observed that "We are happy to have reason to believe that . . . no distinctions any longer exist upon any of the Railways of Massachusetts." [35]

One last incident in this drama of the railroads took place in November, 1843. Nathaniel Barney of Nantucket, a member of the Society of Friends, and an Abolitionist, was a stockholder of the New Bedford and Taunton railroad. As long as the company maintained its regulation, Barney refused to accept his dividends. With the regulation abandoned, Barney ordered the company to pay the sum due him—$22.50—"to the order of Francis Jackson for William Lloyd Garrison, in view of his faithful and undeviating advocacy of the rights of humanity." Garrison accepted the sum as a contribution to the *Liberator*, thanked Barney, and noted that "no odious proscription now obtains on that railroad." [36]

NOTES

1. *An Appeal in Favor of That Class of Americans Called Africans* (New York, 1836), p. 195.

2. Reprinted in the *Liberator* 8 (December 14, 1838): 197.

3. For a summary of the proceedings and the ruling see the *New Bedford Mercury*, July 22, 1841; also the *Liberator* 11 (August 6, 1841): 165.

4. *Liberator* 11 (October 15, 1841): 165.

5. Ibid.

6. Ibid., 11 (November 5, 1841): 180.

7. Massachusetts Anti-Slavery Society, *Tenth Annual Report*, January 26, 1842.

8. *Liberator* 11 (November 5, 1841): 180.

9. Massachusetts Anti-Slavery Society, *Tenth Annual Report*, January 26, 1842.

10. Even before railroads had come into use, Abolitionists had condemned segregation on public conveyances. In 1834, the *Liberator* had characterized the treatment of Negroes on stagecoaches and steamboats as "vulgar and shameful in the extreme." (*Liberator* 4 [June 4, 1834]: 91.) In 1836, Lydia María Child, the prominent Abolitionist author, had asked in her famous *Appeal*: "Will any candid person tell me why respectable colored people should not be allowed to make use of public conveyances, open to all who are able and willing to pay for the privilege? Those who enter a vessel, or a stagecoach, cannot select their companions. If they can afford to take a carriage or boat for themselves, then, and then only, they have a right to be exclusive." (*An Appeal in Favor of That Class of Americans Called Africans* [New York, 1836], p. 206.) In the ensuing years, the *Liberator*, from time to time, reported instances of segregation, which it condemned in no uncertain terms. See 8 (December 14, 1838): 197; 9 (July 19, 1839): 116; 9 (October 18, 1839): 167; 9 (October 25, 1839): 170; 10 (June 26, 1840): 101.

11. The marriage law, first enacted in 1705-6, and revised in 1834, forbade the intermarriage of whites with Negroes, Indians or Mulattoes. It was repealed in 1843 after a long struggle which began in 1831.

12. *Liberator* 11 (July 24, 1841): 118.

13. Ibid., 11 (August 6, 1841): 127.

14. Ibid., 11 (October 1, 1841): 157.

15. Ibid., 11 (October 8, 1841): 163.

16. Ibid., 11 (August 20, 1841): 139.

17. Ibid., 11 (October 15, 1841): 166.

18. Ibid.

19. Ibid.

20. Ibid., 11 (October 29, 1841): 175.

21. Ibid.

22. Reprinted in the *Liberator* 11 (November 5, 1841): 177. Similarly, James Buffum, in a letter to the *National Anti-Slavery Standard,* extracts from which were printed in the *Liberator* 11 (November 12, 1841): 184, noted: "Let it be observed that this murderous prejudice, in reality, exists against *condition* more than against *color.* . . . *Slaves* can travel beside their masters in all our public vehicles without offending northern nerves; why, then, is such a fuss made about colored *freemen?* Our merchants and sea captains can trade with Africans for gold dust and ivory, in exchange for rum and trinkets; they do not shudder at striking heads for such profitable bargains; how is it that they bear such hatred to the colored man in their own country? The plain truth is, it arises from contempt for their *condition.*"

23. *Liberator* 11 (November 12, 1841): 182.

24. Ibid.

25. Reprinted in Ibid., 11 (November 12, 1841): 184.

26. Ibid., 12 (February 25, 1842): 32.

27. Ibid., 12 (February 18, 1842): 26.

28. Ibid., 12 (February 25, 1842): 30.

29. Ibid., 12 (March 4, 1842): 34.

30. Ibid., 12 (March 4, 1842): 33.

31. Henry Wilson, *History of the Rise and Fall of the Slave Power in America,* 2 vols. (Boston, 1872), I, p. 494.

32. *Liberator* 13 (February 17, 1843): 21.

33. Ibid., 13 (February 10, 1843): 23.

34. Ibid., 13 (April 28, 1843): 67.

35. Massachusetts Anti-Slavery Society, *Twelfth Annual Report,* January 24, 1844 (Boston, 1844), p. 7.

36. *Liberator* 13 (December 1, 1843): 190.

26. BENJAMIN QUARLES, The Black Underground (1969)*

Professor Benjamin Quarles of Morgan State University in Baltimore is one of the most prolific black historians in the United States. In addition to his most recent book, *The Black Abolitionists,* he is the author of an excellent biography of Frederick Douglass and of comprehensive studies on the role of Afro-Americans in the Civil War and the American Revolution. In this selection, Professor Quarles carefully analyzes the activities of Afro-Americans in the work of the underground railroad. Quarles' account also serves to dispel the erroneous notion that the work of spiriting slaves out of the South was largely in the hands of white abolitionists.

On a day in early August 1850, William Still of Philadelphia was approached by a man who gave his name as Peter Freeman and said that he was looking for his long-lost mother and father, Levin and Sidney, former slaves like himself. William Still was an underground railroad operator and hence familiar with dramatic incidents. But as Peter unfolded his story Still stood almost transfixed. For it happened that Levin and Sidney were his own parents and therefore the man talking to him was an older brother he had never seen before.[1]

Such human interest stories about former slaves who journeyed northward looking for relatives or in pursuit of freedom, or both, made effective propaganda for the abolitionist cause. Fugitive slaves on the wing tended to arouse sympathy and to stir the public conscience. Slavery was weakened far less by the economic loss of the absconding blacks than by the antislavery feeling they evoked by their flight and the attempts to reclaim them.

Sympathy for the runaway slave was created and sustained by the Fugitive Slave Act of 1793. Heavily weighted in favor of the master, this measure offended the popular sense of fair play. Without first obtaining a warrant, a master had only to seize his slave, bring him before any judge, and prove to the court's satisfaction that the person in custody was guilty as charged. The judge would then issue what was in essence a certificate of repossession. The alleged slave was permitted no trial by jury and given no opportunity to present witnesses to give testimony on his behalf.

The abolitionists attacked the measure on the dual grounds that it was unconstitutional and that it legalized kidnaping. The latter contention was the more readily provable, particularly in the instance in which Richard Allen was claimed as a fugitive, much to the subsequent discomfiture of the claimant.[2] The law was one-sided, but, even had it been more fairly drafted, there would still have remained a great reservoir of sympathy for those who made the dash for freedom. A blend of the desperate and the heroic, their actions could hardly fail to win the admiration even of the great mass of people who did not care for the abolitionists and to whom the free Negro was someone to be tolerated rather than welcomed.

Hence the work of assisting runaways was in popular favor in the North, many whites being drawn into the work. Possibly the best known of these was the Quaker, Levi Coffin, whose thirty-five-year record of slaves assisted ran to well over two thousand. Formerly from North Carolina, Coffin's success as a storekeeper in Newport, Indiana, and then in Cincinnati, afforded him the means for underground railroad activities.

Two other abolitionists with long and almost as notable careers in helping fugitives were Thomas Garrett, whose Wilmington home was perhaps the best known station in the East, and Canadian-born Alexander M. Ross, who took time from his career as a physician to recruit escape-minded slaves in Richmond, Nashville, Selma, and New Orleans.[3]

Any balanced analysis of underground railroad operations must include its Negro workers. In Ohio, for example, black people were particularly active. Abolitionist leader James G. Birney noted in February 1837 that slaves were escaping in great numbers to Canada by way of Ohio. And, he added, "such matters are almost uniformly managed by the colored people. I know nothing of them generally till they are past." The fugitive slaves who made their way through Sandusky were aided almost wholly by the town's one hundred Negroes, led by a barbershop owner, Grant Richie. The state numbered not fewer than one hundred Negro underground railroad workers. In Missouri the loose network included a cluster of all-Negro associations in St. Louis which sped the fugitive to Chicago and points north.[4]

The great authority on the underground railroad, Wilbur H. Siebert, points out that the list of towns and cities in which Negroes were co-workers with whites in the movement was a long one. Moreover, he adds, many Negroes in states that bordered the slave regions found numerous ways to help the fugitives without much risk to themselves. Although Siebert is as objective as one could wish in his assessment of the Negro's role in the movement, he unwittingly does not do it full justice. In his monumental "Directory of the Names of Underground Railroad Operators," embracing some 3200 entries, Siebert designates 143 names as Negroes. But in listing the following he did not identify them as colored: James J. G. Bias, Frederick Douglass, George T. Downing, Robert Morris, Robert Purvis, Charles B. Ray, Stephen Smith, and William Whipper. Similarly, in listing the membership of the Vigilance Committee of Boston, Siebert omits the Negro identity of William C. Nell and John T. Hilton, and in the roster of the General Vigilance Committee of Philadelphia, he does not indicate that Charles H. Bustill, Robert Purvis, C. L. Reason, William Still, Josiah C. Wears, and Jacob C. White were colored men.[5]

Of the variety of ways to assist fugitives, one in particular was suited to the Negro operator—that which entailed going into the South and making contact with those who were escape-minded. The slave was more likely to place his trust initially in a black face. Moreover, some Negro conductors were former slaves who were familiar with the territory in which they operated. Some of these secret returnees were willing to run this special risk in order to rescue their wives and children.

The most renowned of these black conductors was Harriet Tubman who, like Nat Turner, was given to dreams and to prayers. Herself an escapee from Dorchester County, Maryland, in 1849, she made some fifteen excursions into slave territory and brought back more than two hundred fugitives. Short and spare, she hardly looked like a person with a price on her head. But she was skillful in avoiding detection, her coolness in a tight spot matching her courage. To her abolitionist associates she became something of a legend, Thomas Wentworth Higginson calling her the greatest heroine of the age.[6]

A less noted and less lucky conductor was Leonard A. Grimes, a free Negro. Grimes became a hackman in Washington, D. C., eventually owning a number of horses and carriages, all as available for rescuing slaves as for conveying paying passengers. In one of his ventures in Virginia, his native state, he was seized after spiriting a slave family away in a hack. Grimes spent two years in the state prison at Richmond. He then went to Boston and became the pastor of the Twelfth Baptist Church. But, as in Washington, he neglected no opportunity to assist a runaway.

Most of the conductors whose names are lodged in the record were based in the free states and hence were engaged in speeding the slave on his way rather than leading him out of the South. These "middlemen" included George L. Burroughs of Cairo, Illinois, whose job as a sleeping-car porter between Cairo and Chicago gave him an unusual opportunity for smuggling slaves. The most enterprising conductor in Salem, Ohio, was George W. C. Lucas, whose false-bottomed wagon conveyed fugitives to Cleveland, Sandusky, and Toledo.[7] At Elmira, New York, former slave John W. Jones secreted slaves in baggage cars bound for Canada.

For some black conductors the water was the freedom route. Slaves were carried across the Ohio on skiffs from Kentucky to Indiana. Negro crewmen might bring slaves aboard as stowaways on vessels leaving Southern ports and bound for the North. Elizabeth Barnes, who worked for a ship captain at Portsmouth, Virginia, hid slaves on vessels sailing for Boston and New Bedford. New Yorkers Edward Smith and Isaac Gansey of the schooner *Robert Centre* were charged by the Virginia Governor Thomas W. Gilmer with having abducted slave Isaac, and $3000 was offered for their delivery to the jailer at Norfolk.[8]

Shipping slaves from one northern port to another was far more common than the intersectional traffic, not to say less hazardous. James Ditcher piloted slaves along the Ohio from Portsmouth to Proctorville. Fugitive slaves were a common sight on the canal boat running from Cleveland to Marietta and owned by Negro abolitionist John Malvin.[9]

It is to be noted that many runaways never left the cotton kingdom, taking refuge either in the towns or the swamp lands. Other slaves preferred Mexico as their destination. A letter from a "free, colored Floridian," in an abolitionist journal in October 1831, urged slaves to turn toward Mexico because of its convenient location, its mild climate, its generous land policy, and its freedom from color prejudice.[10] But to the great majority of footloose slaves, the region above the Ohio River had one irresistible attraction that Mexico lacked—a substantial black population like themselves in language and outlook and one whose feeling of "sympatico" needed no proving.

A prominent feature of the Negro underground was the providing of overnight accommodations for the absconding slave. A white host might well be an object of suspicion to a newly fledged fugitive. Upon reaching Philadelphia, where they revealed their true identities, William and Ellen Craft were placed with Barkley Ivens, a non-Negro, much to Ellen's alarm. "I have no confidence whatever in white people," she told William, "they are only trying to get us back into slavery."

Levi Coffin noted that the fugitives who passed through Newport, Indiana, generally stopped among the colored people, although the latter were not always as skillful in concealing them as they might have been. But carelessness could hardly be charged to Chapman Harris of Jefferson County and his associate, Elijah Anderson, despite the fact that their cabins were well-known stopping places for fugitives.[11]

Coming to Cincinnati in 1847, Levi Coffin found that there, too, most of the fugitives who landed in the city soon vanished into the colored quarter. Some of those who were taken to the Negro section wound up at a place most unlikely to be suspected of harboring fugitives—the well-appointed Dumas House, famous for its ornate saloon where one might find the "biggest colored faro game in the country." At Ross, Ohio, the Reverend William H. Mitchell gave overnight housing to some thirteen hundred fugitives over a span of twelve years. Mitchell's lodging-house activities ceased in 1855 when the American Baptist Free Mission Society engaged his services as a missionary to the former slaves in Toronto. Runaway slaves reaching Detroit could find asylum at the residence of George DeBaptiste, who had worn out his welcome in Madison, Indiana, because of his underground railroad activities. A slave coming to Chicago might be lodged with the well-to-do tailor, John Jones.[12]

At Philadelphia the physician-clergyman James J. G. Bias "gave his bed freely" to slaves directed to his house by the white abolitionist Charles T. Torrey. Not stopping with his bed, Bias also gave to his overnight guests a quick medical checkup. Just outside Philadelphia the Byberry residence of Robert Purvis, a well-known station on the underground, had a special room reached only by a trap door. Another wealthy black abolitionist, William Whipper of Columbia, a port of entry for fugitives from Maryland and Virginia, resided at the end of the bridge leading into the town. He put up as many as seventeen slaves in one night, the next day sending them west by boat to Pittsburgh or by rail to Philadelphia in the false end of a boxcar he owned. In one instance Whipper alerted Jacob C. White at Philadelphia that the fugitive he was dispatching was in a "perilous situation," having seen his master that very day. At West Chester, Abraham D. Shadd, fairly well-off but not in a class with Whipper or Purvis, "entertained and forwarded" black transients.[13]

In New York City, the home of Charles B. Ray was a haven for journeying fugitives, fourteen of them walking up the front steps one summer morning. But Ray was not the only black New Yorker to be so blessed. "One hundred and fifty, in a single year, have lodged under my roof," wrote Henry Highland Garnet, "and I have never asked or received a penny for what I gave them, but divided with them my last crust." [14]

Colored abolitionist leaders in upstate New York knew that run-always would be directed to their doors. Jermain W. Loguen at Syracuse fitted an apartment in his house for these unannounced visitors. Those who came to Rochester made their way to the office of Frederick Douglass on Buffalo Street, early morning arrivals sitting on the steps until opening time. In Albany the home of Stephen Myers was an overnight sanctuary for black drop-ins on the last leg of their northward journey. The Buffalo home of William Wells Brown was a station on the underground railroad, Brown himself conducting sixty-nine to Canada over a period of seven months in 1842.[15]

In the Northeast the best known rendezvous for runaways was the home of Lewis Hayden in downtown Boston. Hayden himself was a fugitive from Kentucky, his rescuer Calvin Fairbank having been arrested and jailed for helping him escape. Hayden had turned down an earlier opportunity to escape because he could not bring his future wife along with him. As if to prove himself worthy of Fairbank's sacrifice, Hayden welcomed fugitives to stop under his roof. When the owner of William and Ellen Craft, Dr. Robert Collins of Macon, Georgia, sent two deputies to reclaim them, William took lodging in the Hayden dwelling, temporarily barricaded for the occasion. One day when Harriet Beecher Stowe visited the Haydens she was surrounded by thirteen escaped slaves.[16] Upon settling in Newport, Rhode Island, in 1855, George T. Downing quickly established himself as the friend of any fugitive alighting in that city.

Individual assistance to runaway slaves was supplemented by the work of vigilance committees, and here too the black people in the North played a distinctive role.[17] A vigilance committee aided the fugitives in a variety of ways—boarding and lodging them for a few days, purchasing clothing and medicine for them, providing them with small sums of money, informing them as to their legal rights and giving them legal protection from kidnapers. A primary function of the vigilance committee was to help a slave establish himself in a new location, to furnish him with letters of introduction, to help him find a job, and to give him guidance and protection while he was thus engaged in getting started. Hence a vigilance committee was a combination underground and upperground railroad, the latter comprising its efforts to help the slave locate within the United States. "The time has come to stop running," announced Jermain W. Loguen, manager of the Fugitive Aid Society of Syracuse.[18]

Many of the vigilance committees had a totally or predominantly Negro membership. The greatest of these Negro-run organizations was the New York Committee of Vigilance, founded in November 1835, with David Ruggles as its secretary and general agent. At its monthly meetings the committee listened to speakers like James Emerson, a seaman who had almost been sold into slavery after accepting work on a ship running to Petersburg, Virginia. Appearing at committee meetings were speakers like the wife of kidnaped Peter John Lee, her fatherless sons at her side.[19]

The committee listened to stories of colored children who had been hired as domestics and then carried into the South and sold. The committee publicized descriptions of missing Negroes, and informed its members as to the arrival and departure dates of ships suspected of harboring slaves. At one of its meetings three destitute Africans were introduced, with a plea for funds to help them return to their native land. On one occasion Isaac Wright told his story of being rescued by an agent of the committee after having been sold into slavery at New Orleans by the captain of the *Newcastle*, J. D. Wilson. It was through the committee that Wilson was arrested and detained for the illegal sale of Wright and two other Negro seamen. To attend a meeting of the Vigilance Committee tended to tear at the heart strings. At the annual meeting in 1837 at the Zion Church, Alvan Steward, founder in 1835 of the New York Anti-Slavery Society, was deeply moved by the strong emotions of gratitude expressed by the fugitives whom the committee had assisted. "I could almost submit to become a slave for the privilege of making such a friendship," he said to the gathering.[20]

Much of the success of the New York Committee of Vigilance could be credited to David Ruggles. "He is a General Marion sort of man," wrote a contemporary editor, "for sleepless activity, sagacity and talent." [21] Ruggles personally gave assistance to hundreds of runaways. The case of Frederick Douglass was a typical one. Ruggles sheltered the young Douglass for nearly two weeks, made his marriage arrangements, and sent the newlyweds to New Bedford, Massachusetts, with a five-dollar bill and a letter of introduction to a locally prominent Negro, Nathan Johnson.

Ruggles boarded incoming ships to see whether slaves were being smuggled in. He went from door to door in fashionable neighborhoods making inquiry as to the status of black domestics, New York law freeing any imported slave after a residence of nine months. In one instance Ruggles went to the Brooklyn home of Daniel K. Dodge and brought away a domestic, Charity Walker, a former slave. Although Ruggles got her a job, the obliging Charity succumbed to a ne'er-do-well and soon became pregnant, opening Ruggles to a volley of criticism, however unjustified, from those hostile to the abolitionists.[22]

Ruggles resigned as secretary and agent in February 1839 because of trouble with his eyes and a clash with the committee. Ruggles kept no books and hence was never able to render an accurate account of monies received and expended. The committee could never tell whether Ruggles overdrew his salary of $400 a year, and Ruggles, secure in his own sense of honesty, resented any probing of it.[23]

With the resignation of Ruggles the New York Committee of Vigilance lost its driving spirit and much of its influence. But its record over a five-year span had been commendable. During its first year it had "protected" 335 Negroes from slavery, and this figure was a sound approximation for each of the succeeding four years. The committee also won public acceptance of its contention that persons claimed as fugitives should have a trial by jury, a measure they had advocated from their opening meeting. In May 1841 Governor William H. Seward signed such a bill, and a month later the Vigilance Committee held a victory celebration at Asbury Church. The presiding officer, Charles B. Ray, hailed the measure for sweeping clean from the statute books the last vestiges of slavery in the state.[24] But the law was not firmly enforced at the outset, and before it could prove itself it was nullified by a Supreme Court decision (*Prigg v. Pennsylvania*, 1842) giving Congress the exclusive right to enforce the Fugitive Slave Law.

Negroes in Boston and Detroit had all-Negro vigilance groups, although neither had as dramatic a figure as Ruggles. Founded in Boston in 1842 and lasting for five years, the New England Freedom Association aimed to "extend a helping hand to all who may bid adieu to whips and chains." It solicited donations of money or clothing for the fugitives and places of residence, temporary or permanent, and advertised in the abolitionist press for persons who would give them jobs. Two of its seven directors were women. Founded in the same year as its Boston counterpart, the Colored Vigilance Commitee of Detroit was headed first by William Lambert and then by George DeBaptiste. In the absence of competing white abolitionist organizations, the Detroit group maintained an independent existence until the Civil War, reaching its peak in the mid-fifties. In one two-week period in 1854 the committee gave assistance to fifty-three freedom-bound blacks, a figure which grew to 1043 for the period from May 1, 1855, to January 1, 1856. Cleveland had an all-colored committee of nine, of whom four were women, which sped 275 slaves to Canada from April 1854 to January 1855.[25]

In Boston and New York the all-Negro vigilance groups were succeeded by racially mixed prototypes. In Boston in September 1846 a committee of vigilance was formed by Samuel Gridley Howe following public indignation over the return of a slave who had secreted himself on a vessel bound from New Orleans to Boston. The committee included Robert Morris and William C. Nell along with many prominent white reformers and literary figures; for example, Ralph Waldo Emerson sent word that if the economic well-being of Massachusetts depended upon making Boston a "slave-port," he would willingly forego such prosperity and "turn to the mountains to chop wood." [26] The Boston Committee of Vigilance performed its most conspicuous services in the early 1850s following the passage of the Fugitive State Law.[27]

New York City was the headquarters of another racially mixed group to assist the runaway slave—the New York State Vigilance Committee. Founded in 1847 with the Quaker Isaac T. Hopper as president, but with a membership over 50 percent Negro, the committee assisted 166 fugitives during its first six months. In 1848 the committee was reorganized with white philanthropist Gerrit Smith as president and Charles B. Ray as corresponding secretary. One of the committee's accomplishments during its first year was the instigation of action in the federal courts in nine cases in which a person was held as a slave in a slave state even though he was entitled to his freedom by the laws of the state. From January 1851 to April 1853 the committee assisted 686 former slaves, many of whom received little more than periodic counseling, but of whom thirty-eight were freed after being brought into New York City by their reputed masters.[28]

Upstate New York had two interracial slave-assisting organizations, although the one in Albany might well have been called the Myers Vigilance Committee. Its guiding spirit, Stephen Myers, held few meetings, although he acted in the name of the committee. That Myers was able and honest muted any criticism. At Syracuse the abolitionists founded the Fugitive Aid Society, with Jermain W. Loguen as its manager. Engaged in helping runaways since 1850, Loguen devoted full time to the work beginning in 1857. He wrote letters to the local newspapers urging their readers to hire fugitives in their shops and on their farms. How many jobs he found for the more than three hundred former slaves that passed through his hand cannot be known, but it earned for Syracuse the title of "the Canada of the United States." [29]

Loguen's good work in Syracuse was overshadowed only by that of William Still in Philadelphia, the secretary of the General Vigilance Committee. This organization had a predecessor, the Philadelphia Vigilance Committee, which was founded in 1838 and was in existence six years. This parent group was interracial on paper; eleven of the thirteen members of the first so-called Standing Committee were whites. But the president was Purvis and the agent (executive secretary) was another Negro, Jacob C. White. After 1839 the monthly meetings were no longer attended by whites, so that the committee was all-Negro in its operations and increasingly Negro in its personnel. This committee assisted some three hundred fugitives a year—its high for one week, the first week in September 1842, running to twenty-six.[30] It dispatched the fugitives to Canada or to David Ruggles in New York.[31] The committee expired in 1844, although many of the former members, Purvis, White, J. J. G. Bias, Daniel Payne, and Stephen H. Gloucester among them, continued to assist slaves in an individual capacity.

The successor of this pioneer organization, the General Vigilance Committee, was more consistently interracial. Robert Purvis was made chairman of the new organization, seven of whose nineteen founders were Negroes. But, most importantly, black William Still was made chairman of the four-member Acting Committee, thus becoming the executive secretary of the organization and its dominant figure.

A more resourceful and hard-working operator could hardly have been found. The full scope of Still's activities may be gleaned from his 780-page work, *The Underground Railroad*, published in 1872. In this fact-crammed, semi-documentary work, Still reproduced scores of letters from workers in the field, such as Joseph C. Bustill from Harrisburg describing the beginnings of the local Fugitive Aid Society. Still exchanged fruitful letters with such white supporters and colleagues as Thomas Garrett in Wilmington, Sidney Howard Gay in New York, Levi Coffin in Cincinnati, and Hiram Wilson at St. Catherine's in Canada. Still received scores of letters from fugitives he had helped, such as the one John J. Hill sent from Toronto: "I am as Free as your President Pearce [*sic*], only I have not been free so long. It is true that I have to work very hard for comfort but I am Happy, Happy." [32]

The general Vigilance Committee aided hundreds of black bondmen, the number running to 495 from December 1852 to February 1857. But the episode that Still was least likely to forget was the delivery of Henry Brown, shipped in a box from Richmond to Philadelphia by Adams

Express. When the shipment reached the antislavery office, Still, one of the four receiving agents, pried off the lid. Whereupon "the marvellous resurrection of Brown ensued," wrote the author of *The Underground Railroad*. "Rising up in his box, he reached out his hand, saying, 'How do you do, gentlemen?' " [33]

It was well that underground railroad work had its rewards. For there was no lack of problems, a need for funds ranking first. As in the case of all other antislavery operations, money was in short supply. The three major sources were Negroes, a sprinkling of whites, and a corps of women's groups on both sides of the Atlantic.

Negro giving was fair to good. The $284.31 raised by the New York Vigilance Committee from January 1, 1839, to May 23 of the same year came almost wholly from Negroes. The racial identity of one of its donors in 1837 could hardly be mistaken—George Jones, who had contributed $12.50, "was dragged to slavery by an order from our City Recorder," according to the committee's first annual report. Many members of the committee pledged themselves to contribute 50¢ a month, and in cases of dire need the members advanced money out of their own pockets. At its annual meetings the committee passed the hat, the average collection running to $75. In Detroit the bulk of the money of the Vigilance Committee seems to have come from collections taken up at meetings, particularly at call meetings growing out of quick-breaking incidents. Some of the funds of the Vigilance Committee of Philadelphia came from small donors, fifty-two of them contributing a total of $95.94½ from September 11, 1839, to January 13, 1840. This committee also solicited from Negro churches and it held soirees, raising $42 at one of these held in June 1841.[34]

At Rochester the Negroes "systematically aided their hunted brethren," wrote William C. Nell to William Lloyd Garrison on February 19, 1852, having just held a "donation festival" on their behalf. At Syracuse in January 1859 the manager of the Fugitive Aid Society, Jermain W. Loguen, received a financial contribution from thirty of the escaped slaves for whom he had gotten jobs, some of them adding a personal gift to him, such as an engraved sugar spoon or butter knife. To put something into its ever-exhausted treasury the New England Freedom Association sponsored juvenile concerts, charging a small fee at the door. On one desperate Sunday in August 1846 the association sent delegates to five of the colored churches in Boston, succeeding in raising a total of $23.19.[35]

Some of the support of the vigilance groups came from white donors. In 1840 the New York Committee received $25 from Arthur Tappan and $10 from John Rankin, both New York merchant-abolitionists. At Albany, Stephen Myers could operate independently of his committee because he had only to call upon three wealthy whites for whatever monies he needed. Upon assuming the presidency of the New York State Vigilance Committee in 1848, Gerrit Smith authorized the committee to draw upon him for $500 for the year's operations. On occasion a collection for underground railroad operations might be taken up at an abolitionist gathering, Harriet Tubman receiving $37 from such a source at Framingham, Massachusetts, in July 1858.[36]

Raising money for fugitive slave assistance had its appeal for wives and mothers. In New York the Negro women held annual fairs at the Broadway Tabernacle for the benefit of the Vigilance Committee. An admission fee of 12½¢ was charged, thus guarding against a poor sale of the "useful and fancy articles" on display. Many of the women who conducted the fair also worked for the committee by collecting a penny a week from friends. At Syracuse a group of women busied themselves in soliciting food, clothing, and money, channeling their collections to J. W. Loguen.

The women of Philadelphia outstripped all others in the work. Over a four-year span the colored Women's Association made donations for fugitive slave work, giving $50 in 1851. The earlier Vigilance Committee had a short-lived women's auxiliary, from which it received $10 in 1839. The interracial Philadelphia Female Anti-Slavery Society generally dipped into its treasury after receiving a touching appeal from the committee, usually to the effect that it had on hand a group of fugitives ready to move northward but had no funds to get them on the road. The society sent $20 in September 1841, $50 in January 1842, and $10 in January 1843, and an additional $25 later that year. In May 1845 the society gave $10 to one of its members, Hester Reckless, to assist fugitives, following her plea on their behalf.[37]

Women in the British Isles lent a sisterly hand in the work. Beginning in 1852, the year of its founding, the Glasgow Female New Association for the Abolition of Slavery held an annual bazaar for the New York Vigilance Committee, designating it as the principal recipient of its funds. The New York group also received grants of $50 each from the women in Dundee and Edinburgh in both 1857 and 1858. The Rochester friends of the fugitive received $100 in 1857 from the Edinburgh Ladies' New Anti-Slavery Association. The Philadelphia Vigilance Committee received remittances from the women of Dundee and Newcastle-on-Tyne, the latter through Anna D. Richardson who in 1846 had been instrumental in raising $700 to purchase the freedom of Frederick Douglass. In the spring of 1858 the Philadelphia Committee and Thomas Garrett in Wilmington each received $50 from Eliza Wigham, on behalf of the Edinburgh Ladies Emancipation Society.[38]

The work of Loguen at Syracuse drew support from women's anti-slavery groups throughout Great Britain—Edinburgh, Aberdeen, Berwick-on-Tweed, Halifax, Liverpool, Barnsley, and Huddersfield. The women from the land of Daniel O'Connell were not to be left out, the Irish Ladies Anti-Slavery Society sending Loguen $72.79 in February 1859 "for the benefit of fugitives coming to his house in Syracuse." [39] It is possible that over the five-year span from 1855 to 1860 Loguen received from the women in the British Isles some $400 a year, a sum which perhaps equalled their combined contributions to the other fugitive aid societies in the United States during the period.

Hundreds of women, British and American, white and black, gave sacrificially to help the fugitive slave. But their efforts fell short of the need, this phase of the abolitionist crusade sharing with the others a chronic lack of funds. The modest salaries of the full-time agent were generally in arrears. Collections were slow, and only the zeal of the workers kept the work going as fruitfully as it did. But even the most dedicated worker might have felt a bit dispirited over the plight of the Philadelphia Vigilance Committee, which as of November 11, 1841, reported that its funds were gone, that it was in debt, and that its total collections over the past month had been "a bundle of clothes, two hats and a bonnet." [40]

Resources that were badly needed to help the fugitive from the South went sometimes to unworthy recipients—those who pretended to be run-aways or their relatives. Since a fugitive aroused sympathy and received aid, it is not surprising that a small corps of impersonators sprung up. Most impostors claimed themselves to be slaves; others put forth the more modest honor of being a slave's relative—husband, father, son, or brother, whose freedom they were allegedly raising money to effect.

During the first week of December 1839 the Philadelphia Committee of Vigilance turned town the requests of two men claiming to be slaves, although one of them looked so woebegone that the committee relented and gave him $20 and some food. Generally the warnings against detected impostors were to be found in the columns of the antislavery journals. At Hartford in the summer of 1845, James W. C. Pennington advised the public to be on guard against one James Thompson, who was passing himself off as a slave from Lynchburg, Virginia. Early in 1850 the abolitionists of New York City were alerted about one William Johnson, an alleged fugitive in search of his alleged spouse. Johnson was all the more reprehensible for having recently deserted a real wife. Late in 1855 an antislavery weekly gave a personal description of one O. C. Gilbert who was pocketing monies he collected for fugitives. Gilbert was a large, robust man, 5 feet, 9 inches, of dark brown hue, practically bald and quite bowlegged: "Let all the papers pass him around," ran the warning.[41]

In January 1858 the inhabitants of Middlesex County, Massachusetts, were warned against a short, slender, light mulatto of twenty-two, who called himself George Thompson. Namesake of the British abolitionist, this "strolling knave" George Thompson had already collected $15 from sympathizers in Leominster. Abolitionists were advised that George was a reckless liar, varying his story according to circumstances. The breed was not unknown in England, Reuben Nixon spending a jail term for falsely soliciting funds as a fugitive.[42]

Elizabeth Buffum Chace, a Quaker at Valley Falls, Rhode Island, encountered only two known imposters in her long career of helping runaways. But one of these impersonators turned out to have been a hardened criminal. The "gentlemanly, light-colored, handsome man" she had protected for ten weeks from the slave catchers allegedly trailing him turned out to be an escapee from the New York state prison at Auburn. Mrs. Chace might have been forgiven, confessing that she had been impressed by his "great desire to learn our ideas about right and wrong, and for the improvement of himself in all directions." [43]

Abolitionist weeklies often advised their readers to be less credulous when approached by someone claiming to be a runaway. Some fugitive aid societies were hesitant about giving assistance unless the alms-seeker could produce a certificate of identification from friends or acquaintances in the border states. But such a precaution could have had little real effect. The counterfeiting of certificates of freedom ("free papers") was common in underground railroad operations; hence, a person who chose to become an imposter would have found it no real obstacle to borrow this technique and proceed to acquire forged letters of introduction.

To the friends of the fugitive slave there was one class more hated than the imposters and this was the informers—those who could be bribed to reveal the whereabouts of a runaway. Levi Coffin, head of the underground railroad at Cincinnati, found that not all Negroes were to be trusted in fugitive slave operations.[44] But such a group of betrayers of the slave remained very small, in part because of the adverse publicity given them and in part due to more forceful action.

Dating from its origin, the Negro press printed the names of black informants, *Freedom's Journal* listing those of Moses Smith, formerly of Baltimore, and Nathan Gooms of New York, in its issue of November 7, 1828. The mere appearance of these names in the columns of the weekly was a sufficient deterrent to the other informers whose identity the editors threatened to reveal. When Martin R. Delany was editor of the *Pittsburgh*

Mystery he was sued on two occasions for charging Negroes with having assisted the slave-catchers.[45]

A Negro who assisted the slave-catchers ran the risk of bodily harm, as two of this ilk found out in Cincinnati. Robert Russell decoyed a fugitive to a wharf where he was seized by his master's agents. But before Russell could enjoy his informant's fee of $10 he was tarred and feathered by a group of young Negro men. In August 1858 two runaways were betrayed by John Brodie, who had promised to assist them in returning to Covington, Kentucky, to effect the liberation of relatives. Brodie's treachery nearly cost him his life. He was seized by a group of Negroes, who proceeded to give him three hundred blows with a paddle, a stroke for each dollar he was supposed to have received from the slave-catchers. Only the presence of the influential Henry Highland Garnet saved Brodie from further punishment. The badly mauled informer delivered himself to the police authorities, to be placed in jail for safe-keeping. In Jefferson County, Indiana, an informer was whipped within an inch of his life. During the court trial it was impossible to get any Negro to testify against his floggers.[46]

Telltale Negroes were dealt with harshly because underground railroad work was hazardous enough as it was. Whether black or white, in the North or South, the benefactor of a fugitive slave ran a variety of risks. Imprisonment was an ever-present threat to those whose theater of activity included the slave states, as some Negro operators could ruefully attest. For journeying into the South to recruit runaways Samuel D. Burris was placed in jail at Dover, Delaware, for fourteen months. He was then auctioned off as a slave to serve for seven years, but his abolitionist friends arranged to have him purchased by a dummy. Elijah Anderson of Indiana died in 1857 at the state prison in Frankfort, Kentucky, where he was serving a term for conducting fugitive slaves across the state line. For the same offense and at the same penitentiary Oswald Wright of Corydon, Indiana, served a five-year term. Samuel Green, a local Methodist preacher at Dorchester County, Maryland, who attracted public attention upon receiving a sentence of ten years for possessing a copy of *Uncle Tom's Cabin*, was actually being punished for his suspected aid to fugitives, the original reason that brought the search party to his house.[47]

David Ruggles, executive secretary of the New York Committee of Vigilance, had to stay on the alert lest any attempt be made to assault him. He took the precaution of changing his lodgings periodically, but this did not save him late one night in January 1837 when a small group attempted to force open his door, possibly with kidnaping in mind. In 1838 Ruggles was jailed for two days on the charge that he had harbored Thomas Hughes, a slave charged with felony. At Columbus, Pennsylvania, Negro businessmen William Whipper and Stephen Smith risked no bodily harm or jail sentence for secreting slaves but two attempts were made to set fire to their lumberyard.[48]

Whites who were made to suffer for assisting fugitives received public expressions of sympathy and esteem from Negroes. Amos Dresser, who had received a public whipping in Nashville in 1836, allegedly for distributing abolitionist literature, received a different reception later that year at Theodore S. Wright's Presbyterian Church and at a crowded call meeting of the New York Committee of Vigilance. Daniel Drayton of the schooner *Pearl*, who spent over four years in jail for making arrangements to smuggle seventy-seven slaves from Washington to New York in April 1843, was an honored name among Negroes. The Colored Ladies' Anti-Slavery Sewing Circle of Canandaigua sent him $7 and an effusive letter, the latter described as being "exceedingly gratifying to the feelings of Captain Drayton." In New Haven at the Temple Street Church of Amos G. Beman he spoke to an overflow audience, many of whom purchased copies of his *Personal Memoirs*.[49] Perhaps there was a touch of self-guilt in the attitude of Negroes toward Drayton, a colored informer having been a contributing factor in his capture.

For assisting runaways Calvin Fairbank served two prison terms, totaling nearly seventeen years. His first stay came to an end in August 1849 when Lewis Hayden, the former slave whose escape had led to Fairbank's arrest, raised $650 from 160 donors to pay Hayden's owners, who thereupon joined in the petition for a pardon for Fairbank. Detroit Negroes, led by George DeBaptiste, took up a collection for Fairbank upon his release.[50] In less than three years, however, Fairbank was back in a Kentucky jail, again for aiding a fugitive. This time he remained behind bars until late in the Civil War, in the meantime sending letters to Frederick Douglass and others, addressed from "Louisville Jail."

The fugitive slave movement had its martyr in Charles T. Torrey, who died in a Maryland penitentiary in May 1846. A clergyman-abolitionist who felt compelled to live out his convictions about the brotherhood of man, Torrey worshiped only in Negro churches while in Washington in the winter of 1841. From his base at Baltimore, Torrey helped to speed some four hundred runaways on the road to freedom over a two-year span. But in 1844 he was charged by a Winchester, Virginia, master with helping his slaves escape, and the court sentenced him to six years at hard labor. At Boston "a Torrey meeting of Negroes" took up a collection of $30 for their jailed friend and called upon the abolitionists in general and the Negroes in particular to rally to his aid.[51] Detroit's black reformers gathered at the First Colored Baptist Church to offer prayers for him.

Torrey's death in May 1846 brought from Negroes many expressions of grief, mingled with indignation and purpose. At Oberlin the colored citizens adopted a series of resolutions drafted and read by William H. Day, tendering sympathy to Torrey's wife and children and condemning the governor of Maryland for not having pardoned him so that he might have "breathed his last among his native hills." Boston Negroes, meeting in Zion Church on June 15, 1846, voted to erect a monument to Torrey and invited the cooperation of colored people throughout New England. On July 31, 1846, the Negroes of the city held a service at Tremont Temple in honor of Torrey, with eulogies by John T. Hilton, William C. Nell, Joshua B. Smith, Henry Weeden, former slaves Samuel Snowden and Lewis Hayden, and a visiting speaker, Methodist minister Lucius C. Matlack, a friend of Torrey's.[52]

Meeting the next day at an August First celebration the colored people of Providence passed a resolution in favor of the Torrey monument proposal made by the Boston Negroes. But the Torrey Monument Association received very few contributions, Garrison having expressed the opinion that abolitionist money might be put to better use. The absence of such a stone did not keep Negroes from visiting Torrey's grave at Mt. Auburn cemetery at Cambridge, Massachusetts, Daniel Payne making a trip there in the summer of 1850.[53]

During the four months he spent in the Moyamemsing Prison in 1855 Passmore Williamson of Philadelphia evoked the sympathy of Negroes throughout the North. Williamson, a member of the General Vigilance Committee, was charged with contempt of court for having refused to reveal the whereabouts of three slaves whom he had persuaded to leave their master, no less a personage than the United States Minister to Nicaragua, John H. Wheeler. In truth Williamson did not know the whereabouts of Jane Johnson and her two boys, Daniel and Isaiah, inasmuch as they had been spirited from the wharf by William Still and five Negro porters. Still and his accomplices were brought to trial, two of them, John Ballard and William Curtis, receiving a week in jail for assault and battery on Colonel Wheeler.[54]

While the trial of the six black rescuers was going on, Williamson remained behind bars. But he received hundreds of letters and scores of visitors. Among the latter was a five-man delegation—George T. Downing, Stephen Myers, Robert Purvis, Charles Lenox Remond, and John S. Rock —from the Colored National Convention, which was meeting in Philadelphia in mid-October 1855. The delegates reported that Williamson had assured them that he would not sacrifice a single principle on the altar of slavery. A month later the highminded Quaker was triumphantly acquitted, his case having been greatly strengthened by Jane's testimony that, in the language of the court record, she had "willingly left the boat, aided in the departure by several colored persons, who took her children, with her consent, and led or carried them off the boat, and conducted your petitioner and her children to a carriage, a short distance from the boat." [55]

The friends of the fugitive included a small corps of lawyers and to these, too, the Negroes found a way to express their gratitude. At Bethel Church in February 1841, a group representing the colored citizens of Philadelphia gave a set of silver plates to David Paul Brown for his services in defending runaways. At Cincinnati, Salmon P. Chase regularly defended fugitives, receiving no fees for his services but acquiring a silver pitcher from the city's grateful blacks. In July 1851, attorneys E. C. Larned and George Maniere each received a silver cup from the colored citizens of Chicago as a token of high regard for their successful services on behalf of Moses Johnson, an alleged fugitive. For their legal services in the Shadrach rescue case in 1851, Richard Henry Dana and John P. Hale received from the Negroes of Boston an eight-volume set of Henry Hallam's *Constitutional History of England* which, as the donors pointed out, was "a history marked by the progress of free institutions and by the virtue of courage of great lawyers." Both recipients sent gracious replies, Dana stating that the set gave him a feeling of pride and gratification and Hale saying that he would cherish his set while he lived and bequeath it to his family when he was gone. [56]

To a Negro abolitionist few things could be so satisfying as helping a runaway. But the great majority of black leaders felt that there was a complementary work to be done—one that would not only strike at slavery but would simultaneously elevate the free Negro. This was the use of political power—getting the ballot and putting it to the proper use.

NOTES

1. Still to J. M. McKim, Aug. 8, 1850, in *Bugle*, Nov. 9, 1850. See also the interesting article, Robert Brent Toplin, "Peter Still Versus the Peculiar Institution," *Civil War History* 13 (Dec. 1967): 340–49.

2. L. Maria Child, *Isaac T. Hopper: A True Life* (Boston, 1853), p. 209.

3. Fred Landon, "A Daring Canadian Abolitionist," *Michigan History Magazine* 5 (July-Oct. 1921): 370.

4. Birney to Tappan, Feb. 27, 1837, Dwight L. Dumond, ed., *Letters of James Gillespie Birney*, 2 vols. (New York: D. Appleton-Century Co., 1938), I, p. 376. Benjamin G. Merkel, "The Underground Railroad and the Missouri Borders, 1840–1860," *Missouri Historical Review* 37 (Apr. 1943): 278. Rush R. Sloane, "The Underground Railroad of the Firelands," *Magazine of Western History* 8 (May 1888): 38. E. Delorus Preston, Jr., "The Underground Railroad in Northwest Ohio," *Journal of Negro History* 17 (Oct. 1932): 411.

5. Wilbur H. Siebert, *The Underground Railroad from Slavery to Freedom* (New York, 1898), p. 32; hereafter cited as *Underground Railroad;* Ibid., pp. 151, 403–36.

6. Earl Conrad, *Harriet Tubman* (Washington, D. C.: Associated Publishers, 1943), p. 232. Mary Thacher Higginson, ed., *Letters and Journals of Thomas Wentworth Higginson, 1846–1906* (New York: Houghton Mifflin Company, 1921), p. 81.

7. Siebert, *Underground Railroad*, pp. 70, 296.

8. Wilbur Siebert, "The Underground Railroad in Massachusetts," *Proceedings of the American Antiquarian Society*, new series 45 (1936): 29. Luther R. Marsh, ed., *Writings and Speeches of Alvan Stewart on Slavery* (New York, 1860), pp. 219–20.

9. Siebert, *Underground Railroad*, p. 95. Allan Peskin, ed., *North into Freedom: The Autobiography of John Malvin, Free Negro, 1795–1880* (Cleveland: Press of Western Reserve University, 1966), pp. 6, 10.

10. Larry Gara, *The Liberty Line: The Legend of the Underground Railroad* (Lexington: University of Kentucky Press, 1961), pp. 27–28; hereafter cited as *Liberty Line. Genius*, Oct. 1831.

11. William Craft, *Running a Thousand Miles for Freedom* (London, 1860), p. 85. Levi Coffin, *Reminiscences of Levi Coffin* (Cincinnati, 1876), p. 107; hereafter cited as *Reminiscences*. Emma Lou Thornbrough, *Negro in Indiana before 1900* (Indianapolis: Indiana Historical Bureau, 1957), p. 41.

12. Coffin, *Reminiscences*, p. 297. Wendell P. Dabney, *Cincinnati's Colored Citizens* (Cincinnati: Dabney Publishing Co., 1926), p. 130. For Mitchell, see William M. Mitchell, *The Underground Railroad* (London, 1860). Siebert, *Underground Railroad*, p. 70. Jones to F. Douglass, Nov. 11, 1853, in *Douglass' Paper*, Nov. 18, 1853.

13. R. C. Smedley, *History of the Underground Railroad in Chester and the Neighboring Counties of Pennsylvania* (Lancaster, 1883), p. 355; hereafter cited as *Underground Railroad in Chester*. William Still, *Underground Railroad* (Philadelphia, 1872), p. 736. Whipper to White, Apr. 26, 1839, Leon Gardiner Collection. Smedley, *Underground Railroad in Chester*, p. 338.

14. Monroe N. Work, "Life of Charles B. Ray," *Journal of Negro History* 4 (Oct. 1919): 371. *Weekly Anglo-African*, Sept. 17, 1859.

15. *Narrative of William W. Brown, A Fugitive Slave. Written by Himself* (Boston, 1847), pp. 107–8.

16. Archibald H. Grimké, "Anti-Slavery Boston," *New England Magazine*, new series 3 (December, 1890): 453. Austin Bearse, *Reminiscences of Fugitive-Slave Days in Boston* (Boston, 1880), p. 8.

17. These abolitionist outfits are not be confused with the horse-thief societies so common to the rural America of that day.

18. *Douglass' Paper*, Apr. 6, 1855.

19. *Emancipator*, Jan. 26, 1837.

20. Wilson's arrest in *Colored American*, July 21, 1838. *Emancipator*, June 1, 1837.

21. *Herald of Freedom*, Mar. 8, 1839.

22. For the Charity Walker affair, see *Mirror of Liberty* (New York), July 1838.

23. In its August 20, 1840, issue, *The Standard* devotes six columns to an airing of the quarrel between Ruggles and the committee.

24. *First Annual Report of the New York Committee of Vigilance* (New York, 1837), p. 84. *Emancipator*, June 1, 1837, Aug. 13, 1840, June 17, 1841.

25. *Liberator*, Dec. 12, 1845. DeBaptiste to Douglass, Nov. 5, 1854, in *Douglass' Paper*, Nov. 17, 1854. *Provincial Freeman*, May 31, 1856. *Douglass' Paper*, Jan. 26, 1855.

26. Emerson to "Dr. S. G. Howe, and Associates of the Committee of Citizens," Sept. 23, 1846, in *Address of the Committee Appointed by a Public Meeting Held in Faneuil Hall, September 24, 1846, for the Purpose of Considering the Recent Case of Kidnaping from our Soil and of Taking Measures to Prevent the Recurrence of Similar Outrages* (Boston, 1846), p. 31.

27. Benjamin Quarles, *Black Abolitionists* (New York: Oxford University Press, 1969), pp. 197–222.

28. *North Star*, May 19, 1848. *Bugle*, May 25, 1849. *Report of the New York State Vigilance Committee made at the Annual Meeting Held in New York, March 19, 1853* (New York, 1853), p. 4.

29. For the constitution of the Fugitive Aid Society, see *Douglass' Weekly*, Apr. 6, 1855. *Weekly Anglo-African*, May 5, 1860.

30. Minutes of the Philadelphia Female Anti-Slavery Society, Sept. 8, 1842, Historical Society of Pennsylvania.

31. See letter of White to Ruggles, Dec. 6, 1838, in Leon Gardiner Collection. On the makeup and operations of this organization see Joseph A. Boromé, "The Vigilant Committee of Philadelphia," *Pennsylvania Magazine of History and Biography* 92 (July 1968): 320–51.

32. Carter Godwin Woodson, *The Mind of the Negro as Reflected in Letters Written During the Crisis, 1800–1860* (Washington, D. C.: Association for the Study of Negro Life and History, Inc., 1926), p. 586.

33. Still, *Underground Railroad*, p. 83.

34. *Colored American*, June 8, 1838. *First Annual Report of the New York Committee of Vigilance*, p. 84. *Emancipator*, Sept. 19, 1839. Figures of donations to Vigilance Committee of Philadelphia compiled from the Minute Book of the Vigilant Committee of Philadelphia, June 4, 1839, to March 20, 1844, which also includes other fund-raising activities of the committee.

35. *Liberator*, Mar. 5, 1852. *Douglass' Monthly*, Mar. 1859. Funds raised at Sunday collections compiled from *Liberator*, Aug. 28, 1846.

36. *Emancipator*, Mar. 19, 1840. *Northern Star and Freeman's Advocate*, Dec. 8, 1842. *North Star*, May 18, 1849. *Liberator*, July 8, 1858.

37. The woman's auxiliary reference is found in the Minute Book of the Vigilant Committee of Philadelphia, June 4, 1839, to March 20, 1844. All other citations may be found in the Minutes of the Philadelphia Female Anti-Slavery Society, 1839–70 (8 vols., handwritten).

38. *Douglass' Paper*, Mar. 11, 1842. *Report of Edinburgh Ladies New Anti-Slavery Association for 1856 and 1857* (Edinburgh, 1858), p. 3. For Richardson's letters to Still (Vigilance Committee of Philadelphia), see Still's *Underground Railroad*, pp. 604–8. *Report of the Edinburgh Ladies New Anti-Slavery Association for 1858*, p. 5.

39. Loguen to "Dear Friend," Feb. 7, 1859, in A.M.A. Papers.

40. Minutes of the Philadelphia Female Anti-Slavery Society, 1839–70, Nov. 11, 1841.

41. Minute Book of the Vigilant Committee of Philadelphia, Dec. 4, 1839. *Liberator*, Aug. 7, 1845. *Standard*, Feb. 21, 1850. *Douglass' Paper*, Dec. 7, 1855.

42. *Standard*, Jan. 2, 1858. Thomas Franklin Harwood, "Great Britain and American Antislavery," (unpublished doctoral dissertation, University of Texas, 1959), p. 712.

43. E. B. Chace, *Anti-Slavery Reminiscences* (Central Falls, R.I., 1891), p. 89.

44. Coffin, *Reminiscences*, p. 298.

45. W. Montague Cobb, "Martin Robinson Delany, 1812–1855," *Journal of the National Medical Association* 44 (May 1952): 234.

46. Laura Haviland, *Woman's Life Work* (Grand Rapids, Mich., 1881), p. 135. *Liberator*, Sept. 11, 1858. Thornbrough, *Negro in Indiana*, p. 42.

47. *Standard*, Sept. 21, 1848. Still, *Underground Railroad*, pp. 746–47. Thornbrough, *Negro in Indiana*, p. 42. Still, *Underground Railroad*, pp. 246–50.

48. *Liberator*, Dec. 21, 1849. *Weekly Advocate*, Jan. 14, 1837. Still, *Underground Railroad*, p. 739.

49. *Emancipator*, Dec. 8, 15, 1836. *Pennsylvania Freeman*, Jan. 6, 1853. Beman to Douglass, Sept. 10, 1855, in *Douglass' Paper*, Sept. 14, 1855.

50. *Standard*, Sept. 13, 1849. Calvin Fairbank, *How the Way Was Prepared* (Chicago, 1890), p. 63.

51. J. C. Lovejoy, *Memoir of Charles T. Torrey* (Boston, 1847), p. 89. *Emancipator*, Aug. 14, 1844.

52. *Liberator*, July 10, Aug. 7, 1846.

53. Ibid., Daniel A. Payne, *Recollections of Seventy Years* (Nashville, 1888), p. 98.

54. For a good contemporary account of the Williamson episode, see William Still's lengthy article in *Provincial Freeman*, Aug. 22, 1855.

55. *Proceedings of Colored National Convention of 1855*, p. 25. *Case of Passmore Williamson. Report of the Proceedings . . .* (Philadelphia, 1856), p. 165.

56. *Colored American*, Feb. 20, 1841. Albert Bushnell Hart, *Salmon Portland Chase* (Boston, 1899), pp. 82, 84. *Liberator*, July 11, 1851. Robert Morris to Dana, Jan. 1, 1852; Morris to Hale, Jan. 1, 1852; Hale to Morris, Jan. 18, 1852, and Dana to Morris, Jan. 1, 1852, all in *Liberator*, Mar. 19, 1852.

27. HOWARD H. BELL, Search for a Place: Black Separatism and Africa, 1860 (1969)*

Black resistance to white oppression in the United States took several forms. In addition to protesting against discrimination in the North and to assisting fugitive slaves in escaping bondage in the South, a few prominent Afro-Americans were advocates of Black Separatism. Howard H. Bell, a white historian at Morgan State University, is a specialist on Black Nationalism during the ante-bellum period. Author of several valuable articles on black militancy, he has also written a detailed account of the Negro Convention Movement. In this selection, Professor Bell describes the activities of Martin R. Delany and Alexander Campbell, who became promoters of the most extreme form of separatism: a Back to Africa Movement in the 1850s.

* From Howard H. Bell, "Introduction" in M. R. Delany and Robert Campbell, *Search for a Place: Black Separatism and Africa, 1860* (Ann Arbor: University of Michigan Press, 1969), pp. 1–22. Reprinted by permission.

Often, present-day black separatists look for ways to restore the balance of justice for centuries of oppression by penalizing the white man. Their counterparts a century ago looked often for a place beyond the borders of the United States where they might develop a powerful black nation, the products of which would compete economically with those of the slave South, and where the Negro's genius for politics and government would be unhampered by meddling whites.

Mindful always of their responsibility to those still in slavery, the Negro separatists of that era reasoned that uplift of the black race, whether in Canada, the Caribbean, Central America, or Africa would have a "reflex influence" on the plight of those still held in bondage and on those only partly removed from its curse in America. A black nation would in time accomplish the goals which an oppressed people could not accomplish for themselves. To support this thesis they pointed to such examples as the Puritans who had been unable to throw off the yoke of oppression in England until some of their number had braved the dangers of a new land and had established a viable government of their own. Of such conviction were Martin R. Delany and Robert Campbell, two black Americans who penetrated into the Egba and Yoruba areas of what is now western Nigeria in the search for a place where, in the Biblical language so meaningful to Americans of the mid-nineteenth century, "Ethiopia might stretch forth her hand."

Campbell begins his narrative at Liverpool, England, June 24, 1859, and ends it at the same city, May 12, 1860. Delany's *Report* is only briefly narrative and is concerned chiefly with conditions that the immigrant would encounter. Delany arrived in Liberia in July 1859; from there he sailed to Lagos, and not until November 5 did he meet Campbell at Abbeokuta, the starting point for their expedition inland as far as Illorin. Thereafter, they remained together except for short intervals.

When the expedition began, Delany was forty-seven years old; Campbell probably twenty years younger. Delany, born in northern Virginia in 1812 to parents who traced their ancestry to African chieftains, grew up with a great pride in all things black—a pride that was to be the sorrow and the joy of an action-packed life. Perennial student, editor, and publisher, Harvard student of medicine, dentist, doctor, orator, explorer, dabbler "in absentia" in Central American politics, army officer, and politician, Delany was ever changing in his career, but it was always associated with the black man and his place in history. In the words of an eminent contemporary, Delany was "the intensest embodiment of black Nationality to be met with outside the valley of the Niger" (*Douglass' Monthly*, August, 1862, p. 695).

Campbell, born in the British West Indies of Negro-Caucasian ancestry (he stated that he was three-fourths white), received a good education, traveled in Central America, and became a teacher of science in the Institute for Colored Youth in Philadelphia. Unlike Delany, he developed no reputation as a militant or separatist, but did develop an interest in Africa as the secrets of that continent began to be revealed through the works of missionaries in the 1850s.

The interest of American blacks in Africa was not new when Delany and Campbell, representing the "General Board of Commissioners" of the colored people, explored the Niger area. As early as 1770 young Negroes had been in training to go to Africa in something of a missionary capacity. The Revolutionary War and its aftermath saw thousands of American blacks being dispersed to various British possessions, with some making their way to Africa. Periodically thereafter certain Negro Americans thought of Africa as a land of opportunity, as a world to which they owed a debt of loyalty for having been the land of their forebears, as a land for missionary effort, or as an area of economic opportunity for which blacks were qualified physically, mentally, and emotionally in greater degree than whites. A number of Negroes from Boston expressed an interest in emigration to Africa in 1787, and before the end of the century a Rhode Island group had asked permission to enter the British colony of Sierra Leone. But the first American Negro to make an individual attempt to tie Africa and North America together commercially by cords of black was Paul Cuffee, a Quaker of Negro-Indian ancestry, a self-made fisherman, whaler, merchant. Cuffee sought with some degree of success to persuade American blacks to take an interest in his joint scheme for emigration and commercial exploitation, but it was brought to a halt by the War of 1812. After the war he did transport a group of emigrants, but died soon afterward.

When in 1816 the American Colonization Society presented its plan for expatriation of free Negroes to the land that was to become Liberia, the great mass of Negro Americans quickly labeled the enterprise as destructive of the black heritage in America and would have nothing to do with it. Of Cuffee's top echelon of former supporters (James Forten, the clergymen Peter Williams, and Daniel Coker) only Coker supported the new effort. Resentment against the plan for expatriation, for whatever reason, and knowledge of the high mortality rate in Liberia were strong influences against any emigration or colonization project for many years. A further deterrent was the widely held abolitionist doctrine that the free Negro should stand by to see the deliverance of the slave from bondage in America. Finally, the expulsive forces were just not strong enough in America to drive many blacks overseas.

The attention of free blacks was eventually turned to lands beyond the borders (except for runaway slaves who found refuge chiefly in Canada) by economic opportunities and Negro nationalism—a kind of militant black unity—which developed concurrently in the decade of the 1850s. Meantime, the foundations for these developments were being laid by evolvement of Negro leadership, capital, and education at home. Before 1830 black leadership had been confined largely to Negro churches, lodges, and self-help associations and had not been noticeable on the national level. Determined to play a larger role in American society, Negroes in 1827 started a new periodical, *Freedom's Journal;* and by 1830 they had begun a series of national conventions, which were to have a telling effect on America—both black and white.

Thereafter, the voice of the Negro gained rapidly in authority as the younger and usually the better educated gained positions of leadership. By 1840 the able young men who boasted a college education were not as prejudiced against emigration as their parents had been. They were willing to consider all avenues of progress, even if it meant leaving their immediate surroundings, and even adventuring on foreign soil. Canada, Haiti, Central America, Liberia had each its appeal to the more venturesome. On the whole, however, the invisible cords of a self-imposed loyalty to those still in bondage, an indefinable reluctance to gamble life and goods in a new land, and a firm belief in their rights as native-born Americans to all of the privileges of free birth and citizenship kept blacks from emigrating for many years.

So long as the Negro community considered emigration as part and parcel of a diabolical scheme of the American Colonization Society to rid the country of free Negroes, there could be no strong support for overseas projects. Occasionally, a minister like Daniel Coker or an editor like John Russwurm would brave the wrath of Negro public opinion to make his home in Africa, but their number was never large nor particularly influential. During these decades it was more acceptable to go to Canada, Haiti, or the British West Indies, where, so the reasoning went, the Negro American could influence the government of his adopted home in the cause of eliminating American slavery, where, so far as the Caribbean area was concerned, he could compete with the South in the production of cotton for the world market, and where, hopefully, he would have a place in the highest ranks of government. So it was that several thousand black Americans made their way to the Caribbean regions during the 1820s and 1830s and some, like Hezekiah Grice and F. E. Dubois, rose to prominence in their adopted lands. Also, substantial communities of free blacks developed in Canada.

Meanwhile, voices began to be raised in defense of the right to choose individually where one would cast his lot. Writing in *The Colored American* for May 3, 1838, "Augustine" contended that animosity of the black community to emigration was simply a reaction to the effort of the American Colonization Society to exile the free Negroes and that this was not a legitimate reason for the opposition. A few months later (September 28) he was examining the belief expressed by some blacks that they should face death rather than allow themselves to be removed from America for any cause whatsoever. "After much reflection upon this highly important point, I am free to acknowledge that I am not one of that number." Noting that too many blacks were "just beginning to live happily in the West Indies, and in Canada, for me to think of dying just now," he suggested that he would "rather be a *living freeman,* even in one of these places, than a 'dead nigger' in the United States."

Another voice in favor of breaking the tie that bound the free Negro to the area close to the slave came from Cleveland, where the Young Men's Union Society labored over a plan to found a colony either within the United States or on its borders. In a series of reports in *The Colored American* for March 2 and 9 and May 18, 1839, the youthful group defended their plan, which called for minimal separation from home territory and for emphasis upon strengthening the black community so that it could withstand pressures exerted toward expatriation to Africa. James M. Whitfield, reporter and defender of the project, would be heard from again. In fact, he became during the 1850s one of the most ardent advocates of Negro emigration, which, to him and his compatriots, was an integral part of Negro nationalism. This movement encompassed a strong pride in the African heritage and a kind of militant unity distrustful of white leadership in projects pertaining to the black community, sought to bypass social and political controls within the nation by setting up black-dominated controls, and planned to establish or support a black nation somewhere beyond the bounds of the United States. Negatively, Negro nationalism may be seen in the unified opposition to the American Colonization Society's effort in Liberia; more positively its embryonic structure may be found in the Negro's defiance in 1840 of the whites who had for a decade made themselves conspicuous in Negro conventions or in the growing feeling expressed openly by the editor of the *Ram's Horn* in 1847 when he suggested that a proposition could be considered legitimately by the Negro community because it was being put forward by a Negro. The black unity—so ready to reject a project proposed by whites and so willing to accept, at least for investigation, a proposition by Negroes—was to become pronounced during the 1850s.

No one year can be singled out as the beginning of a new era in Negro interest in areas beyond the borders of the United States, but the birth of the government of Liberia in 1847 was significant. No longer to be considered only as a white man's attempt to siphon off the free black, Liberia now emerged as a black nation and therefore a place to which the Negro American could look with hope—even with pride. Henry Highland Garnet launched one of the most spectacular challenges to the philosophy of staying at home while black governments were being born, and black men could be building for a brighter future. In articles in the *North Star* for January 26 and March 2, 1849, he made it clear that he still opposed the American Colonization Society in its philosophy that the Negro could never rise to equality in America, but he was now ready to accept the long-suspect society's ministrations "to the land of my fathers," and like "Augustine" a decade earlier he would rather be free in lands beyond the borders than a slave in the United States. He now looked to Liberia to become of great commercial and political benefit to Africa, and he expected the new government to check the slave trade "by the diffusion of light and knowledge, and by turning the attention of the black traders to some other and honorable business, and by sweeping off the white ones as with the hands of an avenging God."

Garnet's new stand on emigration was followed by a feverish decade of proposals and counterproposals relating to emigration, always with the view that emigration and Negro nationalism went hand in hand. Information on politics and on the agricultural or horticultural potential of Liberia and news of educational advances in the new nation, which hitherto had always been rebuffed by the abolitionist press, now received a respectful hearing by at least some Negro editors; other blacks, especially the younger generation, put their new interest to practical account by trying their luck on foreign soil.

Martin R. Delany with his great pride in the black race was not slow to accept the new interest, and once having done so he became the embodiment of Negro separatism to the great discomfiture of those dedicated to leading the Negro into full equality in the United States. In 1852 he published a booklet entitled *The Condition, Elevation, Emigration, and Destiny of the Colored People of the United States*. Here he claimed credit for having planned at an earlier date an East African commercial-colonization project based on a transcontinental railway reaching from the Red Sea to the west coast. Now willing to suspend the original venture, so long as the black man got credit for the plan, he turned his attention to the more urgent need for developing a powerful and respected Negro nation in the tropics of the Western Hemisphere. But whether his interests lay in the American tropics early in the decade or in Africa in the latter part, he saw the need to develop a strong support from black America. He must change the philosophy which had bound the black man to the area where he could be a symbol of hope to the enslaved and a threat to the enslaver. He must persuade blacks to change an attitude which made them reluctant to lead in any venture, but willing to follow if the white man led the way. He must persuade Negro Americans that once the colored people got together in the American tropics they would be beyond the grasp of the United States. And above all he must persuade them that it was the will of God. He warned against resisting lest "[God's] protecting arm and fostering care . . . be withdrawn from us."

As to those who remained in bondage in America, Delany recognized that blacks must ever be mindful of their condition, but the "reflex influence" would be at work to mitigate their plight. In his words "the redemption of the bondmen depends entirely upon the elevation of the freeman; therefore, to elevate the free colored people of America, anywhere upon this continent, forbodes the speedy redemption of the slaves."

Within a few months Delany was emphasizing the necessity for having access to all means of progress. In a communication to *Frederick Douglass' Paper* of July 23, 1852, he insisted that the black man must take the lead in developing projects for black people. "We must have a position," he wrote, "independently of anything pertaining to white men or nations." It was time to quit "whimpering, whining, and snivelling at the feet of white men." Still later (April 1, 1853), after Douglass had been in consultation with Harriet Beecher Stowe concerning an educational project, Delany insisted that Douglass had not acted properly. Blacks, not whites, must make plans for blacks. In regard to Mrs. Stowe, Delany insisted "she *knows nothing about us* . . . neither does any other white person—and, consequently can contrive no successful scheme for our elevation." He wanted it clearly understood that "no enterprise, institution, or anything else, should be commenced *for us*, or our general benefit, without first consulting us."

Delany's booklet appeared in 1852. In 1853 the great national Negro convention met at Rochester and set up the Negro National Council, probably in an effort to capitalize on the growing militancy in the Negro community, which was fueling the separatist trend. It was anticipated that this National Council would supervise a national educational institution, a national consumer's union, a national system of arbitration of disputes, a national information agency—all to be formed in the hope of keeping problems of blacks as much as possible in the hands of blacks and out of the hands of whites.

In a countermove the emigrationists were to meet at Cleveland in 1854. Meanwhile, a running literary battle developed between James M.

Whitfield, for the separatists, and Frederick Douglass and William J. Watkins, for those favorable to remaining in the United States. These articles were drawn together by M. T. Newsome in a pamphlet entitled *Arguments, Pro and Con, on the Call for a National Emigration Convention* [1854], with an introduction by emigrationist J. Theodore Holly. They ably develop the opposing viewpoints and are especially valuable in seeking to understand the separatist philosophy.

Holly referred to the recently created National Council as "an informal national organization of a denationalized people, whereby an organic, though premature and sickly birth was given to the idea of [Negro] national independence." Whitfield, writing on the same subject, suggested that the effort at Rochester had been "to create a union of sentiment and action among the colored people, and give it efficiency, by forming a kind of national organization here, under the overshadowing influence of their oppressors." Like Delany and most other separatists, Whitfield contended that respect and equality for colored men in America or elsewhere would come only after blacks could show "men of their own race occupying a primary position instead of a secondary and inferior one."

These men knew their history and they knew their times. "Manifest Destiny" had been much in the public mind as the United States relieved neighboring countries of territorial possessions on its trek west and south. But black men were seldom welcome as participants in the American manifest destiny in an age when slavery still existed in nearly half of the states. Whitfield looked beyond the narrow confines of the continent and proclaimed: "I believe it to be the destiny of the negro, to develop a higher order of civilization and Christianity than the world has yet seen." Like Delany he saw manifest destiny for the Negro in the American tropics, beyond the reach of the United States. Then, challenging the discomfited proponents of the National Council, he portrayed emigration as merely the continuation of a logical forward movement begun by them at the great Rochester National Convention. "The child who has ventured to stand alone, must, of necessity, either step on or fall down again and crawl in the dust." Though forward movement might be feeble, it was, in Whitfield's estimation, preferable to "crawling again in the dust to the feet of our oppressors."

Whitfield had shared with Delany an early interest in emigration. Like Delany he suffered for his people when he saw them slow to move into unoccupied or thinly populated lands when they could possess the land for themselves, and then quick to rush in as menials when those lands had fallen to the westward surge of white Americans. "If such a course as this is pursued," inquired the disconsolate Whitfield, "what stronger proof could be desired by our enemies in support of their favorite argument, that the negro is incapable of self-government, and aspires no higher than to be a servant to the whites?"

Repeatedly, the emigrationists were accused of seeking to emigrate en masse, and repeatedly they denied it. Whitfield dealt with the problem more than once in exchanges with opponents in the months between the formation of the National Council at Rochester in 1853 and the emigration convention at Cleveland in 1854. He insisted that emigration en masse was impossible in a society which had passed beyond the pastoral stage, and that mass emigration was not a prerequisite for achieving their goals. He was just as firmly of the opinion that emigration of some of the proscribed group was necessary and that those who did emigrate "should go forth and build up their own institutions, and conduct them in such a manner as to furnish ocular proof of their . . . capacity . . . to fulfill ably all the duties of the highest as well as the lowest positions of society."

The Cleveland National Convention on emigration ruled out opponents of emigration and any who were looking toward Africa. Those interested in emigration to the West Indies, Central America, and South America and those with an interest in Canada were to be given a hearing. They reminded each other that they must always remember the slave, but in so doing they remained firmly of the opinion that by congregating in the American tropics they could be building a new home and a new nation while competing with the American South and thus cutting the slave system down.

In his prepared document on "The Political Destiny of the Colored Race," published as a part of the *Proceedings of the National Emigration Convention,* Delany denied that the blacks were either free men or citizens; he contended that his people could not be free unless they constituted a majority of the ruling class and that emigration was the answer to the plight of the black. Here as elsewhere in his writings, Delany cited the fact that world population was predominantly colored. "The white races," he wrote, "are but one-third of the population of the globe—or one of them to two of us—and it cannot much longer continue that two-thirds will passively submit to the universal domination of this one-third." He recognized readily the great accomplishments of the Caucasian, but unlike earlier blacks in the United States who had "admitted themselves to be inferior, we barely acknowledge the whites as equals." And if equals, or even superiors in some areas of endeavor, the whites were definitely inferior in certain physical qualities: "the whites in the southern part of the United States have *decreased* in numbers, *degenerated* in character, and become mentally and physically imbecile." On the other hand Delany saw the "blacks and colored" as having "steadily *increased* in numbers, *regenerated* in character, and grown mentally and physically vigorous."

Along with the physical ability to live and thrive where the whites could not, Delany saw the darker races as having "the highest traits of civilization." "They are," he said, "civil, peaceable, and religious to a fault." This group would most surely prove their leadership "in the true principles of morals, correctness of thought, religion, and law or civil government."

The ideas of Delany and Whitfield must be related to those of J. Theodore Holly, a former shoemaker, in order to get a clear picture of Negro separatism which so vitally affected the 1850s and which culminated in separate drives toward Africa and Haiti. Holly investigated possibilities of going to Liberia in 1850, but in the following year he attended the North American Convention at Toronto, where the emphasis was on activities in the Western Hemisphere. Holly's principal ideas on Negro nationalism are presented in a series of articles in *The Anglo-African Magazine* from June to November 1859. Although his emphasis is on Haiti, the Negro separatist philosophy is orthodox and applicable to other areas. He saw the Haitian government as the "most irrefragable proof of the equality of the negro race." He would direct American Negroes to Haiti so that they might offer their skills to a less-developed people, but people with whom they could find easy assimilation. He saw American Negro emigration as a necessity "for the political enfranchisement of the colored people of the United States," but also as the only logical source from which Haiti could draw in its effort to improve.

Turning his attention to the significance of a Negro nation, Holly contended, as did most other separatists, that the black man was exploited on a world-wide basis because there was no powerful Negro nation to call a halt to such abuse. The appearance of such a nation would stop the African slave trade and portend the end of slavery itself. From this nation "a reflex influence will irradiate, not only to uproot American slavery, but also to overthrow African slavery and the slave-trade throughout the world."

In a pamphlet publication, *A Vindication of the Capacity of the Negro for Self-Government* (1857) Holly stated his views on the comparative qualities of white and black. "I have made no allowance," he wrote, "for the negroes just emerging from a barbarous condition and out of the brutish ignorance of West Indian slavery." His reason for not making any allowance was his "fear that instead of proving negro equality only, I should prove negro superiority."

Between 1854 and 1858 Holly and Delany worked together through the Board of Commissioners of colored people organized at the Cleveland emigration convention in 1854. Their emphasis was on a black empire in the American tropics. New interest in Africa from various sources, including missionary accounts, was becoming more pronounced as the decade progressed, and Delany's earlier interest in that continent was renewed to the extent that he transferred his efforts from the American tropics to Africa.

The year 1858 is important in the African phase of Negro separatism. The African Civilization Society was launched at Philadelphia, with Henry Highland Garnet, veteran of many a battle within and without the Negro community for the betterment of the race, as president of the new organization. This new organization was the outgrowth of a great deal of planning and support from Philadelphia whites, notably Benjamin Coates, Christian and colonizationist in sympathy, but a member of the American Colonization Society, and therefore suspect to most blacks even in 1858. The society began immediately to plan for an expedition to Africa, and there is some reason to suspect that Delany's decision to go to the Niger River area was dictated by the prior decision of the African Civilization Society to seek to exploit that district. Delany had earlier considered territory farther south. Garnet knew how to arouse the interest of the black community in his new project, and he proceeded to do so by public debates and by provoking Frederick Douglass into editorializing on the disadvantages of going to Africa in language no longer convincing.

Also in 1858, Delany and his colleagues met in convention for the third time to deliberate on what course to follow. Delany surrendered the presidency to William H. Day, but remained in a position of responsibility by being accorded the office of foreign secretary. Delany demanded immediate and specific action on Africa. His colleagues were willing to seek money to build up a press, schools, and churches in Canada and use these facilities to train young people to go as missionary teachers to Africa. At his own insistence Delany was authorized to be a commissioner to explore Africa and to name his own colleagues. He was also given the dubious privilege of raising the funds necessary for the expedition. It was characteristic of Delany that he assumed the arduous task willingly and went to work with his usual optimism. The funds would be available, and it was important that they come from the black community.

Thus, Delany and Garnet became rivals in an effort to explore within the Niger area. Delany had the formidable task of selecting capable members for the expedition, with no organizational backing for either men or money. Garnet had the support of the African Civilization Society, with access to money from interested whites. But if the two men were rivals, they still had much in common. Both had had an honorable career in efforts to improve the position of the blacks in America. Both had opposed emigration. Both had come to believe in emigration as a legitimate way of progress and to believe in a Negro nation. Both now looked to Africa as the land of promise.

Neither man expected miracles in planning for a home in Africa. They did not expect to lead a mass emigration. Both expected to develop small settlements of American blacks in Africa—people carefully chosen who would demonstrate Christianity, morality, and good character. They should have skills in agriculture, the mechanical arts, and commerce; they should come well recommended. It was expected that these enclaves of Americans would influence the people of Africa to accept their way of life. Meantime, the new community would raise cotton or other crops to compete with the American South and thus hasten the day when slavery would be no more. And if there were still slaves being put on board ship from Africa, that curse could also be eliminated by the influence of the new settlers.

Delany's unwillingness to use money from whites quickly got him into financial difficulties which Garnet's easier acceptance of proffered aid allowed him to avoid. In fact, it was Garnet's organization, the African Civilization Society, which put up the money necessary to send one of Delany's chosen colleagues on his way to Africa via England. This was, of course, without Delany's consent. The man in question was Robert Campbell. Campbell's residence at Philadelphia made him a natural target for those interested in the African Civilization Society, for Philadelphia was also the home of Benjamin Coates, to whom Frederick Douglass once referred as the real head of the African Civilization Society. When Delany had trouble raising funds for the expedition, which was to have lasted for three years and to have had five members, Campbell was induced to accept aid from the rival organization and departed for England. In so doing Campbell not only violated a trust, he also offended Delany's black nationalism, even compounding the offense by accepting more money—this time from Englishmen—on his way to Africa.

With Campbell already on his way, Delany had to secure emergency financing and betake himself to Africa in order to maintain some semblance of control. The men were gone about a year. They visited England together on their way home and were accorded a hero's welcome.

Their separate reports, though partly covering the same material, are in most respects highly individualistic. Of the two accounts, Delany's is the more mission-minded; Campbell's the more practical and factual. Both were familiar with Thomas Jefferson Bowen's *Central Africa* (1857) and seem to have used information from it to some extent. Delany was familiar with David Livingstone's *Missionary Travels and Researches in South Africa,* first published in London in 1857, and this work seems to have influenced his thinking on Africa, but bears little relation to the printed report. Campbell appreciated Charlotte Tucker's *Abbeoukuta,* which by 1854 had reached a fourth edition. Miss Tucker, unlike Bowen and Livingstone, had not lived in Africa but had drawn her information from missionary sources and from her familiarity with the lives of some of the missionaries.

Bowen, a white Southern Baptist missionary, had the advantage of having spent some seven years in the interior of Africa, mostly in the Egba-Yoruba country. He was a missionary first, a rather good observer second. But he had one overwhelming disadvantage. He was a white man in a black society that had not been cowed by colonialism, nor was it a society particularly receptive to the Christian religion which Bowen was seeking to propagate. His observations were from the outside, sometimes so literally from the outside that he was not allowed to sleep within the walls of the town. Delany and Campbell, though classified as "white men" because they had accepted the Euro-American way of life, had the great advantage of being considered as relatives of the Africans, even though Campbell had to make a point of explaining that he was indeed of African ancestry. Delany was never troubled by any such necessity for explanations. His face was proof positive that Africa was indeed the land of his fathers.

In reporting on their sojurn in Africa, whether in Liberia or in Egba-Yoruba area from Lagos to Ilorin, Delany seldom forgets his mission. He must develop a Negro nation. He must read into the record the achievement of the black man and his plans for the future, for white historians had deprived the Negro of his rightful place in history by simply failing to record the accomplishments of other groups than their own. He suffered for the race when he recounts how his young colleague had taken things into his own hands and had, in his estimation, sullied the banner of Negro nationalism by accepting money from, and thereby an obligation to, the Africa Civilization Society.

Delany reports courteous treatment at the hands of the Liberians, even though his fame as an opponent of the American Colonization Society's child had preceded him. He found it possible to explain his position to their satisfaction and his role as an emissary from American blacks to inspect the land for future settlement. He gives an account of the climate, soil, plants, animals, and people of Liberia and offers suggestions for improvement of health, welfare, housing, government, and crops. Continuing his journey to meet Campbell who had preceded him to Africa and who had moved on to the Niger area, Delany again gives brief details on the land, the products, way of life, diseases, and treatment. He devotes a section to missionaries, where his anti-Catholic bias is noticeable, and suggests that the correct kind of missionary effort would quickly bring positive results. Such missionaries should be black. He discusses commerce, transportation, crops—including cotton—and sees in this and other tropical or semitropical crops the hope of competing successfully with the economy of the American South. The "reflex influence" could work also in Africa. And of course there is the reproduction of a treaty with the African kings calling for black settlements in the Niger area.

By page count slightly more than one-third of Delany's report is devoted to details of the history of the movement before the African experience itself or to the visit to England on the way home. Only about one-half of his report pertains to the Niger Valley experience. Delany can be described as forceful and positive in his writings—as indeed he was in life—but he was not well organized or polished in his literary style. The great merit of his report is that it conveys in a most positive manner the dreams and ambitions of a man who hungered for a place for his people and a recognition of their contribution to man and to civilization.

Campbell's account is devoted entirely to the African experience. It is far more readable, better arranged, and more detailed insofar as Yoruban Africa is concerned. The report plunges immediately into the recital of the sojourn in Africa and closes with the treaty between the explorers and the African kings. If there is a Negro nationalist in Campbell it is quietly implicit in the last paragraph of his preface: "I have determined, with my wife and children, to go to Africa to live." His determination is evinced in *The Anti Slavery Reporter* for April 18, 1863, which reports Mr. R. Campbell to be operating a new paper, the *Anglo-African*, at Lagos.

Campbell comments regularly on social and economic conditions, war and peace, religion and politics, geography and climate, and health and housing. Indeed, these topics were covered again and again by both men. Of the two, Campbell was much more likely to record the fact, perhaps in greater detail, but he was much less inclined to rebuild African society on the spot. While Delany offers suggestions on how to improve coffee tree culture or how to improve ventilation, or on why horses did not live in Liberia, Campbell is more likely to give a description of people, of a social gathering, or of a dramatic confrontation between his party and a wandering band of soldiers.

On the way home the two explorers stopped off in England in May 1860 and were assured of the interest of Englishmen in developing the cotton industry in Africa. They were told that the African Aid Society would be at their service in exploiting the resources of the continent. What neither report records is that within a few months the African kings reneged on their treaty, the British government began to pressure the African Aid Society into withholding further succor for the would-be immigrants, and Delany made a kind of peace with the African Civilization Society after he had dictated some modification of the constitution requiring that blacks be in command. By that time the American Civil War had begun, and the interest in Africa had to take second place in the lives, though perhaps not in the hearts, of men like Martin Delany. When he died in 1885, somewhat past the Biblical three score years and ten, he was once again involved in an enterprise concerning blacks beyond the borders of the United States.

Delany's report preserves information on the history of the separatist movement, culminating in the effort to transfer Christian black communities from America to Africa. Delany remained defensively aware of his own place in history and defensively aware of the Negro's struggle for recognition and fulfillment. To the end of his life he saw black men as a noble race and the only source from which the regeneration of Africa might be achieved. Campbell, less defensive, less volatile, recorded more of Africa and less of the history of a movement to vindicate the black man's place in history. Together the two throw valuable light on a facet of history little known to a generation which has developed its own brand of black nationalism.

These two black nationalist movements, separated by the Civil War and more than a century of unkept promises, have more in common than at first meets the eye. Both have elements of pride in race, which has been too often lacking among the oppressed. Both look to the Negro as the means of salvation, not only for Africa but also for America. Both are aggressively aware of black unity which scoffs at claims of white superiority, but is ready to accept black superiority. Both demand the fulfillment of economic and social equality. Both are disdainful of white-led, or even white-participating efforts at betterment of conditions for the Negro. Both demand black leadership for black projects.

Black nationalism of the 1960s is, however, better educated, more aggressive, more sophisticated, more ruthless than the Negro nationalism of the 1850s. Whitfield and Holly and Delany looked for a place where the black man might prove his capacity for government; the black nationalist of today is more likely to suggest that a substantial portion of the United States be assigned to Negroes for past misdeeds of the nation.

Perhaps one of the greatest differences, and one of the happiest, between the nationalists of the 1850s and those of today is the greater confidence which the twentieth century has brought to the black man. One cannot read Delany without being painfully aware of his great sense of hurt and frustration, but there were relatively few who believed him when he spoke of the great soul and the potentially great accomplishments of the blacks. Today there are literally millions of people in the United States and in Africa who do believe what only the few believed about the black man's greatness a century ago.

This new confidence is in part due to the development of Africa during the intervening years. The Negro nationalists of the 1850s had to persuade themselves, and seek to persuade others, that their confidence in the black man would be vindicated. It is somewhat ironic that the "reflex influence" which was cited so often by Negro nationalists of the past century came to fruition only in the 1960s after Africa had suddenly spawned its independent members of the family of nations. It is even more ironic that, except for Liberia, the reflex influence came not from the emigrant American black men, but from the native population which had emerged to independence under the aegis of European powers.

Even though Delany and Campbell failed to lead many emigrants to Africa, the back-to-Africa movement of the period should not be written off as inconsequential. There were in Africa at that time thousands of blacks who had made their way back from the Western Hemisphere and had settled in Liberia, or Sierra Leone, or the Niger River area. They had come not only from the United States but from Latin America and British American areas as well.

This return to Africa was nationalistic, as portrayed in the lives of men like Delany and Campbell. It had a strong economic bent as demonstrated by a Negro emigrationist's reference to the meeting between Diogenes and Alexander the Great, when Diogenes had asked the great one to get out of his light: "We, too, asked this [of the whites] a long time; finding, however, they wouldn't mind us, we came around to the east, so as to get between them and the sun, and get the early sun on our sugar, coffee, and cotton, that by and by we may somewhat obstruct their view" (*African Repository*, February, 1860, p. 56). Finally, the return to Africa was never devoid of the religious element. The bondage and redemption of the children of Israel had too many similarities to the later bondage and hopeful redemption of the blacks to escape notice.

It was Alexander Crummell, emigrationist in Liberia, who pointed up these similarities. Recalling the centuries of suffering and servitude of the Israelites he yet saw that bondage as a time of preparation, for God was always with them and led them into new knowledge and acquaintance with a high civilization. So it was for the Negro in the Americas, where God had been preparing him for new duties. "The day of preparation for our race is well nigh ended; the day of duty and responsibility on our part, to suffering, benighted, Africa, is at hand" [Alexander Crummel, *Africa and America* (1891), p. 421].

IX

The Afro-American in the Civil War

William E. Woodward, a popular writer of the 1920s, expressed the belief of many Americans about the role of Afro-Americans in the Civil War. In 1928, in his biography of General Ulysses S. Grant, he wrote that "The American Negroes are the only people in the history of the world . . . that ever became free without any effort of their own." Despite the surfeit of contrary evidence, laymen and historians alike persist in accepting the myth that the Negro was a passive recipient of his freedom in 1865 rather than the fact that he was an active participant both in the Civil War itself and in the controversy which led to this conflict.

As previous selections have indicated, black protest from without as well as black opposition from within the slave system were immensely important in educating white Americans about the evils of slavery. Black gains were more often the result of black aggressiveness than they were of white humanitarianism or moral concern. Although historians are again seeing slavery as the fundamental cause of the Civil War, they have not recognized properly the importance of Afro-Americans in bringing to the attention of the nation the necessity for abolishing slavery. It was not coincidental that the American Anti-Slavery Society was launched after rather than before David Walker's *Appeal*, Nat Turner's insurrection, and the establishment of the Negro Convention Movement. It hardly seems likely that the crusade to rid the nation of slavery would have been pushed with the same vigor if it had not been for the strong pressure of Afro-Americans who constantly pricked the moral conscience of Anglo-Americans. Since the Civil War would never have occurred without the controversy over slavery, black Americans were then active agents in bringing on this conflict and not passive recipients of white beneficence.

In contrast to the national administration, Afro-Americans recognized from the beginning that the Civil War was a war for Black Liberation and that it could not be restricted to the narrow objective (as President Abraham Lincoln hoped) of preserving the Union. On the other hand, the South never doubted that it was fighting the war to preserve slavery and not to divide the nation. Its quest for independence was entirely related to its desire to maintain the institution of slavery. Pressure from Afro-Americans and white abolitionists as well as the realities of the situation finally compelled Lincoln and the North to add emancipation to the list of wartime objectives. If black Americans were misinformed, it was not in misunderstanding the cause of the war but in misinterpreting the meaning of emancipation. Afro-Americans were soon to realize emancipation did not spell Black Liberation.

At the outbreak of the Civil War, both the Confederacy and the Union tried to restrict the war to a white man's fight by excluding Afro-Americans from military service. Neither side succeeded. In 1862, the North altered its policy of exclusion and before the war was over more than 200,000 Afro-Americans wore the Union blue. The northern decision to use black troops was the result of several considerations. The flood of black refugees from the South, most of whom were anxious to join the northern army, as well as the demands of black leaders for emancipation and the employment of black soldiers, guaranteed that Lincoln could not disregard the fate of over four million Afro-Americans. Black spokesmen and white abolitionists constantly reminded Lincoln that victory without emancipation was impossible and that the Union could be preserved only if Lincoln augmented the Union Army with black soldiers and crippled the southern war effort by guaranteeing freedom to black slaves. By the summer of 1862, Lincoln and the Congress accepted both arguments. After Congress had prepared the way in the second Confiscation Act of July, 1863, President Lincoln allowed the Secretary of War to recruit a regiment of black soldiers from the Sea Islands of South Carolina. In September, the President issued the preliminary Emancipation Proclamation which became effective the first day of 1863. In retrospect, the participation of Afro-Americans in the Civil War was just as crucial to northern victory in 1865 as French aid in 1778 was to the outcome of the American Revolution. From beginning to end, Afro-American slavery had been the principal issue of the Civil War. The adoption of the Thirteenth Amendment in 1865 left Brazil and Cuba as the only areas in the New World where African slavery was still legal.

The situation in the South was both similar and different. The differences were largely the result of the fact that black Southerners could never support the southern cause as black Northerners did the Union efforts. Since the Confederate government openly endorsed slavery as the paramount reason for fighting the war, black Southerners were hardly anxious to participate on the southern side. Instead they grabbed every opportunity to flee the plantation and join up with the Yankees. While Lincoln reluctantly consented to use black troops, most Confederate leaders adamantly opposed the arming of Afro-Americans for obvious reasons. While the northern problem in the beginning of the war had been to keep Afro-Americans out of the military, the southern problem was how to prevent Afro-Americans from joining the enemy forces.

As the war dragged on, however, the Confederate government began to face a serious manpower shortage. As early as 1862, it became apparent that military needs of the South could not be met by white volunteers alone. Consequently the southern states enacted laws providing for the conscription of whites into military service and the impressment of black laborers into noncombat service. The employment of Afro-Americans as military labor meant that whites would be free for combat service.

After Lee's defeat at Gettysburg in 1863, Confederate strategy was no longer aimed at winning the war but merely at avoiding defeat. Convinced that Northerners were unwilling to finance an expensive war for Negro freedom, Confederate officials planned to prolong the conflict long enough to allow resentment and dissatisfaction to build up in the North. Execution of this policy required total utilization of all manpower from white planters to black slaves. Had the South been able to depend completely on the loyalty of the four million Afro-Americans, this strategy might have succeeded. Even though black Southerners prayed for a northern victory, they nevertheless played a role in keeping the Confederacy alive for over four years. Therefore Afro-Americans were a vital part of the struggle for Black Liberation on both sides of the battle front and were hardly the only people to contribute nothing to the winning of their freedom.

The two essays in this section cover the activities of Afro-Americans during the Civil War. William E. B. DuBois, the grand intellect of Black America, provides a classic description of their role in the North. James H. Brewer, one of the numerous young historians working in the field, gives a brief description of the efforts by Virginia, in conjunction with the Confederate government, to make use of Afro-Americans.

28. W. E. B. DUBOIS, Black Reconstruction in America (1935)*

This selection by the dean of Afro-American scholars is taken from W. E. B. DuBois' classic, *Black Reconstruction*. DuBois was not only the first Afro-American to earn a Ph.D. from Harvard University, but he was also for years the intellectual voice of Black America. From its inception in 1910 until his resignation from the National Association for the Advancement of Colored People in 1934, DuBois was editor of *The Crisis*, which he made into the most influential black journal in the United States. Both as a scholar and as a propagandist, DuBois was unexcelled as a race conscious champion of black people. In this selection, DuBois stresses the part played by Afro-Americans in the war for black freedom.

* From W. E. B. Dubois, *Black Reconstruction in America: An Essay Toward a History of the Part Which Black Folk Played in the Attempt to Reconstruct Democracy in America, 1860–1880* [1935] (New York: Russell & Russell, 1956.) Reprinted by permission.

Three movements, partly simultaneous and partly successive, are treated in different chapters. In the last chapter, we chronicled the swarming of the slaves to meet the approaching Union armies; in this we consider how these slaves were transformed in part from laborers to soldiers fighting for their own freedom; and in succeeding chapters, we shall treat the organization of free labor after the war.

In the ears of the world, Abraham Lincoln on the first of January, 1863, declared four million slaves "thenceforward and forever free." The truth was less than this. The Emancipation Proclamation applied only to the slaves of those states or parts of states still in rebellion against the United States government. Hundreds of thousands of such slaves were already free by their own action and that of the invading armies, and in their cases, Lincoln's proclamation only added possible legal sanction to an accomplished fact.

To the majority of slaves still within the Confederate lines, the proclamation would apply only if they followed the fugitives. And this Abraham Lincoln determined to induce them to do, and thus to break the back of the rebellion by depriving the South of its principal labor force.

Emancipation had thus two ulterior objects. It was designed to make easier the replacement of unwilling northern white soldiers with black soldiers; and it sought to put behind the war a new push toward northern victory by the mighty impact of a great moral ideal, both in the North and in Europe.

This national right-about-face had been gradually and carefully accomplished only by the consummate tact of a leader of men who went no faster than his nation marched but just as fast; and also by the unwearying will of the Abolitionists, who forced the nation onward.

Wendell Phillips said in Washington in 1862:

"Gentlemen of Washington! You have spent for us two million dollars per day. You bury two regiments a month, two thousand men by disease without battle. You rob every laboring man of one-half of his pay for the next thirty years by your taxes. You place the curse of intolerable taxation on every cradle for the next generation. What do you give us in return? What is the other side of the balance sheet? The North has poured out its blood and money like water; it has leveled every fence of constitutional privilege, and Abraham Lincoln sits today a more unlimited despot than the world knows this side of China. What does he render the North for this unbounded confidence? Show us something; or I tell you that within two years the indignant reaction of the people will hurl the cabinet in contempt from their seats, and the devils that went out from yonder capital, for there has been no sweeping or garnishing, will come back seven times stronger; for I do not believe that Jefferson Davis, driven down to the Gulf, will go down to the waters and perish as certain brutes mentioned in the Gospel did."

Horace Greeley was at Lincoln's heels. He wrote in August, 1862, his editorial, "Prayer of Twenty Millions," which drew Lincoln's well-known reply: "If there be those who would not save the Union unless they could at the same time save slavery, I do not agree with them. If there be those who would not save the Union unless they could at the same time destroy slavery, I do not agree with them. My paramount object in this struggle is to save the Union and is not either to save or to destroy slavery. If I could save the Union without freeing any slaves, I would do it; and if I could save it by freeing all the slaves, I would also do that. What I do about slavery and the colored race, I do because I believe it would help to save the Union. . . ."

"Suppose I do that," said Lincoln to Greeley, discussing general emancipation. "There are now 20,000 of our muskets on the shoulders of Kentuckians who are bravely fighting our battles. Every one of them will be thrown down or carried over to the rebels."

"Let them do it," said Greeley. "The cause of the Union will be stronger if Kentucky should secede with the rest, than it is now."

In September, 1862, Lincoln said to representatives of the Chicago Protestants:

"I admit that slavery is at the root of the rebellion, or at least its sine qua non. . . . I will also concede that Emancipation would help us in Europe. . . . I grant, further, that it would help somewhat at the North, though not so much, I fear, as you and those you represent imagine. . . . And then, unquestionably, it would weaken the Rebels by drawing off their laborers, which is of great importance; but I am not so sure we could do much with the Blacks. If we were to arm them, I fear that in a few weeks the arms would be in the hands of the Rebels. . . .

"What good would a proclamation of Emancipation from me do, especially as we are now situated? I do not want to issue a document that the whole world will see must necessarily be inoperative, like the Pope's bull against the comet. . . ." [1]

Nevertheless, just nine days later, Lincoln issued his preliminary Emancipation Proclamation. What caused the sudden change? Was it the mounting mass of Negroes rushing into Union lines? Was it the fighting of Negro soldiers which showed that weapons given to them were never found in the hands of Confederates, or was it the curious international situation?

The failure or success of the war hung by a thread. If England and France should recognize the Confederacy, there was little doubt that the

Union cause would be beaten; and they were disposed to recognize it. Or did Lincoln realize that since a draft law was needed to make unwilling northern soldiers fight, black soldiers were the last refuge of the Union? The preliminary proclamation came in September, and in October and November mass meetings in New York and Brooklyn denounced the proposal as inexpedient and adopted resolutions against it with jeers. Ministers, like the Reverend Albert Barnes of Philadelphia, preached against emancipation, declaring that the control of slavery ought to be left absolutely and exclusively to the states. The New York *Herald* pointed out that even if the proclamation was effective, slave property would have to be restored or paid for eventually by the United States government. "The *Herald* is correct. The slaves taken from our citizens during the war have to be accounted for at its end, either by restoration or indemnity." [2] The New Orleans *Picayune* pointed out in November that abolition would flood the North with Negroes, and that this would "tend to degrade white labor and to cheapen it."

The final proclamation was issued January 1, 1863, and carried a special admonition to the colored people:

"And I hereby enjoin upon the people so declared to be free to abstain from all violence, unless in necessary self-defense; and I recommended to them that, in all cases when allowed, they labor faithfully for reasonable wages.

"And I further declare and make known that such persons, of suitable condition, will be received into the armed service of the United States to garrison forts, positions, stations, and other places, and to man vessels of all sorts in said service.

"And upon this act, sincerely believed to be an act of justice, warranted by the Constitution upon military necessity, I invoke the considerate judgment of mankind, and the gracious favor of Almighty God."

The Charleston *Courier* jeered:

"The Pope's bull against the comet has been issued, and I suppose Mr. Lincoln now breathes more freely. The wonderful man by a dash of his wonderful pen has set free (on paper) all the slaves of the South, and henceforth this is to be in all its length and breadth the land of liberty! . . .

"Meanwhile, I would invite his own and the attention of all his deluded followers to a paragraph in the late number of the New Orleans *Picayune*, wherein it is stated that inquests had been held upon the bodies of 21 contrabands in one house alone in that city. These poor Negroes had been stolen or enticed away from the comfortable homes of their masters, and left to starve and rot by these philanthropic (?) advocates of liberty for the slave." [3]

The Savannah *Republican* in March declared:

"In our judgment, so far as the Border States are concerned, his proposition will have exactly the opposite effect to that for which it was designed. Those states, who have held on to the Union with the belief that their Southern sisters were hasty and wrong in the belief that they were about to be brought under an abolition government, will now see that they were right and that all their worst apprehensions have been justified by the acts of that government."

Beauregard sent an impudent telegram to Miles at Richmond:

"Has the bill for the execution of abolition prisoners, after January next, been passed? Do it, and England will be stirred into action. It is high time to proclaim the black flag after that period; let the execution be with the garrote."

The reaction to emancipation in the North was unfavorable so far as political results indicated, although many motives influenced the voters. The elections of 1862 in New York, New Jersey, Pennsylvania, Ohio, Indiana and Illinois went Democratic, and in other parts of the West, Lincoln lost support. In the Congress of 1860, there were seventy-eight Republicans and thirty-seven Democrats, and in 1862, the administration had only fifty-seven supporters, with sixty-seven in the opposition.

Only among Negroes and in England was the reaction favorable, and both counted. The Proclamation made four and a half million laborers willing almost in mass to sacrifice their last drop of blood for their new-found country. It sent them into transports of joy and sacrifice. It changed all their pessimism and despair into boundless faith. It was the Coming of the Lord.

The Proclamation had an undoubted and immediate effect upon England. The upper classes were strongly in favor of the Confederacy, and sure that the Yankees were fighting only for a high tariff and hurt vanity. Free-trade England was repelled by this program, and attracted by the free trade which the Confederacy offered. There was strong demand among manufacturers to have the government interfere and recognize the Southern States as an independent nation. The church and universities were in favor of the Confederacy, and all the great periodicals. Even the philanthropists, like Lord Shaftesbury, Carlyle, Buxton and Gladstone, threw their sympathies to the South. Carlyle sneered at people "cutting each other's throats because one-half of them prefer hiring their servants for life, and the other by the hour." [4]

As Henry Adams assures us:

"London was altogether beside itself on one point, in especial; it created a nightmare of its own, and gave it the shape of Abraham Lincoln. Behind this it placed another demon, if possible more devilish, and called it Mr. Seward. In regard to these two men, English society seemed demented. Defense was useless; explanation was vain; one could only let the passion exhaust itself. One's best friends were as unreasonable as enemies, for the belief in poor Mr. Lincoln's brutality and Seward's ferocity became a dogma of popular faith." [5]

Confederate warships were being built and harbored in English ports and in September, 1862, Palmerston, believing that the Confederates were about to capture Washington, suggested intervention to members of his cabinet. Lord John Russell wanted to act immediately, but the rebels were driven back at Antietam the same month, and the preliminary Emancipation Proclamation appeared. Gladstone and Russell still tried to force intervention, but Palmerston hesitated.

There was similar demand in France, but not as strong, because cotton did not play so large a part. Nevertheless, the textile workers in both France and England were hard-pressed by the cotton famine. Napoleon III was in favor of the South, but the mass of the French nation was not. Napoleon was assured by the Confederate government that a Southern alliance with French Mexico and a guaranty of Cuba could be had for the asking, if France would recognize the Confederacy. No danger from the North was anticipated, for Seward was certain to accept Napoleon's assurances of France's neutrality.

Public opinion stood back of the English government and was, on the whole, in favor of the South; but Garrison and Douglass by their visits, and later Harriet Beecher Stowe, had influenced the opinion of the middle and laboring classes. Nevertheless, it was reported in 1862: "We find only here and there among the Englishmen one who does not fanatically side with the slave states." Various meetings in favor of the South were arranged by the workingmen and the General Council of Workingmen's Associations opposed the pro-Southern movement. The war had created a great scarcity of cotton, and in addition to this, there had already been an over-production of the cotton industry in England in 1860, so that the effect of the blockade was not felt until later, so far as the sale of goods was concerned. But the factories closed, and more than half the looms and spindles lay idle. Especially in Lancashire there was great distress among laborers. Fever and prostitution were prevalent in 1865.

Notwithstanding this, the English workers stood up for the abolition of Negro slavery, and protested against the intervention of the English. Up until 1863, it was argued with some show of right that the North was not fighting to free the slaves; but on the contrary, according to Lincoln's own words, "was perfectly willing to settle the war and leave the Negroes in slavery." But as soon as Lincoln issued the Emancipation Proclamation, the workingmen of England held hundreds of meetings all over the country and in all industrial sections, and hailed his action.

Ernest Jones, the leader of the Chartist movement, raised his eloquent voice against slavery. During the winter of 1862–1863, meeting after meeting in favor of emancipation was held. The reaction in England to the Emancipation Proclamation was too enthusiastic for the government to dare take any radical step. Great meetings in London and Manchester stirred the nation, and gave notice to Palmerston that he could not yet take the chance of recognizing the South. In spite of Russell and Gladstone, he began to withdraw, and the imminent danger of recognition of the South by England and France passed.

In the monster meeting of English workingmen at St. James' Hall, London, March 26, 1863, John Bright spoke; and John Stuart Mill declared that: "Higher political and social freedom has been established in the United States." Karl Marx testified that this meeting held in 1863 kept Lord Palmerston from declaring war against the United States. On December 31, 1863, at meetings held simultaneously in London and Manchester, addresses were sent to Lincoln, drafted by Karl Marx. The London address said:

"Sir: We who offer this address are Englishmen and workingmen. We prize as our dearest inheritance, bought for us by the blood of our fathers, the liberty we enjoy—the liberty of free labor on a free soil. We have, therefore, been accustomed to regard with veneration and gratitude the founders of the great republic in which the liberties of the Anglo-Saxon race have been widened beyond all the precedents of the old world, and in which there was nothing to condemn or to lament but the slavery and degradation of men guilty only of a colored skin or an African parentage. We have looked with admiration and sympathy upon the brave, generous and untiring efforts of a large party in the Northern States to deliver the Union from this curse and shame. We rejoiced, sir, in your election to the Presidency, as a splendid proof that the principles of universal freedom and equality were rising to the ascendant. We regarded with abhorrence the conspiracy and rebellion by which it was sought at once to overthrow the supremacy of a government based upon the most popular suffrage in the world, and to perpetuate the hateful inequalities of race." [6]

The Manchester address, adopted by six thousand people, said among other things:

"One thing alone has, in the past, lessened our sympathy with your country and our confidence in it; we mean the ascendancy of politicians who not merely maintained Negro slavery, but desired to extend and root it more deeply. Since we have discerned, however, that the victory of the free North in the war which has so sorely distressed us as well as afflicted you, will shake off the fetters of the slave, you have attracted our warm and earnest sympathy.

"We joyfully honor you, as the President, and the Congress with you, for the many decisive steps towards practically exemplifying your belief in the words of your great founders: 'All men are created free and equal.' . . .

"We assume that you cannot now stop short of a complete uprooting of slavery. It would not become us to dictate any details, but there are broad principles of humanity which must guide you. If complete emancipation in some states be deferred, though only to a predetermined day, still, in the interval, human beings should not be counted chattels. Women must have rights of chastity and maternity, men the rights of husbands; masters the liberty of manumission. Justice demands for the black, no less than for the white, the protection of the law—that his voice may be heard in your courts. Nor must any such abomination be tolerated as slave-breeding States and a slave market—if you are to earn the high reward of all your sacrifices in the approval of the universal brotherhood and of the Divine Father. It is for your free country to decide whether anything but immediate and total emancipation can secure the most indispensable rights of humanity, against the inveterate wickedness of local laws and local executives.

"We implore you, for your own honor and welfare, not to faint in your providential mission. While your enthusiasm is aflame, and the tide of events runs high, let the work be finished effectually. Leave no root of bitterness to spring up and work fresh misery to your children. It is a mighty task, indeed, to reorganize the industry, not only of four millions of the colored race, but of five millions of whites. Nevertheless, the vast progress you have made in the short space of twenty months fills us with hope that every stain on your freedom will shortly be removed, and that the erasure of that foul blot upon civilization and Christianity—chattel slavery—during your Presidency, will cause the name of Abraham Lincoln to be honored and revered by posterity." [7]

Lincoln in reply said that he knew the suffering of the workingmen in Manchester and Europe in this crisis, and appreciated the action of the English workingmen as an example of "sublime Christian heroism," which "has not been surpassed in any age or in any country." He declared that the Civil War was "the attempt to overthrow this government, which was built upon a foundation of human rights, and to substitute one which should rest exclusively on the basis of human slavery."

In the North, the Emancipation Proclamation meant the Negro soldier, and the Negro soldier meant the end of the war.

"We have come to set you free!" cried the black cavalrymen who rode at the head of the Union Army as it entered Richmond in 1864. These soldiers were in the division of Godfrey Weitzel; when Ben Butler first assigned Negro troops to Weitzel's command in Louisiana, Weitzel resigned. It was a good thing for him that he recalled this resignation, for his black soldiers at Port Hudson wrote his name in history.

Here was indeed revolution. At first, this was to be a white man's war. First, because the North did not want to affront the South, and the war was going to be short, very short; and secondly, if Negroes fought in the war, how could it help being a war for their emancipation? And for this the North would not fight. Yet scarcely a year after hostilities started, the Negroes were fighting, although unrecognized as soldiers; in two years they were free and enrolling in the army.

Private Miles O'Reilly expressed in the newspapers a growing public opinion:

"Some say it is a burnin' shame
    To make the naygurs fight,
An' that the thrade o' bein' kilt
    Belongs but to the white;

"But as for me 'upon me sowl'
    So liberal are we here,
I'll let Sambo be murthered in place o' meself
    On every day in the year."

In December, 1861, Union officers were ordered not to return fugitive slaves on pain of court-martial. In 1862 came Hunter's black regiment in South Carolina.

In the spring of 1862, General Hunter had less than eleven thousand men under his command, and had to hold the whole broken seacoast of Georgia, South Carolina and Florida. He applied often and in vain to the authorities at Washington for reinforcements. All the troops available in the North were less than sufficient for General McClellan's great operations against Richmond, and the reiterated answer of the War Department was: "You must get along as best you can. Not a man from the North can be spared."

"No reinforcements to be had from the North; vast fatigue duties in throwing up earthworks imposed on our insufficient garrison; the enemy continually increasing, both in insolence and numbers; our only success the capture of Fort Pulaski, sealing up Savannah; and this victory offset, if not fully counterbalanced, by many minor gains of the enemy; this was about the condition of affairs as seen from the headquarters fronting Port Royal bay, when General Hunter one morning, 'with twirling glasses, puckered lips and dilated nostrils' [he had just received another "don't-bother-us-for-reinforcements" dispatch from Washington] announced his intention of 'forming a Negro regiment, and compelling every able-bodied black man in the department to fight for the freedom which could not but be the issue of our war.' " [8]

Hunter caused all the necessary orders to be issued, and took upon himself the responsibility for the irregular issue of arms, clothing, equipments and rations involved in collecting and organizing the first experimental Negro regiments.

Reports of the organization of the First South Carolina Infantry were forwarded to headquarters in Washington, and the War Department took no notice. Nothing was said, nor was any authority given to pay the men or furnish them subsistence. But at last a special dispatch steamer plowed her way over the bar with word from the War Department, "requiring immediate answer."

It was a demand for information in regard to the Negro regiment, based on a resolution introduced by Wickliffe of Kentucky. These resolutions had been adopted by Congress. Hunter laughed, but as he was without authority for any of his actions in this case, it seemed to his worried Adjutant-General that the documents in his hands were no laughing matter. But Hunter declared:

"That old fool has just given me the very chance I was growing sick for! The War Department has refused to notice my black regiment; but now, in reply to this resolution, I can lay the matter before the country, and force the authorities either to adopt my Negroes, or to disband them." [9]

So Hunter wrote: "No regiment of 'fugitive slaves' has been, or is being, organized in this department. There is, however, a fine regiment of loyal persons whose late masters are fugitive rebels." He said that he did this under instructions given by the late Secretary of War, and his general authority to employ "all loyal persons offering their service in defense of the Union." He added:

"Neither have I had any specific authority for supplying these persons with shovels, spades, and pickaxes, when employing them as laborers; nor with boats and oars, when using them as lighter-men; but these are not points included in Mr. Wickliffe's resolutions. To me it seemed that liberty to employ men in any particular capacity implied and carried with it liberty, also, to supply them with the necessary tools; and, acting upon this faith, I have clothed, equipped and armed the only loyal regiment yet raised in South Carolina, Georgia or Florida. . . .

"The experiment of arming the blacks, so far as I have made it, has been a complete and even marvelous success. They are sober, docile, attentive, and enthusiastic; displaying great natural capacities in acquiring the duties of the soldier. They are now eager beyond all things to take the field and be led into action; and it is the unanimous opinion of the officers who have had charge of them that, in the peculiarities of this climate and country, they will prove invaluable auxiliaries, fully equal to the similar regiments so long and successfully used by the British authorities in the West India Islands.

"In conclusion, I would say, it is my hope—there appearing no possibility of other reinforcements, owing to the exigencies of the campaign in the Peninsula—to have organized by the end of next fall, and be able to present to the government, from forty-eight to fifty thousand of these hardy and devoted soldiers."

When the reply was read in the House of Representatives: "Its effects were magical. The clerk could scarcely read it with decorum; nor could half his words be heard amidst the universal peals of laughter in which both Democrats and Republicans appeared to vie as to which should be the more noisy. . . . It was the great joke of the day, and coming at a moment of universal gloom in the public mind, was seized upon by the whole loyal press of the country as a kind of politico-military champagne cocktail."

When the Confederate Government heard of this, it issued an order reciting that "as the government of the United States had refused to answer whether it authorized the raising of a black regiment by General Hunter or not," said general, his staff, and all officers under his command who had directly or indirectly participated in the unclean thing, should hereafter be outlaws not covered by the laws of war; but to be executed as felons for the crime of "inciting Negro insurrection wherever caught."

In Louisiana, the colored creoles in many cases hesitated. Some of them had been owners of slaves, and some actually fought in the Confederate Army, but were not registered as Negroes. On November 23, 1861, the Confederate grand parade took place in New Orleans, and one feature of the review was a regiment of free men of color, 1,400 in number. The *Picayune* speaks of a later review on February 9, 1862:

"We must pay deserved compliment to the companies of free men of color, all well-dressed, well-drilled, and comfortably uniformed. Most of these companies have provided themselves with arms unaided by the administration."

When Butler entered the city in 1862, the Confederates fled tumultously or laid aside their uniforms and stayed. The free Negro regiment did neither, but offered its services to the Federal army. Butler at first was in a quandary.

"The instructions given by General McClellan to General Butler were silent on this most perplexing problem. On leaving Washington, Butler was verbally informed by the President, that the government was not yet prepared to announce a Negro policy. They were anxiously considering the subject, and hoped, ere long, to arrive at conclusions." [10]

Butler found the Negroes of great help to him, but he could not, as in Virginia, call them "contraband," because he had no work for them. He wanted to free them, but on May 9, the news came that Hunter's proclamation in South Carolina had been revoked. Butler, however, abolished the whipping houses, and encouraged the Negroes who called on him. "One consequence was that the general had a spy in every house, behind each rebel's chair, as he sat at table."

General Butler asked for reinforcements all summer on account of the growing strength of Vicksburg and Port Hudson, the condition of Mobile and camps near New Orleans. The answer from Washington was: "We cannot spare you one man; we will send you men when we have them to send. You must hold New Orleans by all means and at all hazards."

Earlier, General Phelps, who commanded the Federal forces about seven miles from New Orleans, had received a number of refugees, some of them in chains and some of them bleeding from wounds. Butler ordered him May 23, 1862, to exclude these from his lines. He replied at length:

"Added to the four millions of the colored race whose disaffection is increasing even more rapidly than their number, there are at least four millions more of the white race whose growing miseries will naturally seek companionship with those of the blacks."

He demanded that the President should abolish slavery, and that the Negroes be armed. Butler forwarded Phelps' reply to Washington. Phelps again demanded the right to arm Negro troops. He was ordered July 1, 1862, to use the Negroes to cut wood. He immediately handed in his resignation, saying:

"I am willing to prepare African regiments for the defense of the government against its assailants. I am not willing to become the mere slave-driver which you propose, having no qualifications in that way." [11]

The use of Negro troops was precipitated by the attack which Breckenridge made August 5, 1862, on Baton Rouge. Butler had to have troops to defend New Orleans, and had applied to Washington, but none could be sent. Therefore, by proclamation, August 22, 1862, Butler "called on Africa," accepted the free Negro regiment which had offered its services, and proceeded to organize other Negro troops. He recited at length the previous action of the Confederate Governor in organizing the Negro regiment, April 23, 1861, and quoted directly from the Confederate Governor's proclamation:

"Now, therefore, the Commanding General, believing that a large portion of this militia force of the State of Louisiana are willing to take service in the volunteer forces of the United States, and be enrolled and organized to 'defend their homes' from 'ruthless invaders'; to protect their wives and children and kindred from wrong and outrage; to shield their property from being seized by bad men; and to defend the flag of their native country, as their fathers did under Jackson at Chalmette against Packenham and his myrmidons, carrying the black flag of 'beauty and booty':

"Appreciating their motives, relying upon their 'well-known loyalty and patriotism,' and with 'praise and respect' for these brave men—it is ordered that all the members of the 'Native Guards' aforesaid, and all other free colored citizens recognized by the first and late governor and authorities of the State of Louisiana, as a portion of the militia of the State, who shall enlist in the volunteer service of the United States, shall be duly organized by the appointment of proper officers, and accepted, paid, equipped, armed and rationed as are other volunteer troops of the United States, subject to the approval of the President of the United States." [12]

Thousands of volunteers under Butler's appeal appeared. In fourteen days, a regiment was organized with colored line officers and white field officers. More than half of the privates were not really free Negroes but fugitive slaves. A second regiment with colored line officers was enlisted, and a third, with colored mess officers.

In the Kansas Home Guard were two regiments of Indians, and among them over four hundred Negroes; and 2,500 Negroes served in the contingent that came from the Indian nations. Many of them enlisted early in 1862.

In the meantime, the war was evidently more than a dress parade or a quick attack upon Richmond. One hundred thousand "three months" soldiers were but a "drop in the bucket." More and more troops must be had. The time of enlistment for many of the white troops was already expiring, and at least Negro troops could be used on fatigue duty in the large stretches of territory held by the Federal armies down the Atlantic coast, and in the Mississippi Valley, and in the Border States.

Senator Henry Wilson of Massachusetts, Chairman of the Senate Committee on Military Affairs, introduced a bill in July, 1862, which empowered the President to accept Negroes for constructing entrenchments, or any other war service for which they might be found competent. If owned by rebels, such Negroes were to be freed, but nothing was said of their families. Thaddeus Stevens championed the bill in the House, and it was signed by Lincoln, July 17, 1862.

The debate was bitter; Senator Sherman of Ohio said:

"The question rises, whether the people of the United States, strug-

gling for national existence, should not employ these blacks for the maintenance of the Government. The policy heretofore pursued by the officers
of the United States has been to repel this class of people from our lines,
to refuse their services. They would have made the best spies; and yet they
have been driven from our lines."

Fessenden of Maine added: "I tell the generals of our army, they
must reverse their practices and their course of proceeding on this subject. . . . I advise it here from my place—treat your enemies as enemies, as
the worst of enemies, and avail yourselves like men, of every power which
God has placed in your hands, to accomplish your purpose within the rules
of civilized warfare." Race, of Minnesota, declared that "not many days can
pass before the people of the United States North must decide upon one or
two questions: we have either to acknowledge the Southern Confederacy as
a free and independent nation, and that speedily; or we have as speedily to
resolve to use all the means given us by the Almighty to prosecute this war
to a successful termination. The necessity for action has arisen. To hesitate
is worse than criminal." The Border States demurred, and Davis of Kentucky was especially bitter with threats. The bill finally was amended so
as to pay the black soldier's bounty to his owner, if he happened to be a
slave!

All that was simply permissive legislation, and for a time the War
Department did nothing. Some of the commanders in the field, however,
began to move. On the other hand, Senator Davis of Kentucky tried in
January, 1863, to stop the use of any national appropriations to pay Negro
soldiers. This attempt was defeated, and on January 6, 1863, five days
after the Emancipation Proclamation, the Secretary of War authorized
the Governor of Massachusetts to raise two Negro regiments for three
years' service. These were the celebrated 54th and 55th Negro regiments—
the first regularly authorized Negro regiments of the war.

The recruiting of the 54th Massachusetts Regiment of colored men
was completed by the 13th of May. It had been planned to have the
regiment pass through New York, but the Chief of Police warned that
it would be subject to insult, so that it went by sea to South Carolina.

In October, the Adjutant-General of the United States issued a
general order permitting the military employment of Negroes. The
Union League Club of New York appointed a committee to raise Negro
troops, and after some difficulty with Governor Seymour, they received
from Washington authority to raise a regiment. One thousand Negroes
responded within two weeks, and by January 27, 1864, a second regiment
was raised. No bounty was offered them, and no protection promised
their families. One of the regiments marched through the city.

"The scene of yesterday," says a New York paper, "was one which marks an era of progress in the political and social history of New York. A thousand men with black skins and clad and equipped with the uniforms and arms of the United States Government, marched from their camp through the most aristocratic and busy streets, received a grand ovation at the hands of the wealthiest and most respectable ladies and gentlemen of New York, and then moved down Broadway to the steamer which bears them to their destination—all amid the enthusiastic cheers, the encouraging plaudits, the waving handkerchiefs, the showering bouquets and other approving manifestations of a hundred thousand of the most loyal of our people." [13]

Pennsylvania was especially prominent in recruiting Negro troops. A committee was appointed, which raised $33,388, with which they proposed to raise three regiments. The committee founded Camp William Penn at Shelton Hill, and the first squad went into camp June 26, 1863. The first regiment, known as the Third United States, was full July 24, 1863. The third regiment, known as the Eighth United States, was full December 4, 1863. Two more regiments were full January 6 and February 3. The regiments went South, August 13, October 14, 1863, and January 16, 1864.

In the Department of the Cumberland, the Secretary of War authorized George L. Stearns of Massachusetts to recruit Negroes. Stearns was a friend of John Brown, and a prominent Abolitionist. He took up headquarters at Nashville, and raised a number of regiments. In the Department of the Gulf, General Banks, May 1, 1863, proposed an army corps to be known as the Corps d'Afrique. It was to consist of eighteen regiments, infantry, artillery and calvary, and to be organized in three divisions of three brigades each, with engineers and hospitals, etc. He said in his order:

"The Government makes use of mules, horses, uneducated and educated white men, in the defense of its institutions. Why should not the Negro contribute whatever is in his power for the cause in which he is as deeply interested as other men? We may properly demand from him whatever service he can render."

In March, 1863, the Secretary of War sent the Adjutant-General, Lorenzo Thomas, into the South on a tour of inspection. Stanton's orders said:

"The President desires that you should confer freely with Major-General Grant, and the officers with whom you may have communication, and explain to them the importance attached by the Government to the use of the colored population emancipated by the President's Proclamation, and particularly for the organization of their labor and military strength. . . .

"You are authorized in this connection, to issue in the name of this department, letters of appointment for field and company officers, and to organize such troops for military service to the utmost extent to which they can be obtained in accordance with the rules and regulations of the service." [14]

Thomas spoke to the army officers in Louisiana, and expressed himself clearly.

"You know full well—for you have been over this country—that the Rebels have sent into the fields all their available fighting men—every man capable of bearing arms; and you know they have kept at home all their slaves for the raising of subsistence for their armies in the field. In this way they can bring to bear against us all the strength of their so-called Confederate States; while we at the North can only send a portion of our fighting force, being compelled to leave behind another portion to cultivate our fields and supply the wants of an immense army. THE ADMINISTRATION HAS DETERMINED TO TAKE FROM THE REBELS THIS SOURCE OF SUPPLY— TO TAKE THEIR NEGROES AND COMPEL THEM TO SEND BACK A PORTION OF THEIR WHITES TO CULTIVATE THEIR DESIRED PLANTATIONS—AND VERY POOR PERSONS THEY WOULD BE TO FILL THE PLACE OF THE DARK-HUED LABORER. THEY MUST DO THIS, OR THEIR ARMIES WILL STARVE. . . .

"All of you will some day be on picket duty; and I charge you all, if any of this unfortunate race come within your lines, that you do not turn them away, but receive them kindly and cordially. They are to be encouraged to come to us; they are to be received with open arms; they are to be fed and clothed; they are to be armed." [15]

It would not have been American, however, not to have maintained some color discrimination, however petty. First, there was the matter of pay. The pay of soldiers at the beginning of the war was $13 a month. Negro soldiers enlisted under the same law. In the instructions to General Saxton, August 25, 1862, it was stated that the pay should be the same as that of the other troops. Soon, however, this was changed, and Negro soldiers were allowed but $10 a month, and $3 of this was deducted for clothing. Many of the regiments refused to receive the reduced pay. The 54th Massachusetts Infantry refused pay for a whole year until the regiment was treated as other regiments. The State of Massachusetts made up the difference to disabled and discharged soldiers until June 15, 1864, when the law was changed. In the Department of the Gulf, white troops who did provost duties about the city were paid $16 a month, while the Negro regiments were paid $7. At one time, this came near causing a mutiny.

But the Negroes did not waver. John M. Langston in a speech in Ohio in August, 1862, said:

"Pay or no pay, let us volunteer. The good results of such a course are manifold. But this one alone is all that needs to be mentioned in this con-nection. I refer to thorough organization. This is the great need of the colored Americans."

With regard to officers, the people of Pennsylvania secured from the Secretary of War permission to establish a free military school for the education of candidates for commissioned officers among the colored troops. The school was established, and within less than six months, examined over 1,000 applicants and passed 560. In the Department of the Gulf, Butler was in favor of colored officers, because in the First Colored Regiment there were a number of well-trained and intelligent Negro officers. But Banks was very much against colored officers, and would not use them. There was at first a very great distaste on the part of white men for serving in colored regiments. Hunter found this difficulty with his first regiment, but he quickly cured it by offering commissions to com-petent non-commissioned officers. Later, when the black troops made their reputation in battle, the chance to command them was eagerly sought.

Congress finally freed the wives and children of enlisted soldiers; a measure which Davis of Kentucky quickly opposed on the ground that "The government had no power to take private property except for public use, and without just compensation to the owner."

Abraham Lincoln, under a fire of criticism, warmly defended the enlistment of Negro troops. "The slightest knowledge of arithmetic will prove to any man that the rebel armies cannot be destroyed with Demo-cratic strategy. It would sacrifice all the white men of the North to do it. There are now in the service of the United States near two hundred thousand able-bodied colored men, most of them under arms, defending and acquiring Union territory. . . .

"ABANDON ALL THE POSTS NOW GARRISONED BY BLACK MEN; TAKE TWO HUNDRED THOUSAND MEN FROM OUR SIDE AND PUT THEM IN THE BATTLEFIELD OR CORNFIELD AGAINST US, AND WE WOULD BE COMPELLED TO ABANDON THE WAR IN THREE WEEKS. . . .

"My enemies pretend I am now carrying on this war for the sole purpose of abolition. So long as I am President, it shall be carried on for the sole purpose of restoring the Union. But no human power can subdue this rebellion without the use of the emancipation policy, and every other policy calculated to weaken the moral and physical forces of the rebellion. Freedom has given us two hundred thousand men raised on Southern soil. It will give us more yet. Just so much it has subtracted from the enemy." [16]

The question as to whether Negroes should enlist in the Federal army was not nearly as clear in 1863 as it seems today. The South still refused to believe that the Civil War would end in the emancipation of slaves. There not only were strong declarations to the contrary in the North, but there was still the determined opposition of the Border States. The Confederates industriously spread propaganda among slaves, alleging that Northerners mistreated the Negroes, and were selling them to the West Indies into harsher slavery. Even in the North, among the more intelligent free Negroes, there was some hesitancy.

Frederick Douglass spoke for the free and educated black man, clear-headed and undeceived: "Now, what is the attitude of the Washington government towards the colored race? What reasons have we to desire its triumph in the present contest? Mind, I do not ask what was its attitude towards us before this bloody rebellion broke out. I do not ask what was its disposition, when it was controlled by the very men who are now fighting to destroy it, when they could no longer control it. I do not even ask what it was two years ago, when McClellan shamelessly gave out that in a war between loyal slaves and disloyal masters, he would take the side of the masters against the slaves—when he openly proclaimed his purpose to put down slave insurrections with an iron hand—when glorious Ben Butler, now stunned into a conversion to anti-slavery principles (which I have every reason to believe sincere), proffered his services to the Governor of Maryland, to suppress a slave insurrection, while treason ran riot in that State, and the warm, red blood of Massachusetts soldiers still stained the pavements of Baltimore.

"I do not ask what was the attitude of this government when many of the officers and men who had undertaken to defend it openly threatened to throw down their arms and leave the service if men of color should step forward to defend it, and be invested with the dignity of soldiers. Moreover, I do not ask what was the position of this government when our loyal camps were made slave-hunting grounds, and United States officers performed the disgusting duty of slave dogs to hunt down slaves for rebel masters. These were all the dark and terrible days for the republic. I do not ask you about the dead past. I bring you to the living present.

"Events more mighty than men, eternal Providence, all-wise and all-controlling, have placed us in new relations to the government and the government to us. What that government is to us today, and what it will be tomorrow, is made evident by a very few facts. Look at them, colored men. Slavery in the District of Columbia is abolished forever; slavery in all the territories of the United States is abolished forever; the foreign slave trade, with its ten thousand revolting abominations, is rendered impossible; slavery in ten States of the Union is abolished forever; slavery in the five remaining States is as certain to follow the same fate as the night is to follow the day. The independence of Haiti is recognized; her Minister sits beside our Prime Minister, Mr. Seward, and dines at his table in Washington, while colored men are excluded from the cars in Philadelphia; showing that a black man's complexion in Washington, in the presence of the Federal Government, is less offensive than in the city of brotherly love. Citizenship is no longer denied us under this government.

"Under the interpretation of our rights by Attorney General Bates, we are American citizens. We can import goods, own and sail ships and travel in foreign countries, with American passports in our pockets; and now, so far from there being any opposition, so far from excluding us from the army as soldiers, the President at Washington, the Cabinet and the Congress, the generals commanding and the whole army of the nation unite in giving us one thunderous welcome to share with them in the honor and glory of suppressing treason and upholding the star-spangled banner. The revolution is tremendous, and it becomes us as wise men to recognize the change, and to shape our action accordingly.

"I hold that the Federal Government was never, in its essence, anything but an antislavery government. Abolish slavery tomorrow, and not a sentence or syllable of the Constitution need be altered. It was purposely so framed as to give no claim, no sanction to the claim of property in man. If in its origin slavery had any relation to the government, it was only as the scaffolding to the magnificent structure, to be removed as soon as the building was completed. There is in the Constitution no East, no West, no North, no South, no black, no white, no slave, no slaveholder, but all are citizens who are of American birth.

"Such is the government, fellow-citizens, you are now called upon to uphold with your arms. Such is the government, that you are called upon to coöperate with in burying rebellion and slavery in a common grave. Never since the world began was a better chance offered to a long enslaved and oppressed people. The opportunity is given us to be men. With one courageous resolution we may blot out the handwriting of ages against us. Once let the black man get upon his person the brass letters U. S.; let him get an eagle on his button, and a musket on his shoulder, and bullets in his pocket, and there is no power on the earth or under the earth which can deny that he has earned the right of citizenship in the United States." [17]

In the meantime, two fateful occurrences took place. First, the white workers of New York declared in effect that the Negroes were the cause of the war, and that they were tired of the discrimination that made workers fighters for the rich. They, therefore, killed all the Negroes that they could lay their hands on. On the other hand, in Louisiana and South Carolina, Negro soldiers were successfully used in pitched battle.

The opposition to the war in the North took various forms. There was the open sedition, led by Vallandingham and ending in the mass opposition of the working classes. This Copperhead movement was pro-slavery and pro-Southern, and was met in part by closer understanding and alliance between the Abolitionists and the Republican administration. But the working class movement was deeper and more difficult. It was the protest of the poor against being compelled to fight the battles of the rich in which they could conceive no interest of theirs. If the workers had been inspired by the sentiment against slavery which animated the English workers, results might have been different. But the Copperheads of the North, and the commercial interests of New York, in particular, were enabled to turn the just indignation of the workers against the Negro laborers, rather than against the capitalists; and against any war, even for emancipation.

When the draft law was passed in 1863, it meant that the war could no longer be carried on with volunteers; that soldiers were going to be compelled to fight, and these soldiers were going to be poor men who could not buy exemption. The result throughout the country was widespread disaffection that went often as far as rioting. More than 2,500 deserters from the Union army were returned to the ranks from Indianapolis alone during a single month in 1862; the total desertions in the North must have been several hundred thousands.

It was easy to transfer class hatred so that it fell upon the black worker. The end of war seemed far off, and the attempt to enforce the draft led particularly to disturbances in New York City, where a powerful part of the city press was not only against the draft, but against the war, and in favor of the South and Negro slavery.

The establishment of the draft undertaken July 13 in New York City met everywhere with resistance. Workingmen engaged in tearing down buildings were requested to give their names for the draft; they refused, and drove away the officers. The movement spread over the whole city. Mobs visited workshops and compelled the men to stop work. Firemen were prevented from putting out fires, telegraph wires were cut, and then at last the whole force of the riot turned against the Negroes. They were the cause of the war, and hence the cause of the draft. They were bidding for the same jobs as white men. They were underbidding white workers in order to keep themselves from starving. They were disliked especially by the Irish because of direct economic competition and difference in religion.

The Democratic press had advised the people that they were to be called upon to fight the battles of "niggers and Abolitionists"; Governor Seymour politely "requested" the rioters to await the return of his Adjutant-General, whom he had dispatched to Washington to ask the President to suspend the draft.

The report of the Merchants' Committee on the Draft Riot says of the Negroes: "Driven by the fear of death at the hands of the mob, who the week previous had, as you remember, brutally murdered by hanging on trees and lamp posts, several of their number, and cruelly beaten and robbed many others, burning and sacking their houses, and driving nearly all from the streets, alleys and docks upon which they had previously obtained an honest though humble living—these people had been forced to take refuge on Blackwell's Island, at police stations, on the outskirts of the city, in the swamps and woods back of Bergen, New Jersey, at Weeksville, and in the barns and out-houses of the farmers of Long Island and Morrisania. At these places were scattered some 5,000 homeless men, women and children." [18]

The whole demonstration became anti-Union and pro-slavery. Attacks were made on the residence of Horace Greeley, and cheers were heard for Jefferson Davis. The police fought it at first only half-heartedly and with sympathy, and finally, with brutality. Soldiers were summoned from Fort Hamilton, West Point and elsewhere.

The property loss was put at $1,200,000, and it was estimated that between four hundred and a thousand people were killed. When a thousand troops under General Wool took charge of the city, thirteen rioters were killed, eighteen wounded, and twenty-four made prisoners. Four days the riot lasted, and the city appropriated $2,500,000 to indemnify the victims.

In many other places, riots took place, although they did not become so specifically race riots. They did, however, show the North that unless they could replace unwilling white soldiers with black soldiers, who had a vital stake in the outcome of the war, the war could not be won.

It had been a commonplace thing in the North to declare that Negroes would not fight. Even the black man's friends were skeptical about the possibility of using him as a soldier, and far from its being to the credit of black men, or any men, that they did not want to kill, the ability and willingness to take human life has always been, even in the minds of liberal men, a proof of manhood. It took in many respects a finer type of courage for the Negro to work quietly and faithfully as a slave while the world was fighting over his destiny, than it did to seize a bayonet and rush mad with fury or inflamed with drink, and plunge it into the bowels of a stranger. Yet this was the proof of manhood required of the Negro. He might plead his cause with the tongue of Frederick Douglass, and the nation listened almost unmoved. He might labor for the nation's wealth, and the nation took the results without thanks, and handed him as near nothing in return as would keep him alive. He was called a coward and a fool when he protected the women and children of his master. But when he rose and fought and killed, the whole nation with one voice proclaimed him a man and brother. Nothing else made emancipation possible in the United States. Nothing else made Negro citizenship conceivable, but the record of the Negro soldier as a fighter.

The military aid of the Negroes began as laborers and as spies. A soldier said: "This war has been full of records of Negro agency in our behalf. Negro guides have piloted our forces; Negro sympathy cared for our prisoners escaping from the enemy; Negro hands have made for us naval captures; Negro spies brought us valuable information. The Negroes of the South have been in sympathy with us from the beginning, and have always hailed the approach of our flag with the wildest demonstrations of joy." [19]

All through the war and after, Negroes were indispensable as informers, as is well known. The southern papers had repeated notices of the work of Negro spies. In Richmond, a white woman with dispatches for the Confederate army was arrested in 1863 on information given by a Negro. At the Battle of Manassas, the house of a free Negro was used as a refuge for the dead and wounded Union men. Negro pilots repeatedly guided Federal boats in southern waters, and there were several celebrated cases of whole boats being seized by Negro pilots. A typical instance of this type was the action of William F. Tillman, a colored steward on board the brig *S. J. Waring*, which carried a cargo valued at $100,000. He had succeeded, by leading a revolt, in freeing the vessel from the Confederates who had seized it, and with the aid of a German and a Canadian had brought the vessel into port at New York. This action brought up the question of whether a Negro could be master of a vessel. In the Official Opinions of the Attorney-General for 1862, it was declared that a free colored man if born in the United States was a citizen of the United States and that he was competent to be master of a vessel engaged in the coasting trade.

The case of Smalls and the *Planter* at Charleston, South Carolina, became almost classic. "While at the wheel of the *Planter* as Pilot in the rebel service, it occured to me that I could not only secure my own freedom, but that of numbers of my comrades in bonds, and moreover, I thought the *Planter* might be of some use to Uncle Abe. . . .

"I reported my plans for rescuing the *Planter* from the rebel captain to the crew (all colored), and secured their secrecy and coöperation.

"On May 13, 1862, we took on board several large guns at the Atlantic Dock. At evening of that day, the Captain went home, leaving the boat in my care, with instruction to send for him in case he should be wanted. . . . At half-past three o'clock on the morning of the 14th of May, I left the Atlantic Dock with the *Planter*, went to the *Ettaoue*; took on board my family; and several other families, then proceeded down Charleston River slowly. When opposite . . . Fort Sumter at 4 A.M., I gave the signal, which was answered from the Fort, thereby giving permission to pass. I then made speed for the Blockading Fleet. When entirely out of range of Sumter's guns, I hoisted a white flag, and at 5 A.M., reached a U. S. blockading vessel, commanded by Capt. Nicholas, to whom I turned over the *Planter*." [20]

After Lincoln was assassinated, General Hancock appealed to Negroes for help in capturing his murderers:

"Your President has been murdered! He has fallen by the assassin and without a moment's warning, simply and solely because he was your friend and the friend of our country. Had he been unfaithful to you and to the great cause of human freedom he might have lived. The pistol from which he met his death, though held by Booth, was held by the hands of treason and slavery. Think of this and remember how long and how anxiously this good man labored to break your chains and make you happy. I now appeal to you, by every consideration which can move loyal and grateful hearts, to aid in discovering and arresting his murderer." [21]

This was issued on the 24th of April. On the next day, the cavalry and police force, having crossed the Potomac, received information from a colored woman that the fugitives had been seen there. They were followed toward Bowling Green, and then toward Port Royal. There an old colored man reported that four individuals, in company with a rebel Captain, had crossed the river to Bowling Green. This information brought the police to Garrett's house, where Booth was found.

Negro military labor had been indispensable to the Union armies. "Negroes built most of the fortifications and earth-works for General Grant in front of Vicksburg. The works in and about Nashville were cast up by the strong arm and willing hand of the loyal Blacks. Dutch Gap was dug by Negroes, and miles of earth-works, fortifications, and corduroy-roads were made by Negroes. They did fatigue duty in every department of the Union army. Wherever a Negro appeared with a shovel in his hand, a white soldier took his gun and returned to the ranks. There were 200,000 Negroes in the camps and employ of the Union armies, as servants, teamsters, cooks, and laborers." [22]

The South was for a long time convinced that the Negro could not and would not fight. "The idea of their doing any serious fighting against white men is simply ridiculous," said an editorial in the Savannah *Republican*, March 25, 1863.

Of the actual fighting of Negroes, a Union general, Morgan, afterward interested in Negro education, says:

"History has not yet done justice to the share borne by colored soldiers in the war for the Union. Their conduct during that eventful period, has been a silent, but most potent factor in influencing public sentiment, shaping legislation, and fixing the status of colored people in America. If the records of their achievements could be put into shape that they could be accessible to the thousands of colored youth in the South, they would kindle in their young minds an enthusiastic devotion to manhood and liberty." [23]

Black men were repeatedly and deliberately used as shock troops, when there was little or no hope of success. In February, 1863, Colonel Thomas Wentworth Higginson led black troops into Florida, and declared: "It would have been madness to attempt with the bravest white troops what successfully accomplished with black ones." [24]

In April, there were three white companies from Maine and seven Negro companies on Ship Island, the key to New Orleans. The black troops with black officers were attacked by Confederates who outnumbered them five to one. The Negroes retreated so as to give the Federal gunboat *Jackson* a chance to shell their pursuers, But the white crew disliked the Negro soldiers, and opened fire directly upon the black troops while they were fighting the Confederates. Major Dumas, the Negro officer in command, rescued the black men; repulsed the Confederates, and brought the men out safely. The commander called attention to these colored officers: "they were constantly in the thickest of the fight, and by their unflinching bravery, and admirable handling of their commands, contributed to the success of the attack, and reflected great honor upon the flag." [25]

The first battle with numbers of Negro troops followed soon after. Banks laid siege to Port Hudson with all his forces, including two black regiments. On May 23, 1863, the assault was ordered, but the various cooperating organizations did not advance simultaneously. The Negro regiments, on the North, made three desperate charges, losing heavily, but maintained the advance over a field covered with recently felled trees. Confederate batteries opened fire upon them. Michigan, New York and Massachusetts white troops were hurled back, but the works had to be taken. Two Negro regiments were ordered to go forward, through a direct and cross fire.

"The deeds of heroism performed by these colored men were such as the proudest white men might emulate. Their colors are torn to pieces by shot, and literally bespattered by blood and brains. The color-sergeant of the 1st Louisiana, on being mortally wounded, hugged the colors to his breast, when a struggle ensued between the two color-corporals on each side of him, as to who should have the honor of bearing the sacred standard, and during this generous contention, one was seriously wounded.

One black lieutenant actually mounted the enemy's works three or four times, and in one charge the assaulting party came within fifty paces of them. Indeed, if only ordinarily supported by artillery and reserve, no one can convince us that they would not have opened a passage through the enemy's works.

"Captain Callioux of the 1st Louisiana, a man so black that he actually prided himself upon his blackness, died the death of a hero, leading on his men in the thickest of the fight." [26]

"Colonel Bassett being driven back, Colonel Finnegas took his place, and his men being similarly cut to pieces, Lieutenant-Colonel Bassett reformed and recommenced; and thus these brave people went on, from morning until 3:30 P.M., under the most hideous carnage that men ever had to withstand, and that very few white ones would have had nerve to encounter, even if ordered to. During this time, they rallied, and *were ordered to make six distinct charges*, losing thirty-seven killed, and one hundred and fifty-five wounded, and one hundred and sixteen missing,— the majority, if not all, of these being in all probability, now lying dead on the gory field, and without the rites of sepulture; for when, by flag of truce, our forces in other direction were permitted to reclaim their dead, the benefit, through some neglect, was not extended to these black regiments!" [27]

In June, came the battle of Milliken's Bend. Grant, in order to capture Vicksburg, had drawn nearly all his troops from Milliken's Bend, except three Negro regiments, and a small force of white cavalry. This force was surprised by the Confederates, who drove the white cavalry to the very breastworks of the fort. Here the Confederates rested, expecting to take the fortifications in the morning. At three o'clock, they rushed over with drawn bayonets, but the Negroes drove them out of the forts and held them until the gunboats came up. One officer describes the fight:

"Before the colonel was ready, the men were in line, ready for action. As before stated, the rebels drove our force toward the gunboats, taking colored men prisoners and murdering them. This so enraged them that they rallied, and charged the enemy more heroically and desperately than has been recorded during the war. It was a genuine bayonet charge, a hand-to-hand fight, that has never occured to any extent during this prolonged conflict. Upon both sides men were killed with the butts of muskets. White and black men were lying side by side, pierced by bayonets, and in some instances transfixed to the earth. In one instance, two men, one white and the other black, were found dead, side by side, each having the other's bayonet through his body. If facts prove to be what they are now represented, this engagement of Sunday morning will be recorded as the most desperate of this war. Broken limbs, broken heads, the mangling of bodies, all prove that it was a contest between enraged men; on the one side from hatred to a race; and on the other, desire for self-preservation, revenge for past grievances and the inhuman murder of their comrades." [28]

The month of July, 1863, was memorable. General Meade had driven Lee from Gettysburg, Grant had captured Vicksburg, Banks had captured Port Hudson, and Gilmore had begun his operations on Morris Island. On the 13th of July, the draft riot broke out in New York City, and before it was over, a Negro regiment in South Carolina, the 54th Massachusetts, was preparing to lead the assault on Fort Wagner. It was a desperate, impossible venture, which failed, but can never be forgotten.

The black 54th Massachusetts regiment was to lead the assault. "Wagner loomed, black, grim and silent. There was no glimmer of light. Nevertheless, in the fort, down below the level of the tide, and under roofs made by huge trunks of trees, lay two thousand Confederate soldiers hidden. Our troops advanced toward the fort, while our mortars in the rear tossed bombs over their heads. Behind the 54th came five regiments from Connecticut, New York, New Hampshire, Pennsylvania and Maine. The mass went quickly and silently in the night. Then, suddenly, the walls of the fort burst with a blinding sheet of vivid light. Shot, shells of iron and bullets crushed through the dense masses of the attacking force. I shall never forget the terrible sound of that awful blast of death which swept down, battered or dead, a thousand of our men. Not a shot had missed its aim. Every bolt of iron and lead tasted of human blood.

"The column wavered and recovered itself. They reached the ditch before the fort. They climbed on the ramparts and swarmed over the walls. It looked as though the fort was captured. Then there came another blinding blaze from concealed guns in the rear of the fort, and the men went down by scores. The rebels rallied, and were reinforced by thousands of others, who had landed on the beach in the darkness unseen by the fleet. They hurled themselves upon the attacking force. The struggle was terrific. The supporting units hurried up to aid their comrades, but as they raised the ramparts, they fired a volley which struck down many of their own men. Our men rallied again, but were forced back to the edge of the ditch. Colonel Shaw, with scores of his black fighters, went down struggling desperately. Resistance was vain. The assailants were forced back to the beach, and the rebels drilled their recovered cannons anew on the remaining survivors."

When a request was made for Colonel Shaw's body, a Confederate Major said: "We have buried him with his niggers." [29]

In December, 1863, Morgan led Negro troops in the battle of Nashville. He declared a new chapter in the history of liberty had been written. "It had been shown that marching under a flag of freedom, animated by a love of liberty, even the slave becomes a man and a hero." Between eight and ten thousand Negro troops took part in the battles around Nashville, all of them from slave states.

When General Thomas rode over the battlefield, and saw the bodies of colored men side by side with the foremost on the very works of the enemy, he turned to his staff, saying: "Gentlemen, the question is settled: Negroes will fight."

How extraordinary, and what a tribute to ignorance and religious hypocrisy, is the fact that in the minds of most people, even those of liberals, only murder makes men. The slave pleaded; he was humble; he protected the women of the South, and the world ignored him. The slave killed white men; and behold, he was a man!

The New York *Times* said conservatively, in 1863:

"Negro soldiers have now been in battle at Port Hudson and at Milliken's Bend in Louisiana, at Helena in Arkansas, at Morris Island in South Carolina, and at or near Fort Gibson in the Indian territory. In two of these instances they assaulted fortified positions, and led the assault; in two, they fought on the defensive, and in one, they attacked rebel infantry. In all of them, they acted in conjunction with white troops, and under command of white officers. In some instances, they acted with distinguished bravery, and in all, they acted as well as could be expected of raw troops."

Even the New York *Herald* wrote in May, 1864:

"The conduct of the colored troops, by the way, in the actions of the last few days, is described as superb. An Ohio soldier said to me today, 'I never saw men fight with such desperate gallantry as those Negroes did. They advanced as grim and stern as death, and when within reach of the enemy struck about them with pitiless vigor, that was almost fearful.' Another soldier said to me: 'These Negroes never shrink, nor hold back, no matter what the order. Through scorching heat and pelting storms, if the order comes, they march with prompt, ready feet.' Such praise is great praise, and it is deserved."

And there was a significant dispatch in the New York *Tribune* July 26th:

"In speaking of the soldierly qualities of our colored troops, I do not refer especially to their noble action in the perilous edge of the battle; that is settled, but to their docility and their patience of labor and suffering in the camp and on the march."

Grant was made Lieutenant-General in 1864, and began to reorganize the armies. When he came East, he found that few Negro troops had been used in Virginia. He therefore transferred nearly twenty thousand Negroes from the southern and western armies to the army of Virginia. They fought in nearly all the battles around Petersburg and Richmond, and officers on the field reported:

"The problem is solved. The Negro is a man, a soldier, a hero. Knowing of your laudable interest in the colored troops, but particularly those raised under the immediate auspices of the Supervisory Committee, I have though it proper that I should let you know how they acquitted themselves in the late actions in front of Petersburg, of which you have already received newspaper accounts. If you remember, in my conversations upon the character of these troops, I carefully avoided saying anything about their fighting qualities till I could have an opportunity of trying them." [30]

When the siege of Petersburg began, there were desperate battles the 16th, 17th and 18th of June. The presence of Negro soldiers rendered the enemy especially spiteful, and there were continual scrimmages and sharp shooting. Burnside's 9th Corps had a brigade of black troops, who advanced within fifty yards of the enemy works. There was a small projecting fort which it was decided to mine and destroy. The colored troops were to charge after the mine was set off. An inspecting officer reported that the "black corps was fittest for the perilous services," but Meade objected to colored troops leading the assault. Burnside insisted. The matter was referred to Grant, and he agreed with Meade. A white division led the assault and failed. The battle of the Crater followed. Captain McCabe says: "It was now eight o'clock in the morning. The rest of Potter's (Federal) division moved out slowly, when Ferrero's Negro division, the men beyond question, inflamed with drink [There are many officers and men, myself among the number, who will testify to this], burst from the advanced lines, cheering vehemently, passed at a double quick over a crest under a heavy fire, and rushed with scarcely a check over the heads of the white troops in the crater, spread to their right, and captured more than two hundred prisoners and one stand of colors."

General Grant afterward said: "General Burnside wanted to put his colored troops in front. I believe if he had done so, it would have been a success." [31]

The following spring, April 3rd, the Federal troops entered Richmond. Weitzel was leading, with a black regiment in his command—a long blue line with gun-barrels gleaming, and bands playing: "John Brown's body lies a-moldering in the grave but his soul goes marching on."

President Lincoln visited the city after the surrender, and the Connecticut colored troops, known as the 29th Colored Regiment, witnessed his entry. One member of this unit said:

"When the President landed, there was no carriage near, neither did he wait for one, but leading his son, they walked over a mile to General Weitzel's headquarters at Jeff Davis' mansion, a colored man acting as guide. . . . What a spectacle! I never witnessed such rejoicing in all my life. As the President passed along the street, the colored people waved their handkerchiefs, hats and bonnets, and expressed their gratitude by shouting repeatedly, 'Thank God for His goodness; we have seen His salvation.' . . .

"No wonder tears came to his eyes, when he looked on the poor colored people who were once slaves, and heard the blessings uttered from thankful hearts and thanksgiving to God and Jesus. . . . After visiting Jefferson Davis' mansion, he proceeded to the rebel capitol, and from the steps delivered a short speech, and spoke to the colored people, as follows:

" 'In reference to you, colored people, let me say God has made you free. Although you have been deprived of your God-given rights by your so-called masters, you are now as free as I am, and if those that claim to be your superiors do not know that you are free, take the sword and bayonet and teach them that you are—for God created all men free, giving to each the same rights of life, liberty and the pursuit of happiness.' " [32]

The recruiting of Negro soldiers was hastened after the battle of Fort Wagner, until finally no less than 154 regiments, designated as United States Negro troops, were enlisted. They included 140 infantry regiments, 7 cavalry regiments, 13 artillery regiments, and 11 separate companies and batteries.[33] The whole number enlisted will never be accurately known, since in the Department of the Gulf and elsewhere, there was a practice of putting a living Negro soldier in a dead one's place under the same name.

Official figures say that there were in all 186,017 Negro troops, of whom 123,156 were still in service, July 16, 1865; and that the losses during the war were 68,178. They took part in 198 battles and skirmishes. Without doubt, including servants, laborers and spies, between three and four hundred thousand Negroes helped as regular soldiers or laborers in winning the Civil War.

The world knows that noble inscription on St. Gaudens' Shaw Monument in Boston Common written by President Eliot:

THE WHITE OFFICERS

Taking Life and Honor in their Hands—Cast their lot with Men of a Despised Race Unproved in War—and Risked Death as Inciters of a Servile Insurrection if Taken Prisoners, Besides Encountering all the Common Perils of Camp, March, and Battle.

THE BLACK RANK AND FILE

Volunteered when Disaster Clouded the Union Cause—Served without Pay for Eighteen Months till Given that of White Troops—Faced Threatened Enslavement if Captured—Were Brave in Action—Patient under Dangerous and Heavy Labors and Cheerful amid Hardships and Privations.

TOGETHER

They Gave to the Nation Undying Proof that Americans of African Descent Possess the Pride, Courage, and Devotion of the Patriot Soldier—One Hundred and Eighty Thousand Such Americans Enlisted under the Union Flag in MDCCCLXIII–MDCCCLXV.

Not only did Negroes fight in the ranks, but also about 75 served as commissioned officers, and a large number as subalterns. Major F. E. Dumas of Louisiana was a free Negro, and a gentleman of education, ability and property. He organized a whole company of his own slaves, and was promoted to the rank of Major. Many of the other Louisiana officers were well-educated. Among these officers were 1 Major, 27 Captains and 38 Lieutenants, and nearly 100 non-commissioned officers. In the other colored regiments, most of the officers were whites; but Massachusetts commissioned 10 Negro officers, and Kansas 3. There were, outside Louisiana, 1 Lieutenant-Colonel, 1 Major, 2 Captains, 2 Surgeons, and 4 Lieutenants, whose records are known. There were a number of mulattoes who served as officers in white regiments; one was on the staff of a Major-General of Volunteers.[34] Medals of honor were bestowed by the United States government for heroic conduct on the field of battle upon 14 Negroes.

The Confederates furiously denounced the arming of Negroes. The Savannah *Republican* called Hunter "the cold-blooded Abolition miscreant, who from his headquarters at Hilton Head, is engaged in executing the bloody and savage behests of the imperial gorilla, who from his throne of human bones at Washington, rules, reigns and riots over the destinies of the brutish and degraded North." The officers in command of black troops were branded as outlaws. If captured, they were to be treated as common felons. To be killed by a Negro was a shameful death. To be shot by the Irish and Germans from northern city slums was humiliating, but for masters to face armed bodies of their former slaves was inconceivable. When, therefore, black men were enrolled in northern armies, the Confederates tried to pillory the government internationally on the ground that this was arming barbarians for servile war.

In a message to the Confederate Congress, Jefferson Davis asked "our fellowmen of all countries to pass judgment on a measure by which several millions of human beings of an inferior race—peaceful and contented laborers in their sphere—are doomed to extermination, while at the same time they are encouraged to a general assassination of their masters by the insidious recommendation to abstain from violence unless in necessary defense. Our own detestation of those who have attempted the most execrable measures recorded in the history of guilty men is tempered by profound contempt for the impotent rage which it discloses. So far as regards the action of this government on such criminals as may attempt its execution, I confine myself to informing you that I shall—unless in your wisdom you deem some other course expedient—deliver to the several State authorities all commissioned officers of the United States that may hereafter be captured by our forces in any of the States embraced in the Proclamation, that they may be dealt with in accordance with the laws of those States providing for the punishment of criminals engaged in exciting servile insurrection." [35]

In December, 1862, he issued a proclamation, "that all Negro slaves captured in arms be at once delivered over to the executive authorities, of the respective States to which they belonged and to be dealt with according to the law of the said States," which, of course, meant death. The same month, the Confederate Congress passed resolutions confirming in the main the President's Proclamation ordering that commissioned officers commanding Negro troops be put to death by the Confederate government, while the Negroes be turned over to the states.

The fire of the Confederates was always concentrated upon the black troops, and Negroes captured suffered indignities and cruelties. Frederick Douglass, who visited the White House in the President's carriage "to take tea," appealed in behalf of his fellow blacks. If they served in Federal uniform, he said that they should receive the treatment of prisoners of war. This treatment of Negro soldiers brought rebuke from Abraham Lincoln; but worse than that, it brought fearful retaliation upon the field of battle.

The most terrible case of Confederate cruelty was the massacre at Fort Pillow. When Major Booth refused to surrender the fort the Confederate General Forrest gave a signal, and his troops made a fierce charge. In ten minutes, they had swept in. Federal troops surrendered; but an indiscriminate massacre followed. The black troops were shot down in their tracks; pinioned to the ground with bayonets and saber. Some were clubbed to death while dying of wounds; others were made to get down upon their knees, in which condition they were shot to death. Some were burned alive, having been fastened inside the buildings, while still others were nailed against the houses, tortured, and then burned to a crisp.

The dilemma of the South in the matter of Negro troops grew more perplexing. Negroes made good soldiers; that, the northern experiment had proven beyond peradventure. The prospect of freedom was leading an increasing stream of black troops into the Federal army. This stream could be diverted into the southern army, if the lure of freedom were offered by the Confederacy. But this would be an astonishing ending for a war in defense of slavery!

In this first year of the war large numbers of Negroes were in the service of the Confederates as laborers. In January, at Mobile, numbers of Negroes from the plantations of Alabama were at work on the redoubts. These were very substantially made, and strengthened by sand-bags and sheet-iron. Elsewhere in the South Negroes were employed in building fortifications, as teamsters and helpers in army service. In 1862, the Florida Legislature conferred authority upon the Governor to impress slaves for military purposes, if so authorized by the Confederate Government. The Confederate Congress provided by law in February, 1864, for the impressment of 20,000 slaves for menial service in the Confederate army. President Davis was so satisfied with their labor that he suggested, in his annual message, November, 1864, that this number should be increased to 40,000, with the promise of emancipation at the end of their service.[36]

In Louisiana, the Adjutant-General's Office of the Militia stated that "the Governor and the Commander-in-Chief relying implicitly upon the loyalty of the free colored population of the city and state, for the protection of their homes, their property and for Southern rights, from the pollution of a ruthless invader, and believing that the military organization which existed prior to February 15, 1862, and elicited praise and respect for the patriotic motives which prompted it, should exist for and during the war, calls upon them to maintain their organization and hold themselves prepared for such orders as may be transmitted to them."

These "Native Guards" joined the Confederate forces but they did not leave the city with these troops. When General Butler learned of this organization, he sent for several of the prominent colored men and asked why they had accepted service under the Confederate government. They replied that they dared not refuse, and hoped by serving the Confederates to advance nearer to equality with the whites.

In Charleston on January 2, 150 free colored men offered their services to hasten the work of throwing up redoubts along the coast. At Nashville, Tennessee, April, 1861, a company of free Negroes offered their services to the Confederates, and at Memphis a recruiting office was opened. The Legislature of Tennessee authorized Governor Harris, on June 28, 1861, to receive into military service all male persons of color between the ages of fifteen and fifty. A procession of several hundred colored men marched under the command of Confederate officers and carried shovels, axes, and blankets. The observer adds, "they were brimful of patriotism, shouting for Jeff Davis and singing war songs." A paper in Lynchburg, Virginia, commenting on the enlistment of 70 free Negroes to fight for the defense of the State, concluded with "three cheers for the patriotic Negroes of Lynchburg."

After the firing on Fort Sumter, several companies of Negro volunteers passed through Augusta on their way to Virginia. They consisted of sixteen companies of volunteers and one Negro company from Nashville. In November of the same year, twenty-eight thousand troops passed before Governor Moore, General Lowell and General Ruggles at New Orleans. The line of march was over seven miles, and one regiment comprised 1,400 free colored men. The Baltimore *Traveler* commenting on arming Negroes at Richmond, said: "Contrabands who have recently come within the Federal lines at Williamsport, report that all the able-bodied men in that vicinity are being taken to Richmond, formed into regiments, and armed for the defense of that city."

In February, 1862, the Confederate Legislature of Virginia considered a bill to enroll all free Negroes in the state for service with the Confederate forces.

While then the Negroes helped the Confederates as forced laborers and in a few instances as soldiers, the Confederates feared to trust them far, and hated the idea of depending for victory and defense on these very persons for whose slavery they were fighting. But in the last days of the struggle, no straw could be overlooked. In December, 1863, Major-General Patrick R. Cleburne, who commanded a division in Hardee's Corps of the Confederate Army of the Tennessee, sent in a paper in which the employment of the slaves as soldiers of the South was vigorously advocated. Cleburne urged that "freedom within a reasonable time" be granted to every slave remaining true to the Confederacy, and was moved to this action by the valor of the 54th Massachusetts, saying: "If they [the Negroes] can be made to face and fight bravely against their former masters, how much more probable is it that with the allurement of a higher reward, and led by those masters, they would submit to discipline and face dangers?"

President Davis was not convinced, and endorsed Cleburne's plea with the statement: "I deem it inexpedient at this time to give publicity to this paper, and request that it be suppressed."

In September, 1864, Governor Allen of Louisiana wrote to J. A. Seddon, Secretary of War in the Confederate government: "The time has come to put into the army every able-bodied Negro as a soldier. The Negro knows he cannot escape conscription if he goes to the enemy. He must play an important part in the war. He caused the fight, and he will have his portion of the burden to bear. . . . I would free all able to bear arms, and put them in the field at once." In that year, 1864, 100,000 poor whites deserted the Confederate armies. In November, 1864, Jefferson Davis in his message to the Confederate Congress recognized that slaves might be needed in the Confederate army. He said: "The subject is to be viewed by us, therefore, solely in the light of policy and our social economy. When so regarded, I must dissent from those who advise a general levy and arming of slaves for the duty of soldiers. Until our white population shall prove insufficient for the armies we require and can afford to keep the field, to employ as a soldier the Negro, who has merely been trained to labor, and as a laborer under the white man accustomed from his youth to the use of firearms, would scarcely be deemed wise or advantageous by any; and this is the question before us. But should the alternative ever be presented of subjugation or of the employment of the slave as a soldier, there seems no reason to doubt what should be our decision."

In response to an inquiry from the Confederate Secretary of War, as to arming slaves, Howell Cobb of Georgia opposed the measure to arm the Negroes. "I think that the proposition to make soldiers of our slaves is the most pernicious idea that has been suggested since the war began . . . you cannot make soldiers of slaves or slaves of soldiers. The moment you resort to Negro soldiers, your white soldiers will be lost to you, and one secret of the favor with which the proposition is received in portions of the army is the hope when Negroes go into the army, they [the whites] will be permitted to retire. It is simply a proposition to fight the balance of the war with Negro troops. You can't keep white and black troops together and you can't trust Negroes by themselves. . . . Use all the Negroes you can get for all purposes for which you need them but don't arm them. The day you make soldiers of them is the beginning of the end of the revolution."

J. P. Benjamin, Secretary of State, on the other hand, declared that the slaves would be made to fight against the South, if Southerners failed to arm them for their own defense. He advocated emancipation for such black soldiers at a large meeting at Richmond: "We have 680,000 blacks capable of bearing arms, and who ought now to be in the field. Let us now say to every Negro who wishes to go into the ranks on condition of being free, go and fight—you are free." [37]

In a letter to President Davis, another correspondent added: "I would not make a soldier of the Negro if it could be helped, but we are reduced to this last resort." Sam Clayton of Georgia wrote: "The recruits should come from our Negroes, nowhere else. We should away with pride of opinion, away with false pride, and promptly take hold of all the means God has placed without our reach to help us through this struggle—a war for the right of self-government. Some people say that Negroes will not fight. I say they will fight. They fought at Ocean Pond [Olustee, Florida], Honey Hill and other places. The enemy fights us with Negroes, and they will do very well to fight the Yankees."

In January, 1865, General Lee sent his celebrated statement to Andrew Hunter:

"We should not expect slaves to fight for prospective freedom when they can secure it at once by going to the enemy, in whose service they will incur no greater risk than in ours. The reasons that induce me to recommend the employment of Negro troops at all render the effect of the measures I have suggested upon slavery immaterial, and in my opinion the best means of securing the efficiency and fidelity of this auxiliary force would be to accompany the measure with a well-digested plan of gradual and general emancipation. As that will be the result of the continuance of the war, and will certainly occur if the enemy succeeds, it seems to me most advisable to do it at once, and thereby obtain all the benefits that will accrue to our cause." [38]

This letter was discussed by the Confederates, and February 8, Senator Brown of Mississippi introduced into the Confederate Congress a resolution which would have freed 200,000 Negroes and enrolled them in the army. This was voted down.

Jefferson Davis in a letter to John Forsythe, February, 1865, said that "all arguments as to the positive advantage or disadvantage of employing them are beside the question, which is simply one of relative advantage between having their fighting element in our ranks or in those of the enemy."

On February 11, another bill to enroll 200,000 Negro soldiers was introduced, and for a while it looked as though it would pass. General Lee again wrote, declaring the measure not only expedient but necessary, and that "under proper circumstances, the Negroes will make efficient soldiers."

The Richmond *Whig* of February 20, 1865, declared "that the proposition to put Negroes in the army has gained rapidly of late, and promises in some form or other to be adopted. . . . The enemy has taught us a lesson to which we ought not to shut our eyes. He has caused him to fight as well, if not better, than have his white troops of the same length of service."

Jefferson Davis discussed the matter with the Governor of Virginia, and said that he had been in conference with the Secretary of War and the Adjutant-General. He declared that the aid of recruiting officers for the purpose of enlisting Negroes would be freely accepted. March 17, it was said: "We shall have a Negro army. Letters are pouring into the departments from men of military skill and character asking authority to raise companies, battalions, and regiments of Negro troops." [39]

Thus on recommendation from General Lee and Governor Smith of Virginia, and with the approval of President Davis, an act was passed by the Confederate Congress, March 13, 1865, enrolling slaves in the Confederate army. Each state was to furnish a quota of the total 300,000. The preamble of the act reads as follows:

"An act to increase the Military Force of the Confederate States: The Congress of the Confederate States of America so enact, that, in order to provide additional forces to repel invasion, maintain the rightful possession of the Confederate States, secure their independence and pre-serve their institutions, the President be, and he is hereby authorized to ask for and accept from the owners of slaves, the services of such number of able-bodied Negro men as he may deem expedient, for and during the war, to perform military service in whatever capacity he may direct. . . ." The language used implied that volunteering was to be rewarded by freedom.

General Lee cooperated with the War Department in hastening the recruiting of Negro troops. Recruiting officers were appointed in nearly all southern states. Lieutenant John L. Cowardin, Adjutant, 19th Battalion, Virginia Artillery, was ordered April 1, 1865, to recruit Negro troops according to the act. On March 30, 1865, Captain Edward Bostick was ordered to raise four companies in South Carolina. Other officers were ordered to raise companies in Alabama, Florida, and Virginia. "It was the opinion of President Davis, on learning of the passage of the act, that not so much was accomplished as would have been, if the act had been passed earlier so that during the winter the slaves could have been drilled and made ready for the spring campaign of 1865."

It was too late now, and on April 9, 1865, Lee surrendered.

Negroes well within the Confederate lines were not insensible of what was going on. A colored newspaper said:

"Secret associations were at once organized in Richmond, which rapidly spread throughout Virginia, where the venerable patriarchs of the oppressed people prayerfully assembled together to deliberate upon the proposition of taking up arms in defense of the South. There was but one opinion as to the rebellion and its object; but the question which puzzled them most was, how were they to act the part about to be assigned to them in this martial drama? After a cordial interchange of opinions, it was decided with great unanimity, and finally ratified by all the auxiliary associations everywhere, that black men should promptly respond to the call of the Rebel chiefs, whenever it should be made, for them to take up arms.

"A question arose as to what position they would likely occupy in an engagement, which occasioned no little solicitude; from which all minds were relieved by agreeing that if they were placed in front as soon as the battle began the Negroes were to raise a shout about Abraham Lincoln and the Union, and, satisfied there would be plenty of supports from the Federal force, they were to turn like uncaged tigers upon the rebel hordes. Should they be placed in the rear, it was also understood, that as soon as firing began, they were to charge furiously upon the chivalry, which would place them between two fires; which would disastrously defeat the army of Lee, if not accomplish its entire annihilation." [40]

Of the effect of Negro soldiers in the northern army, there can be no doubt. John C. Underwood, resident of Virginia for twenty years, said before the Committee on Reconstruction:

"I had a conversation with one of the leading men in that city, and he said to me that the enlistment of Negro troops by the United States was the turning-point of the rebellion; that it was the heaviest blow they ever received. He remarked that when the Negroes deserted their masters, and showed a general disposition to do so and join the forces of the United States, intelligent men everywhere saw that the matter was ended. I have often heard a similar expression of opinion from others, and I am satisfied that the origin of this bitterness towards the Negro is this belief among the leading men that their weight thrown into the scale decided the contest against them. However the fact may be, I think that such is a pretty well settled conclusion among leading Rebels in Virginia." [41]

A Union general said: "The American Civil War of 1861–1865 marks an epoch not only in the history of the United States, but in that of democracy, and of civilization. Its issue has vitally affected the course of human progress. To the student of history it ranks along with the conquests of Alexander; the incursions of the Barbarians; the Crusades; the discovery of America, and the American Revolution. It settled the question of our National unity with all the consequences attaching thereto. It exhibited in a very striking manner the power of a free people to preserve their form of government against its most dangerous foe, Civil War. It not only enfranchised four millions of American slaves of African descent, but made slavery forever impossible in the great Republic, and gave a new impulse to the cause of human freedom." [42]

It was not the Abolitionist alone who freed the slaves. The Abolitionists never had a real majority of the people of the United States back of
them. Freedom for the slave was the logical result of a crazy attempt to
wage war in the midst of four million black slaves, and trying the
while sublimely to ignore the interests of those slaves in the outcome of
the fighting. Yet, these slaves had enormous power in their hands. Simply
by stopping work, they could threaten the Confederacy with starvation.
By walking into the Federal camps, they showed to doubting Northerners
the easy possibility of using them as workers and as servants, as farmers,
and as spies, and finally, as fighting soldiers. And not only using them thus,
but by the same gesture, depriving their enemies of their use in just these
fields. It was the fugitive slave who made the slaveholders face the alternative of surrendering to the North, or to the Negroes.

It was this plain alternative that brought Lee's sudden surrender.
Either the South must make terms with its slaves, free them, use them to
fight the North, and thereafter no longer treat them as bondsmen; or
they could surrender to the North with the assumption that the North,
after the war, must help them to defend slavery, as it had before. It was
then that Abolition came in as a determining factor, and itself was transformed to a new democratic movement.

So in blood and servile war, freedom came to America. What did it
mean to men? The paradox of a democracy founded on slavery had at last
been done away with. But it became more and more customary as time
went on, to linger on and emphasize the freedom which emancipation
brought to the masters, and later to the poor whites. On the other hand,
strangely enough, not as much has been said of what freedom meant to the
freed; of the sudden wave of glory that rose and burst above four million
people, and of the echoing shout that brought joy to four hundred thousand fellows of African blood in the North. Can we imagine this spectacular revolution? Not, of course, unless we think of these people as
human beings like ourselves. Not unless, assuming this common humanity,
we conceive ourselves in a position where we are chattels and real estate,
and then suddenly in a night become "thenceforward and forever free."
Unless we can do this, there is, of course, no point in thinking of this
central figure in emancipation. But assuming the common humanity of
these people, conceive of what happened: before the war, the slave was
curiously isolated; this was the policy, and the effective policy of the
slave system, which made the plantation the center of a black group with
a network of white folk around and about, who kept the slaves from
contact with each other. Of course, clandestine contact there always was;
the passing of Negroes to and fro on errands; particularly the semi-

freedom and mingling in cities; and yet, the mass of slaves were curiously provincial and kept out of the currents of information.

There came the slow looming of emancipation. Crowds and armies of the unknown, inscrutable, unfathomable Yankees; cruelty behind and before; rumors of a new slave trade; but slowly, continuously, the wild truth, the bitter truth, the magic truth, came surging through.

There was to be a new freedom! And a black nation went tramping after the armies no matter what it suffered; no matter how it was treated, no matter how it died. First, without masters, without food, without shelter; then with new masters, food that was free, and improvised shelters, cabins, homes; and at last, land. They prayed; they worked; they danced and sang; they studied to learn; they wanted to wander. Some for the first time in their lives saw Town; some left the plantation and walked out into the world; some handled actual money, and some with arms in their hands, actually fought for freedom. An unlettered leader of fugitive slaves pictured it: "And then we saw the lightning—that was the guns! and then we heard the thunder—that was the big guns; and then we heard the rain falling, and that was the drops of blood falling; and when we came to git in the craps it was dead men that we reaped."

The mass of slaves, even the more intelligent ones, and certainly the great group of field hands, were in religious and hysterical fervor. This was the coming of the Lord. This was the fulfillment of prophecy and legend. It was the Golden Dawn, after chains of a thousand years. It was everything miraculous and perfect and promising. For the first time in their life, they could travel; they could see; they could change the dead level of their labor; they could talk to friends and sit at sundown and in moonlight, listening and imparting wonder-tales. They could hunt in the swamps, and fish in the rivers. And above all, they could stand up and assert themselves. They need not fear the patrol; they need not even cringe before a white face, and touch their hats.

To the small group of literate and intelligent black folk, North and South, this was a sudden beginning of an entirely new era. They were at last to be recognized as men; and if they were given the proper social and political power, their future as American citizens was assured. They had, therefore, to talk and agitate for their civil and political rights. With these, in thought and object, stood some of the intelligent slaves of the South.

On the other hand, the house servants and mechanics among the freed slaves faced difficulties. The bonds which held them to their former masters were not merely sentiment. The masters had stood between them and a world in which they had no legal protection except the master. The masters were their source of information. The question, then, was how far they could forsake the power of the masters, even when it was partially overthrown? For whom would the slave mechanic work, and how could he collect his wages? What would be his status in court? What protection would he have against the competing mechanic?

Back of this, through it all, combining their own intuitive sense with what friends and leaders taught them, these black folk wanted two things—first, land which they could own and work for their own crops. This was the natural outcome of slavery. Some of them had been given by their masters little plots to work on, and raise their own food. Sometimes they raised hogs and chickens, in addition. This faint beginning of industrial freedom now pictured to them economic freedom. They wanted little farms which would make them independent.

Then, in addition to that, they wanted to know; they wanted to be able to interpret the cabalistic letters and figures which were the key to more. They were consumed with curiosity at the meaning of the world. First and foremost, just what was this that had recently happened about them—this upturning of the universe and revolution of the whole social fabric? And what was its relation to their own dimly remembered past of the West Indies and Africa, Virginia and Kentucky?

They were consumed with desire for schools. The uprising of the black man, and the pouring of himself into organized effort for education, in those years between 1861 and 1871, was one of the marvelous occurrences of the modern world; almost without parallel in the history of civilization. The movement that was started was irresistible. It planted the free common school in a part of the nation, and in a part of the world, where it had never been known, and never been recognized before. Free, then, with a desire for land and a frenzy for schools, the Negro lurched into the new day.

Suppose on some gray day, as you plod down Wall Street, you should see God sitting on the Treasury steps, in His Glory, with the thunders curved about him? Suppose on Michigan Avenue, between the lakes and hills of stone, and in the midst of hastening automobiles and jostling crowds, suddenly you see living and walking toward you, the Christ, with sorrow and sunshine in his face?

Foolish talk, all of this, you say, of course; and that is because no American now believes in his religion. Its facts are mere symbolism; its revelation vague generalities; its ethics a matter of carefully balanced gain. But to most of the four million black folk emancipated by civil war, God was real. They knew Him. They had met Him personally in many a wild orgy of religious frenzy, or in the black stillness of the night. His plan for them was clear; they were to suffer and be degraded, and then afterwards by Divine edict, raised to manhood and power; and so on January 1, 1863, He made them free.

It was all foolish, bizarre, and tawdry. Gangs of dirty Negroes howling and dancing; poverty-stricken ignorant laborers mistaking war, destruction and revolution for the mystery of the free human soul; and yet to these black folk it was the Apocalypse. The magnificent trumpet tones of Hebrew Scripture, transmuted and oddly changed, became a strange new gospel. All that was Beauty, all that was Love, all that was Truth, stood on the top of these mad mornings and sang with the stars. A great human sob shrieked in the wind, and tossed its tears upon the sea,— free, free, free.

There was joy in the South. It rose like perfume—like a prayer. Men stood quivering. Slim dark girls, wild and beautiful with wrinkled hair, wept silently; young women, black, tawny, white and golden, lifted shivering hands, and old and broken mothers, black and gray, raised great voices and shouted to God across the fields, and up to the rocks and the mountains.

A great song arose, the loveliest thing born this side the seas. It was a new song. It did not come from Africa, though the dark throb and beat of that Ancient of Days was in it and through it. It did not come from white America—never from so pale and hard and thin a thing, however deep these vulgar and surrounding tones had driven. Not the Indies nor the hot South, the cold East or heavy West made that music. It was a new song and its deep and plaintive beauty, its great cadences and wild appeal wailed, throbbed and thundered on the world's ears with a message seldom voiced by man. It swelled and blossomed like incense, improvised and born anew out of an age long past, and weaving into its texture the old and new melodies in word and in thought.

They sneered at it—those white Southerners who heard it and never understood. They raped and defiled it—those white Northerners who listened without ears. Yet it lived and grew; always it grew and swelled and lived, and it sits today at the right hand of God, as America's one real gift to beauty; as slavery's one redemption, distilled from the dross of its dung.

The world at first neither saw nor understood. Of all that most Americans wanted, this freeing of slaves was the last. Everything black was hideous. Everything Negroes did was wrong. If they fought for freedom, they were beasts; if they did not fight, they were born slaves. If they cowered on the plantations, they loved slavery; if they ran away, they were lazy loafers. If they sang, they were silly; if they scowled, they were impudent.

The bites and blows of a nation fell on them. All hatred that the whites after the Civil War had for each other gradually concentrated itself on them. They caused the war—they, its victims. They were guilty of all the thefts of those who stole. They were the cause of wasted property and small crops. They had impoverished the South, and plunged the North into endless debt. And they were funny, funny—ridiculous baboons, aping man.

Southerners who had suckled food from black breasts vied with each other in fornication with black women, and even in beastly incest. They took the name of their fathers in vain to seduce their own sisters. Nothing—nothing that black folk did or said or thought or sang was sacred. For seventy years few Americans had dared say a fair word about a Negro.

There was no one kind of Negro who was freed from slavery. The freedmen were not an undifferentiated group; there were those among them who were cowed and altogether bitter. There were the cowed who were humble; there were those openly bitter and defiant, but whipped into submission, or ready to run away. There were the debauched and the furtive, petty thieves and licentious scoundrels. There were the few who could read and write, and some even educated beyond that. There were the children and grandchildren of white masters; there were the house servants, trained in manners, and in servile respect for the upper classes. There were the ambitious, who sought by means of slavery to gain favor or even freedom; there were the artisans, who had a certain modicum of freedom in their work, were often hired out, and worked practically as free laborers. The impact of legal freedom upon these various classes differed in all sorts of ways.

And yet emancipation came not simply to black folk in 1863; to white Americans came slowly a new vision and a new uplift, a sudden freeing of hateful mental shadows. At last democracy was to be justified of its own children. The nation was to be purged of continual sin not indeed all of its own doing—due partly to its inheritance; and yet a sin, a negation that gave the world the right to sneer at the pretensions of this republic. At last there could really be a free commonwealth of freemen.

Thus, amid enthusiasm and philanthropy, and religious fervor that surged over the whole country, the black man became in word "henceforward and forever free."

NOTES

1. George Washington Williams, *A History of the Negro Race in America from 1619 to 1880*, 2 vols. (New York: G. P. Putnam's Sons, 1883), II, pp. 265–66.

2. Charleston *Daily Courier*, January 8, 1863.

3. Ibid., February 16, 1863.

4. Donaldson Jordan and Edwin J. Pratt, *Europe and the American Civil War* (Boston and New York: Houghton Mifflin Company, 1931), p. 78.

5. Henry Adams, *The Education of Henry Adams* (New York: Houghton Mifflin Company, 1907), pp. 130–31.

6. Herman Schlüter, *Lincoln, Labor and Slavery; a Chapter from the Social History of America* (New York: Socialist Literature Company, 1913), p. 158.

7. Ibid., pp. 161, 162, 163.

8. Joseph T. Wilson, *The Black Phalanx: A History of the Negro Soldiers of the United States in the Wars of 1775–1812, 1861–'65* (Hartford, Connecticut: American Publishing Company, 1888), pp. 146–47.

9. Ibid., pp. 151–54.

10. James Parton, *General Butler in New Orleans* (New York: Mason Brothers, 1864), pp. 491, 493.

11. Wilson, *History of the Black Phalanx*, p. 192.

12. Ibid., p. 195.

13. Williams, *History of the Negro Race in America*, II, pp. 292, 293.

14. Wilson, *History of the Black Phalanx*, p. 120.

15. Williams, *History of the Negro Race in America*, pp. 289, 290. (Italics ours.)

16. Emanuel Hertz, *Abraham Lincoln, A New Portrait*, 2 vols. (New York: H. Liveright, 1931), II, pp. 931–32.

17. Carter Woodson, *Negro Orators and Their Orations* (Washington, D. C.: Associated Publishers, 1925), pp. 249, 251.

18. *Report of the Merchants Committee*, p. 7.

19. Wilson, *History of the Black Phalanx*, p. 394.

20. Story told by Smalls to the A. M. E. General Conference, Philadelphia, May 1864.

21. *New Orleans Tribune*, May 4, 1865.

22. Williams, *History of the Negro Race in America*, II, p. 262.

23. Wilson, *History of the Black Phalanx*, p. 305.

24. Williams, *History of the Negro Race in America*, II, p. 314.

25. Wilson, *History of the Black Phalanx*, p. 211.

26. Williams, *History of the Negro Race in America*, II, p. 321.

27. Ibid., II, pp. 320, 321.

28. Ibid., II, p. 327.

29. Wilson, *History of the Black Phalanx*, p. 256.

30. Williams, *History of the Negro Race in America*, II, pp. 338, 339.

31. *Testimony Before Congressional Committee;* cited in Wilson, *History of the Black Phalanx*, p. 428.

32. Isaac J. Hill, *A Sketch of the 29th Regiment of Connecticut Colored Troops* (Baltimore: Daugherty, Maguire & Co., 1867), pp. 26, 27.

33. Nicholay and Hay give 149 regiments. John G. Nicolay and John Hay, eds., *Complete Works of Abraham Lincoln*, 12 vols. (New York: Francis D. Tandy Company, 1905), VI, p. 468.

34. Cf. Wilson, *History of the Black Phalanx*, ch. 4; and Williams, *History of the Negro Race in America*, II, pp. 299–301.

35. Wilson, *History of the Black Phalanx*, pp. 316, 317.

36. Charles H. Wesley, "Lincoln's Plan for Colonizing the Emancipated Negroes," *Journal of Negro History* 4 (January 1919): 7–21.

37. Wilson, *History of the Black Phalanx*, pp. 491, 492.

38. Ibid., p. 490.

39. Ibid., p. 494.
40. New Orleans *Tribune*, February 25, 1865.
41. *Report of the Joint Committee on Reconstruction*, 1866, p. 8.
42. General T. J. Morgan, in Wilson, *History of the Black Phalanx*, p. 289.

29. JAMES H. BREWER, The Confederate Negro (1969)*

Professor James H. Brewer of North Carolina Central University, located in Durham, is representative of the younger group of black scholars. In this selection, Professor Brewer describes the efforts of the Confederacy to make full use of black labor during the Civil War. Concentrating on Virginia where records are more extensive than in other Confederate states, the author discusses the legislative measures passed to conscript Afro-Americans into non-combatant service. The author is seriously handicapped by the scarcity of adequate research material pertaining to individual Afro-Americans and by the availability of only white sources.

The presence of over 500,000 Negroes in Virginia at the outset of the Civil War raises the question of their involvement in and their importance to the Confederate war effort. Part of the answer is to be found in legislation enacted by both the General Assembly of Virginia and the Confederate Congress; and part of the story is told in Confederate war records which reflect the extent to which Negroes, with their brawn and skills, were effectively mobilized to meet the Confederacy's technological, military, and agricultural demands.[1]

As an auxiliary labor force, the total slave population of Virginia on the eve of the Civil War numbered over 491,000, while the state's free Negro population numbered only some 58,000. Translated into percentages of the total white population 1,048,000 Negroes equaled approximately 51 percent of the white population in Virginia. An estimate of the geographical distribution of the state's Negro population is shown in Table 1.

Table 1. *Distribution of Negro population
in Virginia on the eve of the Civil War*

Section	Free Negroes	Slaves
Tidewater	59%	39%
Piedmont	30%	46%
Appalachian	11%	15%

*From James H. Brewer, *The Confederate Negro* (Durham, N.C.: Duke University Press, 1969), pp. 3–16. Reprinted by permission.

The immense demands of armed conflict were such that they could not be borne by whites alone. Many skilled laborers, for example, were needed to fabricate the weapons of war in machine shops, arsenals, and ironworks. Many other workers were needed to procure raw materials. Building new transportation lanes, or improving upon existing ones, to facilitate the movement of troops, war materials, and other supplies essential to the war effort demanded a number of laborers. Likewise, Virginia's vulnerability necessitated the extensive use by Confederate engineers of a massive labor force for the construction of fortifications and defensive works to protect industrial centers, strategic areas, and the endangered routes of communication within the state. Finally, an ample supply of labor was imperative to sustain and to increase the production of foodstuffs and to make possible the wholesale conversion of the use of land to corn, wheat, potatoes, and cereal grains such as oats and barley. Black manpower throughout the war was called upon not only by military authorities but by private industry as well to offset the dwindling pool of white civilian war workers.

By the late fall of 1862 Virginia was confronted with a serious problem. The impressment of slaves and free Negroes to labor on fortifications and river batteries, coupled with the slaveowners' practice of hiring out a large percentage of their slaves to the quartermaster, ordnance, and other bureaus of the War Department, tended to exhaust the supply of available Negro manpower which was necessary for the agricultural and industrial needs of the state. This labor shortage was one of the knottiest problems facing Confederate and state authorities. As the war became more critical, open conflict ensued between these two groups, even though it was apparent that if the South were to increase its military potential, Virginia would have to commit to the Confederate government as noncombat workers an even larger proportion of its Negro population.

Negro labor had been used extensively in Virginia's industrial growth for several decades before the conflict of 1861.[2] In the forties and fifties, for example, the expanding practice of slave hiring was exceptionally well suited for supplying labor force to meet the mounting needs of manufacturing, transportation, mining, and public works.[3] There emerged a new class of brokers, usually known as "agents," who specialized in hiring and supplying slaves for industrial and urban employment. In the tobacco-growing regions they also supplied slaves to serve as a supplementary labor force during both the planting and harvesting seasons. The agent's fees were usually 7½ percent for "hiring-out, bonding, collecting the hire, and attention to the physical needs of the slave during the period of hire."

Throughout Virginia many owners had hired out their slaves for annual payments, according to Clement Eaton, that averaged "from 10 to 15 percent of their value." This practice permitted employers to secure the labor of slaves by hire instead of investing money to purchase them. The state's businessmen considered this a sound procedure; and Richmond, Petersburg, Danville, and Lynchburg became the principal centers for slave hiring. The practice afforded profitable returns to Tidewater and Piedmont slaveowners.

Prewar Virginia history, especially during the 1850s, includes typical scenes in which slaves were hired out by their owners as sawyers, coopers, quarrymen, millers, wheelwrights, and wagonmakers; they were also hired to mine coal, limestone, lead, salt, and iron ore; and they worked as pilots, boathands, and fishermen. Hundreds of slaves were employed in the construction and maintenance of canals and railroads. Town slaves were hired out to work in flour mills, tobacco factories, shoe shops, foundries, sawmills, and stores. On the docks they labored as stevedores, and at railroad depots they loaded and unloaded freight. There were hundreds of slave and free Negro craftsmen engaged in such trades as boatmaker, ropemaker, caulker, blacksmith, shoemaker, and carpenter. Virginia's railroads procured a large labor force of slaves to work as firemen, track hands, brakemen, machinists, boilermakers, and blacksmiths.

According to Clement Eaton, "the growing practice of obtaining the service of slave labor by hire instead of by purchase" was an important aspect of the institution in the upper South.[4] It was inevitable that the condition of servitude would be affected by the nature of the bondsman's employment. Some slaves were permitted to receive wages, make contracts, and maintain their own homes.[5] Urban slaves possessed a greater degree of mobility and quite often at least a limited choice as to the place of their employment. Increasing numbers of slaves were allowed to hire their own time and to pay their masters an annual fee from their wages.

Prewar slave hiring, with its greater flexibility of labor supply, contributed to the upgrading of slave labor and was an important factor in the industrial development of ante-bellum Virginia. In 1846, for example, there were 5,667 slaves employed in Richmond's business enterprises such as cotton and flour mills, and a decade later the number had increased to 6,326. In many instances such slaves were hired rather than owned by manufacturers.[6]

Prewar slave hiring not only contributed to the upgrading of slave labor, it also augmented the industrial development of the state. Ante-bellum slave hiring also greatly increased the number of slave technicians who were to be available for service as war workers, thereby contributing to the success of the state's program of mobilization of Negro labor for the Civil War.

The responsibility for effectively assembling Negro manpower became that of the Virginia lawmakers and the Confederate Congressmen. Speaking on this point, President Jefferson Davis stated, "Much of our success was due to the much abused institution of African servitude." This opinion was shared by General Ulysses S. Grant, who was well aware of the need to remove from the South her vast army of Negro noncombatants. Grant said, "The 4,000,000 colored noncombatants were equal to more than three times their numbers in the North, age for age, sex for sex." Both President Davis and General Grant early recognized that the mobilization of the Negro constituted an extremely valuable military resource. The Virginia legislature found it necessary, however, to pass impressment laws forcing slaveholders to send their chattel to labor for the military. Statutes were also enacted to draft free Negroes for military work.

From February 1862 to February 1864, five impressement laws constituted the most significant acts dealing with the mobilization of Virginia's Negro population for noncombat purposes. Three of the five laws were passed by the General Assembly of the state, while the other two were enacted by the Confederate Congress. The first state law subjected the free Negro to the draft as a laborer, the second placed a ceiling on the number of slaves that could be impressed, and the third exempted the slaves from counties where impressment would materially affect agricultural production. The two wartime regulations passed by the Confederate Congress not only made provision for tapping Virginia's Negro reservoir but were also designed to minimize conflicts between Confederate and state authorities over the impressment of slaves and to correct glaring defects of state impressment laws.

Such impressment legislation was prompted by the collapse, nine months after the beginning of hostilities, of the voluntary recruiting efforts for Negro labor. At the call to repel the Yankee invaders, for example, Virginia looked to its Negro population as a major source of civilian workers. Yet, by the late fall of 1861 the fervor of free Negroes for volunteering had largely subsided. The early months of war had also taught the folly of depending upon slaveholders to comply willingly with military requisitions for the labor of their slaves. Consequently, the state by January 1862 was in no mood to continue its voluntary recruiting efforts for Negro workers. Nevertheless the hiring-out of slaves and the hire of free colored persons by contracts with military authorities and private war industries were to continue throughout the war. This was particularly true with respect to the state's railroads, ironworks, factories, and public works. Likewise the majority of Negroes employed by the quartermaster, ordnance, niter and mining bureaus, and military hospitals were hired through voluntary contracts with free Negroes and the owners of bondsmen.

The realities of war and the mounting demands of the Confederate armies forced Virginia actively to recruit Negroes as military laborers. At first, legal provision was made for tapping only the free Negro reservoir. In February 1862 the state legislature passed an act which required the local courts to register all male free Negroes within their jurisdiction who were between the ages of eighteen and fifty. Such registration lists were to be sent to the Adjutant General, and whenever a commanding officer of any post or department wanted laborers he was to submit his requisition to the local court. A board of three justices was authorized to select the workers from the registration list. The local sheriff was responsible for notifying the free Negroes of their call, and if he failed to perform his duty he was subject to a fine of from $50 to $100. The selected free persons were not required to serve longer than 180 days without their consent. They were also entitled to such compensation, rations, quarters, and medical attention as any white laborers of similar character. Their pay, rations, and allowances were borne by the Confederate States, unless the services rendered were exclusively for the state.[7]

After authorizing the impressment of free Negroes for military service, Virginia lawmakers next considered the slave. By the late summer of 1862, it was apparent that ample slave labor could not be obtained without specific legislative action. Therefore, on October 3, 1862, the legislature passed an act providing for the public defense of the state. The act required that a census be taken of all slaves between the ages of eighteen and forty-five. Upon requisition from the President of the Confederate States, the Governor of Virginia would impress slaves to work on entrenchments and to do other labor necessary for the defense of the state. The number that could be impressed should not exceed 10,000 or more than 5 percent of the slave population from any county, city, or town. The sheriff was to receive the slaves from their masters for delivery to the proper government agents. Such slaves were not allowed to remain in the employment of the government longer than sixty days. A penalty of thirty days was invoked for cases in which steps had to be taken against the local authorities who refused to comply with the act. The law further provided that $16 per month was to be paid to the slaveowner, plus a soldier's ration, medicine, and medical care for the slave. All expenses were to be borne by the Confederate States government. If the owner furnished his slaves' subsistence he would be given 60 cents per day for each one. Slaves working on farms devoted exclusively to the production of grains were to be exempt from impressment. Owners were to be paid by the government for the loss of bondsmen who escaped to the Union lines, were killed by the enemy, or were injured because of negligence on the part of the military.[8]

Military officers violated this law from time to time. Occasionally military commanders took steps to impress more slaves after receiving all that had been made available for public defense. Governor Letcher accordingly turned down a request by Major General Jones to draft slaves to work at Saltville in the salt mines. The governor also received protests from many owners about the seizure of their slaves by military officers without the owners' authorizations. The Virginia lawmakers finally made unauthorized impressment a misdemeanor, and the violator was subject to a fine double the value of the slave impressed.

In March 1863 the General Assembly passed a third act which exempted agricultural counties where slave impressment would materially affect production. This law also increased to $20 per month the maximum pay to owners. Any owner sending thirty to forty slaves to a receiving station was expected to provide an overseer to guard his property. Legal exemption was expanded to include counties near the enemy lines, where owners could prove to the court that they had lost one third of their slaves through escape. Still other exemptions from impressment included any soldier in the army having only one slave, and a widow having a son in the army or whose husband had died in the service. The act of 1863 also extended to fifty-five the age limit for the impressment of slaves. Any owner who refused to send a slave was subject to a maximum fine of $10 for each day of recalcitrance. Failure of the sheriff to deliver a drafted bondsman carried a fine of from $50 to $200. Thus in 1862 and in 1863 the state's lawmakers enacted these laws to put a portion of its large Negro labor market in readiness for effective war service.

As the conflict entered the twenty-third month, the Confederate Congress was forced to take more drastic steps to procure Negro labor. On March 26, 1863, it passed its first significant act to achieve access to the Confederacy's Negro military labor force. No longer was the state governor to be the chief enforcing agent in procuring Negro labor, but instead he was to be replaced by President Davis. The act of March 1863, designed to correct the defects of state impressment laws, specifically legalized slave impressment by Confederate authorities "according to the rules and regulations provided in the laws of the state wherein they are impressed." [9] At times, however, military officers were obliged to find ways to evade the more annoying state provisions. For example, one section of the law of 1863 gave army officers the right to impress "other property" whenever the exigencies were such as to make impressment absolutely necessary. Supported by this "other property" phrase, military commanders resorted to impressment of slaves, in some instances in violation of Virginia law. Such action, however, was immediately challenged by state officials. During the months to follow, Virginia lawmakers wrote to the Secretary of War protesting such action. J. B. Baldwin of Staunton urged the importance of returning slaves and free Negroes to the Valley district to aid in harvesting the large crop. Virginia lawmakers openly questioned the legality of "any law authorizing a draft of slaves in the state except according to state law and through the Governor and the county courts." [10] Early in 1864 a joint resolution of the General Assembly directed the Confederate government to refrain, if possible, from drafting slaves from agricultural areas because they were needed for food production.

Throughout 1863 demands to impress or conscript free blacks as military laborers were intensified. Occasionally a military officer expressed similar sentiments. On November 11, 1863, Major Samuel W. M. Melton, the Assistant Adjutant General, suggested to War Secretary Seddon that conscription might be extended to free Negroes. He insisted that their services were "as clearly due as those of any other class in the Confederacy." [11] Confederate authorities, however, were more concerned about finding means to utilize fully the vast reservoir of slave laborers. The Secretary of War frequently reminded President Jefferson Davis that "to command slaves . . . in anything like the number required for the many works of the government . . . compulsion in some form would be necessary." Seddon also pointed out: "There may be difficulties and embarrassments in enforcing the services of slaves, but they might be overcome on the principle of impressing them as property, or requiring contributions from their owners of certain quotas for public service, as has been done for works of public defense." [12]

Unfortunately, the first impressment act of March 1863 was inadequate, and southern leaders considered more stringent measures. President Davis acknowledged the shortcomings of existing impressment laws in his message to Congress on December 7, 1863.[13] Consequently the 1863 law was supplemented by an amendatory act of February 17, 1864, which authorized a levy of 20,000 slaves throughout the Confederacy between the ages of eighteen and fifty, when conditions should require. Slaves were to be impressed, however, only if the supply of free Negroes failed to meet the needs of the War Department. If the owner had but one male bondsman between the ages of ten and fifty, that one was not to be taken without the owner's permission. Only one fifth of the male slaves were to be taken, and credit was to be given for slaves already impressed by the government. By September 1864 the War Secretary had issued a requisition for 14,500 slaves, of which Virginia was expected to furnish her quota of 2,500.

The second slave impressment act was not altogether successful, and within a few months a new levy was contemplated. President Davis, in November, 1864, asked the Confederate Congress for additional legislation to employ 40,000 slaves.

The Confederate Congress's second impressment act of February 17, 1864, was also designed to make all male free Negroes between the ages of eighteen and fifty liable "to service in war manufactories, in erecting defensive works, and in military hospitals." The act, moreover, required that they be taken in preference to the 20,000 slaves eligible to be impressed, and that such free Negroes should receive the same pay and subsistence as soldiers. The 1864 conscription act allowed the creation of the Bureau of Conscription to administer the drafting of persons. A bureaucracy of officers, medical examiners, and other agents was authorized to handle the task of enrolling or exempting white males between the ages of seventeen and fifty. The Bureau was also entrusted with the task of procuring Negroes, free and slave. In the spring of 1864 War Secretary Seddon instructed Brigadier General John S. Preston, Chief of the Bureau of Conscription, to bring into service the free Negroes authorized by the act of Congress.

Subsequently A. R. Lawton, the Quartermaster General, commented about the issuing of clothing and suggested that blankets, shoes, and woolen garments be provided by bureaus employing Negroes. Lawton stated that his department could provide some summer clothing and cotton pants, shirts, drawers, socks, and caps. In November 1864 a directive from the Quartermaster General's office ran:

> Each bureau will also provide such Negroes and all other employees in service with the necessary woolen shirts, jackets, and pants, and blankets, overcoats, and shoes. Cotton pants, shirts, drawers, socks, and caps will be provided by the Quartermaster Department on requisitions made quarterly. . . .[14]

Among the 27,771 free Negro males in Virginia, there were approximately 5,000 who were between the ages of eighteen and forty-five, and thus liable for military service. Well over 50 percent, however, were already usefully employed in transportation, mining, and industrial pursuits as well as in government shops, depots, and yards. Also to be included were free Negroes working in arsenals, armories, salt works, niter works, and military hospitals. This helps to explain why the Assistant Adjutant General was informed by the Bureau of Conscription: "The orders for the enrollment and assignment of free blacks have been carried out as effectively as could be done under the circumstances." On September 19, 1864, the Bureau of Conscription reported:

> Upon a general examination of the returns of the enrolling officers it is manifest that all the labor of this class which could well be has been withdrawn from the agricultural districts.
>
> The Niter and Mining Bureau desires every one that can be found. Colonel Corley, Chief Quartermaster Army of Northern Virginia, calls for 500, and the Engineer Bureau makes a requisition for a large force on the line of the Richmond and Danville and the South Side Railroads. General Walker, commanding defenses on the Richmond and Danville Railroad, also calls for assistance from this class. The officers of the Quartermaster Department collecting forage in the Valley have received assistance, but are demanding more. Major J. G. Paxton, in charge of extensive operations for the Quartermaster's Department at Lynchburg and in the Piedmont counties, is asking for aid. All the demands are pressing and of the most vital importance, and the number required by the officers making the requisitions for them approximates, if does not exceed, the whole number of free Negroes within the military lines of the prescribed ages.[15]

There were, moreover, a number of free Negroes who either deserted or successfully managed to evade the enrolling officers. The Bureau of Conscription was informed that several free Negroes in Culpeper escaped conscription with the aid of their white friends. The matter was referred to Colonel J. C. Porter, enrolling officer of the Eighth District, with instructions to enroll the Culpeper Negroes. Such free persons were to be employed in saving the large crop of government forage and in obtaining fuel for the army.

The complete story of the impressment of free Negroes and their war experiences in Virginia can never be told, because the records were imperfectly kept, and no returns were sent from some sections of the state. Late in February 1864 the Bureau of Conscription reported the occupations of a large portion of the conscripts as listed in Table 2.

From February 1864 to March 1865, when the Conscription Bureau was abolished, no fewer than 1,818 free Negroes were enrolled, and of

Table 2. *Conscription Act of 1864: free Negroes enrolled, 1864–1865* [16]

Occupation	Number	Occupation	Number
Ambulance driver	2	Mason	48
Baker	9	Mechanic	31
Barber	23	Messenger	7
Carpenter	25	Miller	4
Coffin maker	2	Miner	1
Collier	1	Nurse	1
Cook	15	Ostler	1
Cooper	12	Packer	2
Depot hand	18	Painter	4
Drayman	3	Plaster	4
Engineer	2	Porter	7
Engine cleaner	12	Railroad hand	29
Engine hand	20	Sawyer	32
Farmer	175	Shearer	1
Farm hand	129	Shoemaker	61
Fireman (train)	24	Striker	6
Fisherman	17	Tanner	36
Gardner	1	Teamster	29
Grave digger	1	Tobacco hand	38
Groom	2	Tobacco factory	47
Hackman	2	Tobacconist	3
House servant	16	Wagoner	11
Huckster	4	Wagon maker	13
Laborer	440	Waiter	10
Lumber man	47	Wheelwright	14
Machinist	16	Wood house hand	2
		Total	1,464

this number 45 were reported as deserters.[17] To meet the demands of the state's diversified war economy the versatility of its free colored population was exploited. A free Negro had to be just as much at home in the cornfield as in collecting forage; he had to be prepared not only to care for stock, act as a sawyer, repair a wagon, serve as a teamster or boatman, and procure raw materials, but even to furnish skilled and unskilled labor for the South's war industries and defensive works. To the Confederate States Navy at Richmond, for example, the Bureau of Conscription assigned 83 Negroes to alleviate the scarcity of both skilled and ordinary labor for naval ordnance, naval works, shipyards, and depots. The Conscription Bureau also responded to the urgent appeals of Virginia railroads, ironworks, flour mills, niter works, tanneries, and mines. Although several hundred free Negroes were assigned to the aforementioned areas, the engineers, quartermaster, and ordnance consumed more than 70 percent of the free Negro conscripts. Throughout 1864 there was a mounting need for the labor of free Negroes, and to meet such crises they were impressed, gathered, and turned over to the enrolling officers, usually located at camps of instruction. Then the conscripts were detailed to areas where their labor was needed.

Much of Virginia's war effort was effected by the legal machinery devised for the mobilization and the regulation of slave and free Negro labor. Although impressment by the state and the Confederate government prompted bitter criticism by slaveholders, it produced tangible and significant results. Negro labor, for example, became a key factor in the mechanism of Virginia's wartime economy. Mobilization of the state's colored manpower considerably enhanced Confederate fighting strength, as whites were freed to swell the southern armies. Mobilization eventually made available a greater variety of foodstuffs and manufactured commodities for military and civilian needs.

Mobilization also attracted the attention of the North and the South. As early as October 1862 James S. Wadsworth stated the value of assembling Negro labor. As he accepted the Republican nomination for governor of New York, Wadsworth stated, "Six million whites, having had time to organize their government and arm their troops, fed and supported by the labor of 4,000,000 slaves, present the most formidable rebellion in recorded history." He added, "Strike from the rebellion the support which it derives from the unrequited toil of these slaves, and its foundations will be undermined." [18] Seven months later the Richmond *Examiner* asserted that the North had discovered from this war the value of the slave to the South as a military laborer, and "Lincoln's proclamation is designed to destroy this power in our hands." [19]

Once mobilized, Virginia was able to minimize, until the closing months of the war, the number of Negroes who were captured by Federal raiding parties or who escaped into Union lines. No doubt, the presence of Lee's armies as well as Confederate patrols, at points accessible to Union lines, sealed off possible avenues of escape for the Negro. [20] After thirty-two months of warfare, in December 1863, J. M. Bennett, Auditor of Public Accounts, reported to the General Assembly of Virginia that the loss of slaves to the enemy by flight or seizure by Federal raiding parties was not as large as expected. Bennett indicated that the loss of slaves, based on tax returns, totaled less than 10 percent (exclusive of West Virginia) of the slave population, or 31,551 slaves. The auditor's report also disclosed that in 1860 the proportion of slaves (exclusive of free Negroes) was 47 to every 100 whites, and by 1863 there were 71 slaves to every 100 white persons in the 78 countries and 5 cities included in his report to the Virginia lawmakers.

It would appear that Virginia was not faced with a serious break-down of its holding power over the Negro noncombatants until the closing days of the war. Flight into Union lines, however, or seizure by Union troops, though seemingly less extensive than in other parts of the Confederacy, was a cause of concern. In countless ways, the war came closer to the Virginia Negro than to other Negroes within the South. Both of the war governors, John Letcher and William Smith, encouraged and supported Negro mobilization and war measures whereby the labor of Negroes contributed to the ability of the Confederacy to keep an army in the field. The Virginia Negro resided in what was not only the industrial heart of the South but also the major battleground of the Civil War. Armed conflict greatly increased the technological and military demand for his

Table 3. *Loss of slaves from Virginia, 1861–1863* [21]

Year	Total in Counties	Total in Corporations	Total
1860	355,632	22,767	378,399
1863	331,537	15,311	346,848
Loss	30,250	7,456	37,706
Gain	6,155	0	6,155

brawn and his skills. Virginia's coal mines, ironworks, lead-smelting works, nitriaries, harness shops, arsenals, naval yards, and machine shops offer unique examples of the state's efforts to match Negro manpower to the need for increased production. The many and diversified needs of the war involved the Virginia Negro in a correspondingly wide variety of tasks—procurement operations, processing of minerals, fabrication of the weapons of war, transportation of war materials by land and by river, and construction of fortifications and defensive works. Probably no other southern state offers a better example of the premium placed upon Negro manpower.

NOTES

1. See Tinsley Lee Spraggins, "Mobilization of Negro Labor for The Depart-ment of Virginia and North Carolina, 1861–1865," *North Carolina Historical Review* 24 (April 1947): 173.

2. From 1840 to 1861 the rapidly changing pattern of the state's economic growth and life resulted from the rapid development of urban areas and industries. In 1860 the South contained only 10 of the 102 American cities with a population of more than 10,000 people, and 30 percent of the southern cities in this category were

located in Virginia (Richmond had a population of about 40,000). Virginia also ranked first among the southern states, with its 5,385 manufacturing establishments.

3. See Clement Eaton, "Slave-Hiring in the Upper South: A Step Toward Freedom," *Mississippi Valley Historical Review* 46 (March 1960): 663 ff.

4. Ibid., p. 663.

5. See James H. Brewer, "Legislation Designed to Control Slavery in Wilmington and Fayetteville," *North Carolina Historical Review* 30 (April 1953): 155–66.

6. See Luther P. Jackson, *Free Negro Labor and Property Holding in Virginia, 1830–1860* (New York: D. Appleton-Century Company, 1942), p. 55.

7. Spraggins, "Mobilization of Negro Labor," p. 171. In order to avoid the Impressment Act of 1862, some free Negroes took advantage of a Virginia statute enacted in 1853 which allowed any free Negro of mixed blood to have himself legally declared "not a Negro by the testimony of a white person." Subsequently, the Virginia courts certified many free Negroes, claiming less than one fourth Negro blood, to be "persons of mixed blood and not Negroes." In December 1862 Albert S. Gentry, a free Negro of Richmond, was arrested "for want of a register, and brought before the court on a writ of habeas corpus." After hearing the argument of Gentry's lawyer (Virginia Code, 17th Section, chapter 107), the judge ruled that "Gentry had less than ¼ Negro blood" and discharged him. On January 26, 1863, Gentry was again arrested and his case was tried in the Richmond hustings court. Gentry's counsel again argued that his client was not a Negro and secured his release. After the trial the mayor of Richmond questioned whether "the legislature had the constitutional right to make white men out of mixed bloods." See the Richmond *Examiner,* December 5, 1862; January 26, 1863. Also see Jackson, *Free Negro Labor and Property Holding.*

8. Spraggins, "Mobilization of Negro Labor," p. 173.

9. *Journal of the Congress of the Confederate States of America, 1861–1865,* 7 vols. (Washington: Government Printing Office, 1904–1905), III, p. 191. See Brewer, *The Confederate Negro,* ch. 6 for a full discussion of slaves impressed to labor on fortifications and defensive works. Even before this law, the Confederate Congress in 1862 authorized the employment of Negroes as cooks and musicians in the army. Subsequently the majority of cooks in southern armies were Negroes; each company was entitled to four cooks. Owners were paid $15 monthly for slave furnished, and their chattels were entitled to clothing and rations.

10. *The War of the Rebellion: A Compilation of the Official Records of the Union and Confederate Armies* (Washington, 1880–1901), ser. IV, vol. III, p. 547.

11. Ibid., II, p. 947.

12. Ibid., p. 998.

13. Ibid., p. 208.

14. Ibid., pp. 716–17.

15. Ibid., p. 665.

16. *War Department Collection of Confederate Records,* Record Group 109, vol. 241, ch. 1, Register of Free Negroes Enrolled, 1864–1865. See also vol. 240, ch. 1.

17. Ibid.

18. Richmond *Whig,* October 10, 1862.

19. Richmond *Examiner,* May 5, 1863.

20. Existing records indicate that the greatest loss of slaves occurred in the western counties of Virginia. Most historians agree that slaves usually fled whenever a reasonable chance presented itself. Some evidence exists to sustain this point of

view, especially during the last sixteen months of the war. There is, however, little evidence to sustain the position that Virginia Negroes, free and slave, showed an appreciable disposition to desert or to impair the war effort. Virginia's desertion problem or slave losses did not contribute to the general breakdown of Confederate industry. This study is not designed to treat thoroughly the question of slave losses, although such a study should be made to ascertain the effect desertion had upon the Confederate war effort.

21. See "Communication from the Auditor of Public Accounts, Virginia State Library, Richmond, Virginia." *Documents of the Senate, 1863–1864*, No. 19.

X

Northern Opinion and Black Freedom

With the announcement of Lincoln's Emancipation Proclamation, the "Negro Question" eclipsed the slavery issue as a topic of public debate. Only the question of how to conduct the war absorbed more of the nation's attention from 1862 to 1865. Although the proclamation itself freed only those slaves still in the hands of southern rebels, almost everyone recognized that it signaled the end of legal slavery in the United States. The Thirteenth Amendment, which freed the remaining slaves in the southern and northern border states, was adopted in 1865 without serious debate since by that time public opinion centered on the more important matter of the freedman's future status. Experience based on state laws and federal court decisions during the period from 1830 to 1860 indicated that freedom did not necessarily entitle a person to the full rights of citizenship. In many northern states, Afro-Americans possessed few rights that the white man was obliged to respect.

The struggle for black equality began when the controversy over slavery ended. Pleased with their initial victory, the abolitionists immediately launched a new campaign to persuade the nation that black people should receive full equality before the law. Aware that one of the principal obstacles to full acceptance of Afro-Americans was the myth of Negro inferiority, abolitionists conducted an educational program to make the public understand that racial distinctions were the result of environmental conditions and not of inherent racial characteristics.

Their purpose was to persuade Anglo-Americans that blacks were potentially as intelligent and resourceful as any race of people. Afro-Americans appeared to be otherwise, they insisted, only because slavery had reduced them to a state of dependency which had robbed them of ambition. Once the yoke of slavery had been removed, Afro-Americans would quickly become useful citizens, making valuable contributions to American society.

One important reason for the failure of the abolitionists' campaign was the rising tide of race prejudice that inflicted the North. Lincoln's proclamation not only gave new direction to the abolitionists, it also brought forth the first set of racial demagogues who raised the specter of an imminent black peril. They frightened many Northerners into believing that emancipation might result in a mass exodus of Afro-Americans out of the South; they predicted that a flood of cheap black labor would undermine the economic position of northern workers; and they warned that hordes of "savage Africans" would transform peaceful and picturesque northern communities into teaming urban centers festering with crime and violence. They filled the columns of racist newspapers with false and exaggerated accounts of unbelievable Negro atrocities. In fact, the viciousness of their racial hatred would be exceeded only by the most blatant racists of twentieth-century America. One immediate result of this hate campaign was a renewal of racial disturbances in northern cities. The worst of these occurred in July, 1863, in New York City where bands of angry whites killed or injured scores of innocent and defenseless Afro-Americans.

Most Northerners, however, fitted into neither group. Unable to accept the abolitionist arguments of equality of all races and unwilling to join the corps of outspoken racists, they occupied a position in the broad middle somewhere between the two extremes. They recognized the need for momentary federal assistance to southern freedmen but worried lest the practice linger too long and make the Afro-American a permanent ward of the nation. On the other hand, they refused to accept the abolitionists' proposition that slavery was largely responsible for the Negro's behavior. Because they still looked upon blacks as inferiors, most Northerners were reluctant to extend voting rights or the privilege of office holding to them. Since most southern blacks were both unskilled and uneducated, they also feared the social consequences of a mass black invasion of the North. Consequently, the vast majority of Northerners, including some Afro-Americans, wished to keep the newly freed blacks in the South.

The most obvious way of preventing an influx of black migrants into the North—state and federal legislation—was not viewed with much favor. Those states which had earlier enacted such laws hastily repealed them during the war in order not to appear too bigoted. A second alternative had greater appeal, especially among those earlier advocates of anti-slavery who were masters of equivocation. If the South should be transformed from a slave dungeon into a free society, perhaps many Afro-Americans would want to remain in their old homeland where their labor had largely created the wealth of the South.

By favoring fundamental changes in the South, they again would appear progressive rather than prejudiced. By no means all of the northern support for radical reconstruction came from those moderates who feared a black peril but who wished to avoid the label of racial extremists. Many who acquiesced in the establishment of southern governments where Afro-Americans participated on an equal basis with Anglo-Americans were motivated by a desire to prevent the same thing from occurring in the North.

The essays in this section provide a good summary of the arguments at both extremities. Professor McPherson discusses the arguments in favor of racial equality expressed by abolitionists and indicates how close their position was to that of twentieth-century social scientists. On the other hand, the selection by Professor V. Jacque Voegeli reveals that many northern Anglo-Americans harbored feelings of Negrophobia. By demonstrating the parallel between the arguments of race haters during the Civil War and those of southern demagogues in the twentieth century, Voegeli reveals how little Anglo-Americans have changed over the last century.

30. V. JACQUE VOEGELI, The Northwest and the Race Issue, 1861–1862 (1963)*

Emancipation of southern slaves was viewed with mixed emotions by many Northerners. In his perceptive study entitled *Free But Not Equal,* Professor V. Jacque Voegeli of Vanderbilt University carefully analyzed the attitudes of residents in the Midwest during the Civil War. In this particular selection, Professor Voegeli devotes attention only to the views of Northwesterners. There he finds widespread prejudice against Afro-Americans despite the fact that most people in the Northwest opposed the extension of slavery and supported the Civil War.

In a recent essay, C. Vann Woodward wrote critically of those writers—"myth-makers" he called them—who have created "the legend that the Mason-Dixon Line not only divided slavery from freedom in ante-bellum America," but also "set apart racial inhumanity in the South from benevolence, liberality and tolerance in the North." In this "North Star Legend," the pre-Civil War North emerges as the practicing champion of racial equality.[1] This myth is related to and becomes, in fact, a part of a current interpretation of the Civil War. In this interpretation, which emphasizes the moral conflict, slavery appears not primarily as a political or emotional issue but as a thing of evil against which men must fight. Since the evil was sectional, the forces of good and evil appear divided along sectional lines. "Human dignity and freedom" as well as "democracy" were to be restored to the South. The North thus went to war in 1861 fighting for human dignity, freedom, and democracy.[2] Yet how deeply committed to human dignity and democracy for the Negro was the North? How deeply was it committed to equality for the Negro?

The northern commitment to equality cannot be measured by the amount of antislavery sentiment. Outrage over slavery and belief in white supremacy were two seemingly discordant strains of thought that

* From V. Jacque Voegeli, "The Northwest and the Race Issue, 1861–1862," *Mississippi Valley Historical Review* 50 (September, 1963): 235–51. Reprinted by permission.

were often harmonized in the antislavery intellect. In the section of the country then popularly called the Northwest, the coexistence of these two strains was perhaps most apparent. In that portion of the North, at any rate, humanitarian pity for the slaves did not always spring from a desire to confer equal rights on all men. Antislavery men did not necessarily understand that equality for the Negro would inexorably follow emancipation. In that section, when war broke out, opposition to the evil of slavery did not carry with it a commitment to equality for the Negro.

The Northwest comprised the seven states of Ohio, Indiana, Illinois, Michigan, Wisconsin, Minnesota, and Iowa. In 1861 it was a stronghold of white supremacy. As the nation girded for war, state constitutions and statutes reflected the racism that flourished in the region. The severity of the discriminatory legislation varied, but every state imposed legal disabilities upon its black residents. All seven states limited service in the militia to white males and barred Negroes from the suffrage. In Illinois and Indiana there were no provisions for the education of colored children, and Negroes were not recognized as competent witnesses in court trials where a white person was a party to the case. Iowa and Ohio excluded Negroes from jury service. Interracial marriages were forbidden in Michigan, Ohio, Indiana, and Illinois. Ohio denied Negroes the benefits of poor relief and provided for racially segregated public schools. Exclusion laws carrying severe penalties prohibited Negroes from settling in Indiana, Illinois, and Iowa.

Early in the war, the fate of the Negro race became a source of great concern to the Northwest. Armed conflict brought the realization that war could loosen the bonds of slavery and this in turn raised the question: What can be done with the freed slaves? This was not a new question; it had, of course, long troubled the friends of emancipation, both North and South. Now, with slavery in jeopardy for the first time, the most disturbing aspect of this problem in the Northwest was the apprehension that the freedmen would throng into the area and become social, economic, and political competitors of the whites.[3]

Apprehension became alarm as a result of legislation of the second session of the Thirty-seventh Congress, for by the time of adjournment on July 17, 1862, Republican party members had pushed through a series of measures designed to shatter the cornerstone of the Confederacy. Both houses approved a joint resolution offering financial aid to slave states that would adopt gradual emancipation. Bondsmen in the District of Columbia and in the territories were declared free. The use of military power in returning fugitive slaves to their masters was prohibited, and a militia act liberated Union slave-soldiers and their families owned by rebels. Climaxing this program, the Confiscation Act of July 17, 1862, provided that slaves owned by persons supporting the rebellion should be forever free.[4] If enforced, this law would have freed practically every slave in the Confederacy. The congressional drive toward emancipation stirred violent partisan conflict, in and out of Congress, as Democrats and Republicans debated the consequences of freeing the slaves and plumbed the depths of the race problem. The northwestern attitude toward the Negro now received its fullest exposition.

Among the most implacable foes of emancipation were the northwestern Democrats. Although they had many constitutional and political objections to slave liberation, much of their resistance to the assault on slavery sprang from the fear that emancipation would deluge the Northwest with Negroes and challenge white supremacy there. These Democrats attacked every proposal to free the slaves or improve the lot of the free Negro. They did not defend slavery as a positive good, and they seemed ready to tolerate the institution rather than to increase the number of Negroes in the Northwest. Their attitude was that expressed by an Iowa newspaperman. He opposed "slavery *per se*"; yet he was confident that slaves would not benefit from freedom and that there was "little doubt of the demoralizing effect it will have upon the white race in the North . . . to have these emancipated blacks introduced among them." Representative Samuel S. Cox of Ohio observed, "If slavery is bad, the condition of . . . Ohio, with an unrestrained black population, only double what we now have partly subservient, partly slothful, partly criminal, and all disadvantageous and ruinous, will be far worse." [5]

Skillfully exploiting the dread of a Negro invasion of the Northwest, Democrats protested that slave confiscation and emancipation would send the freed slaves surging into the Northwest, and that ruin and degradation would follow in their wake. They argued, in part, from reasons of economic interest. The withdrawal of the southern laboring force would destroy the prosperity of the South, thereby depriving the Northwest of its market for surplus goods. Bills calling for federal compensation to slave states which would adopt emancipation were scored as projects for taxing the whites to build black communities in the North. Negro immigrants, they said, would drain the northern economy because they were thieves and chronic paupers.[6] Wage earners were warned that hordes of unskilled competitors would inundate the Northwest to degrade society, reduce wages, and drive the whites from their jobs.[7]

Professing to believe that the Republicans intended to "equalize" the races, Democrats assailed the specter of racial equality with an appeal to white superiority. Because the Negro was inherently inferior, said the Democrats, equality for the black man would contaminate northwestern society and politics and debase the American people.[8] A Republican bill authorizing the exchange of diplomatic representatives with Haiti and Liberia drew a stream of abuse from alarmed Democrats who suspected that this was an instrument for forcing equality. Representative Cox objected to receiving colored diplomats in Washington, he said, because history taught that "these Commonwealths and this Union were made for white men; that this Government is a Government of white men; that the men who made it never intended by anything they did to place the black race upon an equality with the white." To Representative William A. Richardson of Illinois, the Republicans were mocking the Almighty: "God made the white man superior to the black, and no legislation will undo or change the decrees of Heaven . . . and unlike the abolition equalizationists I find no fault and utter no complaint against the wisdom of our Creator." [9]

While the Democrats protested emancipation and vilified the Negro, Republicans slowly pushed their antislavery program through Congress. When Congress convened in December, 1861, there was no consensus on slavery within the Republican party. A deep gulf separated those abolitionists who interpreted the war as a divine command to destroy slavery from the moderate and conservative men, most of whom advanced haltingly to the position that the confiscation of slaves could sap the strength of the rebels. Emancipationists from the Northwest presented an appealing case for confiscating Confederate slaves. Confiscation and emancipation, they maintained, would cripple or crush the southern war effort, save the Union, insure future national unity, and punish the South.[10] Seldom, however, was the plight of the enslaved given as the chief justification for emancipation.

Many considerations determined this approach to the slavery problem. To most Republican Congressmen in 1862 the war was being waged for the restoration of the Union, with or without slavery. Besides this, sound political tactics demanded that "Union," not "abolition," be the cry to unify the North. The party in power was especially sensitive to Democratic accusations that rabid abolitionists had caused the South to secede, seized control of the Republican party, and were forcing unconstitutional abolition measures upon Congress. The plea that slave liberation was the price of military victory was partially designed to overcome the constitutional scruples of those strict constructionists who doubted the constitutionality of the slave confiscation proposals. There was still another reason for not converting the war into an avowed abolition crusade: Republicans of every persuasion knew that the Northwest would not shed blood solely in behalf of a race it despised. Excessive emphasis upon the humanitarian objectives of emancipation would have lent truth to the Democratic complaint that the Republicans were fighting a war to free the Negro. Consequently, although they denounced slavery as a crime against God, humanity, morality, and natural rights, northwestern Republicans made it clear that they were primarily concerned with restoring the Union.[11]

The Democratic outcry that emancipation would inundate the Northwest with Negroes gravely disturbed the Republicans, for they knew of the deep-seated opposition in the Northwest to the entry of colored persons. Republican members of Congress warned of this feeling. When Senator Jacob M. Howard of Michigan was told by a colleague that if the slaves were freed and distributed among the various states in proportion to the white population, Michigan would have about 123,000 blacks instead of the 6,800 it then had, Howard retorted, "Canada is very near us, and affords a fine market for 'wool'." Senator Lyman Trumbull of Illinois candidly told the Senate, "There is a very great aversion in the West—I know it to be so in my state—against having free negroes come among us. Our people want nothing to do with the negro." [12] Time and time again Republicans voiced these sentiments.[13] Some party leaders arraigned the section for its hostility toward Negroes, but no one questioned the prevalence or intensity of this feeling.

This Negrophobia impeded and imperiled the passage of slave confiscation and emancipation measures in 1862. Senator Trumbull, who was himself the chief draftsman of the confiscation bill, discerned that hostility to Negroes posed one of the most potent objections to his proposal. The people of the Northwest, Trumbull said, were asking the supporters of confiscation: "What will you do with them [slaves]; we do not want them set free to come in among us; we know it is wrong that the rebels should have the benefit of their services to fight us; but what do you propose to do with them?" An Ohio congressman put it more bluntly. Incensed by the slow progress of confiscation proposals, he cried: "The nation has been led astray quite long enough by the miserable partisan war cry that emancipation means 'to turn the niggers loose'." [14]

To overcome these objections, a number of Republican leaders— both radicals and conservatives—brought forth a theory destined to become a Republican panacea for all the ills of emancipation. According to this theory, slave liberation would not only remove slavery from the South but would take the Negro from the Northwest. It was slavery, both the Republican press and politicians emphasized, that caused the flight of blacks from the cotton kingdom. Free the slaves, they said, and a warm climate, abundant land, a demand for their labor, a sentimental attachment to the South, and northern race prejudice would induce the freedmen to stay on southern soil.[15] Furthermore, the same forces would send northern Negroes rushing southward.[16] Republicans from the middle states joined their northwestern brethren in this refrain. Two sanguine emancipationists, George W. Julian of Indiana and Albert G. Riddle of Ohio, expected freedom in the South to drain both the North and Canada of their colored residents.[17]

To what extent these Republicans actually believed that northern Negroes would go South to freedom is difficult to ascertain. But such pronouncements were certainly more than Machiavellian utterances fashioned to deceive the people of the North. The idea that the Negro was a creature of the tropics was a part of the stereotype of the black race. In private correspondence as well as in public statements, antislavery men declared their belief that slavery alone prevented northern Negroes from moving to the South. David Noggle, a Wisconsin judge who boasted of his radicalism, censured Senator James R. Doolittle for espousing the colonization of the slaves. "With all due deference to your wild notions of colonization," he wrote, "I think you can't but believe that [by] abolishing Slavery in the Southern States the Northern States would be speedily cleared of their present free colored population." This same belief led Secretary of the Treasury Salmon P. Chase of Ohio to advocate military emancipation in the Deep South. In a letter to Major General Benjamin F. Butler, then the Union Commander of the Department of the Gulf, Chase wrote that "many honest men really think they [Negroes] are not to be permitted to reside permanently in the Northern States." While he said he had no objection to the presence of colored people in his state, Chase felt that they would prefer the southern climate. "Let, therefore, the South be opened to negro emigration by emancipation along the Gulf, and it is easy to see that the blacks of the North will slide southward, and leave behind them no question to quarrel about as far as they are concerned." [18]

Although many Republicans expressed such views, the party adhered officially to colonization as the answer to the problems which would be created by emancipation. The slaves that were to be freed were to be colonized in foreign lands. In the vanguard of the deportation movement were prominent northwestern Republicans—President Abraham Lincoln, Senators John Sherman of Ohio, James R. Doolittle of Wisconsin, Trumbull and Orville H. Browning of Illinois, and Henry S. Lane of Indiana.

These men were convinced that physical differences between the races created racial antagonism that would not be dispelled by emancipation. Senator Doolittle, a chief advocate of colonization, wrote that "the question of race is a more troublesome one than the question of condition." The colonizationists urged—since history and evidence on every hand indicated that white Americans would not admit black men to the equality to which all men aspired—that emancipation be followed by removal of the freedman from the United States. Such a course would benefit both races. The whites would profit from the departure of an alien race, and the blacks would escape from domination and oppression. The most concise statement of the philosophy of colonization came from President Lincoln. On August 14, 1862, shortly after Congress adjourned, Lincoln addressed a deputation of colored men and pointed out that both humanitarianism and racial antipathy nourished the colonization movement. Lincoln stated that the broad physical difference between the two races was disadvantageous to both. "I think your race suffer very greatly, many of them by living among us," he said, "while ours suffer from your presence. . . . If this is admitted, it affords a reason at least why we should be separated." He reminded his audience that freedom did not bring equality to the Negro; for "on this broad continent, not a single man of your race is made the equal of a single man of ours." [19]

Similar pleas for deportation were advanced by Republican congressmen from the Northwest. They emphasized the point that as long as the Negro race resided in the United States, it was doomed to subordination and ostracism. In bestowing freedom upon a proscribed people, the nation was obligated to resettle the outcasts in foreign lands where they could enjoy equal rights and govern themselves.[20] Many Congressmen, especially those from New England, protested that colonization was inhumane, impractical, uneconomic, and un-Christian. With the strong support of the Northwest and the middle states, Congress overrode these objections. It incorporated into both the confiscation act and the District of Columbia emancipation act provisions for colonizing those slaves, liberated by that legislation, who were willing to leave the United States.[21]

There were also stern political exigencies that turned the Republican party to colonization in 1862. Some Republican strategists, including Lincoln, hoped that the adoption of deportation would persuade the loyal slave states to move toward emancipation. But it was the political situation in the North that insured Republican support for colonization. In the Northwest, Pennsylvania, and New Jersey, insistent voices clamored for positive action to shield the North from a Negro invasion. Colonization became a key part of the program to make slave confiscation and emancipation more palatable to the free states. Deportation would blunt the threat of a Negro ingress and thus would relieve emancipation of a dreaded burden.

Republicans, in fact, openly avowed that deportation was designed to keep the freedmen out of the North. When Senator Trumbull placed a confiscation measure before the Senate, he said that the colonization proposal in the bill would answer those northwesterners who wanted the slaves freed but objected to having them brought into their section. Republican Senator John C. Ten Eyck of New Jersey, a member of the committee which considered the confiscation bill, announced that the committee thought the colonization section to be "of the utmost importance." He contended that the North's opposition to an influx of Negroes called for a declaration of the government's policy on colonization.[22] After Congress had passed the acts containing provisions for voluntary colonization, Assistant Secretary of the Interior John P. Usher of Indiana pressed President Lincoln to accept a plan for colonizing the freedmen in Chiriqui. On August 2, 1862, Usher advised the President that such action would allay apprehensions that the North was going to be overrun by free Negroes. Twelve days later, at his widely publicized conference with the colored men, the President noted that hopes for freedom would be greatly enhanced if some free Negroes would accept colonization. "There is an unwillingness on the part of our people, harsh as it may be, for you free colored people to remain with us," he said. "Now, if you could give a start to the white people, you would open a wide door for many to be made free." [23]

Throughout the congressional discussion of colonization and other measures relating to the condition of the Negro, it was apparent that northwestern Republicans were not advocating racial equality. If any of them were egalitarians, they pondered their principles in silence. They had joined with other Republicans in enacting legislation intended to improve the lot of the black man, particularly in the District of Columbia.[24] They were, in this respect, considerate of the humanity of the black man; but at the same time they disclaimed any goal of racial equality. They agreed that political and social rights were outside the province of federal law; only the states could confer political privileges, and each individual could regulate his own social relations.[25] Charity and humanity, not equality, were their watchwords. Sympathy for the victims of slavery, a spirit of noblesse oblige, and an urge to do justice to the oppressed inspired their benevolence. Representative John Hutchins of Ohio said: "These measures have no relation to political or social equality. . . . Because we are willing to do justice to the humblest in society, does it follow that we are bound to extend to them the same social and political privileges which we enjoy?" To Senator James Harlan, an Iowa Republican, civilized society was obligated to protect the Negroes, "another feeble people," but their freedom would neither bring nor require equality with the whites.[26]

Meanwhile, Republicans at home in the Northwest displayed much the same attitude. Although the Ohio state legislature Republicans withstood the demand for Negro-exclusion legislation, discriminatory laws continued to prevail. Republican-dominated legislatures in Iowa and Ohio met and adjourned without altering the anti-Negro laws on their statute books. The heavily Republican Iowa legislature amended its militia law, but continued to limit the enrollment to white males.[27]

There were some Northwesterners who wished to grant equal political rights to the Negro. The referendum on a new state constitution for Illinois indicated the size of this minority in that state. In a direct vote on the franchise, the people of Illinois, by a majority of over five to one, chose to continue its ban on Negro suffrage and office holding.[28] In such an atmosphere, no political party and few, if any, politicians could admit egalitarian principles and survive.

As they talked at home and in Congress, many northwestern Republican stalwarts spoke the language of white supremacy. Governor William Dennison, a founder of the Republican party in Ohio, referred to the "superior [white] race." Because of the Negro's "kindly and affectionate" nature, remarked the Chicago *Tribune*, he is "rarely agitated by the profound passions which belong to his superiors." [29] Republican Senators Sherman, Browning, Doolittle, and Harlan were certain that a higher law transcended man-made rules and governed race relations. They stressed that natural instincts implanted by the Creator forbade equality of the races. God and nature, not prejudice, accounted for racial antipathy, and what God had decreed they did not propose to deny. The law of caste, asserted Sherman, was the unchangeable "law of God. . . . The whites and the blacks will always be separate, or where they are brought together, one will be inferior to the other." [30] According to Browning and Doolittle, human instincts caused white resistance to social and political equality. Doolittle stated that "in the temperate zone, the Caucausian race has always been dominant, and always will be. In the torrid zone the colored man dominates and will forever. . . . The Creator has written it upon the earth and upon the race." [31] Responding to a query about the possibility of interracial marriages, Senator Harlan asked, "Has the hand of nature fixed no barrier to such loathsome associations?" [32]

Events in the summer of 1862 warned of intensifying hostility toward the black race. In a June referendum on a new state constitution, Illinois voters refused to ratify the proposed constitution, but they overwhelmingly approved an article that prohibited Negroes from settling in the state and denied suffrage and public office to Negroes and mulattoes. Voting on these two provisions separately, the people endorsed the exclusion section by a vote of 171,896 to 71,806. Since the defeat of the constitution, reputedly a Democratic party document, was hailed as a Republican victory, the vote for the anti-Negro article was obviously drawn from both parties.[33] Later that summer anti-Negro sentiment became even more apparent, when in July and August serious race riots flared in New Albany (Indiana), Chicago, Toledo, and Cincinnati.[34]

The campaign which began in the summer of 1862 for the fall congressional elections found both emancipation and the status of the Negro as major political issues in the Northwest. Militant Democratic state conventions drafted caustic resolutions condemning emancipation as an unconstitutional, impractical measure that portended ruin for the region. The Iowa Democrats resolved that "this is a Government of white men, and was established exclusively for the white race; that the negroes are not entitled to, and ought not to be admitted to political or social equality with the white race." To halt economic competition between the races, the Democrats of Ohio opposed emancipation and demanded a ban on Negro immigration into the Buckeye State.[35] Excoriating slave liberation, the Illinois and Indiana Democratic conventions demanded enforcement of their exclusion laws on the grounds that white men alone were suited to the free institutions of their states. Wisconsin Democrats adopted and published an address which asserted that social equality of the races was contrary to the laws of nature: "Nature never placed the races together; when brought together the servitude of the inferior is the best condition for both races." [36]

Standing upon these party platforms, Democratic candidates and newspapers fired their familiar barrage of social, political, and economic objections at emancipation. If the slaves were liberated, they would fly to the North where their contact with a superior race would degrade white society, their economic rivalry would reduce wages, and their political competition would contaminate politics. Democrats spied the spirit of "equalization" lurking within every scheme of the Republicans. The preliminary Proclamation of Emancipation, issued by Lincoln on September 22, 1862, served as a prime target for the Democrats. In order to preserve white supremacy and repel the black invaders, the Democrats argued, the Republican party should be turned out of power before the President could execute his Emancipation Proclamation.[37]

On the emancipation and Negro issues, the campaign strategy of the Republican and Union party organizations in the Northwest usually followed a well-established line: slave confiscation and emancipation were desperately needed to win the war and restore the Union. Humanitarian goals were generally shunted aside while the voters were reassured that Union, not abolition, was the object of the war. On one point the Republicans concurred with the Democrats—Negroes were not wanted in the Northwest. Instead of extending an invitation to the slaves to seek their freedom in the free states, they made it clear that they neither desired nor expected any increase in the colored population of the area. From the press, pulpit, and political rostrum radicals and conservatives sounded the familiar cliché: slavery was driving southern Negroes into the Northwest, but emancipation in the Confederate states would hold the freedmen in the land of their labor and lure northern Negroes to the congenial South. Colonization, too, was proffered as a means of reducing the Negro population.[38] Democratic charges of Republican egalitarianism were either ignored or dismissed as malicious slander. Irritated by the allegation that Republican policies would lead to equality of the races and that "our volunteers are periling their lives to make niggers the equal of whites," the Indianapolis *Journal* exclaimed, "what a monstrous and villainous lie." [39]

In the elections of October and November, 1862, the Democrats swept to victory in the Northwest. They carried Ohio, Illinois, and Indiana, and registered impressive gains in Michigan and Wisconsin. For the federal House of Representatives, the Democrats elected fourteen out of nineteen members from Ohio, seven of eleven in Indiana, nine of fourteen in Illinois, and divided six Wisconsin seats with their rivals. The next Congress would contain thirty-four Democrats out of a total of sixty-four northwestern representatives, a gain of eighteen seats for the resurgent party.[40]

Many factors inspired the political revolt against the party of Lincoln in the 1862 elections. In the Northwest, arbitrary arrests by federal authorities, suspension of the habeas corpus privilege, the Emancipation Proclamation, and a disappointing military situation plagued the nominees of the Republican and Union parties.[41] The emancipation issue with its many ramifications played a leading role in the Democratic victory. Many northwestern Republicans conceded its impact. Senator Browning informed Lincoln that the proclamation suspending the writ of habeas corpus and the emancipation edict had defeated the party. John Sherman wrote that the "ill timed proclamation contributed to the general result." According to Unionist Thomas Ewing, a former United States senator, Lincoln had ruined the Union party in Ohio by issuing the proclamations. A clarion of radical Republicanism, the Cleveland *Leader*, asserted that Ohio and Illinois had voted against emancipation.[42]

This opposition to emancipation was primarily the product of Negrophobia aggravated by the threat of a massive influx of Negroes. H. S. Bundy, an unsuccessful Union party aspirant for Congress from Ohio, wrote Salmon P. Chase that the emancipation proclamation had been delivered just in time to defeat him and many other Union candidates in the Indiana and Ohio elections. "I had thought until this year the cry of 'nigger' & 'abolitionism,' were played out but they never had as much power & effect in this part of the state as at the recent elections." [43] The dis-

gruntled Chicago *Tribune* interpreted the political reverses as a signal
for the Republican party to re-emphasize its devotion to the "white race."
It counseled fellow Republicans to justify the emancipation proclamation
in terms of its effect upon "the happiness, the freedom and the prosperity
of the white men of the North. . . . We need not go beyond that; if we
do we bring the prejudices of caste and races into full play, and by
weakening the efforts of the North, impair the good the proclamation
promises." [44]

Elated Democrats hailed the elections of 1862 as a repudiation of the
emancipation heresy. To the Democratic Columbus *Crisis* the elections,
a contest of "*black vs. white*," had resolved that Ohio would never become
the refuge for southern Negroes. Representative Cox said the victory of
his party had brought forth a new commandment, "Thou shalt not degrade the white race by such inter-mixtures as emancipation would bring."
"The people," an Illinois Democrat told the House of Representatives,
"are sick and tired of this eternal talk upon the negro, and they have
expressed their disgust unmistakably in the recent elections." [45]

Impressed by the North's persistent hostility toward the free Negro,
President Lincoln strove to assuage the fears of the people. In his annual
message to Congress in December, 1862, he contended that liberation
and deportation of the slaves would benefit northern white men. He
strongly recommended the adoption of a constitutional amendment calling
for compensated emancipation and voluntary colonization of the freedmen. The claim that liberated Negroes would displace white labor the
President termed "largely imaginary, if not sometimes malicious." If the
freedmen should remain where they were, "they jostle no white laborers;
if they leave their old places, they leave them open to white laborers."
Emancipation alone would probably improve the wages of whites, and
the deportation of colored workers would certainly increase the earnings
of white men.

The President then turned to the fear "that the freed people will
swarm forth, and cover the whole land":

Equally distributed among the whites of the whole country . . . there would
be but one colored to seven whites. Could the one, in any way, greatly disturb
the seven? . . . But why should emancipation south, send the free people
north? People, of any color, seldom run, unless there be something to run
from. *Heretofore* colored people, to some extent, have fled north from bondage; and *now*, perhaps, from both bondage and destitution. But if gradual
emancipation and deportation be adopted, they will have neither to flee from.
Their old masters will give them wages . . . till new homes can be found
for them in congenial climes, and with people of their own blood and race.
. . . And, in any event, cannot the north decide for itself, whether to receive
them? [46]

Under the skillful pen of Lincoln, emancipation, colonization, and exclusion became deterrents to a Negro invasion of the North. By the end of 1862, the Northwest had amply demonstrated that ultimate equality for the Negro had not been a war aim when the conflict began.[47] The concept of the innate superiority of the "white race" cut across party lines and pervaded the mind of the Northwest. Moral opposition to slavery helped kindle the "irrepressible conflict," but moral principle had not abated the Northwest's determination to preserve white supremacy.

NOTES

1. C. Vann Woodward, "The Antislavery Myth," *American Scholar* 31 (Spring 1962): 316.

2. Arthur M. Schlesinger, Jr., "The Causes of the Civil War: A Note on Historical Sentimentalism," *Partisan Review* 16 (October 1949): 968–81.

3. Columbus (Ohio) *Crisis*, July 11 and August 22, 1861; Detroit *Free Press*, June 28, 1861; Chicago *Times*, October 8 and November 28, 1861. The most complete work on the treatment of the Negro in the North is Leon F. Litwack, *North of Slavery: The Negro in the Free States, 1790–1860* (Chicago: University of Chicago Press, 1961). An excellent study of the same subject in a single state is in Emma Lou Thornbrough, *The Negro in Indiana: A Study of a Minority* (Indianapolis: Indiana Historical Bureau, 1957), pp. 1–182. See also Henry C. Hubbart, *The Older Middle West, 1840–1880* (New York: D. Appleton-Century Company, 1936), pp. 11, 13, 28, 45–51, 151–52.

4. James G. Randall and David Donald, *The Civil War and Reconstruction*, 2nd ed. (Boston: D. C. Heath, 1961), pp. 372–75. It is not the purpose of this article to trace the course of this session of Congress, but, rather, to be concerned with the Northwest's views of the Negro, with some consideration of the influence of these attitudes on political policies.

5. Dubuque *Herald*, April 13 and 29, 1862; *Congressional Globe*, 37 Cong., 2 Sess., Appendix, pp. 244–45. See also Chicago *Times*, March 18, 1862. In 1860 the number and percentage of Negroes in each state were as follows: Illinois, 7,628 (0.4); Indiana, 11,428 (0.9); Ohio, 36,673 (1.3); Wisconsin, 1,171 (0.2); Minnesota, 259 (0.1); Michigan, 6,799 (0.9); and Iowa, 333 (0.2). *Negro Population: 1790–1915* (Washington: Government Printing Office, 1918), pp. 44, 51.

6. Dubuque *Herald*, April 29, 1862; Milwaukee *News* cited in Dubuque *Herald*, April 20, 1862; Detroit *Free Press*, December 10, 1861, and April 13, 1862; Cairo *Gazette*, April 19, 1862; Chicago *Times*, May 22, 1862; *Cong. Globe*, 37 Cong., 2 Sess., p. 1647 (April 11, 1862) and Appendix, pp. 247–48. For more information on the Democrats' use of Negrophobia as a political weapon in 1861 and 1862, see Wood Gray, *The Hidden Civil War: The Story of the Copperheads* (New York: Viking Press, 1942), pp. 23, 29, 30, 79, 89, 90, 97–100; Frank L. Klement, *The Copperheads in the Middle West* (Chicago: University of Chicago Press, 1960), pp. 12–17, 25, 45; and Emma Lou Thornbrough, "The Race Issue in Indiana Politics during the Civil War," *Indiana Magazine of History* 47 (June 1951): 169–80.

7. Cairo *Gazette*, April 3, 1862; Chicago *Times*, April 8 and 18, 1862; Columbus *Crisis*, January 29, 1862; Portsmouth (Ohio) *Times* cited in Columbus *Crisis*,

May 7, 1862; Cincinnati *Enquirer* cited in Dubuque *Herald*, June 26, 1862; Dubuque *Herald*, April 16, 19, and June 1, 13, and 22, 1862; Detroit *Free Press*, June 15, 1862; Indianapolis *Sentinel*, April 29, 1862, cited in Thornbrough, *The Negro in Indiana*, p. 189; *Cong. Globe*, 37 Cong., 2 Sess., p. 573 (January 30, 1862), p. 1468 (April 1, 1862), and Appendix, pp. 120, 240, 243–48, 285.

8. Detroit *Free Press*, June 14, 1862; Cairo *Gazette*, April 3, 1862; *Cong. Globe*, 37 Cong., 2 Sess., Appendix, p. 245.

9. Columbus *Crisis*, May 7, 1862; *Cong. Globe*, 37 Cong., 2 Sess., p. 60 (December 11, 1861), p. 2207 (May 19, 1862), p. 2502 (June 2, 1862).

10. *Cong. Globe*, 37 Cong., 2 Sess., p. 195 (January 6, 1862), pp. 327–28 (January 14, 1862), pp. 858–59 (February 17, 1862), and Appendix, pp. 319–20.

11. Ibid., p. 76 (December 12, 1861), pp. 194–95 (January 6, 1862), pp. 327–32 (January 14, 1862), pp. 348–49 (January 15, 1862), pp. 858–59 (February 17, 1862), p. 1816 (April 24, 1862).

12. Ibid., p. 1780 (April 23, 1862), p. 944 (February 25, 1862).

13. Ibid., p. 1357 (March 25, 1862), p. 1491 (April 2, 1862), p. 1606 (April 10, 1862), p. 2243 (May 20, 1862), p. 2923 (June 5, 1862), and Appendix, pp. 84, 297. See also J. M. Burgess to John Fox Potter, April 16, 1862, John Fox Potter Papers (Wisconsin State Historical Society, Madison).

14. *Cong. Globe*, 37 Cong., 2 Sess., p. 944 (February 23, 1862) and Appendix, p. 118. See also ibid., p. 2301 (May 22, 1862).

15. Milwaukee *Sentinel*, December 11, 1861, and June 28, 1862; Springfield *Illinois State Journal*, April 26, 1862; Peoria *Transcript* cited in Chicago *Tribune*, April 22, 1862; *Cong. Globe*, 37 Cong., 2 Sess., p. 332 (January 14, 1862), p. 2243 (May 20, 1862), and Appendix, pp. 212, 327.

16. Chicago *Tribune*, March 24 and April 22, 1862; Milwaukee *Sentinel*, February 27 and May 10, 1862; *Cong. Globe*, 37 Cong., 2 Sess., p. 441 (January 22, 1862), p. 1107 (March 6, 1862), p. 1495 (April 2, 1862), p. 2301 (May 22, 1862).

17. *Cong. Globe*, 37 Cong., 2 Sess., p. 332 (January 14, 1862), p. 2243 (May 20, 1862).

18. David Noggle to James R. Doolittle, May 30, 1862, James R. Doolittle Papers (Wisconsin State Historical Society); Salmon P. Chase to Benjamin F. Butler, July 31, 1862, Jessie Ames Marshall, ed., *Private and Official Correspondence of General Benjamin F. Butler during the Period of the Civil War*, 5 vols. (Norwood, Mass.: The Plimpton Press, 1917), II, pp. 132–33. The same belief was expressed by J. T. Worthington, an Ohio Unionist of unknown party affiliation, in Worthington to Rufus King, June, 1862, Rufus King Papers (Historical and Philosophical Society of Ohio, Cincinnati).

19. Doolittle to Mary Doolittle, April 19, 1862, Doolittle Papers; "Address on Colonization to a Deputation of Negroes," August 14, 1862, Roy P. Basler, ed., *The Collected Works of Abraham Lincoln*, 9 vols. (New Brunswick: Rutgers University Press, 1953), V, pp. 371–72. Lincoln's interest in colonization has been elaborately discussed. See Richard N. Current, *The Lincoln Nobody Knows* (New York: McGraw-Hill Book Co., 1958), pp. 221–22; James G. Randall, *Lincoln the President: Springfield to Gettysburg*, 2 vols. (New York: Dodd, Mead & Co., 1945), II, pp. 137–41; Walter L. Fleming, "Deportation and Colonization: An Attemptel Solution of the Race Problem," J. G. de Roulhac Hamilton, ed., *Studies in Southern History and Politics Inscribed to William Archibald Dunning* (New York: Columbia University Press, 1914), pp. 3–30; Warren A. Beck, "Lincoln and Negro Colonization in Central America," *Abraham Lincoln Quarterly* 6 (September 1950): 162–83; Paul J.

Scheips, "Lincoln and the Chiriqui Colonization Project," *Journal of Negro History* 37 (October 1952): 418–53; Frederic Bancroft, "The Colonization of American Negroes, 1801–1865," in Jacob E. Cooke, *Frederic Bancroft, Historian* (Norman: University of Oklahoma Press, 1957), pp. 186–87, 193, 196–97, 202–3, 209, 211–13.

20. *Cong. Globe,* 37 Cong., 2 Sess., p. 332 (January 14, 1862), pp. 1491–92 (April 2, 1862), p. 1520 (April 3, 1862), p. 1604 (April 10, 1862), p. 2923 (June 25, 1862), and Appendix, pp. 83–84, 297.

21. Ibid., Appendix, pp. 348, 412–13. In a key vote in the Senate, Republicans from the Northwest, New York, Pennsylvania, and New Jersey voted thirteen to three for colonization while New England senators voted against it, six to five. Ibid., pp. 1522–23 (April 3, 1862).

22. Ibid., pp. 944–46 (February 25, 1862). See also ibid., Appendix, p. 297.

23. John P. Usher to Lincoln, August 2, 1862, Robert Todd Lincoln Collection (Manuscript Division, Library of Congress); "Address on Colonization to a Deputation of Negroes," August 14, 1862, Basler, ed., *Collected Works of Lincoln,* V, pp. 371–72. The timing of this interview seems to indicate that Lincoln publicly reaffirmed his faith in colonization at this time to allay northern fears of a Negro influx.

24. *Cong. Globe,* 37 Cong., 2 Sess., Appendix, pp. 356–57, 361, 397.

25. Ibid., p. 3131 (July 5, 1862) and Appendix, pp. 156, 322.

26. Ibid., p. 1359 (March 25, 1862), p. 3131 (July 5, 1862), and Appendix, p. 322.

27. George H. Porter, *Ohio Politics during the Civil War Period* (New York: Columbia University Press, 1911), pp. 96–97; Columbus *Crisis,* April 30, 1862; *Acts and Resolutions Passed at the Regular Session of the Ninth General Assembly of the State of Iowa* (Des Moines, 1862), p. 231.

28. Springfield *Illinois State Journal,* August 16, 1862.

29. Columbus *Ohio State Journal,* January 7, 1862; Chicago *Tribune,* March 24, 1862.

30. *Cong. Globe,* 37 Cong., 2 Sess., p. 3199 (July 9, 1862).

31. Ibid., p. 1521 (April 3, 1862) and Appendix, pp. 83–84.

32. Ibid., Appendix, p. 321.

33. Springfield *Illinois State Journal,* August 5, 1862; Arthur C. Cole, *The Era of the Civil War, 1848–1870* (*The Centennial History of Illinois,* Vol. III, Springfield: Centennial Commission, 1919), pp. 268–72.

34. Chicago *Times,* July 15, 1862; Chicago *Tribune,* August 10, 1862; Columbus *Crisis,* July 16, 1862; Thornbrough, *The Negro in Indiana,* pp. 185–86; Charles R. Wilson, "Cincinnati's Reputation during the Civil War," *Journal of Southern History* 2 (November 1936): 478–79.

35. Dubuque *Herald,* July 22, 1862; Columbus *Crisis,* July 9, 1862.

36. Springfield *Illinois State Journal,* September 11, 1862; Indianapolis *Journal,* July 31, 1862. *Address to the People by the Democracy of Wisconsin, Adopted in State Convention at Milwaukee, Sept. 3d, 1862* ([Madison, 1862]), p. 3, pamphlet, in Moses M. Strong Papers (Wisconsin State Historical Society).

37. For examples, see Detroit *Free Press,* September 28, October 23, 28, 31, and November 2, 1862; Chicago *Times,* September 23, 25, 27, and October 3, 1862; Cairo *Gazette,* August 21, September 27, and October 30, 1862; Columbus *Crisis,* August 13, 27, September 3, 24, and October 15, 1862; Dubuque *Herald,* September 30, and October 3, 7, 8, 10, 11, 12, and 14, 1862.

38. A number of Republican and Unionist newspaper editors contented themselves with the observation that the emancipation proclamation was a "war measure" and then ignored it until after the elections. But the majority followed the course

indicated above. See Joseph A. Wright Papers (Indiana Division, Indiana State Historical Library, Indianapolis); Terre Haute *Express*, September 16, 1862; Columbus *Ohio State Journal*, September 4 and October 8, 1862; Milwaukee *Sentinel*, October 10, 31, and November 3, 1862; Dubuque *Times*, August 21 and September 2, 3, and 6, 1862; Howard (Ind.) *Tribune*, August 21, 1862; Chicago *Tribune*, August 7, September 21, 23, and October 8 and 19, 1862. In a sermon at Terre Haute on September 7, 1862, Lyman Abbott declared that emancipation would turn the tide of Negro immigration southward. Terre Haute *Express*, September 16, 1862.

39. Indianapolis *Journal*, October 6, 1862.

40. Gray, *Hidden Civil War*, p. 108.

41. The issues and the elections of 1862 are treated in ibid., pp. 97–112; Hubbart, *Older Middle West, 1840–1880*, ch. 11; Thornbrough, "The Race Issue in Indiana Politics," pp. 176–79; Porter, *Ohio Politics during the Civil War Period*, pp. 101–9, 139–44; Cole, *Era of the Civil War, 1848–1870*, pp. 296–98, 334–35; Allan Nevins, *The War for the Union: War Becomes Revolution* (*The Ordeal of the Union*, VI, New York: C. Scribner & Sons, 1960), pp. 299–322.

42. Theodore C. Pease and James G. Randall, eds., *The Diary of Orville Hickman Browning*, 2 vols. (Springfield: The Trustees of the Illinois State Historical Library, 1927–1933), I, pp. 588–89; John Sherman to William T. Sherman, November 16, 1862, W. T. Sherman Papers (Manuscript Division, Library of Congress); Cleveland *Leader*, November 10, 1862.

43. H. S. Bundy to Chase, October 18, 1862, Salmon P. Chase Papers (Manuscript Division, Library of Congress).

44. Chicago *Tribune*, November 3, 1862.

45. Columbus *Crisis*, October 22 and 29, 1862; *Cong. Globe*, 37 Cong., 3 Sess., p. 95 (December 15, 1862) and Appendix, p. 39.

46. "Annual Message to Congress," December 1, 1862, Basler, ed., *Collected Works of Lincoln*, V, pp. 533–37.

47. A study of the continuing pattern of prejudice against the Negro can be found in Thornbrough, *The Negro in Indiana*.

31. JAMES M. MCPHERSON, A Brief for Equality: The Abolitionist Reply to the Racist Myth, 1860–1865 (1965)*

In contrast to the study by Voegeli, which concentrates on the attitudes of northern racists, James McPherson's essay deals with the arguments of liberal Northerners of abolitionist persuasion. This article is from a collection of "new essays on the abolitionists" by a group of revisionist historians. In this selection McPherson, professor of history at Princeton University and author of *The Struggle for Equality*, stresses the efforts of abolitionists to counteract the flood of racist

* From James M. McPherson, "A Brief for Equality: The Abolitionist Reply to the Racist Myth, 1860–1865," in *The Antislavery Vanguard: New Essays on the Abolitionists*. Copyright © 1965 by Princeton University Press; Princeton Paperback, 1968, pp. 156–77. Reprinted by permission of Princeton University Press.

propaganda during the Civil War when the nation first debated the question of what provisions should be made for Afro-Americans. According to McPherson, the former abolitionists attempted to prove "the essential equality of the races" and to demonstrate that "the vices and disabilities of the American Negro" resulted from unfavorable environmental conditions and not from an inherent racial inferiority. They failed in this campaign largely because their defense of racial equality was at least a hundred years ahead of its time. McPherson concludes that "the abolitionists had perhaps a deeper understanding of the racial problem than any other men of their time—and many of ours."

One of the most formidable obstacles to the abolition of slavery and the extension of equal rights to free Negroes was the widespread popular and scientific belief, North as well as South, in the innate inferiority of the Negro race. Most white Americans believed that Negroes were by nature shiftless, slovenly, childlike, dullwitted, savage, and thus incapable of assimilation as equals into white society. Since the beginning of the antislavery movement, abolitionists had been confronted by arguments that Negroes belonged to a servile and indolent race; that they would work only under compulsion; that they could not take care of themselves in freedom and would revert to barbarism; and that emancipation would bring economic and social ruin to the South and to the nation.[1]

For thirty years many abolitionists worked tirelessly but without much success to combat these beliefs. When Civil War came in 1861 and emancipation became an imminent possibility, the debate about the Negro's racial character was sharpened by a new urgency and a heightened relevance. Abolitionist attempts to make the war a crusade for emancipation and equal rights were handicapped by the prevailing belief in the Negro's genetic inferiority. During the war, abolitionists redoubled their efforts to show that slavery and a hostile environment, not innate inferiority, had caused the degradation of the American Negro. They declared that if this environment was transformed by the abolition of slavery and of racial discrimination, the Negro would prove himself a constructive, capable, and creative member of society.

Abolitionists were well aware that the common belief in the Negro's racial inferiority constituted one of the main justifications for slavery. In the final analysis, wrote Sydney Howard Gay [2] in 1860, slavery was based "upon the assumed fact that the negroes are an inferior race, over whom the whites possess not merely an artificial superiority dependent upon the existing circumstances of their mutual position, but a natural superiority, which exists and ever must exist." "In truth," said Frederick Douglass, "this question is at the bottom of the whole [slavery] controversy." Until the doctrine of the diversity and inequality of races was discredited, abolitionists reasoned, the theory and practice of slavery would remain strongly entrenched in America. "We cannot expect," said Gilbert Haven, the militant, red-headed Methodist clergyman, "the complete removal of this curse from our land until we stand boldly and heartily upon the divine foundation—the perfect unity of the human race." [3]

The abolitionist attack on the concept of racial inequality centered on two fronts: (1) an attempt to demonstrate, from the Bible, from science, from history, and from observed facts, the essential equality of the races; and (2) an attempt to show that the unfavorable environmental conditions of slavery and segregation, rather than natural inferiority, had caused the vices and disabilities of the American Negro.

The ante-bellum generation had been fond of quoting the Bible as a weapon in the slavery controversy, and abolitionists could point to several passages of scripture which "proved" the unity of the human race. The book of Genesis told the story of the creation of *man* (not men) in God's own image. In his famous sermon on Mars Hill, St. Paul told the people of Athens that God "hath made of one blood all nations of men for to dwell on the face of the earth." Gilbert Haven contended that the Bible sanctioned the complete equality and fraternity of the races. Solomon treated the Queen of Sheba, an Ethiopian, "with the utmost respect and cordiality"; Moses married an Ethiopian; a Negro was called by God to be one of the prophets and teachers of the Church at Antioch. "More than this," declared Haven, "the Bible constantly proclaims the absolute oneness of the race of man, in Adam, Noah, and Christ." [4]

By 1860, however, the Bible argument was pretty well played out. Thirty years of controversy had only shown that the Bible could be quoted effectively on both sides of the slavery issue. Science, especially ethnology and anthropology, commanded a large and growing influence in the mid-nineteenth century. Ethnology in the hands of Josiah Nott, Louis Agassiz, Samuel G. Morton, and George Gliddon (a group which came to be known as the "American School" of Anthropology), who taught that the various races of mankind constituted separate and distinct species with the Negro at the bottom of the scale, had become a major weapon in the defense of slavery.[5] Abolitionists realized that to combat these teachings they must themselves use the weapons of ethnology. Few abolitionists had any formal anthropological training, but as a group they were well educated and highly literate; and given the rather crude state of nineteenth century ethnological knowledge, the industrious layman could become almost as well informed as the professional scientist.

Several abolitionists made intensive studies of the question of race. To refute the American School of Anthropology, abolitionists quoted prominent European naturalists who argued for the unity of origin and equality of races. In 1861, for example, the *Anti-Slavery Standard* published a review of *L'Unité de l'Espèce Humaine*, by M. de Quatrefarges, Professor of Natural History and Ethnology at the Museum of Natural History in Paris. Using the classifications of Linnaeus and Lamarck, M. de Quatrefarges defined mankind as a single species; racial differences were the result of variety within the species developed by conditions of environment and transmitted by heredity. M. de Quatrefarges used his vast knowledge to deny the existence of any fundamental and immutable differences in the mental capacities of various races.[6]

Abolitionists cited several other prominent European scientists who maintained the unity and equality of races: Dr. R. G. Latham, the British ethnologist; Dumont d'Urville, the great French geographer and navigator; George Louis Leclerc Buffon, the brilliant naturalist; and finally, the renowned Alexander von Humboldt, who wrote: "Whilst we maintain the unity of the human species, we at the same time repel the depressing assumption of superior and inferior races of men." Through Humboldt, said Charles Sumner, "Science is enlisted for the Equal Rights of All." [7]

Sumner may have overstated the case, since American science, at least, spoke overwhelmingly for inequality. But the ethnologists of the world spoke with a discordant and divided voice on the subject of race in 1860. Abolitionists argued forcefully (and accurately) that science had failed to *prove* the innate inferiority of the Negro. "You may read Prichard, and Pinkerton, and Morton, and Pickering, and Latham, and all the rest—the whole library of Ethnology," said Theodore Tilton in 1863, "and in the confusion of knowledge you will find one thing clear—and that is, science has not yet proved, in advance, that the negro race is not to be a high-cultured, dominant race—rulers of their own continent, and perhaps dictators to the world." [8]

The endless refinements of the scientific racial arguments probably passed over the heads of the general public. The average man was more interested in concrete examples; and the advocates of Negro inferiority thought they had one incontrovertible example to show him: the supposed barbarous and uncivilized condition of Africa. What contribution to civilization and progress had Africa ever made, asked proslavery writers derisively?

This was a potentially damaging argument, and abolitionists advanced boldly to meet it. Negro abolitionists were in the forefront of the struggle to vindicate Africa. The central theme of their argument was that the ancient Egyptians, fountainhead of Western civilization, were a Negroid or partially Negroid race. "The ancient Egyptians were not white people," declared Frederick Douglass, "but were, undoubtedly,

just about as dark in complexion as many in this country who are considered Negroes." Their hair "was far from being of that graceful lankness
which adorns the fair Anglo-Saxon head." "I claim that the blacks are the
legitimate descendants of the Egyptians," said William Wells Brown,
a prominent Negro abolitionist, lecturer, and author, in 1862. While the
ancestors of the proud Anglo-Saxons were roaming the forests of
Northern Europe as savages, declared Brown, Africa had created the
foundations of Western civilization and passed on this precious heritage
to the Jews, Greeks, Romans, and ultimately to Western Europe. In
reply to a derisive reference to Negroes by William L. Yancey of Alabama, Brown told a group of Boston abolitionists in 1860: "When Mr.
Yancey's ancestors were bending their backs to the yoke of William the
Conqueror, the ancestors of his slaves were revelling in the halls of science
and learning. If the Hon. Senator from Alabama wants antecedents, he
shall have them; and upon such, I claim a superiority for the negro. (Loud
applause.)" [9]

But the glories of ancient Ethiopia were not sufficient to convince
many skeptics of the inherent equality of Negroes. Modern Africa stood
in the way. Most nineteenth century Americans considered Africa a
backward, barbaric continent, devoid of any trace of civilization or culture. Most world travelers who visited the dark continent concurred with
Bayard Taylor's opinion that the Negro was "the lowest type of humanity
on the face of the earth." Not being world travelers themselves, abolitionists perforce obtained much of their information about Africa from such
unflattering sources. Consequently they admitted that contemporary
Africa stood low in the scale of civilization, but they advanced a cyclical
theory of history, by which nations rose and fell, and would rise again,
to explain Africa's temporary eclipse. At one time Africa was the center
of learning and culture, said Gerrit Smith, but in the course of events she
declined in importance. Africa's "inherent, inborn faculties," however,
"are neither multiplied nor diminished because developed in one age, and
undeveloped in another. . . . Changes of circumstances, along with other
causes, alternately lift up and depress a people." "Do you call the negro
race inferior?" asked Theodore Tilton in 1863.

No man can yet pronounce that judgment safely. How will you compare
races, to give each its due rank? . . . You must compare them in their fulfill-
ments, not in their beginnings. . . . How will you estimate the rank of the
Roman people? By its beginnings? By its decline? By neither. You rank it
at the height of its civilization. . . . The Germans, today, give philosophy
to Europe—but you can count the years backward when the Germans, now
philosophers, were barbarians. . . . No man can now predict the destiny of
the negro race. That race is yet so undeveloped—that destiny is yet so unful-

filled—that no man can say, and no wise man pretends to say, what the negro race shall finally become.[10]

Some abolitionists, moreover, did not entirely accept the dark portrait of modern Africa drawn by most travelers. Several months after the outbreak of the Civil War a remarkable little book, written anonymously and entitled *Record of an Obscure Man*, was published in Boston. It purported to be the memoir of a man who had visited a friend in the South in 1842 and had talked with him about the capabilities of the Negro race. In reality it was a fictional essay by Mrs. Mary Putnam, elder sister of James Russell Lowell. Mrs. Putnam asserted that most travelers who visited Africa penetrated no farther than the coastal areas, whose inhabitants had been subjected to debasing contact with rapacious slave traders, "to which their degradation is to be attributed, rather than to inherent depravity or stupidity." Travelers who had ventured into the interior of Africa had found people of finer appearance, gentler manners, greater industry and honesty. "When Central Africa has been fully laid open to the world," she argued, "we shall be called upon to revise many of our opinions." [11]

Displaying great learning, Mrs. Putnam quoted from world-famous explorers who had ventured into Central Africa: Hugh Clapperton, Mungo Park, and Dixon Denham. "Read what Denham says of the inhabitants of the interior," she urged; "of their industry, their skill in weaving and dyeing, of their love of music and poetry." Denham described the natives as "hospitable, kind-hearted, honest, and liberal." Anticipating the findings of modern scholars by nearly three generations, Mrs. Putnam decried the notion that Negroes had been civilized and uplifted by slavery and Christianity. Slavery, she said, had only suppressed their native virtues and intelligence.[12]

In one of the best expressions of "cultural relativism" to come out of the nineteenth century, Mrs. Putnam warned against accepting at face value the somber descriptions of Africa by certain Westerners. "All men are prone to judge the manners of other countries by the standard of their own," she wrote, "and the civilized world views from its own stand-point that which it calls savage. We find the Africans barbarians, wherever customs differ from ours; but they are on the road to civilization, when their nonsense suits our nonsense." [13]

Abolitionists warmly praised Mary Putnam's little book. "Such a studied tribute to the negro, in this way, we have never had the fortune to see," said Garrison in his review of *Record of an Obscure Man*. "The African is contemplated as a man apart from his accidents, and heavy must be the load of prejudice against color that is not lightened by the spirit and the truthfulness with which his claims are urged." The *Anglo-*

African, a Negro newspaper in New York City, declared that Mrs. Putnam had provided "the best, the fullest and most satisfactory record" of the Negro "it has been our fortune to meet with. . . . She recognizes in the negro an original, inherent germ force of his own, solemn, grand, endowed with energy and vitality enough to develop civil, social, and intellectual greatness out of his own resources." [14] Abolitionists adopted many of Mrs. Putnam's arguments in their crusade for emancipation and equal rights.

Some abolitionists, although they argued vigorously for the essential *equality* of the Negro race, nevertheless believed in inherent racial *differences.* James Freeman Clarke had declared that "it is a mistake to speak of the African as an inferior race to the Caucasian. It is doubtless different from this, just as this is also different from the Malay, the Indian, the Mongolian. There are many varieties in the human family." [15] By today's ethnological standards this was an accurate statement, but Clarke and several other abolitionists parlayed it into a more questionable thesis: that the Negro was inferior to the Caucasian in certain aspects of the hard-headed, practical business and professional world, but superior in the realm of religion and the arts. In 1862, for example, Moncure Conway, the son of a Virginia slaveholder and an abolitionist exile from his own state, penned an article for the Boston *Commonwealth.* Negroes were a graceful people, he said, full of exuberance and picturesque charm. It was the Negro who gave to the South its warmth and radiance. The colored people had fertile, poetic imaginations. They had contributed much to southern culture, and would contribute more in freedom. "In our practical, anxious, unimaginative country, we need an infusion of this fervid African element, so child-like, exuberant, and hopeful," wrote Conway. "We ought to prize it, as we do rare woods and glowing gems imported from the gorgeous tropics." One year later, writing for an English audience, Conway stated that Negroes

seem to me to be weaker in the direction of the understanding, strictly speaking, but to have strength and elegance of imagination and expression. Negro sermons, fables, and descriptions are in the highest degree pictorial, abounding in mystic interpretations which would delight a German transcendentalist. My belief is, that there is a vast deal of high art yet to come out of that people in America. Their songs and hymns are the only original melodies we have.[16]

In his widely publicized speech on *The Negro,* Theodore Tilton proclaimed the Negro "the most religious man among men. Is not the religious nature the highest part of human nature? Strike out the negro then, and you destroy the highest development of the highest part of human nature." It was a mistake, thought Tilton, to rank men only by a superiority of intellectual faculties. God has given to man a higher dignity than the reason. It is the moral nature. . . . In all those intellectual activities which take their strange quickening from the moral faculties—processes which we call instincts, or intuitions—the negro is superior to the white man—equal to the white woman. The negro race is the feminine race of the world. . . .

We have need of the negro for his . . . aesthetic faculties. . . . We have need of the negro for his Music. . . . But let us stop questioning whether the negro is a man. In many respects he is a superior man. In a few respects, he is the greatest of man. I think he is certainly greater than those men who clamor against giving him a chance in the world, as if they feared something from the competition.[17]

Among American natural scientists of the mid-nineteenth century, Louis Agassiz was foremost in prestige and authority. His adherence to the "American School" of Anthropology gave it an influence it could not otherwise have commanded. As a Harvard Professor Agassiz had many acquaintances in Boston's intellectual circles; several of these acquaintances were abolitionists, and Agassiz's racial ideas could not help but have some effect on their thinking. Samuel Gridley Howe was one such friend. In 1863–64 Howe served as a member of the American Freedmen's Inquiry Commission (a body created by the Lincoln Administration to investigate the condition and needs of the freed slaves). In connection with his research for this Commission, Howe asked Agassiz for his views on the effect of race on the problems of emancipation and reconstruction. Agassiz replied that he welcomed the prospect of emancipation, but warned against granting equal political and social rights to freedmen. He reviewed the history of the Negro and concluded that colored people were "indolent, playful, sensual, imitative, subservient, good-natured, versatile, unsteady in their purpose, devoted and affectionate." The Negro had never shown himself qualified for self-government. "I cannot," concluded Agassiz, "think it just or safe to grant at once to the negro all the privileges which we ourselves have acquired by long struggles. . . . Let us beware of granting too much to the negro race in the beginning, lest it become necessary hereafter to deprive them of some of the privileges which they may use to their own and our detriment." [18]

Howe was torn between his respect for Agassiz's learning and his own equalitarian principles. "I would not only advocate entire freedom, equal rights and privileges," he told Agassiz, but "open competition for social distinction." Howe was nevertheless influenced by some of Agassiz's notions regarding the mental inferiority of Negroes. In a book on Canadian Negroes published in 1864, Howe lamented that the younger generation, who had never known slavery and who enjoyed equal civil and political rights in Canada, had failed to produce as many outstanding individuals, in proportion to their numbers, as the white community. Howe took into account the prejudice, discrimination, and lack of opportunity which might have accounted for this failure, but concluded that even with these disabilities the Negro community should have produced more superior men. Teachers to whom he talked testified that Negroes learned just as fast. as whites in the lower grades, but fell behind at the higher levels "when they come to studies which tax the higher mental powers, or the reasoning and combining faculties." Colored people, thought Howe, were "quick of perception; very imitative; and they rapidly become intelligent. But they are rather knowing, than thinking people. They occupy useful stations in life; but such as require quick perceptions, rather than strong sense." [19]

To the modern reader familiar with the view of contemporary anthropology that there is no proof of significant differences in the mental capacities of various races, the opinions of Howe and other abolitionists who thought like him appear to border on racism. Even the belief of Tilton, Conway, and others in the inherent superiority of the Negro in the "feminine" virtues—religion and the arts—implies an assumption of Negro *inferiority* in the "masculine" virtues of reason and enterprise. Thus a case of modified racism could be made out against certain of the abolitionists, but only by ignoring the fact that in the contemporary spectrum of opinion on race, even these abolitionists were far in the liberal vanguard. The extraordinary thing about the abolitionists as a group was not that some of them believed in racial differences, but that in a nation where popular belief *and* scientific learning overwhelmingly proclaimed the Negro's absolute inferiority, there were other abolitionists who dared to declare their faith in the essential equality of all men, regardless of race.

Most abolitionists agreed that the adverse environmental effects of slavery and discrimination, rather than innate deficiencies, were responsible for the practical inferiority of the Negro in American society. "What stone has been left unturned to degrade us?" asked James McCune Smith, a leading Negro abolitionist of New York City, in 1860. "What hand has refused to fan the flame of popular prejudice against us? What American artist has not caricatured us? . . . What press has not ridiculed and condemned us? . . . No other nation on the globe could have made more progress in the midst of such a universal and stringent disparagement. It would humble the proudest, crush the energies of the strongest, and retard the progress of the swiftest." Theodore Tilton agreed that discrimination was responsible for the Negro's disabilities. "We put a stigma upon the black man's color, and then plead that prejudice against the commonest fair dealing," he stated. "We shut him out of schools, and then bitterly inveigh against the ignorance of his kind. We shut up all learned professions from his reach, and withhold the motives for ordinary enterprise, and then declare that he is an inferior being, fitted only for menial services." [20]

Prejudice and discrimination against the free Negro were debilitating enough, but the effects of slavery were worse still. "Take any race you please, French, English, Irish, or Scotch," said Frederick Douglass; "subject them to slavery for ages—regard and treat them every where, every way, as property. . . . Let them be loaded with chains, scarred with the whip, branded with hot irons, sold in the market, kept in ignorance, . . . and I venture to say that the same doubt would spring up concerning either of them, which now confronts the negro." It was little wonder that "the colored people in America appear stupid, helpless and degraded. The wonder is that they evince so much spirit and manhood as they do." Tilton conceded that "slavery has reduced the blacks to the lowest point of ignorance and humiliation of which humanity . . . is capable." The peculiar institution had produced some singular effects on the Negro, making him childlike and dependent, lacking in initiative and self-respect. "Man is, to a certain extent, the creature of circumstances," argued Tilton, "and two centuries of slavery must needs have molded the character of the slave. . . . The faults of the slave . . . come of training, rather than of natural endowment." [21]

In the New York *Tribune* of February 5, 1863, Sydney Gay presented a cogent and eloquent summary of the environmentalist argument. "We have never supposed that the liberation of so many human beings, heretofore irresponsible, would be without some embarrassments," he wrote in reply to proslavery arguments that slaves were not fit for freedom. "It is Freedom that fits men for Freedom. . . . The crime of slavery has been that it has found the incapacity of its victims an argument for the continuation of its emasculating influences, and has continually pointed to the ruin it has wrought as an apology for postponing reparation." Nobody in his right senses, continued Gay,

has expected to find the Freedman . . . a model of possible excellence, a miracle of virtue, a wonder of wit, a paragon of prudence, and a marvel of industry. In him who was yesterday a Slave, we should expect to find the vices of the Slave—the traces of that falsehood which heretofore had been his sole protection against cruelty—of that thievishness which may have saved him from the pangs of hunger, or guarded him from the inclemency of the elements —of that insubordination of the animal passions which his superiors in society have encouraged for their own profit and by their own example. . . . Emancipation will not remove the scars which Slavery has inflicted. There is many a brow from which the brand can never be erased. So much the sooner should we, with all the courage of a genuine repentance, dock this entail of human misery, and at least turn the faces of future generations toward kindlier opportunities and less discouraging vicissitudes! [22]

The effects of slavery and racial discrimination on the Negro's character, according to abolitionists, were felt primarily in three areas: intelligence, industry, and morals. The Negro's defects of intelligence, remarked Frederick Douglass, could be found among the peasants, laborers, and lower classes of all races. "A man is worked upon by what *he* works on. He may carve out his circumstances, but his circumstances will carve him out as well." Douglass recalled his trip to Ireland in the 1840s, where he found the population of the poorer districts much like plantation slaves in every respect save color. "The open, uneducated mouth—the long, gaunt arm—the badly formed foot and ankles—the shuffling gait—the retreating forehead and vacant expression—and, their petty quarrels and fights—all reminded me of the plantation, and my own cruelly abused people." [23]

Moncure Conway, born and raised on a Virginia plantation, recounted the story of a companion of his youth, a slave boy who was popular with the white boys of the neighborhood and excelled in telling stories, playing games, etc. The boy had great native intelligence. He accompanied young Moncure to school every day, but of course was not allowed in the schoolroom. He wanted to know what happened in there, and when he found out, he too wanted to learn to read. He could not understand why he was denied this privilege, and grew bewildered, then saddened, and finally rebellious, forcing Moncure's father to sell him South. Conway never forgot the boy. "I have dwelt upon this case," he wrote in his *Testimonies Concerning Slavery*, "because it is that which represents, in my own experience, one of the most tragical forms in which Slavery outrages human nature." On the basis of his experience Conway also denied the theory that because of some natural disability, Negroes learned quickly until the age of ten or twelve, and then fell behind. "It has been my lot to have much to do with the poor whites of the South, and I have observed precisely the same arrest of development, both physical and mental, in those poor whites. . . . They learn well at first, even with a kind of voracity; but, at about the same age with the Negro child, they become dull." This was the result, not of inherent inferiority, but of the sudden realization at age ten or twelve of the cramped circumstances, limited opportunities, and unhappy future that faced the downtrodden of both races. [24]

The lazy, shiftless Negro who would work only under compulsion was a byword among those who defended slavery and ridiculed the idea of emancipation. Of course slaves were lazy, wrote Lydia Maria Child in her study of emancipation in the West Indies. Slavery "takes away the motive power from the laborers, who naturally desire to shirk as much as possible of the work, which brings them no pay. . . . It makes them indifferent to the destruction of property on estates, in whose prosperity they have no interest. . . . It kills their ingenuity and enterprise." She cited the testimony of planters and missionaries in the West Indies, who said that emancipation had "almost wholly put an end to sulking, or pretending to be sick. . . . Planters treat their laborers more like fellow-men, and that leads them to be respectful in their turn. They have now a growing regard for character; a feeling unknown to them in the days of slavery." [25]

The alleged immorality, dishonesty, and untruthfulness of the Negro were cited by proslavery writers as additional proofs of his inferiority. Of course the slave was immoral, replied abolitionists. Under slavery promiscuity was encouraged, marriage had no legal validity, and the father had no personal responsibility for his children, who belonged, not to their parents, but to their master. "Being regarded as animals, and treated like live-stock, [slaves] unavoidably lived like animals," wrote Mrs. Child. "Modesty and self-respect were impossible to their brutalized condition." In the West Indies, she contended, there was much less immorality a generation after emancipation than there had been under slavery.[26]

"To tell us that Slavery fosters in the enslaved habits of deception, is not to communciate to us any startling novelty," wrote Sydney Gay in 1862. Gay and Conway admitted that Negroes were prone to petty thievery, "but it should be remembered that the rights of property involve some very refined problems," said Conway. "If the Negro is inclined to sympathise with the views of Rousseau on such questions more than the English schools would approve, it must be admitted that the systematic disregard of his own right to his earnings is scarcely the best method of giving him better views. I have never heard yet of a slave who had managed to filch back so much as had been filched from him." [27]

"The difference between the Black and White," thought Sydney Gay, "is no other than the difference between the White and the White—differences occasioned by the accidents of location, and susceptible of removal by the opportunities of culture." Abolitionists realized, however, that these differences would not be wiped out in a year or two. "Men going from slavery to freedom cannot change their habits as they change their garments," wrote Samuel Gridley Howe. "The effects of Slavery will last more than one generation or even two," predicted Wendell Phillips. "It were a very slight evil if they could be done away sooner." The Negro was potentially the equal of the white man, but he had a long, hard road to travel before he reached that potentiality.[28]

During the Civil War and Reconstruction, abolitionists had an opportunity to test their theories of racial equality against the actual experiences of the freedmen. Hundreds of abolitionists went to the South in the 1860s and 1870s as teachers and missionaries of the northern freedmen's aid societies, which were formed during the war to bring education and economic assistance to the emancipated slaves. A few abolitionists were disillusioned by the immensity of the task, and soon returned to their homes. Others, for the sake of propaganda or self-justification, extravagantly praised the virtues and nobility of the freedmen. But most abolitionists who went South to help the freedmen entered the work with their eyes open, reinforced by their belief in the essential innate equality of the Negro race and the corrosive effects of slavery on the Negro's character.[29]

Several abolitionists kept diaries, wrote letters, and published articles and books describing and reflecting upon their experiences with the freedmen. These writings expressed various shadings in points of view, of course, but most abolitionists would have agreed with the sober and thoughtful analysis of William Channing Gannett, who went to the South Carolina Sea Islands as a teacher of the freedmen in 1862. "I feel no doubt," Gannett wrote from the Sea Islands in 1863, "that under conditions of peace, three years would find these people, with but very few exceptions, a self-respecting, self-supporting population." [30] In 1865 Gannett presented a cautiously optimistic view of the future. But the road to freedom would not be smooth. "Not only do their old habits cling to the freedmen as they rise, but their ignorance will betray them into new and perilous mistakes. We look for slow progress and much disappointment. . . . For a time discouragement and failure await the eager restorer." The final outcome of this experiment of freedom, however, could not be in doubt. "Judging from the activity already shown, the improvement already made, we feel certain that this 'institution' of freedom will at once be far more than self-supporting, and that, with the paralysis of slavery fairly thrown off, the negro will eventually contribute to the strength and honor of the country in relations far more important than that of simply furnishing its cotton, sugar, and rice." [31]

In spite of countless discouragements, most abolitionists, like Gannett, who worked directly with the freedmen maintained their faith in the innate equality of the Negro race. The abolitionists' argument for racial equality and their analysis of the effects of environment on the Negro's personality were perhaps their most sophisticated and significant contributions to the discussion of the racial problem in the United States. But in the final analysis they emphasized that the question was not one of race, but of human rights. "I think races are of secondary importance," said Wendell Phillips in 1863. "I despise an empire resting its claims on the blood of a single race. My pride in the future is in the banner that welcomes every race and every blood, and under whose shelter all races stand up equal." "Looked at through centuries," proclaimed Theodore

Tilton, "the question of races sinks into insignificance. The only generalization that will stand is, not that there are five races of men, or seven, or twelve, but only one—the universal human race in which all men are brothers, and God is father over all!" [32]

The abolitionist movement was essentially a direct response to the existence of slavery in America. But many strains of Western thought converged and focused in the nineteenth century to produce the particular emotional and intellectual intensity of the antislavery movement in the United States. The rational liberalism of the Enlightenment was synthesized with the romantic mysticism of Transcendentalism; Evangelical Protestantism absorbed elements of both systems and added to them a crusading, unquenchable fervor. In America, all three intellectual traditions—the Enlightenment, Transcendentalism, and Evangelical Protestantism—were basically equalitarian. The Enlightenment produced the Declaration of Independence; Transcendentalism emphasized the innate goodness and ultimate perfectibility of man; Evangelical Protestantism taught that injustice was a sin, and that every Christian had a duty to cleanse society of its sins.

This equalitarianism was at the heart of the abolitionist movement. Slavery and the denial of equal rights were violations of the Declaration of Independence, of Christianity, and of human dignity. Abolitionists insisted that the Negro was a human being, and that he was entitled to all the rights enjoyed by other men in America. Slavery and inequality could be justified only by denying the equal manhood of the Negro, and the supporters of slavery were finally forced to take this position. They maintained that the Negro was a separate and inferior species of human being; in the scale of creation he was higher than the ape, but lower than the Caucasian. The dispute about the Negro's biological capacities was at the core of the slavery controversy. Abolitionists were driven by the whole ideology and logic of their movement to defend the Negro's equality. Although slavery was finally abolished, the abolitionists' racial equalitarianism was ahead of its time. Not until the twentieth century was the validity of the abolitionist argument confirmed. The history of our own time has demonstrated that the abolitionists had perhaps a deeper understanding of the racial problem than any other men of their time—and many of ours.

NOTES

1. The following studies treat this subject in considerable detail: William S. Jenkins, *Pro-Slavery Thought in the Old South* (Chapel Hill: University of North Carolina Press, 1935), pp. 242–84; Guion G. Johnson, "A History of Racial Ideologies in the United States with Reference to the Negro," MS. in the Schomburg Collection of the New York Public Library; William R. Stanton, *The Leopard's Spots: Scientific*

Attitudes Toward Race in America, 1815-59 (Chicago: University of Chicago Press, 1960). For a good example of the many pamphlets and books arguing the innate inferiority of the Negro, see J. H. Van Evrie, *Negroes and Negro "Slavery"; The First an Inferior Race—the Latter its Normal Condition* (New York, 1853).

2. Gay was a veteran Garrisonian abolitionist. He had edited the New York *National Anti-Slavery Standard*, organ of the American Anti-Slavery Society, from 1843 to 1857. In the latter year he joined the editorial staff of the New York *Tribune*. In 1862 Gay became managing editor of the *Tribune*, a position of great influence.

3. New York *Tribune*, December 1, 1860; Philip S. Foner, *The Life and Writings of Frederick Douglass*, 4 vols. (New York: International Publishers, 1950-55), II, p. 294; Gilbert Haven, *National Sermons, Speeches, and Letters on Slavery and Its War* (Boston, 1869), p. 150.

4. Ibid., p. 137.

5. For a discussion of the American School of Anthropology, see Stanton, *Leopard's Spots.*

6. *National Anti-Slavery Standard*, November 9, 1861.

7. Charles Sumner, *Works of Charles Sumner*, 15 vols. (Boston, 1870–73), XIII, pp. 155–57.

8. Theodore Tilton, *The Negro* (New York, 1863), p. 5. This was a speech delivered by Tilton at the annual convention of the American Anti-Slavery Society in 1863. Several thousand copies were published by the Society. Tilton was a young and eloquent abolitionist who in 1863 became editor of the *Independent*, largest religious-political weekly in the world.

9. Foner, *Life and Writings*, II, p. 296; Brown's statements published by *The Liberator*, June 6, 1862, and October 26, 1860. These concepts of Afro-American equality were most vigorously stated by William Wells Brown in a book entitled *The Black Man, His Antecedents, His Genius, and His Achievements*, published in 1863.

10. Gerrit Smith to Montgomery Blair, April 2, 1862, public letter published in *The Liberator*, April 18; Tilton, *The Negro*, pp. 4–5.

11. [Mary Putnam], *Record of an Obscure Man* (Boston, 1861), pp. 91–92.

12. Ibid., pp. 92–96.

13. Ibid., p. 123.

14. *The Liberator*, November 29, 1861; *Anglo-African*, February 15, 1862.

15. James Freeman Clarke, *Slavery in the United States: A Sermon Delivered on Thanksgiving Day, 1842* (Boston, 1843), p. 24. See also James Freeman Clarke, "Condition of the Free Colored People of the United States," *The Christian Examiner*, 5th Ser., 4 (1859): 246–65; and Clarke to Senator Henry Wilson, April 17, 1860, Clarke Papers, Houghton Library, Harvard University.

16. Boston *Commonwealth*, October 18, 1862; Moncure D. Conway, *Testimonies Concerning Slavery*, 2d ed. (London, 1865), p. 71.

17. Tilton, *The Negro*, pp. 11–13.

18. Howe to Agassiz, August 3, 1863, Agassiz to Howe, August 9, 10, 1863, in Elizabeth C. Agassiz, *Louis Agassiz: His Life and Correspondence*, 2 vols. (Boston, 1885), II, pp. 591–608.

19. Howe to Agassiz, August 18, 1863; ibid., p. 614; Samuel G. Howe, *The Refugees from Slavery in Canada West* (Boston, 1864), pp. 81–82.

20. Smith's statement printed in *The Liberator*, November 2, 1860; Tilton's statement published in *Independent*, May 29, 1862.

21. Speech by Douglass at Cooper Union, February 12, 1862, published in New York *Tribune*, February 13; article by Tilton in *Independent*, August 20, 1863.

22. New York *Tribune*, February 5, 1863. See also J. M. McKim to Gay, January 28, 1863, Gay Papers, Columbia University Library.

23. Foner, *Life and Writings*, II, pp. 304–5. This is taken from a speech first delivered by Douglass in 1854, and repeated several times during the Civil War years.

24. Conway, *Testimonies Concerning Slavery*, pp. 4–7, 65–66.

25. Lydia M. Child, *The Right Way the Safe Way*, 2d ed. (New York, 1862), pp. 5–6, 15–16.

26. Ibid., p. 6. See also Charles K. Whipple, *The Family Relation, as Affected by Slavery* (Cincinnati, 1858); and [William C. Gannett], "The Freedmen at Port Royal," *North American Review* 101 (July 1865): 11–13.

27. New York *Tribune*, January 13, 1862; Conway, *Testimonies Concerning Slavery*, p. 70.

28. New York *Tribune*, September 17, 1863; Howe, *Refugees in Canada West*, p. 86; speech by Wendell Phillips in Boston Music Hall, December 16, 1860, in New York *Tribune*, December 18.

29. See Willie Lee Rose, *Rehearsal for Reconstruction: The Port Royal Experiment* (Indianapolis: Bobbs-Merrill, 1964); and James M. McPherson, *The Struggle for Equality: Abolitionists and the Negro in the Civil War and Reconstruction* (Princeton: Princeton University Press, 1964), chs. 7, 17.

30. Elizabeth W. Pearson, ed., *Letters from Port Royal, Written at the Time of the Civil War* (Boston: W. B. Clarke Company, 1906), p. 178. See also William H. Pease, "Three Years Among the Freedmen: William C. Gannett and the Port Royal Experiment," *Journal of Negro History* 42 (April 1957): 98–117.

31. Gannett, "The Freedmen at Port Royal," p. 28.

32. *The Liberator*, May 29, 1863; Tilton, *The Negro*, p. 8.

79
81
83
85
88